# RACIAL AND ETHNIC GROUPS

### Fifth Edition

### Richard T. Schaefer
*Western Illinois University*

# HarperCollins *College Publishers*

*To my son, Peter*

Acquisitions Editor: Alan McClare
Project Coordination and Text Design: Marie Gangemi
Cover Design: Kay Petronio
Cover Illustration: Anthony Russo
Photo Researcher: Mira Schachne
Production/Manufacturing: Michael Weinstein/Paula Keller
Compositor: Ampersand Graphics Ltd.
Printer and Binder: R. R. Donnelley & Sons Company
Cover Printer: The Lehigh Press, Inc.

RACIAL AND ETHNIC GROUPS, Fifth Edition

**Library of Congress Cataloging-in-Publication Data**

Schaefer, Richard T.
    Racial and ethnic groups / Richard T. Schaefer. — 5th ed.
        p. cm.
    Includes bibliographical references and index.
    ISBN 0–673–52241–5
    1. Minorities—United States. 2. United States—Race relations.
3. United States—Ethnic relations. 4. Prejudices. I. Title.
E184.A1S3   1992                                    92-20465
305.8′00973—dc20                                    CIP

92   93   94   95   9   8   7   6   5   4   3   2   1

# Contents

Preface *xi*

## PART ONE
## Perspectives on Racial and Ethnic Groups

## 1
## Aspects of Minority-Majority Relations   2

What Is a Minority Group?   *5*
Types of Minority Groups   *7*
Race   *10*
Sociology and the Study of Minority Groups   *14*
The Creation of Subordinate Group Status   *18*
The Consequences of Subordinate Group Status   *23*
The Pluralist Perspective   *31*
Glancing Back and Looking Ahead   *33*
Key Terms   *34*
For Further Information   *35*

*LISTEN TO THEIR VOICES*
*Problem of the Color-Line*
William E. B. DuBois   *8*

## 2
## Prejudice   37

Prejudice and Discrimination   *39*
Theories of Prejudice   *42*
The Content of Prejudice: Stereotypes   *46*
The Extent of Prejudice   *49*
Mood of the Minority   *55*
Reducing Prejudice   *58*
Glancing Back and Looking Ahead   *64*
Key Terms   *64*
For Further Information   *65*

*LISTEN TO THEIR VOICES*
*A Case of "Severe Bias"*
Patricia Raybon   *62*

# 3
## Discrimination 66

Understanding Discrimination 67
Institutional Discrimination 69
Dual Labor Market 71
The Underclass 72
Discrimination in American Society 75
Affirmative Action 83
Glancing Back and Looking Ahead 88
Key Terms 89
For Further Information 89

*LISTEN TO THEIR VOICES*
**Tally's Corner**
Elliot Liebow 74

# PART TWO
## Ethnic and Religious Sources of Conflict

# 4
## Immigration and the United States 92

Early Immigration 94
Restrictionist Sentiment Increases 99
Contemporary Concerns 103
Illegal Immigration 104
Refugees 108
Glancing Back and Looking Ahead 112
Key Terms 114
For Further Information 114

*LISTEN TO THEIR VOICES*
**Casting a Vote for Freedom of Conscious**
Nien Cheng 110

# 5
## Ethnicity and Religion in American Life 116

Ethnic Diversity 117
Religious Pluralism 118

The Rediscovery of Ethnicity   *121*
The Price Paid by White Ethnics   *126*
Case Example: Italian Americans   *130*
Ethnicity, Religion, and Social Class   *133*
Religion and American Society   *135*
Glancing Back and Looking Ahead   *144*
Key Terms   *145*
For Further Information   *145*

*LISTEN TO THEIR VOICES*
***What It Means to Be Italian-American***
Richard Gambino   *132*

## PART THREE
## Major Racial and Ethnic Minority Groups in the United States

## 6
## American Indians: The First Americans   148

Before the United States   *149*
Treaties and Warfare   *150*
Legislating for the American Indian People   *153*
Reservation Life and Federal Policies   *157*
American Indians in Urban Settings   *164*
Position of American Indians   *166*
Pan-Indianism   *173*
Natural Resources: The New Battleground   *179*
Glancing Back and Looking Ahead   *181*
Key Terms   *182*
For Further Information   *183*

*LISTEN TO THEIR VOICES*
***I Won't Be Celebrating Columbus Day***
Suzan Shown Harjo   *154*

## 7
## The Making of Black Americans in a White America   185

Slavery   *187*
Slavery's Aftermath   *191*
The Challenge of Black Leadership   *192*

The Exodus Northward   *194*
Reemergence of Black Protest   *196*
The Civil Rights Movement   *198*
Explaining Urban Violence   *203*
Black Power   *207*
Black Nationalism   *210*
Glacing Back and Looking Ahead   *213*
Key Terms   *214*
For Further Information   *215*

**LISTEN TO THEIR VOICES**
***Letter from Birmingham Jail***
Martin Luther King, Jr.   *202*

# 8

## African Americans Today   217

Education   *219*
Employment and Income   *224*
Family Life   *230*
Housing   *237*
Criminal Justice   *240*
Health Care   *243*
Politics   *245*
Glancing Back and Looking Ahead   *247*
Key Terms   *248*
For Further Information   *248*

**LISTEN TO THEIR VOICES**
***The Declining Significance of Race: Revisited but Not Revised***
William Julius Wilson   *236*

# 9

## Hispanic Americans   250

The Language Barrier   *252*
Cuban Americans   *262*
Central and South Americans   *267*
Glancing Back and Looking Ahead   *270*
Key Terms   *271*
For Further Information   *271*

**LISTEN TO THEIR VOICES**
***USA Needs to Have an "Official" Language***
S. I. Hayakawa   *261*

# 10

## Chicanos: The Nation's Largest Ethnic Group  273

Legacy of the Nineteenth Century  *275*

The Immigrant Experience  *277*

Organizations Within the Chicano Community  *281*

Education  *290*

Family Life  *293*

Health Care  *296*

Prejudice and Discrimination  *298*

Glancing Back and Looking Ahead  *299*

Key Terms  *301*

For Further Information  *301*

### LISTEN TO THEIR VOICES
*1969 Proclamation of the Delano Grape Workers*
César Chávez  *286*

# 11

## Puerto Ricans: Divided Between Island and Mainland  303

The Island of Puerto Rico  *305*

Bridge Between Island and Mainland  *311*

Race in Puerto Rico and on the Mainland  *313*

El Barrio  *314*

Glancing Back and Looking Ahead  *322*

Key Terms  *323*

For Further Information  *323*

### LISTEN TO THEIR VOICES
*Who is the Terrorist? The Making of a Puerto Rican Freedom Fighter*
Oscar López-Rivera  *310*

# 12

## Asian Americans: Growth and Diversity  325

Korean Americans  *327*

Filipino Americans  *332*

Indochinese Americans  *334*

Hawaii and Its People  *336*

The "Model Minority" Image Explored  *340*

Asian American Identity  *349*

Glancing Back and Looking Ahead  *350*

Key Terms  *351*

For Further Information  *351*

*LISTEN TO THEIR VOICES*
*Eggs, Twinkies and Ethnic Stereotypes*
Jeanne Park   *341*

# 13

## Chinese Americans: Continued Exclusion   353

Legacy of the Yellow Peril   *354*
Chinatowns Today   *355*
Industry and Occupations   *360*
Family and Religious Life   *361*
Politics   *363*
Militancy and Resistance   *365*
Remnants of Prejudice and Discrimination   *366*
Glancing Back and Looking Ahead   *370*
Key Terms   *371*
For Further Information   *371*

*LISTEN TO THEIR VOICES*
*Are Asian GIs Gooks?*
Sam Choy   *368*

# 14

## Japanese Americans: Overcoming Exclusion   373

Early Immigration   *374*
The Anti-Japanese Movement   *375*
The Wartime Evacuation   *377*
Postwar Success   *387*
Assimilation Accomplished, Almost   *388*
Comparing Chinese and Japanese American Experiences   *391*
Glancing Back and Looking Ahead   *392*
Key Terms   *392*
For Further Information   *393*

*LISTEN TO THEIR VOICES*
*Pearl Harbor and Japanese Americans*
Norman Mineta   *380*

# 15

## Jewish Americans: Quest to Maintain Identity   395

The Jewish People: Race or Religion or Ethnic Group?   *397*
Migration of Jews to the United States   *399*

Anti-Semitism Past and Present   *404*
Position of Jewish Americans   *412*
Religious Life   *416*
Jewish Identity   *420*
Glancing Back and Looking Ahead   *424*
Key Terms   *425*
For Further Information   *426*

**LISTEN TO THEIR VOICES**
*The Agony of the Yarmulka—A Confession*
Julian Ungar-Sangon   *400*

## PART FOUR
## Other Patterns of Dominance

# 16
## Women: The Oppressed Majority   430

Gender Roles and Gender Identity   *432*
Sociological Perspectives   *434*
The Feminist Movement   *435*
The Position of American Women   *439*
Double Jeopardy: Minority Women   *456*
Glancing Back and Looking Ahead   *459*
Key Terms   *459*
For Further Information   *460*

**LISTEN TO THEIR VOICES**
*Tomorrow's Tomorrow: The Black Woman*
Joyce A. Ladner   *458*

# 17
## Beyond the United States: The Comparative Perspective   462

Brazil: Not a Racial Paradise   *464*
Great Britain: Former Colonial Subjects Not Welcomed   *468*
Northern Ireland   *473*
Israel and the Occupied Territories   *477*
Republic of South Africa   *481*
Glancing Back and Looking Ahead   *489*
Key Terms   *491*
For Further Information   *491*

**LISTEN TO THEIR VOICES**
*Africa, It Is Ours*
Nelson Mandela   *486*


**Glossary   493**
**References   500**
**Acknowledgments   575**
**Index   577**

# Preface

Relations among racial and ethnic groups change at an accelerating rate. We have increasingly seen social concerns more and more defined by somber economic realities. The Black lower class is now an "underclass." The poverty line now marks the "feminization of poverty." Amid these troubles, we witness Haitian refugees seeking to live in the United States. Besides these economic issues, many Americans, who are themselves the descendants of poor immigrants, argue for proclaiming English the official language. Korean and Filipino Americans are now among the largest minority groups, yet are invisible to most Americans and are rarely portrayed even in a stereotyped way in the media. Beyond the United States, tribalism and nationality continue overwhelmingly to shape the events of which we read in newspapers. This book, as have earlier editions, reflects the changes accompanying recent events and displays how useful theoretical orientations and social science concepts can be in unraveling social relationships in a culturally diverse nation like the United States.

The information in this edition has been thoroughly updated. Relevant scholarly findings in a variety of disciplines have been incorporated. "Listen to Their Voices," appears in every chapter. These selections include excerpts from the writings or speeches of noted members of racial and ethnic groups such as Martin Luther King, Jr., Joyce A. Ladner, and Nelson Mandela. Their writings will help students appreciate both the emotional and intellectual energies felt by subordinate groups.

The changing social fabric of race and ethnic relation is apparent in the revisions since the fourth edition. Some examples of these are the following:

- political correctness controversy (Chapter 1)
- hostility toward Arab Americans during the 1991 Persian Gulf War (Chapter 2)
- the debate over hiring quotas (Chapter 3)
- the plight of Haitian refugees (Chapter 4)
- a case study on Italian Americans (Chapter 5)
- the growth of casino gambling on Indian reservations (Chapter 6)
- creation of public schools for African American boys only (Chapter 8)
- a new wave of Cuban immigrants (Chapter 9)
- health care and Chicanos (Chapter 10)
- a provocative "Listen to Their Voices" entitled "Who is the Terrorist" (Chapter 11)
- the highly-publicized confrontations between inner city Blacks and Korean American merchants (Chapter 12)
- exploitation of women workers in Chinatown (Chapter 13)
- renewed anti-Japan sentiment (Chapter 14)
- results of the 1990 National Jewish Population Study (Chapter 15)
- the debates over Schwartz's "mommy track" and Hochschild's "second shift" (Chapter 16)

- Mandela's release and the 1992 White South African referendum (Chapter 17)
- the Israeli handling of the intifada (Chapter 17)

In addition photographs, maps, and political cartoons have been updated.

Any constructive discussion of racial and ethnic minorities must do more than merely describe events. Part I, "Basic Perspectives on Racial and Ethnic Groups," includes the relevant theories and operational definitions that ground the study of race and ethnic relations in the social sciences. We specifically present functionalist, conflict, and labeling theories of sociology related to the study of race and ethnicity. We show the relationship between subordinate groups and the study of stratification. You will find not only sociology. You will be introduced to the dual labor market theory and the irregular economy from economics and reference group theory from psychology. Extensive treatment of prejudice and discrimination covers anti-White prejudice as well as the more familiar topic of bigotry aimed at subordinate groups. Discrimination is analyzed from an economic perspective, the discussion including the latest efforts to measure discrimination empirically and the continuing legal saga to define affirmative action's role.

In Part II, "Ethnic and Religious Sources of Conflict," we examine some often-ignored sources of intergroup conflict in the United States: White ethnic groups and religious minorities. Diversity in the United States is readily apparent when we look at the ethnic and religious groups that have been formed primarily by immigration. Even refugees, now primarily from Haiti and Central America, continue to be a major issue.

Any student needs to be familiar with the past to understand present forms of discrimination and subordination. Part III, "Major Racial and Ethnic Minority Groups in the United States," brings into sharper focus the history and contemporary status of American Indians, African Americans, Hispanics, Asian Americans, and Jews in the United States. Social institutions such as family, education, politics, and the economy receive special attention for each group. It is only appropriate that institutions are given special notice, because the author contends that institutional discrimination rather than individual action is the source of conflict between the subordinate and dominant elements in American society.

Part IV, "Other Patterns of Dominance," includes topics definitely related to American race and ethnic relations. The author recognizes, as have Gunnar Myrdal and Helen Mayer Hacker before, that relations between women and men resemble those between Blacks and Whites. Therefore, in this volume we consider the position of women as a subordinate group. Since the first edition of "Racial and Ethnic Groups," published 14 years ago, debates over equal rights and abortion have shown no sign of resolution. For women of color, we document the double jeopardy they suffer because of their subordinate status twice over—race and gender. Perhaps we can best comprehend intergroup conflict in the United States by comparing it to the ethnic hostilities in other nations. The similarities and differences between the United States and other societies treated in this book are striking. Again, as in the fourth edition, we examine the tensions of Brazil, Great Britain, Northern Ireland, and South Africa to document further the diversity of intergroup conflict. In addition, we now also consider Israel and the occupied territories from a perspective of ethnic relations.

Several features are included in the text to facilitate student learning. A "Chapter Outline" appears at the beginning of each chapter and is followed by "Highlights," a short section alerting students to important issues and topics to be addressed. To help students review, each chapter concludes with a summary, "Glancing Back and Looking Ahead." A bibliography, "For Further Information," provides references for additional research. The "Key Terms" are highlighted in italics when they are first introduced in the text and are listed with understandable definitions at the conclusion of each chapter. In addition there is an end-of-book "Glossary" with full definitions referenced to text-pages. An extensive illustration program, which includes maps and political cartoons, expands the text discussion and provokes thought. For the instructor, an "Instructor's Resource Manual," written by the author, serves as an effective reference and teaching aid. The manual includes a chapter overview, identification terms with page references, multiple choice questions, essay questions, discussion questions/class topics, and a listing of audio-visual material.

Changes in race and ethnic relations will continue, because these relations are a part of our constantly changing behavior. "Racial and Ethnic Groups" gives the reader a firm knowledge of the past and present, and a sufficient conceptual understanding to prepare for the future.

## *ACKNOWLEDGMENTS*

This revision creating a fifth edition benefited from the thoughtful reaction of my students at Western Illinois University, where special programs enabled me to teach the course in race and ethnicity to older students through independent home study and inmates at a maximum security prison, as well as to undergraduates. This edition benefits from my past collaborative writing experiences on other projects with Robert P. Lamm. The manuscript for the fifth edition was improved by the suggestions of Reginald Clark, California State University, Fullerton; Karen Lynch Fredericks, St. Anselm College; Norman Friedman, California State University, Los Angeles; Donna Hess, South Dakota State University; Walter Konetschni, Shippensburg University; Alvaro Nieves, Wheaton College; Michael Pearson, University of North Carolina, Charlotte; Han Huy Phan, Mankato State University; Fernando Rodriguez, University of Texas, El Paso; and Gary Sandefor, University of Wisconsin, Madison. My relationship with the publisher has been particularly gratifying because of the professional assistance I received from Alan McClare.

The task of writing and researching is often a lonely one. I have always found it an enriching experience, mostly because of the supportive home I share with my wife, Sandy, and our son, Peter. They know my appreciation and gratitude now as in the past and the future.

Richard T. Schaefer

## Part One

# PERSPECTIVES ON RACIAL AND ETHNIC GROUPS

## Chapter One

# ASPECTS OF MINORITY–MAJORITY RELATIONS

*Chapter Outline*

**What is a Minority Group?**
**Types of Minority Groups**
Racial Groups
Ethnic Groups
Religious Groups
Gender Groups
**Race**
Biological Significance
Social Significance
**Sociology and the Study of Minority Groups**
Stratification
Theoretical Perspectives
**The Creation of Subordinate Group Status**
Voluntary Migration

Involuntary Migration
Annexation
Colonialism
**The Consequences of Subordinate Group Status**
Extermination
Expulsion
Secession
Segregation
Fusion
Assimilation
**The Pluralist Perspective**
**Glancing Back and Looking Ahead**
**Key Terms**
**For Further Information**

---

**❋ HIGHLIGHTS ❋**

*Minority* groups are subordinated in terms of power and privilege to the *majority*, or dominant group. A minority is defined not by being outnumbered but by having five characteristics: distinguishing physical or cultural traits, involuntary membership, in-group marriage, awareness of subordination, and unequal treatment. Minority groups are classified in terms of *race, ethnicity, religion,* and *gender.* The *social* importance of race is significant; its *biological* significance is uncertain. The theoretical perspectives of *functionalism, conflict theory,* and *labeling* offer insights into the sociology of intergroup relations.

Social processes such as *immigration* can be identified as bringing about the existence of subordinate groups. Other processes such as *expulsion* may remove the presence of a subordinate group. Especially significant for race and ethnic relations in the United States today is the distinction between *assimilation* and *pluralism.* The former demands minority group conformity to the dominant group, and the latter implies mutual respect among diverse groups.

---

Eighteen states proclaimed English the official language in a clear reaction to the growing influence of Hispanics. David Duke, a former Klansman, captured 55 percent of the White vote in his unsuccessful effort to become governor of Louisiana. In 1992 a jury freed four White Los Angeles policemen accused of the videotaped beating of Rodney King, a Black man. In response, African-American and Hispanic South-Central Los Angeles residents erupted in violence and hundreds of Korean-owned stores were damaged. Pro-football star Roger Staubach received death threats when he suggested that the Dallas city council election rules should be changed to guarantee minorities a few seats. In Boston, Charles Stuart, a White man who claimed that his pregnant wife had been murdered by a Black male, turned out to be the actual killer, but not before massive police raids had taken place in African-American neighborhoods. Despite the United States being allied with several Arab nations, the U.S. Commission on Civil Rights documented an unprecedented rise in harassment of Arab Americans during the 1991 Persian Gulf War.

These tensions arise in an extremely diverse nation as shown in the accompanying Table 1.1. Presently, 15 percent of the population are members of racial minorities and another 9 percent are Hispanic. This represents 1 out of 4 without counting White ethnic groups. Already in 15 of the largest 28 cities Whites are outnumbered by African Americans, Hispanics, and Asian Americans. The trend is toward even greater diversity. Between 1990 and 2010, the population in the United States is expected to grow by 42 million. Hispanics will account for 47 percent of this growth, Blacks 22 percent, Asians and other minorities 18

**TABLE 1.1**  Racial and Ethnic Groups in the United States, 1990

| Classification | Number in Thousands | Percent of Total Population |
| --- | --- | --- |
| *Racial Groups* | | |
| Whites | 199,686 | 80.3 |
| Blacks/African Americans | 29,986 | 12.1 |
| American Indians, Eskimos, Aleuts | 1,959 | 0.8 |
| Chinese | 1,645 | 0.7 |
| Filipinos | 1,407 | 0.6 |
| Japanese | 848 | 0.3 |
| Asian Indians | 815 | 0.3 |
| Koreans | 799 | 0.3 |
| Vietnamese | 615 | 0.2 |
| Laotians | 149 | 0.1 |
| Cambodians | 147 | 0.1 |
| *Ethnic Groups* | | |
| White ancestry | | |
| Germans | 17,160 | 7.9 |
| British and Scottish | 13,116 | 6.1 |
| Irish | 9,760 | 4.5 |
| Italians | 6,110 | 2.8 |
| Poles | 3,498 | 1.6 |
| French | 3,047 | 1.4 |
| Jews | 5,935 | 2.6 |
| Hispanics | 22,354 | 9.1 |
| Chicanos/Mexican Americans | 13,496 | 5.4 |
| Puerto Ricans | 2,728 | 1.0 |
| Cubans | 1,044 | 0.4 |
| Other | 5,086 | 2.0 |
| Total (all groups) | 248,710 | — |

*Note*: Percentages do not total 100 percent since overlap between groups exists (e.g., White Hispanics or Polish American Jews). Data on White ancestry are for 1979. Data on Jews are for 1988.

*Sources*: Bureau of the Census, 1982a, 1991a, 1991b.

47 percent of this growth, Blacks 22 percent, Asians and other minorities 18 percent, and Whites 13 percent (Mullins, 1991).

Race and ethnicity even emerges outside the worlds of politics and economics. The 1991 World Series pitted the Atlanta Braves against the Minnesota Twins. Despite protests by Native American groups, Braves' fans continued their "tomahawk chop" gesture to show support for their professional baseball team. A review of high school nicknames revealed the following derisive terms used by high schools in 1991: Redskins, Orientals, Wops, Sheiks, and Savages to name a few (Dorsey, 1991).

These tensions between racial and ethnic groups are a worldwide phenomenon. Neo-Nazis in Germany are openly seeking advice from the Ku Klux Klan in the United States on driving out foreigners who seek asylum in that European nation. In Japan, Koreans legally residing there are barred from being schoolteachers or holding government jobs. In Montreal, although long the head-quarters for restoring rights to the French-speaking minority in Canada, the Black Coalition has been formed to end police injustices to that city's 200,000 Blacks from Caribbean countries. In the People's Republic of China, Chinese university students rioted, protesting the dating of local women by African students.

Dealing with intergroup hostility is becoming increasingly complex. By 1990, people in the United States were speaking out against racial hatred and laws were passed giving special penalties to actions reflecting racial or ethnic bias. Critics of these efforts created the label *politically correct* to refer to many of the efforts on behalf of racial, ethnic, and religious minorities, and women. The controversy emerged especially on college campuses where courses were introduced and sometimes required on issues of racial diversity. Opponents said these "PC" moves were watering-down the curriculum. In some instances students and even faculty were punished for offensive racist and sexist comments or actions raising serious concerns about freedom of expression. Where does the First Amendment protecting the freedom of speech end and unacceptable bigotry begin?

It is within this complex social context both in the United States and throughout the world that we will examine the nature of racial and ethnic groups.

## WHAT IS A MINORITY GROUP?

Identifying a minority in a society would seem to be a simple enough task—single out the group with fewer members. In the United States, those groups readily identified as minorities—Blacks and American Indians, for example—are outnumbered by non-Blacks and non-American Indians. But minority status is not necessarily the result of being outnumbered. A social minority need not be a mathematical one. A *minority group* is a subordinate group whose members have significantly less control or power over their own lives than the members of a dominant or majority group. Although reference to size and relative concentrations of peoples will be made, for our purposes *minority* should be taken as synonymous with *subordinate* and *dominant* will be used interchangeably with *majority*.

Confronted with evidence that a particular minority in the United States is subordinate to the will and whim of the majority, some individuals will respond, "Why not? After all, this is a democracy, and so majority rules." The subordination of a minority, however, is more than its inability to rule over society. A member of a subordinate or minority group experiences a narrowing of life's opportunities—for success, education, wealth, the pursuit of happiness—that goes beyond any personal shortcoming he or she may have. A minority group does not share in proportion to its numbers in what a given society, such as the United States, defines as valuable.

Being superior in numbers does not guarantee a group control over its destiny and assure it of majority status. In many societies the numerical majority is dominated by the numerical minority. In the Republic of South Africa, fewer than one in five people are White, but they dominate the Black and Asian people. Since 1948, the descendants of White Europeans have erected a system that subjugates more than 80 percent of the population politically, economically, socially, and legally. Particularly in countries that until recently have been colonies (such as those in Africa, Asia, and the islands of the Caribbean and Oceania), the indigenous peoples who constitute the minority outnumber the dominant Europeans. But we do not even have to leave the United States to find a few creating inequality for the many. In 1920, the majority of people in Mississippi and South Carolina were African American, but in no way did African Americans have as much significant control over their lives as Whites, let alone control of the states of Mississippi and South Carolina. Throughout the United States are counties or neighborhoods today in which the majority of people are African American or Native American or Hispanic, but White Americans are the dominant force. Nationally, 51.2 percent of the population is female, but males still dominate the positions of authority and wealth well in excess of their numbers.

A minority or subordinate group has five characteristics: distinguishing physical or cultural traits, unequal treatment, involuntary membership, awareness of subordination, and in-group marriage (Wagley and Harris, 1958, pp. 4–11).

1. Members of a minority group share physical or cultural characteristics that distinguish them from the dominant group such as skin color or language. Each society has its own arbitrary standard for determining which characteristics are most important in defining dominant and minority groups.

2. Members of a minority experience unequal treatment and have less power over their lives than members of a dominant group have over theirs. Social inequality may be created or maintained by prejudice, discrimination, segregation, or even extermination.

3. Membership in a dominant or minority group is not voluntary: people are born into the group. A person does not chose to be an African American or White.

4. Minority group members have a strong sense of group solidarity. William Graham Sumner, writing in 1906, noted that individuals make distinctions between members of their own group (the *in-group*) and everyone else (the *out-group*). When a group is the object of long-term prejudice and discrimination, the feeling of "us versus them" can and often does become extremely intense.

5. Members of a minority generally marry others from the same group. A member of a dominant group is often unwilling to join a supposedly inferior minority by marrying one of its members. In addition, the minority group's sense of solidarity encourages marriages within the group and discourages marriages to outsiders.

# TYPES OF MINORITY GROUPS

There are four types of minority groups. All four, except where noted, have the five properties outlined in the previous section. The four criteria for classifying minority groups are race, ethnicity, religion, and gender.

## Racial Groups

The term *racial groups* is reserved for those minorities, and corresponding majorities, who are classified according to obvious physical differences. Notice the two crucial words in the definition, *obvious* and *physical*. What is obvious? Hair color? Shape of an earlobe? Presence of body hair? Each society defines that which is obvious. In the United States, skin color is one obvious difference. On a cold winter day with clothing covering all but one's face, however, skin color may be less obvious than hair color, but people in the United States have learned informally that skin color is important and hair color is unimportant. We need to say more than that. In the United States a person is classified and classifies himself as either Black or White; there is no in-between except for people readily identified as Native Americans or Asians.

Other societies use skin color as a standard but may have a more elaborate system of classification. In Brazil, where hostility among races is less than in the United States, numerous categories identify people on the basis of skin color. In the United States, a person is Black or White; in Brazil a variety of terms, such as *cafuso, mazombo, preto,* and *escuro,* are applied to describe various combinations of skin color, facial features, and hair texture. That which makes differences obvious is subject to a society's definition (van den Berghe, 1978, p. 71).

The designation of a racial group emphasizes physical differences as opposed to cultural distinctions. For the next type of minority group, culture is the primary distinguishing feature. In the United States, minority races include Blacks, American Indians, Japanese Americans, Chinese Americans, Filipinos, Hawaiians, and other Asian peoples. The issue of race and racial differences has been an important one, not only in the United States but throughout the sphere of European influence. Later in this chapter, we will examine race and its significance more closely.

## Ethnic Groups

Minority groups who are designated by their ethnicity are differentiated from the dominant group on the basis of cultural differences such as language, attitudes toward marriage and parenting, food habits, and so forth. *Ethnic groups,* therefore, are groups set apart from others because of their national origin or distinctive cultural patterns.

Ethnic groups in the United States include a grouping that we refer to collectively as Hispanics or Latinos, including Chicanos, Puerto Ricans, Cubans, and

### ❖ LISTEN TO THEIR VOICES ❖

#### Problem of the Color-Line

*William E. B. DuBois*

*William E. B. DuBois made the following remarks in his address to the Pan-African Conference in London in 1900.*

In the metropolis of the modern world, in this the closing year of the nineteenth century, there has been assembled a congress of men and women of African blood, to deliberate solemnly upon the present situation and outlook of the darker races of mankind. The problem of the twentieth century is the problem of the color-line, the question as to how far differences of race—which show themselves chiefly in the color of the skin and the texture of the hair—will hereafter be made the basis of denying to over half the world the right of sharing to their utmost ability the opportunities and privileges of modern civilization . . .

Let the world take no backward step in that slow but sure progress which has successively refused to let the spirit of class, of caste, of privilege, or of birth, debar from life, liberty and the pursuit of happiness a striving human soul.

Let not color or race be a feature of distinction between white and black men, regardless of worth or ability. . . .

Thus we appeal with boldness and confidence to the Great Powers of the civilized world, trusting in the wide spirit of humanity, and the deep sense of justice of our age, for a generous recognition of the righteousness of our cause.

From *An ABC of Color*, pp. 20–21, 23, by W. E. B. DuBois. Copyright 1969 by International Publishers. Reprinted by permission.

---

other Latin Americans in the United States. White ethnics are also included in this category—Irish Americans, Polish Americans, Norwegian Americans.

The cultural traits that make groups distinctive usually originate from the "homeland" or, for Jews, from a long history of being segregated and prohibited from becoming a part of the host society. Once in the United States, an ethnic group may maintain distinctive cultural practices through associations and clubs. Ethnic enclaves such as a Little Italy or a Greektown in urban areas also perpetuate cultural distinctiveness.

Racial groups discussed in the preceding section may also have distinctive not their cultural differences generally prove to be the barrier to acceptance by the host society. For example, Chinese Americans who are faithful Protestants and know the names of all the members of the Baseball Hall of Fame may well be bearers of American culture, but they are still a minority, because they are seen as physically different.

Ethnicity has proven to be less significant than race in contemporary societies. Almost a century ago, African American sociologist W. E. B. DuBois, addressing an audience in London, called attention to the overwhelming importance of the color-line throughout the world. In "Listen to Their Voices" we hear the words of the first Black person to receive a doctorate from Harvard, who later helped to organize the NAACP. DuBois' observations give us a historical perspective on the struggle for equality. In the chapters to come, we will learn more about this struggle and, from this vantage point, we can look ahead—knowing how far we have come and speculating how much further we have yet to go (Stanfield, 1988).

## Religious Groups

The third basis for minority group status is association with a religion other than the dominant faith. In the United States, Protestants outnumber members of all other religions, although Protestantism is divided into numerous denominations and splinter groups. Roman Catholics form the largest minority religion, and it may seem inappropriate to consider them as a minority. Chapter 5, focusing on Roman Catholics and other minority faiths, details how all five properties of a minority group apply to such faiths in the United States. Other religious minorities include such groups as the Church of Jesus Christ of Latter-Day Saints (the Mormons), the Hutterites, the Amish, and cults or sects associated with such things as doomsday prophecy, demon worship, or use of snakes in a ritualistic fashion. Jews are excluded from this category and placed among ethnic groups because in their case, culture is a more important defining trait than religious dogma. Jewish Americans, discussed in Chapter 15, share a cultural tradition that goes beyond theology. In this sense, it is appropriate to view them as an ethnic group rather than as members of a religious faith.

## Gender Groups

The final attribute that divides dominant and subordinate groups is gender—males are the social majority; females, although more numerous, are relegated to the position of the social minority. Women are a minority even though they do not exhibit all the characteristics outlined earlier (there is, for example, little in-group marriage). Women encounter prejudice and discrimination and are physically visible. Group membership is involuntary, and many women are developing a sense of sisterhood.

Women who are members of racial and ethnic minorities face a special challenge to achieving equality. They suffer from "double jeopardy" because they

Women who are members of racial and ethnic minorities face a special challenge to achieving equality. They suffer from "double jeopardy" because they belong to two separate minority groups—a racial or ethnic group plus a subordinate gender group. Even this may not totally define their deprivation since many women in racial minorities are also fixed in the lowest economic segment of society, placing them in "triple jeopardy."

## RACE

*Race* has many meanings for many people. Probably the only thing about race that is clear is that we are confused about the origins and proper use of the term.

### Biological Significance

Race has a precise biological meaning. A *biological race* is a genetically isolated group characterized by a high degree of inbreeding that leads to distinctive gene frequencies. This distinctiveness is made most apparent by the presence of hereditary physical characteristics that differentiate members of a group from other human groups. This definition corresponds closely to that adopted in the 1950 UNESCO Statement on Race (Montagu, 1972, p. 40).

It is very difficult to consider race in a strictly biological sense. Even among proponents in the past, there were endless debates over what were the races of the world. Given people's frequent migration, exploration, and invasions, pure genetic types have not existed for some time, if they ever did. There are no mutually exclusive races. Skin color among African Americans varies tremendously, as it does among White Americans. There is even an overlapping of dark-skinned Whites and light-skinned African Americans.

Biologically there are no pure, distinct races. For example, blood type cannot determine racial groups with any accuracy. Furthermore, applying pure racial types to humans is problematic because of interbreeding. Despite raised eyebrows about Black-White marriages, a large number of Whites have African-American ancestry. Scientists, using various techniques, maintain that the proportion of African Americans with White ancestry is between 20 to 75 percent (Herskovits, 1930, p. 15; Roberts, 1955). Despite the wide range of these estimates, the mixed ancestry of today's Blacks and Whites is part of the biological reality of race.

Though race is not a useful biological category, it is clear that certain sizeable groups of humans share similar physical traits. Do members of such groups have different innate abilities to think or reason? Is there a relationship between intelligence and race? Much of the scientific discussion begins with the difficulty in measuring intelligence through some form of test.

A test of intelligence must depend on some verbal or written ability. The concern about so-called IQ tests is that they reward a person who has a particular economic or cultural background. One example of culture bias from an IQ test is the question, "Your mother sends you to the store to get a loaf of bread. The store is closed. What should you do?" The "correct" answer is to go to the nearest store and try again. For a rural youth, however, the next store may be miles away, and for the inner-city youth, the next store may not be willing to extend his family credit. Unlike the middle-class child, for both the farm and inner-city youths the proper response might be to return home—an answer that would be marked incorrect (Kagan, 1971, pp. 92–93).

The term IQ stands for *intelligence quotient,* that is, the ratio of an individual's mental age (as computed by an IQ test) divided by his or her chronological age. This quotient is multiplied by 100 to eliminate the decimals. Thus, a young woman with a mental age of 24 who is 20 years old would be evaluated as having an IQ of 120 ($24 \div 20 = 1.20 \times 100 = 120$). An IQ of 100 is the average or norm because it would be the result of one's mental age equaling one's chronological age.

Of course, intelligence cannot be observed directly in the same way that we observe height or measured precisely in the way that we compute time. In practice, intelligence is defined operationally by the measurement procedure used to assess it. In other words, intelligence is whatever intelligence tests measure. There is, therefore, continuing uncertainty about whether intelligence tests measure intelligence or simply skill in taking such tests.

In addition, performance on standardized tests, including IQ tests themselves, does reflect a certain cultural upbringing. These tests have less predictive value for children who are in any way alienated from the cultural mainstream. Children, for example, who come from lower-income households or whose parents do not speak English are at a distinct disadvantage in taking tests that are more suitable for children raised in middle-class families. Scores have been shown to change significantly due to environmental influences such as parenting skills and educational programs, which argues against the argument of innate inheritability of intelligence (R. Weinberg, 1989).

Intelligence tests have been scrutinized because of the role they often play in evaluation of students. To base any type of judgment on placement in school or counseling for a future job on the alleged link between race and IQ would be foolish as well as unscientific. Such judgments would lead one to mistakenly select a person from a so-called superior group who actually is less able to perform than a person from an imputed inferior group. After reviewing many studies of heritability of intelligence, the great majority of scientists contend that within-group differences are greater than between-group differences.

Standardized testing has been accepted in the twentieth century, with such examinations as the ACT and SAT being used in the last 40 years in the United States as a major criterion for admission to colleges. In the late 1980s testing grew in importance despite criticisms of cultural, linguistic, and class biases. Under the guise of "education reform," state governments have taken up the use of "measures" and "outcomes" that provide "accountability" and "assessment." While the direction of this reform is unclear, it has meant reliance on test-based profiles even greater than had been the case before standardized tests were called into question.

## Social Significance

Whatever significance race has biologically is overwhelmed by the effect that membership in a certain race has on the interaction of people. The 1950 UNESCO Statement on Race maintained that, "for all practical social purposes 'race' is not so much a biological phenomenon as a social myth" (Montagu, 1972, p. 118). Adolph Hitler expressed concern over the "Jewish race" and translated this concern into Nazi death camps. Winston Churchill spoke proudly of the "British race" and used that pride to spur a nation to fight. Evidently race was a useful political tool for two rather different leaders in the 1940s.

People speculate that if human groups have obvious physical differences, then they must have corresponding mental or personality differences. No one disagrees that people differ in temper, potential to learn, sense of humor, and so on. But in its social sense race implies that groups that differ physically also bear distinctive emotional and mental abilities or disabilities. Such beliefs are based on the notion that humankind can be divided into distinct groups, and we have already seen the difficulties associated with pigeonholing people into racial categories. Despite these difficulties, belief in the inheritance of behavior patterns and in an association between physical and cultural traits is widespread. When this belief is coupled with the feeling that certain groups or races are inherently superior to others it is called *racism*. Racism is a doctrine of racial supremacy, that one race is superior.

We questioned the biological significance of race in the previous section. In modern complex industrial societies we find little adaptive utility in the presence or absence of prominent chins, epicanthic folds of the eyelids, or the comparative amount of melanin in the skin. What is important is not that people are genetically different but that they approach one another with dissimilar perspectives. It is in the social setting that race is decisive. It is significant because people have given it significance.

Racist ideology reached its peak in the nineteenth century, when European empires stretched throughout Africa and Asia. Racism is not to be confused with colonialism, or, for that matter, with slavery, although it was a convenient rationalization for both. Slavery and colonialism predated the development of a racist ideology. People fought, killed, and enslaved other people, but did so out of a sense of national or tribal pride. Only in the last 150 years has the objection to people on the basis of race been forcibly expressed as an allegedly scientifically based idea.

The popularity of the theory of evolution, replacing the belief in the biblical or special creation of humankind, led in the late nineteenth century to *Social Darwinism*—the belief that societies and races (in place of species) are engaged in a struggle for existence in which the more fit will survive. According to Social Darwinism, certain races have survived because of their superiority and there-

*The social significance of race is particularly evident when the result is death. The NAACP staged a protest parade in New York City in 1917 to demonstrate against violence toward Blacks. Banners in the parade read, "Mothers, do lynchers go to heaven?" and "Mr. President, why not make America safe for democracy?"*

fore are destined to maintain their dominance over other, allegedly inferior, human races. Europeans thought that the most fit to survive were, as one might expect, Europeans. Racism led to proposals for multiplication of superiors, race cleansing, race building, and the elimination of inferiors.

Although such notions were supposedly based on his theory of evolution, Darwin himself gave little scientific support to the belief that some races had outdistanced others in evolution. Darwin's first work, *Origin of Species* (1859), touched off much of the "scientific expression" of racial differences. In his later work, *The Descent of Man,* he rejected classifying humankind, because he saw no way to give names (racial classifications) to objects (races) he could not define (1874, p. 203). More recently, the 1950 UNESCO statement concluded that there is no proof that human groups "differ in their innate mental characteristics, whether in respect of intelligence or temperament" (Montagu, 1972, p. 121).

Fear that any societal change will lead to a lowering of living standards finds expression in concern over the mixing of races. Racist theorists maintain that the mixing of races led to the eventual decline of humankind. This belief is contrary to the truth; the offspring from racial mixing are just as likely to be superior in genetic makeup to their parents as if their parents were of the same race. History indicates that the contact and subsequent interbreeding of different peoples, not their separation, contributed to the emergence of the ancient Egyptian culture, built by a mixture of Mediterranean, Negroid, and Armenoid peoples, among others. Similar mixing of peoples led to the Incan, Mayan, Mesopotamian, and Greek civilizations.

Race cannot be used in a scientific or biological manner. Human beings cannot be classified into mutually exclusive categories, nor is there evidence that physical differences make some groups of people more talented than others. Racists steadfastly maintain that certain races are superior to others in order to justify exploiting those people they identify as inferior.

## SOCIOLOGY AND THE STUDY OF MINORITY GROUPS

Before proceeding further with our study of racial and ethnic groups, let us consider several sociological perspectives that provide insight into understanding minority-majority relationships.

### Stratification

All societies are characterized by members having unequal amounts of wealth, prestige, or power. Sociologists observe that entire groups may be assigned to have less or more of what a society values. The hierarchy that emerges is *stratification.* Stratification, therefore, is the structured ranking of entire groups of people that perpetuates unequal rewards and power in a society.

Much discussion of stratification identifies the *class,* or social ranking of people who share similar wealth, according to sociologist Max Weber's classic definition (Gerth and Mills, 1958). While boundaries between classes may not be clearly defined, mobility from one class to another is not necessarily easy. Movement into classes of greater wealth may be particularly difficult for subordinate group members faced with lifelong prejudice and discrimination.

Recall that the second property of subordinate group standing is unequal treatment from the dominant group in the form of prejudice, discrimination, and segregation. Stratification is intertwined with subordination of racial, ethnic, religious, and gender groups. Sociologist Thomas Pettigrew (1981) refers to the *interactive effect* of race and class. Race has implications for the way people are treated; so does class, but one also has to add the two together. For example, being poor *and* Black is not the same as being either one. Similarly, a wealthy Chicano is not the same as an affluent Anglo or Chicanos in general. The *interactive effect* requires that the race, class, and race and class acting together most accurately explain the total condition of individual members of subordinate groups.

## Theoretical Perspectives

Sociologists view society in different ways. Some see the world basically as a stable and ongoing entity. They are impressed with the endurance of a Chinatown, the relative sameness of male-female roles over time, and other aspects of intergroup relations. Some sociologists see society as composed of many groups in conflict, competing for scarce resources.

Within this conflict, some people or even entire groups may be labeled or stigmatized in a way that blocks access to obtaining what a society values. We will examine three theoretical perspectives that are widely used by sociologists today—functionalist, conflict, and labeling perspectives.

*Functionalist Perspective.* In the view of a functionalist, society is like a living organism in which each part contributes to the survival of the whole. Therefore, the *functionalist perspective* emphasizes the way in which parts of a society are structured to maintain its stability. According to this approach, if an aspect of social life does not contribute to society's stability or survival—if it does not serve some identifiably useful function—it will not be passed on from one generation to the next.

It would seem reasonable to assume that bigotry between races offers no such positive function, and so why, we ask, does it persist? The functionalist, although agreeing that racial hostility is hardly to be admired, would point out that it does serve some positive functions from the perspectives of racists. Manning Nash (1962) describes four functions that racial beliefs have for the dominant group. First, such ideologies provide moral justification for maintaining a society that routinely deprives a group of its rights and privileges. Southern Whites justified slavery by believing that Africans were physically and spiritually subhuman and devoid of souls (Hoebel, 1949, pp. 85–86). Second, racist beliefs discourage subordinate people from attempting to question their lowly status, for to do so is to question the very foundations of the society. Third, racial beliefs provide a cause to which political action can be allied and focus social uncertainty on a specific threat. Racial ideologies not only justify existing practices but serve as rallying cries for social movements, as seen in the rise of the Nazi party. Fourth, racial myths encourage support for the existing order by introducing the argument that if there were any major societal change, the minority would suffer greater poverty and the majority would suffer lower living standards. As a result, Nash feels racial ideology grows when a value system (for example, that underlying a colonial empire or slavery) is being threatened.

There are also definite *dysfunctions* to prejudice and discrimination. Dysfunctions are an element of society that may disrupt a social system or tend to decrease its stability. Arnold Rose outlined seven ways in which racism is dysfunctional to a society and even its dominant group (1951, pp. 19–24).

1. A society that practices discrimination fails to use the resources of all individuals. Discrimination limits the search for talent and leadership to the dominant group.

2. Discrimination aggravates social problems such as poverty, delinquency, and crime and places the financial burden to alleviate these problems on the dominant group.
3. Society must invest a good deal of time and money to defend its barriers to full participation of all members.
4. Goodwill and friendly diplomatic relations between nations are often undercut by racial prejudice and discrimination.
5. Communication between groups restricted. Little accurate knowledge of the minority and its culture is available to the society at large.
6. Social change is inhibited since it may contribute to assisting the minority.
7. Discrimination promotes disrespect for law enforcement and peaceful settlement of disputes.

These costs may seem small compared to the price paid for subordinate group membership. They do, however, remind us that intergroup conflict is exceedingly complex.

*Conflict Perspective.* In contrast to the functionalists' emphasis on stability, conflict sociologists see the social world as in continual struggle. The *conflict perspective* assumes that social behavior is best understood in terms of conflict or tension among competing groups. Such conflicts need not be physically violent, and may take the form of immigration restrictions, real estate practices, or disputes over cuts in the federal budget.

The conflict model is often selected today when examining race and ethnicity, because it readily accounts for the presence of tension between competing groups. The competition, according to the conflict perspective, takes place between groups with unequal amounts of economic and political power. The minorities are exploited by the dominant group or, at the very best, ignored. The conflict perspective also tends to be viewed as more radical and activist than functionalism, because conflict theorists emphasize social change and redistribution of resources. Functionalists are not necessarily in favor of such inequality; rather their approach, as with Nash's analysis of racial beliefs, helps us to understand why such systems persist.

Those who follow the conflict approach in race and ethnicity have repeatedly remarked that the subordinate group is criticized for its low status, whereas the responsibilities of the dominant group for the subordination are often ignored. William Ryan (1976) calls this an instance of "blaming the victim": portraying the problems of racial and ethnic minorities as their fault rather than recognizing society's responsibility. This idea is not new. Gunnar Myrdal, a Swedish social economist of international reputation, headed a project that produced the classic 1944 work on Blacks in the United States, *The American Dilemma.* Myrdal concluded that the plight of the subordinate group is the responsibility of the dominant majority. It is not a Black problem, but a White problem. Similarly, it is not a Hispanic problem or a Haitian refugee problem, but a White problem. He and others since then have reminded the public and policy makers alike that the ultimate responsibility for society's problems must rest with those who possess the most authority and economic resources (Southern, 1987).

*Labeling Approach.* Related to the conflict perspective and its concern over the victim's taking the blame is labeling theory. *Labeling theory,* introduced by sociologist Howard Becker, is an attempt to explain why certain people are viewed as different or less worthy and others are not. Students of crime and deviance have relied heavily on labeling theory. A youth who misbehaves, according to labeling theory, may be considered a delinquent if he comes from the "wrong kind of family," whereas another youth, this time one from a middle-class family, who commits the same sort of misbehavior will be given another chance.

The labeling perspective directs our attention to the role that stereotypes play in race and ethnicity. The image that prejudiced people maintain of a group toward which they hold ill feelings is called a *stereotype.* Stereotypes are exaggerated images of the characteristics of a particular group. The term stereotype was coined by columnist Walter Lippmann (1922, pp. 95–156), who called them pictures in our heads. In Chapter 2, we will review some of the research on the stereotyping of minorities. This labeling is not limited to racial and ethnic groups, however. Age, for instance, can be used to exclude a person from an activity in which he or she is actually qualified to engage. Groups are subjected to stereotypes and discrimination in such a way that they resemble social minorities. Social prejudice exists toward ex-convicts, gamblers, alcoholics, lesbians, homosexual men, prostitutes, and marijuana smokers (Spiegel and Keith-Spiegel, 1973; Simmons, 1969).

People who deviate physically or mentally from a society's standards also are seen as different and are generally subjected to second-class treatment, such as being labeled as unemployable. The physically handicapped, the blind, the deformed, the epileptic, the diabetic, the deaf, the mentally ill, and the mentally retarded are cast out from the mainstream of society. It is important to remember that racial and ethnic minority groups are not the only ones who encounter prejudice and discrimination. Although we here limit ourselves to discussing dominant and subordinate groups, we must, in our daily lives, be mindful of other groups who suffer from arbitrary placement in our social hierarchy.

The labeling approach points out that stereotypes, when applied by people in power, can have very negative consequences for people or groups falsely identified. A crucial aspect of the relationship between dominant and subordinate groups is the prerogative of the dominant group to define society's values. American sociologist William I. Thomas (1923, pp. 41–44), an early critic of racial and sexual differences, saw that the "definition of the situation" could mold the personality of the individual. In other words, Thomas observed that people respond not only to the objective features of a situation (or person) but also to the meaning it has for them. In this manner, we can create false images or stereotypes that become real in their consequences.

In certain situations, we may respond to stereotypes and act on them, with the result that false definitions become accurate. This is known as a *self-fulfilling prophecy.* A person or group described as having particular characteristics begins to display the very traits that were said to exist. Thus, a child who is praised for being a "natural comic" may focus on learning to become funny in order to gain approval and attention.

Self-fulfilling prophecies can be especially devastating for minority groups (see Figure 1.1). Such groups often find that they are allowed to hold only low-paying jobs with little prestige or opportunity for advancement. The rationale of the dominant society is that these minority individuals lack the ability to perform in more important and lucrative positions. Minority-group individuals are then denied the training needed to become scientists, executives, or physicians and are locked into society's inferior jobs. As a result, the false definition becomes real; in terms of employment, the minority has become inferior because it was defined at the start as inferior and prevented thereby from achieving equality.

Because of this vicious circle, a talented minority individual may come to see the worlds of entertainment and professional sports as his or her only hopes for achieving wealth and fame. Thus, it is no accident that successive waves of Irish, Jewish, Italian, African American, and Hispanic performers and athletes have made their mark on American culture. Unfortunately, these very successes may convince the dominant group that its original stereotypes were valid—that these are the only areas of society in which minorities can excel. Furthermore, athletics and arts are well known in our society as highly competitive areas. For every Michael Jordan and Oprah Winfrey who makes it, many, many more will end up disappointed.

In the 1960s and 1970s, many subordinate minorities in the United States rejected traditional definitions and replaced them with feelings of pride, power, and strength. "Black is beautiful" and "Red power" movements were efforts by African Americans and Native Americans to take control of their own lives and self-images. Although a minority can make a determined effort to redefine a situation and resist stereotypes, the definition or label that remains most important is the one used by society's most powerful groups. In this case, the traditional White, Anglo-Saxon, Protestant norms of the United States still shape American definitions and stereotypes of racial and ethnic minorities (Allport, 1958, pp. 155–166; Merton, 1968, pp. 475–490; Myrdal, 1944, pp. 75–78, 1065–1070).

## THE CREATION OF SUBORDINATE GROUP STATUS

Four situations are likely to lead to the formation of a subordinate group–dominant group relationship. A subordinate group emerges through (1) voluntary migration, (2) involuntary migration, (3) annexation, and (4) colonialism (Mack, 1968, pp. 227–228).

### Voluntary Migration

People who immigrate to a new country often find themselves a minority in that new country. The immigrant is set apart from the dominant group by cultural or physical traits or religious affiliation. Immigration from Europe, Asia, and

---

**FIGURE 1.1**   Self-Fulfilling Prophecy

The self-validating effects of majority-group definitions are shown in this figure. The minority-group individual (MGI) attends a poorly financed school and is left unequipped to perform jobs that offer high status and pay. He or she then gets a low-paying job and must settle for a standard of living far short of society's standards. Since the person shares these standards, he or she may begin to feel self-doubt and self-hatred.

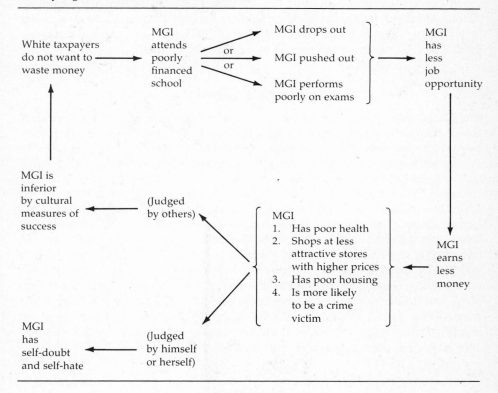

---

Latin America has been a powerful force in shaping the fabric of life in the United States. *Migration* is the general term to describe any transfer of population. *Emigration* (by emigrants) describes leaving a country to settle in another; *immigration* (by immigrants) denotes coming into the new country. From Vietnam's perspective the boat people were emigrants to the United States, where they were counted among this nation's immigrants.

Although people may come voluntarily, leaving the home country is not always voluntary. Throughout human history, people have been displaced by conflict or war. In the twentieth century we have seen huge population movements caused by two world wars; revolutions in Spain, Hungary, and Cuba; the partition of British India; conflicts in Southeast Asia, Korea, and Central America; and the confrontation between Arabs and Israelis. Economic disasters can also lead to human migrations. The potato crop failure of the 1840s (commonly referred to as the potato famine) forced millions of Irish and German people out of their home countries.

In all types of movement, even those that cause an American family to move from Ohio to Florida, two sets of forces operate—*push* factors and *pull* factors. Push factors discourage a person from remaining where he or she lives. Religious persecution and economic factors such as dissatisfaction with employment opportunities are possible push factors. Pull factors, such as a better standard of living, friends and relatives who have already emigrated, and a promised job, attract an immigrant to a particular country.

## Involuntary Migration

The forced movement of people into another society guarantees a subordinate role. Because they have been brought as slaves or indentured servants, their position as minority group members it understood from the beginning. Involuntary migration is no longer common; although enslavement has a long history, all industrial societies today prohibit such practices. Of course, many contemporary societies bear today the legacy of enforced labor.

In some instances we might include contract laborers and indentured servants among involuntary migrants. Such workers generally participate in the transfer freely, but coercion is at times involved. Unlike slaves, contract laborers and indentured servants could return home at the end of a specified period, but historically many remained, forming the beginnings of a new group with minority status. Despite the possibility of freedom, life for these people was hardly ideal. Importation of laborers from India to British Guiana and Trinidad and from China, Japan, Portugal, and the Philippines to Hawaii often involved conditions little better than those that afflicted people in bondage (Harrell-Bond, 1988; Petersen, 1958; Schermerhorn, 1970, pp. 98–99).

## Annexation

Nations, particularly during wars or as a result of war, will incorporate or attach land. This new land is *contiguous* to the nation, as in the German occupation of Europe in the 1940s and the Louisiana Purchase of 1803. The Treaty of Guadalupe Hidalgo that ended the Mexican-American War in 1848 gave the United States California, Utah, Nevada, most of New Mexico, and parts of Arizona, Wyoming, and Colorado. The indigenous people in some of this huge territory were dominant in their society one day only to become minority group members the next.

When annexation occurs, the dominant power generally suppresses the language and culture of the minority. Such was the practice of Russia with the Ukrainians and Poles, and Prussia with the Poles. Minorities try to maintain their cultural integrity despite annexation. The area inhabited by the Poles was

*Haitian "boat people" pictured after having been picked up by the Coast Guard as they sought refuge in Florida in 1992.*

## Colonialism

Colonialism has been the most frequent way for one people to dominate another. *Colonialism* is the maintenance of political, social, economic, and cultural domination over a people by a foreign power for an extended period (W. Bell, 1981). In simple terms, it is rule by outsiders, but unlike annexation does not involve actual incorporation into the dominant people's nation. The long control exercised by the British Empire over much of North America, parts of Africa, and India is an example of colonial domination. The pattern of colonialism on the continent of Africa is illustrated in Figure 1.2.

Societies gain power over a foreign land through military strength, sophisticated political organization, and the massive use of investment capital. The extent of power can also vary according to the extent of settlement by the dominant group in the colonial land. Relations between the colonial nation and the colonized people are similar to those between a dominant group and exploited subordinate groups. The colonial subjects are generally limited to menial jobs, and the profits from their labor and from the natural resources of their land benefit the members of the ruling class.

**FIGURE 1.2** Colonialism in Africa, 1914

With the exceptions only of independent Ethiopia and Liberia, the African continent was
divided among seven European countries in 1914.

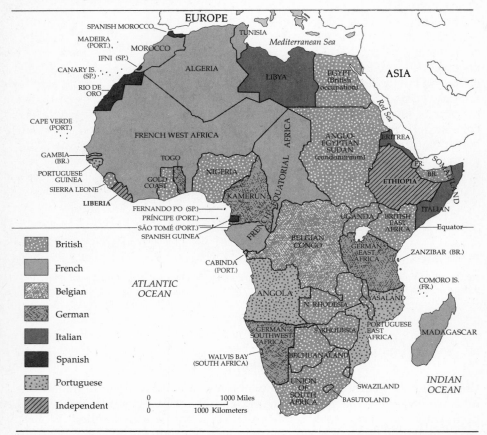

Source: Robert W. July, *A History of the African People*, 3rd ed., New York: Charles Scribner's Sons, 1980, p. 380.

ploited subordinate groups. The colonial subjects are generally limited to menial
jobs, and the profits from their labor and from the natural resources of their land
benefit the members of the ruling class.

By the 1980s, colonialism had largely become a phenomenon of the past. Most
of the world's peoples who were in colonies prior to World War I have achieved
political independence and established their own governments. For many of
these countries, however, the transition to genuine self-rule is not yet complete.
Colonial domination had established patterns of economic exploitation that
continued even after nationhood was achieved, in part because former colonies

were unable to develop their own industry and technology. Their dependence on more industrialized nations, including their former colonial masters, for managerial and technical expertise, investment capital, and manufactured goods kept former colonies in a subservient position. Such continuing dependence and foreign domination is known as *neocolonialism* (Wallerstein, 1979).

The economic and political consequences of colonialism and neocolonialism are quite evident, but these forms of domination also have an important cultural component. Conflict theorists, as we saw earlier, stress the way in which groups are exploited, and this influence can easily reach across national boundaries. The colonized people lose their native values and distinctive identity and begin to identify with the culture of the colonial power. The mother tongue of the country is not used and is even hidden as people attempt to emulate the colonizers (Memmi, 1967, pp. 105–108). Therefore, in the view of opponents of contemporary neocolonialism, every consumer product, film, or television program exported or designed by an industrial nation is an attack on the traditions and cultural autonomy of the dependent people in less-developed countries (Emerson, 1968; McPhail, 1981, pp. 244–245; Schramm et al., 1981).

## THE CONSEQUENCES OF SUBORDINATE GROUP STATUS

There are several consequences for a group of subordinate status. These differ in their degree of harshness, ranging from physical annihilation to absorption into the dominant group. In this section we will examine six consequences of minority group status: extermination, expulsion, secession, segregation, fusion, and assimilation.

### Extermination

The most extreme way of dealing with a subordinate group is eliminating the group itself. One historical example is the British destruction of the people of Tasmania, an island off the coast of Australia. There were 5,000 Tasmanians in 1800, but as the result of being attacked by settlers and forced to die on less habitable islands, the last full-blooded Tasmanian died in 1876. A human group had become extinct, totally eliminated.

Today the term *genocide* is used to describe the deliberate, systematic killing of an entire people or nation. This term is frequently used in reference to the Holocaust—Nazi Germany's extermination of 12 million European Jews and other ethnic minorities during World War II. Genocide, however, also appropriately describes White policies toward Native Americans in the nineteenth century. In 1800 the American Indian population in the United States was about 600,000; by 1850 it had been reduced to 250,000 through warfare with the U.S. cavalry, disease, and forced relocation to inhospitable environments.

*Extermination is the most extreme way to remove minority group members. As a prelude to the "Final Solution" that took more than 6 million lives, Nazi soldiers seize Jews in Warsaw, Poland.*

## Expulsion

Dominant groups may choose to force a specific minority to leave certain areas or even vacate the country. Expulsion is therefore another extreme consequence of minority group status. European colonial powers in North America and eventually the United States government itself drove Native Americans out of their tribal land into territory unfamiliar to the tribes.

More recently, Vietnam in 1979 expelled nearly one million ethnic Chinese from the country, partly as a result of centuries of hostility between the two Asian neighbors. These "boat people" were abruptly eliminated as a minority within Vietnamese society. This expulsion meant, though, that they were now uprooted and a new minority group in many nations from Australia to France, the United States, and Canada. Thus, expulsion may remove a minority group from one society; however, the expelled people merely go to another nation, where they again are a minority group.

## Secession

A group ceases to be a minority when it secedes to form a new nation or moves to an already established nation where it becomes dominant. After Great Britain withdrew from Palestine, Jewish people achieved a dominant position in 1948, attracting Jews from throughout the world to the new state of Israel. In a similar fashion, Pakistan was created in 1947, when India was partitioned. The predominantly Muslim areas in the north became Pakistan, making India predominantly Hindu. Throughout this century minorities have repudiated dominant customs. In this spirit, Estonian, Latvian, Lithuanian, and Armenian peoples, not content with mere toleration by the majority, all seceded to form independent states following the demise of the Soviet Union in 1991.

Some African Americans have called for secession. Suggestions dating back to the early 1700s supported the recolonization of Blacks as a solution to racial problems. The target for colonization of the American Colonization Society was Liberia, but proposals were advanced to establish settlements of freed slaves in Canada, Haiti, South America, and the western United States. Territorial separatism and the emigrationist ideology are recurrent and interrelated themes among African Americans from the late nineteenth century well into the 1980s. The Black Muslims, or Nation of Islam, once expressed the desire for complete separation in their own state or territory within the present borders of the United States. Although secession of Blacks from the United States has not taken place, it has been considered and even attempted in many ways (Bracey, et al., 1970; Butterfield, 1986).

## Segregation

*Segregation* refers to the physical separation of two groups of people in residence, workplace, and social functions. Generally, it is imposed by a dominant group on a subordinate group. Segregation is rarely complete, however; intergroup contact inevitably occurs even in the most segregated societies. South Africa, which we will discuss in detail in Chapter 16, is such a case. Despite rigid residential segregation, South African Blacks and Whites work together and are now beginning to enjoy leisure time activities together.

Housing practices in the United States have often forced subordinate racial and ethnic groups into specific, usually undesirable neighborhoods. In addition, members of a minority group may voluntarily seek to separate themselves from the dominant majority because they fear reprisals.

The extent of racial isolation is staggering especially between Whites and African Americans. Analysis of the 1990 census showed that neighborhood segregation was just as pervasive as in 1960. It is not limited to impoverished inner cities, there are also segregated all-Black middle-class, or affluent, or suburban neighborhoods as well.

In Table 1.2, we present the ten most segregated metropolitan areas, along with selected other major areas, using an index value. This segregation index is a measure of how closely the racial and ethnic makeup of each neighborhood resembles the population mix of the entire metropolitan area. For instance, Detroit has a segregation index of 83 that means that 83% of either minority or White residents would have to move from segregated neighborhoods to achieve

**TABLE 1.2**    Segregation in Metropolitan Areas

The 1990 census provided information on 219 metropolitan areas with the first 10 being the most segregated. The segregation index indicates the percentage of either White or minority residents who would have to move to achieve integration.

| Metropolitan Area | Rank | Segregation Index | Minority Population |
|---|---|---|---|
| Detroit | 1 | 83 | 25% |
| Cleveland | 2 | 82 | 23 |
| Gary-Hammond | 3 | 79 | 28 |
| Buffalo | 4 | 78 | 15 |
| Flint | 5 | 78 | 23 |
| Birmingham | 6 | 76 | 28 |
| Milwaukee | 7 | 76 | 19 |
| Chicago | 8 | 76 | 38 |
| Cincinnati | 9 | 76 | 15 |
| St. Louis | 10 | 76 | 20 |
| New York | 19 | 73 | 52 |
| New Orleans | 38 | 68 | 41 |
| Atlanta | 40 | 67 | 30 |
| Boston | 72 | 62 | 15 |
| Los Angeles-Long Beach | 74 | 62 | 59 |
| Houston | 83 | 60 | 44 |
| Dallas | 86 | 60 | 33 |
| Washington, D.C. | 90 | 59 | 37 |
| Miami-Hialeah | 103 | 58 | 70 |
| San Francisco | 132 | 54 | 42 |

*Source: USA Today,* November 11, 1991, p. 3A.

integration. The residential patterns in the least segregated cities are greatly influenced by the presence of military bases or college housing.

Residential segregation exists for other minorities such as Hispanics and Asians but usually is less pronounced than that for African Americans. One should be cautious not to read too much into this since relatively speaking Hispanics and Asians are more recent migrants to urban areas which may explain some of the present differences. The pattern of segregation is growing also among these minorities. In any event, as shown in Table 1.2, even in Miami which ranks near the middle at 103, 58% of its mostly Hispanic minority would have to relocate to overcome current segregation patterns (Massey and Denton, 1989; Usdansky, 1991).

Residential segregation patterns are not unique to the United States. In Germany today they speak of "Ghettoisierung" (or "ghettoization") as concentrations of Turkish immigrants are emerging. Social scientists in Sweden have used the segregation index to document the isolation of Greek, Chilean, and Turkish immigrants from the rest of the population. Segregation is present in virtually all multiracial societies (Andersson-Brolin, 1988; Nelse, 1988).

## Fusion

Fusion describes the result of a minority and a majority group combining to form a new group. This combining can be expressed a $A + B + C = D$, where $A$, $B$, and $C$ represent the groups present in a society and $D$ signifies the result, a cultural-racial group unlike any of the initial groups. Fusion theoretically does not require intermarriage, but it is very similar to *amalgamation*, or the cultural and physical synthesis of various groups into a new people. In everyday speech the words fusion and amalgamation are rarely used, but the concept is expressed in the notion of a human *melting pot*, in which diverse groups form a new creation (Newman, 1973, p. 63 Schaefer, 1992).

The analogy of an alchemist's cauldron, the "melting pot," is appropriate. In the Middle Ages, the alchemist attempted to change less costly metals into gold and silver. Similarly, the human melting pot implied that the new group would represent only the best qualities and attributes of the different cultures contributing to it. The belief in the United States as a melting pot became widespread in the first part of the twentieth century, particularly because it suggested that America had an almost divinely inspired mission to destroy artificial divisions and create a single humankind. The dominant group, however, had indicated its unwillingness to welcome American Indians, Blacks, Hispanics, Jews, Asians, and Irish Roman Catholics into the melting pot.

This is not to say fusion does not take place elsewhere. A rather atypical case is that of Pitcairn Island in the South Pacific. The mutineers of a British naval vessel landed on Pitcairn in 1790, bringing with them Polynesian men and women from Tahiti. Conflict ultimately arose over the allocation of land and women, ending with all the Polynesian men and most of the British dead. Despite the violent beginnings, fusion took place in the second generation, leading to a mixed culture shared by people with mixed blood. Fusion usually but not always takes place with relatively small groups, as in Pitcairn (H. Shapiro, 1936). A much more significant example can be seen in Mexico whose people today reflect several generations of the merging of the Spaniards and Native Americans.

It is a mistake to think of the United States as an ethnic mixing bowl. While there are superficial signs of fusion as in a cuisine that includes sauerkraut and spaghetti, virtually all contributions of subordinate groups are ignored.

Marriage patterns indicate the resistance to fusion. People are unwilling, in varying degrees, to marry out of their own ethnic, religious, and racial group. Surveys still show 20–50 percent of various White ethnic groups reporting single ancestry. When White ethnics do cross boundaries they tend to marry within one's religion and one's social class. For example, Italians are more likely to marry Irish who are still Roman Catholic than a Protestant Swede.

There is certainly little evidence in the United States of fusion of races. Racial intermarriage has been increasing, but still in 1989, about 0.4 percent of married couples were interracial compared to 0.1 percent in 1970. Spike Lee's 1991 movie

*Jungle Fever* was influenced by his own father's marrying a White woman after his mother died. Yet intermarriage is still the exception involving a small fraction of households in the United States (Bureau of the Census, 1982a, p. 7; 1991a, p. 44; Kalmijn, 1991).

## Assimilation

Assimilation is the process by which a subordinate individual or group takes on the characteristics of the dominant group and is eventually accepted as part of that group. Assimilation is a majority ideology in which $A + B + C = A$. The majority *(A)* dominates in such a way that minorities *(B* and *C)* become indistinguishable from the dominant group. Regardless of how many racial, ethnic, or religious groups are involved, assimilation dictates conformity to the dominant group (Bash, 1979; Hirschman, 1983; Newman, 1973, p. 53).

To be complete, assimilation must entail not only an active effort by the minority group individual to shed all distinguishing actions and beliefs, but also the complete, unqualified acceptance of that individual by the dominant society. In the United States assimilation is encouraged by dominant White society. The assimilationist perspective tends to devalue alien culture and treasure the dominant. For example, an assimilationist assumes that whatever is admirable among Blacks was adapted from Whites, and whatever is bad is inherently Black. The assimilationist's solution to Black-White conflict is the development of a consensus around White American values (Broom, 1965, p. 23).

Assimilation is difficult. The individual must forsake his or her cultural tradition to become part of a different, often antagonistic, culture. Members of the minority group who choose not to assimilate look upon those who do as deserters. Many Hindus in India complained of their compatriots who copied the traditions and customs of the British. Those who assimilate must totally break with the past. Australian aborigines who become part of dominant society conceal their origin by ignoring darker-skinned relatives, including their immediate family. As one assimilated aborigine explained, "Why should I have anything to do with them? I haven't anything in common with them, and I don't even like most of them." These conflicting demands leave an individual torn between two value systems (Berndt and Berndt, 1951, p. 264; McCully, 1940, p. 204).

Assimilation does not occur at the same pace for all groups or for all individuals in the same group. Assimilation tends to take longer in the following situations:

1. Differences between the minority and the majority are large.
2. Majority is not receptive, or if the minority retains its own culture.
3. Arrival of minority group occurs in a short period of time.
4. Minority group residents are concentrated rather than dispersed.
5. Recentness of arrival and accessibility of the homeland.

Assimilation is not an even process (Warner and Srole, 1945).

The last factor deserves special attention, because length of residence indicates the multifaceted nature of assimilation. Sociologist Won Moo Hurh explains the process in terms of seven critical phases in the adaptation of an immigrant to a new culture. The initial phase of *excitement* is short-lived and soon followed by *exigency,* or disenchantment. The immigrant's unhappiness comes as he or she is confronted by the language barrier, employment difficulties, social isolation, and general culture shock. Because many individuals may wish to return to their homeland at this stage, it is an especially critical phase. Those remaining in the United States go through a period of *resolution* during which the newcomer decides to "make it" regardless of difficulties. A sense of accomplishment, the *optimum* stage, soon gives way to the immigrant's awareness that he or she is discriminated against or at least underemployed— the stage of *relative deprivation.* This refers to the conscious feeling of a negative discrepancy between legitimate expectations (such as a nice job and home) and present actualities (such as a menial job and modest living quarters). In short, the immigrants perceive themselves not advancing as they would wish. The immigrant now becomes aware of the limits of assimilation, especially for members of racial minorities. The *identification crisis* stage marks the immigrant's awareness that the melting pot is a fiction. The immigrant then charts a course that either places him or her in a *marginal* acceptance of a role between foreigner and citizen or a *new identity* such as Italian American that somewhat reaffirms both their national origin and their new citizenship. Even with a new identity, however, the immigrant has to settle for less than the optimum stage. Figure 1.3 suggests the length of these stages, but each varies greatly in length and is, in turn, influenced by the other factors of assimilation (Hurh 1977a; 1977b, pp. 46–52; Hurh and Kim, 1984, 1990a).

The concept of *marginality* noted by Hurh was first coined over sixty years ago to refer to the status of being between two cultures at the same time. It may result from birth as in the case of an individual whose mother is a Jew and whose father is a Christian. It may result from incomplete assimilation as in a Korean woman's migrating to the United States. While she may take on the characteristics of her new host society, she may not be fully accepted, thereby being neither Korean or American. From the labeling perspective, the marginal person finds himself or herself being perceived in very different terms with changing expectations. In the family circle, the ethnic heritage may be clearly fixed, but in the workplace a different label is applied (Billson, 1988; Park, 1928; Stonequist, 1937).

Marginality is not as unusual as you might think. Many people coexist in two cultural traditions, often never completely comfortable in either. Walter M. Gerson (1969) examined the cross-pressures experienced by 29 Jewish American families at Christmas—identified by other writers as the "December dilemma," another "coping with Christmas" (B. Berg, 1988; Brozan, 1973; Graham, 1975; N. Kantrowitz, 1987; Porter, 1981; Rothman, 1990). The pressures vary with age (the Jewish child versus adult), residence (living in a Jewish or Gentile community), type of business, and type of Jewish faith. Gerson describes the "culturally

**FIGURE 1.3**    Critical Phases in the Adaptation Process: A Hypothetical Model

Adaptation by an immigrant to a new culture is not an even process. As shown in this graph, immigrants pass through varying periods of time when they perceive their situation as either improving or deteriorating.

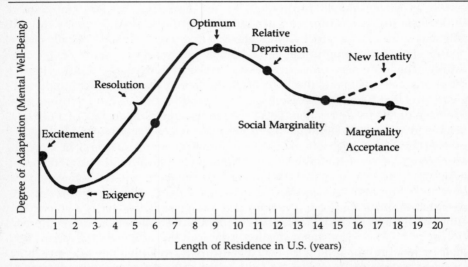

Source: From Won Moo Hurh and Kwang Chung Kim, "Adaptation Stages and Mental Health of Korean Male Immigrants in the United States," *International Migration Review* 24 (Fall 1990), pp. 456–479. Copyright © 1990 by Center for Migration Studies. Reprinted by permission of Center for Migration Studies.

produced cross-pressures for contemporary American Jews," and details the strain-reducing mechanisms Jewish people use to deal with the cross-pressures.

1. Value hierarchy. The Jewish community minimizes role conflict by socializing their children to the relative significance of Hanukkah and Christmas.
2. Insulation. By remaining in predominantly Jewish neighborhoods or traveling in December to areas that cater to Jews, the Jewish American can minimize interaction with Christians during the holiday season.
3. Compartmentalization. Some Jews resolve cross-pressures by participating in Christmas festivities at some levels (for example, sending Christmas cards), while still maintaining their traditional beliefs.
4. Redefinition. Some Jews simply see most aspects of the Christmas celebration as social, not religious symbols.
5. Patterned evasions. Children especially may evade seasonal signs of Christianity by skipping school on the day of classroom Christmas parties. Such actions usually are done with the tacit approval of school officials.
6. Hanukkah. The Jewish festival of Hanukkah takes on much greater significance in societies dominated by Christians. It provides an alternative occasion for exchanging gifts, sending cards, and decorating homes.

These adjustments vary with the individual and are not the same for the entire marginal group.

Most accounts of marginality focus on racial or ethnic groups that take on White, middle-class culture but are not fully accepted and still desire to retain their identity. Helen Hacker (1974) drew attention to "the marginal woman" who is torn between "being feminine" and "being a success," generally defined in male terms, and confronting the rejection or acceptance of traditional sex roles.

## THE PLURALIST PERSPECTIVE

Thus far we have concentrated on ways in which minority groups cease to exist (removal) or take on the characteristics of the dominant group (assimilation). The alternative to these relationships between the majority and minority is pluralism. *Pluralism* implies mutual respect between the various groups in a society for one another's cultures, a respect that allows minorities to express their own culture without suffering prejudice or hostility. Whereas the assimilationist or integrationist seeks elimination of ethnic boundaries, the pluralist believes in maintaining many of them.

There are limits to cultural freedom. A Romanian immigrant to the United States could not expect to avoid learning English and still move up the occupational ladder. In order to survive, a society must have a consensus among its members on basic ideals, values, and beliefs. Nevertheless, there is still plenty of room for variety. Earlier, fusion was described as $A + B + C = D$ and assimilation as $A + B + C = A$. Using this same scheme, we can think of pluralism as $A + B + C = A + B + C$, where groups coexist in one society (Higham, 1974; Hurh and Kim, 1984; Newman, 1973).

In the United States cultural pluralism is more an ideal than a reality. Though there are vestiges of cultural pluralism—in the various ethnic neighborhoods in major cities, for instance—the general rule has been for subordinate groups to assimilate. The cost of cultural integrity has been high. The various Native American tribes have succeeded to a large extent in maintaining their heritage, but it has been in exchange for bare subsistence on reservations dominated by federal control.

Several writers argue that Switzerland exemplifies a pluralist state. The absence of a national language and a dominant religious faith leads to a tolerance of cultural differences. Various political devices were adopted to safeguard the interests of various ethnic groups in a way unparalleled in the United States. But even though there is a spirit of pluralism, the 4 million Swiss are not without their prejudices, as indicated by a separatist movement of one group that has caused violent disturbances. Nevertheless, for the most part there is considerable respect and, in some instances, encouragement of cultural diversity in Switzerland.

The initial expression of pluralism in the United States came in the earlier part

*Classrooms in the United States are increasingly populated by immigrants, both school-age and adult, who are learning English as a second language.*

of this century as an alternative to assimilation, or Americanization. Social worker Jane Addams and educator John Dewey spoke out against the destruction of cultural values in the name of conformity. Horace Kallen, seeing evidence of pluralism in the persistence of cultural identity in the settlements of Norwegians in Minnesota, Germans in Wisconsin, and Irish in Massachusetts, called attention to how Americanization threatened his goal, a federation or commonwealth of national cultures. A multiracial, multicultural society of people getting along with one another and learning from each other is an attractive notion. But the maintenance of largely separate cultural identities may only increase their visibility and encourage discrimination and other socially disabling mechanisms. Pluralism may also detour minorities from challenging their subordinate position because they are satisfied with their distinctive cultures (Kallen, 1915a, 1915b, 1924, p. 11; P. Rose, 1981, p. 65).

Today, 80 years after Kallen drew attention to cultural pluralism, Americans see a reemergence of ethnic identification by groups that long since had expressed little interest in their heritage. In fact, groups that make up the dominant majority are also reasserting their ethnic heritage. Various nationality groups are rekindling interest in almost forgotten languages, customs, festivals, and traditions. In some instances this expression of the past has taken the form of protest against exclusion from dominant society. Chinese youths, for example, chastise their elders for forgetting the old ways and accepting White American influence and control.

Representative of the reassertion of one's cultural heritage is the *Afrocentric perspective*. African-studies scholar Molefi Asante (1987) has called for an *Afro-centric perspective* that emphasizes the customs of African cultures and how they have penetrated the history, culture, and behavior of Blacks in the United States and around the world. The Afrocentric approach could begin in our school curriculum, which has not adequately acknowledged the importance of this heritage. In a very real sense Afrocentrism is meant to counter Eurocentrism and to work toward a multiculturalist or pluralist orientation where no viewpoint is suppressed.

## GLANCING BACK AND LOOKING AHEAD

In the first chapter, we have attempted to organize our approach to minority-majority relations. We observed that minorities do not necessarily have fewer people than the dominant group. Social minorities can be classified into racial, ethnic, religious, and gender groups. Racial classification has been of interest but scientific findings do not explain contemporary race relations. Biological differences of race are relatively unimportant. Yet continuing debates demonstrate that attempts to establish a biological basis of race have not been entirely swept into the dustbin of history. The *social* meaning given to physical differences, however, is very significant. People have defined racial differences in such a way as to encourage or discourage the progress of certain groups.

The confinement of certain people in subordinate groups may function to serve *some* people's vested interests. This denial of opportunities or privileges to an entire group, however, only leads to conflict between dominant and subordinate groups.

An identifiable minority group appears in a society in one of four ways: voluntary migration, involuntary migration, annexation, or colonialism. Once a group is given subordinate status it does not necessarily keep it indefinitely. Extermination, expulsion, secession, segregation, fusion, and assimilation remove the status of subordination.

Subordinate group members' reactions include an alternate avenue to acceptance and success: "Why should we forsake what we are to be accepted by them?" In response to this question there is a resurgence of ethnic identification. Pluralism describes a society in which several different groups coexist, with no dominant or subordinate groups. The hope for such a society remains unfulfilled, except perhaps for isolated exceptions, like Switzerland. But even Switzerland has not entirely lived up to the ideal of mutual respect and cultural diversity.

The two significant forces that are absent in a truly pluralistic society are prejudice and discrimination. In an assimilationist society, prejudice disparages outgroup differences and discrimination financially rewards those who shed their past. In the next two chapters we will explore the nature of prejudice and discrimination.

## *KEY TERMS*

**amalgamation**   The process by which a dominant group and a subordinate group combine through intermarriage to form a new group.

**assimilation**   The process by which an individual forsakes his or her own cultural tradition to become part of a different culture.

**biological race**   A genetically isolated group characterized by a high degree of inbreeding that leads to distinctive gene frequencies.

**class**   As defined by Max Weber, persons who share similar levels of wealth.

**colonialism**   The maintenance of political, social, economic, and cultural dominance over a people by a foreign power for an extended period.

**conflict perspective**   A sociological approach that assumes that social behavior is best understood in terms of conflict or tension among competing groups.

**dysfunction**   Elements of society that may disrupt a social system or led to a decrease in its stability.

**emigration** Leaving a country to settle in another.

**ethnic group**   A group set apart from others because of its national origin or distinctive cultural patterns.

**functionalist perspective**   A sociological approach emphasizing the way in which parts of a society are structured in the interest of maintaining the system as a whole.

**genocide**   The deliberate, systematic killing of an entire people or nation.

**immigration**   Coming into a new country as a permanent resident.

**intelligence quotient (IQ)**   The ratio of an individual's mental age (as computed by an IQ test) divided by his or her chronological age.

**interactive effect**   Pettigrew's view that race and class act together to place an individual in a stratification system.

**labeling theory**   An approach introduced by Howard Becker that attempts to explain why certain people are viewed as deviants and others engaging in the same behavior are not.

**marginality**   Status of being between two cultures at the same time, such as Jewish immigrants to the United States.

**melting pot**   Diverse racial or ethnic groups or both forming a new creation, a new cultural entity.

**migration**   General term to describe any transfer of population.

**minority group**   A subordinate group whose members have significantly less control or power over their own lives than that held by the members of a dominant or majority group.

**neocolonialism** Continuing domination of former colonies by foreign countries.

**pluralism** Mutual respect between the various groups in a society for one another's cultures, allowing minorities to express their own culture without experiencing prejudice or hostility.

**politically correct** Efforts on behalf of racial, ethnic, and religious minorities as well as women. Phrase is often used in criticism of such measures.

**racial group**    A group that is socially set apart from others because of obvious physical differences.

**racism**    A doctrine that one race is superior.

**relative deprivation**    The conscious experience of a negative discrepancy between legitimate expectations and present actualities.

**segregation**    The act of physically separating two groups; often imposed on a subordinate group by the dominant group.

**self-fulfilling prophecy**    The tendency of individuals to respond to and act on the basis of stereotypes, a predisposition that can lead to the validation of false definitions.

**Social Darwinism**    The belief that societies and races are engaged in a struggle for existence in which the fit survive.

**stereotypes**    Unreliable generalizations about all members of a group that do not take into account individual differences within the group.

**stratification**    A structured ranking of entire groups of people that perpetuates unequal rewards and power in a society.

## FOR FURTHER INFORMATION

Richard A. Alba, ed. *Ethnicity and Race in the U.S.A.* New York: Routledge, 1985.

The articles in this collection assess how far a variety of minorities have come and how much further they must go.

James Paul Allen and Eugene James Turner. *We the People: An Atlas of America's Ethnic Diversity.* New York: Macmillan, 1988.

This superb atlas presents the distribution and migration patterns in 110 maps of 67 ethnic groups.

James E. Blackwell and Morris Janowitz, eds. *Black Sociologists: Historical and Contemporary Perspectives.* Chicago: University of Chicago Press, 1974.

A fine collection of contributions to the study of race relations by such scholars as W. E. B. DuBois, Charles S. Johnson, and E. Franklin Frazier.

Hubert M. Blalock, Jr. *Toward a Theory of Minority-Group Relations.* New York: Capricorn Books, 1967.

Ninety-seven theoretical propositions, presented to outline the dynamics of intergroup relations, are stated in such a way as to be directly or indirectly testable. Interesting discussions of African Americans in labor unions and professional sports, racial minorities that mediate between other groups, and the relationship of competition to discrimination.

Milton M. Gordon. *Assimilation in American Life: The Role of Race, Religion, and National Origins.* New York: Oxford University Press, 1964.

The paradigm of assimilation is presented in this book, along with critical discussions of three theories of assimilation—Anglo-conformity, the melting pot, and cultural pluralism. Gordon revises the paradigm slightly in *Human Nature, Class, and Ethnicity* (New York: Oxford University Press, 1978).

Ashley Montagu. *Statement on Race.* London: Oxford University Press, 1972.

The 1950 UNESCO Statement on Race is presented with the anthropologist's annotated remarks. In addition Montagu discusses three other UNESCO statements on race differences and racial prejudice.

William Ryan. *Blaming the Victim,* rev. ed. New York: Random House, 1976.

The poor in general and African Americans in particular are incorrectly blamed for their social and economic inequality. Ryan critically looks at societal institutions that perpetuate this deprivation and ideology. The text of the 1976 edition is the same as the 1971 publication, but a thirty-nine page appendix updates the original book.

Don Spiegel and Patricia Keith-Spiegel, eds. *Outsiders, U.S.A.* San Francisco: Rinehart Press, 1973.

The editors bring together a series of articles that discuss not only racial and ethnic minorities but other outsiders as well—the elderly, the fetus, the consumer (by Ralph Nader), and the soldier.

Stephan Thernstrom, ed. *Harvard Encyclopedia of American Ethnic Groups.* Cambridge, MA: Harvard University Press, 1980.

This monumental reference book is the single best source on the hundreds of ethnic groups in the United States today.

# Chapter Two

# PREJUDICE

## Chapter Outline

**Prejudice and Discrimination**

**Theories of Prejudice**

Exploitation Theory

Scapegoating Theory

The Authoritarian Personality Theory

Structural Approach

**The Content of Prejudice: Stereotypes**

**The Extent of Prejudice**

The Social Distance Scale

**Attitude Change**

**Mood of the Minority**

**Reducing Prejudice**

Mass Media and Education

Equal-Status Contact

**Glancing Back and Looking Ahead**

**Key Terms**

**For Further Information**

## ❋ *HIGHLIGHTS* ❋

*Prejudice* is a negative attitude rejecting an entire group; *discrimination* is behavior depriving a group of certain rights or opportunities. Prejudice does not necessarily coincide with discrimination, as made apparent by a typology developed by Robert Merton. Several theories have been advanced to explain prejudice. The explanations rest on *structural, economic,* and *personality* factors. These explanations examine prejudice in terms of content (*stereotypes*) and its extent. Prejudice is not limited to the dominant group; minority groups often dislike one another. It has been argued that the subordinate people may suffer low self-esteem due to their low status. Mass media seem to be of limited value in reducing prejudice, and may even intensify ill feeling. Equal-status contact and the shared-coping approach may reduce hostility among groups.

Prejudice and discrimination are so prevalent that it is tempting to consider them inevitable or, even more loosely, "just part of human nature." Such a view ignores their variability from individual to individual and society to society. The acceptance of Asians in Hawaii contrasts to their treatment in California and British Columbia. At one time or another intermarriage has been condoned or condemned between virtually all racial and ethnic groups. Finally, the fact that children must learn prejudice before they exhibit it as adults emphasizes the idea that prejudice is a *social* phenomenon, an acquired characteristic. Only a truly pluralistic society would not make unfavorable distinctions through prejudicial attitudes and discriminatory actions among racial and ethnic groups.

Ill feeling among groups can result from ethnocentrism. *Ethnocentrism* is the tendency to assume that one's culture and way of life are superior to all others. The ethnocentric person judges other groups or even other cultures by the standards of his or her own group. This attitude leads the person quite easily into prejudice against cultures he or she views as inferior.

Hostility toward groups different from one's own is not unusual. A 1991 study sponsored by the American Jewish Committee asked a nationwide sample what they thought was the "social standing" of a variety of racial and ethnic groups. Whites did well, racial and ethnic minorities were shown to be held in low social standing. However, fully 39 percent were willing to evaluate the "Wisian Americans"—a nonexistent group made up by the researchers. Not only was this fictitious group rated, but it received one of the lowest evaluations. Obviously, fear of those who are different extends to imaginary groups that sound strange (T. Smith, 1991).

While prejudice is certainly not new in the United States, it is receiving renewed attention as it occurs in neighborhoods, meetings, and on college campuses. In 1990, President George Bush signed into law the Hate Crime

Statistics Act, which directs the Department of Justice to gather data on crimes motivated by the victim's race, religion, ethnicity, or sexual orientation. This created a national mandate to identify such crimes where previously only 12 states monitored hate crimes.

What causes people to dislike entire groups of people? Is it possible for such attitudes to be changed? This chapter will try to answer these questions about prejudice; Chapter 3 will focus on discrimination.

## PREJUDICE AND DISCRIMINATION

Prejudice and discrimination are related concepts, but not the same. *Prejudice* is a negative attitude toward an entire category of people. The two important components in this definition are *attitude* and *entire category*. Prejudice involves attitudes, thoughts, and beliefs, not actions. Frequently prejudice is expressed through the use of *ethnophaulisms* or ethnic slurs, which include derisive nicknames such as "honkie," "gook," or "wetback." Ethnophaulisms also include speaking about or to members of a particular group in a condescending way— "José does well in school for a Chicano"—or referring to a middle-aged woman as "one of the girls."

A prejudiced belief leads to categorical rejection. Prejudice is not disliking someone you meet because you find his or her behavior objectionable. It is disliking an entire racial or ethnic group, even if you have had little or no contact. A college student who requests a room change after three weeks of enduring his roommate's sleeping all day, playing loud music all night, and piling garbage on his desk is not prejudiced. He would be displaying prejudice, however, if he requested a change upon arriving at school and learning from his roommate's luggage tags that his new roommate is of a different nationality group.

Prejudice is a belief or attitude; but discrimination is action. *Discrimination* involves behavior that excludes all members of a group from certain rights, opportunities, or privileges. Like prejudice, it must be categorical. If an individual refuses to hire as a typist an Italian American who is illiterate, it is not discrimination. If an individual refuses to hire any Italian Americans because she thinks they are incompetent, and does not make the effort to see if an applicant is qualified, it is discrimination.

Prejudice does not necessarily coincide with discriminatory behavior. Sociologist Robert Merton (1949, 1976, pp. 189–216), in exploring the relationship between negative attitudes and negative behavior, has identified four major categories (see Figure 2.1). The folk label added to each of Merton's categories may more readily identify the type of individual being described. These are

1. The unprejudiced nondiscriminator: all-weather liberal;
2. The unprejudiced discriminator: reluctant liberal;
3. The prejudiced nondiscriminator: timid bigot;
4. The prejudiced discriminator: all-weather bigot.

**FIGURE 2.1** Prejudice and Discrimination

As sociologist Robert Merton's formulation shows, prejudice and discrimination are related to each other, but are not the same.

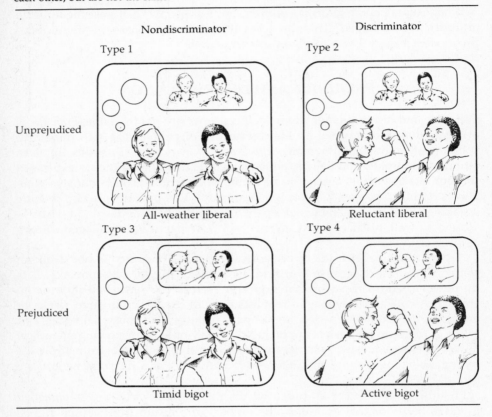

Liberals, as the term is employed in types 1 and 2, are committed to equality among people. The all-weather liberal believes in equality and practices it. Merton was quick to observe that all-weather liberals may be far removed from any real competition with African Americans or women. Furthermore, such people may be content with their own behavior and do little to change. The reluctant liberal is not even this committed to equality among races. Social pressure may cause such a person to discriminate. Fear of losing employees may cause a manager to avoid promoting women to supervisory capacities. Equal opportunity legislation may be the best way to influence the reluctant liberals.

Types 3 and 4 do not believe in equal treatment for racial and ethnic groups, but they vary in their willingness to act. The timid bigot, type 3, will not discriminate if discrimination costs money or reduces profits or if he or she is pressured not to by peers or the government. The all-weather bigot unhesitatingly acts on the prejudiced beliefs he or she holds.

Merton's typology points out that attitudes should not be confused with behavior. People do not always act as they believe. More than half a century ago, Richard LaPiere (1934, 1969) measured the relationship between racial attitudes and social conduct. From 1930 to 1932, LaPiere traveled throughout the United States with a Chinese couple. Despite a climate of alleged intolerance of Asians, LaPiere observed that the couple was treated courteously at hotels, motels, and restaurants. He was puzzled by the good reception they received, for all the conventional attitude surveys showed extreme prejudice by Whites toward the Chinese.

It was possible that LaPiere had been fortunate during his travels and consistently stopped at placed operated by the tolerant minority. To test this possibility he sent questionnaires asking the very establishments at which they had been served, if the owner would "accept members of the Chinese race as guests in your establishment." More than 90 percent responded no, even though LaPiere's Chinese couple had been treated politely at all the establishments. How

*According to sociologist Robert Merton, an "active bigot" is prejudiced and discriminates.*

can this inconsistency be explained? People who returned questionnaires reflecting prejudice were unwilling to act based on those asserted beliefs—they were timid bigots.

The LaPiere study is not without its flaws. First, he had no way of knowing whether the respondent to the questionnaire was the same person who served him and the Chinese couple. Second, he accompanied the couple, but the questionnaire suggested that the arrival was unescorted (and in the minds of some, uncontrolled) and perhaps consisted of many Chinese individuals. Third, personnel may have changed between the time of visit and the mailing of the questionnaire (Deutscher, 1973, pp. 122–123).

Even with these shortcomings, the LaPiere technique has been replicated with similar results (DeFleur and Westie, 1958; Kutner et al., 1952). This technique raised the question of whether attitudes are important if they are not completely reflected in behavior. But if attitudes are not important in small matters, they are important in other ways: lawmakers legislate and courts may reach decisions based on what the public thinks (Allport, 1958, pp. 437–442; Bettelheim and Janowitz, 1950, p. 281).

This is not just a hypothetical possibility. Legislators in the United States are often persuaded to vote in a certain way by what they perceive as changed attitudes toward open housing, school busing, nuclear wastes, and capital punishment. The same is true in other countries. In Great Britain, the first national survey of racial attitudes was conducted in 1969. Because it showed only 10 percent of White Britons highly prejudiced, members of Parliament cited it during the campaign for legislation outlawing discrimination (E. Rose, 1969; Schaefer, 1976a).

Though prejudice is related to behavior, it is not the same. But that does not mean it is harmless. The schoolyard chant "Sticks and stones may break my bones, but names will never hurt me" is not true. Names do hurt people. To be subjected to ridicule is in itself detrimental.

Sociologists Jack and William C. Levin (1982) have enumerated some of prejudice's functions. For the majority group, it serves to maintain privileged occupations and more power for their members. Although this effect seems self-evident, Levin and Levin go on to point out that prejudice may be viewed as having some functions even for subordinate groups. These functions include maintaining in-group solidarity and reducing competition in some areas of employment, admittedly those with lower status or smaller rewards.

The following sections examine the theories of why prejudice exists, and discuss the content and extent of prejudice today.


## THEORIES OF PREJUDICE

The previous section pointed out that prejudice is learned. Friends, relatives, newspapers, books, movies, and television all teach it. Awareness that there are differences among people that society judges to be important begins at an early age. Several theories have been advanced to explain the rejection of certain groups in a society.

## Exploitation Theory

Racial prejudice is frequently used to justify keeping a group in a subordinate position, such as a lower social class. Conflict theorists in particular stress the role of racial and ethnic hostility as a way for the dominant group to keep its position of status and power intact. Indeed this approach maintains that even the less affluent White working class uses prejudice to minimize competition from upwardly mobile minorities.

This exploitation approach clearly is part of the Marxist tradition in sociological thought. Just as Karl Marx emphasized exploitation of the lower class as an integral part of capitalism, the exploitation or conflict approach explains how racism can stigmatize a group as inferior so that the exploitation of that group can be justified (Cox, 1948; Hunter and Abraham, 1987; C. Johnson, 1939; Willhelm, 1980).

The exploitation theory of prejudice is persuasive. Japanese Americans were the object of little prejudice until they began to enter jobs that brought them into competition with Whites. The movement to keep Chinese out of the country (described in Chapter 4) became strongest during the latter half of the nineteenth century, when Chinese immigrants and Whites fought over dwindling numbers of jobs. Both the enslavement of African Americans and removal westward of Native Americans were to a significant degree economically motivated.

Related to the exploitation theory is the *caste approach* to race relations in the United States. The term *caste* describes a system of social inequality in which status is inherited and people have little, if any, opportunity to change their social positions. As we have seen through exploitation theory, economic subordination benefits the dominant group's financial interests. The caste approach, however, does not rely on Marxist theory for theoretical support. The caste explanation for racial subordination sees race and social class as closely related, because Blacks and other non-Whites are destined by the social structure to occupy a castelike position. Membership in the subordinate group is inherited and permanent. W. Lloyd Warner (1937; see also Davis et al., 1965) asserted that the similarities between the caste system of India and race relations in the United States (especially the South) were great enough to make the analogy appropriate.

The caste approach is basically descriptive and not very analytical; for example, sociologists using it make less effort to explain why caste relations originated than does the general exploitation approach of Oliver C. Cox. The caste approach, although acknowledging the importance of social class, argues that race is more important; whereas Cox's 1942 general exploitation theory sees racial discrimination as merely an example of class differences. The caste explanation seems somewhat limited. In a caste system, as strictly defined, the lower castes accept the system and their low status. But the increased numbers of Blacks in high-paying occupations and the continuous struggle for equal rights indicate that African Americans not acquiesce (Berreman, 1960, 1973).

Although some cases support the exploitation theory, it is too limited to explain prejudice in all its forms. First, not all minority groups are exploited economically to the same extent. Second, many groups that have been the victims of prejudice have not been persecuted for economic reasons, for example the Quakers and Mormons. Nevertheless, as Gordon Allport concludes, the exploitation theory correctly points a finger at *one* of the factors in prejudice, that is, the rationalized self-interest of the upper classes (1958, pp. 205–206).

## Scapegoating Theory

Scapegoating theory says that prejudiced people believe they are society's victims. Exploitation theory maintains that intolerant individuals abuse others, whereas scapegoaters feel they are being abused themselves. The term *scapegoat* comes from a biblical injunction telling the Hebrews to send a goat into the wilderness to symbolically carry away the people's sins. Similarly, the theory of scapegoating suggests that an individual, rather than accepting guilt for some failure, will transfer the responsibility for failure to some vulnerable group. In the tragic twentieth century example, Adolph Hitler used the Jews as the scapegoat for all of the social and economic ills of Germany in the 1930s. This premise led to the passage of laws restricting Jewish life in pre-war Germany and eventually escalated into the mass extermination of Europe's Jews.

Bettelheim and Janowitz (1964) studied prejudice in the United States and found that the downwardly mobile usually are more prejudiced. People who lose a job and are forced to accept a lower-status occupation experience increased tension and anxiety. Who is responsible, they ask, for their misfortune? At this time a scapegoat, in the form of a racial, ethnic, or religious group, may enter the picture.

Like exploitation theory, scapegoating theory adds to our understanding of why prejudice exists, but does not explain all its facets. For example, scapegoating theory offers little explanation of why a specific group is selected or why frustration may not be taken out against the real object when it is possible (Allport, 1958, pp. 332–333). Also, both the exploitation and scapegoating theories suggest that every individual sharing generally the same experiences in society would be equally prejudiced, but that is not the case. Prejudice varies among individuals who would seem to benefit equally from the exploitation of a subordinate group or who have experienced equal frustration. In an effort to explain these personality differences, social scientists developed the concept of the *authoritarian personality*.

## The Authoritarian Personality Theory

A number of social scientists do not see prejudice as an isolated trait that anyone can have. Several efforts have been made to detail the prejudiced personality, but the most comprehensive effort culminated in a volume entitled *The Authoritarian Personality* (Adorno et al., 1950). Using a variety of tests and relying on more than 2,000 respondents, ranging from middle-class Whites to inmates of San Quentin State Prison, the authors claimed they had isolated the characteristics of the authoritarian personality.

The basic characteristics of the authoritarian personality included adherence to conventional values, uncritical acceptance of authority, and concern with power and toughness. With obvious relevance to development of intolerance, the authoritarian personality was also characterized by aggressiveness toward people who did not conform to conventional norms or obey authority. According to the authors, this personality type develops from an early childhood of harsh discipline. A child with an authoritarian upbringing obeys, and later treats others as he or she was raised.

This study has been widely criticized, but the very existence of criticism indicates the influence of the study (Kirscht and Dillehay, 1967; Selznick and Steinberg, 1969). Critics have attacked the study's equation of authoritarianism with right-wing politics (liberals can also be rigid), its failure to see that prejudice is more closely related to other individual traits such as social class than to authoritarianism as it was defined, and the research methods employed. Kinloch, discussing personality in general and not just this study, added a fourth criticism: the authors concentrate on factors behind extreme racial prejudice, rather than more common expressions of hostility (1974, p. 167).

Kinloch's emphasis on the everyday reinforcement of prejudice is perhaps the most compelling criticism. Surrendering to authority may be similar to giving in to social pressure that endorses intolerance of racial, ethnic, or religious groups (Couch and Keniston, 1960). The failure of this effort to define the prejudiced personality suggests that we should study societal differences in prejudice, that is, prejudice's structural component.

## *Structural Approach*

Although personality factors are important contributors to prejudice, structural or situational factors must also be given serious consideration. Analysis reveals how societal influences shape a climate for tolerance of intolerance. Societies develop social norms that dictate not only what foods are desirable (or forbidden) but also what racial and ethnic groups are to be favored (or despised). Social forces operate in a society to encourage or discourage tolerance. The force may be widespread—for example, the pressure on Southerners to oppose racial equality while there was slavery; or it may be limited—for example, one male who finds himself becoming more sexist as he competes with three females for a position in a prestigious law firm.

Social psychologist Thomas Pettigrew (1958, 1959; see also Kimmel, 1986; Middleton, 1976) collected data that substantiated the importance of such social norms in developing a social climate conducive to the expression of prejudice. Pettigrew found that Whites in the South were more anti-Black than Whites in the North, and Whites in the United States were not as prejudiced as Whites in the Republic of South Africa.

Personality alone cannot account for such differences. Pettigrew's research revealed no significant variation between the two societies in terms of the presence of authoritarian individuals. He therefore concluded that structural factors explained differences in the levels of prejudice between these two regions. In the Republic of South Africa and the American South, Whites were socialized to have highly prejudiced attitudes toward Blacks. Not all Whites in these areas accepted prevailing racist ideas, however. Personality factors offer the best explanation for these differences in the degrees of prejudice among individuals living in the same region (Louw-Potgieter, 1988).

The four approaches to prejudice should not be viewed as mutually exclusive. Social circumstances provide cues for a person's attitudes; personality determines the extent to which people follow social cues and the likelihood that they will encourage others to do the same. Societal norms may promote or deter tolerance; personality traits suggest the degree to which a person will conform to norms of intolerance (Allport, 1962; T. Wilson, 1986).

## THE CONTENT OF PREJUDICE: STEREOTYPES

In Chapter 1, we saw that stereotypes play a powerful role in how people come to view dominant and subordinate groups. These exaggerated images have been subjected to numerous scientific studies.

The systematic study of stereotypes began with David Katz and Kenneth Braly's (1933) use of the *checklist approach*. College students were presented with a list of eighty-four adjectives (sly, cruel, neat, and so on) and were asked to list which traits they considered most characteristic of ten groups—Germans, Italians, Irish, English, Blacks, Jews, Americans, Chinese, Japanese, and Turks. The students' selection of traits for each group consistently agreed with one another, especially for Blacks and Jews. This technique has been confirmed by several other researchers. Table 2.1 presents the traits most frequently assigned to Blacks and Jews by students in 1932, 1950, 1969, and 1982 (Gardner et al., 1988; Gilbert, 1951; L. Gordon, 1973, 1985, 1986; Karlins et al., 1969; Katz and Braly, 1933; Maykovich, 1972b; A. G. Miller, 1982).

Research on stereotyping provides information on the content of prejudice but tells us little about the amount of prejudice. People may know what the stereotypes of a group are without believing them, or they may believe the stereotypes but also know that it is increasingly improper to use them, even on a questionnaire. Another limitation of this research is that some traits may be positive, or at least neutral, depending on individual interpretation (materialistic or pleasure loving, for instance). Studies indicate that members of younger generations show more care in thinking about racial and ethnic groups; but this tendency in itself does not mean they are less prejudiced (Brigham, 1973; Sigall and Page, 1971). The fading of one stereotype may only mean it has been

**TABLE 2.1**   Change in Stereotype Traits, 1932–1982

The compared responses of college students over a 50-year period show a softening of the stereotypes applied to Black and Jewish Americans.

| Blacks | 1932 | 1950 | 1969 | 1982 |
|---|---|---|---|---|
| *Negative trait selections* | | | | |
| Superstitious | 84% | 42% | 10% | 9% |
| Lazy | 75 | 32 | 18 | 18 |
| Happy-go-lucky | 39 | 17 | 5 | 1 |
| Ignorant | 38 | 24 | 8 | 9 |
| Ostentatious | 26 | 11 | 14 | 10 |
| Stupid | 22 | 10 | 2 | 1 |
| Physically dirty | 17 | — | 1 | 1 |
| Naive | 14 | — | 0 | 0 |
| Sly | — | — | 1 | 15 |
| Aggressive | — | — | 6 | 13 |
| Loud | — | — | 9 | 11 |
| Arrogant | — | — | 1 | 10 |
| Unreliable | — | — | 10 | 6 |
| *Other trait selections* | | | | |
| Musical | 26 | 33 | 25 | 11 |
| Intelligent | — | — | 13 | 13 |
| Materialistic | — | — | 8 | 11 |
| Sportsmanlike | — | — | 6 | 9 |
| Pleasure-loving | — | 19 | 12 | 4 |
| Sensitive | — | — | 8 | 4 |
| **Jews** | | | | |
| *Negative trait selections* | | | | |
| Shrewd | 79 | 47 | 37 | 15 |
| Mercenary | 49 | 28 | 8 | 2 |
| Grasping | 34 | 17 | 1 | 1 |
| Sly | 20 | 14 | 8 | 9 |
| Aggressive | 12 | — | 10 | 6 |
| Ostentatious | — | — | 9 | 3 |
| Extremely nationalistic | — | — | 8 | 2 |
| *Other trait selections* | | | | |
| Industrious | 48 | 29 | 25 | 9 |
| Intelligent | 29 | 37 | 33 | 21 |
| Ambitious | 21 | 28 | 20 | 10 |
| Loyal to family | 15 | 19 | 22 | 11 |
| Persistent | 13 | — | 2 | 2 |
| Talkative | 13 | — | 9 | 2 |
| Very religious | 12 | — | 12 | 14 |
| Materialistic | — | — | 19 | 11 |
| Sophisticated | — | — | 5 | 9 |
| Alert | — | — | 10 | 4 |

*Source:* L. Gordon, 1986, p. 201. Reprinted by permission of *Sociology and Social Research, 70,* August 1988.

replaced by another. The image of many groups as docile and lazy was shattered by the social protest of the 1960s. Now rather than being seen as weak, such groups are viewed as too aggressive.

Are stereotypes held only by dominant groups of subordinate groups? The answer is clearly no. White Americans even believed generalizations about themselves, although admittedly these were rather positive. Minority groups also hold exaggerated images of themselves. Studies before World War II showed a tendency for Blacks to assign to themselves many of the same negative traits that Whites assigned them. Now such stereotypes of themselves are largely rejected by African Americans, Jews, Asians, and other minority groups, although subordinate groups will to some degree stereotype each other (M. Clark, 1985; L. Gordon, 1985). The nature of the subordinate group's self-image is explored later in this chapter. The subordinate group also develops stereotyped images of the dominant group. Anthony Dworkin (1965) surveyed Chicanos and found that the majority agreed that Anglos were prejudiced, snobbish, hypocritical, tense, anxious, neurotic, and had little family loyalty. Research has documented the worldwide existence of stereotypes. Whether it be attitudes toward the Chinese in Malaysia and Indonesia, East Indians in Africa and Britain, or Armenian Christians in Turkey, people develop powerful mental images of other groups (Brewer and Kramer, 1985; Driedger and Clifton, 1984; Lieberson, 1982; Pettigrew, 1966, 1971; Schaefer, 1976a; Stryker, 1959).

If stereotypes are exaggerated generalizations, why are they so widely held and why are some traits more often assigned than others? First, evidence for traits may arise out of real conditions. For example, more Puerto Ricans live in poverty than Whites, and so the prejudiced mind associates laziness with Puerto Ricans. According to the New Testament, some Jews were responsible for the crucifixion of Jesus, and so to the prejudiced mind, all Jews are Christ-killers. Some activists in the women's liberation movement are lesbians, and so all feminists are lesbians. From a kernel of fact, faulty generalization creates a stereotype.

A second aspect of stereotypes is their role in the self-fulfilling prophecy discussed in Chapter 1. The dominant group creates barriers, making it difficult for a minority group to act differently from the stereotype. It also applies pressure toward conformity to the stereotype. Conformity to the stereotype, although forced, becomes evidence of the validity of the stereotype. Some evidence suggests that even today people accept to some degree negative stereotypes of themselves. The labeling process becomes complete as images are applied and in some cases accepted by those being stereotyped.

Labels take on such strong significance that people ignore evidence to the contrary. People who believe Italian Americans to be members of the Mafia disregard law-abiding Italian Americans (Pettigrew et al., 1982, p. 9). Several psychologists asked University of Connecticut students to evaluate the attractiveness of thirty women as depicted in black-and-white photographs. The students were also asked to identify those whom they felt "support women's liberation." True to the stereotype conveyed of feminists, the students identified less attractive women as supporters of the women's movement. Interestingly, even those students who indicated they were feminists themselves were just as likely to label less attractive women as feminists as were those student evaluators who were not supportive of women's liberation (Goldberg et al., 1975).

And even as stereotypes continue to serve as self-fulfilling prophecies, stereotypes are reinforced by representations of the subordinate group in the mass media. Native Americans are shown as savages and Mexicans as lazy, for instance. Gradually the mass media—movies, television, newspapers, and periodicals—are moving to present a more accurate, evenhanded portrayal of racial groups; there is, however, still much room for improvement. The United States Commission on Civil Rights (1977b, 1979), in two exhaustive studies of television programming, found that women are still more likely than men to be shown without any identifiable occupation. If employed women are shown they are most frequently presented as nurses, homemakers, and household workers—positions that reflect traditional notions of "women's work." Of special concern for the Commission was that women are portrayed most stereotypically in the early evening, during the "family hour."

## THE EXTENT OF PREJUDICE

Interest in developing theories of prejudice or studying its concept has been exceeded only by interest in measuring it. From the outset, efforts to measure prejudice have suffered from disagreement over exactly what constitutes intolerance, what differentiates prejudice from nonprejudice, and whether there is such a phenomenon as no prejudice. Add to these dilemmas the methodological problems of attitude measurement, and the empirical study of prejudice becomes an undertaking fraught with difficulty (Brigham and Weissbach, 1972, pp. 77–83).

The extent of prejudice can be measured only in relative, rather than absolute, differences. We cannot accurately say, for example, that prejudice toward Puerto Ricans is four times greater than that toward Portuguese Americans. We can conclude that prejudice is greater toward one group than the other; we just cannot quantify how much greater. To assess differences in prejudice, the social distance scale is especially appropriate.

### The Social Distance Scale

Robert Park and Ernest Burgess first defined social distance as the tendency to approach or withdraw from a racial group (1921, p. 440). A few years later, Emory Bogardus (1925, 1928, 1933, 1968) conceptualized a scale that could empirically measure social distance. So widely used is his social distance scale that it is frequently referred to as the *Bogardus scale*.

The scale asks people how willing they would be to interact with various racial and ethnic groups in specified social situations. The situations describe different degrees of social contact or social distance. The seven items used, with their corresponding distance scores, follow.

To close kinship by marriage (1.00)

To my club as personal chums (2.00)

To my street as neighbors (3.00)

To employment in my occupation (4.00)

To citizenship in my country (5.00)

As visitors only to my country (6.00)

Would exclude from my country (7.00)

A score of 1.00 toward any group would indicate no social distance, therefore no prejudice. The social distance scale has been administered to many different groups, even in other countries (Banton, 1967, pp. 315–325; Cowgill, 1968; Triandis and Triandis, 1960; Westie, 1952; Westie and Howard, 1954). Despite some

*Asian Americans protest the limited, stereotypical portrayal they receive in Hollywood movies. As in this 1980 release "Fiendish Plot of Dr. Fu Manchu," a non-Asian (Peter Sellers) plays the part of an Asian.*

minor flaws and certain refinements in the scale, the results of studies are useful and can be compared.

The data in Figure 2.2 summarize the results of studies using the social distance scale in the United States over a 65-year period. In the top third of the hierarchy are White Americans and northern Europeans. In the middle are eastern and southern Europeans, and generally near the bottom are racial minorities. This prestige hierarchy resembles the relative proportions of the various groups in the population. The arrows indicate some of the dramatic changes in the ranking. For example, the Japanese dropped from twenty-third to thirtieth during World War II, rose to twenty-fifth by 1966 only to fall again to twenty-ninth in 1991 as they became economic competitors. Two groups made marked upward progress between 1966 and 1991—Russian and Black Americans. The stability of rankings over more than half a century, however, is remarkable.

The similarity in the hierarchy during the past 65 years is not limited to White respondents. Several times the scale has been administered to Jewish, Chicano, Asian, Puerto Rican, Black African, and Black American groups. These groups generally share the same hierarchy, although they place their own group at the top. The extent of prejudice as illustrated in the ranking of racial and ethnic groups seems to be widely shared (Bogardus, 1959; Carlson and Iovini, 1985; Crull and Bruton, 1985; Derbyshire and Brody, 1964; R. Hartley, 1946; Hensley, 1989; Dyer, 1989; Kinloch, 1973; Kinloch and Borders, 1972; Schaefer, 1987; Thornton and Taylor, 1988).

A tentative conclusion we can draw from these studies is that the extent of prejudice is decreasing. At the bottom of Figure 2.2 is the arithmetic mean of the racial reactions, on the scale of 1.0 to 7.0. Although the change is slight from survey to survey, it is consistently downward for the entire group. Many specific nationalities and races, however, have experienced little change. The spread in social distance (the difference between the top- and bottom-ranked groups) also decreases or holds steady from 1926 to 1991, indicating that fewer distinctions are being made, although some are still being made. This result has been confirmed empirically in research on stereotypes also (Crull and Bruton, 1985; Owen et al., 1981).

## Attitude Change

Nationwide surveys over the years have consistently shown growing support by Whites for integration, even during the southern resistance and northern turmoil of the 1960s. Table 2.2 lists six questions that have appeared on several opinion polls from 1942 to 1991. With few exceptions, responses show an increase in the number of Whites responding positively to hypothetical situations of increased contact with African Americans. For example, 30 percent of the Whites sampled in 1942 felt that Blacks should not attend separate schools (statement 3), but by 1970 74 percent supported integrated schools, and fully 93 percent responded in that manner in 1991. Of course, this is what Whites *say* they will do. As Andrew Greeley and Paul Sheatsley observe, "attitudes are not

**FIGURE 2.2** Changes in Social Distance, 1926–1991

The social distance scale developed by Emory Bogardus has been a useful measure of people's feelings of hostility toward different racial and ethnic groups.

| | I 1926 | | II 1946 | | III 1966 | | IV 1977 | | V 1991 | |
|---|---|---|---|---|---|---|---|---|---|---|
| 1 | English | 1.06 | Americans (U.S. white) | 1.04 | Americans (U.S. white) | 1.07 | Americans (U.S. white) | 1.25 | Americans (U.S. white) | 1.00 |
| 2 | Americans (U.S. white) | 1.10 | Canadians | 1.11 | English | 1.14 | English | 1.39 | English | 1.08 |
| 3 | Canadians | 1.13 | English | 1.13 | Canadians | 1.15 | Canadians | 1.42 | French | 1.16 |
| 4 | Scots | 1.13 | Irish | 1.24 | French | 1.36 | French | 1.58 | Canadians | 1.21 |
| 5 | Irish | 1.30 | Scots | 1.26 | Irish | 1.40 | Italians | 1.65 | Italians | 1.27 |
| 6 | French | 1.32 | French | 1.31 | Swedish | 1.42 | Swedish | 1.68 | Irish | 1.30 |
| 7 | Germans | 1.46 | Norwegians | 1.35 | Norwegians | 1.50 | Irish | 1.69 | Germans | 1.36 |
| 8 | Swedish | 1.54 | Hollanders | 1.37 | Italians | 1.51 | Hollanders | 1.83 | Swedish | 1.38 |
| 9 | Hollanders | 1.56 | Swedish | 1.40 | Scots | 1.53 | Scots | 1.83 | Scots | 1.50 |
| 10 | Norwegians | 1.59 | Germans | 1.59 | Germans | 1.54 | American Indians | 1.84 | Hollanders | 1.56 |
| 11 | Spanish | 1.72 | Finns | 1.63 | Hollanders | 1.54 | Germans | 1.87 | Norwegians | 1.66 |
| 12 | Finns | 1.83 | Czechs | 1.76 | Finns | 1.67 | Norwegians | 1.93 | Indians (U.S.) | 1.70 |
| 13 | Russians | 1.88 | Russians | 1.83 | Greeks | 1.82 | Spanish | 1.98 | Greeks | 1.73 |
| 14 | Italians | 1.94 | Poles | 1.84 | Spanish | 1.93 | Finns | 2.00 | Finns | 1.73 |
| 15 | Poles | 2.01 | Spanish | 1.94 | Jews | 1.97 | Jews | 2.01 | Poles | 1.74 |
| 16 | Armenians | 2.06 | Italians | 2.28 | Poles | 1.98 | Greeks | 2.02 | Russians | 1.76 |
| 17 | Czechs | 2.08 | Armenians | 2.29 | Czechs | 2.02 | Negroes | 2.03 | Spanish | 1.77 |
| 18 | Indians (American) | 2.38 | Greeks | 2.29 | Indians (American) | 2.12 | Poles | 2.11 | Jews | 1.84 |
| 19 | Jews | 2.39 | Jews | 2.32 | Japanese Americans | 2.14 | Mexican Americans | 2.17 | Mexicans (U.S.) | 1.84 |
| 20 | Greeks | 2.47 | Indians (American) | 2.45 | Armenians | 2.18 | Japanese Americans | 2.18 | Czechs | 1.90 |
| 21 | Mexicans | 2.69 | Chinese | 2.50 | Filipinos | 2.31 | Armenians | 2.20 | Americans (U.S. black) | 1.94 |
| 22 | Mexican Americans | — | Mexican Americans | 2.52 | Chinese | 2.34 | Czechs | 2.23 | Chinese | 1.96 |
| 23 | Japanese | 2.80 | Filipinos | 2.76 | Mexican Americans | 2.37 | Chinese | 2.29 | Filipinos | 2.04 |
| 24 | Japanese Americans | — | Mexicans | 2.89 | Russians | 2.38 | Filipino s | 2.31 | Japanese (U.S.) | 2.06 |
| 25 | Filipinos | 3.00 | Turks | 2.89 | Japanese | 2.41 | Japanese | 2.38 | Armenians | 2.17 |
| 26 | Negroes | 3.28 | Japanese Americans | 2.90 | Turks | 2.48 | Mexicans | 2.40 | Turks | 2.23 |
| 27 | Turks | 3.30 | Koreans | 3.05 | Koreans | 2.51 | Turks | 2.55 | Koreans | 2.24 |
| 28 | Chinese | 3.36 | Indians (from India) | 3.43 | Mexicans | 2.56 | Indians (of India) | 2.55 | Mexicans | 2.27 |
| 29 | Koreans | 3.60 | Negroes | 3.60 | Negroes | 2.56 | Russians | 2.57 | Japanese | 2.37 |
| 30 | Indians (from India) | 3.91 | Japanese | 3.61 | Indians (from India) | 2.62 | Koreans | 2.63 | Indians (India) | 2.39 |
| | Arithmetic mean | 2.14 | Arithmetic mean | 2.12 | Arithmetic mean | 1.92 | Arithmetic mean | 1.93 | Arithmetic mean | 1.76 |
| | Spread in distance | 2.85 | Spread in distance | 2.57 | Spread in distance | 1.56 | Spread in distance | 1.38 | Spread in distance | 1.39 |

*Sources:* Adapted from Emory S. Bogardus, "Comparing Racial Distance in Ethiopia, South Africa, and the United States," *Sociology and Social Research,* 52, January 1968, p. 152; Carolyn A. Owen, Howard C. Eisner, and Thomas R. McFaul, "A Half-Century of Social Distance Research: National Replication of the Bogardus Studies," *Sociology and Social Research,* 66, October 1981, p. 89; and Tae H. Song, "Social Contact and Ethnic Distance Between Koreans and the U.S. Whites in the United States," Unpub. paper. Macomb, IL: Western Illinois University, 1991. Reprinted by permission.

necessarily predictive of behavior. A man may be a staunch integrationist and still feel his neighborhood is 'threatened' " (1971, p. 9). Attitudes are still important, apart from behavior. A change of attitude may create a context in which legislative or behavioral change can occur. Such attitude changes leading to behavior changes did, in fact, occur in some areas during the 1960s. Changes in intergroup behavior mandated by law in housing, schools, public places of accommodation, and on the job appear to be responsible for making some new kinds of interracial contact a social reality. Attitudes translate into votes, peer pressure, and political clout, each of which can facilitate or hinder efforts to undo racial inequality (Oskamp, 1977; Schaefer, 1986).

The trend toward tolerance was not limited to any subgroup of Whites. The 1960s witnessed an increase in support for integration in all regions (including the South), age groups (especially those under twenty-five), income levels, levels of education, and occupational groups. The rise of support was a nationwide phenomenon (Greeley and Sheatsley, 1971). Table 2.3 displays still further evidence of improved attitudes toward Blacks. The proportion of Whites who would vote for an African American presidential candidate more than doubled between 1958 and 1991. This same table also displays the hard core of White resistance that remains. Nearly one in seven White adults would not even vote for a qualified Black person nominated by their own political party.

During the civil disorders from 1965 to 1968, many people talked about a *White backlash*. The militancy of the Black Power movement had allegedly caused a hardening and reversal of White attitudes. The data in Tables 2.2 and 2.3 and other surveys, however, present little evidence of a reversal of attitudes on the part of previously tolerant Whites. If that is so, how did the term White backlash become so widely used? The tumult of the 1960s made race more important for Whites in all regions, not just the South. Race also became important in many political issues, meaning that anti-Black feelings could not only be voiced as bigoted outbursts but could also be used as a political force to oppose open housing, affirmative action, and school busing. Over the years, Whites have shown greater resistance to new advances by African Americans while gradually accepting past advances. This change seems to be verified in Table 2.2: Whites increasingly support accomplishments of the civil rights movement while consistently agreeing that Blacks should not push themselves where they are not wanted; and also Whites display, begrudgingly, very slow acceptance of busing. This resistance to further change came to be called the White backlash (for a different view, see Smith and Sheatsley, 1984).

Surveying White attitudes toward Blacks makes two conclusions inescapable. First, attitudes are subject to change, and in periods of dramatic social upheaval dramatic shifts can occur in one generation. Second, there is no consensus among Whites.

A third conclusion is that less progress has been made in the latter part of the twentieth century than was in the 1950s and 1960s. Economically less successful groups like African Americans and Hispanics tend to be credited with negative traits. In effect, we have another instance of "blaming the victim." Of concern is

**TABLE 2.2**  Attitudes of Whites Toward Blacks, 1942–1991 (percentage affirmative)

Over the last 50 years attitudes of White Americans toward African Americans have improved; however, most of this change took place in the 1950s and 1960s. There has been relatively little change in the last 30 years.

| | Year 1942 | 1956 | 1963 | 1965 | 1967 | 1970 | 1972 | 1976 | 1977 | 1978 | 1982 | 1985 | 1991 |
|---|---|---|---|---|---|---|---|---|---|---|---|---|---|
| 1. Negroes/Blacks have the same intelligence as White people given the same education and training. | 42 | 77 | 78 | | | | | 72 | | 75 | | | |
| 2. Negroes/Blacks should not push themselves where they are not wanted. | | | 75 | | | 84 | 76 | 71 | 73 | | 59 | 61 | |
| 3. White students and Negroes/Blacks should go to the same schools, not separate ones. | 30 | 49 | 63 | 67 | | 74 | 86 | 85 | 86 | | 91 | 93 | |
| 4. Do you favor the busing of Negro/Black and White school children from one district to another? | | | | | | | 14 | 13 | 13 | 17 | 16 | 19 | 32 |
| 5. If a Negro/Black came to live next door, you would move. | 67 | | 45 | 35 | 35 | | 19 | | | 13 | | 7 | |
| 6. If Negroes/Blacks came to live in great numbers in your neighborhood, you would move. | | | 78 | 69 | 71 | | | | | 51 | | | |

*Note:* Percentages indicate the proportion of the nationwide sample who agreed with the statement. The remaining respondents did not necessarily disagree: some did not answer and some expressed no opinion. The wording of the questions may change slightly from one year to the next. Questions not asked in a particular year are indicated by a blank. *Sources:* Campbell and Schuman, 1968; Gallup, 1972; Greeley and Sheatsley, 1971; Hyman and Sheatsley, 1964; National Opinion Research Center, 1991; *Newsweek,* 1979; M. Schwartz, 1967; Skolnick, 1969; Smith and Sheatsley, 1984.

TABLE 2.3   White Support for a Black Presidential Candidate, 1958–1991

An increasing proportion of White Americans are willing to vote for an African American Presidential candidate.

| Year | *Percentage willing to vote for a qualified Black nominated by their own political party* |
|------|------|
| 1958 | 38 |
| 1961 | 50 |
| 1963 | 47 |
| 1965 | 59 |
| 1967 | 54 |
| 1969 | 67 |
| 1972 | 67 |
| 1978 | 81 |
| 1983 | 86 |
| 1985 | 83 |
| 1991 | 81 |

*Sources:* Gallup, 1972; National Opinion Research Center, 1991.

that this view comes at a time when the willingness of government to address domestic ills is limited by increasing opposition to new taxes. While there is some evidence that fewer Whites are consistently prejudiced on all issues from interracial marriage to school integration, it is also apparent that Whites continue to endorse some anti-Black statements, and that negative images of people of color are widespread (Bobo and Kluegel, 1991; Tuch, 1981).

## MOOD OF THE MINORITY

Opinion pollsters have been interested in White attitudes on racial issues longer than they have in the views of subordinate groups. This neglect of minority attitudes reflects, in part, the bias of the White researchers. It also stems from the contention that the dominant group is more important to study because it is in a better position to act out beliefs (Marx, 1969, p. xxv; Schuman et al., 1985).

The results of a 1991 nationwide survey of youth in the United States ages 15–24 offer insight into the sharply different attitudes of African Americans, Hispanics, and Whites (see Table 2.4). Of course, each racial and ethnic group is not homogeneous and does not speak with one voice. Yet we are able to identify some significant differences. Young Whites are more optimistic about the future. Hispanics and African Americans are more likely to have experienced discrimination, but nearly half of the White youth feel they are denied scholarships, jobs, and promotions because of special preferences they feel are extended to minorities.

*Efforts to move ahead often bring prejudice to the surface. Young men of Dubuque, Iowa, began sporting shirts of the National Association for the Advancement of White People, a racist group, in response to that virtually all-White city's efforts to attract Black families to live there.*

Particularly noteworthy is the view that young people hold for integration. Half of the Whites see neighborhood and school integration as very important, with an even greater proportion of Hispanics and African Americans concurring. The three groups seem to come together on one question—one-third feel that integration is unlikely to happen, but two-thirds of Whites, Blacks, and Hispanics alike believe that racial integration "could happen."

Racial attitudes were reassessed in the aftermath of the 1992 Los Angeles riots. The worst civil disturbance in the 20th century, with 52 dead, gave racism frontpage attention throughout the United States. The riots were precipitated by a jury's failing to find four Los Angeles police officers guilty of beating a Black man, Rodney King. Since the beating had been videotaped and reshown numerous times on television, most people felt the police were guilty. In fact a survey taken after the rioting began found 100 percent of African Americans and

**TABLE 2.4**   Views of the United States

Results of a December 1991 national survey of American youth, ages 15–24

|  | *Blacks* | *Hispanics* | *Whites* |
|---|---|---|---|
| America's best years are ahead | 27% | 28% | 42% |
| Race relations are generally good | 35 | 46 | 44 |
| Is personally a victim of racial or ethnic discrimination | 41 | 36 | 18 |
| Qualified minorities are denied scholarships, jobs, and promotions because of racial prejudice | 68 | 52 | 34 |
| Qualified Whites are denied scholarships, jobs, and promotions because minorities get special preference | 19 | 29 | 49 |
| Racial integration in neighborhood, schools, and work is very important | 71 | 72 | 51 |
| Racial integration is unlikely to happen | 36 | 28 | 32 |

*Source:* People for the American Way, 1992, pp. 47, 155, 158, 161.

86 percent of Whites believing that the jury's verdict was wrong. Yet on other issues there was more disagreement. Two-thirds of Whites compared to 90 percent of Blacks saw the Rodney King beating as evidence of widespread racism. Blacks definitely saw race relations worsening in the wake of the riots. Fully 43 percent felt they were poor, compared to 17 percent of Whites questioned (M. Baumann, 1992).

Annual surveys giving respondents an opportunity to identify what they feel to be the nation's major problems consistently show "civil rights" to be among the top six worries for African Americans. It barely makes the top 20 among White respondents, however (M. Gates, 1986). One might wonder whether this continued subordination has led Blacks to have anti-Black feelings as well, as some people contend.

We have focused so far on what usually comes to mind when we think about prejudice: one group's hating another group. But there is another form of prejudice: a group may come to hate itself. Members of groups held in low esteem by society may, as a result, have low self-esteem themselves. Many social scientists believe that members of minority groups hate themselves or, at least, have low self-esteem. Similarly, they argue that Whites have high self-esteem. High self-esteem means that an individual has fundamental respect for him- or herself, appreciates his or her merits, and is aware of personal faults and will strive to overcome them. The research literature of the 1940s through the 1960s emphasized the low self-esteem of minorities. Usually the subject has been African Americans, but the argument was also generalized to include any subordinate racial or ethnic group (Porter, 1985; Rosenberg and Simmons, 1971, p. 9).

Is this assessment true? Leonard Bloom (1971, pp. 68–69) cautions against assuming that minority status influences, either in a good or a bad way, personality traits. First, Bloom says, doing so may create a stereotype. We cannot accurately describe a Black personality, any more than we can a White personality. Second, characteristics of minority group members are not completely the result of subordinate racial status but are influenced by low incomes, poor neighborhoods, and so forth. Third, many studies of personality imply that certain values are normal or preferable, but the values chosen are those of dominant groups.

If, as Bloom suggests, assessments of a minority group's personality are so prone to misjudgments, why is the belief in low self-esteem so widely held? Much of the research rests on studies with pre-school age Black children asked to express preferences among dolls with different facial color. Indeed, one such study by psychologists Kenneth and Mamie Clark (1947) was cited in the arguments before the Supreme Court in the landmark 1954 case, *Brown* v. *Board of Education*. While subsequent doll studies (Powell-Hopson and Hopson, 1988) have sometimes shown Black children's preference for white-faced dolls, other social scientists contend this shows a realization of what most commercially-sold dolls look like rather than documenting low self-esteem.

The fact that African-American, as well as other subordinate groups' children, can realistically see that Whites have more power and resources and thereby rate them higher does not mean that they personally feel inferior. Indeed studies, even with children, show that when the self-images of middle class or affluent African Americans are measured, their feelings of self-esteem are more positive than those of comparable Whites (Cross, 1991; Hughes and Demo, 1989; Martinez and Dukes, 1991; Raymond, 1991; Rosenberg and Simmons, 1971).

## REDUCING PREJUDICE

Focusing on how to eliminate prejudice involves an explicit value judgment: prejudice is wrong and causes problems for those who are prejudiced and for their victims. The obvious way to eliminate prejudice is to eliminate its causes— the desire to exploit, the fear of being threatened, and unacceptable personal failure. These might be eliminated by personal therapy, but therapy, even if it worked for everyone, is no solution. Such a program would not be feasible because of prohibitive cost and because it would have to be compulsory, which would violate civil rights. Furthermore, many of those in need of such therapy would not acknowledge their problem—the first step in effective therapy (Banfield, 1974, p. 260).

The answer would appear to rest with programs directed at society as a whole. Prejudice is indirectly attacked when discrimination is attacked. Despite prevailing beliefs to the contrary, you can legislate against prejudice; statutes and decisions do affect attitudes. In the past, people firmly believed that laws could not defy norms, especially racist ones. Recent history, especially after the civil rights movement began in 1954, has challenged that common wisdom. Laws and court rulings that equalize the treatment of Blacks and Whites have led people to reevaluate their beliefs about what is right and wrong. The increasing tolerance of Whites during the civil rights period from 1954 to 1965 (see Table 2.2), seems to support this conclusion.

Much research has been done to determine how to change negative attitudes toward groups of people. The most encouraging findings point to mass media, education, and intergroup contact.

## Mass Media and Education

The research on mass media and education consists of two types—research performed in artificially (experimentally) created situations, and studies examining the influence on attitudes of motion pictures, television, and advertisements.

Leaflets, radio commercials, comic books, billboards, and classroom posters bombard people with the message of racial harmony. Television audiences watch a public service message that for thirty seconds shows smiling White and African American infants reaching out toward each other. Law enforcement and military personnel attend in-service training sessions that preach the value of a pluralistic society. Does this publicity do any good? Do these programs make any difference?

Most but not all studies show that well-constructed programs do have some positive effect in reducing prejudice, at least temporarily. The reduction is rarely as much as one might wish, however. The difficulty is that a single program is insufficient to change lifelong habits, especially if little is done to reinforce the program once it ends. Persuasion to respect other groups does not operate in a clear field because, in their ordinary environments, individuals are still subjected to pro-prejudice arguments. Children and adults are encouraged to laugh at Polish jokes, or a Black adolescent may be discouraged by peers from befriending a White youth. All this serves to undermine the effectiveness of prejudice reduction programs (Allport, 1958, pp. 444–458).

Study results examine the influence of educational programs specifically designed to reduce prejudice. However, studies consistently document that increased formal education, regardless of content, is associated with racial tolerance. Research data show that more highly educated people are more likely to indicate respect and liking for groups different from themselves. Why should more years of schooling have this effect? It could be that more education gives a more universal outlook and makes a person less likely to endorse myths that sustain racial prejudice. Formal education teaches the importance of qualifying statements and the need at least to question rigid categorizations, if not reject them altogether. Bagley suggests that "education gives training in objective and dispassionate thought, dispositions which are obviously inimical to prejudice" (1970, p. 72). An alternative explanation is that education does not actually reduce intolerance but simply makes individuals more careful about revealing it. Formal education may simply instruct individuals in the proper responses, which in some settings, could even be prejudiced views. Regardless of a clear-cut explanation, either theory suggests that the continued trend to a better-educated population will contribute to a reduction of overt prejudice (Case et al., 1989; Glock et al., 1966, p. 51; Schaefer, 1976a, pp. 127–128; M. Schwartz, 1967, p. 119; Stouffer, 1955, pp. 94–95; Weil, 1983).

Education is not limited to formal schooling; increasingly, many forms of instruction are offered in the workplace. Remedies for intolerance can be taught there as well. With the entry of women and minority men into nontraditional work settings, training and support programs take on increased importance. Generally, when minorities enter an organization, they are thinly represented. Education programs have begun so that management does not treat these pioneers as "golden" (can do no wrong) or as hopeless cases doomed to failure (Pettigrew and Martin, 1987).

The mass media, like schooling, may reduce prejudice without the need for specially designed programs. Television, radio, motion pictures, newspapers, and magazines present only a slice of real life, but what effect do they have on prejudice if the content is racist or antiracist, sexist or antisexist? As with measuring the influence of antiprejudice programs, making strong conclusions on the mass media's effect is hazardous, but the evidence points to a measurable effect. The 1915 movie *The Birth of a Nation* depicts African Americans unfavorably and glorifies the Ku Klux Klan. A study of Illinois schoolchildren has shown that watching the movie made them more unfavorably inclined toward African Americans, a negative effect that persisted even five months later when the children were retested. Conversely, the 1947 movie *Gentleman's Agreement*, which took a strong stand against anti-Semitism, appears to have softened the anti-Semitic feelings of its audience (Ball-Rokeach et al., 1984; Commission on Civil Rights, 1977b, 1980b; Middleton, 1960).

No minority group is immune from mistreatment in the media. The nearly 3 million Arab Americans, mostly Lebanese, Syrian, and Egyptian, receive little attention in discussion of multiculturalism in the United States. Yet they continue to be categorized in a negative fashion. Shaheen (1984, p. 52), a professor of mass communication, is critical of prime-time television for perpetuating four myths about Arabs: "They are fabulously wealthy; they are barbaric and uncultured; they are sex maniacs with a penchant for white slavery; and they are prone to terrorist acts." While the use of stereotyping can promote in-group solidarity, conflict theorists point out that stereotypes contribute to prejudice and thereby assists the subordination of minority groups. For example during the 1990–1991 Persian Gulf War, Arab-American citizens were barred for a period from flying on a United States airline and anti-Arab American incidents escalated in general nationwide (S. Johnson, 1991; Michalek, 1989).

Recent research has examined the influence of television because it commands the widest viewing audience among children and adolescents. A 1988 study found that almost a third of high school students feel that television entertainment is "an accurate representation" of African-American "real life" (Lichter and Lichter, 1988). Many programs, like "Amos 'n' Andy" or films with "dumb Injuns," which depict minority groups in stereotyped, demeaning roles no longer are shown. Blacks and members of other subordinate groups are now more likely than before to appear in programs and commercials. As a result of the networks' greater sensitivity to the presentation of minority groups, people now see more balanced portrayals. Television programs showing positive African American family life such as "Family Matters," "The Cosby Show," and "227" are quite a change from "Diff'rent Strokes" and "Webster" which promoted the notion that African American orphans are best off in White homes. Even the news with its emphasis on crime and corruption contributes to the negative stereotype as noted by Patricia Raybon in "Listen to Their Voices."

But how far have the mass media really come? This chapter has already mentioned the research of the Commission on Civil Rights on the portrayal of women in television. Expert on communications George Gerbner concluded that the image of other minorities is not much better. The overwhelming majority of Black actors on television are employed in comedic roles; no Black dramatic series has lasted a season and very few are even given a chance. Asians and Hispanics have a similar image problem in contemporary television. The problem has been further complicated by the home-video revolution, which has led video cassette marketers to exhume many of the most stereotypic films. Even professional wrestling stars of the 1980s such as the Iron Sheik, the Ugandan Giant, Mr. Fuji, and Chief Jay Strongbow firmly reinforce stereotypes (Gates, 1989; B. Maguire and Wozniak, 1987).

The image of minorities in motion pictures is equally poor. The 1980s witnessed major movies distorting the image of minority groups. For example, *The Fiendish Plot of Dr. Fu Manchu,* starring Peter Sellers, appeared in 1980; and in the next year Paul Newman was featured in *Fort Apache, the Bronx,* which stereotypes the portrayal of both Black Americans and Puerto Ricans. The 1987 Oscar-winning film *Platoon* failed to show Black soldiers' leadership in the Vietnam War. By looking at the past, we can detect progress, but certainly the mass media image of women and racial groups does not uniformly cause people to discard the old definitions, the old stereotypes.

Because prejudice is acquired from our social environment, it follows that the mass media and educational programs, as major precipitates of that environment, influence the level of prejudice. The movement to eliminate stereotyping of minorities and the sexes in textbooks and on television recognizes this influence. Most of the effort has been to avoid contributing to racial hostility; less

## A Case of "Severe Bias"

### Patricia Raybon

*Former editor of* The Denver Post's *Sunday Contemporary* magazine, *Patricia Raybon expresses concern about the one-sided presentation that African Americans receive in the media.*

This is who I am not. I am not a crack addict. I am not a welfare mother. I am not illiterate. I am not a prostitute. I have never been in jail. My children are not in gangs. My husband doesn't beat me. My home is not a tenement. None of these things defines who I am, nor do they describe the other black people I've known and worked with and loved and befriended over these 40 years of my life.

Nor does it describe most of black America, period.

Yet in the eyes of the American news media, this is what black America is: poor, criminal, addicted and dysfunctional. Indeed, media coverage of black America is so one-sided, so imbalanced that the most victimized and hurting segment of the black community—a small segment, at best—is presented not as the exception but as the norm. It is an insidious practice, all the uglier for its blatancy.

In recent months, oftentimes in this very magazine, I have observed a steady offering of media reports on crack babies, gang warfare, violent youth, poverty and homelessness— and in most cases, the people featured in the photos and stories were black. At the same time, articles that discuss other aspects of American life—from home buying to medicine to technol-

ogy to nutrition—rarely, if ever, show blacks playing a positive role, or for that matter, any role at all.

Day after day, week after week, this message—that black America is dysfunctional and unwhole—gets transmitted across the American landscape. Sadly, as a result, America never learns the truth about what is actually a wonderful, vibrant, creative community of people.

Most black Americans are *not* poor. Most black teenagers are *not* crack addicts. Most black mothers are *not* on welfare. Indeed, in sheer numbers, more *white* Americans are poor and on welfare than are black. Yet one never would deduce that by watching television or reading American newspapers and magazines. . . .

I am reminded, for example, of the controversial Spike Lee film, "Do the Right Thing," and the criticism by some movie reviewers that the film's ghetto neighborhood isn't populated by addicts and drug pushers—and thus is not a true depiction.

In fact, millions of black Americans live in neighborhoods where the most common sights are children playing and couples walking their dogs. In my own inner-city neighborhood in Denver—an area that the local press consistently describes as "gang territory"—I have yet to see a recognizable "gang" member or any "gang" activity (drug dealing or drive-by shootings), nor have I been the victim of "gang violence."

Yet to students of American culture—in the case of Spike Lee's film, the movie reviewers—a black, inner-city neighborhood can only be one thing to be real: drug-infested and dysfunctioning. Is this my ego talking? In part, yes. For the millions of black people like myself—ordinary, hard-working, law-abiding, tax-paying Americans—the media's blindness to the fact that we even exist, let alone to our contributions to American society, is a bitter cup to drunk. And as self-reliant as most black Americans are—because we've had to be self-reliant—even the strongest among us still crave affirmation.

I want that. I want it for my children. I want it for all the beautiful, healthy, funny, smart black Americans I have known and loved over the years.

And I want it for the rest of America, too.

I want America to know us—all of us—for who we really are. To see us in all of our complexity, our subtleness, our artfulness, our enterprise, our specialness, our loveliness, our American-ness. That is the real portrait of black America—that we're strong people, surviving people, capable people. That may be the best-kept secret in America. If so, it's time to let the truth be known.

From "A Case for 'Severe Bias' " by Patricia Raybon. *Newsweek* 114 (October 2, 1989), p. 11. Reprinted by permission of Patricia Raybon.

effort has been made to attack prejudice actively, primarily because no one knows how to do that effectively. Looking for a way of directly attacking prejudice, many people advocate intergroup contact.

## Equal-Status Contact

An impressive number of research studies has been made of the *contact hypothesis*. This hypothesis, reflecting an interactionist perspective, states that interracial contact between people of equal status in harmonious circumstances will cause them to become less prejudiced and abandon previously held stereotypes. Most studies indicate that such contact also improves the attitude of minority group members. The importance of equal status in the interaction cannot be stressed enough. If a Puerto Rican is abused by his employer, little interracial harmony is promoted. Similarly, the situation in which contact occurs must be pleasant, making a positive evaluation likely for both individuals. Contact between two nurses, one Black and the other White, competing for one vacancy as a supervisor, may lead to greater racial hostility (Schaefer, 1976a, pp. 107–126).

The key factor in reducing hostility in addition to equal-status contact is the presence of a common goal. If people are in competition as already noted, contact may heighten tension. However, bringing people together to share a common task has been shown to reduce ill-feelings even when bringing together different racial, ethnic, or religious groups (Sherif and Sherif, 1969, pp. 228–268; Slavin, 1985).

As African Americans and other minorities slowly gain access to better-paying and more responsible jobs, the contact hypothesis takes on greater significance. Usually the availability of equal-status interaction is taken for granted. Yet how often does intergroup contact in everyday life conform to the equal-status idea of the contact hypothesis? Probably not as often as assured by researchers hoping to see a lessening of tension (Ford, 1986).

## GLANCING BACK AND LOOKING AHEAD

This chapter has examined theories of prejudice and measurements of its extent. Prejudice should not be confused with discrimination. The two concepts are not the same: prejudice refers to negative attitudes, and discrimination to negative behavior toward a group.

Several theories try to explain why prejudice exists. Some emphasize economic concerns (the exploitation and scapegoating theories), whereas other approaches stress personality or structural factors. No one explanation is sufficient. Surveys conducted in the United States during the past 40 years point to a reduction of prejudice, but they also show that many Whites and Blacks are still intolerant of each other. Equal-status contact and the shared-coping approach may reduce hostility among groups. Mass media seem to be of limited value in reducing discrimination, and may even intensify ill feeling through promoting stereotypic images.

Chapter 3 outlines the effects of discrimination. Discrimination's costs are high to both dominant and subordinate groups. With that in mind we will examine some techniques to reduce discrimination.

## KEY TERMS

**authoritarian personality** A psychological construct of a personality type likely to be prejudiced and to use others as scapegoats.

**caste approach** An approach that views race and social class as synonymous, with disadvantaged minorities occupying the lowest social class and having little, if any, opportunity to improve their social position.

**contact hypothesis** An interactionist perspective stating that interracial contact between people with equal status in noncompetitive circumstances will reduce prejudice.

**discrimination** The denial of opportunities and equal rights to individuals and groups because of prejudice or other arbitrary reasons.

**ethnocentrism** The tendency to assume that one's culture and way of life are superior to all others.

**ethnophaulism** Ethnic or racial slurs, including derisive nicknames.

**exploitation theory** A Marxist theory that views racial subordination in the United States as a manifestation of the class system inherent in capitalism.

**prejudice** A negative attitude toward an entire category of people, such as a racial or ethnic minority.

**scapegoat** A person or group blamed irrationally for another person's or group's problems or difficulties.

**structural approach** The view that prejudice is influenced by societal norms and situations that serve to encourage or discourage tolerance of minorities.

**White backlash** White resistance to further improvement in the status of Black people.

## FOR FURTHER INFORMATION

Gordon W. Allport. *The Nature of Prejudice*, 25th Anniversary Edition. Reading, MA: Addison-Wesley, 1979.

The various theories of prejudice are presented and all the relevant studies available at the time this classic work was published are summarized.

John Brigham and Theodore Weissbach, eds. *Racial Attitudes in America: Analyses and Findings of Social Psychology*. New York: Harper and Row, 1972.

A complete anthology with well-written introductions to previously published articles. Among those included are some cited in this chapter: Allport (1962), Brigham (1973), Hraba and Grant (1970), Karlins et al. (1969), Pettigrew (1959), and Triandis and Triandis (1960).

Arthur G. Miller, ed. *In the Eye of the Beholder: Contemporary Issues in Stereotyping*. New York: Praeger, 1982.

This comprehensive collection of ten articles covers stereotyping based on race, ethnicity, sex, mental disorders, age, and physical attractiveness.

Philip Perlmutter. *Divided We Fall: A History of Ethnic, Religious, and Racial Prejudice in America*. Ames: Iowa State University Press, 1991.

An examination of bigotry in the United States from the beginning of the country to the present, considering groups such as Native Americans, Scotch Irish, Catholics, Mormons, Jews, Huguenots, and Japanese.

William Peters. *A Class Divided. Then and Now* (expanded edition). New Haven: Yale University Press, 1987.

A description of the well-publicized effort of an elementary school teacher to sensitize children to the impact of prejudice and discrimination by dividing her class into privileged brown-eyed children and inferior blue-eyed children.

Thomas F. Pettigrew, George M. Frederickson, Dale T. Knobel, Nathan Glazer, Reed Ueda. *Prejudice*. Cambridge, MA: The Belknap Press of Harvard University Press, 1982.

This paperback concisely summarizes social psychological perspectives on prejudice, a history of discrimination in the United States, and efforts to eradicate it. The three essays are taken from the *Harvard Encyclopedia of American Ethnic Groups*.

James Ridgeway. *Blood on the Face*. New York: Thunder's Mouth Press, 1990.

A journalistic look at the rise of militant White groups including the Ku Klux Klan, Posse Comitatus, and Nazi Skinheads.

Howard Schuman, Charlotte Steeh, and Lawrence Bobo. *Racial Attitudes in America: Trends and Interpretations*. Cambridge, MA: Harvard University Press, 1985.

Traces the changes, or lack thereof, in White and Black American attitudes toward racial issues.

# DISCRIMINATION

## Chapter Outline

**Understanding Discrimination**
Relative Versus Absolute Deprivation
Total Discrimination
**Institutional Discrimination**
**Dual Labor Market**
**The Underclass**
**Discrimination in American Society**
Measuring Discrimination

Eliminating Discrimination
**Affirmative Action**
Affirmative Action Explained
Legal Debates
**Glancing Back and Looking Ahead**
**Key Terms**
**For Further Information**

---

**✳ HIGHLIGHTS ✳**

Just as social scientists have advanced theories to explain why people are prejudiced, they have presented explanations of why discrimination occurs. Social scientists look more and more at the manner in which institutions, not individuals, discriminate. *Institutional discrimination* describes the pattern in social institutions which produces or perpetuates inequalities, even if individuals in the society do not intend to be racist or sexist. Data document that gaps do exist among racial and ethnic groups. Historically, attempts have been made to reduce discrimination, usually as a result of strong lobbying efforts by minorities themselves. More recently, *affirmative action* guidelines have been employed in an effort to equalize opportunity.

---

The agents of conflict, prejudice and discrimination, take their toll on people. Despite apparent reductions in prejudice and legislative efforts to eliminate discrimination, members of dominant and subordinate groups pay a price for continued intolerance.

## UNDERSTANDING DISCRIMINATION

Discrimination is the denial of opportunities and equal rights to individuals and groups because of prejudice or for other arbitrary reasons. Some Americans find it difficult to see discrimination as a widespread phenomenon. "After all," it is often said, "these minorities drive cars, hold jobs, own their homes, and even go to college." This does not mean that discrimination is rare. An understnading of discrimination in modern industrial societies such as the United States must begin by distinguishing between relative and absolute deprivation.

### Relative Versus Absolute Deprivation

Conflict theorists have correctly said that it is not absolute, unchanging standards that determine deprivation and oppression. It is crucial that although minority groups may be viewed as having adequate or even good incomes, housing, health care, and educational opportunities, it is their position *relative* to some other group that offers evidence of discrimination.

The term *relative deprivation* is defined as the conscious feeling of a negative discrepancy between legitimate expectations and present actualities (J. Wilson, 1973, p. 69). We first encountered the term "relative deprivation " in Chapter 1 as we described Hurh and Kim's (1990a) phases of adaptation by an immigrant to a new culture. After settling in the United States, immigrants often enjoy better material comforts and more political freedom than possible in their old country. If they compare themselves to most other people in the United States, however, they will feel deprived, because while their standard has improved, the immigrants still perceive relative deprivation.

*Absolute deprivation*, on the other hand, implies a fixed standard based on a minimum level of subsistence below which families should not be expected to exist. Discrimination does not necessarily mean absolute deprivation. A Japanese American who gets promoted to a management position may still be a victim of discrimination, if he or she had been passed over for years because of corporate reluctance to place an Asian American in such a visible position.

Dissatisfaction is also likely to arise from feelings of relative deprivation. Those members of a society who feel most frustrated and disgruntled by the social and economic conditions of their lives are not necessarily "worst off" in an objective sense. Social scientists have long recognized that what is most significant is how people *perceive* their situation. Karl Marx pointed out that although the misery of the workers was important in reflecting their oppressed state, so too was their position relative to the ruling class. In 1847, Marx wrote that

> although the enjoyment of the workers has risen, the social satisfaction that they have has fallen in comparison with the increased enjoyment of the capitalist. (Marx and Engels, 1955, p. 94).

This statement explains why the groups or individuals who are most vocal and best organized against discrimination are not necessarily in the worst economic and social situation. They are likely, however, to be those who most strongly perceive that relative to others they are not receiving "their fair share."

## Total Discrimination

Social scientists, and increasingly policy makers, have begun to use the concept of total discrimination. *Total discrimination* refers to current discrimination operating in the labor market *and* past discrimination. Past discrimination includes the relatively poorer education and job experience of racial and ethnic minorities compared to that of White Americans. It is not enough, therefore, when considering discrimination to focus only on what is being done to people now. Sometimes a person may be dealt with fairly but still be at a disadvantage, because he or she suffered from poorer health care, inferior counseling in the school system, less access to books and other educational materials, a poor job record resulting from absences to take care of brothers and sisters, and so forth.

We find another variation of this past-in-present discrimination when apparently nondiscriminatory present practices have negative effects because of prior intentionally biased practices. Although unions that purposely discriminated against minority members in the past may no longer do so, some people are still prevented from achieving higher levels of seniority because of those past practices. A study of personnel records in the military shows that the cumulative record is vital in promotion and selection for desirable assignments. Blatantly discriminatory judgments and recommendations in the past, however, remain a part of a person's record (E. Davis, 1977; Feagin and Eckberg, 1980).

Only recently have social scientists tried to measure discrimination itself. Their attempt at measurement is plagued by the difficulty of separating current discrimination from past discrimination. Current discrimination includes refusing qualified people jobs or hiring them at wages below what they should be paid. Past discrimination refers to the processes that decrease the number of qualified people by either encouraging individuals to drop out of school or discouraging them from pursuing nontraditional careers (that is, discouraging an African American from becoming a civil engineer or a woman from becoming a carpenter).

## INSTITUTIONAL DISCRIMINATION

Individuals practice discrimination in one-to-one encounters, while institutions practice discrimination through their daily operations. Indeed, today consensus is growing that this institutional discrimination is more significant than that committed by prejudiced individuals.

Social scientists are particularly concerned with the ways in which patterns of employment, education, criminal justice, housing, health care, and government operations maintain the social significance of race and ethnicity. *Institutional discrimination* refers to the denial of opportunities and equal rights to individuals and groups that results from the normal operations of a society.

Civil rights activist Stokely Carmichael and political scientist Charles Hamilton are credited with introducing the concept of *institutional racism*. Individual discrimination refers to overt acts of individual Whites against individual Blacks; Carmichael and Hamilton reserved the term *institutional racism* for covert acts collectively committed against an entire group (1967, p. 4). James M. Jones provided this definition:

> Those established laws, customs, practices which systematically reflect and produce racial inequities in American society. If racist consequences accrue to institutional laws, customs, or practices, the institution is racist *whether or not the individuals maintaining those practices have racist intentions.* (1972, p. 131)

Under this definition discrimination can take place without an individual's intending to deprive others of privileges, even without the individual's being aware that others are being deprived (Benokraitis and Feagin, 1977; Feagin and Eckberg, 1980; J. Williams, 1985).

How can discrimination be widespread and unconscious at the same time? Knowles and Prewitt (1969) documented many examples.

1. Standards for assessing credit risks work against potential African Americans in business who lack conventional credit references. Blacks in business also usually operate where insurance costs are much greater.

*The residents of nearly all-White Dearborn, a suburb of Detroit, encountered the wrath of civil rights lawyers when they created restrictions for use of their city's parks that could be viewed as a thinly veiled anti-Black gesture.*

2. IQ testing favors middle-class children, especially the White middle class, because of the type of questions included.
3. The entire criminal justice system, from the patrol officer to the judge and jury, is dominated by Whites who find it difficult to understand ghetto life.

In some cases, even apparently "neutral" institutional standards can turn out to have discriminatory effects. In 1966, Chicago's Puerto Rican neighborhood was torn apart by riots. The complaint of police brutality was voiced frequently in the Puerto Rican community. After the riots, the Chicago Police Department admitted that it had no Puerto Rican officers.

Why? Subsequent investigation revealed that the police maintained a height requirement for officers that kept many otherwise qualified Puerto Ricans from applying. As a group, Puerto Ricans are shorter of stature than Whites or African Americans, and they found this arbitrary requirement impossible to overcome. In effect, through this ostensibly neutral standard, the Chicago police were saying, "Puerto Ricans need not apply." Later, the height requirement was revised, allowing Puerto Ricans to enter the police force, and there was some improvement in relations between police and community.

Institutional discrimination continuously imposes more hindrances on and awards fewer benefits to certain racial and ethnic groups than it does to others. This is the underlying and painful context of American intergroup relations.

## DUAL LABOR MARKET

The secondary labor market affecting many members of racial and ethnic minorities has come to be called the *irregular economy*. The irregular economy refers to transfers of money, goods, or services that are not reported to the government. This label describes much of the work in inner-city neighborhoods and poverty-stricken rural areas, in sharp contrast to the rest of the marketplace. Workers are employed in the irregular economy seasonally or infrequently. The work they do may resemble the work of traditional occupations such as mechanic, cook, or electrician, but these workers lack the formal credentials to enter such employment. Indeed, workers in the irregular economy may work sporadically or moonlight in the regular economy. The irregular economy also includes unregulated child care services, garage sales, and the unreported income of craftspeople and street vendors.

The irregular economy, sometimes referred to as the *informal* or *underground economy*, exists worldwide. Conflict sociologists in particular note that a significant level of commerce occurs outside traditional economies. Individually the transactions are small, but they can be significant when taken together. They comprise perhaps as much as 10 to 20 percent of all economic activity in the United States (Denton, 1985, Schaefer and Lamm, 1992, pp. 295–296).

According to the *dual labor market* model, minorities have been relegated to the irregular economy. While the irregular economy may be profitable, it provides few safeguards against fraud or malpractice and gives little attention to the so-called fringe benefits of health insurance and pension that are taken for granted in the conventional marketplace. To be consigned to the irregular economy is therefore yet another example of social inequality.

Sociologist Edna Bonacich (1972, 1976) outlined the dual or split labor market that divides the economy into two realms of employment, with the secondary one populated primarily by minorities working at menial jobs. Labor, even when not manual, is still rewarded less when performed by minorities. In keeping with the conflict model, this dual market model emphasizes that minorities fare unfavorably in the competition between dominant and subordinate groups.

The workers in the irregular economy are ill prepared to enter the regular economy permanently or to take its better-paying jobs. Frequent changes in employment or lack of a specific supervisor leaves them without the kind of job resume that employers in the regular economy expect before they hire. Some of the sources of employment in the irregular economy are illegal, such as fencing,

*As symbolically shown by this rider in a Chicago public housing project elevator, members of the underclass are trapped and unable to enter the conventional economy.*

narcotics pushing, pimping, and prostitution. More likely the work is legal but not transferable to a more traditional job, such as that of an "information broker," who receives cash in exchange for such information as where to find good buys or how to receive maximum benefits in public assistance programs (Ferman and Ferman, 1973; Fusfeld, 1973, pp. 34–36; Pedder, 1991).

Many members of the irregular economy, along with some employed in traditional jobs, compose what has come to be called "the underclass" of American society.

## THE UNDERCLASS

The *underclass* consists of the long-term poor who lack training and skills. Conflict theorists, among others, have expressed alarm at the proportion of the nation's society living in this social stratum. Sociologist William Wilson (1987a, 1987b, 1988, p. 15, 1991) drew attention to the growth of this varied grouping of families and individuals who are outside the mainstream of the occupational structure. While estimates vary depending upon the definition, in 1990 the underclass included more than 3 million adults of working age not counting children or the elderly. In the central city, about 49 percent of the underclass in 1990 comprised African Americans, 29 percent Hispanic, 17 percent White, and 5 percent other (O'Hare and Curry-White, 1992).

The discussion of the underclass has refocused attention on society's inability to address the problems facing the truly disadvantaged—many of whom are Black or Hispanic. Some scholars expressed the concern that the portrait of the underclass seems to "blame the victim," making the poor responsible. Wilson and others have stressed it is not because of bad behavior but structural factors such as the loss of manufacturing jobs that have hit ghetto residents so hard. As the labor market has become tighter, the minorities within the underclass are at a significant disadvantage. Associated with this structural problem is service social isolation. The disadvantaged lack contact or sustained interaction with the individuals or institutions that represent the regular economy. It is the economy, not the poor, that needs reforming. (DeParle, 1991b; Kornblum, 1991; M. Morris, 1989; Reardon, 1991; Schaefer and Lamm, 1992, pp. 240–245; Steinberg, 1989; S. Wright, 1992).

As part of a national survey of race relations commissioned by the NAACP Legal Defense and Educational Fund (1989), researchers conducted face-to-face interviews in mid-1988 with 347 chronically poor Blacks in eight American cities. Among the findings were the following.

- Women constitute 78 percent of the Black underclass.
- The median income of chronically poor Black households over the previous five years was $4,900.
- At least 61 percent of those surveyed had not held a job in the last two years.
- Some 44 percent of those surveyed had either never held a job or never received any training for work.

At the same time, members of the African American underclass were found to share many of the most basic goals and aspirations of American society. For example, 55 percent of respondents stated that they hoped their children would go to college.

Poverty is not new. Yet the concept of underclass describes a very chilling development: workers, whether employed or not in the irregular economy, are beyond the reach of any safety net provided by existing social programs. In addition, membership in the underclass is not an intermittent condition but a long-term attribute. The underclass is understandably alienated and engages sporadically in illegal behavior. Alienation and illegal acts gain the underclass little support from the larger society to address the problem realistically.

In "Listen to Their Voices," urban antropologist Elliot Liebow describes his participant-observation research of lower-class African American men on a street corner in Washington, D.C. The selection documents the problems of working in the irregular economy. The problems have worsened in the 25 years

## ❖ LISTEN TO THEIR VOICES ❖

### Tally's Corner

*Elliot Liebow*

*Tally's Corner is an intersection in Washington, D.C. where Black men congregate. By observing their behavior, Liebow was able to describe their coping strategies.*

In summary of objective job considerations, then, the most important fact is that a man who is able and willing to work cannot earn enough money to support himself, his wife, and one or more children. A man's chances for working regularly are good only if he is willing to work for less than he can live on, and sometimes not even then. On some jobs, the wage rate is deceptively higher than on others, but the higher the wage rate, the more difficult it is to get the job, and the less the job security. Higher-paying construction work tends to be seasonal and, during the season, the amount of work available is highly sensitive to business and weather conditions and to the changing requirements of individual projects. Moreover, high-paying construction jobs are frequently beyond the physical capacity of some of the men, and some of the low-paying jobs are scaled down even

lower in accordance with the self-fulfilling assumption that the man will steal part of his wages on the job. . . .

A crucial factor in the streetcorner man's lack of job commitment is the overall value he places on the job. *For his part, the streetcorner man puts no lower value on the job than does the larger society around him.* He knows the social value of the job by the amount of money the employer is willing to pay him for doing it. In a real sense, every pay day, he counts in dollars and cents the value placed on the job by society at large. He is no more (and frequently less) ready to quit and look for another job than his employer is ready to fire him and look for another man. Neither the streetcorner man who performs these jobs nor the society which requires him to perform them assesses the job as one "worth doing and worth doing well." Both employee and employer are contemptuous of the job. The employee shows his contempt by his reluctance to accept it or keep it, the employer by paying less than is required to support a family. Nor does the low-wage job offer prestige, respect, interesting work, opportunity for learning or advancement, or any other compensation. With few exceptions, jobs filled by the streetcorner men are at the bottom of the employment ladder in every respect, from wage level to prestige. Typically, they are hard, dirty, uninteresting and underpaid. The rest of the society (whatever its ideal values regarding the dignity of labor) holds the job of the dishwasher or janitor or unskilled laborer in low esteem if not outright contempt. So does the street-corner man. He cannot do otherwise. He cannot draw from a job those so-cial values which other people do not put into it. . . .

The streetcorner man is under con-tinuous assault by his job experience and job fears. His experiences and fears feed on one another. The kind of job he can get—and frequently only after fighting for it, if then—steadily confirms his fears, depresses his self-confidence and self-esteem until fin-ally, terrified of an opportunity even if one presents itself, he stands defeated by his experiences, his belief in his own self-worth destroyed and his fears a confirmed reality.

From *Tally's Corner: A Study of Negro Streetcorner Men* by Elliot Liebow. Copyright © 1967 by Little, Brown and Company (Inc.). Reprinted by per-mission of Little, Brown and Company.

since Liebow wrote. Thousands fewer manufacturing jobs are available to the day laborers that Liebow observed. Working-class Blacks who provided a kind of social buffer are not a part of the exodus to better residential areas. In 1985, 43 percent of all Black male high school dropouts in their early twenties reported earning no money whatsoever. As recently as 1973, that figure was just 12 percent (W. Shapiro, 1987, p. 19). It is the relatively privileged Blacks who benefit from most public policies and private philanthropy while the underclass remains virtually untouched. Social policies such as urban renewal, industrial relocation, gentrification, and unavailability of quality child care and health care serve to exacerbate the situation.

## DISCRIMINATION IN AMERICAN SOCIETY

Discrimination is widespread in the United States. It sometimes results from prejudices held by individuals. More significantly it is found in institutional discrimination and the presence of a dual labor market. It is even present in a subtle fashion among the affluent because, as we have just seen, more members of minority families must work in order to reach the type of moderately high incomes enjoyed by Whites.

Not so subtly, the face of discrimination shows itself even when people are prepared to be customers. A 1990 study had Black and White men and women follow a script to buy new cars in the Chicago area. After 164 visits, the results showed a White woman could be expected to pay $142 more for a car than a White man, a Black man $421 more, and for a Black woman it was $875 more. African Americans and women were perceived as less knowledgeable and therefore, there could be more markup in prices. A similar study in housing, only nationwide in 25 metropolitan areas, showed that African Americans and

Hispanics face discrimination in a majority of their responses to advertisements. Discrimination took the forms of failure to be shown real estate presented to Whites, and less favorable terms, such as higher rents or higher fees for parking and utilities (Ayres, 1991; Turner, Struyck, and Yinger, 1991).

Discrimination emerges when we look at data for groups other than Blacks and Hispanics. Sociologists Richard D. Alba and Gwen Moore (1982) conducted interviews with 545 top position holders in powerful political, economic, and social institutions in the United States. Table 3.1 summarizes the representation of several ethnic groups compared to Wasps (White Anglo-Saxon Protestants). This dominant group accounts for 43 percent of the elite, but Wasps comprise only 22.9 percent of men born before 1932 and 31 percent of the college-educated. Evidently they are overrepresented.

Racial and ethnic minorities tend to do relatively well in some areas of the elite structure. Examining Table 3.1, we see that Irish Catholics are well represented among labor leaders; Jewish Americans and racial minorities compare favorably in voluntary organizations. These results are similar to two detailed studies of leadership in metropolitan Chicago. Harold Baron (1968, 1975), focusing on Blacks, found them to be grossly underrepresented in both the public and private sectors. Those Blacks who did occupy policy-making positions usually had a Black constituency—as would a director of a bank in a Black neighborhood. Most Black constituencies, however, were headed by Whites. Also in

**TABLE 3.1**    Ethnic Representation in the Elite

Americans who are not White or Protestant tend to be underrepresented in positions of decision-making authority. Although the situation is improving, the disparity still remains.

|  | Wasps | Other Protes- tants | Irish Catho- lics | Other Catho- lics | Jews | Minor- ities |
|---|---|---|---|---|---|---|
| Overall elite | 43.0% | 19.5% | 8.5% | 8.7% | 11.3% | 3.9% |
| Business | 57.3 | 22.1 | 5.3 | 6.1 | 6.9 | 0.0 |
| Labor | 23.9 | 15.2 | 37.0 | 13.0 | 4.3 | 2.2 |
| Political parties | 44.0 | 18.0 | 14.0 | 4.0 | 8.0 | 4.0 |
| Voluntary organizations | 32.7 | 13.5 | 1.9 | 7.7 | 17.3 | 19.2 |
| Mass media | 37.1 | 11.3 | 4.8 | 9.7 | 25.8 | 0.0 |
| Congress | 53.4 | 19.0 | 6.9 | 8.6 | 3.4 | 3.4 |
| Political appointees | 39.4 | 28.8 | 1.5 | 13.6 | 10.6 | 3.0 |
| Civil servants | 35.8 | 22.6 | 9.4 | 9.4 | 15.1 | 3.8 |
| National population |  |  |  |  |  |  |
| Men born before 1932 | 22.9 | 22.5 | 4.2 | 17.2 | 2.9 | 14.4 |
| College-educated men born before 1932 | 31.0 | 19.8 | 6.0 | 15.5 | 8.9 | 5.2 |

*Source:* From Richard D. Alba and Gwen Moore, "Ethnicity in the American Elite," *American Sociological Review,* 47, June 1982, p. 377. Reprinted by permission of the American Sociological Association and the authors.

Chicago, sociologist Russell Barta (1974) examined the ethnic background of officers of the 106 largest corporations. Not only Blacks and Hispanics but also Poles and Italians were underrepresented.

## *Measuring Discrimination*

How much discrimination is there? As in measuring prejudice, problems arise in quantifying discrimination. Measuring prejudice is hampered by the difficulties in assessing attitudes and by the need to take many factors into account.

Some tentative conclusions about discrimination can be made, however. Figure 3.1 uses government income data to show vividly the disparity in income between African Americans and Whites, men and women. The first comparison is of all workers. White men with a median income of $21,170 earn almost 65 percent more than Black man and 2.4 times as much as Black women, who earn

**FIGURE 3.1**   Median Income in 1990 by Race and Sex

Even casual analysis reveals the significant differences in earning power between men and women, and between Black men and White men. Furthermore, the "double jeopardy" of subordinate status due to race and gender is apparent for Black women.

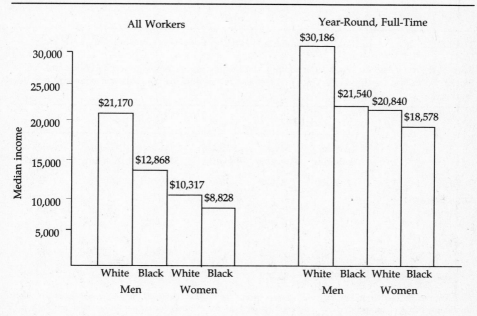

*Note:* Median income is from all sources.
*Source:* Bureau of the Census, 1991c, pp. 104–107.

only $8,828 in wages. As you can see, White males earn most, followed by Black males, White females, and Black females. The sharpest drop is between White and Black males. This disparity means that Black males earn 61 cents for every White male dollar. Even worse, relatively speaking, is the plight of women. Black women earn less than half of what White males in American society earn. This disparity between Black women and White men has remained unchanged over the more than 50 years such data has been tabulated. It illustrates yet another instance of the double jeopardy experienced by minority women.

Also in Figure 3.1 are data for only full-time, year-round workers and therefore excludes housewives or the unemployed. Even in this comparison the deprivation of Blacks and women is confirmed again. White men earn $8,600 more a year than Black men with women of both races earning even less.

Are these differences completely the result of discrimination in employment? No; individuals within the four groups are not equally prepared to compete for high-paying jobs. Past discrimination is a significant factor in a person's present social position. Education is clearly an appropriate variable to control. In Table 3.2, median income is compared, holding education constant, which means we can compare Blacks and Whites and men and women with approximately the same amount of formal schooling. The disparity remains. The gap between races does narrow as education increases. Women, however, lag behind men to the

**TABLE 3.2**   Median Income by Race and Sex, Holding Education Constant

Even at the very highest levels of schooling, the income gap remains between Whites and Blacks. Education has little effect, apparently, also on the income gap between male and female workers.

|  | Race, 1987 | | Ratio | Sex, 1990 | | Ratio |
|---|---|---|---|---|---|---|
|  | White Families | Black Families | Black to White | Male Workers | Female Workers | Women to Men |
| Total | $41,000 | $30,523 | .74 | $29,987 | $20,556 | .69 |
| High School | | | | | | |
| 1–3 years | 31,640 | 23,926 | .76 | 20,452 | 13,858 | .68 |
| 4 years | 36,443 | 30,001 | .82 | 25,872 | 17,412 | .67 |
| College | | | | | | |
| 1–3 years | 41,867 | 32,162 | .77 | 30,865 | 21,324 | .69 |
| 4 years | 51,470 | 36,183 | .70 | 37,283 | 26,828 | .72 |
| 5 years or more | 59,981 | 53,240 | .89 | 47,131 | 31,969 | .68 |

*Note:* Figures are median income from all sources except capital gain. Included are public assistance payments, dividends, pension, unemployment compensation, and so on. Incomes for males and females are limited to year-round full-time workers over 25 years of age.
*Source:* Bureau of Census, 1989a, 1991c, pp. 128, 142.

*Black families in which at least one member has a college degree can typically expect to earn $16,000 per year less than their White counterparts.*

same extent (they earn 69 percent of what men earn). The contrast is dramatic: women with graduate work ($31,969) earn little more than men who fail to finish college ($30,865).

Now that education has been held constant, is the remaining gap caused by discrimination? No, not necessarily. Table 3.2 measured only the amount of schooling, not its quality. Racial minorities are more likely to attend inadequately financed schools. Some efforts have been made to eliminate disparities among school districts in the amount of wealth available to tax for school support, but with little success. In a 1973 case, *San Antonio Independent School District* v. *Rodriquez,* The Supreme Court ruled that attendance at an underfinanced school in a poor district does not constitute a violation of equal protection (Schaefer and Lamm, 1992, pp. 502–504). The inequality of educational opportunity may seem less important in explaining sex discrimination. Even though women are usually not segregated from men, educational institutions encourage talented women to enter fields that pay less (home economics or elementary education).

## Eliminating Discrimination

Two main agents of social change work to reduce discrimination: voluntary associations organized to solve racial and ethnic problems, and the federal government. The two are closely related: most efforts initiated by the government were urged by associations or organizations representing minority groups, following vigorous protests against racism by African Americans.

All racial and ethnic groups of any size are represented by private organizations that are to some degree trying to end discrimination. Some groups originated in the first half of the twentieth century, but most were either founded since World War II or have become significant forces in bringing about change only since then. These include church organizations, fraternal social groups, minor political parties, legal defense funds, as well as more militant organizations operating under the scrutiny of law enforcement agencies. The purposes, membership, successes, and failures of these voluntary associations dedicated to eliminating discrimination are discussed throughout the balance of this book.

Government action toward eliminating discrimination is also part of only relatively recent history. Antidiscrimination actions have been generated by each branch of the government: the executive, the judicial, and the legislative.

The first antidiscrimination action at the executive level was President Franklin D. Roosevelt's 1943 creation of the Fair Employment Practices Commission (FEPC), which handled thousands of complaints of discrimination, mostly from African Americans. Despite strong opposition to the FEPC by powerful economic and political leaders and many southern Whites, it had little actual power. The FEPC had no authority to compel employers to stop discriminating but could only ask for voluntary compliance. Its jurisdiction was limited to federal government employees, federal contractors, and labor unions. State and local governments and any business without a federal contract were not covered. Furthermore, the FEPC never enjoyed vigorous support from the White House, was denied adequate funds, and was part of larger agencies that were hostile to the Commission's existence. This weak antidiscrimination agency was finally dropped in 1946, succeeded by an even weaker one in 1948.

A second executive action to end racial inequality came in 1948 when President Truman issued Executive Order 9981, ending segregation in the armed forces. This order ended the practice of all-Black, all-White, or all-Japanese American units, but charges of racial bias in military assignments and promotions continue to the present. Whatever the limits of their effectiveness, the short-lived FEPC and the military desegregation order set the pattern for future action by presidents.

The judiciary, charged with interpreting laws and the Constitution, has a much longer history of involvement in the rights of racial, ethnic, and religious minorities. Its early decisions, however, protected the rights of the dominant group, as in the 1857 *Dred Scott* decision, which ruled that slaves remained slaves even when living or traveling in states where slavery was illegal. Not until the 1940s did the Supreme Court revise earlier decisions and begin to grant African Americans the same rights as those held by Whites. The 1954 *Brown* v. *Board of Education* decision heralded a new series of rulings arguing, in effect, that to distinguish among races in order to segregate was inherently discriminatory. Unfortunately, the immediate effect of many such rulings was minimal because the executive branch and Congress did not wish to violate the principle of *states' rights,* which holds that each state is sovereign in most of its affairs and has the right to order them without interference from the federal government.

Gradually, United States society became more committed to the rights of individuals. There was also an inherent fallacy in the states' rights argument. It perceived power as a finite quantity, where increased national power automatically meant reduced state and local authority. In reality, government activity expanded at all levels; those who lost power were individuals or businesses that wished to maximize their personal gain at the expense of others' rights. The proponents of states' rights sought to minimize federal government activity by keeping power in the state capitals, where the prospects of inaction were greatest because these proponents had greater influence to protect their own interests. The legislation of the 1960s committed the federal government to actively protecting civil rights, rather than merely leaving it up to state and local officials (Carr et al., 1971, pp. 78–79).

The most important legislative effort to eradicate discrimination was the Civil Rights Act of 1964. This act led to establishment of the Equal Employment Opportunity Commission (EEOC), giving it the power to investigate complaints against employers and recommend action to the Department of Justice. If the Justice Department sued and discrimination was found, the court could order appropriate compensation. The act covered employment practices of all businesses with more than 25 employees, and nearly all employment agencies and labor unions. A 1972 amendment broadened the coverage to employers with as few as 15 employees.

The act also prohibited the application of different voting registration standards to White and Black voting applicants. It prohibited as well discrimination in public accommodations, that is, hotels, motels, restaurants, gasoline stations, and amusement parks. Publicly owned facilities such as parks, stadiums, and swimming pools were also prohibited from discriminating. Another important provision forbade discrimination in all federally supported programs and institutions, such as hospitals, colleges, and road construction.

The Civil Rights Act of 1964 covers discrimination based on race, color, creed, national origin, and sex. Although the inclusion of sex in employment criteria had been forbidden in the federal civil service since 1949, most laws and most groups pushing for change showed little concern for sex discrimination. There was little precedent for attention to sex discrimination, even at the state level. Only Hawaii and Wisconsin had enacted laws against sex discrimination prior to 1964. As first proposed, the act did not include sex. One day before the final vote, opponents of the measure offered the amendment in an effort to defeat the entire act. The act did pass with sex bias included—an event that can only be regarded as a milestone for women seeking equal employment rights with men (Commission on Civil Rights, 1975, pp. 19–20; R. Miller, 1967).

It is easy to overstate the significance of the Civil Rights Act of 1964; it was not perfect. Since 1964, several acts and amendments to the act itself have been added to compensate for the many areas of discrimination it left untouched, such as criminal justice and housing. Even in those areas singled out for enforcement in the Civil Rights Act of 1964, discrimination still occurs. Federal agencies charged with its enforcement complain that they are underfunded or are denied wholehearted support by the White House. Also, regardless of how much the EEOC may want to act in a case, the individual who has been discriminated against has to pursue the complaint over a long time, marked by long periods of inaction.

While civil rights laws often established rights for other minorities, the Supreme Court made this explicit in two 1987 decisions involving groups other than African Americans. In the first of the two cases, an Iraqi-American professor asserted that he had been denied tenure because of his Arab origins; in the second, a Jewish congregation brought suit for damages in response to the defacing of its synagogue with derogatory symbols. The Supreme Court ruled unanimously that, in effect, any member of an ethnic minority may sue under federal prohibitions against discrimination. These decisions paved the way for virtually all racial and ethnic groups to invoke the Civil Rights Act of 1964 (*St. Francis College* v. *Al-Khazraji; Shaare-Tefila Congregation* v. *Cobb;* S. Taylor, 1987b).

A particularly insulting form of discrimination seemed to be finally on its way out in the latter 1980s. Social clubs typically had limitations on their membership forbidding minorities, Jews, and women. For years, exclusive clubs agreed they were merely selecting friends, but, in fact, these clubs have as a principal function providing a forum where business is transacted. Denial of membership meant more than the inability to attend a luncheon, it also seemed to exclude one from part of the marketplace. The Supreme Court ruled unanimously in the 1988 case *New York State Clubs Association* v. *City of New York* that states and cities may ban sex discrimination by large private clubs where business lunches and similar activities take place. While the ruling does not apply to all clubs and leaves the issue of racial and ethnic barriers unresolved, it did serve to chip away at the arbitrary exclusiveness of private groups (S. Taylor, 1988).

The historical record of combating discrimination has not been uniformly positive in recent years. In the controversial 1984 Supreme Court *Grove City College* v. *Bell* decision, the justices held that federal law barring sex discrimination in federally supported educational activities applied only to the specific programs that directly received the aid, not to the entire institution. This meant a biology department might still receive a federal research grant even if the admissions office openly discriminated. Civil rights supporters were outraged by this decision. Eventually, in 1988, Congress passed the Civil Rights Restoration Act which expanded earlier legislation so that all funds could be cut off from an offending organization. However, the act had to be passed over President Ronald Reagan's veto, which he based on a concern that the act would unjustifiably expand the power of the federal government (J. Johnson, 1988).

The inability of the Civil Rights Act, similar legislation, and court decisions to end discrimination is not due entirely to poor financial and political support. Even if the EEOC had been given top priority, discrimination would remain. The civil rights legislation attacked the most obvious forms of discrimination. Many discriminatory practices, such as those described as institutional discrimination, are seldom obvious.

## AFFIRMATIVE ACTION

*Affirmative action* is the positive efforts to recruit minority group members or women for jobs, promotions, and educational opportunities. The phrase *affirmative action* first appeared in an executive order issued by President Kennedy in 1963. The order called for contractors to "take affirmative action to ensure that applicants are employed, and that employees are treated during employment, without regard to their race, creed, color, or national origin." Four years later, the order was amended to prohibit discrimination on the basis of sex, but affirmative action was still vaguely defined.

### Affirmative Action Explained

Affirmative action has become the most important tool toward reducing institutional discrimination. Whereas previous efforts had been aimed at eliminating individual acts of discrimination, federal measures under the heading of affirmative action have been aimed at procedures that deny equal opportunities even if they were not intended to be overtly discriminatory. This policy has been implemented to deal with both the current discrimination and past discrimination outlined earlier in this chapter.

The Commission on Civil Rights (1981, pp. 9–10) has given some examples of areas where affirmative action has been aimed at institutional discrimination:

- Height and weight requirements that are unnecessarily geared to the physical proportions of White males without regard for the actual requirements needed to perform the job, and, therefore, exclude females and some minorities.
- Seniority rules, when applied to jobs historically held only by White males, that make more recently hired minorities and females more subject to lay-off—the "last hired, first fired" employee—and less eligible for advancement.
- Nepotism-based membership policies of some referral unions that exclude those who are not relatives of members who, because of past employment practices, are usually White.
- Restrictive employment leave policies, coupled with prohibitions on part-

time work or denials of fringe benefits to part-time workers, which make it difficult for the heads of single-parent families, most of whom are women, to get and keep jobs and meet the needs of their families.
• Rules requiring that only English be spoken at the workplace, even when not a business necessity, which result in discriminatory employment practices toward individuals whose primary language is not English.
• Standardized academic tests or criteria, geared to the cultural and educational norms of middle-class or White males, when these are not relevant indicators of successful job performance.
• Preferences shown by law and medical schools in the admission of children of wealthy and influential alumni, nearly all of whom are White.
• Credit policies of banks and lending institutions that prevent granting of mortgages and loans in minority neighborhoods or prevent granting of credit to married women and others who have previously been denied the opportunity to build good credit histories in their own names.

Employers have also been cautioned against asking leading questions in interviews, such as "Did you know you would be the first Black to supervise all Whites in that factory?" or "Does your husband mind your working on weekends?" Furthermore, the lack of minority group (Blacks, Asians, Native Americans, and Hispanics) or female employees may in itself represent evidence for a case of unlawful exclusion (Commission on Civil Rights, 1975, p. 12).

### Legal Debates

How far can an employer go in encouraging women and minorities to apply for a job before it becomes unlawful discrimination against White males? In the last fifteen years, a number of bitterly debated cases on this difficult aspect of affirmative action reached the Supreme Court. These are summarized in Table 3.3.

In the 1978 *Bakke* case (*Regents of the University of California* v. *Bakke*), by a narrow 5–4 vote, the Court ordered the medical school of the University of California at Davis to admit Allen Bakke, a White engineer who originally had been denied admission. The justices ruled that the school had violated Bakke's constitutional rights by establishing a fixed quota system for minority students. The Court added, however, that it was constitutional for universities to adopt flexible admissions programs that use race as one factor in making decisions. In the following year, in the *Weber* case (*United Steelworkers of America* v. *Weber*), the Supreme Court ruled, by a vote of 5–2, that the labor union did not have to admit White laboratory technician Brian Weber to a training program in Louisiana. The justices held that it was constitutional for the union to run a program for training skilled technicians which, to promote affirmative action, admitted one Black for every White.

Defenders of affirmative action insist that it is needed to counter continuing discrimination against women and minorities. White males still hold the overwhelming majority of prestigious and high-paying jobs. In fact, despite

**TABLE 3.3** Key Affirmative Action Decisions

In a series of split and often very close decisions, the Supreme Court has been supportive of affirmative action as implemented, although it has had reservations in specific situations.

| Year | Favorable/ Unfavorable to Policy | Case | Vote | Ruling |
|------|------|------|------|--------|
| 1978 | – | Regents of the University of California v. Bakke | 5–4 | Prohibited specific number of places for minorities in college admissions |
| 1979 | + | United Steelworkers of America v. Weber | 5–2 | OK for union to favor minorities in special training programs |
| 1984 | – | Firefighters Local Union No. 1784 (Memphis, TN) v. Stotts | 6–1 | Seniority means recently hired minorities may be laid off first in staff reductions |
| 1986 | + | International Association of Firefighters v. City of Cleveland | 6–3 | May promote minorities over more senior Whites |
| 1986 | + | New York City v. Sheet Metal Workers' Union | 5–4 | Approved specific quota of minority workers for union |
| 1987 | + | United States v. Paradise | 5–4 | Endorsed quotas for promotions of state troopers |
| 1987 | + | Johnson v. Transportation Agency, Santa Clara, CA | 6–3 | Approved preference in hiring for minorities and women over better qualified men and Whites |
| 1989 | – | Richmond v. Croson Company | 6–3 | Ruled a 30 percent set-aside program for minority contractors unconstitutional |
| 1989 | – | Martin v. Wilks | 5–4 | Ruled Whites may bring reverse discrimination claims against court-approved affirmative action plans |
| 1990 | + | Metro Broadcasting v. F.C.C. | 5–4 | Supported Federal programs aimed at increasing minority ownership of broadcast licenses |

affirmative action, the gap in earning power between White males and others remained unchanged throughout the 1970s (Roark, 1977).

Nevertheless, the majority of Americans doubt that everything done in the name of affirmative action is desirable. White public opinion appears united against hiring or admissions programs that offer preferential treatment to women and racial minorities. Surveys throughout the 1980s and as recently as 1991 consistently showed that very few Americans favored such preferential efforts. Many respondents insisted that these programs unfairly penalize White males and should properly be viewed as "reverse discrimination." Furthermore, people who supported affirmative action were ridiculed as merely voicing "politically correct" views (Colasanto , 1989; L. Harris, 1987, pp. 188–193; Swoboda, 1990).

In recent years, the Supreme Court, increasingly dominated by a conservative majority, has issued many critical rulings concerning affirmative action programs. In a key case in early 1989, the Court invalidated, by a 6–3 vote, a Richmond, Virginia, law that had guaranteed 30 percent of public works funds to construction companies owned by minorities. In ruling that the Richmond statute violated the constitutional right of White contractors to equal protection under the law, the Court held that affirmative action programs are constitutional only when they serve the "compelling state interest" of redressing "identified discrimination" by the government or private parties.

Has affirmative action actually helped to alleviate employment inequality on the basis of race and gender? Sociologist Dula Espinosa (1987) studied the impact of affirmative action on a California municipal work force whose hiring practices were traced from 1975 through 1985. As a federal contractor, the city was required to comply with federal guidelines regarding employment practices, including making "good faith efforts" to increase employment opportunities for women and minorities. Espinosa found that employment inequality by gender and ethnicity did indeed decrease during the 10-year period studied.

Espinosa adds, however, that most of the reduction in the city's level of employment inequality occurred just after the affirmative action policy was first introduced. In Espinosa's view, once immediate progress can be seen, an organization may then become less inclined to continue to implement an affirmative action policy. Moreover, while high levels of inequality may be relatively easy to address initially, sustaining positive results may take longer because of institutional discrimination. Espinosa concludes that affirmative action was successful to some degree in reducing employment inequality in the city studied, but clearly had its limitations as well.

A study of income data and occupational mobility among Black and White male workers in the period 1974–1981 examined possible class polarization among Blacks. The researchers found that while Black college graduates made substantial gains as a result of affirmative action, less-advantaged Blacks apparently did not benefit from it. The researchers (Son et al., 1989, p. 325) conclude that the "racial parity achieved by young college-educated Blacks in the 1970s

*Despite the* Bakke *decision, colleges maintained special programs to increase the presence of minorities in higher education. Pictured here are two Hispanic students participating in a summer program intended to encourage minorities to enter medical programs at the University of California at Davis, the plaintiff in the* Bakke *decision.*

will be maintained only if the government's commitment to affirmative action does not slacken."

As state and national election campaigns got underway in the 1990s, affirmative action emerged as an issue. Generally, it was specifically the use of quotas, or the "Q-word" as it came to be referred, in hiring practices. Supporters of affirmative action argue that goals establish "floors" for minority inclusion but do not exclude the truly qualified candidate. Opponents argue that these targets are in fact quotas leading to "reverse discrimination." However, research studies do not confirm its presence, at least in any significant manner. A 1991 survey of employers in Chicago and Washington, D.C. using similarly skilled African American and White applicants found 15 percent of the Whites received job offers compared to only 5 percent of African Americans. Despite such studies, confusion about the merits of affirmative action continues in part due to the bewildering array of Supreme Court decisions and pronouncements by both the Reagan and Bush administrations that while they are opposed to quotas, they are generally supportive of affirmative action (Cohn, 1991; Turner, Fix, and Struyck, 1991).

## GLANCING BACK AND LOOKING AHEAD

Discrimination takes its toll, whether a person who is discriminated against is a part of the irregular economy or not. Even members of minority groups who are not today being overtly discriminated against continue to fall victim to past discrimination.

From the conflict perspective, it should not be surprising to find the widespread presence of a dual labor market and even an underclass. Rev. Jesse Jackson captured this social reality eloquently when he said to a group of poor people, "You are not the bottom. You are the foundation." Wealth and privilege are built upon the suffering of the poor, many of whom are people of color (Bonacich, 1989, pp. 79–80).

Women are a particularly vulnerable group, for whether the comparisons are within or across racial and ethnic grouping, they face significant social disparities. This inequality will be a reoccurring theme throughout this book, but we can note the observations of two distinguished sociologists. Alice Rossi (1988), notes that as a child during the Depression, she learned that homemaking tasks force a woman to think of employment as "a contingency" rather than "continuous." She goes on to recollect how opportunities, including federal research funds, went to aid the careers of men rather than women. More recently, Theda Skocpol has experienced difficulties she attributes to her gender. She notes that in 1984 she "was offered the Harvard tenured professorship that I am convinced would have been mine in 1981 if I had been 'Theodore' rather than 'Theda'" (Skocpol, 1988, p. 155). Whether it is among the underclass or college classes, women are at a disadvantage.

The surveys presented in Chapter 2 show gradual acceptance of the earliest efforts to eliminate discrimination, but that support may be failing. Governmental programs are increasingly aimed at institutional discrimination, a form that some people feel is not really discrimination at all. As one might expect, attempts to attack institutional discrimination have met with staunch resistance. Partly as a result of this outcry from some of the public, especially White Americans, the federal government gradually deemphasized its efforts in affirmative action during the 1980s and early 1990s.

As we turn to examine the various groups that make up the American people, and later focus on intergroup relations in other societies, look for the types of programs meant to reduce prejudice and discrimination that were discussed here. Most of the material in this chapter has been about racial groups, especially Black and White Americans. It would be easy to see intergroup hostility as a racial phenomenon, but that would be incorrect. Throughout the history of the United States, relations among White groups have been characterized by resentment and violence. The next two chapters examine the nature and relations of White ethnic groups.

## KEY TERMS

**absolute deprivation** The minimum level of subsistence below which families or individuals should not be expected to exist.

**affirmative action** Positive efforts to recruit minority group members or women for jobs, promotions, and educational opportunities.

**dual labor market** Division of the economy into two areas of employment, the secondary one of which is populated primarily by minorities working at menial jobs.

**institutional discrimination** A denial of opportunities and equal rights to individuals or groups resulting from the normal operations of a society.

**irregular economy** Transfers of money, goods, or services that are not reported to the government. Common in inner-city neighborhoods and poverty-stricken rural areas.

**relative deprivation** The conscious experience of a negative discrepancy between legitimate expectations and present actualities.

**states' rights** The principle, reinvoked in the 1950s, which holds that each state is sovereign and has the right to order its own affairs without interference from the federal government.

**total discrimination** The combination of current discrimination with past discrimination created by poor schools and menial jobs.

**underclass** Lower-class members not a part of the regular economy whose situation is not changed by conventional assistance programs.

## FOR FURTHER INFORMATION

Gary S. Becker. *The Economics of Discrimination,* 2nd ed. Chicago: University of Chicago Press, 1971.

This is the best statement of a once widely-accepted model of discrimination.

Stephen Carter. *Reflections of an Affirmative Action Baby.* New York: Basic Books, 1991.

A Black law professor at Yale offers an anecdotal account of his life that is critical of life as an African American in higher education under affirmative action and liberalism.

Robert Cherry. *Discrimination.* Lexington, MA: Lexington Book, 1989.

An economist reviews the economic impact of discrimination on Blacks, Women, and Jews.

Philomena Essed. *Understanding Everyday Racism.* Newbury Park, CA: Sage, 1991.

Interviews of 2,000 Black women in the United States and the Netherlands documenting personal and institutional racism.

Daniel R. Fusfeld. *The Basic Economics of the Urban Racial Crisis.* New York: Holt, Rinehart and Winston, 1973.

In a brief book, Fusfeld examines the ghetto economy and its relationship to the larger economy. He lucidly describes theories of discrimination advanced by economists.

Douglas G. Glasgow, *The Black Underclass: Poverty, Unemployment, and Entrapment of Ghetto Youth.* San Francisco: Jossey Bass, 1980.

Glasgow, a professor of social welfare, looks at the special problem facing Blacks between ages eighteen and thirty-four, who constitute a significant segment of the secondary labor market—the irregular economy.

Louis L. Knowles and Kenneth Prewitt. *Institutional Racism in America.* Englewood Cliffs, NJ: Prentice-Hall, 1969.

This book documents institutional racism in economic life, education, the courts, and the political process, and describes how it is expressed in prejudice and discrimination.

William J. Wilson. *The Truly Disadvantaged: The Inner City, the Underclass, and Public Policy.* Chicago: University of Chicago Press, 1987.

A sociologist analyzes the continuing deterioration of conditions facing African American urban poor.

## Statistical Sources

Hundreds of federal government publications provide statistical data comparing racial and ethnic groups to each other and women to men. The Current Population Report Series P–20 and P–60 and the annual *Statistical Abstract of the United States* are among the best sources.

## Part Two

# ETHNIC AND RELIGIOUS SOURCES OF CONFLICT

## Chapter Four

# IMMIGRATION AND THE UNITED STATES

## Chapter Outline

**Early Immigration**
The Anti-Catholic Crusade
The Anti-Chinese Movement
**Restrictionist Sentiment Increases**
The National Origins System
The McCarran-Walter Act
The 1965 Immigration and Naturalization Act
**Contemporary Concerns**
The Brain Drain

Population Growth
Illegal Immigration
Scope of the Problem
Reform and Amnesty
**Refugees**
The Sanctuary Movement
**Glancing Back and Looking Ahead**
**Key Terms**
**For Further Information**

---

**❋ HIGHLIGHTS ❋**

The diversity of the American people is unmistakable evidence of the variety of places from which immigrants came. The different immigrating people did not necessarily welcome one another. Instead they brought their European rivalries to the New World. The Chinese were the first to be singled out for restriction with the passage of the 1882 *Exclusion Act*. The Chinese became, in effect, the scapegoat for America's sagging economy in the last half of the nineteenth cen-

tury. Growing fears that more un-American types were immigrating motivated the creation of the *national origins system* and the quota acts of the 1920s. These acts gave preference to certain nationalities, until the passage of the *Immigration and Naturalization Act* in 1965 ended that practice. Concern about illegal immigration led to passage in 1986 of the *Immigration Reform and Control Act*. Controversy continues to surround the policy of the United States toward refugees.

---

In the summer of 1986, a Taiwanese student arrived at Chicago O'Hare Airport for her first time in the United States. She entered the customs and immigration area knowing there were two sections: one for Americans and the other for foreigners. She recalled, "At that moment, I felt that I had chosen the right line because in the line were a lot of Oriental people and I thought that we are all foreigners who came to the United States. Later, I found that I was wrong because I saw everyone in this line carried American passports. So, from this event I suddenly realized that I could not judge a person's nationality by his appearance, especially in the United States" (S. Tree Feng, 1988).

The diversity of ethnic and racial backgrounds of Americans today is the living legacy of immigration. Except for descendants of Native Americans or of Africans brought here enslaved, today's population is entirely the product of individuals who chose to leave familiar places to come to a new country. Historian Oscar Handlin wrote, "Once I thought to write a history of the immigrants in America. Then I discovered that the immigrants *were* American history" (1951, p. 3). Although this statement may ignore the role of Native Americans , it correctly acknowledges the role of the dominant Europeans.

The forces that cause people to emigrate are complex. The most important have been economic—financial failure in the old country and perception of higher incomes and higher standards of living in the new homeland. Other factors included dislike of new regimes, racial or religious bigotry, and desire to reunite families. All these factors push individuals from their homelands and pull them to other nations such as the United States. Immigration to the United States in particular has at times been facilitated by cheap ocean transportation and by other countries' removal of restrictions on emigration.

The reception given to immigrants in this country, however, has not always been friendly. Open bloodshed, restrictive laws, and the eventual return of some immigrants to their home country attest to the uneasy feeling toward strangers who wish to settle here. Nevertheless, vast numbers of immigrants have still come. Figure 4.1 indicates the high but fluctuating number of immigrants that have arrived during every decade from 1820 to the present.

## EARLY IMMIGRATION

European explorers of North America were soon accompanied by settlers, the first immigrants to the Western Hemisphere. The Spanish founded St. Augustine in Florida in 1565 and the English, Jamestown in Virginia in 1607. White

**FIGURE 4.1**    Immigration in the United States, 1820–1990

Except during a period of tightening immigration policy in the 1930s and 1940s, the United States has received a consistent, sizable flow of immigrants, dominated since 1950 by non-Europeans.

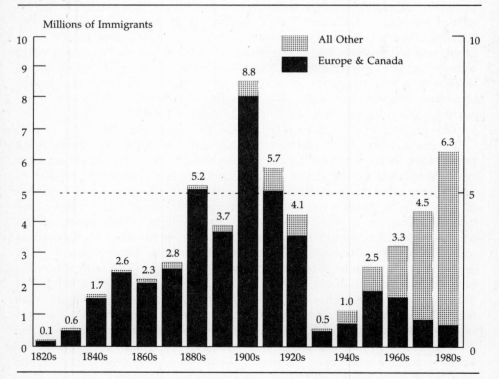

*Source:* The Urban Institute in Fix and Passel, 1991, based on Immigration and Naturalization Service statistics. Data for 1980s adjusted by author based on Bureau of the Census, 1991a, p. 9.

Protestants from England emerged from the colonial period as the dominant force numerically, politically, and socially. The English accounted for 60 percent of the three million White Americans in 1790. Although exact statistics are lacking for the early years of the United States, the English were soon outnumbered by other nationalities, as the numbers of Scotch-Irish and Germans, in particular, swelled. The English colonists, however, maintained their dominant position, as Chapter 5 will examine.

Throughout American history, immigration policy has been a controversial political topic. The policies of George III were criticized in the Declaration of Independence for obstructing immigration to the colonies. Toward the end of the nineteenth century, the American republic itself was criticized for enacting just such policies. But in the beginning the country encouraged immigration. At first, legislation fixed the residence requirement for naturalization at five years, although briefly under the Alien Act it was 14 years and "dangerous" people could be expelled. Despite this brief harshness, through most of the 1800s immigration was unregulated, and naturalization was easily available.

## The Anti-Catholic Crusade

The absence of federal legislation from 1790 to 1881 does not mean that all new arrivals were welcomed. *Xenophobia* (the fear or distrust of strangers or foreigners) led naturally to *nativism* (beliefs and policies favoring native-born citizens over immigrants). Roman Catholics in general, and the Irish in particular, were among the first Europeans to be ill treated. Anti-Catholic feeling originated in Europe and was brought by the early Protestant immigrants. The Catholics of colonial America, although few, were subject to limits on civil and religious rights.

From independence until around 1820 little evidence appeared of the anti-Catholic sentiment of colonial days, but the cry against "popery" grew as Irish immigration increased (Billington, 1938). Prominent Americans encouraged hatred of these new arrivals. Samuel F. B. Morse, inventor of the telegraph and an accomplished painter, wrote a strongly worded anti-Catholic work in 1834 entitled *A Foreign Conspiracy Against the Liberties of the United States*. Morse felt the Irish were "shamefully illiterate and without opinions of their own" (1835, p. 61). In the mind of the prejudiced American, the Irish were particularly unwelcome because they were Roman Catholics. Many Americans readily believed Morse's warning that the Pope planned to move the Vatican to the Mississippi River Valley (Duff, 1971, p. 34). Even poet and philosopher Ralph Waldo Emerson wrote of "the wild Irish . . . who sympathized, of course, with despotism" (Kennedy, 1964, p. 70).

This antagonism was not limited to harsh words. From 1834 to 1854, mob violence against Catholics across the country led to death, the burning of a Boston convent, the destruction of a Catholic church and the homes of Catholics, and the use of Marines and state militia to bring peace to American cities as far west as St. Louis..

THE AMERICAN RIVER GANGES.
THE PRIESTS AND THE CHILDREN.—[See Page 912.]

*Thomas Nast, a political cartoonist who was himself an immigrant from what is now Germany, prepared this cartoon showing invading bishops with mitres like alligators.*

A frequent pattern saw minorities striking out against each other, rather than at the dominant class. Irish Americans opposed the Emancipation Proclamation and the freeing of the slaves because they feared Blacks would compete for the unskilled work open to them. This fear was confirmed when free Blacks were used to break a longshoremen's strike in New York. Hence much of the Irish violence during the 1863 riot was directed against Blacks, not against the Whites who were most responsible for the conditions in which immigrants found themselves (Duff, 1971, pp. 33–34; S. Warner, 1968, pp. 148–152).

In retrospect, the reception given to the Irish is not difficult to understand. Many came following the 1845–48 potato crop failure and famine in Ireland. They fled not so much to a better life as from almost certain death. The Irish Catholics brought with them a celibate clergy, who struck the New England aristocracy as strange and reawakened old religious hatreds. The Irish were worse than Blacks, according to the dominant Whites, because unlike the slaves and even the freedmen who "knew their place" the Irish did not suffer their maltreatment in silence. In the coal fields of Pennsylvania, for instance, the Irish formed the Molly Maguires, a clandestine organization that threatened and killed bosses and destroyed coal trains. Elsewhere in the Pennsylvania coal fields, Slavic miners organized and fought, occasionally with violence, their employers' attempts to take advantage of them. Employers balanced minorities by judiciously mixing immigrant groups to prevent unified action by laborers.

For the most part nativist efforts only led the foreign born to emphasize their ties to Europe.

By the 1850s, nativism became an open political movement pledged to vote only for native Americans, to fight Roman Catholicism, and to demand a 21-year naturalization period. Party members were instructed to divulge nothing about their program and to say that they knew nothing about it. As a result, they came to be called the Know-Nothings. Although the Know-Nothings soon vanished, the antialien mentality survived and occasionally became formally organized into such societies as the Ku Klux Klan in the 1860s and the anti-Catholic American Protective Association in the 1890s. Revivals of anti-Catholicism continued well into the twentieth century. The most dramatic outbreak of nativism in the nineteenth century, however, was aimed at the Chinese. If there had been any doubt that the idea that the United States could harmoniously accommodate all was a fiction by the mid-1800s, debate on the Chinese Exclusion Act would settle the question once and for all (Adamic, 1931, pp. 17–20; Curran, 1966; Greeley, 1972, pp. 118–119; V. Greene, 1968; Schaefer, 1971).

## The Anti-Chinese Movement

Prior to 1851, official records show that only 46 Chinese had immigrated to the United States. In the next 30 years more than 200,000 came to this country, lured by the discovery of gold and the opening of job opportunities in the West. Overcrowding, drought, and warfare in China also encouraged them to take a chance in the United States. Another important factor was improved trans-oceanic transportation; it was actually cheaper to travel from Hong Kong to San Francisco than from Chicago to San Francisco. The frontier communities of the West, particularly in California, looked upon the Chinese as a valuable resource to fill manual jobs. As early as 1854, so many Chinese desired to come that ships had difficulty in handling the volume.

During the 1860s railroad work provided the greatest demand for Chinese labor, until the Union Pacific and Central Pacific railroads were joined at Promontory, Utah, in 1869. The Union Pacific relied primarily on Irish laborers, but 90 percent of the Central Pacific labor force was Chinese, because Whites generally refused the back-breaking work over the Western terrain. Despite the contribution of the Chinese, White workers physically prevented their even being present when the golden spike was driven to mark the joining of the two railroads (Commission on Civil Rights, 1986; Hsu, 1971, p. 104).

A variety of factors, rather than a single cause, motivated the anti-Chinese movement. The movement itself was twofold, including both legislative restrictions on the rights of Chinese immigrants and mob violence, vigilante groups, and spur-of-the-moment tribunals intended to intimidate the new arrivals. Although the legislators often chastised the mobs and vigilantes for their actions, both groups were inspired by the same fears.

Reflecting their xenophobia, White settlers found the Chinese immigrants and their customs and religion difficult to understand. Indeed, relatively few people actually tried to understand these immigrants from Asia. Easterners and legislators, although they had no first-hand contact with Chinese Americans, were soon on the anti-Chinese bandwagon, as they read sensationalized accounts of the way of life of the new arrivals.

Even before the Chinese immigrated, stereotypes of them and their country appeared. American traders returning from China, European diplomats, and Protestant missionaries consistently emphasized the exotic and sinister aspects of life in China. The sinophobes, people with a fear of anything associated with China, appealed to the racist theory developed during the slavery controversy. Similarly, Americans were beginning to be more conscious of biological inheritance and disease, and so it was not hard to conjure up fears of alien genes and germs. The only real challenge the anti-Chinese movement had was to convince people that the consequences of unrestricted Chinese immigration outweighed any possible economic gain from their presence. Perhaps briefly, racial prejudice was subordinated to industrial dependence on Chinese labor for the work that Whites shunned (Schrieke, 1936, p. 16), but such positive feelings were short-lived. The fear of the "yellow peril" overwhelmed any desire to know more about Oriental people and their customs (S. Miller, 1969).

Another nativist fear of Chinese immigrants was based on the threat they posed as laborers. Californians found support throughout the nation as organized labor feared that the Chinese would be used as strikebreakers. By 1870 Chinese workers had been used for that purpose as far east as Massachusetts. When Chinese workers did unionize they were not recognized by major labor organizations. Samuel Gompers, founder of the American Federation of Labor, consistently opposed any effort to assist Chinese workers and refused to consider having a union of Chinese restaurant employees admitted into the AFL (H. Hill, 1967). Gompers worked effectively to see future Chinese immigration ended and produced a pamphlet entitled *Chinese Exclusion: Meat vs. Rice, American Manhood Against Asiatic Coolieism—Which Shall Survive?* (Gompers and Gutstadt, 1908). Although employers were glad to pay the Chinese low wages, laborers came to loathe the Chinese rather than resenting their fellow countrymen's willingness to exploit the Chinese. Only a generation earlier the same concerns had been felt about the Irish, but with the Chinese the hostility was to reach new heights because of another factor.

From the sociological perspective of conflict theory, we can explain how the Chinese immigrants were desirable only when their labor was necessary to maintain growth in the western United States. When the need for laborers was perceived to have lessened, however, the presence of so many job seekers was no longer desired. Conflict theorists would further point out that a greater than necessary influx of workers may lead to some form of restriction, but such restriction would not have to focus on any specific nationality in order to reduce the number of foreign workers in the nation. Because decision making at that time rested in the hands of the descendants of European immigrants, though, the steps to be taken were most likely to be directed against those least powerful—immigrants from China who, unlike Europeans seeking entry, had few allies among legislators and other policymakers.

In 1882 Congress enacted the Chinese Exclusion Act, which outlawed Chinese immigration for ten years. It also explicitly denied naturalization rights to those Chinese in the United States, that is, they were not allowed to become citizens. There was little debate in Congress, and discussion concentrated on *how* suspension of Chinese immigration could best be handled. No allowance was made for spouses and children to be reunited with their husbands and fathers in the United States. Only Chinese government officials, teachers, tourists, and merchants were exempted.

The balance of the nineteenth century saw the remaining loopholes allowing Chinese immigration closed. In 1884 Chinese laborers were not allowed to enter the United States from any foreign place, a ban that lasted ten years. Two years later the Statue of Liberty was dedicated, with the poem of Emma Lazarus inscribed on its base. To the Chinese, the poem welcoming the tired, the poor, the huddled masses must have seemed a hollow mockery.

In 1892 Congress extended the Exclusion Act for another ten years and added that Chinese laborers had to obtain certificates of residence within a year or face deportation. After the turn of the century the Exclusion Act was extended again. Two decades later the Chinese were not alone; the list of people restricted by immigration policy expanded manyfold.

## RESTRICTIONIST SENTIMENT INCREASES

As Congress closed the door to Chinese immigration, debate to restrict immigration turned in new directions. Prodded by growing anti-Japanese feelings, the United States entered into the so-called Gentlemen's Agreement, completed in 1908. Japan agreed to halt further immigration to the United States and the United States agreed to end discrimination against those Japanese who had already arrived. The immigration ended, but anti-Japanese feelings continued. Americans were growing uneasy that the "new immigrants" would overwhelm the culture established by the "old immigrants." The earlier immigrants, if not Anglo-Saxon or similar groups like the Scandinavians, the Swiss, and French Huguenots, were more experienced in democratic political practices and had greater affinity with the dominant Anglo-Saxon culture (Marden and Meyer, 1978, p. 76). But by the end of the nineteenth century more and more immigrants were neither English-speaking nor Protestant, and came from dramatically different cultures.

For four years the United States Immigration Commission, known popularly as the Dillingham Commission, exhaustively studied the effects of immigration. The findings, presented in 1911 in 41 volumes, were determined by the commission's assumption that there were types of immigrants. The two types were the old immigrants, mostly Anglo-Saxons, who were characterized as hard-working pioneers, and the new immigrants from southwestern Europe, who were branded as opportunists (Fermi, 1971, p. 20; Handlin, 1957, pp. 78–110). Not surprisingly, pressure for a more restrictive immigration policy became insurmountable. A literacy test was one of the results of hostility against the new immigrants.

In 1917, Congress finally overrode President Wilson's veto and enacted an immigration bill that included the controversial literacy test. Critics of the bill, including Wilson, argued that illiteracy does not signify inherent incompetency but reflects lack of opportunity for instruction (*New York Times*, 1917a). Such arguments were not heeded, however. The act seems innocent at first glance—it merely required immigrants to read 30 words in any language—but it was the first attempt to restrict immigration from places other than Western Europe. The act also prohibited immigration from the South Sea islands and other parts of Asia not already excluded. Curiously, this law that closed the door on non-Anglo-Saxons permitted waiver of the test if the immigrants came as a result of their government's discrimination against a race (*New York Times*, 1917b).

## The National Origins System

Beginning in 1921 a series of measures was enacted that marked a new era in American immigration policy. Anti-immigration sentiment combined with the isolationism that followed World War I caused Congress to severely restrict entry privileges not just to the Chinese and Japanese but to Europeans as well. The national origins system was begun in 1921 and remained the basis of immigration policy until 1968. This system used the country of birth to determine whether an individual could enter as a legal alien, and the number of previous immigrants and their descendants was used to set the quota of how many from a country could enter annually.

The 1921 measure was temporary and used the 1910 census for determining quotas. It was revised in 1924 to use the 1890 census, a sleight of hand that further reduced the number admitted annually. In 1929 the permanent system went into effect, based on the 1920 census.

To understand the effect the 1929 act had on immigration it is necessary to clarify the quota system. The quotas were deliberately weighted in favor of immigration from Northern Europe. Because of the ethnic composition of the country in 1920, the quotas placed severe restrictions on immigration from the rest of Europe and other parts of the world. Immigration from the Western Hemisphere (that is, Canada, Mexico, Central and South America, and the Caribbean) continued unrestricted. The quota for each nation was set at 3 percent of the number of people descended from each nationality recorded in the 1920 census. Once the statistical manipulations were completed, almost 70 percent of the quota for the Eastern Hemisphere went to just three countries, Great Britain, Ireland, and Germany.

The absurdities of the system soon became obvious, but the system continued. Britain was no longer a source of immigration and so most of its quota of 65,000

**FIGURE 4.2** Legal Immigrants Admitted to the United States, by Region of Last Residence: 1820–1990

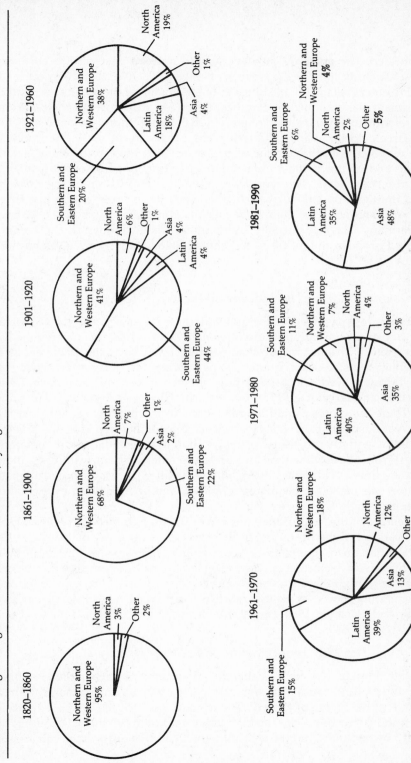

*Source:* From Leon F. Bouvier and Robert W. Gardner, *Immigration to the U.S.: The Unfinished Story* (Washington, DC: Population Reference Bureau, 1986). Reprinted by permission. Data for 1981–1990 are author's estimate based on Population Reference Bureau cited in *USA Today,* January 16, 1990, p. 3A.

went unfilled. The openings, however, could not be transferred, even though countries such as Italy with a quota of only 6,000 had 200,000 people who wished to enter (Belair, 1970). However one rationalizes the purpose behind the act, the result was obvious: any English person, regardless of skill and regardless of any relation to anyone already here, could enter the country more easily than, say, a Greek doctor whose children were American citizens. The quota for Greece was 305, with the backlog of people wishing to come reaching 100,000.

By the end of the 1920s annual immigration dropped to one-fourth of its pre-World War I level. The worldwide economic depression of the 1930s decreased immigration still further. A brief upsurge in immigration just before World War II reflected the flight of Europeans from the oppression of expanding Nazi Germany. The war virtually ended trans-Atlantic immigration. The era of the great European migration to the United States had been legislated out of existence.

## The McCarran-Walter Act

In 1952 Congress passed, over President Harry S Truman's veto, the McCarran-Walter Act, or the Immigration and Nationality Act of 1952. This act retained the quota system with only minor changes, but it still used the 1920 census for determining the size of the quotas. Some concessions to common sense were made—Japanese were for the first time allowed to become citizens and were awarded an annual quota of 115—but the principle of national origins remained intact. There were other small liberalizations of immigration policy. Just after World War II, special provisions were enacted to allow some 120,000 soldiers to return home with their foreign-born wives and to permit displaced persons (or refugees) from Western Europe and Russia to enter without waiting to qualify under the quota (Veidmanis, 1963). Five years after the McCarran-Walter Act, legislation was passed to facilitate reunion of families hampered by the nationality quotas.

One feature of the McCarran-Walter Act remains in force today, even following the passage of the Immigration Reform and Control Act of 1986. The 1952 legislation has provisions that bar entry to the United States for Communists and subversives, including anyone deemed to have advocated Communist ideas. Even though these provisions are regularly waived, occasional cases do arise generating protest by observers who argue that it is too arbitrarily enforced (Bouvier and Gardner, 1986, pp. 12–13; Lacayo, 1986; Scanlan, 1987).

## The 1965 Immigration and Naturalization Act

The national origins system was abandoned with the passage of the 1965 Immigration and Naturalization Act, signed into law by President Lyndon B. Johnson at the foot of the Statue of Liberty. The primary goals of the act were reuniting families and protecting the American labor market. After the act, immigration increased by one-third, but the act's influence was primarily on the composition rather than the size of immigration. The sources of immigration now included Italy, Greece, Portugal, Mexico, the Philippines, the West Indies, and South America. The effect is apparent when we compare the changing sources of immigration over the last hundred years, as in Figure 4.2. The most recent period shows that Asian and Latin American immigrants combined to account for 80 percent of the people who were permitted entry. This figure compares to the national origins system period, reflected approximately in the figure by the years 1931 to 1960, when 60 percent of the legal arrivals came from northern and western Europe and North America.

The liberalization of eligibility rules also brought a backlog of applications from relatives of American citizens who earlier had failed to qualify under the more restrictive national origins scheme. Backlogs of applicants throughout the world still existed, but the equal treatment for all underlying the 1965 legislation gave them greater hope of eventually entering the United States (Belair, 1970; Dinnerstein and Reimers, 1975, pp. 88–89; Reimers, 1983).

## CONTEMPORARY CONCERNS

While our current immigration policies compare favorably to other nations' restrictions, there are four continuing criticisms of our immigration policy—the brain drain, population growth, illegal immigration, and refugees. The first two, which have not been subject to specific legislation, will be examined first. We will then take an extended look at the concerns about illegal immigration and refugees.

### The Brain Drain

The term *brain drain* refers to the immigration to the United States of skilled workers, professionals, and technicians who are desperately needed by their home countries. During the mid-twentieth century many scientists and other professionals from industrial nations, principally Germany and Great Britain, came to the United States. More recently, however, the brain drain has pulled emigrants from developing nations, including India, Pakistan, and newly independent African states. A study in 1977 revealed that nearly two-fifths of the foreign doctors in this country had come from India or Pakistan—two nations that have a chronic shortage of physicians (Shribman, 1981).

The brain drain controversy was evident long before passage of the 1965 Immigration Act. The 1965 act seemed, though, to encourage such immigration by placing the professions in one of the categories of preference. As a result, professionals account for some 9 percent of legal immigrants. For some nationalities, the figure is much higher. In 1979, 12 percent of Filipino immigrants, 19 percent of African immigrants, and 18 percent of Indian immigrants to the United States were professionals (Fortney, 1972; Immigration and Naturalization Service, 1982).

Conflict theorists see the current brain drain as yet another symptom of the unequal distribution of world resources. In their view, it is ironic that the United States gives foreign aid to improve the technical resources of African and Asian countries, simultaneously maintaining an immigration policy that encourages professionals in such nations to migrate to our shores. These are the very countries that have unacceptable public health conditions and need native scientists, educators, technicians, and other professionals.

Some of the effects of the brain drain have been lessened since 1982, when the entry of foreign-born and foreign-educated physicians was greatly restricted. Yet the United States continues to beckon to professionals and to retain highly motivated students, who remain in the United States after completing their education.

One proposed solution to continuing international concern over the brain drain is to limit the number of professionals from a nation who may enter the United States in a year. Such legislation has not received widespread support within Congress, and the brain drain from developing countries continues.

## Population Growth

The United States is almost alone among industrial nations in continuing to accept large numbers of permanent immigrants and refugees. Although such immigration has increased since passage of the 1965 Immigration and Naturalization Act, the nation's birthrate has decreased. Consequently, the contribution of immigration to population growth has become more significant. Legal immigration accounted for one-third of the nation's growth in the 1980s. The impact is not evenly felt throughout the United States. If California had attracted no immigrants, it would have gained two seats in the U.S. House of Representatives instead of seven. Illinois and New York both would have lost population in the 1980s rather than experiencing modest gains due to immigration (Vobejda, 1991).

Contrary to popular belief, immigrant women actually have a lower birthrate than native-born women, yet their contribution to population growth remains sizable. It is projected that immigrants who come to the United States in the period 1990 to 2080 and their descendants will add 72 million more people, or 25 percent, to the population. Assuming that native-born Americans maintain a low birthrate and the immigrant contribution to the population of the United States is just 50 percent higher than at present, the contribution could run as high as 37 percent (Bouvier and Gardner, 1986, p. 27; National Commission on Population Growth, 1972, p. 115).

## ILLEGAL IMMIGRATION

The most bitterly debated aspect of United States immigration policy has been the control of illegal or undocumented immigrants. These immigrants and their

*Illegal immigration is not limited to any ethnic group as evidenced by this lawyer who works on behalf of undocumented workers from Ireland.*

families come to the United States in search of higher paying jobs than are available in their home countries. Their manner of entry, though, is also in defiance of the law.

## Scope of the Problem

A 1990 estimate places the number of illegal immigrants between 2 and 3 million, increasing by 100,000 annually. While Mexican nationals make up about 55 or 60 percent of this total, undocumented immigrants are here from throughout the world (Espenshade, 1990).

That the number of illegal aliens in areas in the United States is substantial is illustrated by the move among unions to actively recruit illegal aliens as members. For many years, labor unions ignored the flood of aliens or sought to prevent them from entering the nation. Unions showed little concern for these people as workers. Now in the West, however, where illegal entrants make up a growing proportion of the work force, several unions are trying to represent these workers in agriculture and the garment industry (Lindsey, 1979).

The cost of the federal government's attempt to police the nation's borders and locate illegal immigrants is sizable. There are significant costs for aliens and for other citizens as well. Civil rights advocates have expressed concern that the procedures used to apprehend and deport people are discriminatory and deprive many aliens of their legal rights. American citizens of Hispanic origin, some of whom were born in the United States, may be greeted with prejudice and distrust, as if their Spanish surnames automatically implied that they were "illegals." Furthermore, such American citizens may be unable to find work because employers wrongly believe that their documents are forged (Domestic Council Committee on Illegal Aliens, 1976; Farber, 1975).

## Reform and Amnesty

In the context of this illegal immigration, Congress approved the Immigration Reform and Control Act of 1986, after debating it for nearly a decade. The act marked a historic change in immigration policy. For the first time, hiring illegal aliens became illegal, so that employers are subject to fines and even prison sentences. Just as significant was the extension of legal status to illegal aliens who entered the United States before January 1, 1982 and have lived here continuously since then. After two years as lawful temporary residents of the United States, 3.1 million previously illegal aliens can become permanent residents eligible for American citizenship after another five years.

Support for the act was not unanimous. Some members of Congress, including Hispanic representatives, felt that employers might discriminate against Hispanics, fearing they were in the country illegally. Others opposed granting amnesty to people who entered the country illegally, even if they had been here for several years. Some wondered about the millions of relatives of the now-legal aliens who may secure passage into the United States as permanent residents. It has been a bureaucratic challenge to determine which illegal immigrants have been in the United States long enough to qualify for legal status. Many people may be deported after unsuccessfully trying to document their residency in the United States.

The 1986 plan to deal with a complex problem was a compromise. It provided monies for local governments to supply increased public assistance, health care, and education to the millions of newly-legal immigrants. The Border Patrol's budget was increased by 50 percent to prevent future illegal immigration. Lobbyists of agricultural employers were assured that they would be guaranteed an adequate labor pool of seasonal workers.

There remains uncertainty as to whether the 1986 act has had its intended effect on illegal immigration. The Immigration and Naturalization Service had been deporting up to 1.6 million illegal immigrants annually. In 1989 the number was under 900,000, yet was back close to the 1.6 million rate in 1991. The Border Patrol is increasingly involved in hunting for drug smugglers and thereby diverting attention from the apprehension of illegal immigrants (Espenshade, 1990; Nichols, 1991).

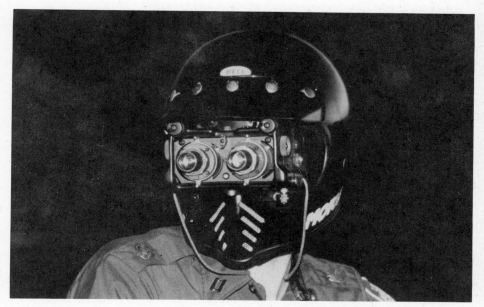

*U.S. Border Patrol agent in southern California, wearing infrared glasses for night vision.*

Although the Immigration Reform and Control Act prohibited employers from discriminating against legal aliens because they were not American citizens, a 1990 report by the General Accounting Office revealed that the law had produced a "widespread pattern of discrimination" against people who looked or sounded like foreigners. The report estimates that some 890,000 employers initiated one or more discriminatory practices in response to the 1986 immigration law. Although these firms employ nearly 7 million workers, fewer than 1,000 complaints of discrimination have been filed with government agencies—in good part because most employees are unaware of the protections included in the Immigration Reform and Control Act (C. Brown, 1990, p. 3).

Critics of the new immigration law emphasize that while it has been extremely beneficial for many immigrants who qualified for amnesty, it has had a devastating impact on those who could not qualify. Many aliens in this situation are being overworked or underpaid by unscrupulous employers, who are well aware that these workers have few options. Consequently, millions of illegal immigrants continue to live in fear and hiding, subject to even more severe harassment and discrimination than before. From a conflict perspective, these immigrants—primarily poor and Hispanic—are being firmly entrenched at the bottom of the nation's social and economic hierarchies.

These issues were left unresolved with the passage of the 1990 Immigration Act, which eased restrictions for foreigners with relatives in the United States. There was little opposition to the measure but it did have the unusual provision

*Ethnic succession through immigration is apparent in many lines of work. The International Ladies' Garment Workers Union was originally formed by immigrant Jewish and Italian garment workers early in this century. Today most of its members are either Hispanic or Asian, like these Puerto Rican members of a New York City local.*

of allowing automatic entry if a potential immigrant would establish a business with $1 million and that would employ at least 10 workers. Clearly money talks when it comes to immigration. These "yacht people" (as contrasted to the Vietnamese and Haitian "boat people") are quite a departure from the nation's commitment to the tired, the poor, and the oppressed (Fix and Passel, 1991; Mydans, 1991b; M. Thompson, 1990).

## REFUGEES

An entire unsettled nation exists. There are approximately 17 million refugees, people who fear prosecution in their homeland. That makes the nation of refugees larger than Belgium or Sweden or Cuba. Table 4.1 illustrates major encampments of the world's uprooted peoples.

The United States has touted itself as a haven for political refugees. For many individuals it has offered a life-saving haven. Nien Cheng was an upper-class widow when the Chinese charged her with espionage and held her without trial. She writes in "Listen to Their Voices" of her poignant feelings on August 16, 1988, when Judge Mark Americus Constantino, the son of Greek immigrant parents, confirmed upon her citizenship.

**TABLE 4.3**  Refugees Worldwide

As of December 31, 1991, there were an estimated 16,650,000 refugees and asylum seekers. This table identifies countries with at least 60,000 refugees and lists refugee groups over 20,000. Refugees are a worldwide phenomenon but are most significant in Africa, the Middle East, and South Asia.

| | Source-group Total | Country-wide Total | Regional Total |
|---|---|---|---|
| **Africa** | | | 5,340,800 |
| Algeria | | 204,000 | |
|   W. Sahara | 165,000 | | |
|   Mali | 35,000 | | |
| Burundi | | 107,000 | |
|   Rwanda | 80,600 | | |
|   Zaire | 25,900 | | |
| Djibouti | | 120,000 | |
|   Somalia | 105,000 | | |
| Ethiopia | | 534,000 | |
|   Somalia | 519,000 | | |
| Ivory Coast | | 240,400 | |
|   Liberia | 240,000 | | |
| South Africa | | 201,000 | |
|   Mozambique | 200,000 | | |
| Sudan | | 717,200 | |
|   Ethiopia | 690,000 | | |
|   Chad | 20,000 | | |
| Tanzania | | 251,100 | |
|   Burundi | 131,000 | | |
|   Mozambique | 72,000 | | |
|   Rwanda | 22,300 | | |
| Uganda | | 165,450 | |
|   Rwanda | 87,000 | | |
|   Sudan | 75,500 | | |
| Zaire | | 482,300 | |
|   Angola | 310,000 | | |
|   Sudan | 104,000 | | |
|   Burundi | 45,000 | | |
| Zambia | | 140,500 | |
|   Angola | 103,000 | | |
|   Mozambique | 25,000 | | |
| **East Asia and the Pacific** | | | 688,500 |
| Hong Kong | | 60,000 | |
|   Vietnam | 60,000 | | |
| Thailand | | 512,700 | |
|   Cambodia | 370,000 | | |
|   Burma | 70,000 | | |
|   Laos | 59,000 | | |
| **Europe and North America** | | | 677,700 |
| Germany | | 256,100 | |
| United States | | 68,800 | |
| **Latin America and the Caribbean** | | | 119,600 |
| **Middle East and South Asia** | | | 9,820,950 |
| Gaza Strip | | 528,700 | |
|   Palestinians | 528,700 | | |
| India | | 402,600 | |
|   Sri Lanka | 210,000 | | |
|   China | 100,000 | | |
|   Bangladesh | 65,000 | | |
| Iran | | 3,150,000 | |
|   Afghanistan | 3,000,000 | | |
|   Iraq | 150,000 | | |
| Jordan | | 960,000 | |
|   Palestinians | 960,200 | | |
| Lebanon | | 314,200 | |
|   Palestinians | 310,600 | | |
| Pakistan | | 3,594,000 | |
|   Afghanistan | 3,591,000 | | |
| Syria | | 293,900 | |
|   Palestinians | 289,900 | | |
| West Bank | | 430,100 | |
|   Palestinians | 430,100 | | |

*Source:* U.S. Committee for Refugees, *World Refugee Survey, 1992* (Washington, DC: U.S. Committee for Refugees, 1992) pp. 32–33.

### ❖ LISTEN TO THEIR VOICES ❖

## Casting a Vote for Freedom of Conscience

*Nien Cheng*

... As I stood with the Statue of Liberty towering over me, I realized again what many have felt before—that America is another name for freedom.

Yet many Americans take their freedom for granted. I cannot. For 6½ years I was in solitary confinement in a Communist Chinese prison, falsely accused of being a spy for the West. My ordeal began on a very different August day 22 years ago, when 30 or 40 Red Guards came to destroy my house. I had been alone in my study reading, and though I knew it was a futile gesture, I picked up a copy of the Chinese constitution. "It's against the constitution of the People's Republic of China to enter a private house without a search warrant," I challenged.

The young Red Guards grabbed the constitution from my hands and tore it up. "The Constitution is abolished," they said. "We recognize only the teaching of our Great Leader Chairman Mao."

Last year and this one have been a time of American constitutional celebration. The people's knowledge of our great historical document has been refreshed. However, mere knowledge of a document is hardly adequate to preserve democratic freedom.

A constitution is only as strong as the beliefs of its people. The American Constitution is not a machine that can run on its own. Laws have no power apart from the conviction of people to follow and enforce them. Military might does not guarantee the security of a nation. Intellectual ignorance and moral apathy are the seedbed of political anarchy. Finally, it is only our beliefs that make America strong. . . .

I am 73. On November 8, I will cast the first free vote of my life. I will be voting for more than a presidential candidate. I will be voting for freedom—freedom of conscience.

From *Life and Death in Shanghai* by Nien Cheng. Copyright © 1987 by Nien Cheng. Reprinted by permission.

The United States, insulated by distance from wars and famines in Europe and Asia, has been able to be selective as to which and how many refugees are welcomed. Since the arrival of refugees uprooted by World War II, the United States has allowed three groups of refugees to enter in numbers greater than regulations would ordinarily permit—Hungarians, Cubans, and Indochinese. Compared to the other two groups, the nearly 40,000 Hungarians who arrived following the abortive revolt of November 1956 were few indeed. At the time, however, theirs was the fastest mass immigration to this country since before 1922. With little delay, the United States amended the laws so that the Hungarian refugees could enter. Their small numbers and their dispersion throughout this country has left the Hungarians little in evidence four decades later. The much larger and longer period of movement of Cuban and Indochinese refugees into the United States has had a profound social impact. We will look at these refugee groups and their descendants in later chapters—Cuban Americans in Chapter 9 and the Indochinese Americans in Chapter 12.

Despite periodic public opposition, the United States government is officially committed to accepting refugees from other nations. According to the United Nations treaty on refugees, which our government ratified in 1968, countries are obliged to refrain from forcibly returning people to territories where their lives or liberty might be endangered. It is not always clear, though, whether an individual is fleeing for his or her personal safety or to escape poverty. Although persons in the latter category may be of humanitarian interest, they do not meet the official definition of refugees and are subject to deportation.

It is the practice of deporting people fleeing poverty that has been the subject of criticism. There is a long tradition in the United States of facilitating the arrival of people leaving communist nations. Mexicans who are refugees from poverty, Liberians fleeing civil war, and black Haitians running from despotic rule are not similarly welcomed. The plight of Haitians became of particular concern in the 1990s as sometimes as many as 2,000 arrived in one week. The United States has consistently contended that Haitians are not victims of political persecution. Several members of Congress have argued that the policy is racist and the stance would be quite different if those seeking refugee status were coming from Ireland, for example. Upon arrival Haitians are interviewed to determine if they are eligible for refugee status, but more than 97 percent are ruled as subject to deportation. In 1992, the Supreme Court, in a 6–3 ruling, supported the government's policy of forcibly repatriating perhaps as many as 10,000 of the recent refugees back to Haiti. The controversy does not appear near resolution as the economic and political situation in Haiti remains unsettled and the official United States position remains opposed to acceptance of more Haitians (Crossette, 1992; Waite, 1991).

## The Sanctuary Movement

A symbol of the frustration surrounding refugees is the growing sanctuary movement. Begun in 1982, a loosely connected organization offers asylum, often in churches, to those seeking refugee status but regarded by the Immigration and Naturalization Service as illegal aliens. *Asylees* are defined as persons who fear persecution if forced to return to their homeland, but unlike refugees, are already in the United States. This category was first created by the Refugee Act of 1980. The refugees given comfort by the sanctuary movement tend to be escaping governments of which the United States officially approves; they are therefore unlikely to be granted asylum status. Participants in the sanctuary movement, by giving shelter to those violating immigration laws, are themselves subject to stiff fines and jail sentences.

About 23 percent of people who apply for political asylum receive it. The objects of the sanctuary movement's aid have most often been immigrants from Central America and Haiti said by leaders of the movement to be in danger if forced to return to their home country. Not only churches participate. Some municipalities, including Chicago, Los Angeles, and San Francisco, have voted to transform their entire city limits into sanctuaries. Such steps may be mostly symbolic, but they do reflect the strong feelings of many Americans that the status of asylee is too narrowly defined. In 1987, the Supreme Court in a 6–3 decision (*Immigration and Naturalization Service* v. *Cardoza-Fonseca*) ruled that the government was required to lessen the difficulty of the requirement for asylees who were trying to document their fear of persecution if they were forced home. The plight of people unsuccessfully seeking political asylum contrasts with the reception afforded Cuban Americans, which is discussed in Chapter 9 (Bouvier and Gardner, 1986, pp. 41–43; Pear, 1987; Silk, 1986; S. Taylor, 1987a).

The sanctuary movement initially focused on offering asylum to persons who seek refugee status in the United States but are viewed by the government as illegal aliens. However, in mid-1988, when immigration officials implemented full enforcement of the employer sanctions provisions of the Immigration Reform and Control Act of 1986, some activists in the sanctuary movement began harboring undocumented workers. Catholic clergy have taken the lead in this effort to protect the undocumented. By late 1988, three Los Angeles priests were under criminal investigation by the Immigration and Naturalization Service; they faced possible felony charges for offering assistance to illegal aliens. Reverend Luis Olivares, one of the priests under investigation, openly defends such assistance: "This is an outgrowth of the sanctuary movement. We've expanded it to include the undocumented. It doesn't make any difference to us whether you die by a bullet or by hunger; you're still dead" (B. Hérandez, 1988).

## GLANCING BACK AND LOOKING AHEAD

For its first hundred years the United States allowed all immigrants to enter and become permanent residents. The federal policy of welcome did not mean, however, that immigrants would encounter no discrimination and prejudice. With the passage of the Chinese Exclusion Act, discrimination against immigrants became law. The Chinese were soon joined by the Japanese as peoples forbidden by law to enter and prohibited from becoming naturalized citizens. The development of the national origins system in the 1920s created a hierarchy of nationalities, with people from Northern Europe encouraged to enter while other Europeans and Asians encountered long delays. The melting pot, which had always been a fiction, was legislated out of existence even as a possibility.

In the 1960s, the policy was liberalized so that the importance of nationality was minimized, and a person's work skills and relationship to an American were emphasized. This liberalization came at a time when most Europeans no longer desired to emigrate to the United States. The legacy of the arrival of nearly 50 million immigrants since 1820 is apparent today.

What about the future? What will be the effect of continued immigration? Figure 4.3 presents two projections of the United States population for the year 2080. One assumes an annual immigration rate of 500,000 persons (somewhat below the recent level of about 600,000). The other projection assumes a higher annual immigration rate: 1 million persons per year. As these projections illustrate, the Hispanic population of the United States will increase dramatically in

**FIGURE 4.3**  Population of the United States, 1990 and 2080

Assuming continuing high rates of immigration over the next 100 years—either 500,000 or 1 million immigrants per year—the proportion of Americans who are White and non-Hispanic will decrease substantially by the year 2080. By contrast, the proportion of both Hispanics and Asian Americans will rise strikingly.

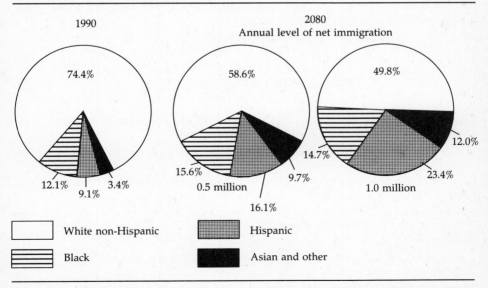

*Source:* From Bouvier and Davis, *The Future Racial Composition of the United States* (Washington, D.C.: Population Reference Bureau, 1982.) Reprinted by permission. Also from Bureau of the Census, 1991a and 1991b.

the next 100 years. By 2080, Hispanics will outnumber African Americans and could account for more than 23 percent of the nation. Similarly, the proportion of Americans classified as "Asian or other" will rise substantially, perhaps to as much as 12 percent of the population. These figures could easily be underestimates, for they do not take into account the possible results of the Immigration Reform and Control Act of 1986.

Because of these population shifts, the proportion of White, non-Hispanic Americans will decrease significantly. In fact, by the year 2080, the combined Black, Hispanic, and Asian populations may be approximately equal to the number of Whites. This balance does not necessarily mean that the White population will lose its historic social dominance, but it certainly suggests that the United States of 2080 will be a vastly different society.

This chapter has shown that the majority of Americans are not descended from the English, and that Protestants are outnumbered by other worshipers. This diversity of religious and ethnic groups will be examined next.

## KEY TERMS

**asylee**   A person already in the United States who fears persecution if forced to return to his or her homeland.

**brain drain**   Immigration to the United States of skilled workers, professionals, and technicians who are desperately needed by their home countries.

**nativism**   Beliefs and policies favoring native-born citizens over immigrants.

**sanctuary movement**   A movement of loosely connected organizations that offer asylum, often in churches, to those who seek refugee status but are regarded by the Immigration and Naturalization Service as illegal aliens.

**xenophobia**   The fear or hatred of strangers or foreigners.

## FOR FURTHER INFORMATION

Frank D. Bean, Barry Edmonston, and Jeffrey S. Passel. *Undocumented Migration to the United States*. Santa Monica, CA: Rand Corporation, 1990.

A detailed look at the 1980s in terms of illegal immigration including the impact of the 1986 Immigration Reform and Control Act.

Ray Allen Billington. *The Protestant Crusade, 1800–1860*. 1963; reprinted. Gloucester, MA: Peter Smith, 1963.

Historian Billington traces American nativism from the anti-Catholicism of the 1820s to the rise and fall of the Know-Nothings in the 1850s.

Ted Conover. *Coyotes*. New York: Vintage, 1986.

A poignant look at illegal immigration, including the smugglers of aliens (known as *coyotes*).

Ann Crittenden. *Sanctuary: A Story of American Conscience*. New York: Weidenfeld and Nicholson, 1988.

A detailed account of the movement in the 1980s to provide asylum to refugees who were not granted legal status by the government.

Roger Daniels. *A History of Immigration and Ethnicity in American Life.* New York: Harper Perennial, 1990.

Historian Daniels provides a comprehensive history of the waves of immigration from 1500 to the present.

Stanley Feldstein and Lawrence Costello, eds. *The Ordeal of Assimilation.* Garden City, New York: Anchor Books, 1974.

This collection of speeches, magazine articles, and newspaper accounts presents a documentary history of European immigration from 1840 to the present. The concluding section stresses the recently renewed ethnic consciousness.

Elmer Clarence Sandmeyer. *The Anti-Chinese Movement in California.* 1939: reprinted, Urbana, IL: University of Illinois Press, 1973.

This book, originally published in 1939, was the first modern account of the development of anti-Chinese racism in the West. Roger Daniels in his introduction to the present edition places Sandmeyer's effort in the context of later research.

Bernard A. Weisberger. *The American People.* New York: American Heritage, 1971.

Immigration to the United States is traced pictorially through paintings, pictures, and political cartoons from pre-Revolutionary days to the brain drain controversy and post-World War II immigration from Latin America.

## *Periodicals*

Both the *International Migration Review* (formerly the *International Migration Digest),* begun in 1966, and *Migration Today,* begun in 1972, are published by the Center for Migration Studies. The *Journal of Refugee Resettlement* (1981), the *Journal of Refugee Studies* (1988), and *Refugee Reports* (1979) were inaugurated in response to renewed interest in refugees.

## Chapter Five

# ETHNICITY
# AND RELIGION
# IN AMERICAN LIFE

*Chapter Outline*

**Ethnic Diversity**

**Religious Pluralism**

**The Rediscovery of Ethnicity**

The Third-Generation Principle

The Nature of Ethnicity

The Rise and Fall of the Ethnic Revival

**The Price Paid by White Ethnics**

Prejudice Toward White Ethnic Groups

Income and Housing

The Prejudice of Ethnics

**Case Example: The Italian Americans**

**Ethnicity, Religion, and Social Class**

**Religion and American Society**

The New Denominationalism

Women and Religion

Religion and the Supreme Court

Limits of Religious Freedom: Mormonism

**Glancing Back and Looking Ahead**

**Key Terms**

**For Further Information**

---

## ❋ HIGHLIGHTS ❋

The United States encompasses a multitude of ethnic and religious groups. Do they coexist in harmony or in conflict? How significant are they as sources of identity for their members? British Americans and Protestants may be the largest ethnic and religious groups, but both are outnumbered by all other groups combined. There was a resurgence of ethnicity among Whites in the 1960s and well into the 1970s, partly the result of the renewed ethnicity of Blacks, Hispanics, and Native Americans. White ethnics are the victims of humor (or "respectable bigotry") that many still consider socially acceptable and find themselves with little power in big business. Religious minorities have also experienced bigotry in the past; and conflicts between groups occasionally are taken to the Supreme Court.

---

The complexity of relations between dominant and subordinate groups in the United States is partly the result of its heterogeneous population. No one ethnic origin or religious faith enfolds the inhabitants of the United States. Even with its period of largest sustained immigration two generations past, an American today is surrounded by remnants of cultures and practitioners of religions whose origins are foreign to this country. Religion and ethnicity continue to be significant in defining an individual's identity.

## ETHNIC DIVERSITY

The ethnic diversity of the United States in the 1990s is a social fact of life apparent to almost everyone. Passersby in New York City were undoubtedly surprised once, when two street festivals met head-to-head. The procession of San Gennaro, the patron saint of Naples, marched through Little Italy to run directly into a Chinese festival originating in Chinatown. Teachers in many public schools frequently face students who speak only one language, and it is not English. In Chicago there are many possibilities. Besides Spanish, students may know only Greek, Italian, Polish, German, Creole, Japanese, Cantonese, or the language of a Native American. In the Detroit metropolitan area, 21 languages are taught, including Arabic, Portuguese, Ukrainian, Latvian, Lithuanian, and Serbian. Recognition of different ethnic groups has led to the creation of White ethnic studies programs at 135 colleges. The 230 foreign-language papers and periodicals published in the United States are joined by 708 English-language or bilingual publications aimed at ethnics and having a total circulation of 6 million (Cummings, 1973; Fishman et al., 1966; Herman, 1973; Komives and Goodel, 1971; Maeroff, 1974; Toth, 1972).

## RELIGIOUS PLURALISM

The more than 130 organized religions in the United States range from the over 50 million members of the Roman Catholic Church to sects with fewer than a thousand adherents. In addition there are growing numbers of non-Christian followers. Besides the long Jewish tradition in the United States, Muslims number close to 5 million. A smaller, but also growing, number of people adhere to such Eastern faiths as Hinduism, Confucianism, and Taoism. The diversity of American religious life is apparent from Figure 5.1, which shows the Christian faiths that numerically dominate areas of the country. For most nations of the world a map of religions would hardly be useful, because one faith accounts for almost all religious followers in the country. The diversity of beliefs, rituals, and experiences that characterizes religious life in the United States reflects both the nation's immigrant heritage and the First Amendment prohibition against establishing a state religion.

Sociologists use the word *denomination* for a large, organized religion not officially linked with the state or government. By far the largest denomination in the United States is Roman Catholicism, yet at least 23 other religious faiths have 1 million or more members (see Table 5.1). Protestants collectively accounted for about 56 percent of the nation's adult population in 1991, compared with 26 percent for Roman Catholics and about 3 percent for Jews. (Princeton Religion Research Center, 1992b).

The diversity of faiths in the United States sharply contrasts with European countries, where a handful of faiths dominate. Religious statistics should be used with caution, however. Because census takers have not asked about religious affiliation since 1957, information about religious membership is supplied by the churches themselves (Bureau of the Census, 1958; Petersen, 1962). Churches vary as to whom they count as members—some count only baptized or confirmed members, others count only those in good standing.

One notable characteristic of religious practice in the United States is the almost completely separate worship by Blacks and Whites. During the 1976 presidential campaign an unusual amount of attention was directed at the segregation practiced by churches in the United States. The church attended by Jimmy Carter in Plains, Georgia, captured headlines as it closed its doors to a Black civil rights activist seeking membership. The Plains church later opened its membership to African Americans at Carter's urging. Such formal racial restrictions are unusual, but today the church hour on Sunday mornings still fits Dr. Martin Luther King, Jr.'s description as "the most segregated hour of the week." Of all major Protestant denominations, the United Methodist Church boasts the largest Black constituency, but that is only 3 percent. Overall, no more than 10 percent of Black Christians belong to predominantly White denomina-

**FIGURE 5.1**  Predominant Christian Faiths, by Counties, of the United States, 1980

The diversity of Christian religious life in the United States is apparent in the figure. Many Christian faiths account for 25 percent or more of the church members in a county. Among non-Christian faiths, only Judaism may figure so significantly—in New York County (Manhattan) of New York City and Dade County Florida (which includes Miami Beach).

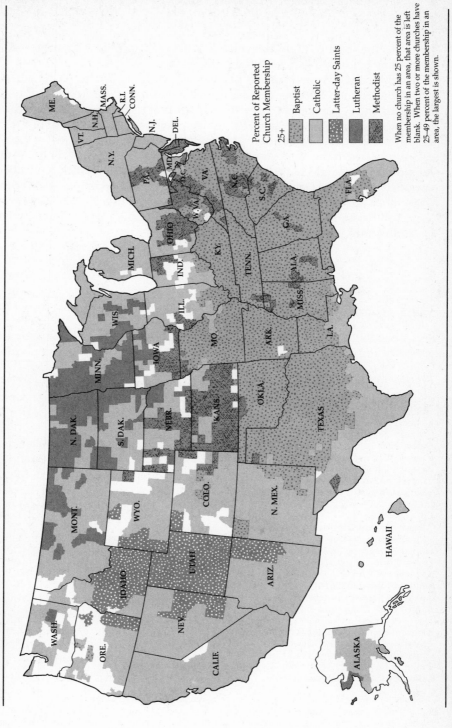

Percent of Reported
Church Membership

25+

◻ Baptist
◻ Catholic
◻ Latter-day Saints
◻ Lutheran
◻ Methodist

When no church has 25 percent of the membership in an area, that area is left blank. When two or more churches have 25–49 percent of the membership in an area, the largest is shown.

Source: Quinn et al., 1982. Copyright © 1982 by the National Council fo Churches of Christ in the U.S.A. Adapted by permission.

tions. At the local or church level, it is estimated that only 1 percent of Black Christians belong to White churches (K. Briggs, 1976; Stark, 1987).

Nearly 7 in 10 Americans (68 percent) are counted as church members, but great confusion exists over the degree of religiosity or the strength of religious commitment. A persuasive case can be made that religious institutions continue to grow stronger through an influx of new members despite mounting secularism in society. Some observers think that after reaching a low in the 1960s, religion is becoming important to people again. The upheavals in American religious life are reflected in the covers of *Time* magazine, which have cried out variously: "Is God Dead?" (April 8, 1966), "Is God Coming Back to Life?" (December 26, 1969), and "The Jesus Revolution" (June 21, 1971). At present, there is little statistical support for the view that influence of religion on society is diminishing.

---

**TABLE 5.1**    Churches with More than a Million Members, 1989–1990

Several hundred religions are practiced in the United States. Of these, 24 have at least 1 million members.

| *Religious Body* | *Membership* |
| --- | --- |
| Roman Catholic Church | 54,918,949 |
| Southern Baptist Convention | 15,038,049 |
| United Methodist Church | 8,904,824 |
| National Baptist Convention, U.S.A.* | 5,500,000 |
| Evangelical Lutheran Church in America | 5,240,739 |
| Church of Jesus Christ of Latter-Day Saints | 4,267,000 |
| Presbyterian Church (U.S.A.) | 3,788,009 |
| Church of God in Christ* | 3,709,661 |
| National Baptist Convention of America* | 2,668,779 |
| Lutheran Church-Missouri Synod | 2,602,849 |
| Episcopal Church | 2,446,050 |
| African Methodist Episcopal Church | 2,210,000 |
| Assemblies of God | 2,181,502 |
| United Synagogue of America | 2,000,000 |
| Greek Orthodox Church* | 1,950,000 |
| Churches of Christ | 1,683,346 |
| United Church of Christ | 1,599,262 |
| American Baptist Churches in the U.S.A. | 1,535,971 |
| Baptist Bible Fellowship, International | 1,405,900 |
| Union of American Hebrew Congregations | 1,300,000 |
| African Methodist Episcopal Zion Church | 1,200,000 |
| Christian Churches and Churches of Christ | 1,070,616 |
| Christian Church (Disciples of Christ) | 1,039,692 |
| Union of Orthodox Jewish Congregations of America | 1,000,000 |
| Orthodox Church in America* | 1,000,000 |

*Data are for 1982 or earlier and therefore may not be comparable to the most recent data.
*Source:* From *Yearbook of American and Canadian Churches 1992,* edited by Constant Jacquet, Jr. Copyright © (1992) by the National Council of Churches of Christ in the U.S.A. Used by permission of the publisher, Abingdon Press.

Religion is important to Americans. According to a 1991 report, only 8 percent of the adults in the United States described themselves as "nonreligious." When residents of 11 nations were asked to indicate the importance of God in their lives, Americans registered the third-highest score, slightly behind Mexicans and South Africans and far ahead of Hungarians, Japanese, Danes, and Swedes (Kosmin, 1991; Princeton Religion Research Center, 1986, p. 5).

In reviewing data on church attendance and feelings about organized religion, however, we surmise that religion is not uniformly on the upswing. There is a great deal of switching of denominations and, as in the past, considerable interest in new ways of expressing spirituality. Some new groups encounter hostility from organized, established faiths that question the tactics used to attract members and financial support. It would be incorrect to conclude either that religion is slowly being abandoned or that Americans are turning to religion with the zeal of new converts. The future may not only bring periods of religious revivalism but times of decline in religious fervor as well (Chalfant et al., 1987).

One of the most common religious rituals in the Protestant and Catholic faiths is church attendance. The Gallup poll has provided the only regular measurement of such attendance; in 1991, it reported that during an average week, 43 percent of adult Americans attended church. As is apparent in Figure 5.2, Protestant attendance has remained relatively constant over the period 1958 to 1991. By contrast, Catholic attendance suffered a dramatic decline, beginning in 1964, which began to level off only in the 1970s (Princeton Religion Research Center, 1991, p. 3).

The sharp decline in Catholic churchgoing has been attributed to the influence of Vatican II and the *Humanae Vitae* encyclical. Vatican II was an ecumenical convention brought together by Pope John XXIII that met from 1962 to 1965. It issued a series of sweeping reforms affecting Catholic rituals, including termination of the exclusive use of Latin during the Mass.

A large proportion of Roman Catholics (though not a majority) opposed these changes. *Humanae Vitae,* issued in 1967, reaffirmed the traditional family planning teachings of the Catholic church. This document disturbed many communicants who had expected, or at least hoped for, a more liberal stance on issues of birth control and sexuality (Greeley, 1989).

## THE REDISCOVERY OF ETHNICITY

Ethnic groups seldom forget their heritage, and society reminds them of their strangeness in numerous, hardly subtle ways. The mass media and scholars, however, had forgotten but have now rediscovered the White ethnics.

Robert Park (1950, p. 205), a prominent early sociologist, wrote in 1913 that "a Pole, Lithuanian, or Norwegian cannot be distinguished, in the second generation, from an American, born of native parents." At one time, sociologists saw the end of ethnicity as practically a foregone conclusion. W. Lloyd Warner and Leo Srole (1945) wrote in their often-cited Yankee City series that "the future of

**FIGURE 5.2**   Church Attendance of Protestants and Catholics in a Typical Week, 1958–1991

Church attendance among American Protestants and Catholics began to stabilize in the late 1970s after two decades of decline.

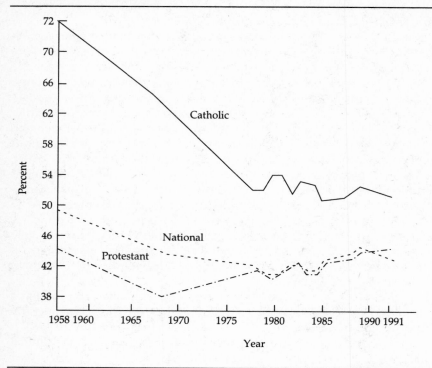

*Sources:* Gallup, 1982, p. 44; Princeton Religion Research Center, 1990b, 1991, 1992a. Reprinted by permission of *The Gallup Poll.*

American ethnic groups seems to be limited; it is likely that they will be quickly absorbed." Oscar Handlin's *The Uprooted* (1951) told of the destruction of immigrant values and their replacement by American culture. Although Handlin was among the pioneers in investigating ethnicity, assimilation was the dominant theme in his work (Cinel, 1969; Vecoli, 1970).

Many writers have shown almost a fervent hope that ethnicity would vanish. The persistence of ethnicity was for some time treated by sociologists as dysfunctional, for it meant continuation of old values that interferred with allegedly superior new values (Metzger, 1971; Novak, 1973, p. 271). Ethnicity was expected to disappear not only because of assimilation but also because higher social class and status demanded that it vanish (Abramson, 1973, p. 11; Yancey et al., 1976; J. M. Yinger, 1976, pp. 206–211).

*Ethnicity cannot be ignored by politicians even by those who themselves are members of minorities. Rev. Jesse Jackson is shown soliciting Chicano support at a San Francisco parade during his 1988 campaign for the Democratic presidential nomination.*

### The Third-Generation Principle

Historian Marcus Hansen's *principle of third-generation interest* was an exception to the assimilationist approach to White ethnic groups (1937, 1952, 1987). Simply stated, Hansen maintained that in the third generation—the grandchildren of the original immigrants—ethnic interest and awareness would actually increase; said Hansen, "what the son wishes to forget the grandson wishes to remember." Will Herberg (1983) and Gerhard Lenski (1961) made similar arguments on religious participation among descendants of immigrants—arguments that with qualification have been confirmed by survey research (Lazerwitz and Rowitz, 1964). Hansen's principle has been tested several times since it was first put forth. Although less research has been done on assimilation among third-generation women compared to men (Vecoli, 1987), in interviewing Irish and Italian Catholics, John Goering (1971) found that ethnicity was more important to members of the third generation than it was to the immigrants themselves (Roche, 1984).

Myrdal (1974, p. 28), who, as we saw in Chapter 1, wrote from an assimilationist perspective, contended that the resurgence in ethnicity is merely an intellectual movement articulated by a few professors and writers. Wendell Bell argues that separate ethnic identification is diminishing and is "coalescing into a single class manifestation with supra-ethnic overtones" (1974, p. 63). Increasingly, however, social scientists accept the importance of ethnicity.

Nathan Glazer and Daniel Moynihan admitted in the second edition of *Beyond the Melting Pot* (1970, p. viii) that perhaps they had been too hasty in concluding the first edition by saying "religion and race define the next stage in the evolution of the American peoples" (1963, p. 315). Social-scientific dismissal of ethnic awareness by blue-collar workers had begun the academic minimizing of the importance of ethnicity. Ethnicity was viewed as merely another aspect of White ethnics' alleged racist nature, an allegation that will be examined later in this chapter. Curiously, the very same intellectuals and journalists who bent over backward to understand the growing solidarity of Blacks, Hispanics, and Native Americans refused to give White ethnics the academic attention they deserved (Wrong, 1972).

The new assertiveness of Blacks and other non-Whites about their rights in the 1960s unquestionably presented White ethnics with the opportunity to reexamine their own position. "If solidarity and unapologetic self-consciousness might hasten Blacks' upward mobility, why not us?" asked the White ethnics, who often were only a half step above the Blacks in social status. The African American movement pushed other groups to reflect on their past. The increased consciousness of Blacks and their positive attitude toward African culture and the contributions worldwide of African-Americans are embraced in what we termed earlier (Chapter 1) as the Afrocentric perspective. The mood, therefore, was set in the 1960s for the country to be receptive to ethnicity (Blackwell, 1976). By legitimating Black cultural difference from White culture, along with that of Native Americans and Hispanics, the country's opinion leaders legitimated other types of cultural diversity.

## The Nature of Ethnicity

The persistence of ethnic consciousness does not depend upon foreign birth, distinctive language, and a unique way of life. When the American dream of full acceptance does not materialize for many White ethnics, they reexamine their own roots. Appreciation of one's individual heritage is not automatic. Just because a person is of Italian descent and lives in an Italian neighborhood does not mean he or she is acquainted with the writings of Dante, the thirteenth-century poet. Frequently the tradition that American ethnics preserve has little in common with life in the old county. Instead, it reflects experience in the United States as a unique group that developed a cultural tradition distinct from that of the mainstream (Glazer, 1971; Glazer and Moynihan, 1970, p. xxxiii).

Ethnicity gives continuity with the past, an affective or emotional tie. The significance of this sense of belonging cannot be emphasized enough. Whether reinforced by distinctive behavior or by what Milton Gordon (1964) called a sense of "peoplehood," ethnicity is an effective, functional source of cohesion. Proximity to fellow ethnics is not necessary for a person to maintain social cohesion and in-group identity. Even the ethnic neighborhoods that do exist are not ethnically homogeneous; most contain outsiders within their boundaries (Suttles, 1972, pp. 27, 251). Fraternal organizations or sports-related groups can preserve associations among ethnics who are separated geographically. Members of ethnic groups may even maintain their feelings of in-group solidarity after leaving ethnic communities in the central cities for the suburban fringe (Gallo, 1974, p. 121; Lieberson, 1962; Parenti, 1967, pp. 720–721, 1970, p. 175; Wood, 1959).

## The Rise and Fall of the Ethnic Revival

A vast amount of evidence pointed to the revival of ethnicity in the United States beginning in the mid-1960s (Roche, 1984). We have seen that social scientists then began to reconsider the inevitable disappearance of ethnic identity. Statistical evidence pointed to growth in non-English-language homes that could not be explained by immigration alone. Non-English-language publications, churches, radio stations, and television programs grew throughout the 1960s. Even the conventional media seemed more sensitive to ethnic interests. By the 1980s, however, if not the late 1970s, the ethnic revival seemed to have subsided considerably, perhaps not to the levels of the 1950s, but the emergent ethnicity had peaked (Fishman, 1985, pp. 490–491).

The ethnicity of the 1980s embraced by English-speaking Whites typically is more symbolic. It does not include active involvement in ethnic activities or participation in ethnic-related organizations. In fact, sizable proportions of White ethnics have gained large-scale entry into almost all clubs, cliques, and fraternal groups. Such acceptance is a key indicator of assimilation (M. Gordon, 1964). Ethnicity has become increasingly peripheral to the lives of members of the ethnic group. Although they may not relinquish their ethnic identity, other identities become more important.

According to sociologist Herbert Gans (1979), ethnicity today increasingly involves the symbols of ethnicity such as food, acknowledging ceremonial holidays, and supporting specific political issues or the issues confronting the "old country." This *symbolic ethnicity* may be more visible, but this type of ethnic heritage does not interfere with what they do, read, say, or even whom they befriend or marry. Richard Alba (1990) surveyed Whites in the Albany, New York, area in the mid-1980s and found that while there had been a decline in distinctions among ethnic groups, ethnic identity was still acknowledged. Heritage may not have disappeared, yet the present and future seem more relevant to today's White Americans (Alba, 1985; Roche, 1984).

## THE PRICE PAID BY WHITE ETHNICS

Many White ethnics shed their past and wish only to be Americans, with no ancestral ties to another couuntry. Boris Shlapak, who played forward on a professional soccer team, changed his name to Ian Stone because "American kids need to identify with soccer players as Americans" (C. Terry, 1975). Stone, who by his own admission "never felt ethnic," was not concerned about being a figure to whom Slavic Americans would look for a hero. But some ethnics do not wish to abandon their heritage. To retain their past as a part of their present, however, they must pay a price, because of prejudice and discrimination.

### Prejudice Toward White Ethnic Groups

Our examination of immigration to the United States in Chapter 4 pointed out the mixed feelings that have greeted European immigrants. They are apparently still not well received. In 1944, well after most immigration from Poland had ended, the Polish-American Congress, an umbrella organization of 40 Polish fraternities, was founded to defend the image of Polish Americans. Young Polish Americans are made to feel ashamed of their ethnic origin when teachers find their names unpronounceable, and when they hear Polish jokes bandied about in a way that anti-Black or anti-Semitic humor is not. One survey found that half of second-generation Polish Americans encounter prejudice. Curiously, it was socially proper to condemn the White working class as racist, but quite improper to question the negative attitude of middle-class people toward White ethnics. Michael Lerner (1969) calls this hostility toward White ethnics *respectable bigotry*. Polish jokes are acceptable, whereas anti-Black humor is considered in poor taste (Krug, 1974; Polzin, 1973, p. 220; Sanders and Morawska, 1975, pp. 91–92).

An important component of Lerner's respectable bigotry is not race prejudice but class prejudice. In 1973 researchers surveyed Whites living in areas of Florida that had undergone school desegregation. After identifying whether or not a respondent protested against school desegregation, the researchers sought to determine if the opposition was caused by racial prejudice. The affluent and well-educated, the researchers found, were more disturbed by the possibility of interacting more with working-class people. Although not conclusive, the study suggests that even if the more affluent Whites are more tolerant of racial minorities, they may be less accepting of class differences (Giles et al., 1976).

White ethnics in the early 1970s felt that the mass media unfairly ridiculed them and their culture while celebrating Black Power and African culture. Italian Americans, for instance, are concerned that their image is overwhelmed by stereotypes of organized crime, spaghetti, overweight mothers, and sexy women. Even television's Italian policemen seem to conform to the old stereotypes. In response to such stereotyping, the Columbian Coalition, founded in 1971, employs lawyers to handle cases of Italian Americans claiming they are victims of bigotry (Gambino, 1974a, 1974b; Greeley, 1975; *New York Times,*

1974b). Italian Americans are also not pleased with their conspicuous absence from the Roman Catholic Church hierarchy in the United States and in high political office. The Italians are well aware that another ethnic group, the Irish, dominates the American Catholic hierarchy, with 57 percent of the bishops in the country, although it only has 17 percent of the Catholic population. Not all Italian Americans are convinced that such self-help organizations as the Columbian Coalition, the Italian American Civil Rights League, or the Americans of Italian Descent are the answer. Despite disagreement over methods, most would agree that attitudes need changing. Italians are just an example, however. Across the country and among all ethnic groups appreciation for ethnic heritage is increasing (Gambino, 1974a, p. 283; Glazer and Moynihan, 1970, p. lxvii; Novak, 1973, p. 55; Pileggi, 1971; Severo, 1970).

## Income and Housing

Harsh words toward ethnics translate into lower incomes. A hierarchy of ethnic groups coinciding with a hierarchy of social classes has long been documented: disparities do exist among ethnic groups in socioeconomic status. A study of 1962 census data showed that national origin is not as important an explanation of the variance in education and occupation among contemporary ethnic men as it was for their parents. For some ethnic groups, however, such as the Irish, Polish, and Italians, occupational success falls short of what would be expected for men of similar background and education. Other statistical analyses have not been clear as to which disparities are caused by ethnic discrimination. Lower incomes do not necessarily mean that a group is the victim of discrimination. But in general, studies point to lower income and less likelihood of upward social mobility for White ethnic groups (Blau and Duncan, 1967, pp. 231–241, 407; Duncan and Duncan, 1968; Duncan et al., 1972, pp. 51–55; Levine and Herman, 1972; Warner and Srole, 1945, pp. 67–102).

The disparity between ethnics and other Whites is most apparent at the top rungs of the ladder of success in business. In 1972, Russell Barta (1974) examined the ethnic background of the officers of the 106 largest Chicago-area corporations. African Americans and Hispanics were grossly underrepresented as directors and officers. The two groups accounted for 22 percent of the area population but only 0.5 percent of the directorships and 0.2 percent of the officerships. White ethnics seemed to face exclusion as well. Poles made up 6.9 percent of the area population but comprised only 0.3 percent of the directorships and 0.7 percent of the officerships. Italians fared somewhat better, with 1.9 percent of the directorships and 2.9 percent of the corporation officerships, but they comprised nearly 5 percent of the area population. Of the 106 corporations' boards, 102 had no Poles and 84 had no Italians. The figure for Italians, which suggested that they have fared better, was inflated by one individual who served on the board of nine companies. Further evidence of White ethnics' underrepresentation came in sociologists Richard Alba and Gwen Moore's 1982 study described in

Chapter 3 (see Table 3.2) and in an analysis by the Order of Sons of Italy of the *Forbes* magazine list of top corporations (Ruffini, 1983).

Some forms of discrimination were overt, as in housing. As recently as 1963, realtors in Michigan employed a point handicap system that made it difficult for Poles and Italians to purchase homes in better neighborhoods by penalizing people for being White ethnics (Bufalino, 1971). The result of such practices has been an ethnic segregation not unlike racial segregation. Ethnic groups form a Little Italy, Greektown, or Scandinavian "Andersonville" mostly because they want to stay together, but the difficulty of finding housing elsewhere has contributed as well. Many statistical studies have documented the ethnic segregation in American cities and the surrounding suburbs. Besides being segregated, ethnic neighborhoods are ripe for urban renewal programs and disruptive highway construction. White ethnics, like African Americans and Hispanics, have lacked the political power to prevent their neighborhoods from being physically destroyed (Bufalino, 1971; Guest and Weed, 1976; Kantrowitz, 1973; Krickus, 1976, p. 272; Lieberson, 1962, 1963; Taeuber and Taeuber, 1964).

An additional price was paid by White ethnics in the 1970s. They became labeled as typical bigots. The stereotype of the prejudiced "hard hat" has rarely been questioned. The danger of such a stereotype is that it becomes indistinguishable from fact. David Matza refers to these mental pictures, which "tend to remain beyond the reach of such intellectual correctives as argument, criticism and scrutiny. . . . Left unattended, they return to haunt us by shaping or bending theories that purport to explain major social phenomena" (1964, p. 1). This picture of ethnics and the degree of truth behind it will be examined next.

## The Prejudice of Ethnics

In the 1960s, as the civil rights movement moved northward, White ethnics replaced the Southern redneck as the typical bigot portrayed in the mass media. The chanting of protesters resulted in ugly incidents that made White ethnics and bigots synonymous. In 1951 Harvey Clark, an African American war veteran, moved into a $60-a-month apartment in Cicero, Illinois. Cicero adjoins Chicago's Black ghetto but no Blacks live in the heavily Polish, Italian, and Czech town. Clark fled after being greeted by a mob aided by the local police. The Cicero police chief warned Clark, "Get out of Cicero and don't come back to town or you'll get a bullet through you." A grand jury handed down indictments against Clark's NAACP attorney, the apartment house owner, her lawyer, and her rental agent. The indictments, subsequently dropped, charged them all with conspiracy to injure property by causing "depreciation in the market selling price" (Epstein, 1972; Gremley, 1952; Margolis, 1972, p. 254). Does this sort of incident typify White ethnic attitudes and justify the hard-hat image?

The first issue to resolve is whether White ethnic groups are more prejudiced than other Whites. Greeley (1974a, pp. 187–216; 1977, pp. 90–125; Nie et al. 1974; see also Schlozman, 1977) examined attitudes toward race, social welfare, and American involvement in Vietnam. The evidence pointed to minimal differences between ethnics and nonethnics. Some of the differences actually showed greater tolerance and liberalism among White ethnics. White ethnics were more in favor of welfare programs and more opposed to this country's participation in the Vietnam War.

Even when more sophisticated statistical analysis is introduced, the overall finding remains unchanged. When income and region are accounted for, some differences between ethnics and nonethnics are reduced, because White southerners are overwhelmingly nonethnics. Still there is no evidence to support the hard-hat image. Greeley concludes, "Our argument is not that ethnics are the last bastion of liberalism in America today, but rather that it is a misrepresentation of the facts to picture them as a vanguard of conservatism" (1974a, p. 202). Working-class ethnic neighborhoods, however, have undeniably been the scene of ugly racial confrontations. If ethnics are no more bigoted than nonethnics, how have such incidents occurred and how has the hard-hat reputation developed? For that answer, the unique relationship between White ethnic groups and African Americans must be understood.

In retrospect, it should be no surprise that one group antagonistic to Blacks has been the White ethnics. For many citizens, including White ethnics, the America they had known seemed to change. When politicians told Americans "we must fight poverty and discrimination," this translated to White ethnics as "share your job, share your neighborhood, pay your taxes" (Novak, 1973, p. 15; Sanders and Morawska, 1975, pp. 79–84; G. Tyler, 1972, p. 196). Whites reflected on their movement several generations before from membership in a poor immigrant group to become part of the prosperous working class. Government assistance to the poor was virtually nonexistent then, public education was more restricted, and subsidized training programs were absent (Glazer and Moynihan, 1970, p. lv). Why is it different now? Many White ethnics found it difficult to understand why African Americans seem to be singled out for cause for concern.

White ethnics went so far as to turn their backs on federal aid offered them, because they did not wish to have their neighborhoods marked as "poverty pockets," nor did they wish to be associated with Black-oriented programs. In Newark, New Jersey, Italians successfully prevented an antipoverty office from being established and thereby cut off the jobs that its programs would have created (Barbaro, 1974). This ethnic opposition to publicly sponsored programs was not new. James Wilson and Edward Banfield (1964) studied elections in seven major cities between 1956 and 1963 for referenda to build new hospitals, parks, and schools. The results indicated that the least support came from White ethnics, who would have paid the least and benefited the most.

The prevailing conception of urban America is that the city is Black and the suburbs are White. Although the latter is almost true, the former is definitely not. Along with poor Blacks and Hispanics in the big city are many White ethnics who are "economically unmonied and geographically immobile" (G. Tyler, 1972, p. 195). White ethnics thought they were being made to pay for past injustices even though they were not making the decisions or evaluating their consequences. White ethnics found it difficult to be happy with minority-group gains. The upward movement of Blacks would not have disturbed White ethnics if the ethnics had kept pace, but given the absence of economic-based programs for White ethnics, they have not even kept pace with the modest gains by Blacks (Conforti, 1974; H. Goldstein, 1971).

The real grievances of White ethnics were overlooked and reformist bureaucrats of the 1960s neglected nationality groups, thinking they would fade into the White middle class. When residents of an ethnic neighborhood were threatened or when they perceived a potential threat (as in Cicero), they rose to defend themselves.

White ethnics have not only separated themselves from Blacks, but have chosen to distinguish themselves from Wasps as well, as the next section indicates. White ethnics have learned that they are not considered part of the dominant group and that in order to achieve a larger slice of government benefits they must function as a self-interest group, just as racially subordinate groups have.

## CASE EXAMPLE: THE ITALIAN AMERICANS

While each European country's immigration to the United States has created its own social history, the case of Italians, while not typical of each, offers insight into the White ethnic experience. Italians immigrated even during the colonial period and they played prominent roles during the American Revolution and the early days of the republic. Mass immigration, however, began in the 1880s peaking in the first 20 years of the twentieth century when Italians accounted for one-fourth of the European immigration. Not only was the immigration concentrated in time, but also geographically. The majority of the immigrants were landless peasants from rural southern Italy, the Mezzogiorno.

Many Italians, especially in the early years of mass immigration in the nineteenth century, received their jobs through ethnic labor contractors, the *padrone*. Similar arrangements have been used with Asian, Hispanic, and Greek immigrants, where the labor contractor, most often an immigrant, had mastered sufficient English to mediate for his fellow countryman. Exploitation was common within the padrone system through kickbacks, provision of inadequate housing, and withholding of wages. By the time of World War I, 90 percent of Italian girls and 99 percent of Italian boys in New York City left school at the age of 14 to work, but by that time Italian Americans were sufficiently fluent in English to seek out work on their own and the padrone system had disappeared.

Along with manual labor, the Roman Catholic church was a very important part of the Italian American's life at this time. Yet, they found little comfort in a Catholic church dominated by an earlier immigrant group—the Irish. The traditions were different, weekly attendance for Italian Americans was overshadowed by the religious aspects of the *feste* (or festivals) in honor of saints throughout the year (which the Irish viewed as practically a form of paganism). These initial adjustment problems were overcome as the establishment of ethnic parishes—a pattern repeated by other non-Irish immigrant groups. Thus, parishes would be staffed by Italian priests, sometimes imported for that purpose. While the hierarchy of the church would adjust more slowly, Italian Americans were increasingly able to feel at home in their local parish church. Today, nearly 90 percent of Italian Americans are raised as Catholics (Alba, 1985; Rolle, 1972).

The most controversial aspect of the Italian American experience involves organized crime as typified by Al Capone (1899–1947). Arriving in the United States society in the bottom layers, Italians lived in decaying, crime-ridden neighborhoods that became known as "Little Italies." For a minority of these immigrants, crime did serve as a significant means of upward social mobility. In effect, entering and leading criminal activity is one aspect of assimilation— admittedly not a positive one. Complaints linking ethnicity and crime actually began in colonial times with talk about the criminally-inclined Irish and Germans and continues with contemporary stereotyping about Colombian drug dealers and Vietnamese street gangs. Yet the image of Italians as criminals has persisted from Prohibition Era gangsters to the view of mob families today. The fact that Italians can be so consistently characterized as criminal, even in the mass media, is another example of what we have termed as respectable bigotry toward White ethnics. The persistence of linking Italians, or any other minority group, with crime is probably attributable to explaining a problem with a single, naive cause—the presence of perceived undesirables (Alba, 1985, pp. 95–99; Bell, 1953; Daniels, 1990a, pp. 198–199; Gambino, 1974a, pp. 274–312; O'Kane, 1992).

The immigration of Italians was halted by the national origins system described in the previous chapter. As Italian Americans settled permanently, the mutual aid societies that had grown up in the 1920s to provide basic social services began to dissolve. More slowly, education came to be valued as a means of upward mobility. Politics was another means of success, at least at the local level, where family and community ties could be translated into votes. National politics have been much more difficult for Italian Americans to break into—it was not until 1962 that an Italian American was named to a cabinet-level position. Geraldine Ferraro's being named the Democratic vice-presidential candidate in 1984 was every bit an achievement for Italian Americans as it was for women (Alba, 1985).

People of Italian ancestry account today for about 5 percent of the population, but how Italian are they? The majority of older people are not of mixed ancestry but among children of Italian ancestry perhaps only one in ten is not of mixed ancestry. In other words, by the 1990s, a scant century after the beginning of mass Italian immigration, most Italian Americans are individuals who have one non-Italian parent. Do young people of Italian descent have a clear idea of what it means to be Italian American? According to Richard Gambino in "Listen to Their Voices" this identity is fuzzy to say the least for today's young adults of Italian background.

## ❖ *LISTEN TO THEIR VOICES* ❖

### *What It Means to Be Italian-American*

*Richard Gambino*

*Richard Gambino, chair of the Italian-American Studies program at Queens College in New York City, shares his effort to have college students reflect on what Italian-American identity is.*

In the past months I have asked people not of Italian background what comes to mind when they think of Italian-Americans. The responses have been standard ones to which we are all accustomed. The same words are repeated with remarkable uniformity—the Mafia; pizza and other food; hard hats; blue collar; emotional, jealous people; dusky, sexy girls; overweight mammas; frightening, rough, tough men; pop singers; law and order; pastel-colored houses; racists; nice, quiet people. I told a group of Italian-American college students of these views. As I recited the litany of familiar pictures, the group's responses ranged from sounds of exasperation (Mafia, pizza, and hard hats) to titters (law and order, unchic homes, and jealous passions), to out-right laughter (sexy girls, fat mammas, frightening men). They reacted to the other images with interest and bemusement.

When I asked the group whether the composite picture accurately reflected their sense of Italian-American identity, they answered strongly and unanimously in the negative. Upon my asking them what it means to be Italian-American, an initial period of silence was followed by an increasingly intense but confused discussion which produced no consensus or even any clear directions.

Trying another approach, I asked a different group of Italian-American students whether they thought of themselves as Italian. Their response was decidedly affirmative. Then I listed five questions on a blackboard and suggested they respond to them:

1. Do you instinctively think of yourself as Italian, American, or Italian-American?
2. Have you ever felt conflict between the Italian part of you and American demands on your nature?
3. What particular insights, nerve endings, advantages, do you have from your Italian background?
4. If there is one thing that you think you as an Italian-American do not share with others, what is it?
5. Name some Italian-Americans of whom you are privately most proud.

The questions left the students in absorbed thought. They tentatively offered only a few vaguely formulated answers. After a period of mostly silence, I asked them whether they thought the five questions were significant. The answer was a quick and firm yes. When I next repeated my question of whether they identified themselves as Italian, the response was even more assertively affirmative than the first time. I then asked why they thought they had difficulty forming answers to the five questions. The group again fell into silence, until one girl said, "The questions are too complicated," a response to which the others instantly gave accord. When I suggested that they were too complicated because we had a deep identity problem, they quickly agreed. They relaxed. Their paralyzing puzzlement turned into eagerness to discuss the question of their identity.

If this was consciousness-raising, it was easily accomplished because their consciousness wanted to be raised. . . .

From *Blood of My Blood*, pp. 352–353. Copyright 1974. Reprinted by permission of Harold Matson and Company, Inc.

Assimilation has clouded the ethnic picture. While symbolic ethnicity is certainly present in many Italian American households, it is sporadic at best. This is not to say success has been accomplished for the people from the Mezzogiorno. Richard Alba's (1985, 1988) analyses show Italian Americans lagging notably behind Protestants of British ancestry in terms of education and occupational status. The gap is closing but this is happening as today's Italian-American household composed of mixed ancestry is already at some distance from the immigrant experience and the culture of Southern Italy. Ethnicity, for Italian Americans, has not disappeared but it is steadily receding. A little over ten years ago, a researcher found little agreement among Italian Americans except for one area—nearly 90 percent were opposed to changing one's name to sound less Italian. Ethnic identity that is so limited is unlikely to sustain a sense of ethnic in-group solidarity very far into the twenty-first century (Alba, 1985, p. 1974; Crispino, 1980).

## ETHNICITY, RELIGION, AND SOCIAL CLASS

Generally, several social factors influence a person's identity and life chances. Pioneer sociologist Max Weber described *life chances* as people's opportunities to provide themselves with material goods, positive living conditions, and favorable life experiences (Gerth and Mills, 1958, p. 181). Either religion or ethnicity or both may affect life chances.

Religion and ethnicity do not necessarily operate together. Sometimes they have been studied as if they were synonymous. Groups have been described as Irish Catholic, Swedish Lutheran, or Russian Jewish, as if religion and ethnicity had been merged into some type of national church. Religious and ethnic divisions may reinforce each other, but they also may operate independently.

In the 1960s, sociologists felt that religion was more important than ethnicity in explaining behavior (Glazer and Moynihan, 1963; Herberg, 1983). They based this conclusion not on data but on the apparently higher visibility of religion in society. Using survey data collected between 1963 and 1972, Andrew Greeley came to different conclusions (1974a, pp. 111–120, 1974b; for a different perspective, see Yancey et al., 1976). He attempted to clarify the relative importance of religion and ethnicity by measuring four areas.

1. Personality characteristics, such as authoritarianism, anxiety, and conformity.
2. Political participation, such as voting and civic activity.
3. Civil liberties and civil rights, such as support for legislation.
4. Family structure, such as the role of women, marital happiness and sexual adjustment.

The sample consisted of German and Irish Americans, both Protestant and Catholic. If religion was more significant than ethnicity, Protestants, whether of German or Irish ancestry, and Catholics regardless of ethnicity would be similar in outlook. Conversely, if ethnicity was the key, then the similarities would be among the Germans of either faith or among Irish as a distinct group.

On 17 of the 24 items that comprised the four areas measured, the differences were greater between German Catholics and Irish Catholics than between German Catholics and Protestants or Irish Catholics and Protestants. Ethnicity was a stronger predictor of attitudes and beliefs than religion. In one area, political party allegiance, religion was more important, but this was the exception rather than the rule. (The significance of religion will be examined later in this chapter.)

In sum, Greeley found ethnicity to be generally more important than religion in predicting behavior. In reality it is very difficult to separate the influences of religion and ethnicity on any one individual, but Greeley's research cautions against discounting the influence of ethnicity.

In addition, as already noted several times, social class is yet another significant factor. Sociologist Milton Gordon (1978) developed the term *ethclass* (ethnicity and class) to denote the importance of both factors. All *three* factors—religion, ethnicity, and class—combine to form one's identity, determine social behavior, and limit life chances. Using national data gathered from surveys of African Americans from 1982 to 1985 researchers tried to clarify the role of ethclass. They found that more affluent African Americans are more conservative with regard to attitudes toward social welfare spending than lower income African Americans but are significantly more liberal than their White social class peers (Gilliam, 1989).

# RELIGION AND AMERICAN SOCIETY

Divisive conflicts along religious lines are relatively muted in the United States compared with those in, say, Northern Ireland or the Middle East. Although not entirely absent, conflicts in religion in the United States seem to be overshadowed by *civil religion. Civil religion* refers to that religious dimension in American life that merges the state with sacred beliefs.

Sociologist Robert Bellah borrowed the phrase *civil religion* from the eighteenth-century French philosopher Jean-Jacques Rousseau to describe a significant phenomenon in the contemporary United States (Bellah, 1967, 1968, 1970, 1989; see also Marty, 1976, pp. 180–203; Mathisen, 1989). Civil religion exists alongside established religious faiths and embodies a belief system incorporating all religions but not associating with any one. It is the type of faith that presidents refer to in inaugural speeches and to which American Legion posts and Girl Scout troops swear allegiance. In 1954, Congress added the phrase "under God" to the Pledge of Allegiance as a legislative recognition of religion's significance. Bellah sees no sign that the importance of civil religion has diminished, but does acknowledge that it is more conservative than during the 1970s (Marty, 1985, p. 16).

## The New Denominationalism

The public awareness of White ethnicity has coincided with a less publicized recognition of the religious diversity among Christians in the United States— both among Roman Catholics and among Protestants. Herberg (1983) stressed the overall similarity among Americans within the tripartite division of Protestant, Catholic, and Jew. A rival model, focusing on the continued significance of underlying differences among the various groups, more adequately represents the reality of American social life. (For a different perspective, see Laumann, 1969, and Niebuhr, 1929.)

*Diversity Among Catholics.* Social scientists have persistently tended to ignore the diversity within the Catholic church in the United States. Recent research has not sustained Herberg's (1983) conclusion that Catholics are melting into a single group following the traditions of the American Irish Catholic model and that foreign-language churches are long gone. A recent finding of special interest is that religious behavior has been different in each ethnic group. The Irish and French Canadians left a society that was highly competitive culturally and socially. Their religious involvement in the United States is more relaxed than it was in Ireland and Quebec. The influence of American society, however, has increased German and Polish involvement in the Catholic church, but Italians have remained relatively inactive. Variations by ethnic background continue to emerge in studies of contemporary religious involvement in the Roman Catholic church (Abramson, 1973; Alba, 1976; Radzialowski, 1974; Spreitzer and Snyder, 1975). Perhaps the most prominent subgroup in the Catholic church are the

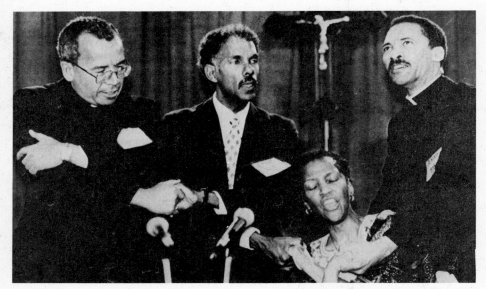

At the 1989 meeting of Roman Catholic bishops, several sessions were held and resolutions passed, as the Church sought to reach out to the growing number of Black and Hispanic members.

Hispanics who, according to a conservative estimate, will constitute the majority of Catholics by 2050. The significance of their participation in the church will be discussed in Chapter 10 (R. Ostling, 1987, p. 48).

The Catholic church, despite its ethnic diversity, has clearly been a powerful force in reducing ethnic ties. There is an irony to this role of Catholicism in that so many nineteenth-century Americans heaped abuse on Catholics in this country for allegedly being un-American and having dual allegiance. The history of the Catholic church in the United States may be portrayed as a struggle within its membership between the Americanizers and the anti-Americanizers, with the former ultimately winning (Greeley, 1977). As a result, unlike the various Protestant churches that accommodated immigrants of a single nationality, the Roman Catholic church had to Americanize a variety of linguistic and ethnic groups. The Catholic church may have been the most potent assimilating force next to the public school system (Fishman, 1966, p. 407). Comparing the assimilationist goal of the Catholic church and the present diversity in it leads us to the conclusion that ethnic diversity has continued in the Roman Catholic church in spite of, and not because of, this religious institution.

***Diversity Among Protestants.*** Protestantism, like Catholicism, is often portrayed as a monolithic entity. Little attention is given to the doctrinal and attitudinal differences that sharply divide the various denominations, in both laity and clergy. Several studies document the diversity (Glock and Stark, 1965a, 1965b; Hadden, 1967, 1969, 1971; Roof and McKinney, 1985; T. Smith, 1984; Stark and Glock, 1968). Unfortunately most opinion polls and surveys are content to learn if a respondent is a Catholic or a Protestant or a Jew. Stark and Glock (1968) in their massive undertaking found sharp differences in religious attitudes within Protestant churches. For example, 99 percent of Southern Baptists had no doubt that Jesus was the divine Son of God, as contrasted to only 40 percent of Congregationalists. Based on the data, Glock and Stark identified four "generic theological camps" among Protestants:

1. Liberals: Congregationalists, Methodists, and Episcopalians;
2. Moderates: Disciples of Christ and Presbyterians;
3. Conservatives: American Lutherans and American Baptists;
4. Fundamentalists: Missouri Synod Lutherans, Southern Baptists, and various small sects (1965a, pp. 120–121).

Roman Catholics generally agreed with conservatives, except on essentially Catholic issues such as papal infallibility (the authority of the Pope in all decisions regarding faith and morals). Whether or not there are four distinct camps is not important. The point is that the familiar practice of contrasting Roman Catholic and Protestant is clearly not productive. Some differences between Catholics and Protestants are inconsequential compared with differences among Protestant sects.

Protestant faiths may be distinguished by secular criteria as well as doctrinal issues. Research has consistently shown that denominations can be arranged in a hierarchy based on social class. As Figure 5.3 reveals, certain faiths, such as Episcopalianism, Judaism, and Lutheranism, have a higher proportion of affluent members. Members of others, including Baptists and Evangelicals, are comparatively poor. Of course, all Protestant groups draw members from each social stratum. Nonetheless, the social significance of these class differences is that religion becomes a mechanism for signaling social mobility. A person who is "moving up" in wealth and power may seek out a faith associated with higher social ranking.

## Women and Religion

Religious beliefs have often placed women in an exalted, but protected, position. As religions are practiced, this has often meant being "protected" from becoming leaders. Perhaps the only major exception in the United States is the Christian Science church, in which the majority of practitioners and readers are women. Women may be evangelists, prophets, and even saints, but they find it difficult to become clergy*men* within their own congregations. Lutherans did not ordain women until 1970, the Episcopalians in 1976, and Conservative Jews in 1985. Even today, the largest denomination in the United States, Roman Catholicism, does not permit women to be priests. The largest Protestant denomination, the Southern Baptist Convention, has voted against ordaining women (even though some of its autonomous churches have women ministers). Other American faiths that do not allow women clergy include the Lutheran Church–

**FIGURE 5.3**    Income and Denominations

Denominations attract different income groups. All groups have both affluent and poor members, yet some have a higher proportion of members with high incomes and others are comparatively poor.

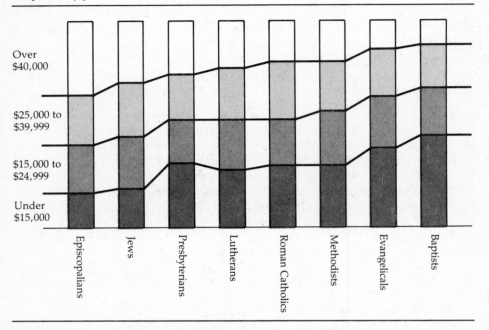

*Source:* Gallup, 1987, pp. 20–27, 29. Reprinted by permission of *The Gallup Poll.*

Missouri Synod, the Greek Orthodox Archdiocese of North and South America, the Orthodox Church in America, the Church of God in Christ, the Church of Jesus Christ of Latter-Day Saints, and Orthodox Judaism.

Despite these restrictions, there has been a notable rise in female clergy in the last 15 years. According to the National Council of Churches, by 1985 about 7.5 percent of all clergy in the United States were women. Female enrollment in American seminaries has steadily increased since the early 1970s. For example, in 1991 women accounted for 30 percent of the total enrollment.

Women clergy are not accepted on an equal basis but tend to go into education, chaplaincies, and administrative positions rather than leading a congregation. Women clergy are well aware that their struggle for equality is far from over. The Reverend Joan Forsberg, an administrator at the Yale Divinity School, tells women graduates that they must view their efforts as part of a larger, long-term process of change. "Even if you don't see change overnight," she notes, "you must remind yourself that you *are* making a difference for future

*Bishop Barbara Morris shows her happiness as she, in 1989, became the first woman ordained in the United States an Episcopal Church bishop.*

generations" (Brooks, 1987, p. 15; A. Goldman, 1986; Hirsley, 1991a; Lehman, 1985; O'Driscoll, 1985; Stump, 1986).

## Religion and the Supreme Court

Civil religion and its accompanying religious pluralism owe their existence to the First Amendment declaration that "Congress shall make no law respecting an establishment of religion, or prohibiting the free exercise thereof." The Supreme Court has consistently interpreted this wording to mean not that government should ignore religion but that it should follow a policy of neutrality to maximize religious freedom. For example, the government may not help religion by financing a new church building, but it also cannot obstruct religion by denying a church adequate police and fire protection. We will examine five issues that continue to require clarification: school prayer, parochial education, secessionist minorities, creationism, and public display of religious symbols (Katz and Southerland, 1967; Oelsner, 1975).

Among the most controversial and continuing disputes has been whether prayer has a role in the schools. Many people were disturbed by the 1962

Supreme Court decision in *Engel* v. *Vitale* that disallowed an allegedly non-denominational prayer drafted for use in New York public schools. The prayer was, "Almighty God, we acknowledge our dependence upon Thee, and we beg Thy blessings upon us, our parents, our teachers, and our country." Subsequent decisions outlawed state laws requiring Bible reading in public schools, laws requiring recitation of the Lord's Prayer, and laws permitting a daily one-minute period of silent meditation or prayer. Despite the rulings, children in many public schools throughout the United States are led in regular prayer recitation or Bible reading.

What about prayers at public gatherings? In 1992, the Supreme Court ruled 5-4 in *Lee* v. *Weisman* that prayer at a junior high school graduation in Providence, Rhode Island violated the Constitution's mandate of separation of church and state. The rabbi had given thanks to God in his invocation. The district court suggested that the invocation would have been acceptable without that reference. The Supreme Court did not agree with the school board that a prayer at a graduation was not coercive. The court did say in its opinion that it was acceptable for a student speaker voluntarily to say a prayer at such a program. Despite such rulings, national surveys show that the majority endorse prayer in schools.

Parochial schools have long been guaranteed the right to function. In 1925 the Supreme Court (*Pierce* v. *Society of Sisters*) declared that parents may not be compelled to send their children to public schools, although they must send them to a properly accredited school. The degree to which the government can assist religious schools has not been resolved, however. Federal grants for lunches in all schools and tax exemption for all religious institutions not engaged in business for profit have been upheld. The Court has refused to review state legislation that denies free bus transportation to parochial school children (Abraham, 1965, p. 64; R. Morgan, 1974). The lack of consensus on the Court was reflected in the May 19, 1975 decision in *Meek* v. *Pittinger* on assistance to parochial schools. Three justices voted against any assistance being given, three voted in favor of all types, and three vot4ed that giving books and maps was acceptable but projectors and lab paraphernalia were not, because they could be "diverted to religious" purposes. The issues generated by the country's commitment to separation of church and state will continue to face the Supreme Court and other judicial bodies.

Among religious groups are several that have been in legal and social conflict with the rest of society. Some can be called *secessionist minorities,* in that they reject assimilation as well as coexistence in some form of cultural pluralism. The Hutterian Brethren, or Hutterites, are one such group of about 5,000 in the United States. Found mostly in South Dakota and Montana, they live in cluster colonies and practice a nineteenth-century way of life. Many Hutterites have moved to Canada in order to expand their communities, but even there they encounter suspicion and resentment from outsiders (Kephart and Zellner, 1991). The Amish, a sect of Mennonites numbering about 100,000, also come in conflict with outside society because of their beliefs and way of life. The Amish shun

"WILL THAT BE THE PRAYING OR NON-PRAYING SECTION?"

*Supreme Court decisions prohibit prayer in public schools, but many citizens oppose such rulings.*

most modern conveniences such as electricity, television, radio, and automobiles. Their primary clash with larger society has been in education, because the Amish operate their own schools, which stop at the eighth grade. On May 16, 1972, the Supreme Court in *Yoder* v. *Wisconsin* upheld a lower court's decision that a Wisconsin compulsory education law violated the Amish right to religious freedom (Hostetler and Huntington, 1971; Kephart and Zellner, 1991; Peters, 1965; Sites, 1975, pp. 239–240; *Time*, 1972a).

The fourth area of contention has been over whether the Biblical account of creation should be or must be present in school curricula and whether to give this account equal weight with scientific theories. In the famous "monkey trial" of 1925, Tennessee schoolteacher John Scopes was found guilty of teaching the scientific theory of evolution in public schools. Since then, however, Darwin's evolutionary theories have been presented in public schools with little reference to the Biblical account in Genesis. Persons who support literal interpretation of the Bible, commonly known as *creationists,* have formed various organizations to crusade for creationist treatment in American public schools and universities. In 1982 a critical defeat of the creationists came in *McLean* v. *Arkansas Board of Education* when a Federal District Court judge overturned an Arkansas law that called for balanced treatment of evolution and the Genesis account. Judge William Ray Overton declared that "creation science . . . has no scientific merit or

*The 1925 "monkey trial" of Tennessee schoolteacher John Scopes was an early test of the legality of teaching evolution. Scopes is pictured here (second from left) as he stands before the judge's bench.*

educational value." He added that the balanced-treatment law was "simply and purely an effort to introduce the Biblical version of creation into the public school curricula" and therefore violated the First Amendment guarantee of separation of church and state (Stuart, 1982, p. A2).

The fifth area of contention has been a battle over public displays. Can manger scenes be erected on public property? Do people have a right to be protected from large displays such as a cross or star atop a water tower overlooking an entire town? In a series of decisions in the 1980s, the Supreme Court ruled that religious displays on public government property may be successfully challenged, but not if they were made more secular. Displays that combine the crèche, the Christmas manger scene depicting the birth of Jesus, or the Hanukkah menorah, with reindeer or even Christmas trees have been ruled to be secular. These decisions have been dubbed "the plastic reindeer rules" and should be viewed as tentative since the Court cases have been by close votes, and changes in the Supreme Court composition may alter the outcome of future cases (Hirsley, 1991b).

## Limits of Religious Freedom: Mormonism

Religious freedom is not absolute and must be balanced against other constitutional rights. The Church of Jesus Christ of Latter-day Saints (Mormons) has encountered severe persecution during its history, dramatizing the limits to which American secular society will tolerate a new religious order. Ironically, the obstacles in the way of the Mormons, as they are commonly called by the

Gentiles (or non-Mormons in this context), strengthened the young church as it grew throughout the nineteenth century. Leadership struggles and disputes over doctrine were forced into the background as the Mormons fought for life as a sect. In this instance intergroup conflict maintained group identity and strengthened group cohesion (Coser, 1956; MacMurray and Cunningham, 1973).

The Mormon faith was founded in 1830 by Joseph Smith, who, by his account, had earlier translated the *Book of Mormon* from a set of gold plates left by the angel Moroni. The followers of Smith encountered several decades of hostility as they moved from New York to Ohio, to Missouri, to Illinois, and finally to the Great Salt Lake basin in Utah. When they first arrived in a new community, the Mormons were usually well received because accounts of their persecution elsewhere created sympathy. But Gentiles soon grew suspicious of a religious group that had a lay priesthood, opposed slavery, and saw their church as the center of a planned community (Braden, 1949, p. 428). The most violent disputes within as well as outside the church community took place in Illinois. They arose in response to the extraordinary political power the Mormons were able to attain in the state and Smith's encouragement of plural marriage. The violence eventually led to Smith's arrest and assassination in 1844 and Brigham Young's assumption of leadership. The majority of Mormons followed Young to Utah.

In Utah, they continued to have conflicts with Gentiles. Anti-Mormon sentiment grew throughout the country to the extent that President Buchanan sent troops in 1857 to replace Young with a non-Mormon as territorial governor. The effort failed, and Young remained, but during this short-lived "Mormon War," 120 Gentiles were allegedly led into an Indian trap by overzealous Mormons in the Mountain Meadows Massacre. The anti-Mormon bandwagon grew and concern grew, as well, over the issue of polygamy (more accurately, polygyny, for Mormons permitted only men to take more than one spouse, and did not practice polyandry, which permits women to have multiple husbands). Estimates of the proportion of polygynous households among Mormons ranged from 10 to 50 percent (O'Dea, 1957, p. 246). In 1862 Congress enacted the Morill "anti-bigamy law," banishing the practice in the territories. In Utah no grand jury would issue indictments for this offense, but the Supreme Court ruled finally in *Reynolds* v. *United States* in 1878 that the Morill Act must be upheld and did not represent an infringement of religious freedom. In 1890, the church officially abandoned polygamy in a manifesto that marked the end of Mormon separatism and the beginning of an uneasy compromise with Gentiles. Six years later Utah was admitted to the Union (O'Dea, 1957, pp. 101–111).

Unlike most Protestant faiths, the Latter-day Saints insist that theirs is the only true church of Christ and that they alone are the church for today's world (Weigel, 1961, p. 62). Mormons send missionaries out to seek converts even among those already associated with another Christian faith. This vigorous proselytizing is deeply resented by many Gentiles. The Mormon church seems to maintain its solidarity as much because of the conflict it encounters as in spite of it. Thomas O'Dea remarks of this solidarity that the Latter-day Saints have come "closer to evolving an ethnic identity on this continent than any other comparable group" (1957, p. 116).

Even today Mormons have to defend their practices, but the charges they defend themselves against are of racism and sexism. The church followed Smith's declaration that black skins are cursed "as pertaining to the priesthood" until 1978. From 1968 to 1970 athletic teams from Brigham Young University, affiliated with the church, encountered boycotts and even riots during intercollegiate competition as students from other schools protested the church's discriminatory policy (De Pillis, 1978; Trillin, 1970; White and White, 1980). The priesthood is still denied to women, who are expected to make their contribution through family-centered activities and auxiliary organizations. Although the church did not take an official position on the Equal Rights Amendment (ERA), the conservative attitude toward women's rights was fundamental to the defeat of the ERA in Utah (Miller and Linker, 1974). The practice of plural marriage by perhaps as many as 30,000 individuals who have been officially excommunicated from the church continues to embarrass church stalwarts (Kephart and Zellner, 1991).

Mormons still follow the strict life set forth over a century ago by Joseph Smith. The faithful are expected to forgo tobacco, liquor, cola drinks, coffee, and tea, and to follow a relatively puritanical code of sexual behavior. The more than 160-year history of the Church of Jesus Christ of Latter-day Saints encompasses a series of conflicts, some violent clashes, others conflicts of social values. These conflicts have contributed to the transformation of a sect into a viable religious faith (Christensen and Cannon, 1978).

## GLANCING BACK AND LOOKING AHEAD

Any study of American life, but especially one focusing on dominant and subordinate groups, cannot ignore religion and ethnicity. The two are closely related, as certain religious faiths predominate in certain nationalities. People have been and continue to be ridiculed or to be deprived of opportunities solely because of their ethnic or religious affiliation. Women, in particular, may be at a disadvantage in organized religion. Reassertion of ethnicity has raised issues, but left them unresolved. How ethnic can a person be before society punishes him or her for the willingness to be different? How will the courts and society resolve the issues of religious freedom and freedom from religion? Today ethnicity remains a viable source of identity for many citizens. Religious institutions may be under attack, but an examination of religious ties is fundamental in completing an accurate picture of a person's social identity.

Is the "new ethnicity" serious? That this question continues to be raised by liberal Whites may in itself be another example of Lerner's "respectable bigotry." Ethnicity is a part of today's social reality. The emotions, disputes, and debate over religion and ethnicity in the United States are powerful indeed. The social conflicts experienced by the groups examined in the chapters that follow, however, are so overwhelming that it is easy to forget the importance of religion and ethnicity.

## KEY TERMS

**civil religion**   The religious dimension in American life in which the state merges with sacred beliefs.

**creationists**   People who support a literal interpretation of the Biblical book of Genesis on the origins of the universe and argue that evolution should not be presented as established scientific thought.

**denomination**   A large, organized religion not officially linked with the state or government.

**ethclass**   The merged ethnicity and class in a person's status.

**life chances**   People's opportunities to provide themselves with material goods, positive living conditions, and favorable life experiences.

**padrone**   Labor contractor who would find work and sometimes homes for the new Italian immigrants.

**respectable bigotry**   Michael Lerner's term for the social acceptance of prejudice against White ethnics, when intolerance against non-White minorities is regarded as unacceptable.

**secessionist minority**   Groups such as the Hutterites, who reject assimilation as well as coexistence.

**symbolic ethnicity**   Herbert Gans's term to describe emphasis on ethnic food and ethnically associated political issues rather than deeper ties to one's heritage.

**third-generation interest principle**   Marcus Hansen's contention that ethnic interest and awareness increase in the third generation, among the grandchildren of immigrants.

## FOR FURTHER INFORMATION

Richard D. Alba. *Ethnic Identity: The Transformation of White America.* New Haven: Yale University Press, 1990.

> An overview of the changing role of ethnicity among European Americans, with particular attention on Italian Americans.

Richard D. Alba, ed. *Ethnicity and Race in the U.S.A.* New York: Routledge, 1988.

> A collection of eight papers that considers the status of race and ethnic minorities and speculates on the outlook for the next two decades.

Charles H. Anderson. *White Protestant Americans: From National Origins to Religious Group.* Englewood Cliffs, NJ: Prentice-Hall, 1970.

> Describes a variety of privileged ethnic groups, including Anglo-Saxons, the Dutch, the Finns, the Germans, the Scandinavians, and the Scotch.

H. Paul Chalfant, Robert E. Beckley, and C. Eddie Palmer. *Religion in Contemporary Society,* 2d ed. Palo Alto, CA: Mayfield, 1987.

> The authors draw upon sociological research in order to study the organization, leadership, and current trends of religious life in the United States.

Robert Coles and Jon Erickson. *The Middle Americans: Proud and Uncertain*. Boston: Little, Brown, 1971.

Erickson's photographs, along with Coles's commentary, describe that segment of the population frequently called, perhaps inaccurately, "the silent majority" or the White, lower-middle class.

Joshua Fishman, ed. *The Rise and Fall of the Ethnic Revival*. Berlin: Mouton, 1985.

Drawing upon language patterns, Fishman critiques claims about the extent of the ethnic revival in the United States.

Andrew Greeley. *Ethnicity in the United States: A Preliminary Reconnaissance*. New York: John Wiley and Sons, 1974.

Greeley summarizes the findings available on the attitudes, politics, religion, and socioeconomic status of White ethnic groups, and stresses the need for further study. In *The American Catholic*, Greeley (1977) brings together similar data on Catholics.

Will Herberg. *Protestant—Catholic—Jew: An Essay in American Religious Sociology*, rev. ed. Chicago: University of Chicago Press, 1983.

Herberg presents his thesis that immigrant ties to the old country have been replaced by religious self-identification along the tripartite scheme of Protestant, Catholic, Jew. Martin Marty provides a new introduction to this revision of the 1960 edition.

William M. Kephart and William M. Zellner. *Extraordinary Groups: The Sociology of Unconventional Life-Styles*, 4th ed. New York: St. Martins Press, 1991.

Kephart and Zellner bring together for the first time in a sociological treatment the Romani (commonly known as the Gypsies), the Amish, the Oneida community, Hasidic Jews, the Shakers, and the Mormons.

Lionel Maldonado and Joan Moore, eds. *Urban Ethnicity in the United States*. Beverly Hills, CA: Sage Publications, 1985.

This collection of ten articles reviews the historical and present situation of ethnics in the United States.

Randall M. Miller, ed. *The Kaleidoscopic Lens: How Hollywood Views Ethnic Groups*. Englewood, NJ: Jerome S. Ozer, 1980.

This illustrated book looks at how Blacks, Native Americans, Hispanics, Irish, Jews, Germans, Slovaks, and Asians have been treated stereotypically in the movies.

Charles H. Mindel, Robert W. Habenstein, and Roosevelt Wright, Jr., eds. *Ethnic Families in America: Patterns and Variations*, 3rd ed. New York: Elsevier, 1988.

The nature of family life is fundamental to comprehending minority groups. The editors of this book have brought together fifteen original articles on family life in different racial and ethnic groups, including Italian Americans, Greek Americans, Mormons, Vietnamese Americans, and Irish American Catholics.

Rodney Stark and William Sims Bainbridge. *The Future of Religion*. Berkeley: University of California Press, 1985.

An examination of contemporary religion, from traditional denominations to cults.

## *Journals*

Among the journals that focus on issues of race and ethnicity is *Ethnic and Racial Studies* (1978). The sociological study of religion is reflected in the *Journal for the Scientific Study of Religion, Review of Religious Research* (1958), *Sociological Analysis* (1940), and *Social Compass* (1954). The monthly newsletter *Emerging Trends*, published by the Princeton Religion Research Center beginning in 1979, provides the latest survey data on religious life.

## Part Three

# MAJOR RACIAL AND ETHNIC MINORITY GROUPS IN THE UNITED STATES

## Chapter Six

# AMERICAN INDIANS: THE FIRST AMERICANS

*Chapter Outline*

**Before the United States**

**Treaties and Warfare**

The Case of the Sioux

**Legislating for the American Indian People**

The Allotment Act

The Reorganization Act

**Reservation Life and Federal Policies**

The Indian Claims Commission

The Termination Act

The Case of the Menominee Tribe

**American Indians in Urban Settings**

**Position of American Indians**

Employment and Income

Education

Health Care

**Pan-Indianism**

Fish-Ins and Alcatraz

The Government Response

American-Indian Protests

Pan-Indianism: An Overview

**Natural Resources: The New Battleground**

**Glancing Back and Looking Ahead**

**Key Terms**

**For Further Information**

---

**❋ HIGHLIGHTS ❋**

The American Indians were the first inhabitants of North America and the first to be subordinated by the Europeans. The Native Americans who survived contact with the White people were removed from their ancestral homes, often far away. The U.S. government weakened tribal institutions through a succession of acts beginning with the *Allotment Act* of 1884. Even efforts to strengthen tribal autonomy, such as the 1934 *Reorganization Act*, did so by encouraging adoption of White society's way of

life. The modern period of Native American-White relations is little different, as shown by such measures as the *Employment Assistance Program* and the *Termination Act*, both of which encourage Indians to assimilate. The *Red Power* and *pan-Indian* movements speak for a diverse Native-American people with many needs—settlement of treaty violations, increased employment opportunities, control over natural resources, improved educational programs, and greater self-rule, to name a few.

---

From Christopher Columbus's incorrect identification of the inhabitants of the Americas as people of India on, the American Indians were misunderstood and ill treated by their conquerors for several centuries. It would be a mistake to assume that the Native Americans understood the Europeans any better than the immigrants from the Old World comprehended the people of the New World. But because the Europeans had superior weaponry, it was the mistakes and misunderstandings of the English, French, Spanish, and Portuguese that became law.

## BEFORE THE UNITED STATES

The first explorers of the Western Hemisphere came long before Columbus and Leif Ericson. Archaeologists estimate that between 25,000 and 40,000 years ago Asians crossed over into North America on a land bridge that joined the two continents near present-day Alaska. The ancestors of today's Native Americans were hunters in search of wild game, including mammoths and long-horned bison. For thousands of years the people spread through the Western Hemisphere, adapting to the many physical environments. Hundreds of cultures evolved, including the complex societies of the Mayas, Incas, and Aztecs.

It is beyond the scope of this book to describe the many American-Indian cultures of North America, let alone the ways of life of Native Americans in Central and South America and the islands of the Caribbean. We must appreciate that the term "Indian culture" is a convenient way of glossing over the diversity of cultures, languages, religions, kinship systems, and political organizations that existed, and in many instances remain, among the peoples collectively referred to as American Indians. For example, an estimated 300 Indian languages were spoken in the area north of Mexico at the time of European contact. At least half are still spoken by some tribal members today. For simplicity's sake we will refer to native Americans as American Indians, but we must be ever mindful of the differences this term conceals. Similarly, we will refer to non-Native Americans as "White people" although in this context, this term encompasses a host of people, including African Americans and Hispanics in some instances (Billard, 1974; Boas, 1966; J. Powell, 1966; Wax, 1968).

Columbus commented in his diary that "It appears to me that the people [of the New World] are ingenious and would be good servants. . . . These people are very unskilled in arms. . . . With fifty men they could all be subjected to do all that one wishes" (*Akwesasne Notes*, 1972a, p. 22). The words of the first European explorer were prophetic. The period between initial European contact and the formation of the United States was characterized by cultural and physical conflict between Native Americans and Whites.

The number of American Indians north of the Rio Grande, estimated at about 7 million in 1500, gradually decreased as their food sources disappeared or they fell victim to diseases like measles, smallpox, and influenza. By 1800, the Native-American population was about 600,000 and by 1900 it had been reduced to 250,000. This loss of human life can only be judged as catastrophic. The United States does not bear total responsibility. The pattern had been well established by the early Spaniards in the Southwest and the French and English colonists who sought to gain control of the eastern seaboard. Not all the initial contacts led to loss of life. Some missionaries traveled well in advance of settlements in an effort to Christianize the Native Americans before they came into contact with other, less "Christian," Europeans. Fur trappers, vastly outnumbered by Native Americans, were forced to learn their customs, but these trappers established routes of commerce that more and more Whites were to follow (Snipp, 1989; Thornton, 1991).

As of the 1990 census, there were just under 20 million American Indians, with 38 percent of them living on reservations. The Cherokee, followed by the Navajo and Sioux are the largest tribes today. The present Native-American population reflects a significant growth in the last 10 or 20 years primarily due to their increased willingness to claim their heritage.


## TREATIES AND WARFARE

The United States formulated a policy toward Native Americans that followed the precedents established during the colonial period. The government policy was to not unnecessarily antagonize the Native Americans, but if the needs of tribes interfered with the needs, or even the whims, of Whites, Whites were to be victorious. The tribes were viewed as separate nations to be dealt with by treaties arrived at through negotiations with the central government. Fair-minded as that policy might seem, it was clear from the very beginning that the American Indians who refused to agree to treaties suggested by the White people's government would be dealt with harshly. Federal relations with the Native Americans were the responsibility of the Secretary of War. Consequently, when the Bureau of Indian Affairs was created in 1824 to coordinate federal relations with the tribes, it was placed on the War Department. The government's primary emphasis was on maintaining peace and friendly relations along the frontier. As settlers moved the frontier westward, though, they encroached more and more on land that Indians had inhabited for centuries.

The Indian Removal Act, passed in 1830, called for relocating all Eastern tribes across the Mississippi River. The act was very popular with Whites because it opened more land to settlement. Almost all Whites felt that the Native Americans had no right to block progress, defining progress as movement by White society. Among the largest groups relocated were the five tribes of the Creek, Choctaw, Chickasaw, Cherokee, and Seminole, who were resettled in Oklahoma. The movement, lasting more than a decade, has been called the "Trail of Tears" because the tribes left their ancestral lands under the harshest conditions. Poor planning, corrupt officials, little attention to those ill from a variety of epidemics, and inadequate supplies characterized the forced migration (Deloria and Lytle, 1983, pp. 6–8).

The Removal Act not only totally disrupted Native-American culture itself but didn't move the tribes far enough or fast enough to stay out of the path of

*Cherokee Indians, carrying their few possesions, are prodded along by cavalry soldiers on the "Trail of Tears." Several thousand Indians died during this forced migration.*

the ever-advancing White settlers. Following the Civil War, settlers moved westward at an unprecedented pace. The federal government found it difficult to maintain any semblance of order in the West, because troop strength was weakened by demobilization at the end of the Civil War. Peace commissions were hastily sent out in 1867 to try to create reserves for the American-Indian nations, apart from the White settlers. It was a half-hearted effort at best, because Congress amended the 1871 Indian Appropriations Act so that the United States abandoned the treaty-making system altogether. Consequently, the federal government negotiated even less with the Native Americans but legislated for them, and rarely consulted them (McNickle, 1973, p. 77; Presidential Commission on Indian Reservation Economics, 1984, p. 5; Wax, 1971, pp. 70–73).

## The Case of the Sioux

The nineteenth century was devastating for every Native-American tribe in the areas claimed by the United States. No tribe was the same after its association with federal policy. The treatment of the Sioux, or Dakotas, was especially cruel and remains fresh in the minds of tribal members even today.

In an effort to safeguard White settlers, the United States signed the Fort Laramie Treaty of 1868 with the Sioux, then under the leadership of Red Cloud. The government agreed to keep Whites from hunting or settling on the newly established Great Sioux Reservation, which included all of the land that is now South Dakota west of the Missouri River. In exchange the Sioux relinquished most of the remaining land they occupied at that time. The first few years saw relative peace, except for some raids by warrior bands under the leadership of the medicine man Sitting Bull. Red Cloud even made a much-publicized trip to Washington and New York in 1870.

The flood of White people eventually infiltrated the Sioux territory in an influx spurred on by Colonel George Custer's 1874 exaggerated reports of gold in the Black Hills. Hostilities followed and bands of Native Americans were ordered to move during the winter, when travel was impossible. When the Sioux failed to move, Custer moved in to "pacify" them and the neighboring Cheyenne. Relying on Crow scouts, Custer underestimated the strength of the Sioux warriors under the leadership of Crazy Horse. The ensuing Battle of the Little Big Horn in 1876 was the last great Sioux victory. After the battle, the large encampment of warriors scattered throughout the plains into small bands that were defeated one by one by a Congress and Army more determined than ever to subdue the Sioux.

In 1876, the Sioux reluctantly sold the Black Hills and agreed to the reduction of the Great Sioux Reservation to five much smaller ones. The Sioux, unable to hunt game as they traditionally had, found life unbearable on the reservation. They sought escape through the supernatural, the Ghost Dance religion. The Ghost Dance was a religion that included dances and songs proclaiming the return of the buffalo and the resurrection of dead ancestors in a land free of the White people. The dance soon became a symbolic movement that social scientists call a *millenarian movement*—a movement founded on the belief that a cataclysmic upheaval will occur in the immediate future, followed by collective salvation. The movement had originated among the Paiutes of Nevada and, ironically, had spread northward to the Plains Indians via the cornerstone of the government's assimilationist policy, the schools. The English that American Indians learned in the mission or government schools gave them the means to overcome the barrier of tribal languages. By 1890, about 65 percent of the tribes in the West, according to sociologist Russell Thornton (1981), were involved in this movement.

From a functionalist perspective, this millenarian movement can be viewed as a means of coping with the domination of White intruders. Although the Ghost Dance was essentially harmless to Whites, Whites feared that the new tribal solidarity encouraged by the movement would lead to renewed warfare. As a result, more troops were summoned to areas where the Ghost Dance had become popular.

In late December 1890, anticipating that a massive Ghost Dance would be staged, a cavalry division arrived at an encampment of Teton Sioux at Wounded Knee Creek on the Pine Ridge, South Dakota, reservation. When the soldiers began disarming the warriors, a random shot was fired at the soldiers, touching off a close-range battle. The cavalry then turned its artillery on men, women, and children. Approximately 300 Sioux and 25 government soldiers were killed in the ensuing fighting, which is now referred to as the Battle of Wounded Knee.

One Sioux witness later recalled: "We tried to run, but they shot us like we were a buffalo. I know there are some good white people, but the soldiers must be mean to shoot children and women" (D. Brown, 1971, p. 417). The Wounded Knee massacre was not the most tragic defeat suffered by Indians during the nineteenth century, but it shattered the Sioux hope for a return, even a supernatural one, to the life they had known (D. Brown, 1964, pp. 277–285; 1971, pp. 389–418; Olson, 1965; Slagle, 1973).

For the federal government, the "Indian problem" remained; it had not vanished. Despite the effects of disease and warfare, nearly 250,000 Indians still lived, according to the 1890 census. The reservation system constructed in the last decades of the nineteenth century to provide settlements for Indian peoples formed the basis of their relationship to the government from then until the present. Given this historical backdrop, it is little wonder that Native Americans express sentiments today such as those by Suzan Shown Harjo in "Listen to Their Voices."

## LEGISLATING FOR THE AMERICAN INDIAN PEOPLE

Accompanying military defeat of the tribes, the federal government tried to limit the functions of tribal leaders. If tribal institutions were weakened, it was felt, the Native Americans would more rapidly assimilate. The government's intention to merge the American Indians into White society was unmistakably dem-

## ❖ LISTEN TO THEIR VOICES ❖

### I Won't Be Celebrating Columbus Day

*Suzan Shown Harjo*

*Harjo, who is Cheyenne and Muskogee, wrote this piece in 1991 anticipating, accurately, the celebration in 1992 that would accompany the 500th anniversary of Christopher Columbus' first voyage to the "New World."*

Columbus Day, never on Native America's list of favorite holidays, became somewhat tolerable as its significance diminished to little more than a good shopping day. But this next long year of Columbus hoopla will be tough to take amid the spending sprees and horn blowing to tout a five-century feeding frenzy that has left Native people and this red quarter of Mother Earth in a state of emergency. For Native people, this half millennium of land grabs and one-cent treaty sales has been no bargain.

An obscene amount of money will be lavished over the next year on parades, statues and festivals. The Christopher Columbus Quincentenary Jubilee Commission will spend megabucks to stage what it delicately calls "maritime activities" in Boston, San Francisco and other cities with no connection to the original rub-a-dub-dub lurch across the sea in search of India and gold. Funny hats will be worn and new myths born. Little kids will be told big lies in the name of education.

The pressure is on for Native people to be window dressing for Quincentennial events, to celebrate the evangelization of the Americas and to denounce the "Columbus-bashers." We will be asked to buy into the thinking that we cannot change history, and that genocide and ecocide are offset by the benefits of horses, cut-glass beads, pickup trucks and microwave ovens.

The participation of some Native people will be its own best evidence of the effectiveness of 500 years of colonization, and should surprise no one. But at the same time, neither should anyone be surprised by Native people who mark the occasion by splashing blood-red paint on a Columbus statue here or there. Columbus will be hanged in effigy as a symbol of the European invasion, and tried in planned tribunals. . . .

We would like to turn our attention to making the next 500 years different from the past ones; to enter into a time of grace and healing. In order to do so, we must first involve ourselves in educating the colonizing nations, which are investing a lot not only in silly plans but in serious efforts to further revise history, to justify the bloodshed and destruction, to deny that genocide was committed here and to revive failed policies of assimilation as the answer to progress. . . .

The United States could start by upholding its treaty promises—as it is bound to do by the Constitution that calls treaties the "Supreme law of the Land." Churches could start by dedicating money to the eradication of those diseases that Native people still die from in such disproportionately high numbers—hepatitis, influenza, pneumonia, tuberculosis.

Church and state could start defending our religious freedom and stop further destruction of our holy places. The general society could help more of our children grow into healthy adults just by eliminating the dehumanizing images of Native people in popular culture. Stereotypes of us as sports mascots or names on leisure vans cannot be worth the low self-esteem they cause.

Native people are few in number—under 2 million in the United States, where there are, even with recent law changes, more dead Indians in museums and educational institutions than there are live ones today. Most of us are in economic survival mode on a daily basis, and many of us are bobbing about in the middle of the mainstream just treading water. This leaves precious few against great odds to do our part to change the world.

It is necessary and well past time for others to amplify our voices and find their own to tell their neighbors and institutions that 500 years of this history is more than enough and must come to an end.

This year, Native people will memorialize those who did not survive the invasion of 1492. It is fitting for others to join us at this time to begin an era of respect and rediscovery, to find a new world beyond 1992.

From "I Won't Be Celebrating Columbus Day," by Suzan Shown Harjo. Originally appeared in *Newsweek,* Special Issue, October 1991. Reprinted by permission of Suzan Shown Harjo.

onstrated in the 1887 Dawes, or General Allotment, Act. This failure to assist Native-American people was followed by a somewhat more admirable effort, the Indian Reorganization Act of 1934. The Allotment Act and the Reorganization Act established the government's paternalistic approach based on legislating for the American Indians.

## The Allotment Act

The Allotment Act bypassed tribal leaders and proposed to make individual landowners of tribal members. Each family was given up to 160 acres, under the government's assumption that with land they would become more like the White homesteaders who were then flooding the not-yet-settled areas of the West.

Those who for years had sought the eviction, if not the extermination, of the Native Americans were not the ones who proposed the Allotment Act. Rather, civic and religious bodies that saw themselves as protecting American Indian interests justified and propounded the parceling of land to individuals rather than tribes. They assumed that it was best for the American Indians to conform to the White people's ways.

The effect on the Native Americans of the Allotment Act was disastrous. In order to guarantee that they would remain homesteaders, the act prohibited their selling the land for 25 years. Yet no effort was made to acquaint them with the skills necessary to make the land productive. Because many tribes were not accustomed to cultivating land, and if anything considered such labor undignified, assistance to the new homesteaders would have been needed for the American Indians to adapt to homesteading, but none was forthcoming.

Much of the land initially deeded under the Allotment Act eventually came into the possession of White landowners. The land could not be sold legally but it could be leased and subsequently transferred through fraudulent procedures. Whites would even go so far as to arrange to become legal guardians of American-Indian youths who had received allotments. The Bureau of Indian Affairs (BIA) vainly tried to close such loopholes, but unscrupulous Whites and their American-Indian allies would inevitably discover new loopholes. For those Native Americans who managed to retain the land, the BIA required that upon the death of the owner the land be equally divided among all descendants, regardless of tribal inheritance customs. In documented cases this division resulted in as many as 30 individuals trying to live off an 80-acre plot of worthless land. By 1934, Native Americans had lost approximately 90 million of the 138 million acres in their possession prior to the Allotment Act. The land left was generally considered worthless for farming and marginal even for ranching (Deloria and Lytle, 1983, pp. 8–11; Hagan, 1961, pp. 140–147; Holford, 1975; S. Tyler, 1973, pp. 95–107; Wax, 1971, pp. 52–53; Witt, 1970, p. 113).

## The Reorganization Act

The assumptions behind the Allotment Act and the missionary activities of the nineteenth century were that (1) it was best for Native Americans to assimilate into the White society, and (2) each individual was best considered apart from his or her tribal identity. Very gradually, in the twentieth century, government officials have accepted the importance of tribal identity. The Indian Reorganization Act of 1934, the Wheeler-Howard Act, recognized the need to use, rather than ignore, tribal identity. But assimilation, rather than movement toward a pluralistic society, was still the goal of the act.

Many provisions of the Reorganization Act, including revocation of the Allotment Act, benefitted American Indians. Still, given the legacy of broken treaties, many tribes distrusted the new policy at first. Under the Reorganization Act, tribes could adopt a written constitution and elect a tribal council with a chairperson. This system imposed foreign values and structures. The elected tribal chairperson actually represented an entire reservation, which might include several tribes, some of whom were hostile to one another. Furthermore, the chairperson had to be elected by majority rule, a concept alien to many tribes. Many full-blooded American Indians resented the provision that mixed bloods were to have full voting rights. The Indian Reorganization Act did facilitate tribal dealings with government agencies, but the use of *Robert's Rules of Order* and formal judicial process impressed many American Indians as unreasonable and dictatorial.

As had been true of earlier government reforms, the Reorganization Act sought to assimilate American Indians into the dominant society on the dominant group's terms. In this case, the tribes were absorbed within the political and economic structure of the larger society. Except for chairpeople who were to oversee reservations that had several tribes, the Reorganization Act served to solidify tribal identity. Unlike the Allotment Act, it recognized the right of Native Americans to approve of some actions taken on their behalf. The act still maintained substantial non-Native-American Indian control over the reservations. As institutions, the tribal governments owed their existence not to their people, but to the BIA. These tribal governments rested at the bottom of a large administrative hierarchy (Cornell, 1984; Deloria, 1971, pp. 99–106; 1974, pp. 187–203; McNickle, 1973, pp. 91–94; Washburn, 1984; Wax and Buchanan, 1975, pp. 36–40).

## RESERVATION LIFE AND FEDERAL POLICIES

Today over 740,000 Native Americans live on reservations throughout the United States. While the majority, 62 percent, live outside these tribal areas, the reservations play a prominent role in the identity of the American Indian peoples (see Figure 6.1).

More than any other segment of the population with the exception of the military, the reservation Native American finds his or her life determined by the federal government. From the condition of the roads to the level of fire protection to the quality of the schools, reservation life is effectively controlled by the federal government and such agencies as the Bureau of Indian Affairs and the Public Health Service. Tribes and their leaders are now consulted more than in the past, but the ultimate decisions rest in Washington, D.C., to a degree that is not true for the rest of civilian population.

An April 1954 editorial in *The Washington Post* expressed sympathy with efforts of the federal government to "get out of the Indian business." Many of the policies instituted by the Bureau of Indian Affairs during the twentieth century have been designed with this purpose in mind. Most American Indians and their organizations do not quarrel with this goal. They may only wish that the government and the White people had never gotten into "Indian business" in the first place. Disagreement between the BIA and the tribes and among American Indians themselves has focused on how to reduce federal control and subsidies, not on whether they should be reduced. The government has taken three steps in this direction since World War II. Two of these measures are the formation of the Indian Claims Commission and the passage of the Termination Act, examined here with special focus on the Menominee of Wisconsin. The section following will show how the third step, the Employment Assistance Program, created a new meeting place for Native Americans in American cities, far from either their native homelands or the reservations (S. Tyler, 1973, p. 175).

**FIGURE 6.1** Indian Lands and Communities

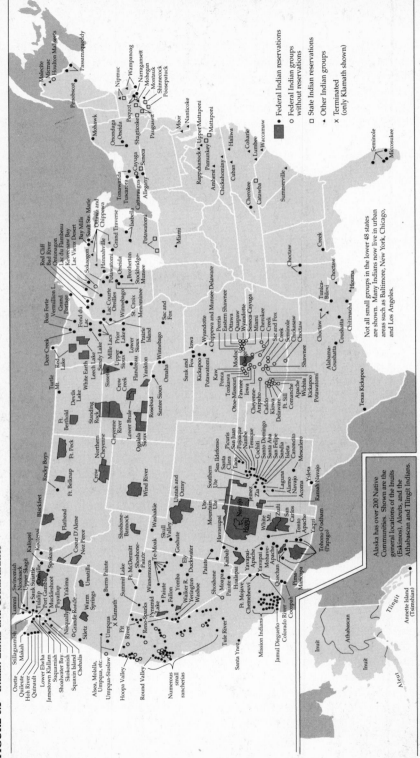

Federal Indian reservations

○ Federal Indian groups without reservations

□ State Indian reservations

▲ Other Indian groups

× Terminated (only Klamath shown)

Not all small groups in the lower 48 states are shown. Many Indians now live in urban areas such as Baltimore, New York, Chicago, and Los Angeles.

Alaska has over 200 Native Communities. Shown are the general locations of the Inuits (Eskimos), Aleuts, and the Athabascan and Tlingit Indians.

*Source: Bureau of Indian Affairs, 1986, pp. 12–13.*

## The Indian Claims Commission

American Indians have had a unique relationship to the federal government. As might be expected, little provision was made for them as individuals or tribes to bring grievances against the government. From 1863 to 1946, Native Americans could bring no claim against the government without a special act of Congress, a policy that effectively prevented most charges of treaty violations. Only 142 claims were heard during those 83 years. In 1946, Congress created the Indian Claims Commission, with authority to hear all tribal cases against the government. The three-member commission was given a five-year deadline. During the first five years, however, nearly three times as many claims were filed as had been filed during the 83 years of the old system. Therefore the commission's term was extended and extended again, and its size expanded. It continues to meet now, more than four decades after its establishment, and it now has five members.

The commission, although not a court, operates somewhat like one, with lawyers presenting evidence for both sides. Witnesses testify as to the legitimacy of land claims. If the commission concurs with the Native Americans, it then determines the value of the land at the time it was illegally seized. Native Americans do not usually receive payment based on present value, nor do they usually receive interest on the money due. Value at time of loss, perhaps a few pennies an acre, is considered "just compensation." Payments are then decreased by setoffs. *Setoffs* are deductions from the money due equal to the cost of federal services provided to the tribe. It is not unusual to have a case decided in favor of the tribe, only to have its settlement exceeded by the setoffs (Deloria, 1971, pp. 220–228; Ellis, 1972, pp. 173–174; Wilkinson, 1966).

One bitter dispute that continues unresolved illustrates the complexity of land claims. In 1882, the United States declared an end to a century-long conflict over which tribe—the Hopi or the Navajo—had the right to some lands in northeastern Arizona. The original inhabitants, the Hopi, were granted sole use of a group of mesas. These lands were surrounded by joint-use land to be used by both tribes, which itself was totally surrounded by the relatively populous Navajo reservation, as shown in Figure 6.2. In 1974, responding to Hopi protests, the federal government partitioned the joint-use area and declared that by 1986 all tribal members had to cross to their own tribe's side of a newly erected 340-mile barbed-wire fence. The eviction of American Indians was unparalleled since Japanese Americans were interred during World War II. American Indians were compensated with housing and resettlement costs, but the emotional costs were high. An Indian Health Service study found 60 percent of the relocatees suffering from depression. The deadline came and went, leaving several hundred Navajo families clinging to their ancestral lands on the "wrong" side of the boundary.

Although today the dispute seems to be between the tribes, the original conflict was created when Navajos fled the U.S. Cavalry in New Mexico, and entered neighboring Arizona. Even after joint use was declared, in the 1930s the government began issuing grazing permits to Navajos in these areas. Opponents

**FIGURE 6.2**    Navajo-Hopi Land Dispute

Approximately 10,000 Navajos and 100 Hopis living within the partition lands were ordered to relocate by a 1974 act of Congress. The partition land is, in turn, surrounded by the Navajo reservation.

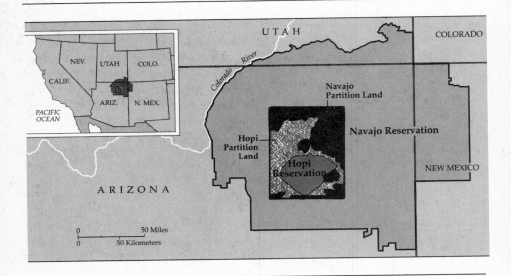

of the present plan contend that multimillion-dollar coal, oil, and uranium development is the real motive for doing away with a joint-use area. Although Native Americans are the continuing victims in this dispute, it has involved non-Natives for the last century (Garitty, 1986).

In legal cases, Native Americans have increasingly succeeded. The Supreme Court has ruled on more and more issues involving Native Americans—handing down 12 decisions in the 1960s, 35 in the 1970s, and 32 from 1980 through 1988. Most of these cases have gone in favor of the tribes, and have reasserted such basic principles as that tribes are separate governments; that states have no jurisdiction over the reservations; that the federal government has a responsibility to the tribes; and that American Indians have substantial rights to the resources on their land. Native-American legal groups have organized to protect these and other legal rights, while various anti-American-Indian groups have organized to oppose what they regard as special privileges to tribes. The anti-American-Indian groups, often linked to conservative extremist groups, argue that recognition of American Indians is a violation of the Constitution. Native Americans express concern as these groups have formed alliances on specific legal cases with such established groups at the National Wildlife Federation and the National Rifle Association (*Akwesasne Notes*, 1988; Schmidt, 1988, p. 85).

*Alice Yazzi, a Navajo who has lived all her life in this hogan, contemplates moving out of the joint-use area into the partitioned Navajo land.*

Native Americans are increasingly expressing a desire to recover their land, rather than accept financial settlements. Following numerous legal decisions favoring the Sioux Indians, including a ruling of the Supreme Court, Congress finally agreed to pay $106 million for the land illegally seized in the aftermath of the Battle of Little Big Horn, described earlier in this chapter. The Sioux rejected the money and lobbied for measures such as the 1987 Black Hills Sioux Nation Act in Congress to return the land to the tribe. No positive action has been taken on these measures. In the meantime, however, the original settlement, subsequent unaccepted payments, and interest brought the 1991 total of funds being held for the Sioux to over $300 million. Despite the desperate need for housing, food, health care, and education the Sioux still wish to regain the land lost in the 1868 Fort Laramie Treaty (Lazarus, 1991).

## The Termination Act

The most controversial government policy toward reservation American Indians during the twentieth century was initiated by the Termination Act of 1953. As might be said of many such policies, termination originated in ideas that were meant to be sympathetic to Native Americans. The BIA Commissioner, John Collier, had expressed concern in the 1930s over extensive governmental control of tribal affairs. In 1947, congressional hearings were held to determine which tribes had the economic resources to be relieved of federal control and assistance. The policy proposed at that time was an admirable attempt to give Native Americans greater autonomy and at the same time reduce federal expenditures, a goal popular among taxpayers.

The special services the tribes received, like medical care and scholarships to college, should not be viewed as making them wards of the government. These services resulted from neither authoritarianism nor favoritism, but merely fulfill treaty obligations. The termination of the Native Americans' relationship to the government could then be viewed as a threat to reduce services rather than a release from arbitrary authority. American Indians might be gaining greater self-governance, but the price was high.

Unfortunately, the Termination Act as finally passed emphasized reducing costs and ignored individual needs. Recommendations for a period of tax immunity were dropped. Federal services such as medical care, schools, and road equipment were supposed to be withdrawn gradually. Instead, when termination was implemented, federal services were stopped immediately, with minimal coordination between local government agencies and the tribes themselves to determine whether services could be continued by other means. The BIA Commissioner who oversaw termination was Dillon Myer, who had supervised Japanese-American internment camps during World War II (see Chapter 14), and as it had been for the Japanese Americans, the effect of the government orders on the Native Americans was disastrous (Deloria, 1969, pp. 60–71; Fixico, 1988; S. Tyler, 1973, pp. 161–188; Wax and Buchanan, 1975, pp. 67–68).

## The Case of the Menominee Tribe

The tragic treatment of the Menominee tribe of Wisconsin under termination is not typical. No other tribe that was terminated was as well organized beforehand and no other tribe was able to convince the federal government it was mistaken. The termination of the Menominees was preceded by a favorable Claims Commission settlement of $8 million from the government as compensation for mismanagement of a forest on tribal land. The money, however, would not be paid unless Congress appropriated it, which was conditional on the Menominees' voting for termination. A vote for termination meant an almost immediate cash payment of $1,500 to each tribal member. Even with such a positive incentive, the Menominees at first overwhelmingly voted against termination. Finally, after six years of campaigning by members of Congress and the BIA, the Menominees voted for termination in 1959.

From the government's point of view, the 3,270 Menominees were prepared to be independent of federal services. They were one of only three tribes able to pay the costs of their own administration, which they could do because of a tribally owned sawmill. Twenty-five percent were unemployed, however, and the majority of tribal members met the standards of eligibility for surplus food. Even mill workers earned only $56 a week to support a typical family of eight.

After termination they would also have to bear the burden of taxation, medical expenses, and utility payments.

On May 1, 1961, termination became final, and Menominee County, formerly a federal reservation, became the newest, smallest, least populated, least educated, most poorly housed county in Wisconsin. To provide the services previously financed by the federal government, the Menominees reluctantly started selling lakeshore property within a year of termination. Even with such drastic actions, the Menominees went without a full-time doctor for 11 years and had no school. Schoolchildren and patients had to be bused into neighboring communities, which did not appreciate the added burden on their limited medical and educational facilities.

In response to the growing problems, the Menominees created a grassroots organization called Determination of Rights and Unity for Menominee Shareholders (DRUMS). Drawing upon the Menominees in the county as well as those who had fled the dismal life for Chicago and Milwaukee, DRUMS struggled to stop the sale of land and the damming of rivers. Beginning in 1972, under the leadership of Ada Deer, DRUMS tried to persuade Congress that it should reverse termination of the Menominees. To outsiders, it seemed puzzling to find the Menominees seeking the aid of the often criticized BIA. Ada Deer herself said that the choice was not easy, but "determination" was the only choice, "because there is no alternative, no other way to hold on to our land" (Raymer, 1974, p. 248). Finally, in 1973, Congress, with the support of President Nixon, overwhelmingly enacted the Restoration Act, making Menominee County once again the Menominee Indian Reservation. The termination policy had been a failure. The BIA estimated the cost had been much greater to the federal government because of the additional economic assistance required once the Restoration Act was passed.

Even the Menominees, who succeeded in holding onto most of their land, have found the post-termination period less than peaceful. From 1974 to 1976, violent disputes broke out between Menominees and Whites who still held lakefront property, as well as Whites near the reservation who resented having had to assist the Menominees during termination. The Menominees themselves are divided over their future. Perhaps the future of the Menominees is unclear, but once again the government failed to get out of the "Indian business" and succeeded only in making the plight of the Native Americans worse (Deloria, 1969, pp. 60–82; Draeger, 1975; Egerton, 1973; Husar, 1976; McNickle, 1973, pp. 103–112; Mullen, 1975; Orfield, 1972; Peroff, 1982; Shames, 1972; Spindler and Spindler, 1984, pp. vii–viii; 193–204; .T. Taylor, 1972, pp. 48–62, 231–232).

The move toward termination came to a halt with the passage in 1975 of the Indian Self-Determination and Education Assistance Act. The act expanded tribal control over reservation programs, without necessarily suggesting that federal assistance would be decreased. The law also provided that parental groups have increased authority over school programs—a special problem, as we will see later in this chapter (Bureau of Indian Affairs, 1981, p. 5; Spicer, 1980).

## AMERICAN INDIANS IN URBAN SETTINGS

The depressing economic conditions of reservation life might lead one to expect government initiatives to attract business and industry to locate on or near reservations. The government could provide tax incentives that would eventually pay for themselves. Such proposals, however, have not been advanced. Rather than taking jobs to the Native Americans, the federal government decided to lead the more highly motivated away from the reservation. This policy has further devastated the reservations' economic potential.

The BIA in 1952 began programs to relocate young American Indians, one of which, after 1962, was called the Employment Assistance Program (EAP). Assistance centers were created in Chicago, Cleveland, Dallas, Denver, Los Angeles, Oakland, San Jose, Oklahoma City, Tulsa, and Seattle. In some cities, the Native-American population increased as much as fivefold in the 1950s, primarily because of the EAP. By 1968 more than 100,000 individuals had participated in the program and 200,000, or one-fourth of the American Indian population, had moved to urban areas. They have tended not to spread out throughout urban areas but remain somewhat segregated. Though not as segregated as African Americans or Hispanics, Native Americans often experience moderate segregation, similar to that of European ethnic groups (Bohland, 1982).

The EAP's primary provision was for relocation, individually or in families, at government expense, to urban areas where job opportunities were greater than those on reservations. The BIA stressed that the EAP was voluntary, but as Bahr correctly states, this voluntary aspect was "a fiction to the extent that the white man has structured the alternatives in such a way that economic pressures force the Indian to relocate" (1972, p. 408). The program was not a success for the many American Indians who found the urban experience unsuitable or unbearable. By 1965, one-fourth to one-third of the people in the EAP had returned to their home reservation. So great was the rate of return that in 1959 the BIA actually stopped releasing data on the percentage of returnees, fearing that these would give too much ammunition to critics of the EAP.

Adjustment to a new way of life was the major challenge facing relocated Native Americans. Two studies (Price, 1968; Weppner, 1971) document the difficulty met by members of an agricultural tribe, the Navajo, in adjusting to urban life in Denver and Los Angeles. If the BIA had provided adequate vocational training and proper instruction in English, many more would undoubtedly have coped better with the new social environment. In the late 1960s, Merwyn Garbarino interviewed relocated Native Americans in Chicago. The 29-year-old man who told Garbarino the following could not be judged one of the EAP's successes.

> I don't like living in Chicago. I'm here on the relocation training program, and I'm glad to learn a trade, but I sure don't like the city. The BIA doesn't give us enough money to live in Chicago. It's awfully expensive here. But it's not just that. People are different here—even the Indians. They don't talk to you. Bus drivers are bastards, and I got lost on the "el" and no one could help me.

City people are in such a hurry. As soon as I finish school, I'm going away—maybe back to the reservation, but to a small town anyhow. I'd rather be in a small town and not have such a good job as stay in the city (1971, p. 182).

Other Native Americans were able to adjust to urban life in Chicago, as this interview with a 49-year-old man documents:

I heard about relocation on the reservation. It's a good idea. Sometimes it doesn't work too well. When I first came, I had some training, and then things got bad and I lost my job. The BIA helped me get another one, but it didn't pay too good, and we had a hard time making out. We had to get some welfare at times. That sort of embarrassed me at first, but then in those days lots of people were out of work. At first it was just my wife and me. That wasn't so bad. She did some day jobs, you know, just line up each morning and see if there's a job for the day. That helped get some money. . . . I heard of a better job from a friend and I changed. No, I didn't think about going back to the reservation. Jobs were even worse there. There are things in the city that I like—the museums, movies, things like that. There are things to do, and the jobs did get better. We have quite a family now. Three girls and two boys, and I can take care of them all. Some people say that it is easier if you are alone, but I am glad that I have my family. I take the children to the zoo, and things. My wife never has to work any more. I think I'd like some other cities too. I like Chicago, but I have visited some smaller cities like Green Bay, and I think I might like to live there. But I can say I like a city (1971, pp. 179–180).

From Merwyn Garbarino, "Life in the City," in Jack O. Waddell and O. Michael Watson, eds., *The American Indian in Urban Society.* Copyright © 1971 by Merwyn Garbarino. Reprinted by permission of the author.

The Employment Assistance Program was not a total failure, but neither did it present an easy solution to the difficulties faced on the reservation.

The movement of American Indians into urban areas has had many unintended consequences. It has further reduced the labor force on the reservation. Because those who leave tend to be better educated, it is the Native-American version of the brain drain described in Chapter 4. It also increased nonresidents' demands for better representation on tribal councils. Urbanization unquestionably contributed to the pan-Indian movement described later in this chapter. The city became the new meeting place of American Indians who learned of their common predicament both in the city and on the federally-administered reservation. Government agencies also had to develop a policy of continued assistance to nonreservation American Indians. Even the tribes themselves recognized the need. By 1986, the Navajos were dispensing $40,000 to urban centers for emergency need of city-dwelling tribal members. Despite such efforts, the problems of Native Americans in the city remain, and the need to address their difficulties will continue to be raised. In 1986, for example, New York City's 14,000 Native Americans were experiencing a 40 percent unemployment rate, with eight out of nine families living below the poverty level. Furthermore, a study published in 1988 revealed little difference between the earning power of migrants to urban areas and those who stayed on the reservations. (American Indian Policy Review Commission, 1976a; Martin, 1987; Medicine, 1973, p. 400; Sorkin, 1969; Steiner, 1968, pp. 175–192; Stewart, 1979; C. Sullivan, 1986b; S. Tyler, 1973, pp. 151, 153; Waddell and Watson, 1973).

## POSITION OF AMERICAN INDIANS

The United States, through the Bureau of Indian Affairs, has removed American Indians westward, restricted their movement, unilaterally severed agreements, created a special legal status for them, and, after World War II, has attempted to move them again. After all this ill treatment, how well have they been compensated? The sections that follow summarize the status of contemporary Native Americans in employment and income, education, and health care.

Any discussion of Native-American socioeconomic status today must begin by emphasizing the diversity of the people. Besides the variety of tribal heritages already noted, the contemporary Indian population is split between those on and off reservations, those living in small towns and in central cities, and those living from one coast to the other. Native-American life has shifted from the several hundred reservations to small towns and big cities. Life in these contrasting social environments is quite different, but there are enough similarities to warrant some broad generalizations on the status of Native Americans in the United States today. (Note: For more information on the census, see Passel and Berman, 1986; Snipp, 1989.)

### Employment and Income

The American Indians are impoverished people. To even the most casual observer of a reservation, the poverty is a living reality and not merely numbers and percentages. Some visitors seem unconcerned, arguing that because they are used to hardship and lived a simple life before Europeans arrived there is no need to worry now (Bureau of Indian Affairs, 1973). In an absolute sense of dollars earned or quality of housing, Native Americans are no worse off now. But in a relative sense, comparing their position to that of Whites, they are dismally behind on all standards of income and occupational status. The 1980 census revealed that American Indian families are three times more likely to be below the poverty level and much less likely to have a wage earner employed full time (Bureau of the Census, 1983). Furthermore, domination by Europeans, sociologist Murray Wax writes, has disrupted the American Indian's "system of economic and social interdependence" a situation not measurable in statistics (1971, p. 194).

Tourism is an important source of employment for many reservation residents, who either directly serve the needs of visitors or provide souvenirs and craft items. Generally such enterprises do not achieve the kind of success that significantly improves the tribal economy. Even if it did, sociologist Murray Wax argues, "it requires a special type of person to tolerate exposing himself and his family life to the gaze of tourists who are often boorish and sometimes offensively condescending in their attitudes" (1971, p. 69). Craft work rarely realizes the profits most Native Americans desire and need. Whites are interested in trinkets, not the more expensive and profitable items. The trading-post business has also taken its toll on American-Indian cultures. Many craft workers have been manipulated by Whites and other Native Americans to produce what the tourists want. Creativity and authenticity have frequently been replaced by mechanical duplication of "genuine Indian" curios. The price of economic survival is high (*Akwesasne Notes*, 1972b; Federal Trade Commission, 1973; M. Smith, 1982; Snipp, 1980; Steiner, 1976, pp. 207–212; Sweet, 1990).

A more recent source of income and some employment has been the introduction of gambling on reservations. Under the 1988 Indian Gaming Regulatory Act, states must negotiate gambling agreements with reservations and cannot prohibit any gambling already allowed under state law. By 1992, tribes in nine states were operating a variety of gambling operations including off-track betting, casino tables such as blackjack and roulette, lotteries, sports betting, video games of chance, telephone betting, slot machines, and high-stakes bingo. The gamblers are almost all non-Native Americans who sometimes travel long distance for the opportunity to wager money. The economic impact on some reservations has been enormous, and nationwide the gambling revenue was $2.5 billion for the now 200 tribes involved. Criticism is not hard to find even among Native Americans who oppose gambling not only on moral grounds but because it is marketed in a form incompatible with Native-American culture. On the Mohawk reservation along the Canada-New York State border the battle over gambling combined with other issues has become extremely violent. Despite this tragic experience, gambling is on the rise (Hornung, 1990; Larrabee, 1991; McGee, 1991).

Another major source of employment is the government, principally the BIA, but also other federal agencies, the military, and state and local government. In 1970, one of every four employed Native Americans worked for the government. More than half the BIA's employees have American Indian ancestry. In fact, since 1854 the BIA has had a policy of giving employment preference to American Indians over Whites. This policy has been questioned, but the Supreme Court (*Morton v. Mancari*) upheld the policy in 1974. Although this is a significant source of employment opportunity, many criticisms have been leveled at Native-American government workers, especially federal employees.

There is little question that government employees form a subculture in Native-American communities. They tend to be Christians, educated in BIA schools, and sometimes the third generation born into government service. Discrimination against American Indians in private industry makes government work attractive, and once a person is employed and has seniority, he or she is virtually guaranteed security. Of course, in some individuals (whether Native Americans or Whites) this security may lead to smugness and less than efficient

*A casino operates on an American Indian reservation in Connecticut. Gambling has become an important revenue source on reservations.*

work. Finally, the large number of "feds," or BIA workers, further divides a community already in desperate need of unity (Bureau of Indian Affairs, 1970, p. 13; Rachlin, 1970, pp. 170–171).

American Indians who move to small towns near reservations frequently encounter strong reactions against their being employed. Ralph Luebben (1964) found that in areas bordering the massive Navajo reservation in Arizona, New Mexico, and Utah, members of the tribe were nearly always hired at the lowest level, regardless of the need for labor or the qualifications of the individual. The Navajos expected prejudice and discrimination, and their expectations in the employment sector were usually borne out. Similarly, a 1972 study of Indians in Seattle found one-third reporting that they had been denied housing because of their race and another one-fourth reporting that they had been discriminated against in hiring (Bahr et al., 1972).

We have examined the sources of employment, such as tourism, government service, legalized gambling, and businesses in towns adjoining reservations, but the dominant feature of reservation life is unemployment. A 1986 report issued by the Full Employment Action Council opened with the statement that such words as "severe," "massive," and "horrendous" are appropriate to describe unemployment among American Indians. Official unemployment figures for reservation Indians range from 23 percent to 90 percent. Unemployment rates for urban-based Indians are equally high; Los Angeles reports more than 40 percent and Minneapolis 49 percent (Cornell and Kalt, 1990; Knudson, 1987; C. Sullivan, 1986a).

The economic outlook for Native Americans need not be bleak. A single program is not the solution; the diversity of both them and their problems demands a multifaceted approach. The solutions need not be unduly expensive; indeed, because the American Indian population is exceedingly small compared to the total population programs with major influence may be financed without significant federal expenditures. Murray Wax observed that reformers often view the depressed position of American Indians economically and quickly seize upon education as the key to success (1971, p. 82). As the next section shows, improving the educational programs for Native Americans would be a good place to start.

## Education

Government involvement in the education of Native Americans dates as far back as a 1794 treaty with the Oneida Indians. In the 1840s the federal government and missionary groups combined to start the first school for American Indians. By 1860, the government operated schools that were free of missionary involvement. Today, laws prohibit federal funds for Native-American education from going to sectarian schools. Also, since the passage of the Johnson-O'Malley Act in 1934, the federal government reimburses public school districts that include Native-American children.

Federal control of the education of American-Indian children has had mixed results from the beginning. Several tribes started their own school systems at the beginning of the nineteenth century, completely financing the schools themselves. The Cherokee tribe developed an extensive school system that taught both English and Cherokee, the latter using an alphabet developed by the famed leader, Sequoyah. Literacy for the Cherokees was estimated by the mid-1800s at 90 percent, and they even published a bilingual newspaper. The Creeks, Chickasaws, and Seminoles also maintained school systems. But by the end of the nineteenth century all these schools were closed by federal order. Not until John Collier became BIA commissioner did the federal government become committed to ensuring an education for Native-American children. Despite the push for educational participation, by 1948 only a quarter of the children on the Navajo reservation, the nation's largest, were attending school. Today, over 90 percent of Navajo children are in school (Adams, 1988; Bureau of Indian Affairs, 1970, pp. 5–6; 1974, p. 5; Fuchs and Havighurst, 1972, pp. 6–7).

*Educational Attainment.* A serious problem in Native-American education has been the unusually high level of underenrollment. Many children never attend school or leave while in elementary school and never return. Enrollment rates are as low as 30 percent for Alaska Eskimos (or Inuits). Another discouraging sign is the high dropout rate, which is at least 50 percent higher than that of Blacks or Hispanics and nearly three times that of Whites. The term *dropout* is misleading, because many American-Indian schoolchildren have found their educational experience so hostile they had no choice but to leave (D. Kelly, 1991).

Rosalie Wax (1967) conducted a detailed study of the education among the Sioux on the Pine Ridge reservation of South Dakota. She concluded that terms like *kickout* or *pushout* are more appropriate. The children are not so much hostile to school as they are set apart from it; they are socialized by parents to be independent and not to embarrass their peers, but teachers reward docile acceptance and expect schoolchildren to correct one another in public. Socialization is not all that separates home from school. Teachers are often happy to find parents not "interfering" with their job. Parents do not visit the school, and teachers avoid the homes, a pattern that only furthers the isolation of school from home. This lack of interaction is partly due to the predominance of non-Native-American professionals, although the situation is improving. American Indians in BIA-funded schools in 1988 account for 26 percent of counselors, 41 percent of teachers, and 54 percent of administrators (Bureau of Indian Affairs, 1988, p. 111).

The fact that some American-Indian children never enter school and others leave school early produces a predictable gap in educational attainment between Whites and Native Americans. In 1970, Whites typically had completed high school, whereas American-Indian adults had not finished their sophomore year of high school. By the 1980 census, Whites had attained 12.5 median years of education compared to 12.2 median years for American Indians. Yet preliminary data published in 1988 suggest that proportionately fewer Native Americans are now enrolling in college. To understand this disturbing trend, we need to consider the quality of the education (Bureau of the Census, 1983, pp. 97–98; Tijerina and Biemer, 1988, p. 88).

*Quality of Schooling.* The qualitative aspect of Native-American education is more difficult to measure than the quantitative. How does one measure excellence? And excellence for what? White society? Tribal life? Both? Chapter 1 discussed the disagreement over measuring intellectual achievement (how much a person has learned) and the greater hazards in measuring intellectual aptitude (how much a person is able to learn). It is not necessary to repeat the arguments. Studies of reservation children, using tests of intelligence that do not require knowledge of English, consistently show levels at or above those for middle-class urban children. Yet in the upper grades, a *crossover effect* appears when the tests used assume lifelong familiarity with English. Native-American students drop behind their White peers and so would be classified by the dominant society as underachievers (Bureau of Indian Affairs, 1988, pp. 69–72; Coleman et al., 1966a, p. 450; Fuchs and Havighurst, 1972, pp. 118–135).

Preoccupation with such test results perhaps avoids the more important question: Educational excellence for what? It would be a mistake to assume that the American Indian peoples have reached a consensus. They do wish, however, to see a curriculum that at the very least considers the unique aspects of their heritage. Charles Silberman (1971, p. 173) reported visiting a sixth-grade English class in a school on a Chippewa reservation where the students were all busily at work writing a composition for Thanksgiving: "Why We Are Happy the

Pilgrims Came." A 1991 Department of Education report entitled "Indian Nations at Risk" still found the curriculum presented from a European perspective. Little wonder that a 1990 national survey found that at 48 percent of all schools American-Indian children attend there is not a single American-Indian teacher.

Some positive changes in education are occurring. About 23 percent of students in BIA-funded schools receive bilingual education but as of yet no coordinator exists in the BIA for this important activity. Although bilingual programs directed at American Indians were underway in 1988, this figure represents an increase from the 17 available in the mid-1970s. There is growing recognition of the need to move away from past policies that suppressed or ignored the native language and to acknowledge that educational results may be maximized by working with the native language (Bureau of Indian Affairs, 1988; R. Wells, 1991).

*Higher Education.* The picture for Native Americans in higher education is decidedly mixed with some progress and some promise. Enrollment in college has been steadily increasing from the mid-1970s through the 1980s, but degree completion, especially for professional degrees, may actually be declining. Their economic and educational background, especially reservation residents, make considering entering a predominantly White college a very difficult decision. Native-American students can soon feel isolated and discouraged, particularly if the college does not help them understand the alien world of Western higher education. Even at campuses with large American-Indian student bodies, there are few Native-American faculty or advisors to serve as role models. Over one-half of the students leave at the end of their first year (Carnegie Foundation for the Advancement of Teaching, 1990; Wells, 1989).

The most encouraging development in higher education in recent years has been the creation of tribally controlled colleges—usually two-year community colleges. The Navajo Community College was established in 1968 and by 1991 there were 24. Besides serving in some rural areas as the only educational institution for many miles, tribal colleges also provide services such as counseling and childcare. Tribal colleges enable the students to maintain their cultural identity while training them to succeed outside the reservation. About 90 percent of American-Indian students who leave the reservation for traditional college drop out, but 35 percent entering tribal colleges go on to complete their bachelor's degree and another 53 percent find jobs after leaving tribal college.

Funding for tribal colleges is a major problem. When Congress passed the Tribally Controlled Community College Assistance Act in 1978, it proposed $5,280 a year in federal funds for every full-time student. Over the years, the assistance has been under $2,000, jeopardizing its future. Full-time faculty make $22,000 a year at some colleges (Kleinhuizen, 1991b; L. McMillen, 1991).

*Summary.* This section has touched upon only a few of the failures in the government's educational programs for Native Americans. These primary problems are as follows.

1. Underenrollment at all levels, from the primary grades through college;
2. The need to adjust to a school with values sometimes dramatically different from those of the home;
3. The need to make the curriculum more relevant;
4. The special difficulties faced by children in boarding schools;
5. The unique hardships encountered by reservation-born American Indians who later live in and attend schools in large cities;
6. The language barrier faced by the many children who have little or no knowledge of English.

Other problems include lack of educational innovations (the BIA had no kindergartens until 1967) and failure to provide special education to children who need it. Health care received by Native Americans is another area in need of reform (Fuchs and Havighurst, 1972, pp. 106–117, 206–213).

### Health Care

For Native Americans "health care" is a misnomer, another broken promise in the array of unmet promises that the government has made. In 1987, one-third of Indians died before age 45, compared with only 11 percent of the general population. This dramatic difference arises out of their poverty, but also out of the lack of health services. There are only 96 doctors per 100,000 Native Americans compared to 208 for the general population. Similarly there are 251 nurses per 100,000 Native Americans contrasted to 672 per 100,000 for the nation as a whole (Coddington, 1991; Kanamine, 1991).

In 1955, the responsibility for health care for American Indians was transferred from the BIA to the Public Health Service (PHS), and although their health has improved markedly in the last three decades, serious problems remain. As is true in industrial development and education, advances in health care are hampered by the poverty and geographical isolation of the reservation. Also, as in the educational and economic sectors, health policies in effect initiate a cultural war in which American Indians must reject their traditions to secure better medical treatment (H. Johnson, 1969).

It is not merely that Native Americans have more disease and shorter life than the rest of the population. Indians have acute problems, in such areas as mental health, nutrition, the needs of the elderly, and alcoholism, that have been documented for generations but have only recently been addressed through innovative programs. Further improvement can be expected, but it will be some time before the gains make health care for them comparable to that of the general population.

Minority groups in the United States, including Native Americans, have made tremendous gains and will continue to do so in the years to come. But the rest of the population is not standing still. As Native-American income rises, so too does White income. As Native-American children stay in school longer, so too do White children. American-Indian health care improves, but so too does

White health care. Advances have been made, but the gap remains between the descendants of the first Americans and those of later arrivals. Testimony before Congress in 1982 was not encouraging. Half the members of the Papago tribe of Arizona are diabetic, for example. Low incomes, inadequate education, and poor health care spurred Native-American/White relations to take a dramatic turn in the 1960s and 1970s, during which time Native Americans demanded a better life in America (American Indian Policy Review Commission, 1976a; 1976b, pp. 71–73; 1976c; Campbell, 1983).

## PAN-INDIANISM

The growth of pan-Indian activism has been an important development in the last decades. *Pan-Indianism* refers to intertribal social movements in which several tribes, joined by culture but not by kinship, unite to confront an enemy. Proponents of this movement see American-Indian tribes as captive nations or internal colonies. They generally see the enemy as the federal government. Until recently, pan-Indian efforts have usually failed to overcome the cultural differences and distrust among tribal groups. There have, however, been successful efforts to unite, even in the past. The Iroquois are a confederation of six tribal groups dating back to the seventeenth century. The Ghost Dance briefly united the plains tribes during the 1880s, some of whom had earlier combined to withstand cavalry attacks. But these were the exceptions. It took nearly a century and a half of BIA policies to accomplish a significant level of unification (Cornell, 1987; Nagel, 1989; Snipp, 1986a, 1986b; Witt, 1970, pp. 94–95).

The National Congress of American Indians (NCAI), founded in 1944 in Denver, Colorado, was the first national organization representing American Indians. The NCAI registered itself as a lobby in Washington, D.C., hoping to make the American-Indian perspective heard. Concern about "White peoples' meddling" is reflected in the NCAI requirement that White members pay twice as much in dues. The NCAI has had its successes. Early in its history, it played an important role in creating the Indian Claims Commission, and later it pressured the BIA to abandon the practice of termination. It is still the most important civil rights organization for American Indians and uses tactics similar to those of the NAACP, although the problems facing African Americans and American Indians are legally and constitutionally different.

A more recent arrival is the more radical American Indian Movement (AIM), the most visible pan-Indian group. The AIM was founded in 1968 by Clyde Bellecourt (of the White Earth Chippewa) and Dennis Banks (of the Pine Ridge Oglala Sioux), both of whom then lived in Minneapolis. Initially AIM created a "patrol" to monitor police actions in order to document charges of police brutality. Eventually it promoted programs for alcohol rehabilitation and school reform. By 1972, AIM was nationally known not for its neighborhood-based reforms but for its aggressive confrontations with the BIA and law enforcement agencies (Jarvenpa, 1985; Lurie, 1971, p. 453; Mencarelli and Severin, 1975, pp. 145–158, 166–168).

## Fish-Ins and Alcatraz

*Fish-ins* began in 1964 to protest interference by Washington state officials with American Indians who were fishing, who, as they argued, in accordance with the 1854 Treaty of Medicine Creek and not subject to fine or imprisonment, even if they did violate White society's law. Protest was initially blocked by disunity and apathy, but several hundred Native Americans were convinced that civil disobedience was the only way. Legal battles followed, and the Supreme Court in 1968 confirmed the treaty rights. Other tribes continue to fight in the courts, but the fish-ins brought increased public awareness about the deprivations of Native Americans. One of the longest battles continues to the present for the Chippewas have rights to 50 percent of the fish, timber, and wildlife across the upper third of Wisconsin. In 1991, Wisconsin agreed with this long-standing treaty right, but Whites continue to demonstrate against what they feel is the unfair advantage extended to the Native Americans (Jolidon, 1990; Steiner, 1968, pp. 48–64).

The fish-ins were only the beginning. After the favorable Supreme Court decision in 1968, other events followed in quick succession. In 1969, members of the San Francisco Indian Center seized Alcatraz Island in San Francisco Bay. The thirteen-acre island was once a maximum-security federal prison that had been abandoned, with the government undecided about how to use it. The American Indians claimed "the excess property" in exchange for $24 in glass beads and cloth, following the precedent set in the sale of Manhattan more than three centuries earlier. They also outlined the striking similarities between Alcatraz and the typical reservation.

1. It is isolated from modern facilities and without adequate means of transportation.
2. It has no fresh running water.
3. It has inadequate sanitation facilities.
4. There are no oil or mineral rights.
5. There is no industry and so unemployment is very great.
6. There are no health care facilities.
7. The soil is rocky and nonproductive, and the land does not support game.
8. There are no educational facilities.
9. The population has always exceeded the land base.
10. The population has always been held as prisoners and kept dependent upon others (Sklansky, 1989, p. 44).

The protesters left the island more than a year later, and their desire to transform it into an American-Indian cultural center was ignored. Despite the outcome, the event gained international publicity for their cause. Red Power was born and those Native Americans who sympathized with the BIA were

*A group of Native Americans moves across Alcatraz, an island in San Francisco Bay and site of an 18-month demonstration in 1969-1970.*

branded either "Uncle Tomahawks" or "apples" (red on the outside, white on the inside).

## The Government Response

The BIA and the White House were not deaf to the cries for a new policy that involved Native Americans in its formulation. Nevertheless, no major breakthroughs came in the 1960s. Under presidents Kennedy and Johnson (1960–1968) reforms were made and an American Indian even became BIA commissioner, but policies remained much the same. The Nixon administration began its interaction with American Indians on a positive, historic note. Within seven months of taking office, President Nixon sent a special message to Congress. It proclaimed a commitment to self-determination for Native Americans and argued against either excessive paternalism or rapid termination. The message was only a declaration, however, and Native Americans waited to see what actions would be taken (Josephy, 1971, pp. 211–230).

In retrospect, the Nixon years (1969–1974) were among the most active and began with many positive moves. Federal expenditures for American Indians increased dramatically and most BIA area directors were American Indians. Several major land restorations took place, although not always with the president's enthusiastic support. In 1970 the Blue Lake of New Mexico was returned to the Taos, to whom it was sacred. Although the tribe viewed this heavily forested area as the holiest of places it had been seized in 1906 and made part of a national forest. As we have seen, Menominee County was restored to federal reservation status during this time, and Nixon dropped termination as a policy (Waugh, 1970).

Another significant step was passage of the Alaska Native Settlement Act of 1971. Alaskan natives—the Eskimos (or Inuits) and Aleuts—have maintained their claim to the land since Alaska was purchased from Russia in 1867. The federal government had allowed the natives to settle on about one-third of the land they claimed, but had not even granted them title to that land. The discovery of huge oil reserves in 1969 made the issue more explosive, as the state of Alaska auctioned off mineral rights, ignoring Eskimo occupation of the land. The Alaskan Federation of Natives (AFN), the major native Alaskan group, which had been organized in 1967, quickly moved to stop "the biggest land grab in the history of the U.S.," as the AFN termed it. The AFN-sponsored bill was revised by the Nixon administration, and a compromise was passed in late 1971. The final act, which fell short of the requests by the AFN, granted control and ownership of forty-four million acres to Alaska's 53,000 Eskimos, Aleuts, and other peoples and gave them a cash settlement of nearly $1 billion. Given the enormous pressures from oil companies and conservationists, however, the Native Claims Settlement Act can be regarded as one of the more reasonable agreements reached between the Native Americans and the government (Langdon, 1982; Nickerson, 1971).

## American-Indian Protests

The relatively sympathetic stance of the Nixon administration makes the militance and violence of American-Indian protest all the more difficult for the uninformed observer to understand. Four factors explain the increased violence of confrontations from 1969 to the present.

1. *Unkept promises.* During the early 1970s, the BIA and the White House made promises of new, innovative programs and greater self-determination that were not carried out.
2. *Indian unity and disunity.* More federal money in American Indians' hands, although put to positive use, also promoted power struggles among pan-Indian groups, among tribes, and within tribes.
3. *Greater militancy in other protests.* Many American Indians, especially the young and urban, felt that more militant actions by welfare and civil rights groups seemed to bring faster results.
4. *Government's reliance on a few token leaders.* The federal government, especially under Nixon, increasingly listened to the more conservative American-Indian leaders, as if they were the only people with legitimate grievances.

The last factor was especially apparent during the 1970s, when the government seemed reluctant to listen to even the long-established NCAI. By closing the door to those presenting grievances, the government ensured that it was only a matter of time before the first Americans would take new steps to be heard.

Little wonder, then, that the 1970s were marked by increasingly militant protests. One moderate group organized a summer-long caravan to reach the nation's capital just when the presidential election was being held in 1972. The Nixon administration, increasingly distrustful of protesting American Indians, refused to meet with them. The militant AIM then emerged as the leader of those frustrated by government unresponsiveness.

The most dramatic confrontation between Native Americans and government came early the next year in the Battle of Wounded Knee II. In January, AIM leader Russell Means led an unsuccessful drive to impeach Richard Wilson as tribal chairman of the Oglala Sioux tribe on the Pine Ridge reservation. In the next month Means, accompanied by some 300 supporters, started a 70-day occupation of Wounded Knee, South Dakota, site of the infamous cavalry assault in 1890 and now a part of the Pine Ridge reservation. The occupation received tremendous press coverage. A Harris nationwide survey in March 1973 found 93 percent of the population had heard of the occupation (*Current Opinion*, 1973). When asked with whom they sympathized more in the Wounded Knee dispute, 51 percent said the Native Americans, 21 percent the federal government, and 28 percent were unsure (Burnette and Koster, 1974).

*The 70-day occupation of Wounded Knee in 1972 reflected the frustration of militant American Indians with the federal government.*

Did this sympathy bring results? Negotiations between AIM and the federal government on the occupation itself brought no tangible results. Federal prosecutions were initiated against most participants. Although AIM leaders Means and Banks were eventually cleared of all charges, they faced prosecution on a number of felony charges. Means himself returned in 1974 to run against Wilson for tribal chairman and was narrowly defeated. After the 1973 protest demonstration in South Dakota, both Means and Banks found themselves facing new charges. Both men were eventually imprisoned. AIM, on the other hand, had less visibility as an organization since then. Russell Means wryly remarked in 1984, "We're not chic now. We're just Indians and we have to help ourselves" (Hentoff, 1984, p. 23; also see Matthiesson, 1983; Nagel, 1988; Roos et al., 1977; Trimble, 1976).

## Pan-Indianism: An Overview

Life on the Pine Ridge, South Dakota, reservation is typical of that on many reservations, with an unemployment and underemployment rate of 63 percent. Added to this are the extremely violent confrontations among conservative Sioux, AIM, and law enforcement officials. Two people died as a result of the Wounded Knee occupation, but in addition, between July 1973 and May 1976, 50 homicides took place on or near the reservation, with only 13 of them officially solved. Native-American life in the United States is not always that violent, nor is pan-Indianism as evident elsewhere as it is on the Pine Ridge reservation. The American-Indian community went through a major change in the late 1960s and 1970s not unlike that among Black Americans. The people also became more pragmatic, more accepting of different approaches. The NCAI, which works through lobbyists and the courts, enjoys the respect of most American Indian leaders. But AIM, even if not a unified, organized force in the late 1980s, has awakened Whites to the real grievances of American Indians and for this step has garnered the begrudging acceptance of many moderates (*Akwesasne Notes*, 1977; Bureau of Indian Affairs, 1973).

The results of pan-Indianism, however, have not all been productive, even when viewed from a perspective sympathetic to Native-American self-determination. National organizations are dominated by plains tribes, not only politically but culturally as well. Powwow styles of dancing, singing, and costuming derived from the Plains tradition are spreading nationwide as common cultural traits. This cultural dominance is not wrong in itself, but some tribes are finding tourists and even their own youths disappointed for failing to live up to misguided expectations of a supposed ethnic ideal (R. Thomas, 1970, pp. 128–143; Wax, 1971, pp. 148–151).

The aspect of the pan-Indian movement most visible to Whites has been violent confrontation with the federal government. To Native Americans, however, in numbers of participants, the most significant aspect of pan-Indianism is its religious, not political, character. Common forms of religious worship are the most powerful bonds among tribes today. The peyote cult or religion is well established and dates back to 1870. First a Southwest-based religion, it has spread since World War II among northern tribes. In 1918, the religious use of peyote, a plant that creates mild psychedelic effects, was organized as the Native American Church (NAC). The use of the substance is a relatively small part of a long and moving ritual. Because peyote is a hallucinogen, however, the government has been concerned about NAC use of it. Several states passed laws in the 1920s and 1930s prohibiting the use of peyote. The federal government and 23 states exempt the religious use of peyote from criminal penalties— a policy that defenders view as an application of the First Amendment guarantee of free exercise of religion. However, the state of Oregon does not accept peyotism; its refusal to do so became the center of a controversy that made its way to the United States Supreme Court in *Oregon* v. *Alfred Smith*, a Sioux. Eventually, in 1990, the Supreme Court held, by a 6–3 vote, that prosecuting people who use illegal drugs as part of religious rituals is not a violation of the First Amendment guarantee of religious freedom. Dissenting justices and civil libertarians worried that this ruling inevitably would be used against the rituals of "minor" (but not "major") religions. Indeed, Justice Sandra Day O'Conner called the majority opinion "incompatible with our nation's fundamental commitment to individual religious liberty" (Greenhouse, 1990, p. A10). The following year Oregon passed a law protecting the American-Indian use of peyote, but the specter of prosecution remains in much of the nation (Lawson and Morris, 1991).

Another area of concern is over the stockpiling of American-Indian relics, including burial remains. Contemporary Native Americans are increasingly seeking return of their ancestor's remains and artifacts, raising alarm among museums and archaeologists. Legislation is proposed which would require an inventory of such collections and provide for the return of materials if a claim can be substantiated. To many scholars, the ancient bones and burial artifacts are valuable clues to humanity's past. Yet, in part, this reflects a difference in cultural traditions. Western scientists have been dissecting cadavers for hundreds of years, but many tribes believe disturbing the graves of ancestors will bring spiritual sickness to the living. Today's Native Americans are asking for their traditions to be recognized as an expression of pluralist rather than assimilationist coexistence (G. Cowley, 1989).

Tribal sovereignty has begun to be recognized because of policy developments at the federal level and in the courts, but it is also under continuous attack because of issues related to economic development and natural resources.

## NATURAL RESOURCES: THE NEW BATTLEGROUND

The Native peoples have always been rooted in their land. It was their land that became the first source of tension and conflict with the Europeans. As the twenty-first century approaches, it is not surprising that land and the natural resources it holds continue to be major concerns.

It is important to realize that development needs to be defined in terms of a tribe's traditions. For example, both the White Mountain Apaches (Arizona) and the Yakima (Washington) have major, potentially marketable wildlife resources. The Apaches see their wildlife as commercial, and therefore operate a profitable tribal enterprise of selling trophy-quality elk hunts to wealthy non-American Indians for $10,000 or more per hunt. The Yakimas, however, argue that the animals were put there by the Creator and carefully regulate hunting by anyone, thereby foregoing potential income. Often the "outsider" who views resources on Native-American land fails to consider the local culture when shaping economic development (Cornell, 1991).

In 1975, the Council of Energy Resource Tribes (CERT) was formed by leaders of 25 of the West's largest tribes. Organized following the crippling oil embargo, CERT soon came to be viewed as a Native-American OPEC (Organization of Petroleum Exporting Countries). Like the international oil cartel, this new council reasoned that it could ensure more revenue from the vast mineral reserves. An estimated one-third of the nation's low-sulfur coal, half the privately owned uranium, 4 percent of the oil and gas, and substantial deposits of oil shale, tar sands, phosphate, and geothermal resources occur on federally recognized reservations. President Jimmy Carter provided a grant of $2 million to help the

THE MILWAUKEE JOURNAL
November 10, 1972

*"I don't think they're interested in colored beads anymore."*

American Indians to organize, open a Washington office, and hire legal help. By 1991, CERT had grown to encompass 45 tribes represented through their tribal chairpeople.

Reservations contain a wealth of resources. In the past, Native Americans have lacked the technical knowledge to negotiate beneficial agreements successfully with private corporations, and when they had such ability, the federal government often stepped in and made the final agreements more beneficial to the non-American Indians than to the residents of the reservations. Some of the early agreements reached by CERT were impressive. Skillful negotiating converted an Atlantic Richfield Company (ARCO) offer of $300,000 for an oil pipeline right-of-way on the Navajo reservation into a contract that will bring the tribe $78 million over 20 years. Recently, CERT has provided services to tribes monitoring nuclear waste management on their lands.

The CERT is not without its detractors even among Native Americans. Some expressed concern that early comparisons by CERT leaders to OPEC may have alienated potential support from the White community. Others question how much of this wealth will actually be seen by the average reservation resident and how much of CERT's activities is only an ego trip for the tribal chairpeople who head it. Furthermore, some feel that unchecked energy development on American-Indian lands could disrupt traditional culture and values and cause environmental pollution. There is even evidence that the federal government has decreased its assistance to American Indians, using as justification this new-found wealth, in a new version of the termination policy. Nevertheless, Native Americans seem to have little choice but to develop their mineral resources, using the increased revenue to diversify the tribal economies (Bureau of Indian Affairs, 1981, pp. 7–9; Cornell, 1987; Council of Energy Resource Tribes, 1986, 1991; Dorris, 1981, p. 63; Fialka, 1978; Jorgensen et al., 1978; LaDuke, 1980; Schmidt, 1982; Snipp, 1986b; R. Taylor, 1982; *Time*, 1979).

## GLANCING BACK AND LOOKING AHEAD

Both Black Americans and American Indians are more likely than Whites to have lower incomes, to suffer from poor health, and to experience prejudice and discrimination. Both groups have protested against these injustices for centuries. Beginning in the 1960s, these protests gained a new sense of urgency. But there the similarities between the nearly 29 million African Americans and the 1.4 million Native Americans in the United States end.

The reservation is not a ghetto. It is economically depressed, but the reservation is the home of the American-Indian people, if not physically, then ideologically. Furthermore, the reservation's isolation means that the frustrations of reservation life and the violent outbursts against them do not alarm large numbers of Whites as do disturbances in Black ghettos. The federal government, since the BIA was created in 1824, has had much greater control over Native Americans than over any other civilian group in the nation. For them, the federal government and White people are virtually synonymous. The typical White, however, tends to be more sympathetic, if not paternalistic, toward Native Americans than toward Blacks. Even during the Second Battle of Wounded Knee in 1973, public opinion polls showed nationwide support for the American-Indian cause (Sterba, 1973).

As Chapter 7 will show, African Americans have achieved a measure of recognition in Washington, D.C., that Native Americans have not. They are only 5 percent as numerous as the Black population, making their collective voice weaker. Only one Native American has served in Congress, and many of the Whites representing states with large numbers of American Indians have been their biggest foes.

Another enemy of the American Indian people is their disunity—full bloods are pitted against mixed bloods, reservation residents against city dwellers, tribe against tribe, conservative against militant. This disunity reflects the diversity of cultural backgrounds and historical experiences represented by the people collectively referred to as American Indians. It is also counterproductive when it comes to confronting a central government. Pan-Indianism has made tremendous strides since the weak alliances formed by a few tribes hundreds of years ago, but the current mood serves as much to split as to unify Native Americans nationally. Symptomatic of this were government hearings in 1989 that, rather than focusing on the BIA bureaucracy, quickly shifted attention to alleged corruption among American Indian leaders. A subject of investigation, Peter MacDonald, one of the founders of CERT, was pressured in 1989 to resign as Navajo Tribal Chairman.

The greatest challenge to and asset of the descendants of the first Americans is their land. Although only a small slice of what they once occupied, the land they still possess is a rich natural resource. It is barren and largely unproductive agriculturally, but it is unspoiled, relatively free of pollution, and often rich in natural resources. No wonder many large businesses and land developers covet their land. For Native Americans, the land they still occupy, as well as much of that occupied by other Americans, represents their roots, their homeland.

On Thanksgiving, 1988 one scholar noted that, according to tradition, at the first Thanksgiving in 1621 the Pilgrims and the Wampanoag ate together. The descendants of these celebrants increasingly sit at distant tables with thoughts of equality equally distant. Today's Native Americans are the "most undernourished, most short-lived, least educated, least healthy." For them, "that long ago Thanksgiving was not a milestone, not a promise. It was the last full meal" (Dorris, 1988).

## KEY TERMS

**crossover effect**  An effect that appears as previously high-scoring American Indian children become "below average" in intelligence when tests are given in English rather than their native languages.

**fish-ins**    Tribal protests over government interference with their traditional rights to fish as they would like.

**kickouts or pushouts**    American-Indian school dropouts, who leave behind an unhealthy academic environment.

**millenarian movements**    Movements, such as the Ghost Dance, that prophesize a cataclysm in the immediate future, followed by collective salvation.

**pan-Indianism**    Intertribal social movements in which several tribes, joined by culture but not by kinship, unite, usually to confront an enemy such as the federal government.

**setoffs**    Deductions from U.S. money due in settlements to Native Americans equal to the cost of federal services provided to the tribe.

## FOR FURTHER INFORMATION

Gretchen Bataille and Kathleen Sands (eds.) *American Indian Women Telling Their Lives.* Lincoln: University of Nebraska Press, 1984.

> Intriguing accounts that largely focus on everyday life, marriage, and the rearing of children.

Dee Brown, *Bury My Heart at Wounded Knee.* New York: Holt, Rinehart and Winston, 1971.

> Focuses on what the author calls the "incredible era of violence, greed, audacity, sentimentality, [and] undirected exuberance" toward Native Americans from 1860 to 1890.

Vine Deloria, Jr. *Custer Died For Your Sins: An Indian Manifesto.* New York: Avon, 1969.

> Although much has happened since Deloria wrote this book, it remains an excellent, readable explanation for non-American Indians about why Native Americans are tired of being oppressed. In often witty writing, he touches on termination policy, missionaries, American-Indian leadership, and the BIA.

Vine Deloria, Jr., and Clifford M. Lytle. *American Indians, American Justice.* Austin: University of Texas Press, 1983.

> The authors examine key legal concepts and decisions in the relationship between Native Americans and the U.S. courts.

Leonard Dinnerstein, Roger Nichols, and David M. Reimers. *Natives and Strangers*, 2nd ed. New York: Oxford University Press, 1990.

> A concise history of African Americans, American Indians, and immigration to the United States.

M. Annette Jaimes (ed.). *The State of Native America.* Boston: South End Press, 1992.

> Drawing mostly on Native American writers, Jaimes, a Juaneño/Yaqui, explores the various circumstances confronted by American Indians in the contemporary United States.

Edward Lazarus. *Black Hills White Justice.* New York: HarperCollins, 1991.

> A detailed account of the on-going legal fight of the Sioux nation from 1755 to the present.

Nicholas C. Peroff. *Menominee Drums.* Norman: University of Oklahoma Press, 1982.

> Political scientist Peroff traces the history of the Wisconsin tribe from termination through to the successful restoration of reservation rights in 1974.

Stephen L. Pevar. *The Rights of Indians and Tribes*, 2nd ed. Carbondale: Southern Illinois University Press, 1992.

> Completed under the auspices of the American Civil Liberties Union, this book summarizes Native American rights without resorting to too much legal jargon.

Linda Shorten. *Without Reserve: Stories from Urban Natives.* Edmonton: NeWest Press, 1991.

A collection of autobiographical profiles of individual Native people who live in urban Canada.

C. Matthew Snipp. *American Indians: The First of This Land.* New York: Russell Sage Foundation, 1989.

A detailed demographic study of American Indians, including analyses of housing, household composition, education, occupation, and migration.

Murray L. Wax. *Indian Americans: Unity and Diversity.* Englewood Cliffs, N.J.: Prentice-Hall, 1971.

Wax examines the contemporary life of the people and focuses on the ideological and assimilationist challenges facing them.

## Periodicals

Many Indian tribes publish regular newspapers and there are two national papers: *Akwesasne Notes* (1969) issued four times a year, and *Wassaja* (1972), which now comes out irregularly. Journals include the *American Indian Culture and Research Journal* (1977), a quarterly published by University of California, Los Angeles, *Indian Historian* (1967), a quarterly published by the American Indian Historical Society, and the *Journal of American Indian Education* (1961), published three times a year by Arizona State University.

## Chapter Seven

# THE MAKING OF
# BLACK AMERICANS
# IN A WHITE AMERICA

*Chapter Outline*

**Slavery**
Slave Codes
African Americans and Africa
The Attack on Slavery
**Slavery's Aftermath**
**The Challenge of Black Leadership**
The Politics of Accommodation
The Niagara Movement
**The Exodus Northward**
**Reemergence of Black Protest**
**The Civil Rights Movement**
Struggle to Desegregate the Schools

Civil Disobedience
The Battle of Birmingham
**Explaining Urban Violence**
Rising Expectations and Relative Deprivation
Developing a National Consciousness
**Black Power**
**Black Nationalism**
Religious Nationalism
Cultural Nationalism
**Glancing Back and Looking Ahead**
**Key Terms**
**For Further Information**

---

### ✷ *HIGHLIGHTS* ✷

The Black presence in America began almost simultaneously with permanent White settlement. Unlike Europeans, however, the African people were brought involuntarily and in bondage. The end of slavery heralded new political rights during Reconstruction, but this was a short-lived era of dignity. The twentieth century witnessed the movement of Blacks northward and the beginning of a Black protest movement that was assisted by some sympathetic Whites.

Despite advocacy of nonviolence by leaders such as the Reverend Martin Luther King, Jr., the civil rights movement was met with violent resistance throughout the South. In the middle 1960s, the nation's attention was diverted to urban violence in the North and West. Blacks responded to the absence of significant change despite years of protest by advocating Black Power and by showing renewed interest in Black nationalism.

---

The United States, with more than 30 million Blacks (or African Americans), has the sixth largest Black population in the world—only Brazil, Ethiopia, Nigeria, South Africa, and Zaire have larger Black populations. Despite their large numbers, Blacks in this country have had virtually no roles in major national and political decisions and have been allowed only a peripheral role in many crucial decisions influencing their own destiny.

To a significant degree the history of African Americans is the history of the United States. Black people accompanied the first explorers, and a Black man was among the first to die in the American Revolution. Their enslavement was responsible for the South's wealth in the nineteenth century and led to the country's most violent domestic strife. Their continued subordination has led to sporadic outbreaks of violence in the rural South and throughout urban America. This chapter will concentrate on the history of Black Americans into the 1990s and on the formation of the social institutions, the subject of Chapter 8.

The Black experience in what came to be the United States began as something less than citizenship yet slightly better than slavery. In 1619, twenty Africans arrived in Jamestown as indentured servants. Their children were born free people. These Blacks in the British colonies were not the first in the New World, however, for some Blacks had accompanied Spanish explorers, perhaps even Columbus. But all this is a historical footnote. By the 1660s, the British colonies had passed laws making Africans slaves for life, forbidding interracial marriages, and making children of slaves bear the status of their mother. Slavery had begun in North America; more than three centuries later we still with its legacy.

# SLAVERY

Slavery seems far removed from the debates over issues that divide Whites and Blacks today. Both contemporary institutional and individual racism, however, which are central to today's conflicts, have their origins in the institution of slavery. Slavery was not merely a single aspect of American society for three centuries, it has been an essential part of our country's life. For nearly half of this country's history, slavery not only was tolerated, but was legally protected by the Constitution and the Supreme Court. Because it was so fundamental to our culture, it continues to exert influence on Black-White relations in the 1990s (Berg, 1975; Noel, 1972, p. 3).

## Slave Codes

Slavery in the United States rested on four central conditions: first, that slavery was for life and was inherited; second, that slaves were considered to be merely property; third, that slaves were denied rights; and fourth, that coercion was used to maintain the system (Noel, 1972, pp. 4, 8). As slavery developed in colonial America and the United States (see Table 7.1), *slave codes* were created to clarify the position of slaves. Although the rules varied from state to state and from time to time, and were not always enforced, the more common features demonstrate how completely subjugated the Africans were.

---

**TABLE 7.1**   Black Population, 1790–2000

Blacks accounted for a decreasing proportion of the total population until the 1940s primarily because White immigration to the United States far outdistanced population growth by Blacks.

| Census | Black Population (in thousands) | Black Percentage of Total Population |
|---|---|---|
| 1790 | 757 | 19.3 |
| 1810 | 1,378 | 19.0 |
| 1830 | 2,329 | 18.1 |
| 1850 | 3,639 | 15.7 |
| 1870 | 4,880 | 12.7 |
| 1890 | 7,489 | 11.9 |
| 1910 | 9,828 | 10.7 |
| 1930 | 11,891 | 9.7 |
| 1950 | 15,042 | 10.0 |
| 1970 | 22,581 | 11.1 |
| 1990 | 29,986 | 12.1 |
| 1995 (projection) | 33,199 | 12.8 |
| 2000 (projection) | 35,129 | 13.1 |

*Source:* Bureau of the Census, 1960, p. 9; 1975; 1985b; 1991a, pp. 16, 22.

1. A slave could not marry or even meet with a free Black.
2. Marriage between slaves was not legally recognized.
3. A slave could not buy or sell anything unless by special arrangement.
4. A slave could not possess weapons or liquor.
5. A slave could not quarrel with or use abusive language with Whites.
6. A slave could not possess property (including money), except as allowed by his or her master.
7. A slave could make no will nor could he or she inherit anything.
8. A slave could not make a contract or hire himself or herself out.
9. Slaves could not leave a plantation without a pass noting their destination and time of return.
10. No one, including Whites, was to teach slaves (and in some areas even free Blacks) to read or write, or to give them books, including the Bible.
11. Slaves could not gamble and had to obey established curfews.
12. A slave could not testify except against another slave (Elkins, 1959, pp. 59–60; Franklin and Moss, 1988; Stampp, 1956, pp. 192–236).

Violations of these rules were dealt with in a variety of ways. Mutilation and branding were not unknown. Imprisonment was rare; most violators were whipped. A master was virtually immune from prosecution for any physical abuse of slaves. Because slaves could not testify in court, a White's actions toward enslaved African Americans was practically above the law.

Slavery, as enforced through the slave codes, controlled and determined all facets of the lives of the enslaved Africans. The organization of family life and religious worship were no exceptions. Naturally, the Africans brought their own cultural traditions. In Africa, people had been accustomed to a closely regulated family life and a rigidly enforced moral code. The slave trade rendered it impossible for them to retain family ties in the New World. The demand for male Africans created an extreme imbalance of the sexes of the slave population. It was not until 1840, two centuries after African slave labor had begun, that the number of Black women equaled the number of Black men in America. Religious life in Africa was rich with rituals and beliefs, but, like family structures, the religious practices of the slaves were to undergo major transformation in the New World (Du Bois, 1970, pp. 18–19; Stampp, 1956, pp. 340, 371).

The slave family had no standing in law. Marriages among slaves were not legally recognized and masters rarely respected them in selling adults or children. Slave breeding—sustained efforts to maximize the number of offspring—was practiced with little attention to the emotional needs of the slaves themselves. The master, not the parents, decided at what age children should begin working in the fields. The slave family could not offer its children shelter or security, rewards or punishments. The man's only recognized family role was that of siring offspring, being the sex partner of a woman. In fact, slave men were often identified as if they were the woman's possession—"Nancy's Tom." Southern law consistently ruled that "the father of a slave is unknown to our law." This is not to imply that the male slave did not occupy an important economic role. Men held virtually all the managerial positions open to slaves (Bryce-Laporte, 1975; Elkins, 1959, p. 55; Record and Record, 1975).

Unlike the family, which slavery victimized, a strong religious tradition survived slavery. In fact, a master wishing to do "God's work on earth" would encourage the slave church, finding it functional in dominating the slaves. Of course, African religions were forbidden and the White people's Christianity flourished, but Blacks still used West African concepts in the totally new way of life caused by slavery. The preacher maintained an intense, dependent relationship with the congregation, similar to the role played by the elder in West Africa. The Christianity to which the slaves were introduced stressed obeying the master. Complete surrender to Whites meant salvation and eternal happiness in the hereafter. To question God's will, to fight slavery, caused everlasting damnation. Obviously this twisted version of Christianity was intended to make slaves acquiesce to their masters' wishes in return for reward after death. However, to some degree religion did keep alive in slaves the desire for freedom and to some extent it formed the basis of their struggle for freedom: nightly prayer meetings and singing gave a sense of unity and common destiny necessary for that struggle. On a more personal level, religion made the slaves' daily lives bearable (Frazier, 1964; Rawick, 1972, pp. 30–52; Stampp, 1956).

## African Americans and Africa

The importance of Africa to Black Americans can be seen in the aspects of African culture that became integral parts of life in the United States for Blacks. There was and still is a great deal of debate over whether and how much African culture survived slavery. Black historians W. E. B. Du Bois (1939) and Carter Woodson (1968), along with the respected White anthropologist Melville Herskovits (1941, 1943), have all argued persuasively for the continued influence of the African heritage.

Participants in the debate over the survival of African culture through slavery concur on several points.

1. Africa not only produced cultures worthy of study, it produced cultures as glorious as those found in Europe.
2. In Brazil and the Caribbean Islands, which also had slavery, it is easier to recognize the continuity of African culture in the lives of African Americans today. The White South put more pressure on slaves to assimilate. Furthermore, a significantly higher proportion of slaves in the United States were born in America and not Africa. As a result slaves in the United States had more limited awareness of African culture (O. Patterson, 1977).
3. The survival of African culture among Black Americans can be most easily documented in folklore, religion, music, and aspects of social organization. African culture, like any other culture, is not like clothing that can be taken off and thrown away. Many new cultures emerged as slaves drew upon the

older culture of Africa and adapted it to their American situation (Rawick, 1972, p. 6; Vass, 1979).

4. Most of the distinctive aspects of Black life today originate in the poverty and segregation created by slavery, not in Africa's rich cultural traditions.

Africa has and will always have an importance to Blacks that many Blacks and most Whites do not appreciate, and this importance is unlikely to be influenced by the continued debate over which aspects of Black life today can be traced back to African culture. The significance of Africa to Black Americans is one of the most easily identifiable themes in the Black experience. During certain periods (the 1920s and the late 1960s), the Black cultural tradition was the rallying point of many Blacks, especially those living in the cities. Recent studies continue to document the survival of African culture in North America. Research on the Sea Islands along the coast of South Carolina and Georgia shows movement and dance among Blacks similar to that in African folklore. The Sea Island inhabitants have been isolated from the mainland and therefore are less assimilated into the rest of society (Toner, 1987; Twining, 1985). The reality of African culture in America rests not in its integrity or availability to scientific study, as in the Sea Islands study, but in the extent to which it becomes real and significant to African Americans (Blauner, 1972, p. 153).

## The Attack on Slavery

Although the slave was vulnerable to his or her owner's wishes, slavery as an institution was vulnerable to outside opinion. For a generation after the American Revolution, restrictions on slaves increased as Southerners accepted slavery as permanent. Slave revolts and antislavery propaganda only accelerated the intensity of oppression. This change led to the ironic situation that as slavery was attacked from within and without, it became harsher and its defenders more outspoken in asserting what they saw as its benefits (Fitzhugh, 1857).

The antislavery or *abolitionist* movement involved both Whites and free Blacks. Many Whites who opposed slavery, such as Abraham Lincoln, did not believe in racial equality. In their minds slavery was a moral evil but racial equality was unimaginable. This apparent inconsistency did not lessen the emotional fervor of the efforts to end slavery. Antislavery societies had been founded even before the American Revolution, but the Constitution dealt the antislavery movement a blow. In order to appease the South, the writers of the Constitution recognized and legitimized slavery's existence. The Constitution even allowed slavery to increase Southern political power. A slave was counted as three-fifths of a person in determining population for representation in the House of Representatives.

Another aspect of Black enslavement was resistance to servitude by the slaves themselves. Slaves did revolt and between 40,000 and 100,000 actually escaped from the South and slavery. Yet fugitive slave acts provided for the return of slaves even in free states. Enslaved Blacks who did not attempt escape, which, in failure, often led to death, resisted slavery through such means as passive resistance. Slaves feigned clumsiness or illness; pretended not to understand, see, or hear; ridiculed Whites with mocking, subtle humor their masters did not comprehend; and destroyed farm implements and committed similar acts of sabotage (Bauer and Bauer, 1942; Bennett, 1966, p. 136).

## SLAVERY'S AFTERMATH

On January 1, 1863, President Lincoln issued the Emancipation Proclamation. The document created hope in slaves in the South, but many Union soldiers resigned rather than participate in a struggle to free slaves. The proclamation freed slaves only in the Confederacy, over which the president had no control. The 800,000 slaves in the border states were unaffected. The proclamation was a war measure effective in gaining the support of European nations for the Union cause. Shortly after the surrender of the Confederacy in 1865, abolition became a fact when the Thirteenth Amendment abolished slavery throughout the nation.

From 1867 to 1877, during the period called Reconstruction, Black-White relations in the South were unlike what they had ever been. The Reconstruction Act of 1867 put each Southern state under a military governor until a new state constitution could be written with Blacks fully participating in the process. Whites and Blacks married each other, went to public schools and state universities together, and rode side by side on trains and streetcars. The Black codes that the former Confederate states passed in 1865 and 1866 to replace the slave codes were set aside. The most conspicuous evidence of the new position of Blacks was their presence in elected office. In 1870, the Fifteenth Amendment was ratified, prohibiting the denial of the right to vote on grounds of race, color, or previous condition of servitude. Black men put their vote to good use; Blacks were elected as six lieutenant governors, sixteen major state officials, twenty congressmen, and two senators. Despite accusations that they were corrupt, Black officials and Black-dominated legislatures created new and progressive state constitutions. Black political organizations, such as the Union League and the Loyal League, rivaled the church as the focus of community organization (Bennett, 1965, pp. 79–80; 1966, pp. 199–200; Du Bois, 1969a, pp. 711–729).

With the fall of Reconstruction governments, segregation became entrenched in the South. Evidence of Jim Crow's reign was apparent by the close of the nineteenth century. The term *Jim Crow* appears to have its origin in a dance tune, but by the 1890s it was synonymous with segregation and referred to the statutes that kept African Americans in an inferior position. Laws, C. Vann Woodward argues, were not always "an adequate index of the extent and prevalence of segregation and discriminatory practices in the South" (1974, p. 102). Segregation often preceded laws and often went beyond their provisions. The institutionalization of segregation gave White supremacy its ultimate authority. In 1896, the Supreme Court ruled in *Plessy* v. *Ferguson* that state laws requiring "separate but equal" accommodations for Blacks were a "reasonable" use of state government power (Bennett, 1966, p. 232; Woodward, 1974, pp. 7, 102).

It was in the political sphere that Jim Crow exacted its price soonest. In 1898, the Court's decision *Williams* v. *Mississippi* declared constitutional the use of poll taxes, literacy tests, and residential requirements to discourage Blacks from voting. In Louisiana that year, 130,000 Blacks were registered to vote. Eight years later only 1,342 were. Even all these measures still did not deprive all African Americans of the vote, and so White supremacists erected a final obstacle. By the turn of the century, the South had a one-party system, making the primary the significant contest and the general election a mere rubber stamp. Beginning with South Carolina in 1896 and spreading to 12 other states within 20 years, statewide Democratic primaries were adopted. The party explicitly excluded Blacks from voting, which was constitutional because the party was defined as a private organization free to define its membership. The *White primary* brought a virtual end to the political gains of Reconstruction (Lacy, 1972, pp. 108–112; Lewinson, 1965; C. Woodward, 1974, pp. 7, 84–85, 102).

## THE CHALLENGE OF BLACK LEADERSHIP

The institutionalization of White supremacy precipitated different responses from African Americans, just as slavery had. In the late 1800s and early 1900s a number of articulate Blacks attempted to lead the first generation of freeborn Black Americans. Most prominent were Booker T. Washington and W. E. B. Du Bois. The personalities as well as the ideas of these two men contrasted with one another. Washington was born a slave in 1856 on a Virginia plantation. He worked in coal mines after emancipation and attended elementary school. Through hard work and driving ambition, Washington became the head of an educational institute for Blacks in Tuskegee, Alabama. Within 15 years his leadership brought Tuskegee Institute national recognition and made him a national figure. Du Bois, on the other hand, was born in 1868 of a free family in Massachusetts. He attended Fisk University and the University of Berlin, and became the first Black to receive a doctorate from Harvard. Washington died in 1915, while Du Bois died in self-imposed exile in Africa in 1963.

### The Politics of Accommodation

Washington's approach to White supremacy is referred to as the *politics of accommodation.* He was willing to forgo social equality until White people saw Blacks as deserving of it. Perhaps his most famous speech was the one made in Atlanta September 18, 1895, to an audience that was mostly White, and mostly wealthy. Introduced by the governor of Georgia as "a representative of Negro enterprise and Negro civilization," Washington made a five-minute speech in which he pledged the continued dedication of Blacks to Whites.

As we have proved our loyalty to you in the past, in nursing your children, watching by the sick-bed of your mothers and fathers, and often following them with tear-dimmed eyes to their graves, so in the future, in our humble way, we shall stand by you with a devotion that no foreigner can approach, ready to lay down our lives, if need be, in defense of yours (1900, p. 221).

The speech catapulted Washington into the public forum, and he became the anointed spokesperson for Blacks for the next 20 years. President Grover Cleveland congratulated Washington for the "new hope" he gave Blacks. Washington's essential theme was compromise. Unlike Frederick Douglass, who demanded for Blacks the same rights as Whites had, Washington asked that Blacks receive more education because it would be a wise investment for Whites to make. Racial hatred he referred to as "the great and intricate problem which God has laid at the doors of the South." Blacks' goal should be economic respectability. Washington's accommodative attitude ensured his popularity with Whites. His recognition by Whites contributed to his large following of Blacks, who were not used to seeing their leaders achieve fame among Whites (Hawkins, 1962; Logan, 1954, pp. 275–313; Pinkney, 1987).

It is easy in retrospect to be critical of Washington and to write him off as simply a product of his times. Booker T. Washington entered the public arena when the more militant proposals of Douglass had been buried. Black politicians were losing political contests and influence. To become influential as a Black, Washington reasoned, required White acceptance. His image as an accommodator allowed him to fight discrimination covertly. He assisted presidents Roosevelt and Taft in appointing Blacks to patronage positions. Washington's goal was for African Americans eventually to have the same rights and opportunities as Whites. Just as people disagree with leaders today, some Blacks disagreed over the means that Washington chose to reach that goal. No African American was more outspoken in his criticism of the politics of accommodation than W. E. B. Du Bois (Harlan, 1970, 1971, 1972; Hawkins, 1962, p. vii; Meier, 1957; Meier and Rudwick, 1966, pp. 180–181; K. Miller, 1903; S. Spencer, 1955, pp. 125–143).

## The Niagara Movement

The rivalry of Washington and Du Bois has been overdramatized. Actually they enjoyed fairly cordial relations for some time. In 1900, Washington recommended Du Bois, at his request, to be superintendent of Black schools in Washington, D.C. By the time the Niagara Movement arose in 1905, however, relations between the two had cooled. Du Bois spoke critically of Washington's influence, arguing that his power was used to stifle African Americans such as himself who spoke out against the politics of accommodation. He also charged that Washington had caused the transfer of funds from academic programs to vocational education. Du Bois's greatest objection to Washington's statements was that they encouraged Whites to place the burden of the Blacks' problems on the Blacks themselves (Du Bois, 1961, pp. 42–54; see also Broderick, 1959, pp. 62–75; Hawkins, 1962, p. vii).

As an alternative to Washington's program, Du Bois advocated the theory of the *talented tenth* (1903), which reflected his atypical educational background. Unlike Washington, Du Bois was not at home with both intellectuals and share-croppers. Although the very words *talented tenth* have an aristocratic ring to them, Du Bois argued that the privileged Blacks must serve the other 90 percent. This argument was also Du Bois's way of criticizing Washington's emphasis on vocational education. He thought education for African Americans should em-phasize academics, which would be more likely to improve their position. Drawing upon the talented tenth, Du Bois invited 29 Blacks to participate in a strategy session near Niagara Falls in 1905. Out of a series of meetings came several demands that unmistakably placed the responsibility for the problems facing African Americans on the shoulders of Whites.

The Niagara Movement, as it came to be called, was closely monitored by Booker T. Washington. Du Bois encountered difficulty gaining financial support and recruiting prominent people, and Du Bois himself was to write: "My leader-ship was solely of ideas. I never was, nor ever will be, personally popular" (1968, p. 303). The movement's legacy was the education of a new generation of African Americans in the politics of protest. After 1910, the Niagara Movement ceased to hold annual conventions. In 1909, however, the National Association for the Advancement of Colored People (NAACP), with White and Black mem-bers, was founded by the Niagara Movement leaders. It was through the work of the NAACP that the Niagara Movement accomplished most of the goals set forth in 1905. The NAACP also marked the merging of White liberalism and Black militancy, a coalition unknown since the end of the abolition movement (Bennett, 1966, p. 281; Rudwick, 1957).

## THE EXODUS NORTHWARD

The most significant event for African Americans during the first half of the twentieth century was not in the realm of legal or social rights, but the demo-graphic change in distribution of the Black people. In 1900, 90 percent of Blacks lived in the South. As shown in Figure 7.1, Blacks have moved out of the South and into the West and North, especially the urban areas in those regions, during the post-Civil War period and continuing through the 1950s and 1960s. How-ever, most African Americans still live in the South as of 1990.

The movement called the "Great Migration of the World War I Era" set in motion in exodus that continued into the 1960s. Life in the North was generally better than it had been in the South, where agricultural conditions had con-siderably worsened. Although the migrants entered the job market at the bottom and lived in the worst housing the North offered, they were still better off than in the rural South. The principal reason for Black migration out of the South was similar to the motivation for the many millions of Europeans who came to the

**FIGURE 7.1** Migration of Black Americans

This map shows the origin of Black Americans based on their residence in 1980. It shows net internal migration out of the southeastern part of the United States.

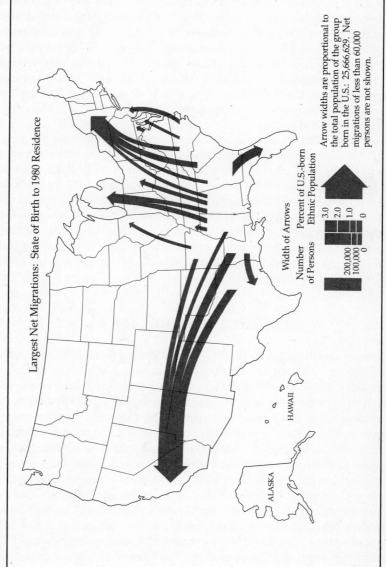

Largest Net Migrations: State of Birth to 1980 Residence

Width of Arrows    Percent of U.S.-born
                   Ethnic Population
                   3.0
                   2.0
                   1.0
                   0

Number             200,000
of Persons         100,000
                   0

Arrow widths are proportional to
the total population of the group
born in the U.S.: 25,666,629. Net
migrations of less than 60,000
persons are not shown.

ALASKA

HAWAII

*Source:* Reprinted with permission of Macmillan Publishing Company from *We the People: An Atlas of Ethnic Diversity,* p. 148, by James Paul Allen and Eugene James Turner. Copyright © 1988 by Macmillan Publishing Company, a Division of Macmillan, Inc.

United States: the search for better economic opportunities (Franklin and Moss, 1988; C. Johnson, 1923; Lacy, 1972, pp. 139–140; Meier and Rudwick, 1966, pp. 191–192).

The debate over problems between the races is not merely academic. The pattern of violence, with Blacks usually the victims, started in the South during Reconstruction, continued into the twentieth century, and moved northward. In 1917 a riot in East St. Louis, Illinois, claimed the lives of 39 Blacks and 9 Whites. The several days of violence resulted from White fear of social and economic gains made by Blacks. The summer of 1919 saw so much violence that it is commonly referred to as the "red summer." Twenty-six riots broke out throughout the country as returning White soldiers feared the new competition that Blacks represented. This period of violence against African Americans also saw a resurgence of the Ku Klux Klan, which at its height had nearly 9 million members (Bonacich, 1976; Grimshaw, 1969, pp. 60–116; Schaefer, 1969, p. 20; 1971, pp. 146–151; 1980).

The Competition between African Americans and Whites for jobs was short-lived. The unionization of industrial plants by the all-white American Federation of Labor (AFL) generally meant expulsion of all Blacks, regardless of skills or seniority. The National Urban League, founded in 1911 by Blacks and Whites allied with Booker T. Washington, wrestled unsuccessfully with the mass unemployment of Blacks. The NAACP did not involve itself at this time with job discrimination. Basically the needs and frustrations of African Americans in the growing ghettos of the North were unmet by the existing organizations (Bennett, 1966, pp. 294–295; Franklin and Moss, 1988; Lacy, 1972, pp. 143–144; Meier and Rudwick, 1966, pp. 196–200).


## REEMERGENCE OF BLACK PROTEST

American involvement in World War II signaled prosperity for both Whites and Blacks. Nearly a million African Americans served in the military in rigidly segregated units. Generally Blacks had a better opportunity to serve in World War II than in previous military engagements, but efforts by Blacks to contribute to the war effort at home were hampered by discriminatory practices in defense plants. A. Philip Randolph (1971), president of the Brotherhood of Sleeping Car Porters, threatened to lead 100,000 Blacks in a march on Washington in 1941 to ensure their employment. Randolph's proposed tactic was nonviolent direct action, which he modeled on Mahatma Ghandi's practices in India. Randolph made it clear that he intended the march to be all Black, because he saw it as neither necessary nor desirable for Whites to lead Blacks to their own liberation. President Franklin Roosevelt responded to the pressure and agreed to issue an executive order prohibiting discrimination if Randolph would call off the march. Although the order and the Fair Employment Practices Commission (FEPC) it set up did not fulfill the original promises, a precedent had been established for federal intervention in job discrimination (Garfinkel, 1959).

*Until 1948, African Americans were forced to serve in segregated units in the armed forces. Most recently, in the 1991 Persian Gulf War, African Americans served in disproportionately large numbers.*

Racial turmoil during World War II was not limited to threatened marches. Racial disturbances occurred in cities throughout the country, with the worst riot in Detroit in June 1943. In that case President Roosevelt sent in 6,000 soldiers to quell the violence that left 25 Blacks and 9 Whites dead. The racial disorders were paralleled by a growth in civil disobedience as a means to achieve equality for Blacks. The Congress of Racial Equality (CORE) was founded in 1942 to fight discrimination with nonviolent direct action. This biracial group used sit-ins to open restaurants to Black patrons in Chicago, Baltimore, and Los Angeles. In 1947, CORE sent "freedom riders" to test a court ruling that prohibited segregation in interstate bus travel. In contrast to the red summer of 1919, the end of World War II was not followed by widespread racial violence, in part, because the continued expansion of the postwar economy reduced competition between Whites and Blacks for employment (Grimshaw, 1969, pp. 136–183; Meier and Rudwick, 1966, pp. 217–219; Rustin, 1942).

The war years and the period following saw several Supreme Court decisions that suggested that the high court was moving away from tolerating racial inequities. The White primary elections endorsed in Jim Crow's formative period were finally challenged in the 1944 *Smith* v. *Allwright* decision. A particularly repugnant legal device for relegating African Americans to second-class status was restrictive covenants. A *restrictive covenant* was a private contract entered into by neighborhood property owners stipulating that property could not be sold or rented to certain minority groups, thus ensuring that they could not live in the area. In 1948, the Supreme Court finally declared in *Shelley* v. *Kramer* that restrictive covenants were not constitutional, although it did not actually attack their discriminatory nature. The victory was in many ways less substantial than symbolic of the new willingness by the Supreme Court to uphold the rights of Black citizens. The effectiveness of the victory was limited, for many states simply passed new devices to frustrate the Black electorate (Commission on Civil Rights, 1963, pp. 109–111, 139; Hornsby, 1975, p. 71; Marshall, 1957).

The Democratic administrations of the late 1940s and early 1950s made a number of promises to Black Americans. The party adopted a strong civil rights platform, but its provisions were not enacted. Once again, union president Randolph threatened Washington, D.C., with a massive march. This time he insisted that as long as Blacks were subjected to a peacetime draft, the military must be desegregated. President Truman responded by issuing Executive Order No. 9981 on July 26, 1948, desegregating the armed forces. The Army abolished its quota system in 1950, and training camps for the Korean War were integrated. Desegregation was not complete, however, especially in the reserves and the National Guard, and even today charges of racial favoritism confront the armed forces. Whatever its shortcomings, the desegregation order offered Blacks an alternative to segregated civilian life (Moskos, 1966).

## THE CIVIL RIGHTS MOVEMENT

It is difficult to say exactly when a social movement begins or ends. Usually a movement's ideas or tactics precede the actual mobilization of people and continue long after the movement's driving force has been replaced by new ideals and techniques. This description applies to the civil rights movement and its successor, the continuing struggle for African American freedom. The civil rights movement gained momentum with a Supreme Court decision in 1954 and ended as a major force in Black America with the civil disorders of 1965 through 1968. Even prior to 1954, there were some confrontations to White supremacy— the CORE sit-ins of 1942 and efforts to desegregate buses in Baton Rouge, Louisiana in 1953. Beginning in 1954, toppling the traditional barriers to full rights for Blacks was the rule, not the exception.

### Struggle to Desegregate the Schools

For the majority of Black children, public school education meant attending segregated schools. Southern school districts assigned children to school by race, rather than by neighborhood, a practice that constitutes *de jure* segregation. It was this form of legal humiliation that was attacked in the landmark decree of *Linda Brown et al.* v. *Board of Education of Topeka*.

Seven-year-old Linda Brown was not permitted to enroll in the grade school four blocks from her home in Topeka, Kansas. Rather, school board policy dictated that she attend the Black school almost two miles from her home. This

*Linda Brown, of* Brown v. Board of Education, *standing in front of the school near her home that she could not attend because the schools of Topeka, Kansas were segregated.*

denial led to the NAACP Legal Defense and Educational Fund to bring suit on behalf of Linda Brown and 12 other Black children. The NAACP argued that the Fourteenth Amendment was intended to rule out segregation in public schools. The NAACP suit was supported by briefs filed by labor, Jewish organizations, and the solicitor general of the United States, who represented the federal government. Chief Justice Earl Warren wrote the unanimous opinion that "in the field of public education the doctrine of 'separate but equal' has no place. Separate educational facilities are inherently unequal."

The freedom that African Americans saw in their grasp at the time of the *Brown* decision essentially amounted to a reaffirmation of American values. What Blacks sought was assimilation into White American society. The motivation for the *Brown* suit came not merely because Black schools were inferior, although they undoubtedly were. Blacks were assigned to poorly ventilated and dilapidated buildings, overcrowded classrooms, and unqualified teachers. Less money was spent on Black schools than on White schools throughout the South, in both rural and metropolitan areas. The issue was not such tangible factors, however, but the intangible factor of not being allowed to go to school with

Whites. All-Black schools could not be equal to all-White schools. Even in this victory, Blacks were reaffirming White society and the importance of an integrated educational experience.

Although *Brown* marked the beginning of the civil rights movement, the reaction to it showed just how deeply held prejudice was in the South. Resistance to court-ordered desegregation took many forms—some people called for impeachment of all the Supreme Court justices, others petitioned Congress to declare the Fourteenth Amendment unconstitutional, cities closed schools rather than comply, and the National Guard was even used to block Black students from entering a previously all-White high school in Little Rock, Arkansas (Commission on Civil Rights, 1963, pp. 152–156). The most enduring resistance was formation of the White Citizens' Councils. Founded in Mississippi, these councils spread throughout the South and claimed up to half a million members. Citizens' Councils assisted in opening private all-White schools to evade the Supreme Court edict. These "freedom schools," as they were called, enrolled an estimated 300,000 White children by 1970 (H. Carter, 1959; N. McMillen, 1971).

The issue of school desegregation was extended to higher education, and Mississippi state troops and federal forces confronted each other over the 1962 admission of James Meredith, the first African American admitted to the University of Mississippi. Scores were injured and two killed in this clash between segregationists and the law. A similar defiant stand was taken a year later by Governor George Wallace, who "stood in the schoolhouse door" to block two Blacks from enrolling in the University of Alabama. President Kennedy federalized the Alabama National Guard in order to guarantee admission of the students (Commission on Civil Rights, 1974c). *Brown* did not resolve the school controversy and questions remain unanswered. More recently the issue of school segregation resulting from neighborhood segregation has been debated. In the next chapter another form of segregation, called *de facto*, is examined more closely.

## Civil Disobedience

The success of a year-long boycott of city buses in Montgomery, Alabama dealt Jim Crow another setback. On December 1, 1955, Rosa Parks defied the law and refused to give her seat on a crowded bus to a White man. Her defiance led to organization of the Montgomery Improvement Association, headed by 26-year-old Martin Luther King, Jr., a Baptist minister with a Ph.D. from Boston University. The bus boycott was the first of many instances in which nonviolent direct action was employed as a means of obtaining for Blacks the rights Whites already enjoyed. Initially the boycott protested discourtesies to Blacks and asked that Black drivers be hired for bus routes in predominantly Black areas. Eventually the demands included the outright end of segregated seating. The *Brown* decision woke up all of America to racial injustice, but the Montgomery boycott marked a significant shift away from the historic reliance on NAACP court battles (Killian, 1975, pp. 49–51).

The belief that individuals have the right to disobey the law under certain circumstances was not new, and it had been used by Blacks before. Under King's leadership, however, *civil disobedience* became a widely used tactic and even gained a measure of acceptability among some prominent Whites. King, in his celebrated "Letter from the Birmingham Jail" clearly distinguished between the laws to be obeyed and disobeyed: "A just law is a man-made law of God. An unjust law is a code that is out of harmony with the moral law" (1963, p. 82). In disobeying unjust laws, King developed this strategy.

1. *Active* nonviolent resistance to evil
2. Not seeking to defeat or humiliate opponents, but to win their friendship and understanding
3. Attacking the forces of evil rather than the people who happen to be doing the evil
4. Willingness to accept suffering without retaliating
5. Refusing to hate the opponent
6. Acting with the conviction that the universe is on the side of justice (1958, pp. 101–107)

King, like other Blacks before him and since, made it clear that passive acceptance of injustice was intolerable. He hoped that by emphasizing nonviolence, southern Blacks would display their hostility to racism but that violent reaction by Whites would be undercut.

The pattern had now been established, and a method devised to confront racism. But civil disobedience did not work quickly. The struggle to desegregate buses in the South, for example, took seven years. Civil disobedience also was not spontaneous. The success of the civil rights movement rested on a dense network of local efforts. People were attracted to the efforts, but organized tactics and targets were crucial to dismantling racist institutions that had existed for generations (A. Morris, 1984).

## The Battle of Birmingham

Beginning in April 1963, the Southern Christian Leadership Conference (SCLC), founded by King, began a series of marches in Birmingham to demand fair employment opportunities, desegregation of public facilities, and release of the 3,000 people arrested for participating in the marches. King, himself arrested, tells in "Listen to Their Voices" why civil disobedience and the confrontation that followed were necessary. In May the Birmingham police, headed by Eugene "Bull" Connor, used dogs and water from high pressure hoses on the marchers, who included many school children. The violence touched off sympathetic demonstrations of support throughout the country. In the next month, Medgar Evers, leader of the Mississippi NAACP, was shot in the back outside his house, touching off nationwide sit-ins, school strikes, and marches. President Kennedy could delay no longer and submitted to Congress legislation to secure voting

## ❖ LISTEN TO THEIR VOICES ❖

### Letter from Birmingham Jail

*Martin Luther King, Jr.*

You may well ask: "Why direct action? Why sit-ins, marches and so forth? Isn't negotiation a better path?" You are quite right in calling for negotiation. Indeed, this is the very purpose of direct action. Nonviolent direct action seeks to create such a crisis and foster such a tension that a community which has constantly refused to negotiate is forced to confront the issue. It seeks so to dramatize the issue that it can no longer be ignored. My citing the creation of tension as part of the work of the nonviolent-resister may sound rather shocking. But I must confess that I am not afraid of the word "tension." I have earnestly opposed violent tension, but there is a type of constructive, non-violent tension which is necessary for growth. Just as Socrates felt that it was necessary to create a tension in the mind so that individuals could rise from the bondage of myths and half-truths to the unfettered realm of creative analysis and objective appraisal, so must we see the need for nonviolent gadflies to create the kind of ten-sion in society that will help men rise from the dark depths of prejudice and racism to the majestic heights of understanding and brotherhood.

The purpose of our direct-action program is to create a situation so crisis-packed that it will inevitably open the door to negotiation. I therefore concur with you in your call for negotiation. Too long has our beloved Southland been bogged down in a tragic effort to live in monologue rather than dialogue. . . .

You express a great deal of anxiety over our willingness to break laws. This is certainly a legitimate concern. Since we so diligently urge people to obey the Supreme Court's decision of 1954 outlawing segregation in the public schools, at first glance it may seem rather paradoxical for us consciously to break laws. One may well ask: "How can you advocate breaking some laws and obeying others?" The answer lies in the fact that there are two types of laws: just and unjust. I would be the first to advocate obeying just laws. One has not only a legal but a moral responsibility to obey just laws. Conversely, one has a moral responsibility to disobey unjust laws. I would agree with St. Augustine that "an unjust law is no law at all."

rights and broaden government protection of Blacks' civil rights. But this initiative was followed by inaction, as Congress delayed.

Following the example of A. Philip Randolph in 1943, Blacks organized the March on Washington for Jobs and Freedom on August 28, 1963. With more than 200,000 people participating, the march was the high point of the civil rights movement. The mass of people, middle-class Whites and Blacks, looking to the federal government for support, symbolized the struggle. A public opinion poll conducted shortly before the march documented the continuing resentment of the majority of Whites—63 percent were opposed to the rally (Gallup, 1972, p. 1836). King delivered his famous "I have a dream" speech before the large crowd; he looked forward to a time when all Americans "will be able to join hands and sing in the words of the old Negro spiritual, 'Free at last! free at last! thank God almighty, we are free at last!' " (1971, p. 351). Just 18 days later a bomb exploded in a Black church in Birmingham, killing 4 little girls and injuring 20 others.

Despair only increased as the November elections saw segregationists successful in their bid for office. Most distressful was the assassination of President Kennedy on November 22, 1963. Kennedy had significantly appealed to Blacks despite his mediocre legislative record. His death left doubt as to the direction and pace of future actions by the executive branch on civil rights. Now no time could be lost. Two months later the Twenty-fourth Amendment was ratified, outlawing the poll tax that had long prevented Blacks from voting. The enactment of the Civil Rights Act on July 2, 1964, was hailed as a major victory and provided for at least a while what historian John Hope Franklin called "the illusion of equality" (Franklin and Moss, 1988, p. 448).

In the months that followed, the pace of the movement to end racial injustice slowed. The violence continued, however, from Bedford-Stuyvesant, in Brooklyn, to Selma, Alabama. Southern courts still found White murderers of Blacks innocent, and they had to be tried and convicted in federal court on the charge that by killing a person one violates that person's civil rights. Government records, which did not become public until 1973, revealed a systematic campaign by the FBI to infiltrate civil rights groups in an effort to discredit them, claiming that such activist groups were subversive (Blackstock, 1976). It was in such an atmosphere that the Voting Rights Act was passed in August 1975, but this significant, positive event was somewhat overshadowed by violence in the Watts section of Los Angeles in the same week.

## EXPLAINING URBAN VIOLENCE

Riots involving Whites and Blacks did not begin in the 1960s. As we saw earlier in this chapter, urban violence occurred after World War I and even during World War II, and violence against Blacks is more than 300 years old. But the urban riots of the 1960s influenced Blacks and Whites in the United States and throughout the world so extensively that they deserve special attention. We must remember, however, that most violence between Whites and Blacks has not been large-scale collective action but involves only a few people (R. Williams, 1975, p. 149).

The summers of 1963 and 1964 were a prelude to riots that were to grip the country's attention. Although most people knew of the civil rights efforts in the South and legislative victories in Washington, everyone realized that the racial problem was national after several Northern cities experienced violent disorders. The riot in Los Angeles in August 1965 first shocked those who thought racial harmony had been achieved. Thirty-four were killed in the Black ghetto of Watts in the worst riot since Detroit in 1943. Americans were used to tension between Whites and Blacks, but in the South, not the North, and certainly not in California (Blauner, 1972, pp. 94–217; Conot, 1967; Degler, 1969; Oberschall, 1968).

The next two years saw major riots in Cleveland, Newark, and Detroit. Violence was not limited to a few urban ghettos, however. One estimate for 1967 alone identifies 257 disorders in 173 cities claiming 87 lives, injuring 2,500 and

*Martin Luther King stands on the balcony of the Memphis Motel at approximately the spot where he was assassinated. This picture was taken April 3, 1968, the day before the shooting, shortly after King arrived in Memphis, Tennessee. Standing next to King, tieless, is Jesse Jackson, to whom King was talking at the instant he was shot. At right is Ralph Abernathy, who would become King's successor as the head of the Southern Christian Leadership Conference (SCLC).*

leading to 19,200 arrests. In April of 1968, after the assassination of Martin Luther King, more cities exploded than had in all of 1967. Even before the summer of 1968 began, there were 369 civil disorders. Communities of all sizes were hit. More than one-fourth of race-related disturbances occurred in cities with populations of less than 25,000. Most of the civil disorders were relatively minor and probably would have received no publicity if the major riots had not created increased awareness (Baskin et al., 1971, 1972).

As the violence continued and embraced many ghettos, a popular explanation was that riot participants were mostly unemployed youths who had criminal records, often involving narcotics, and who were vastly outnumbered by African Americans who repudiated the looting and arson. This explanation was called the *riff-raff* or *rotten-apple* theory because it discredited the rioters and left the barrel of apples, White society, untouched. On the contrary, research shows that the Black community expressed sympathetic understanding toward the rioters and that the rioters were not merely the poor and uneducated but included middle-class, working-class, and educated residents (Sears and McConahay, 1969, 1973; Tomlinson, 1969).

Several alternatives to the riff-raff theory explain why Black violent protest increased in the United States at a time when the nation was committed to civil rights. Two explanations stand out. One ascribes the problem to Black frustration with rising expectations in the face of continued deprivation relative to Whites. The other points to increased national consciousness.

*The failure of a jury to find four Los Angeles policemen guilty of beating Rodney King touched off a riot in South Central Los Angeles in 1992.*

## Rising Expectations and Relative Deprivation

The standards of living of Blacks improved remarkably after World War II, and continued to do so during the civil rights movement. White income and occupation levels, however, did not remain unchanged either. Chapter 3 showed feelings of relative deprivation are often the basis for seeing discrimination. (*Relative deprivation* is the conscious feeling of a negative discrepancy between legitimate expectations and present actualities.)

It is of little comfort to Black Americans that their earning power matches that of Whites eight to ten years earlier. As shown in Figure 7.2 in 1959 the Black median family income was little more than half of White income. Five years later, Black income had jumped 21 percent but White income had increased 16 percent, leaving the gap between the two intact. Most Blacks made no tangible gains in housing, education, jobs, or economic security. African Americans were doing better in absolute numbers, but not relative to Whites. As we consider the effect of this situation on Blacks, we must determine whom they select as an appropriate reference or comparison group. Frustration does not come from a group's absolute level of attainment but from its position relative to the appro-

---

**FIGURE 7.2**    Black-White Income Gap

For the 40 years of available data, Black income has been only a fraction of White income.

---

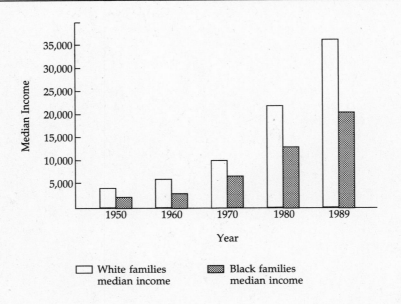

Year

☐ White families    ▨ Black families
median income         median income

---

*Source:* Bureau of the Census, 1991a.

priate comparison group (Merton and Kitt, 1950; Vander Zanden, 1983). David Matza wrote that "profound degradation in an absolute sense may be tolerable or even pass unnoticed if others close at hand fare no better or if one never had any reason to expect better" (1971, p. 607n). Blacks' situation was thus intolerable in both ways, because the continued greater affluence of Whites was apparent to Blacks despite consistent promises of a better life.

Blacks felt that they had legitimate aspirations, and the civil rights movement reaffirmed that discrimination had blocked upward mobility (Geschwender, 1964). The civil rights movement gave higher aspirations to Black America, yet for the majority, life remained basically unchanged. Not only were their lives unchanged, but the feeling was widespread that the existing social structure held no prospect for improvement (Sears and McConahay, 1970, p. 133; also see Thomas and Thomas, 1984).

## Developing a National Consciousness

The first riots in the 1960s were examined in an effort to find causes in the community. Did the chief of police misjudge the situation? Was it crucial that the governor was vacationing out of the country? Would the riot have occurred if the unemployment rate had been slightly lower? As the rioting became a national phenomenon, such localized explanations were replaced by statistical efforts to find similarities among riot cities that contrasted them to nonriot cities.

The nature of the community was not important in explaining the outbreak of racial conflict both because the federal government played a pivotal role, and because of the influence of the mass media in transforming local issues into national ones. The federal government was responsible for promoting or failing to promote racial equality. Blacks in Jacksonville and Boston were in many respects more affected by decisions in the nation's capital than in their own city halls.

Second, coverage of civil rights in the mass media, especially national television newscasts, created national interest and a national racial identity that transcended community boundaries. The mass media were criticized for emphasizing the emotional side of the riots, but the Kerner Commission, established to investigate the riots and their causes, found reporting to be calm and factual. Prior to the riots, however, mass media coverage of the civil rights movement, documenting recognition by Whites of Black leaders, served to develop a national consciousness. Blacks became aware not of deprivation unique to their own neighborhood but of the deprivation common to all ghettos. Given this increased awareness of their low status despite years of promises, almost any Black community could explode (National Advisory Commission on Civil Disorders, 1968).

## BLACK POWER

The riots in the Northern ghettos captured the attention of Whites, and Black Power was what they heard. Appropriately enough, Black Power was born not of Black but of White violence. On June 6, 1966, James Meredith was carrying out a one-person march from Memphis to Jackson, Mississippi, to encourage fellow Blacks to overcome their own fears and vote, following the passage into law of the Voting Rights Act. During that march an unidentified assailant shot and wounded Meredith. Blacks from throughout the country immediately continued the march, led by King of SCLC, Floyd McKissick of CORE, and Stokely Carmichael of the Student Nonviolent Coordinating Committee (SNCC). Responding to King's pressure and his threat to withdraw financial support, McKissick and Carmichael agreed to open up the march to Whites. This was the last integrated effort by all the major civil rights organizations. During the march, Carmichael proclaimed to a cheering Black crowd, "what we need is Black Power." King and others later urged "Freedom Now" as the slogan for the march. A compromise dictated no slogan would be used, but the mood of Black America dictated something else (M. King, 1967; Lomax, 1971, pp. 272–327).

In retrospect it may be puzzling that the phrase Black Power frightened Whites and offended so many Blacks. It was not really new. The National Advisory Commission on Civil Disorders correctly identifies it as old wine in new bottles—Black consciousness was not new even if the phrase was (1968, pp. 234–235). Furthermore, it was the type of umbrella term that can mean everything or nothing. A survey of Detroit Blacks in the following year showed many respondents confused or vague about the concept (Aberbach and Walker, 1970, 1973). But to many Whites the meaning was clear enough. Set against the backdrop of riots in the North, Black Power signaled to many that the civil rights movement was over. And indeed they were right.

By advocating Black Power, Carmichael was distancing himself from the assimilationism of King. Carmichael rejected the goal of assimilation into White middle-class society. Instead, he said, Blacks must create new institutions. To succeed in this endeavor, Carmichael argued that Blacks must follow the same path as the Italians, Irish, and other White ethnic groups. "Before a group can enter the open society, it must first close ranks. . . . Group solidarity is necessary before a group can operate effectively from a bargaining position of strength in a pluralistic society" (Carmichael and Hamilton, 1967, p. 44). Prominent Black leaders opposed the concept; many feared that Whites would retaliate even more violently. King (1967) saw Black Power as a "cry of disappointment" but acknowledged it had a "positive meaning."

Eventually Black Power gained wide acceptance among Blacks and even many Whites. Although it came to be defined differently by nearly every new proponent, support of Black Power generally implied endorsing Black control of the political, economic, and social institutions in Black communities. One reason for its popularity among African Americans was that it gave them a viable option for surviving in a segregated society (Ladner, 1967; Pinkney, 1987). The civil rights movement strove to end segregation, but their response showed how committed White society was to maintaining it. Black Power presented restructuring society as the priority item on the Black agenda.

One aspect of Black Power clearly operated outside the conventional system. The Black Panther party was organized in October 1966 in Oakland, California,

*Bobby Seale was cofounder of the militant Black Panther party, but by 1982 he advocated change using more moderate means. These two pictures of Seale, the first taken in 1969 and the second showing him campaigning in 1982, illustrate the change from revolutionary to advocate of electoral politics.*

by Huey Newton, aged 24, and Bobby Seale, aged 30, to protect Blacks from police abuse. The Panthers were controversial from the beginning. From 1969 to 1972, internal weaknesses, a long series of trials involving most of the leaders, intraparty strife, and several shoot-outs with police combined to bring the organization to a standstill. The Panthers, although they were frequently portrayed as the most separatist of the Black militant movements, were willing to form alliances with non-Black organizations, including Students for a Democratic Society (SDS), the Peace and Freedom party, the Young Lords, the Young Patriots, and the Communist Party of the United States. Despite, or perhaps because of, such coalitions, the Panthers were not a prominent force in shaping contemporary Black America. Newton himself admitted in 1973 that the party alienated Blacks and became "too radical" to be a part of the Black community (Abron, 1986; Cleaver, 1982; Woodward, 1974, p. 105).

The militant Black Panthers encountered severe difficulties during the 1970s, and fell victim to both internal political problems and external surveillance. Finally, their former outspoken leaders moved in new directions. Eldridge Cleaver became a born-again Christian and confined himself to lecturing on the virtues of his evangelical faith. Cofounder Bobby Seale, ran unsuccessfully for mayor of Oakland, California, in the kind of traditional campaign he had formerly denounced as unproductive. Seale, following that unsuccessful bid, became an organizer of moderate community groups. Former Panther defense minister Bobby Rush became deputy chairman of the Illinois State Democratic Party and was successfully elected to the U.S. Congress in 1992. The role of spokesperson for a minority group in the United States is exhausting, and people who have assumed that role for a time often turn to more conventional, less personally demanding roles, especially if public support for their programs wanes.

## BLACK NATIONALISM

Few recent social movements have gained as much attention and reaction as Black nationalism. *Black nationalism* refers to the philosophy that encourages Blacks to see themselves in a positive light as Blacks first, rather than Americans (or "negro americans" as H. Rap Brown wrote in 1969), or New Yorkers, or men and women. An important part of this movement for the individual is the transformation that William Cross (1973), a Black psychologist, called the "Negro-to-Black" conversion experience. This self-actualization leads to greater creativity and productivity. Black nationalists wish Blacks to control their own destiny and resist any attempts to continue their own subordination. In this conversion experience, to be Negro meant to be nobody, to be Black means to be somebody. Regardless of its definition, few Black Americans have escaped the influence of contemporary Black nationalism (Isaacs, 1963; Pinkney, 1970, 1976; Pitts, 1972; Schaefer, 1973a; J. Turner, 1973).

The variety of ways in which to express this nationalism among African Americans can best be summarized under two categories: religious nationalism, and cultural nationalism. Black nationalism has redefined many things for White America, including the conventional definitions of Black religion and culture.

## Religious Nationalism

Religion has influenced the lives of Black Americans throughout history. As we saw earlier in this chapter, because the Africans brought involuntarily to the Western Hemisphere were non-Christian they were seen as heathens and barbarians. To "civilize" the slaves in the period before the Civil War, Southern slaveowners encouraged and often required their slaves to attend church and embrace Christianity. The Christian churches to which Blacks were introduced in the United States encouraged them to accept the inferior status enforced by Whites. Allison Davis, Burleigh Gardner, and Mary Gardner (1965) observed in *Deep South* that Blacks were convinced of the authenticity of their conversion only when they had a vision of a White man or woman, a white horse, or some other white object. The religion the slaves received equated whiteness with salvation and saw whiteness as an acceptable, if not preferred, object of reverence.

Rejecting this White-imposed religion, religious nationalism has, with a few exceptions, embraced non-Christian traditions. A variety of non-Christian groups have attracted followers in the twentieth century. The Nation of Islam, for example, which became known as the Black Muslims, has attracted a large number of followers and received the most attention. The Muslim religion was first introduced to Black Americans in 1930, with the arrival of Wali D. Fard, later called Mr. W. Fard Muhammad, in Detroit.

Under the leadership of Elijah Muhammad, the Nation of Islam became a well-known, controversial organization. While Black Muslims were preaching racial hatred and suffering internal violence, they built a financial empire. Elements of White society have respected the Nation of Islam for its impressive use of capitalism to the organization's advantage and for the ascetic moral code its members follow. The membership of the group now officially called the American Muslim Mission dropped from 250,000 in the mid-1970s to 100,000 a decade later. W. Deen Muhammad, successor and son of Elijah Muhammad, has opened the faith to people of all races, although he acknowledges that it is basically an African-American organization. In 1985, Muhammad dissolved the sect, leaving the 200 mosques and worship centers to operate independently.

During the 1984 presidential campaign, a Muslim sect led by Louis Farrakhan received significant media attention. Farrakhan broke with W. Deen Muhammad in 1977 and named his group Nation of Islam, adopting, along with the name, the more orthodox ideals of Elijah Muhammad, such as Black moral superiority. Farrakhan's endorsement of the candidacy of Rev. Jesse Jackson for the Democratic nomination for president propelled Farrakhan into the limelight, although his public statements about Jews and Israel gave an anti-Semitic taint to Farrakhan's teachings. The split between Farrakhan and Muhammad is not new to the Black followers of Islam, as Malcolm X's life indicates (Bursma and Houston, 1985; J. Howard, 1966; Reed, 1991; Shipp, 1984).

Malcolm X became the most powerful and brilliant voice of the nationalist revival in the 1960s. He was an authentic folk hero to his sympathizers. Besides his own followers, he commanded an international audience, and is still referred to in a manner befitting a prophet. In his autobiography, Malcolm X explained what he understood to be the difference between segregation and the separatism of the Nation of Islam:

> Segregation is when your life and liberty are controlled, regulated, by someone else. To segregate means to control. Segregation is that which is forced upon inferiors by superiors. But separation is that which is done voluntarily, by two equals—for the good of both! (1964, p. 246).

In advocating separatism, Malcolm X subjected the civil rights movement in general and King in particular to harsh abuse. But Malcolm X is not remembered for his stiff attacks on other Black leaders, for his break with the Nation of Islam, or even for his apparent shift to support the formation of coalitions with progressive Whites. Rather, he is remembered for teaching Blacks lessons—which have not been learned by all and which came to haunt the champions of nonviolent direct action—among them, that Blacks must resist violence "by any means necessary." During his last year, Malcolm X (by then known as Malik El-Shabazz) created the nonreligious Organization of Afro-American Unity, which was meant to internationalize the civil rights movement. Malcolm X's life was ended by three assassins in 1964. "His philosophy can be summarized as pride in Blackness, the necessity of knowing Black history, Black autonomy, Black unity, and self-determination for the Black community" (Pinkney, 1975, p. 213; see also Clarke, 1969; Goldman, 1974; Lomax, 1971, p. 292; Pinkney, 1976, pp. 64–75; Woodward, 1974).

## Cultural Nationalism

Cultural nationalism refers to those movements or organizations which encourage and teach the customs, characteristics, and values of a people in a positive light. Just as religious nationalism has two aspects, Christian and non-Christian, cultural nationalism among Blacks has followed two approaches. First is the teaching and practicing of African customs, largely foreign to Black Americans. Some Blacks have overcome immense obstacles to trace their ancestry back to African tribal origins. Writer Alex Haley (1976) spent ten years on such a search, which culminated in his successful identification of Gambian villagers with whom he shared an ancestor, a teenage boy who was captured and sold into slavery in 1767. As noted in Chapter 1, African American studies scholar Molefi Asante (1987; 1991) has called for an *Afrocentric perspective* that emphasizes the customs of African cultures and how they have penetrated the history, culture, and behavior of Blacks in the United States and around the world. The Afrocentric approach could begin in our school curriculum, which has not adequately acknowledged the importance of this heritage.

The second approach to cultural nationalism is the adoption of positive attitudes toward practices developed by Blacks since being brought to this coun-

*Reflecting contemporary cultural nationalism, Harlem youth celebrate Kwanzaa, a seven-day festival based on an African harvest celebration.*

try—an example would be eating "soul food." Both types have taken on a theme of social activism as they have become associated with Black militancy (L. Jones, 1963; Keil, 1966). Although the two approaches are different, it is not always easy to separate one from another. Black American musical styles appear to have been shaped mostly by Black experience in the United States, but do show African influences.

A large controversy has developed in academic circles over whether Black Americans have a unique cultural heritage. It appears that much of what proponents consider part of Black ethnic past is due more to differences from Whites in such respects as geographic and economic background than it is to a common Black experience. Such investigation, although academically useful, is largely irrelevant to the question of cultural nationalism. The existence of positive images that a Black can bring out of the past is a useful and significant counterbalance to the stereotypic portrayals of the African and American Black.

## GLANCING BACK AND LOOKING AHEAD

The dramatic events affecting African Americans as well as their everyday life have their roots in the fact that their ancestors were forcibly brought to the United States as slaves. Blacks had allies among Whites—the abolitionists, the pro-Reconstruction Republicans, and the wealthy benefactors of Tuskegee Institute and the NAACP. In the South, whether as slaves or as victims of Jim Crow, Blacks were not a real threat to any but the poorest Whites, although even affluent Whites feared the potential threat Blacks posed. During the time of slavery, revolts were met with increased suppression, but after emancipation, leaders calling for accommodation were applauded.

As Blacks moved to the urban North, a new social order was being defined. Whites found it more difficult to ignore Blacks in the ghetto than sharecroppers in the rural South. The Black urban voter had potential power, no longer excluded by the "White primary" as in the South. The federal government and city halls slowly began to acknowledge the presence of Blacks. From the Black community came voices that spoke of pride and self-help—Douglass, Washington, and Du Bois.

Black and White Americans dealt with the continued disparity between the two groups by endorsing several ideologies. Assimilation was the driving force behind the civil rights movement, which sought to integrate Whites and Blacks into one society. People who rejected any contact with the other group endorsed separatism. The government and various Black organizations began to recognize cultural pluralism as a goal, at least paying lip-service to the desire of many African Americans to exercise some autonomy over their own lives. Although Blacks differed on their willingness to form coalitions with Whites, but they would have concurred with Du Bois when he wrote that a Black person "simply wishes to make it possible to be both a Negro and an American, without being cursed and spit upon by his fellows, without having the door of opportunity closed roughly in his face" (1903, pp. 3–4). The object of the protest seems simple enough, but for many, including presidents, the point was lost.

Chapter 8 will assess the status of African Americans today. Recall the events chronicled in this chapter as you consider the advances that have been made. These events are a reminder that any progress followed years, indeed generations of struggle by African Americans enlisting the support of Whites sympathetic to the removal of second-class status for African Americans in the United States.

## KEY TERMS

**abolitionists**   Whites and free Blacks who favored the end of slavery.

**Afrocentric perspective**   View that African cultures have penetrated the history, culture, and behavior of Blacks in the United States and throughout the world.

**Black nationalism**   The philosophy that encourages Blacks to see themselves in a positive light as Black people and carriers of a distinctive cultural tradition.

**civil disobedience**   Tactic promoted by Martin Luther King, Jr., based on the belief that individuals have the right to disobey unjust laws under certain circumstances.

**Jim Crow**   Southern laws passed during the latter part of the nineteenth century that kept Blacks in their subordinate position.

**relative deprivation** The conscious feeling of a negative discrepancy between legitimate expectations and present actualities.

**restrictive covenants** Private contracts or agreements that discourage or prevent minority group members from purchasing housing in a neighborhood.

**riff-raff theory** Also called the rotten-apple theory; the belief that the riots of the 1960s were caused by discontented youths, rather than by social and economic problems facing all African Americans.

**slave codes** Laws that delineated the position held by enslaved Blacks in the United States.

**White primary** Legal provisions forbidding Black voting in election primaries, which in one-party areas of the South effectively denied Blacks their right to select elected officials.

## FOR FURTHER INFORMATION

Molefi Kete Asante. *The Afrocentric Idea.* Philadelphia: Temple University Press, 1987.

Historians, philosophers, and others are taken to task for promoting a Eurocentric view of life so rigid that it ignores the experience and the contributions of African Americans.

Molefi Kete Asante and Mark T. Mattson. *The Historical and Cultural Atlas of African Americans.* New York: Macmillan, 1991.

Maps, illustrations, and extended narratives offer an overview of the African-American experience in the United States.

Arthur R. Ashe, Jr. with Kip Branch, Ocania Chalk, and Francis Harris. *A Hard Road to Glory: A History of the African-American Athlete* (3 volumes). New York: Amistad Books, 1989.

A comprehensive examination of African Americans in sports that is both a history and a cry of protest.

Stokely Carmichael and Charles V. Hamilton. *Black Power: The Politics of Liberation in America.* New York: Random House, 1967.

A civil rights activist and a political scientist join in this book to describe a political framework that, as they state, "represents the last reasonable opportunity for this society to work out its racial problems short of prolonged destructive guerilla warfare." The concepts of Black Power, internal colonialism, and institutional racism were presented in a book for the first time here.

Clayborne Carson et al. (eds.). *The Eyes on the Prize Civil Rights Leader.* New York: Penguin Books, 1991.

The documents, speeches, and first-hand accounts of the African American struggle beginning with 1954 through Nelson Mandela's address in Atlanta in 1990.

W. E. B. Du Bois. *The Philadelphia Negro: A Social Study.* New York: Schocken Books, 1967.

This, the first important sociological study of a Black community, was originally published in 1899 and is worth reading today. Du Bois discusses family life, interracial relations, education, occupations, and other aspects of the North's largest Black community just three decades after the end of slavery.

John Hope Franklin and Alfred A. Moss, Jr. *From Slavery to Freedom: A History of Negro Americans*, 6th ed. New York: Alfred A. Knopf, 1988.

The most authoritative historical account of the Black experience in the United States. The 37 pages of bibliographical notes are an excellent initial source for research work.

Alex Haley. *Roots: The Saga of an American Family*. Garden City, NY: Doubleday, 1976.

Drawing upon the knowledge of his relatives and the oral history retold by a *griot* in the Gambian village of Kinte-Kundah plus archival research, Haley managed to trace his ancestry back to Kunta Kinte, who was abducted in 1767 and eventually sold to a Virginia planter.

James H. Jones. *Bad Blood: The Tuskegee Syphilis Experiment*. New York: Free Press, 1981.

Historian James Jones details the horrors of a Public Health Service survey in which 412 Black Alabama men with syphilis were used as experimental subjects from 1932 to 1972. The study's purpose was to assess the long-term effects of syphilis *without* medical treatment. It was not until newspaper publicity in 1972 that the victims, their infected wives, and offspring born with the disease were given any treatment.

C. Eric Lincoln and Lawrence H. Mamiya. *The Black Church in the African American Experience*. Durham, NC: Duke University Press, 1990.

An overview of the role of organized religion from the days of slavery through the challenges experienced today in the United States.

Malcolm X. *The Autobiography of Malcolm X*. New York: Grove Press, 1964.

Just before his assassination, Malcolm X related his experiences leading to his leadership in the nation of Islam and his subsequent disenchantment with that organization.

Kenneth M. Stampp. *The Peculiar Institution: Slavery in the Ante-Bellum South*. New York: Random House, 1956.

An objective, scholarly account of what slavery was like and what effects it had on Blacks, Whites, and the South.

Wallace Terry. *Bloods: An Oral History of the Vietnam War by Black Veterans*. New York: Random House, 1984.

Journalist Terry, who covered the war for *Time*, provides vivid testimony by 20 veterans.

## Periodicals

Numerous mass-circulation magazines deal primarily with Black Americans, including: *Black Collegiate, Black Enterprise, Black World* (formerly *Negro Digest*), *Ebony, Essence,* and *Jet.* Journals include: *Black Politics* (first issued in 1969), *Black Scholar* (1969), *Journal of Negro Education* (1931), *Journal of Negro History* (1916), *Negro History Bulletin* (1946), *Phylon: Journal of Race and Culture* (1940), and *Race Relations Reporter* (1970, formerly *Southern School News,* 1954).

# Chapter Eight

# AFRICAN AMERICANS TODAY

## Chapter Outline

**Education**
Quality and Quantity of Education
School Integration
Higher Education
**Employment and Income**
Black-owned Businesses
The Black White-Collar Worker
**Family Life**
Challenges to Family Stability
Strengths of African American Families

The Black Middle Class and Its Significance
**Housing**
Residential Segregation
The Outlook
**Criminal Justice**
**Health Care**
**Politics**
**Glancing Back and Looking Ahead**
**Key Terms**
**For Further Information**

---

## * HIGHLIGHTS *

African Americans have made significant progress in many areas, but inequality relative to White Americans remains in all sectors. African Americans have advanced in formal schooling to a remarkable degree, although public schools remain mostly segregated. The usual solution to school segregation—busing to achieve racial balance—has met with public opposition and has been supported with decreasing enthusiasm by the federal government as an appropriate remedy. Higher education also reflects the legacy of a nation that has operated two schooling systems—one for Blacks and another for Whites. Gains in earning power have barely kept pace with inflation, and the gap between Whites and Blacks has remained relatively unchanged. African-American families are susceptible to the problems associated with a low-income group that also faces discrimination and prejudice. Housing remains segregated, despite growing numbers of Blacks in suburban areas. African Americans are more likely to be victims of crimes as well as to be arrested for violent crimes, but they have a less powerful role in the judicial system than do Whites. The subordination of Blacks is also apparent in the delivery of health care. African Americans have made substantial gains in elective office, but still are not represented in proportion to their share of the population.

---

By the late 1980s, a superficial sense of complacency about the position of African Americans in the United States was evident. Uninformed, casual observers compared the relative absence of violence in central cities to the situation in the 1960s and saw the increasing presence of African Americans inside city halls rather than marching outside, and some concluded that everything was going well in Black America.

Yet, these episodes served in some respects as a prelude to the events in southern California in 1991 and 1992. Rodney King, a Black construction worker, sustained nearly a dozen head fractures when he was beaten by Los Angeles Police Department officers following a highspeed chase. The beating of 56 blows in 81 seconds happened to be captured on a videotape that shocked the nation as it replayed numerous times on television. Four White officers were tried, a year later, on a variety of charges but were not found guilty by a jury of 10 Whites, 1 Hispanic, and 1 Asian.

The verdict touched off rioting in Los Angeles and smaller disturbances in several cities, but the California riots became the worst in the twentieth century—52 dead, 2,400 injured, and 8,800 arrested. The Los Angeles 1992 riot area of South-Central borders the 1965 Watts riot area. Except for a few government buildings and 500 units of low income housing, Watts remains a ghetto. South-Central was virtually leveled through fires and looting that, like the original

Rodney King beating, also shocked America. Yet the expressions of concern over lawless civilians, police brutality, and insufficient government policies for the ghetto seemed all too familiar (A. Stone, 1992).

Yet Miami's predominantly Black neighborhoods were torn apart with violence, looting, and charges of police brutality and miscarriage of justice during the early 1980s. In 1980, 9 days of rioting resulted in 18 deaths, 1,300 arrests, and nearly $125 million in property damage. Two deaths, 25 injuries, and 45 arrests accompanied rioting in some of the same Miami neighborhoods, in violence that broke out at the end of 1982. The Community Relations Service of the Department of Justice consistently receives more and more reports of racial violence annually, and 92 percent of the victims are Blacks. In 1986 the largest number ever was reported, a 42 percent increase over 1985. Even baseball superstar Henry Aaron lamented that race was a major factor in his lack of success in landing the type of executive position he wanted in baseball after he retired as an active player (Department of Justice, 1980; Dunn and Porter, 1981; B. Staples, 1987; Warfield, 1987).

As you read this chapter, try to keep the profile of Blackness in America today in perspective. This chapter will assess education, employment and income, family life, housing, criminal justice, health care, and politics among the nation's African Americans. Progress has occurred, and some of the advances are nothing short of remarkable. The deprivation of the African American people relative to Whites remains, however, even if absolute deprivation has been softened. A significant gap remains between African Americans and the dominant group, and to this gap a price is assigned—the price of being African Americans in the United States.

## EDUCATION

America's Black population has always placed special importance on acquiring education, beginning within the home of the slave family through the creation of separate, inferior schools for Black children because the regular schools were closed to them by custom or law (Pinkney, 1987). Today, long after the old civil rights coalition disbanded, education remains a controversial issue. Formal schooling is the key to social mobility in the United States. Because racial and ethnic minorities realize that it is, they wish to maximize their opportunities for upward mobility, and so demand better schooling. White Americans also appreciate the value of formal schooling and do not wish to do anything that they perceive will jeopardize their position.

### Quality and Quantity of Education

Several measures document the inadequate education received by African Americans, for example, in the quantity of formal education. Blacks generally drop out of school sooner and therefore are less likely to receive high school diplomas, let alone college degrees. Table 8.1 shows the gap in the amount of schooling African Americans receive compared to Whites. It also illustrates progress in reducing this gap in recent years. Yet despite this progress, the gap remains substantial, with more than twice as many young Whites as Blacks having a college degree in 1990; the gap is widening.

A second aspect of inadequate schooling, many educators argue, is that many students do not drop out of school but are pushed out by the combined inadequacies of their education.

1. Insensitive teachers
2. Poor counseling
3. Unresponsive administrators
4. Overcrowded classes
5. Irrelevant curricula
6. Dilapidated school facilities

Middle- and upper-class children occasionally face these barriers to a high-quality education, but they are more likely than the poor to have a home environment favorable to learning. Because Black students are less likely to have such a home environment, these barriers to learning are particularly damaging to Black students. Even Black schoolchildren who stay in school are not guaranteed success in life. Many high schools do not prepare students who are interested in college for advancing schooling. The problem is that schools are failing students and not just that students are failing in schools.

**TABLE 8.1**  Years of School Completed (Persons 25 years old and over)

Among adults, the gaps remain between Blacks and Whites in the proportion completing high school and college.

|  | 1960 | 1990 |
|---|---|---|
| Completing high school |  |  |
| Black |  |  |
| Male | 18.2% | 65.8% |
| Female | 21.7 | 66.5 |
| White |  |  |
| Male | 41.6 | 79.1 |
| Female | 44.7 | 79.0 |
| Completing college |  |  |
| Black |  |  |
| Male | 2.8% | 11.9% |
| Female | 3.3 | 10.8 |
| White |  |  |
| Male | 10.3 | 25.3 |
| Female | 6.0 | 19.0 |

*Source:* Bureau of the Census, 1988b; 1991g, p. 31.

## School Integration

Almost 40 years ago the Supreme Court declared in *Brown* v. *Board of Education* that "separate educational facilities are inherently unequal." This legal finding was buttressed by a 1966 government-financed study implying that racial integration was desirable in public schools. The document is commonly referred to as the Coleman Report after the principal investigator, sociologist James Coleman (Coleman et al., 1966a, 1966b, 1966c). The data from its nationwide survey of public school systems supported the significance of the home in a pupil's ability to learn. Coleman and others argued that academic achievement by children from lower socioeconomic backgrounds (Black or White) is improved when those children attend schools with children from higher socioeconomic backgrounds (Black or White). The Coleman Report has been used mostly to support racial integration, although its argument is just as persuasive for social-class integration, if not more so. Either way, the data suggest that such arrangements would be advantageous for the low achievers and would not hurt the higher achievers' progress.

The Coleman and subsequent studies have been hotly debated, with the overall result that biracial schooling has been judged as neither a success nor a failure. Little effort, legal or legislative, has been made to eliminate the social-class differences between school districts. Class inequities allow middle-class districts with lower tax levies on a broader property base to spend more on education than poor areas with higher tax levies (Schaefer and Lamm, 1992, pp. 502–504).

With the 1954 *Brown* v. *Board of Education* decision, school segregation was brought to national attention. Initially the focus was on the South and *de jure segregation*, the assignment of children to schools solely because of race. The Supreme Court has consistently ruled that such practices violate the Constitution and that the schools involved must desegregate. Since this beginning, however, the focus has switched to the North and West, to school segregation that results from Blacks and Whites living in separate neighborhoods, called *de facto segregation*.

In 1971, the Supreme Court ruled in *Swann* v. *Charlotte-Mecklenburg Board of Education* that busing was "a normal and accepted tool of educational policy." Prior to *Swann* most court desegregation programs had been in the South and had involved assignment to nearby schools. The *Swann* decision opened the door to noncontiguous pairing of schools, or busing across district lines in order to produce a specific racial balance. Subsequent Supreme Court decisions, however, reversed that direction. In the 1991 *Board of Education of Oklahoma City* v. *Dowell* decision, the Court said that formerly segregated school systems can be released from court-ordered busing even if desegregation had not been accomplished, as was the case in Oklahoma City.

With desegregation efforts stalled, African-American parents continued efforts to improve the quality of education their children received wherever they attended. Some backed state-subsidized voucher programs that would allow them some choice in which schools children were placed. A more controversial

*Forty years after the* Brown v. Board of Education *Supreme Court decision, the vast majority of African-American children do not attend public schools with white children.*

response was to create all-Black or even all-Black male schools with the expectation that separate classes could foster positive self-images and role models (P. King, 1989; J. Morgan, 1991).

## Higher Education

The overall picture for African Americans in higher education is not promising. Black enrollment in colleges and graduate programs reached a plateau in the mid-1970s and has declined ever since. In 1976, 53 percent of Black middle-class high school graduates were enrolled in college; by 1988 only 36 percent were. Why the decline? On one level opportunities have improved. Because of blatant discrimination, 52 percent of African Americans in college in 1976 attended predominantly Black public and private institutions. Through the ending of racial restrictions, this proportion was reduced to about 18 percent in 1992, but they still produce 40 percent of the bachelor's degrees earned by Black college students. It is not because Blacks have lowered their aspirations, since surveys show an actual increase in the number of Black high school seniors (Carter and Wilson, 1991; Farrell, 1992).

Several factors have been identified for the reversal in African-American progress in higher education.

1. Reduction in financial aid and more reliance on loans than on grants-in-aid coupled with rising costs have tended to discourage students who would be the first members of their families to attend college.
2. Pushing for "higher standards" and "excellence" in educational achievement without providing compensatory resources have locked out many minority students.
3. Employment opportunities, though slight for Blacks without some college, have continued to lure young people who must contribute to their family's income.
4. Negative publicity about affirmative action may have discouraged some from even considering college.
5. Increasing attention to what appears to be a growing number of racial incidents of predominantly White college campuses.

Colleges and universities seem uneasy about these problems but publicly are committed to addressing them.

There is little question that special challenges face the African-American student at a college with overwhelmingly White student body, faculty, advisers, coaches, and administrators. The campus culture may, at best, be neutral and is often times hostile to the presence of members of racial minorities. The high attrition rate of African-American students on predominantly White college campuses confirms the need for a positive environment (Carter and Schaefer, 1976a, 1976b; Edwards, 1970; Mallinckrodt, 1988).

*A student at the University of Massachusetts at Amherst reads a statement after ending a five-day occupation of a campus building to protest campus racial problems in 1988.*

As noted above, there have been a growing number of widely publicized racial incidents on college campuses. They have included cross burnings, discrimination, racist literature, physical attacks, derogatory behavior, and racist remarks. In addition, there are more subtle aspects, such as campus bars that discourage minority student patronage by not playing minority-oriented music and local law enforcement officials who more closely monitor the activities of African-American students. As a consequence of the lack of continued success of Blacks in college relatively fewer Blacks are available to fill faculty and administrative positions. This means that there were no more, and perhaps fewer, role models standing in the fronts of college classrooms for minority students to see (Allen et al., 1991; Farrell and Jones, 1988).

In Chapter 1, we said that one of the consequences of subordinate group status was segregation. This is certainly true in education. De facto segregation is present in the public schools and, indeed, there are some state university systems accused of promoting segregation. African Americans who attend predominantly White colleges often encounter a chilly climate where they are isolated from their classmates and even their teachers. The gains of the 1970s in educational advancement have not continued (De Palma, 1991; O'Hare et al., 1991).

## EMPLOYMENT AND INCOME

By almost every measure of employment and income, the lot of African Americans has improved in absolute terms in the last four decades. Progress has not always been even, and the rate of improvement varies considerably by region, education, age, and gender. More important than this overall improvement by Blacks is that Whites have made similar gains. As the discussion of relative deprivation in Chapter 3 showed, the gap between Black and White income remains. Figure 8.1 vividly shows the lack of significant change in the ratio between Black and White family income. Median income, which is the middle level of earnings—half of the families make more and half less—offers a realistic view of the earning power of a particular group. One cannot help but be struck by the lack of progress in closing this gap after four decades.

Much of the apparent gain in African-American incomes is misleading, for it may not signify a "better life," as is usually assumed. First, Black family income is more likely to depend upon two sources of income, with both husband and wife working. Second, Blacks have consistently migrated to areas with higher living costs, say, from farms to cities, where increased income barely keeps pace with the increased costs. Third, Blacks are especially hard hit at times of increased unemployment. As shown in Figure 8.2, higher unemployment rates for Blacks have persisted since 1960 and can be documented even further back. Recessions, such as those during the 1970s, 1980s, and 1990s have taken their toll on Black Americans. The Reverend Joseph Lowery, former aide to Martin Luther King, Jr., appropriately said that "when America catches a cold, the black community gets pneumonia" (Zinsmeister, 1988, p. 41).

**FIGURE 8.1**   Black Median Family Income as Percentage of Median Family Incomes of Whites, 1950–1989

After reaching a "high" of 62 percent of White income in 1974, Black median family income fell to 56 percent of White median family income in 1989.

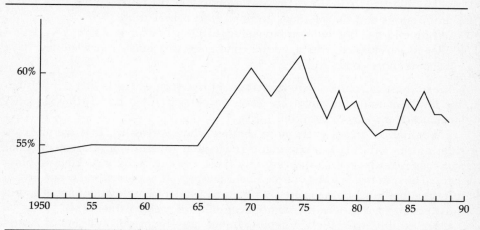

*Note:* Data prior to 1970 is for "Black and others."
*Source:* Bureau of the Census, 1991a, p. 454 and 1980a, p. 451.

**FIGURE 8.2**   Black and White Unemployment Rates, 1960–1991

Even in the healthy economy of the early 1960s, African American unemployment did not fall below 9 percent until 1965.

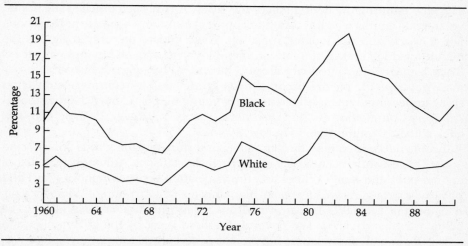

*Note:* Black data for 1960–1971 are for "Blacks and other races."
*Source:* Rates through 1981, from John Reid, "Black America in the 1980s." *Population Bulletin 37* (December 1982). Reprinted by permission of the Population Reference Bureau. Data for 1982–1991 from Bureau of Labor Statistics, 1986, 1988, 1991.

The employment picture is especially grim for young Black workers aged 16–24. Many live in the central cities and fall victim to the unrecorded, irregular economy outlined in Chapter 3. Many factors have been cited by social scientists to explain why official unemployment rates for young Blacks exceed 40 percent.

1. Many Blacks live in the depressed economy of the central cities.
2. Immigrants and illegal aliens are increased competition.
3. White middle-class women have entered the labor force.
4. Illegal activities at which youths find they can make more money have become more prevalent.

None of these factors is likely to change soon, which suggests that depression-like levels of unemployment are likely to persist (Allen and Farley, 1986; F. Jones, 1981, pp. 92–93; Swinton, 1987).

The situation grows even more somber when we realize that we are considering only official unemployment. The federal government's Bureau of Labor Statistics regards as unemployed only those persons *actively* seeking employment. Thus, in order to be counted as unemployed, a person must not hold a full-time job, must be registered with a government employment agency, and must be engaged in writing job applications and seeking interviews.

Quite simply, the official unemployment rate leaves out millions of Americans who are effectively unemployed. It does not count persons so discouraged that they have temporarily given up looking for employment. The problem of unemployment is further compounded by underemployment. The term *underemployment* refers to the practice of working at a job for which one is overqualified, or involuntarily working part-time, or being intermittently employed.

The official unemployment rate for African-American teenagers in a central city is about 40–45 percent, well above the 25 percent jobless rate for the nation as a whole during the depression of the 1930s. Again, such official statistics do not include youths who have dropped out of the system—who are not at school, not at work, and not looking for a job. If we add to the official figures the discouraged job seeker, the rate of unemployment and underemployment for Black teenagers in central-city areas climbs to 90 percent. As discouraging as these data are, the picture becomes even grimmer as we consider studies that show underemployment is increasing for young Blacks (Lichter, 1988; National Advisory Commission on Civil Disorders, 1968, p. 257; Ritzer, 1977, pp. 358–363; Sheler, 1982; Swinton, 1987; Thurow, 1980).

Income data are equally discouraging. Unfortunately the words "Black" and "poor" have always been closely related in these statistics. Although most Blacks are not poor and many Whites are, the association between minority race and poverty is strong. As we have seen, Black income falls far short of White income. As shown in Table 8.2, African Americans are nearly three times as likely to be below the poverty level. The poverty threshold is set by the government and adjusted annually for inflation. In 1990, the poverty level for a family of four was $13,359. This relationship of Blacks to the poverty level has not changed

TABLE 8.2    Persons Below the Poverty Level, 1959–1990 (percentages)

Nearly one in three African Americans is below the poverty level, compared to one in ten Whites.

| Year | Black | White | Ratio of Black to White |
|------|-------|-------|-------------------------|
| 1959 | 55.1% | 18.1% | 3.0% |
| 1965 | 41.8 | 11.3 | 3.7 |
| 1970 | 33.5 | 9.9 | 3.4 |
| 1975 | 31.3 | 9.7 | 3.2 |
| 1980 | 32.5 | 10.2 | 3.2 |
| 1985 | 31.3 | 11.4 | 2.7 |
| 1990 | 31.9 | 10.7 | 3.0 |

*Source:* Bureau of the Census, 1991d, pp. 16–17.

significantly in the last quarter century. Low incomes are counterbalanced to some extent by Medicare, Medicaid, public assistance, and food stamps. The income of the affluent is underestimated, however, because capital gains and other types of income received by the more well-to-do are excluded from census data. That an African-American family in 1990 had a 32 percent probability of being poor showed that the degree of social inequality is staggering.

## Black-Owned Businesses

Many people aspire to run their own businesses, but it is clearly attractive to minorities including African Americans. Going into business alone means the opportunity to make it into the middle class. It is also a way to avoid some of the racism in business—the "glass ceilings" that block the promotion of a qualified worker and the tensions of a multiracial work environment.

Historically the first Black-owned business developed behind the wall of segregation. African Americans provided services that Whites would not provide, such as insurance, hairdressing, legal assistance, and medical help. While this is less true today, African-American entrepreneurs usually first cater to the market demand within their own community in such areas as music and mass media. However, if these new ventures become profitable, the entrepreneur will usually face stiff competition from outside the African-American community.

In the 1970s there were strong cries to help Black-owned businesses. Community leaders launched "Buy Black" campaigns and the government spoke of assisting Black capitalists. Black-owned businesses have increased, but they are relatively few in number. African Americans still own only about 3 percent of the nearly 14 million firms in the United States. They tend to be very small, with 83 percent having no paid employees. Only 189 out of the 400,000 Black-owned firms have 100 or more employees, but these few enterprises account for 14 percent of all receipts (Bureau of the Census, 1991a).

The situation is not improving. Among the factors creating new obstacles are the following:

1. Continuing backlash against affirmative action programs
2. Difficulty in obtaining loans and other capital
3. Changing definition of minority that allows women, veterans, and the disabled to qualify for special small business assistance programs.
4. Reduction in number and scope of set-aside programs

The last item requires further explanation. *Set-aside programs* are stipulations that government contracts must be awarded to a minimum proportion, usually 10–30 percent, of minority-owned businesses. However in 1989, the U.S. Supreme Court determined that the city of Richmond, Virginia, had acted illegally in its set-aside programs (see Table 3.3). Since *City of Richmond* v. *Croson*, cities and government have abandoned such programs jeopardizing already fragile Black-owned businesses.

In the aftermath of the 1992 South-Central Los Angeles riots, President George Bush advanced his policy of creating enterprise zones in urban areas. While not directly aimed at minority-owned businesses, the policy intends to encourage employment and investment in blighted neighborhoods through the use of tax breaks. Ten such zones were proposed to be created in 1993 with a total of 50 by 1997. The idea is not new and has been employed by 30 states with varying degrees of success. Locally in Los Angeles, successful African American business leaders began to develop their own strategies to create business opportunities in the ghetto (Wolf and Benedetto, 1992).

Even if programs that stress increasing the number of Black-owned businesses succeeded, most ghetto Blacks would still be left poor. Writing more than a generation ago, Du Bois mentioned this potentially negative effect of Black capitalism. Encouraging a few African Americans to move up the capitalistic ladder, he said, "will have inserted into the ranks of the Negro race a new cause of division, a new attempt to subject the masses of the race to an exploitating capitalist class of their own people" (1968, p. 208). Du Bois's alternative was a program that would substantially improve the economic conditions of all Blacks, not a few.

## The Black White-Collar Worker

The limits of Black capitalism are evident if one examines how Whites have succeeded. Most Whites achieve upward mobility by climbing the ladder of jobs in established businesses or by entering financially rewarding professions. It is through these methods of economic improvement, rather than by establishing Black-owned businesses, that some Blacks have begun to make progress. Admittedly, the continued dependence on White firms that this method implies does little to assist the large numbers of Blacks relegated to work or unemployment in the ghetto, distant from the high-paying stable jobs in the suburbs or in urban corporate enclaves (O'Hare et al., 1991; Wilson, 1987a).

While few African Americans have crashed the "glass ceiling" and made it into the top echelons of American business or government, more have entered a wider variety of jobs. The taboo against putting Blacks in jobs in which they would supervise Whites has weakened, and many African Americans hold managerial and professional positions. The percentage of African-American men in the professional and managerial occupations rose from 4 percent in 1949 to 13 percent in 1990. A remarkable improvement, but most of it was prior to 1980. There has been little advancement since then. In 1990, White men were still twice as likely as Black men to hold jobs in administration, management, or the professions. Conversely, Black men were more likely to work as semi-skilled laborers and twice as likely as White men to hold service jobs. In Table 8.3 are presented comparative figures for selected occupations.

The differences between African-American and White women are less striking, perhaps because American women are less likely to enter high-level jobs. Considering that 42 percent of Black female employees worked in domestic service in 1949, the change in their occupational profile is dramatic. In 1990, 19 percent of African-American women were in managerial and professional occupations, and 39 percent were in technical or administrative. While these percentages are well below those of White women in higher paying jobs, the gaps are narrower than they are for men (O'Hare et al., 1991, pp. 24–26).

In summary, the economic differences between Whites and Blacks are striking. The same generalizations that were made prior to the civil rights movement are still accurate as the twenty-first century approaches. African Americans have a higher unemployment rate, a greater rate of business failure, and predominate

**TABLE 8.3**  Percentage of Black Employees in Selected Occupations, 1972 and 1989

In professional and managerial positions, progress has been slight since 1972.

| Occupation | 1972 | 1989 |
|---|---|---|
| Professional workers | 6 | 7 |
| Engineers | 2 | 4 |
| Lawyers and judges | 2 | 3 |
| Physicians | 3 | 3 |
| Registered nurses | 6 | 7 |
| College teachers | 4 | 4 |
| Other teachers | 8 | 9 |
| Social workers | 16 | 18 |
| Managers | 3 | 6 |
| Sales workers | 3 | 9 |
| Clerical workers (including administrative support) | 8 | 11 |
| Service workers | 17 | 18 |
| Cleaners and servants | 64 | 37 |
| Firefighters | 4 | 12 |
| Police | 8 | 15 |

*Sources:* Bureau of the Census, 1982b, pp. 419–420; 1991a, pp. 395–397.

in low-paying occupations. As might be expected, this disparity in income takes its toll on family life.

## *FAMILY LIFE*

The family in its role as a social institution providing for the socialization of children is crucial to its members' life satisfaction. The family also reflects the influence, positive or negative, of income, housing, education, and other social factors. For African Americans, the family reflects both amazing stability as well as the woes of racism and low income.

### *Challenges to Family Stability*

In 1989, more than 7 million African-American families lived in the United States. In slightly less than 4 million of them, both a husband and wife were present. But in more than 3 million, a single parent was raising children under age 18 (see Figure 8.3). It is as inaccurate to assume that a single-parent family is necessarily "deprived" as it is to assume that a two-parent family is always secure and happy. Nevertheless, life in a single-parent family can be extremely stressful. Speaking about all single parents, and not just those who are members of racial minorities, Ronald Haskins, Director of the Child Development Institute at the University of North Carolina, observes: "It's a big and risky undertaking when so many parents try to raise so many children alone" (Mann,

*Employment is a key to family stability.*

**FIGURE 8.3**   One-Parent Families among Blacks and Whites, 1970 and 1989

In 1989, 44 percent of African American families and 13 percent of White families were maintained by the mother with no adult male in the home.

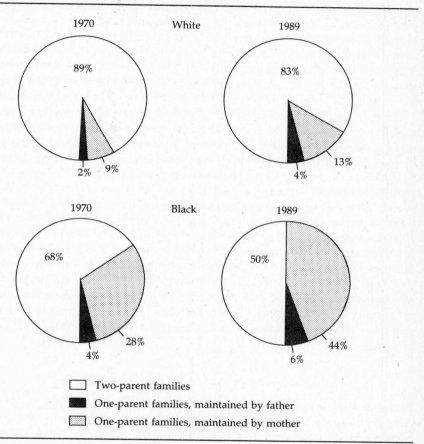

Source: Bureau of the Census, 1991a, p. 38; Bureau of Labor Statistics, 1986.

1983, p. 62). There is also the very real issue that the lack of a male presence, typically the absent parent, means almost always the lack of a male income. This monetary impact of a single-parent household is not to be minimized (Hacker, 1992, p. 73).

Looming behind the woman-headed families is the plight of the Black man. Simply stated, the economic status of Black men is deteriorating. Historically, it has not always been a problem. Despite the absence of legal protection for the slave family, Blacks were able to establish significant kinship relationships. After emancipation, males preferred that their wives remain at home, because a working woman was considered a mark of slavery. But it was hard for Black men to find work as anything other than a strikebreaker, and so women were the more important source of wages. In 1900, about 41 percent of Black women were employed, compared to only 16 percent of White women. The twentieth-century movement from the rural South to the ghettos of the North increased opportunities for employment for Black men, but Black women found job opportunities as well, including relatively high-paid positions in nursing and teaching. Ever since labor statistics on Blacks were first collected, in 1890, Black men have had more jobs than Black women, but when Blacks are compared to Whites, Black women fare better. As we saw in Chapter 3, the employment gap is narrower between Black and White women than it is between Black and White men.

For many African-American women living in poverty, marriage after having a child is only an added burden. The absence of a husband does not mean that no one shares in child care—85 percent of the out-of-wedlock children born to Black teenage mothers live with their grandparents, to form three-generational households. Stronger religious beliefs contribute to teenage Blacks' being almost half as likely to terminate a pregnancy by abortion compared to Whites. A variety of social factors combine to explain the frustration felt by many Blacks beginning to rear a family (Billingsley, 1987; Cummings, 1983; Curry, 1986; Hill, 1987; Ladner, 1986; R. Staples, 1986a, 1986b; Sussman, 1986).

No one explanation accounts for the rise in single-parent households. The rapid expansion is attributed by sociologists primarily to shifts in the economy that kept Black men, especially in urban areas, out of work. The phenomenon of expansion in female-headed families certainly is not limited to Blacks. Increasingly, White and Black women both bear children before they marry. More and more parents, White and Black, divorce, leaving the children with only one parent.

## Strengths of African American Families

In the midst of ever-increased single parenting, another picture of African-American family life becomes visible—success despite discrimination and economic hardship. Robert Hill (1972, 1987) of the National Urban League listed five strengths of African-American families that allow them to function effectively in a hostile (racist) society.

1. *Strong kinship bonds.* Blacks are more likely than Whites to care for children and the elderly in an extended family network.
2. *Strong work orientation.* Poor Blacks are more likely to be working and poor Black families often include more than one wage earner.
3. *Adaptability of family roles.* In two-parent families, the egalitarian pattern of decision making is the most common. The self-reliance of Black women who are the primary wage earners best illustrates this adaptability.
4. *High achievement orientation.* Working-class Blacks indicate greater desire for their children to attend college than working-class Whites. Even a majority of low-income Blacks desire to attend college.

5. *Strong religious orientation.* Black churches since the time of slavery have been the source of many significant grass-roots organizations.

Since Hill's astute observations 20 years ago, social workers and sociologists have confirmed these strengths through actual social research (Gary et al., 1983; Royce and Turner, 1980). Within the African-American community these are the sources of family strengths, just as economic deprivation fosters instability.

Increasingly, social scientists are learning to look at both aspects of African-American family life—the weaknesses and strengths. Expressions of alarm about instability date back to 1965, when the Department of Labor issued the report *The Negro Family: The Case for National Action.* The document, commonly known as the Moynihan Report after its principal author, Daniel Patrick Moynihan, outlined a "tangle of pathology" with the Black family at its core (Rainwater and Yancey, 1967). More recently, two studies, the Stable Black Families Project and the National Survey of Black Americans, sought to learn how Black families encounter problems and resolve them successfully with internal resources. The coping mechanisms paralleled those outlined by Hill in his highly regarded work (Department of Labor, 1965, p. 30; Gary et al., 1983; Hatchett et al., 1991).

The most consistently documented strength of African American families is the presence of an extended family household—the first strength listed above. The most common feature is to have grandparents residing in the home. Even when considering differences in income, extended living arrangements were twice as common among Black compared to White households. These arrangements are recognized as having important economic benefits by pooling limited economic resources. Because of generally lower earnings of African-American heads-of-household, income from second, third and even fourth wage earners is required to achieve a desired standard of living or, in all too many cases, simply to meet daily needs (Farley and Allen, 1987; R. Taylor et al., 1990).

## The Black Middle Class and Its Significance

Many characterizations of African-American family life have been attacked because they overemphasize the poorest segment of the Black community. An opposite error is the exaggeration of the success that Blacks have achieved. Social scientists face the challenge of avoiding a selective, one-sided picture of Black society. The problem is similar to viewing a partially filled glass of water. Does one describe it as half empty and emphasize the need for assistance? Or does one describe the glass as half full to give attention to what has been accomplished? The most complete description would acknowledge both perspectives (Gouldner, 1970, p. 4; also see Feagin, 1991).

A clearly defined Black middle class has emerged. In 1989, one-fourth of African-American families earned above the median income for Whites of that year (Bureau of the Census, 1991a, p. 449). At least 25 percent of Blacks, then, are middle class. Many have debated the character of this middle class. E. Franklin Frazier (1957), a Black sociologist, wrote an often critical study of the Black middle class, in which he identified its overriding goal as achieving petty social values and becoming acceptable to White society.

Yet African Americans are still aware of their racial subordination even when they have superficially achieved economic equality. The Black middle class may not be militant, but neither do its newest members forget their roots. They are more likely than Whites to be first-generation middle class, dependent on two or more sources of income, and precariously close to the lower class both financially and residentially. Yet with their relative success has come a desire to live in better surroundings. The migration of middle-class Blacks out of the ghetto in the 1970s and 1980s has left a vacuum. They may still care about the problems of the Black poor, but they are no longer present as role models (Durant and Louden, 1986; Landry, 1987; Lemann, 1986a, 1986b; Vannemann and Cannon, 1987, pp. 225–251).

Members of the Black middle class do not automatically accept all aspects of the White middle class. For years, for example, Whites have relied on books and magazines on infant and child care, but such materials treated African-American children as if they did not exist. To counter this neglect, Alvin Poussaint and James Comer wrote *Black Child Care* (1975), in which they advise parents on how to deal with questions like "What is Black?" and with a child's first encounter with prejudice.

Directing attention to the Black middle class also requires that we consider the relative importance of the two components in *ethclass*, Milton Gordon's concept introduced in Chapter 5. The degree to which relatively affluent Blacks identify themselves on class terms or racial terms is an important ideological question. Du Bois argued that when racism decreases, class issues become more important (1952, p. 202). As Du Bois saw it, exploitation would remain and many of the same people will continue to be subordinate. Black elites might become economically successful, either as entrepreneurs (Black capitalists) or professionals (Black white-collar workers), but they would continue to identify with and serve the dominant group's interest.

African-American women knowledgeable about the labor market's limited opportunities for people of color, see their jobs as more crucial to success than do White women. To attain and maintain a middle-class lifestyle is quite an achievement for African Americans, and studies show that they view an occupation as a primary concern and that marriage may have to be a secondary concern. Marriage is a goal, but African American women are more likely than their male counterparts to view financial security as an important reason to get married. This reflects again, as noted earlier in the chapter, on the plight of Black men today in both education or the job market (Hatchett, 1991; Higginbotham and Weber, 1991).

Social scientists have long recognized the importance of class. *Class* is a term used by sociologist Max Weber to refer to persons who share a similar level of wealth and income. The significance of class in people's lives is apparent to all. In the United States today, roughly half of the middle-class populations suffers from chronic physical conditions that limit their activity, compared with only one in eleven among the affluent. The poor are more likely to become victims of crime, and they are only about half as likely as the affluent to send their children to colleges or vocational schools (Schaefer and Lamm, 1992, p. 92).

Once the importance of class is recognized, it becomes reasonable to assume that some deprivation that members of minorities experience is due to their membership in a lower social class rather than to prejudice and discrimination based on race and ethnicity. As Chapter 3's examination of total discrimination showed, one element in today's social inequality is past discrimination, including events of the magnitude of slavery. Such past events are important reasons racial and ethnic minorities are disproportionately poor.

The complexity of relative influence of race and class was apparent in the controversy surrounding the publication of sociologist William J. Wilson's *The Declining Significance of Race.* Pointing to the increasing influence of African Americans, Wilson (1980, p. 150) concluded that "class has become more important than race in determining black life-chances in the modern world." The policy implications of his conclusion are that programs must be developed to confront class subordination rather than ethnic and racial discrimination. Wilson does not deny the legacy of discrimination reflected in the disproportionate number of Blacks who are poor, less educated, and residents of inadequate and overcrowded housing. He points, however, to "compelling evidence" that young Blacks are successfully competing with young Whites.

Critics of Wilson comment that focusing attention on this small educated elite ignores vast numbers of African Americans relegated to the lower class (Pinkney, 1984, pp. 13–16; Willie, 1978, 1979). Wilson himself is not guilty of such an oversimplification and indeed expresses concern over lower-class, inner-city Blacks' seemingly falling even further behind, as do those who become a part of the irregular economy discussed in Chapter 3. He points out that the poor are socially isolated and have shrinking economic opportunities (1987a, 1987b). It is easy to conclude superficially, however, that because educated Blacks are entering the middle class, race has ceased to be of concern. You may begin to evaluate for yourself, as you consider Wilson's response to his critics in "Listen to Their Voices."

As a result of controversy, researchers have given increased attention to the relative roles of race and class in accounting for Black subordination in the United States. A 1986 study using national survey data drawn over a four-year period examined how the more affluent African Americans feel on such issues as government spending, assistance for the poor, and police treatment of minorities. There was little evidence of significant attitudinal difference among Blacks in different social classes. Indeed, any differences that were found showed middle-class Blacks actually taking more liberal positions than did the poor (Gilliam, 1986). Similarly, Thomas and Hughes (1986) found little change in the quality of life experienced by African Americans from 1972 to 1985 regardless of social class. The vitality of race in determining a way of life is apparent as we examine Blacks confronting the dominant group's interests in controlling crime and disturbing justice.

### ❖ *LISTEN TO THEIR VOICES* ❖

## *The Declining Significance of Race: Revisited but Not Revised*

*William Julius Wilson*

*Few recent sociology books attracted as much attention as William Julius Wilson's* The Declining Significance of Race, *first published in 1978. In the following selection Wilson, a Black sociologist at the University of Chicago and former president of the American Sociological Association, responds to the criticism of Charles V. Willie, a Black sociologist at Harvard, in which Willie offers the counterhypothesis that race has increased in significance, especially for middle class Blacks who, because of school desegregation and affirmative action, have come into direct contact with Whites for the first time for extended social interaction.*

My book is an attempt to explain race and class in the American experience. I feel that in order to understand the changing issues of race and, indeed, the relationship between class and race in America, a framework that would relate changes in intergroup relations with changes in the American social structure is required. In-dividual mobility is not used as the independent variable in explaining race and class experiences, as Willie's analysis would suggest. Rather I try to show how the economy and state interacted in different historical periods not only to structure the relations between blacks and whites and to produce dissimilar contexts for the manifestation of racial antagonisms, but also to create different situations for racial group access to rewards and privileges. Using this framework, I define three stages of American race relations (the preindustrial, industrial, and modern industrial), stages in which I describe the role of both the system of production and the state in the development of race and class relations.

Although my book devotes considerable attention to the preindustrial and industrial periods of American race relations, it is my description of the modern industrial period that has generated controversy and has provoked Willie to respond. I contend that in the earlier periods, whether one focuses on the way race relations were structured by the economy or by the state or both, racial oppression (ranging from the exploitation of black labor by the economic elite to the elimination of black competition, especially economic competition, by the white masses) was a characteristic and important aspect of life. However, I also maintain that in the modern industrial period the economy and the state have, in relatively independent ways, shifted the basis of racial antagonisms away from black/ white economic contact to social, political, and community issues. The net effect is a growing class division among blacks, a situation, in other words, in which economic class has been elevated to a position of greater importance than race in determining individual black opportunities for living conditions and personal life experiences. . . .

Let me say, first of all, that when I speak of the declining significance of race, I am referring to the role it now plays in determining black life chances—in other words, the changing impact of race in the economic sector and, in particular, the importance of race in changing mobility opportunities. Thus, as I have tried to show, as the barriers to entering mainstream occupations were removed for educated blacks, they began to move away from the lower paying professions such as teaching and social work and began in significant numbers to prepare themselves for careers in finance, management, chemistry, engineering, accounting, and other professional areas. Nowhere in my

book do I argue that race is "irrelevant or insignificant." It is not simply an either-or situation, rather it is a matter of degree. And I strongly emphasized that there is still a strong basis for racial antagonism on the social, community, and political levels.

I do not disagree with the way in which Willie has proposed his counter-hypothesis. Many educated blacks do experience psychological discomfort in new integrated situations. Willie and I could probably draw many personal examples of this. We both are black, and we both teach at elite universities. A few years ago almost no blacks were in such positions. But I am sure that neither of us would trade places with a poor black trapped in the ghetto and handcuffed to a menial, dead-end, and poorly paid job. That is the real problem in the black community, and no cries about the psychological discomfort of the integrated black elite should distract our attention from the abominable and deleterious physical conditions of the isolated black poor.

Published by permission of Transaction Publishers, from *Society*, Vol. 15, No. 5, pp. 11, 21. Copyright © 1978 by Transaction Publishers.

## HOUSING

Housing plays a major role in determining the quality of a person's life. For Blacks as for Whites, housing is the result of personal preferences and amount of income. Blacks differ from Whites, however, in that their housing has been restricted in a manner not employed against Whites. Black housing has improved, as indicated by statistics on home ownership, new construction, density of living units, and quality as measured by plumbing facilities. Despite such gains, Blacks remain behind Whites. The quality of Black housing is inferior to that of Whites at all income levels, yet Blacks pay a larger share of their income for the shelter they have.

Housing was the last major area to be covered by civil rights legislation. The delay was not due to its insignificance; quite the contrary, it was last precisely because housing touches so many parts of the American economy and relates to private property rights that legislators were slow to act. After an executive order by President Kennedy, the government required nondiscrimination in federally-assisted housing, but this ruling included only 7 percent of the housing market. In 1968, the Federal Fair Housing Law (Title VIII of the 1968 Civil Rights Act) and the Supreme Court decision in *Jones* v. *Mayer* combined to outlaw all racial discrimination in housing. Enforcement has remained weak, however, and many aspects of housing, real estate customs, and lending practices remain untouched.

In 1988, new attention was given to persistence of *redlining*, a practice in which financial lenders designated minority and racially changing neighborhoods as poor investments for home and commercial loans. Research documented that in many cities including Atlanta, Baltimore, Chicago, Philadelphia, and Washington, D.C., minority neighborhoods received fewer and smaller loans than White neighborhoods, even when economic factors were taken into account. Particularly compelling data emerged from a 1991 study by the Federal Reserve Board, which showed that White borrowers with the lowest incomes were approved for mortgages more often than Black borrowers with median incomes over $66,000 per year. The disparity continued whether mortgages were sought from local banks, the Federal Housing Administration, or the Veteran's Administration. Redlining exists primarily because of the continuation of the most

" YOU NEED TO SPEAK TO ONE OF OUR LOAN OFFICERS!"

*Marlette* © *1988*, The Atlanta Constitution.

prominent characteristic of Black housing, residential segregation (J. Knight, 1991; J. Schwartz, 1988; Shalay, 1988).

## Residential Segregation

Racial segregation has resulted from the actions of individual property owners supported and even encouraged by real estate organizations, laws, and the Federal Housing Administration (FHA). The motivation behind such action, aside from racial contempt, is fear that racial minorities jeopardize property values. In 1973 the U.S. Commission on Civil Rights surveyed research on this subject over the preceding 20 years and concluded that minority group residency does not inevitably lead to a decline in property values. This conclusion is verified by studies conducted in Baltimore, Chicago, Detroit, Houston, Kansas City, Louisville, Philadelphia, and San Francisco. The myth of instability in property values, however, sometimes becomes the basis for action—appraisers downgrade Black-occupied housing and White homeowners sell in a panic and glut the market. This rush is followed by a surge of African-American buyers willing to pay premium (artificially inflated) prices in the limited new areas for better housing. A study of owner-occupied housing in St. Louis found that wherever they live, whether in the ghetto or in integrated neighborhoods, African Americans pay more. In fact, Blacks pay about 15 percent more than Whites for equivalent housing across the board (Laurenti, 1960; Molotch, 1972; J. Yinger, 1978; see also Aaron, 1972).

The extent of segregation has remained relatively unchanged since the 1950s. Some researchers, using different sample sizes or different definitions, found evidence of a decline in segregation, but this result may have been due to a tight housing market that made it difficult for Whites to move out (Masters, 1975, p. 32; Sorensen et al., 1975; Van Valey et al., 1976). Even at best, such studies have shown only a moderate decline in segregation in some cities, with most Americans living racially apart from one another. All demographic analyses confirm that Blacks continue to live mostly in the central cities and Whites in the suburban fringe. Even cities that have, relatively speaking, lower levels of segregation may not offer greater housing opportunities for Blacks. Generally these lower levels of segregation point only to the presence of several ghettos, rather than just one, increasing the size of fringe areas where Black neighborhoods expand into adjoining White areas. Regardless of the indexes used, Whites and Blacks are unlikely to live near one another (Cortese et al., 1976a, 1976b; Massey et al., 1987; Massey and Denton, 1989; Simkus, 1978; Sorensen et al., 1975; Taeuber, 1975; Taeuber and Taeuber, 1964, 1969, 1976; Van Valey et al., 1976).

Although Black concentration in the central cities has increased, a small but growing number of Blacks have moved into suburban areas. Between 1981 and 1988, the proportion of the nation's African Americans living in suburban areas rose from 17 percent to 25 percent. Yet the most significant growth in the percentage of suburban Blacks has come from movement into suburbs that are predominantly Black or are adjacent to predominantly Black areas. In many instances, therefore, it represents further ghettoization and spillover from city slums. It is not necessarily a signal of two cars and a backyard pool. In many instances, the suburbs with large Black populations are isolated from surrounding White communities and have less satisfactory housing and municipal services (Dunn and Johnson, 1991).

## The Outlook

A dual housing market is part of today's reality, although attacks continue against remaining legal barriers to fair housing. *Zoning laws*, in theory, are enacted to ensure that specific standards of housing construction are satisfied. These regulations can also separate industrial and commercial enterprises from residential areas. Some zoning laws in suburbs, though, have seemed to curb development of low- and moderate-income housing that would attract African Americans who want to move out of the central cities.

For years, construction of low-income public housing in the ghetto has furthered racial segregation. Yet the courts have not ruled consistently in recent years in this matter so that, as with affirmative action and busing, public officials lack clear guidance. In the suburban Chicago community of Arlington Heights, the courts decided in 1977 that a community could refuse to rezone to allow low-income housing, a policy that effectively kept out African Americans. Yet in 1988, the courts fined Yonkers, a city adjoining New York City, for failing to build public housing for low- and middle-income households in a way that would foster integration.

Even if court decisions continue to dismantle exclusionary housing practices, the rapid growth of integrated neighborhoods is unlikely. In the future Black housing (1) will continue to improve, (2) will remain in all-Black neighborhoods, and (3) will remain inferior in quality to White housing. This gap is greater than can be explained by differences in social class.

Remarkably little has changed. Economist John Weicher (1988) looked at seven slums in 1988 to examine the changes that had occurred in the 20 years surrounding the riots of the 1960s. The results were depressing in places such as Bedford-Stuyvesant in Brooklyn, Watts in Los Angeles, and Woodlawn in Chicago. Incomes were actually lower, and the quality of plumbing in housing had deteriorated in the last half of the period studied. Perhaps the most encouraging statistic was that these slums housed only half as many people as they had before.

## CRIMINAL JUSTICE

A complex, sensitive topic affecting African Americans is their role in criminal justice. It encompasses the paucity of lawyers (2.6 percent of attorneys are Black) to the large proportion of inmates facing death sentences (more than 42 percent are Black).

*In an effort to bridge the gap between law enforcement agencies and community residents, police departments have actively recruited both minorities and women.*

Data collected annually in the FBI's *Uniform Crime Report* show that Blacks account for 25 percent of arrests, even though they represent only about 12 percent of the nation's population. Conflict theorists point out that the higher arrest rate is not surprising for a group that is disproportionately poor and therefore much less able to afford private attorneys, who might be able to prevent formal arrests from taking place. Even more significantly, the *Uniform Crime Report* focuses on index crimes (mainly property crimes), which are the type of crimes most often committed by low-income persons (Pinkney, 1987, pp. 132–138).

Interestingly—and in contrast to popular misconceptions about crime—African Americans and the poor are especially likely to be the victims of serious crimes. This is documented in *victimization surveys*, which are systematic interviews of ordinary people carried out annually to learn how much crime occurs. These Bureau of Justice statistics show that Black men have a 1 in 21 chance of being murdered, compared with a 1 in 131 chance for White men (Sargent, 1986).

The videotaped beating of Rodney King and the subsequent not-guilty verdict of four Los Angeles police officers touched off the 1992 South-Central Los

Angeles riots. These events had very different messages to the public. For Blacks, many minorities, and sympathetic Whites, the events called for renewed attention to police procedures and the handling of citizen complaints. For others, the televised looting and arson pointed to the need for a stronger law enforcement presence in the inner city.

Central to the concerns minorities often express about the criminal justice system is *differential* justice; that is, Whites are dealt with more leniently than Blacks whether at time of arrest, indictment, conviction, sentencing, or parole. Several studies demonstrate that police often deal with Black youths more harshly than with White youngsters.

Conflict theorists argue that the criminal justice system, through these differential applications of social control, serves to keep certain groups in their deprived systems. A 1983 report documented that African Americans and Hispanics receive stiffer prison sentences and serve more time in jail than Whites convicted of similar felonies (Petersilia, 1983; also see Bridges et al., 1988; Klein et al., 1988). In this two-year study, prepared for the National Institute of Corrections of the U.S. Department of Justice, data showed that minorities were less able to make bail than Whites and more likely to have court-appointed lawyers. The study surveyed three states—California, Michigan, and Texas—which accounted for 22 percent of the nation's inmates. Although no racial differences were found in the type of prison programs to which inmates were assigned, the study did find significant differences in length of sentences:

- In California, Hispanics' sentences were about six and one-half months longer than Whites'; Blacks' were almost one and one-half months longer than Whites'.
- In Texas, Hispanics' sentences were more than two months longer than Whites'; Blacks' are three and one-half months longer than Whites'.
- In Michigan, Blacks' sentences averaged more than seven months longer than Whites'.
- Differential justice is not limited to adult offenders. Black juveniles appeared to be at greater risk for being charged with more serious offenses than Whites involved in comparable levels of delinquent behavior (Huizinga and Elliott, 1987).

While the racial, ethnic, or social class background of criminal suspects and offenders may lead to differential justice, the background of crime *victims* can achieve the same result. A study by the *Chicago Sun-Times* of 400 randomly-selected crimes (including rapes, stabbings, and shootings) found that crimes against members of minority groups are more likely to be "downgraded" from felonies to minor offenses, thereby reducing the seriousness of the offense and the potential jail sentence. All the downgraded crimes studied involved a victim from a minority group; in most cases, both the victim and the assailant were Black or Hispanic and lived in a low-income neighborhood. One researcher, reflecting on the social hierarchies of the United States, has suggested that this pattern of differential justice was "victim discounting"—that is, "if the victim is worth less, the crime is worth less" (Gibbons, 1985, pp. 1, 18).

Victim discounting also appears to be a factor in the imposition of the death penalty since the key factor is not so much the race or class background of the killer as the race of the victim. In the first four years of administering the death penalty after it was reinstituted in the United States in 1977, state attorneys were twice as likely to seek the death penalty when a Black was convicted of killing a White as when a Black killed a Black or a White killed a White (McManus, 1985, p. 47).

Although some 60 percent of all homicide victims in the United States are African American, 75 percent of the inmates currently on death row were convicted of killing Whites. Viewed from a conflict perspective, such data suggest that, in applying the death penalty, the American judicial system considers Black lives less valuable than White lives. Prosecutors are less likely to argue for a death sentence—and juries and judges less likely to impose it—when the murder victim is Black.

Statistically based arguments against the death penalty suffered a grave blow as a result of the 1987 Supreme Court ruling in the case of *McCleskey* v. *Kemp*. In an appeal of a murder conviction, the defense presented data showing that the murderer of a White person in Georgia was 11 times more likely to receive a death sentence than the murderer of a Black person. However, in a 5-4 decision that provoked bitter dissents, the Court held that such "apparent disparities" in sentencing do not in themselves constitute unlawful racial discrimination. Instead, the defendant in any such criminal case "must prove that the decision makers in *his* case acted with a discriminatory purpose." The ruling in *McCleskey* v. *Kemp* removed one of the last major hurdles restricting application of capital punishment in the United States. In a stinging critique, Benjamin Hooks, executive director of the National Association for the Advancement of Colored People (NAACP), accused the justices of giving a "green light" for "an even broader imposition of the death penalty on Black victims." A cursory view of the criminal justice system finds little evidence to support Wilson's thesis that race is of "declining significance" (Baldus et al., 1986; Elsasser, 1987, p. 8; Radelet, 1989; S. Taylor, 1987c, p. B13).

## HEALTH CARE

The price of being Black in the United States took on new importance with the release in 1990 of a shocking study in a prestigious medical journal that reveals that a man in Harlem, a predominantly Black neighborhood in New York City, is less likely to live to the age of 65 than is a man in Bangladesh, one of the poorest nations of the world. Whereas 55 percent will reach age 65 there, the same will be true for only 40 percent of men in Harlem. According to this study, based on data from the period 1979-1981, the factors contributing to Harlem's high mortality rate, in order, were cardiovascular disease, cirrhosis, homicide, tumors, and drug dependency. However, as the researchers note, the problem of mortality among 25- to 44-year-olds in Harlem has become even more severe since 1980, with acquired immunodeficiency syndrome (AIDS) now established as the most common cause of death in this age group. The researchers add that Harlem's high mortality rate is not unique; they have identified 53 other health areas, predominantly inner-city neighborhoods with high Black or Hispanic populations, that have age-adjusted mortality rates approximately twice the national average for Whites (McCord and Freeman, 1990).

The morbidity and mortality rates for Blacks as a group, and not just Harlem men, are equally distressing. Compared with Whites, Blacks have higher death rates from diseases of the heart, pneumonia, diabetes, and cancer. In 1987, the death rate for strokes was twice as high among African Americans as it was among Whites. Such epidemiological findings reflect in part the higher proportion of Blacks found among the nation's lower classes. According to a study released by the federal government in 1990, White Americans can expect to live 75.6 years. By contrast, life expectancy for Blacks is 69.2 years, while for Black men it is only 64.9 years and has been *decreasing* since the mid-1980s (Hilts, 1990; *New York Times*, 1990).

What accounts for these racial differences? According to a national survey conducted in 1986, African Americans of all income levels are substantially worse off than Whites in terms of access to physicians. For example, African Americans had a lower rate of visits to physicians, despite higher rates of serious illness among Blacks than Whites. The survey points to significantly less use of medical care by Blacks, and adds that Blacks are less likely than Whites to have medical insurance. Finally, in comparison with Whites, Blacks were found to be less satisfied with the health care they received from physicians and hospital personnel (Blendon et al., 1989).

A study in Massachusetts, for example, found that substantial racial inequalities exist in the provision of cardiac care. In comparison with Blacks, a significantly higher proportion of Whites admitted to Massachusetts hospitals with heart problems undergo cardiac bypass operations and cardiac catheterizations. These racial differences are evident even among patients hospitalized with serious heart problems (Wenneker and Epstein, 1989).

Drawing upon the conflict perspective, sociologist Howard Waitzkin (1986) suggests that racial tensions contribute to the medical problems of Black Americans. In his view, the stress resulting from racial prejudice and discrimination helps to explain the higher rates of hypertension found among African Americans (and Hispanics) compared with Whites. Hypertension is twice as common in Blacks as in Whites; it is believed to be a critical factor in Blacks' high mortality rates from heart disease, kidney disease, and stroke. Although there is disagreement among medical experts, some argue that the stress resulting from racism and suppressed hostility exacerbates hypertension among Blacks (Coleman, 1990).

The previous section noted that Blacks are underrepresented in the criminal justice system among lawyers. A similar phenomenon emerges in health care. Blacks constituted about 6 percent of medical school enrollment in 1986—a figure that has remained the same since 1975. Blacks represented only 3 percent of practicing physicians. Black Americans are also underrepresented in other areas of medicine. The fact that Blacks are even underrepresented in clinical and research trials of new drugs suggests that insufficient data have been generated to accurately assess the safety of these chemicals on American Blacks (Lloyd and Miller, 1989; N. Miller, 1987; Svensson, 1989).

Just how significant is the impact of poorer health on the lives of the nation's less educated people, less affluent classes, and minorities? Drawing upon a variety of research studies, population specialist Evelyn Kitagawa (1972) estimated the "excess mortality rate" to be 20 percent. In other words, 20 percent more people were dying than otherwise might have, because of differentially poor health linked to race and class. Using Kitagawa's model, we can calculate that if every African American in the United States were White and had at least 1 year of college education, some 53,000 fewer Blacks would have died in 1990 and in each succeeding year (Bureau of the Census, 1991a, p. 80).

## POLITICS

Blacks have never received an equal share of the political pie. After Reconstruction, it was not until 1928 that a Black was again elected to Congress. Now, over 60 years and several civil rights acts later, there are still only 24 Black congressional representatives (see Table 8.4). Recent years have brought some improvement. In fact, between 1970 and 1990, the number of Black elected officials has increased more than fivefold (see Table 8.5).

In May 1973 Councilman Tom Bradley, a Black sharecropper's son, defeated incumbent Sam Yorty to become mayor of Los Angeles. Bradley's victory was particularly impressive because Los Angeles is only 15 percent Black. By 1991, 330 other cities had Black mayors, including Chicago, Philadelphia, Detroit, Washington, D.C., New Orleans, New York City, and Atlanta.

African Americans, despite the growing number of Black elected officials, are still looking for a national political leader. Also the gains by Blacks in number of elected officeholders are not as great as many Blacks and sympathetic Whites would like to see. Black gains do, however, increase the likelihood that legislative moves to bring about equality will continue. Black officials may find it difficult, if not impossible, to work in a manner of which all Blacks can approve. But Black officials are keenly aware of their responsibility for serving the Black community effectively (Conyers and Wallace, 1976; Lichter, 1985; Rollins, 1977; Sussman, 1985).

The Reverend Jesse Jackson became the most visible Black political figure in the 1980s even though never elected to office. Well known for his civil rights

**TABLE 8.4**   Black Elected Officials, 1991

It is no longer unusual for Blacks to be elected to office at all levels and in all regions of the country.

| | Region | | | | |
|---|---|---|---|---|---|
| Level of Office | Northeast | Midwest | South[a] | West | Total |
| Federal | 7 | 8 | 7 | 4 | 26 |
| State | 76 | 89 | 252 | 27 | 444 |
| Substate, regional | 0 | 0 | 0 | 3 | 3 |
| County | 21 | 85 | 669 | 15 | 790 |
| Mayors | 23 | 58 | 221 | 12 | 314 |
| Municipal[b] | 236 | 589 | 2,467 | 67 | 3,389 |
| Judicial and law enforcement[c] | 116 | 153 | 474 | 104 | 847 |
| Education[d] | 265 | 326 | 924 | 114 | 1,629 |
| Total | 744 | 1,318 | 5,034 | 346 | 7,442 |

[a]Excludes 35 officials in Virgin Islands.
[b]Includes vice-mayors, council members, commissioners, and other local officials.
[c]Includes judges, justices, magistrates, chiefs of police, constables, marshals, sheriffs, justices of the peace, and other law officials.
[d]Includes state and college boards, local school boards, and other educational officials.
*Source:* From data in the *National Roster of Black Elected Officials*, 1992, by the Joint Center for Political Studies. Reprinted by permission.

activity, Jackson campaigned for the 1984 Democratic nomination for president. His expressed goal was to create a "Rainbow Coalition" of disenfranchised Americans, including Blacks, Hispanics, Asian Americans, women, and gay people. Aided by a dramatic turnout of Black voters across the country, Jackson made a strong showing, winning 18 percent of the votes cast in Democratic presidential primaries. His success appeared to encourage more Blacks to run for national and statewide offices. Jackson ran for president again in 1988 and won 29 percent of the votes in Democratic primaries, second only to the 43 percent won by Massachusetts governor Michael Dukakis (*Congressional Quarterly*, 1984; Dionne, 1988). Douglas Wilder, the Black governor of Virginia, mounted a race for the next Democratic presidential nomination, but pulled out before the beginning of the 1992 primaries.

Another positive development that has attracted few headlines as the growth of Blacks in union politics. In 1984, only two of the AFL-CIO's 95 affiliates were headed by Blacks, but by 1989 two more were led by Blacks—two of the larger unions as well. Blacks are even better represented in the second and third echelons of union power (Noble, 1989).

African Americans continue to hold a disproportionately small share of elective and appointive offices in the United States. They usually serve in predominantly Black areas and rarely represent mixed constituencies. White political leaders, however, continue to represent many areas populated by racial minorities. As they have since passage of the Voting Rights Act of 1965, Black Amer-

**TABLE 8.5**    Black Elected Officials, 1970–1990

Although the rate of increase has leveled off, the number of Black elected officials has continued to increase.

| Year | Number | Percentage Change During Preceding 2 Years | Percentage Increase Since 1969 |
|------|--------|--------------------------------------------|--------------------------------|
| 1970 | 1,469 | — | — |
| 1972 | 2,264 | 54 | 54 |
| 1974 | 2,991 | 32 | 104 |
| 1976 | 3,979 | 33 | 171 |
| 1978 | 4,503 | 13 | 207 |
| 1980 | 4,912 | 9 | 234 |
| 1982 | 5,160 | 5 | 251 |
| 1984 | 5,700 | 11 | 288 |
| 1986 | 6,424 | 13 | 337 |
| 1988 | 7,225 | 12 | 392 |
| 1990 | 7,370 | 2 | 402 |

*Source:* From data in *National Roster of Black Elected Officials,* 1991, by the Joint Center for Political Studies.

icans continue to grow as a political force, but still fall far short of parity in elective and appointive office (Pinkney, 1987, pp. 112–115).

## GLANCING BACK AND LOOKING AHEAD

Black and White Americans have dealt with the continued disparity between the two groups by endorsing several ideologies. Assimilation was the driving force behind the civil rights movement, which sought to integrate Whites and Blacks into one society. People who rejected any contact with the other group endorsed separatism. Both Whites and Blacks, as Chapter 2 showed, generally lent little support for separatism. The government and various Black organizations in the latter 1960s began to recognize cultural pluralism as a goal, at least paying lip service to the desire of many African Americans to exercise cultural and economic autonomy. Perhaps in no other issue is this condition more evident than in the schools.

As the future of African-American people in the United States unfolds, one element of the population generally unnoticed thus far may move into prominence. An evergrowing proportion of the Black population consists of people of foreign birth. In the 1980 census, 816,000 foreign-born Blacks were counted, or 3.1 percent of the Black population, the highest ever recorded. Projections suggest that in another 30 years the foreign-born proportion of the Black population will increase to 7–10 percent. English-speaking West Indians have long emigrated to the United States, but such an increase, coupled with growing numbers of Blacks speaking French, Creole, Spanish, Portuguese, Swahili, and other African languages, will add new diversity within the Black community (Farley and Allen, 1987, pp. 302–407; Reid, 1986).

Some measures of progress have registered gains for African Americans in the last ten years—degree of educational attainment, numbers employed in white-collar occupations, and numbers elected to political offices. Other indicators have shown no improvement—income relative to Whites and residential segregation. Still other barometers of progress have registered mixed or disappointing results—the poverty rate, the degree of family stability, and numbers present in higher education. The serious geographic mismatch between the places where Blacks reside—the central cities and rural South—and the locations of better jobs—the outer fringes of metropolitan areas—continue to hinder progress (Pettigrew, 1985; D. Taylor, 1984). The gains that have been made are substantial, and they occur in the socially significant areas of education and occupation. This mixed improvement has occurred in a generation inspired and spurred on to bring about change. If the resolve to continue toward that goal lessens in the United States, the picture may become even bleaker, for the rate of positive change will decline further.

## KEY TERMS

**class** As defined by Max Weber, persons who share similar levels of wealth.

**de facto segregation** Segregation that results from residential patterns, such as use of neighborhood schools in communities in which there is residential segregation.

**de jure segregation** Segregation that results from assignment of children to schools specifically to maintain racial separation in schools.

**redlining** Practice of financial lenders refusing to grant home and commercial loans in minority and racially changing neighborhoods.

**set asides** Programs stipulating a minimum proportion of government contracts that must be awarded to minority-owned businesses.

**underemployment** Work at a job for which the worker is overqualified; involuntary part-time employment instead of full-time; or intermittent employment.

**victimization surveys** Annual attempt to measure crime rates by interviewing ordinary citizens who may or may not have been crime victims.

**zoning laws** Legal provisions stipulating land use and architectural design of housing, often employed to keep racial minorities and low-income persons out of suburban areas.

## FOR FURTHER INFORMATION

Walter R. Allen, Edgar G. Epps, and Nesha Z. Haniff. *College in Black and White.* Albany: State University of New York Press, 1991.

  A series of seventeen articles dealing with African Americans at both predominantly White as well as historically Black universities.

James E. Blackwell. *The Black Community: Diversity and Unity,* 3rd ed. New York: Harper-Collins, 1991.

  An analysis of the contemporary situation of African American social institutions.

George Davis and Glegg Watson. *Black Life in Corporate America: Swimming in the Mainstream.* Garden City, NY: Anchor Press, 1982.

Writer Davis and executive Watson trace the entry of Blacks into executive positions—a world previously inhabited almost entirely by White males.

Reynolds, Farley. *Blacks and Whites: Narrowing the Gap.* Cambridge, MA: Harvard University Press, 1984.

Drawing upon demographic and statistical measures, Farley looks at the mixed success of Black Americans relative to that of Whites.

Andrew Hacker. *Two Nations: Black and White, Separate, Hostile, Unequal.* New York: Charles Scribner's Sons, 1992.

Political scientist Hacker analyzes the relative status of African Americans in terms of family, income, employment, education, criminal justice, and government.

James S. Jackson, ed. *Life in Black America.* Newbury Park, CA: Sage Publications, 1991.

Articles on Black neighborhood life, families, religion, work and unemployment, mental and physical health, and politics.

Gerald David Jaynes and Robin M. Williams, Jr., eds. *A Common Destiny: Blacks and American Society.* Washington, DC: National Academy Press, 1989.

Completed under the auspices of the National Research Council, this report examines the period since 1940 and attempts to provide a comprehensive picture of African Americans today.

Bart Landry. *The New Black Middle Class.* Berkeley: University of California Press, 1987.

Landry considers historical treatments of the Black middle class but concentrates the way of life of contemporary modestly well-off Black Americans.

Alphonso Pinkney. *Black Americans,* 3rd ed. Englewood Cliffs, NJ: Prentice-Hall, 1987.

Pinkney presents an excellent profile of Blacks and devotes a chapter to Black nationalism, although that subject is described in even greater detail in the author's 1976 work. He evaluates Milton Gordon's seven assimilation variables in the context of contemporary Black life.

William Pleasant, ed. *Independent Black Leadership in America.* New York: Castillo International Publications, 1990.

A collection of statements by three controversial African Americans—Minister Louis Farrakhan, Dr. Lenora Fulant, and Rev. Al Sharpton.

Lee Rainwater and William L. Yancey, eds. *The Moynihan Report and the Politics of Controversy.* Cambridge, MA: MIT Press, 1967.

The complete text of the Moynihan Report is accompanied by critical responses by civil rights leaders, government officials, and social scientists.

Robert Staples, ed. *The Black Family: Essays and Studies,* 3rd ed. Belmont, CA: Wadsworth, 1986.

This collection of 32 articles covers all aspects of Black family life, including dating, alternative ways of life, and public policy.

William J. Wilson. *The Declining Significance of Race: Blacks and Changing American Institutions,* 2nd ed. Chicago: University of Chicago Press, 1980.

Although acknowledging Black Americans' disadvantaged position compared to Whites, Wilson argues that for the first time in the nation's history, class is more important than race in determining Black people's access to privilege and power.

## Chapter Nine

# HISPANIC AMERICANS

*Chapter Outline*

**The Language Barrier**
Quality of Hispanic Schooling
Bilingualism
**Cuban Americans**
Immigration Patterns
The Present Picture

**Central and South Americans**
Immigration Patterns
The Present Picture
**Glancing Back and Looking Ahead**
**Key Terms**
**For Further Information**

---

**❊ HIGHLIGHTS ❊**

The group label *Hispanic American* links a diverse population of people who share a common language heritage but otherwise have many significant differences. The language barrier in an assimilationist-oriented society has been of major importance to Hispanics. For generations schools made it difficult for Spanish-speaking children to succeed. The United States has only recently recognized its *bilingual, bicultural* heritage and allowed knowledge of a language other than English to be an asset, rather than a liability. The strength of resistance even to elements of pluralism has been exhibited by the *language purity* movement. Hispanics include several major groups, of which Chicanos, Puerto Ricans, and Cubans are the largest. Cuban Americans constitute a significant presence in southern Florida. Immigrants and refugees from Central and South America have also increasingly established communities throughout the United States.

---

More than 1 out of 12 Americans are of Spanish or Latin American origin. The Census Bureau estimates that by 2080, Hispanics will number 59.6 million and constitute 19.2 percent of the population. Collectively, Hispanics (or Latinos) would outnumber Blacks by that date (Bureau of the Census, 1986b; Exter, 1987). Today, the majority of Hispanics are Chicanos, or Mexican Americans. Puerto Ricans and Cuban Americans account for the largest segment of the remaining 8 million Hispanics (see Table 9.1).

The Hispanic influence is everywhere. Motion pictures of the 1980s such as *La Bamba, Born in East L.A., Stand and Deliver,* and *Salsa* did not cater to Hispanic audiences alone. Cuban-born fashion designer Adolfo was a favorite of Nancy

---

**TABLE 9.1**  Hispanic Population, 1990

The Hispanic population accounts for one out of twenty Americans, with Chicanos forming the largest group.

| Group | Percentage of Hispanics | Percentage of Population | Number (in thousands) |
|---|---|---|---|
| Chicano | 64.0 | 5.4 | 13,305 |
| Puerto Rican | 10.5 | .9 | 2,180 |
| Cuban | 4.9 | .4 | 1,014 |
| Central and South Americans | 13.7 | 1.1 | 2,842 |
| Other | 6.9 | .6 | 1,437 |
| Total | 100.0 | 8.4 | 20,778 |

*Source:* Bureau of the Census, 1991f, p. 6.

Reagan. Politicians acknowledge that they must address the needs and desires of Hispanic Americans. Music groups such as Los Lobos and the Miami Sound Machine attract listeners throughout the United States. Are these significant signs of acceptance or remnants of tolerant curiosity? In this and the next two chapters, we will examine the vibrant, growing group of Hispanic citizens in the United States (Lacayo, 1988).

People of Spanish or Latin origin share the group labels *Hispanic* or *Latino* and a common ancestral home, Central and South America. The *Hispanic* label combines the offspring of colonized natives, the *Hispanos,* with the descendants of foreigners, and with political and economic refugees under one ethnic umbrella (Nelson and Tienda, 1985). The term Hispanic is not universally used and some prefer Latino. Furthermore, sharp differences exist among the cultures of Latin America. In the United States, continued immigration keeps these differences alive. A survey of Hispanics born in the United States showed that 81 percent wanted to be viewed by their Hispanic as well as by their American identity (Ogletree and Ujlaki, 1985, p. 33).

The various segments of the Hispanic population live in different regions— Chicanos are mostly in the Southwest, Puerto Ricans in the Northeast (primarily New York City), and Cuban Americans in Florida (see Figure 9.1). The political strength of Hispanics is felt most in the Southwest. Over 60 percent of the nation's Hispanics are located in Arizona, California, Colorado, New Mexico, and Texas. This Hispanic population is dominated by Chicanos, of course, who account for almost 90 percent of the Southwest's Hispanics and are also a major factor in that region's growth. Chicanos accounted for half of Texas' growth of over 2.7 million during the 1980s (Bureau of the Census, 1991e).

Some prevailing images of Hispanic settlements in the United States are no longer accurate. Hispanics do not live in rural areas but are generally urban dwellers—86 percent of Hispanics live in metropolitan areas, contrasted to 73 percent of the total population. Hispanics have moved away from their traditional areas of settlement. Many Chicanos have left the Southwest and Puerto Ricans have left New York City. In 1940, 88 percent of Puerto Ricans residing in the United States lived in New York City, but by the 1980 census the proportion had dropped to less than half.

## THE LANGUAGE BARRIER

Hispanics, wherever they reside in the United States, share the heritage of the Spanish language. They do not all speak Spanish, but most do, and if they speak English in the larger world, they frequently speak Spanish at home. So identified is the language with the people that such phrases as "Spanish-speaking people" or "people with a Spanish surname" are frequently employed demographically.

The myth of Anglo superiority has rested in part on language differences. (The term *Anglo* in the following text will mean all non-Hispanics, but primarily Whites.) First, criteria for economic and social achievement usually include

**FIGURE 9.1**   Where Most Hispanics Live, 1990

Nearly 86 percent of the 22.4 million Hispanics in the United States in 1990 lived in 9 states. Chicanos, the largest Hispanic group, are concentrated in the Southwest, particularly California and Texas. Most Puerto Ricans live in New York and New Jersey. Cubans are primarily in Florida. The largest numbers of the fourth, more scattered group, "other Hispanic," live in California and New York.

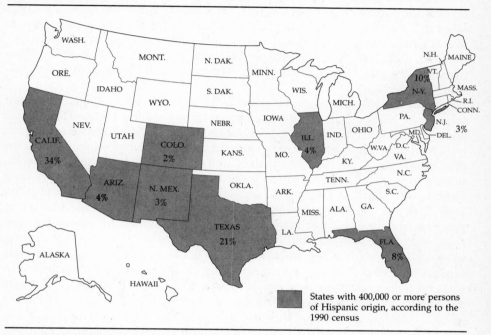

*Source:* Bureau of the Census, 1991e.

proficiency in English. By such standards, Spanish-speaking pupils are judged less able to compete. Many Americans perceive French and German as the only cultured foreign languages. Further, many Anglos believe that occupationally, Spanish is not an asset. Only recently, as government agencies belatedly begin to service Hispanic people, and as businesses recognize the growing Hispanic consumer market, have Anglos recognized that knowing Spanish is not only useful but necessary to carry out certain tasks.

The plight of Spanish-speaking individuals is a product of Anglo ethnocentrism, which ignores the value of any language other than English. In 1979, nearly 18 million people in the United States spoke something other than English at home. Of these, half spoke Spanish. The language barrier is especially daunting for the 2.5 million Spanish-speaking people who cannot speak English or do so with great difficulty (Bureau of the Census, 1976a, 1982a, p. 38; Morrow and Kuvlesky, 1982).

## Quality of Hispanic Schooling

The devaluing of the Spanish language has until recently, resulted in a conscious effort to discourage Hispanics from using it. This intent has been most evident in the schools. In the recent past in the Southwest, Chicanos (or Mexican Americans) were assigned to "Mexican schools," which were substantially underfunded in comparison to the regular public schools. Legal action against such schools dates back to 1945, but it was not until 1970 that the Supreme Court ruled in *Cisneros* v. *Corpus Christi Independent School District* that de jure segregation of Chicanos was unconstitutional. Appeals delayed implementation of that decision, and so not until September 1975 was the de jure plan forcibly overturned in Corpus Christi, Texas (Commission on Civil Rights, 1976a, pp. 106–112).

Even in integrated schools, Hispanic children were given separate, unequal treatment. "No Spanish" was a rule enforced throughout the Southwest, Florida, and New York City by school boards in the 1960s. Children speaking Spanish on school grounds, even on the playground, might be punished with detention after school, fines, physical reprimands, and even expulsion for repeated violations. From 1855 to as recently as 1968, teaching in any language other than English was illegal in California. Such laws existed despite a provision in the 1848 Treaty of Guadalupe Hidalgo between the United States and Mexico that guaranteed the right of Mexicans to maintain their culture. All official publications were to be bilingual, but "English only" became the social norm. Young schoolchildren were not allowed to go to the washroom unless they made their request in perfect English. Spanish-speaking children were then humiliated in front of their classmates as they wet their pants. As late as 1971, 22 states specifically forbade bilingual instruction by law and no state required it. Finally in 1974, the Supreme Court unanimously ruled in *Lau* v. *Nichols* that it is a violation of civil rights to use English to teach pupils who cannot understand it. This ruling opened the way for bilingual instruction of Spanish-speaking schoolchildren. Ironically, this precedent involved Chinese students in San Francisco (Macias, 1973; Sheils, 1977; Stoddard, 1973; Vidal, 1977).

The poor treatment of Hispanic schoolchildren has in part been the result of school staffs having few Hispanics, who might better understand the problems faced by Spanish-speaking youths thrust into an English-language school system. The Commission on Civil Rights (1971b, 1974b) conducted an extensive survey on the education of Chicanos, especially in the Southwest. The study found that although Chicanos accounted for 17 percent of the Southwest's public school enrollment, only 4 percent of the teachers and 3 percent of the principals were Hispanic.

The campaign to discourage the use of Spanish has naturally taken its toll on Hispanic schoolchildren's performance. The devastating fact that most Spanish-speaking Texans spend twice as long as Anglos in the first grade is attributed to the children's speaking only Spanish. Through the twisted logic of dominant society, the children are held responsible and become the victims. As early as the 1930s, George Sanchez (1934) was warning his fellow educators about the fallacy of using tests in English to measure the potential of non-English-speaking children. Many of these pupils were classified as retarded or slow learners when, in fact, their only difficulty was lack of fluency in English. Such mistaken labeling impairs the learning of Hispanics, and perpetuates in their own eyes as well as those of Anglos the notion that they are less qualified to compete (Aspy, 1970; Commission on Civil Rights, 1974b, pp. 28–31; *The New York Times*, 1979; Steiner, 1974, pp. 382–396).

The language barrier extends beyond school into employment. Hispanics are more likely to learn about jobs by word of mouth and less likely than Anglos or Blacks to read job listings in newspapers or use employment agencies. Furthermore, the government has done little to help. Ironically, job training programs designed to help the poor compete are rarely offered in bilingual form (Commission on Civil Rights, 1976c, pp. 58, 69–70).

The importance of Spanish to Hispanics cannot be overstated. Even to English-speaking Hispanics, the language represents a cultural heritage centuries old. This recognition is particularly important because rules against using Spanish have generally extended to suppression of Hispanic cultures. Even in those places without the "no Spanish" rule, positive treatment of the Hispanic experience was still rare. As recently as 1969, California was alone in the Southwest in offering any courses on Mexican-American heritage in schools that were at least 10 percent Chicano. In the Southwest, where two cultures coexist, assimilation is essentially one-way (Commission on Civil Rights, 1972).

### *Bilingualism*

Should the United States place greater emphasis on respect for cultural diversity or should it promote shared cultural standards? Is it essential that English be the

*The growing economic power of the nation's Hispanics shows in this marketing pitch to Spanish-speaking Americans.*

sole language of instruction in American schools and universities? Such questions are part of the passionate debate on *bilingualism* currently under way in the
United States.

*Bilingualism* is the use of two or more languages in places of work or educational facilities, according each language equal legitimacy. Thus, a program of
bilingual education may instruct children in their native language (such as
Spanish) while gradually introducing them to the language of the dominant
society (English). If such a program is also bicultural, it will teach children about
the culture of both linguistic groups. Bilingualism has most often appeared as
an issue in the voting booth and in the classroom.

*Voting Rights.* In 1975, Congress moved toward recognizing the multilingual
background of the American people. Federal law now requires bilingual or even
multilingual ballots where census data show a substantial number of non-
English-speaking people. Even before Congress acted, the federal courts had
been ordering cities like Chicago, Miami, and New York City to provide bilingual ballots where necessary.

Historically, language minorities have not participated in elections to the
extent that Anglos have, and they have produced even fewer officeholders than
the Black community has. Table 9.2 documents the relatively small proportion
of Hispanics, compared to Blacks and to all Americans, who reported being
registered to vote and reported voting in both the 1972 and the 1988 presidential
elections.

The poor turnout was not because Hispanics were not interested in voting.
Many were ineligible because they were noncitizens. In the November 1988
election, 52 percent of Hispanics who did not vote were noncitizens, compared
to only 7 percent of non-Hispanics. This handicap may help to explain why only
29 percent of Hispanics compared to 57 percent of the people as a whole
reported voting in 1988. By contrast, Puerto Rican voters on the island of Puerto

---

**TABLE 9.2**   Voter Participation Reported, 1972 and 1988

Numerical minorities such as Blacks and Hispanics are at a disadvantage in national elections,
but the problem is compounded when they register and vote in smaller proportions than White
Americans.

| Group | 1972 | | 1988 | |
|---|---|---|---|---|
| | *Percent Registered* | *Percent Voted* | *Percent Registered* | *Percent Voted* |
| Whites | 73.4 | 64.5 | 67.9 | 59.1 |
| Hispanics | 44.4 | 37.5 | 35.5 | 28.8 |
| Blacks | 65.5 | 52.1 | 64.5 | 51.5 |
| Total population | 72.3 | 63.0 | 66.6 | 57.4 |

*Source:* Bureau of the Census, 1989b, pp. 1, 3.

Rico turn out in proportions that exceed those for Anglos, but they have a dismal record on the mainland, where they face English ballots (with some exceptions in New York City). Similarly, states with literacy tests had substantially lower voter registration in areas populated by Hispanics than states without such tests. The result of multilingual ballots should be more Hispanic officeholders, from school board members to legislators (Apple, 1975; Barrera et al., 1972; Bureau of the Census, 1989b, pp. 4–5; Commission on Civil Rights, 1971a, 1974a, 1976d, pp. 11–14; Lindsey, 1978; Tostado, 1985).

***Bilingual Education.*** *Bilingual education* allows students to learn academic material in their own language, while they are learning a second language. Ideally bilingual education programs also allow English-speaking pupils to be bilingual, but generally they are directed only to make non-English speakers proficient in more than one language.

Belatedly, bilingualism has become recognized as an asset. In the past, school systems' suppression of Spanish made many Hispanics *aliterate*—illiterate in both languages. Although children were superficially able to speak both English and Spanish, they could not speak and write either language correctly. Finally, in 1965, the Elementary and Secondary Education Act (ESEA) provided for

*A bilingual second-grade classroom in Los Angeles.*

bilingual education. Implementation of the ESEA provisions and subsequent programs has been slow.

Teaching English as a Second Language (ESL) programs have been the cornerstone of bilingual education, but they are limited in approach. For example, ESL programs tend to emphasize bilingual, but not bicultural, education. As a result, the method can unintentionally contribute to ethnocentric attitudes, especially if it seems to imply that a minority group is not really worthy of attention. As conflict theorists are quick to note, the interests of the less powerful—in this case, millions of non-English-speaking children—are those that are least likely to be recognized and respected. One alternative to the ESL approach, viewed with much less favor by advocates of bilingualism, is *English immersion*, through which students are taught primarily in English, using their native languages only when they do not understand their lessons. In practice, such instruction usually becomes an English-only "crash program" (Hechinger, 1987).

Bilingual education has been beset by problems. Its early supporters were disillusioned by the small number of English-speaking children participating and by the absence of a bicultural component in most programs. The frustration has been most clearly visible in the lack of consensus among educators on how best to implement bilingual programs. Even when a consensus is reached in a school district, superintendents find it difficult to get qualified instructors. The problem is further complicated by the presence of children speaking languages other than the predominant second language, so that superintendents must mount multilanguage programs. Indeed, federally supported programs now operate in an estimated 125 languages.

Do bilingual programs help children to learn English? It is difficult to reach firm conclusions on the effectiveness of the bilingual programs in general because they vary so widely in their approach to non-English-speaking children. Research studies evaluating bilingual programs among Navaho-speaking children in Arizona, Chinese-speaking children in New York City, French-speaking children in Louisiana and Minnesota, and Spanish-speaking children in several states have all demonstrated that a quality bilingual program can be effective in improving both general learning skills and performance in reading and speaking English. But some educational researchers seem to agree that studies on bilingual education have been methodologically unsound and thus remain inconclusive (Hakuta and Garcia, 1989; Imhoff, 1990; Ramirez et al., 1991; Willig, 1985).

Drawing upon the conflict sociological perspective, we can understand some of the attacks on bilingual programs. The criticisms do not necessarily result from careful educational research. Rather, they stem from the effort to assimilate children, and deprive them of language pluralism. This view is expressed in those who wish to stamp out "foreignness" wherever it occurs and especially in our schools. Research findings have little influence on those who, holding such ethnocentric views, try to persuade policy makers to follow their thinking. Success in bilingual education may begin to address the problem of high school dropouts and the paucity of Hispanics in colleges and universities.

*Language Purity.*  Attacks on bilingualism both in voting and in education have taken several forms, and have even broadened to question the appropriateness of United States' residents using any language other than English. Federal policy has become more restrictive. Local schools have been given more authority to determine appropriate methods of instruction; they have also been forced to provide more of their own funding for bilingual education. Early in 1981, the federal government decided to scrap new proposals requiring school districts to offer bilingual education to non-English-speaking children. The government's action was bitterly protested by Representative Robert Garcia, a Puerto Rican congressman from New York City, who stated, "This is a signal to the rest of the country that does not want civil rights for Hispanics that school districts can say, 'The hell with it, why should we bother?' It will be back to business as usual, which in many states is back to bigotry" (Barrett and Cooper, 1981, p. 24).

The congressman's warnings were not heeded. Beginning in 1985, federal funds for bilingual education could also be used for alternative types of programs, which include English immersion of Spanish-speaking children in the English-language programs. Furthermore, a 1988 law stipulates that no student

*By 1990, 18 states had declared English the official language. Copyright 1988, USA Today. Reprinted with permission.*

can be in a federally-funded transitional bilingual program for more than three years unless special requirements are met.

Attacks on bilingualism have come on a number of fronts. In 1983, San Francisco voters in a nonbinding referendum approved by a two-to-one vote a proposition opposing the practice of printing city ballots in Spanish and Chinese as well as English. In 1984, Californians passed by almost a three-to-one margin a statewide proposition supporting repeal of a federal requirement that ballots be printed in foreign languages as well as in English. The proposition passed even though a survey in California found that in 1984 about the same proportion of White ethnics used non-English ballots as did Hispanics. In response to this mood and in an overall effort to reduce federal spending, the Reagan admin- istration issued new regulations, beginning with the 1984 general election, sharply reducing the number of counties required to provide bilingual ballots for Hispanic Americans and other voters in need of bilingual services.

Besides these local initiatives, a proposed constitutional amendment was introduced in the Senate to designate English as the "official language of the nation." According to Senator Quentin N. Burdick of North Dakota, one of the English Language Amendment's sponsors, it would discourage both instructing of non-English-speaking students in their native languages and using election ballots printed in languages other than English. By 1990, there were active efforts to pass laws or voter-initiated referenda to declare English the official language in 37 states. Eighteen states already have such laws. These challenges come just as Hispanic voter registration was showing signs of growth. The Census Bureau estimates it grew to 47 percent between 1976 and 1984, com- pared to an increase of 37 percent in Black voter registration and 16 percent among Whites (Broder, 1986; Cain and Kiewiet, 1985; Donahue, 1985; Farrell and Weaver, 1984; Lawlor, 1987; Lindsey, 1986; Pear, 1984).

A major force behind the proposed constitutional amendment and other efforts to restrict bilingualism is U.S. English, a nationwide organization, which by 1990 claimed to have 350,000 members. Its adherents echo the view of Idaho senator Steve Symms that "many Americans now feel like strangers in their own neighborhoods, aliens in their own country." They agree with former Senator S. I. Hayakawa of California as he states in "Listen to Their Voices" that the United States needs English proclaimed as the official language. By contrast, Hispanic, leaders see the U.S. English campaign as a veiled expression of racism. "I wonder whether the movement has as part of its agenda whitening the com- plexion of the country," asks Joe Trevino, head of the League of United Latin American Citizens (D. Bauman, 1985; Bernstein, 1990; Bland and DeQuinne, 1987; Donahue, 1985; J. Ridgeway, 1986, p. 33).

The discouraging lack of movement toward bilingualism in the United States makes this country unusual. Switzerland has four official languages and India more than twenty, and most nations elevate more than one language to some kind of official status. It is depressing to see businesses but not the government or general public recognize as viable more than one language. Again, conflict sociologists would see this condition as an instance of the interests of the

---

### ❖ *LISTEN TO THEIR VOICES* ❖

---

*USA Needs to Have an*
*"Official" Language*

*S. I. Hayakawa*

*Hayakawa, founder and honorary chairman of U.S. English, is a former U.S. senator from California and former president of San Francisco State University. His strong assimilationist stance is in direct confrontation with bilingual ballots and efforts to expand bilingual programs.*

In the last few decades, government has been increasingly reluctant to press immigrants to learn the English language, lest it be accused of "cultural imperialism."

Rather than insisting that it is the immigrant's duty to learn the language of this country, government has instead acted as if it has a duty to permanently accommodate an immigrant in his native language.

A prime example of this can be found in the continuing debate over bilingual education.

Federal policy has come dangerously close to making the main goal of this program the maintenance of the immigrant child's native language, rather than the early acquisition of English.

As a former U.S. senator, I am very familiar with both the rhetoric and reality that lie behind the current debate on bilingual education.

My experience has convinced me that many of these programs are short-changing children in their quest to learn English by keeping them out of English-speaking classes for up to six years.

Another highly visible policy that has strayed from our tradition of one common language is the requirement for bilingual voting ballots.

We cannot continue to overlook the message we are sending to immigrants about the connection between English-language ability and citizenship when we print ballots in other languages. The ballot is the primary symbol of civic duty. When we tell immigrants that they should learn English yet offer them a voting ballot in their native language, I fear our actions will speak louder than our words.

The message that has been sent by these three states and the 14 others that have made English their official language must now be delivered to Washington. The people have spoken, and now Congress must act to strengthen our national commitment to the tradition of one common language for all Americans.

powerful being given primacy. McDonald's touts its "hamburguesas" and An-heuser-Busch insists that "Budweiser es para usted" (is for you). Perhaps at some time in the future teachers and poll watchers will more often offer the greeting, "Se habla inglés y español."

Bilingual education, however, is not just an issue for Spanish-speaking people. The plaintiff Kinney Lau, after all, in the initial landmark ruling *Lau* v. *Nichols* was a Chinese student failing in his San Francisco school because he could not understand the language of instruction. More than 5 million children of immigrants are expected to enter public schools during the 1990s speaking more than 150 languages. While Spanish will be the major minority-language, seven states will have schools where 25 percent or more of the students do not speak English as their primary language (C. Leslie, 1991).

## CUBAN AMERICANS

Third in numbers only to Chicanos and Puerto Ricans, Cuban Americans represent a significant ethnic minority in the United States. Their presence in this country is a relatively long one, with Cuban settlements in Florida dating back as early as 1831. These tended to be small, close-knit communities organized around a single enterprise such as a cigar manufacturing factory.

Until recently, however, the number of Cuban Americans was very modest. The 1960 census showed that 79,000 people who were born in Cuba lived in the United States. By 1990 over a million people of Cuban birth or descent lived in the United States. This tremendous increase followed Fidel Castro's assumption of power after the 1959 Cuban Revolution.

### Immigration Patterns

Cuban immigration to the United States since the 1959 Revolution came in four distinct waves. First, the initial exodus of about 200,000 following Castro's assumption of power lasted for a period of about three years. Regular commercial air traffic continued despite the United States' severing of diplomatic relations with Cuba. This first wave stopped with the missile crisis of October 1962, when all legal movement between the two nations was halted.

The second stage was clandestine, yet significant. Between 1962 and 1965 there was no direct, sanctioned transportation but nearly 30,000 Cubans came via private planes, boats, rafts, and other makeshift vessels.

In the third stage, responding to internal pressures for emigration, the Cuban government permitted twice-daily flights from 1965 until 1973, bringing immigrants who often were reunited with families in the United States. Approximately 300,000 Cubans arrived during this period, which was followed by several years of little immigration (Pérez, 1976).

The fourth wave has been the most controversial. In 1980, more than 124,000 refugees fled Cuba in the "freedom flotilla." In May of that year a few boats from

Cuba began to arrive in Key West, Florida, with people seeking asylum in the United States. President Carter, reflecting the nation's hostility toward Cuba's Communist government, told the new arrivals and anyone else who might be listening in Cuba that they were welcomed "with open arms and an open heart." As the number of arrivals escalated it became apparent that Castro had used the invitation as an opportunity to send prison inmates and addicts. The majority of the refugees, though, were neither marginal to the Cuban economy nor were they social deviants.

This most recent group of Cuban refugees soon was given the derisive name *Marielitos*. The word, meant to suggest that these refugees were undesirable, refers to Mariel, the fishing port west of Havana where Cuban authorities herded people into boats. *Marielitos* became and remains a stigma today in the media and in Florida, suggesting that this group of people is inferior, in surprising agreement with Castro's evaluation of them, and to the embarrassment of the Carter administration that first welcomed them. The refugees negative reception by longer-established Cuban immigrants, coupled with the group's relatively modest skills and little formal education, has made this Latin American group the one with the most difficulty in adjusting effectively to their new life in the United States. Government assistance to these immigrants was limited, but help from some groups of Cuban Americans in the Miami area was substantial. For many children of the "freedom flotilla" a smooth transition has been difficult. Unlike the earlier waves, they grew up in a country bombarded

*The fourth, and most controversial, wave of Cuban migrants were those arriving in southern Florida aboard the "freedom flotilla."*

with anti-American images. Furthermore, 600 of the 8,000 minors who arrived in the boatlift came with no relatives and had none waiting for them here.

Acceptance into the Hispanic community has been impressive and many members of the fourth wave have found employment. Most have applied for permanent resident status. However, for a small core group of 3,700, adjustment was impossible. In 1987 they were still detained in prison facilities. Their legal status was ambiguous because of alleged offenses committed either in Cuba or the United States or both. Major prison riots in Louisiana and Georgia by these detainees violently brought attention to their plight, still largely unresolved (Boswell and Curtis, 1984, pp. 38–60; Hufker and Cavender, 1990; LeMoyne, 1990; Portes and Stepick, 1985; H. Silva, 1985).

Yet another wave may be emerging in the 1990s and is being dubbed a "slow-motion Mariel." Beginning in 1990, Cuban President Castro started lowering the age from 65 for men and 60 for women who wished to leave the country to visit the United States. Now set at 20 years of age, about one-third of those who "visit" overstay their visa and are assumed to be residing permanently in the United States. While the numbers are not enormous, perhaps 20,000 annually, there are many more to come. As Ricardo Perez, caught twice trying to sail to Florida from Cuba, put it, "I don't know what there might be for me (in Miami). It might not be so great. But it's got to better than here" (Hockstader, 1991).

## The Present Picture

Compared to other recent immigrant groups and Hispanics as a whole, Cuban Americans are doing relatively well. As shown in Table 9.3, young Cubans (those 25 to 34 years old) have college completion rates twice those of other Hispanics and comparable to those of Anglos. Unemployment rates are low, especially for Cuban American women who are unlikely to seek employment unless positions are available. The close-knit structure of Cuban American families encourages women to follow traditional roles of homemaker and mother.

The presence of Cubans has been felt in urban centers throughout the United States, but most notably in the Miami, Florida, area. Throughout the various phases, Cubans have been encouraged to move out of southern Florida, but many returned to Dade County (metropolitan Miami), with its warm climate and proximity to other Cubans and Cuba itself. As estimated 90,000 or 72 percent of the Cubans arriving in the "freedom flotilla" settled in Miami. By 1986, Miami was 64 percent Hispanic, two-thirds of these being Cuban American (Bearak, 1982).

Probably no ethnic group has had more influence on the fortunes of a city in a short period of time than have the Cubans on Miami. Some consider the Cubans' influence positive; the president of the University of Miami declared, "Castro is the best thing that ever happened to Miami." Those less enthusiastic include leaders of Miami's Black community, who feel that new job opportunities have gone to Cubans instead of to their people.

**TABLE 9.3**  Selected Social and Economic Characteristics: Cuban Americans, 1990

Compared to Hispanics, Cuban Americans are doing relatively well but still fall behind Anglos.

| Characteristic | Total Anglo | Total Hispanic | Cuban Americans |
|---|---|---|---|
| Median age | 33.5 | 26.0 | 39.1 |
| Percent completing college | | | |
| 25 to 34 years | 25.5 | 9.0 | 20.0 |
| 35 years and over | 22.2 | 9.2 | 20.2 |
| Percent unemployed | | | |
| Male | 5.7 | 8.0 | 6.3 |
| Female | 4.9 | 8.5 | 5.1 |
| Percent living below poverty level | 11.6 | 26.2 | 15.2 |
| Income | | | |
| Male | $22,081 | 14,047 | 19,336 |
| Female | 11,885 | 9,861 | 12,880 |

Source: Bureau of the Census, 1991f, pp. 6–11.

The Cuban immigrants had much to adjust to, such as the language barrier many had to overcome, which kept them from immediately picking up where they had left off in Cuba. The federally funded Cuban Refugee Program gave a transitional grant to resettling refugees of $100 for a family and $60 for an individual. Officials emphasize that only about 8 percent of the refugees end up receiving welfare or other public aid, but as the Cuban Refugee Program has continued, concern has risen that the program has become institutionalized. In 1988, the program was almost 40 years old and had cost $1.5 billion, the costliest program of its kind in the nation's history. Critics argue that continuation of the program had only led to the mistaken belief that all Cubans receive special treatment at taxpayer's expense (Nordheimer, 1988; Volsky, 1976).

Although those who fled Cuba were sometimes forced to give up their life's savings, the earlier immigrants were generally well educated, and many had professional or managerial backgrounds (*Business Week*, 1971; J. Clark, 1970; Rosenhouse, 1970). Generally, the Cubans have met with economic success. There are now 25,000 Cuban-owned businesses in the Miami area, compared to fewer than 1,000 in 1970. Thirty percent of construction, including the city's tallest building, has been financed by the residents of Miami's "Little Havana," which now covers 600 square blocks. More recently, Cubans have begun to move to suburban areas. Cuban family income has increased faster than the national rate; also, their crime rate is well below the norm (Burkholz, 1980; *Business Week*, 1971; DeQuinne, 1986; Jacoby, 1974; Schwirian et al., 1976; Winsberg, 1983).

The long-range prospects for Cubans in the United States depend on several factors. Of obvious importance are events in Cuba, for many Cuban refugees publicly proclaim their desire to return if the Communist government is overturned. As the years pass and as the refugees' prosperity increases, however, fewer and fewer are likely to return even if a political reversal occurs. A hard core of Cubans in the United States remains active anti-Castro militants. Although 68 percent of Miami's Cuban Americans surveyed in 1983 favored an invasion, only 24 percent indicated they would return if Castro were actually ousted (Burkholz, 1980; Elder, 1976; Morin, 1983, p. 7M).

More dramatic than efforts to change Cuba politically has been the transformation in Miami politics. Miami was once a liberal Democratic stronghold, but Cuban Americans' 2 to 1 Republican voter registration has elected a number of conservatives to major offices. Miami elected a Cuban American, Xavier Suarez, as mayor in 1985 over another Cuban American. Hispanics accounted that year for three of the five City Council seats, two of the seven county school board members, including the chair, and eight of the twenty-eight local state legislators (DeQuinne, 1986; Mohl, 1986). In 1989, Havana-born Ileana Ros-Lehtinen became the first Cuban American in Congress, representing Miami. A Republican, she came to the United States during the first wave of immigration following Castro's rise to power.

Cubans have selectively accepted Anglo culture. One especially vulnerable Cuban practice has been the tradition of chaperoning adolescents. But Cuban culture has been tenacious; Cubans do not feel that they need to forget Spanish, as other immigrant children have shunned their linguistic past. Still, a split between the original exiles and their children is evident. As a result, Miami has become the most bilingual of any city in the United States not on the Mexican border. At the annual Orange Bowl Parade on New Year's Eve, tourists are greeted with dual-language signs warning "No se siente en la acera" ("Don't sit on the curb") (*The New York Times*, 1974a).

The Cuban experience in the United States has not been completely positive. Some detractors worry about the Cubans' vehement anticommunism and about the apparent growth of an organized crime syndicate that engages in gang-like violence and lucrative trade in illegal drugs. Miami's Cubans have also expressed concern recently over what they feel is the indifference of Miami's Roman Catholic hierarchy. Cubans, like other Hispanics, are under-represented in the leadership positions throughout the church. Although there is one Anglo priest for every 855 English-speaking Catholics, there is only one Hispanic priest for every 5,000 parishioners. The Catholic leadership counters by affirming their long commitment to assisting the exiles. In addition, Cuban Americans in Miami as a group, despite individual success stories, fall behind Anglos in income, proportion of professionals, and employment rate.

Bilingualism has become an emotional issue in south Florida, where concern over language purity has been strong. In a 1980 election, the electorate by a 3 to 2 vote reversed a 1978 resolution designating Dade County a bilingual county. Through this referendum voters prohibited public expenditure "for the purpose of utilizing any language other than English or promoting any culture other than that of the United States." This vote ended the practice of translating county legal documents into Spanish, although bilingual education programs continue.

*Miami's Cuban American community has spurred that city's economic growth over the last 20 years.*

This 1980 vote was a statement by the overwhelming majority of non-Cubans that they were uncomfortable with the "Latinization" of their area. But it was for the most part an ideological statement; it has had little practical effect. Just as Cubans are at a clear disadvantage if they cannot communicate effectively in English, business people have increasingly realized the value, as reflected in profit statements, of being able to communicate in Spanish as well as English (Mohl, 1986).

Cubans have made a worthwhile contribution to the United States, although their relations with other groups may not be perfect. Some others among Miami's Hispanics such as the Venezuelans, Ecuadorians, and Colombians resent being mistaken for Cubans and feel their own distinctive nationality is submerged (Jacoby, 1974). Perhaps the primary criticism heard in Miami's Anglo community is that the Cubans invest their profits in other Cuban-owned businesses and have little to do with Anglos and Blacks. The Cubans respond that this is not clannishness but self-help.

## CENTRAL AND SOUTH AMERICANS

More than one million immigrants have come from Central and South America, not including Mexico, since 1820. This diverse population has not been closely observed. Indeed, most government statistics treat them collectively as "other," and rarely differentiate by nationality. Yet people from Chile and Costa Rica have little in common other than hemisphere of origin and the Spanish language. Not all Central and South Americans have Spanish as their native tongue—for example immigrants from Brazil speak Portuguese, immigrants from French Guiana speak French, and those from Surinam speak Dutch.

Many of the nations of Central and South America have a *color gradient* differentiating people into a myriad of racial groups. African slaves were brought to almost all of these countries, and these people of African descent, in varying degrees, have intermarried with each other or with indigenous Indians. Rather than placing people in two or three distinct racial groupings, these societies describe skin color in a continuum from light to dark. Terms such as "mestezo Hondurans," "mulatto Columbians," or "African Panamanians" reflect this continuum. Discussion of Puerto Ricans in Chapter 11 and race relations in Brazil in Chapter 17 will consider color gradients in greater detail.

Added to language diversity and the color gradient are social class distinctions, religious differences, urban vs. rural backgrounds, and differences in dialect even among those speaking the same language. We can understand historians Ann Orlov and Reed Veda's (1980, p. 212) conclusion that, "social relations among Central and South American ethnic groups in the United States defy generalization." Central and South Americans do nor form, nor should they be expected to form, a cohesive group, nor do they "naturally" form coalitions with Cuban Americans or Chicanos or Puerto Ricans.

## Immigration Patterns

Immigration from the various Central and South American nations has been sporadic—influenced by both our immigration laws and social forces operating in the home country. Perceived economic opportunities escalated the northward movement in the 1960s. By 1970, Panamanians and Hondurans represented the largest national groupings, with most of them identified in the census as "non-white."

In the last 10 to 20 years, increasing numbers of Central and South Americans have fled unrest. While Hispanics as a whole are a fast growing minority, Central and South Americans have increased even faster than Mexicans or any other group during the 1980s. In particular, since about 1978, war and economic chaos in El Salvador, Nicaragua, and Guatemala prompted many to seek refuge in the United States. Not at all a homogenous group, they range from Guatemalan Indian peasants to wealthy Nicaraguan exiles. These latest arrivals have probably had some economic motivation for migration, but this concern is overshadowed by their fear of being killed or hurt if they remained in their home country. The difficulty that most people in their predicament have in qualifying for official refugee status has contributed to the growth of the *Sanctuary Movement* outlined in Chapter 4. Central American immigrants have been the primary focus of this grassroots effort to shelter those violating immigration law (Allen and Turner, 1988, pp. 168–171; Orlov and Veda, 1980).

## The Present Picture

Contemporary settlement of Central and South Americans has been clouded by two issues familiar in contemporary immigration. First, many of the arrivals are illegal immigrants. Citizens from El Salvador, Guatemala, and Columbia are outnumbered only by Mexican nationals among those seeking asylum under the 1986 Immigration Reform and Control Act (Singer, 1988, p. 9). Second, significant numbers of highly trained and skilled people have left countries which most desperately need their professional workers (Orlov and Veda, 1980, p. 213). While difficult to document, this *brain drain* worsens conditions in the countries that have been left.

Although Central and South Americans in the United States tend to be better educated than other Hispanics, as shown in Table 9.4, they still fall behind Anglos. Similar observations can be made about their poverty level—better than their fellow Hispanics, but still not comparable to Anglos—but not unemployment. This suggests that many work in low-paying jobs that do not provide a living wage.

The diverse Central and South Americans over time have had their settlement patterns in common. They have congregated in urban areas, especially in very large metropolitan areas. This has been true even in earlier historical periods. For example in 1920, when 49 percent of the population in the United States lived in rural areas, 87 percent of the Central and South Americans in the United States were living in cities.

Colombians exemplify this pattern in having primarily settled in New York City and Chicago. The initial arrivals after World War I were educated, middle-class people who quickly assimilated into American life. Rural unrest in Co-

---

**TABLE 9.4**  Selected Social and Economic Characteristics: Central and South Americans, 1990

People in the United States of Central or South American origin have less formal schooling and are more likely to be poor.

| Characteristic | Total Anglo | Total Hispanic | Central and South Americans |
|---|---|---|---|
| Median age | 33.5 | 26.0 | 28.0 |
| Percent completing college | | | |
| 25 to 34 years | 25.5 | 9.0 | 15.4 |
| 35 years and over | 22.2 | 9.2 | 15.6 |
| Percent unemployed | | | |
| Male | 5.7 | 8.0 | 6.9 |
| Female | 4.9 | 8.5 | 6.3 |
| Percent living below poverty level | 11.6 | 26.2 | 18.5 |
| Income | | | |
| Male | $22,081 | 14,047 | 15,067 |
| Female | 11,885 | 9,861 | 10,083 |

*Source:* Bureau of the Census, 1991f, pp. 6–11.

lombia triggered large-scale movement to the United States where the Colombian immigrants had to adapt to a new culture *and* to urban life. The adaptation of this later group has been much more problematic. Some have found success through catering to their fellow countrymen. For example, enterprising immigrants have opened *bodegas* (grocery stores) to supply traditional, familiar foodstuffs. Similarly, Colombians have established restaurants, travel agencies, and realtors catering to other Colombians. Yet many find themselves obliged to take menial jobs and require that several family members combine incomes to stay abreast of the high cost of urban life. Colombians of mixed African descent also face racial as well as ethnic and language barriers (Orlov and Veda, 1980, pp. 213–215).

What is likely to be the future of Central and South Americans in the United States? While much will depend upon future immigration, they could assimilate over the course of generations. One alternative is that they become trapped with Chicanos as a segment of the dual labor market of urban America where they have taken residence. A more encouraging possibility is that they would retain an independent identity, like the Cubans, and establish an economic base. An examination of the urban economy of the San Francisco metropolitan area in the 1980s seemed to show that they were entering the same irregular economy and poverty populated by the Chicanos there. Little evidence of the establishment of a local economic base is found. Whether this initial assessment remains and can be generalized to other cities will await subsequent analysis (S. P. Wallace, 1989).

In 1991 violence broke out in the Hispanic Mount Pleasant area of Washington, D.C., heavily populated by Central American immigrants. El Salvadorans figured prominently in those arrested during the several days of rioting that followed the police shooting of a Salvadoran man being arrested. In the aftermath, many concerns were raised similar to those in the riots in African American neighborhoods in the 1960s—no jobs, police brutality, unresponsive city government, exploitative employers, and uncaring teachers. One difference was that many neighborhood residents have come to our nation's capital fleeing violent warfare in their home country (Raspberry, 1991; A. Sanchez, 1991).

## GLANCING BACK AND LOOKING AHEAD

The signals are mixed. The movies, television programs, and music have a Hispanic flavor. The candidates for political offices seek Hispanic votes and sometimes even speak Spanish to do so. Yet the poverty rate of Hispanic families reported in 1989 was 26.2 percent, compared to 11.6 percent for non-Hispanics (Bureau of the Census, 1991f, p. 10).

The successes are there. Texas Tech University president Lauro Cavazos was named by Ronald Reagan in 1988 to head the Department of Education—the first Hispanic cabinet appointee in this nation's history. George Bush subsequently asked him to continue in that position. Yet the year before, a study found that Hispanic schoolchildren—unlike Black students—are now far more likely to attend segregated schools than they were 20 years ago (Orfield, 1987). Of the 36 schools listed as overcrowded in Chicago, 33 are in Hispanic neighborhoods.

Ballots are printed in Spanish and other languages. Bilingual education at taxpayer expense is available throughout the United States. Yet more and more states are declaring English the "official" language. Many Hispanics feel to be bilingual is not to be less American. Espousing pluralism rather than assimilation is not un-American. This contrast of images and substance will be evident again in the chapters on Chicanos and Puerto Ricans. "In World War II, more Hispanics won Medals of Honor than any other ethnic group," says Democratic Representative Matthew Martinez, a former Marine who represents part of Los Angeles. "How much blood do you have to spill before you prove you are a part of something?" (Whitman, 1987, p. 49).

## KEY TERMS

**bilingual education**   A program designed to allow students to learn academic concepts in their native language while they learn a second language.

**bilingualism**   The use of two or more languages in places of work or in educational facilities, with each language treated as equally legitimate.

**brain drain**   Immigration to the United States of skilled workers, professionals, and technicians who are desperately needed by their home countries.

**color gradient**   The alignment of placing people along a continuum from light to dark skin color rather than in distinct racial groupings by skin color.

**English immersion**   Teaching in English by teachers who know the students' native language, but use it only when students do not understand the lessons.

**Marielitos**   People who arrived from Cuba in the fourth wave of Cuban immigration, most specifically those forcibly deported via Mariel Harbor. The term is generally reserved for those refugees seen as especially undesirable.

**sanctuary movement**   A movement of loosely connected organizations that offers asylum, often in churches, to those who seek refugee status but are regarded by the Immigration and Naturalization Service as illegal aliens.

## FOR FURTHER INFORMATION

M. Beatriz Arias, ed. "The Education of Hispanic Americans: A Challenge for the Future," special issue of the *American Journal of Education* (November 1986).

This collection of ten articles looks at bilingual programs in the larger social context of the education of Hispanic Americans.

Thomas D. Boswell and James R. Curtis. *The Cuban-American Experience*. Totowa, NJ: Rowman and Allanheld, 1984.

A comprehensive look at the history of Cuban immigration and at contemporary Cuban-American social institutions.

Pastora San Juan Cafferty and William C. McCready, eds. *Hispanics in the United States: A New Social Agenda.* New Brunswick, NJ: Transaction Books, 1985.

> A collection of 11 articles that emphasizes the social policy issues connected with demography, identity, language, socioeconomic status, justice, education, and health care.

Terry Doran, ed. *A Road Well Traveled: Three Generations of Cuban American Women.* Fort Wayne, IN: Latin American Educational Center, 1988.

> From a woman who at 57 began studying to be an L.P.N., to a judge who worked as a maid and a factory worker after arriving in the United States, this book tells the intriguing stories of women who immigrated from Cuba.

Jose Llanes. *Cuban Americans: Masters of Survival.* Cambridge, MA: Abt Books, 1982.

> Llanes, a Havana-born social scientist, looks at various components of the Cuban American community and is optimistic about the prospects of this ethnic group.

Joan Moore and Harry Pachon. *Hispanics in the United States.* Englewood Cliffs, NJ: Prentice-Hall, 1985.

> Two sociologists present an analysis of people in the United States whose identity is based on national origins in Mexico, Puerto Rico, Cuba, and other Latin American nations.

Thomas Weyr. *Hispanic U.S.A.* New York: Harper and Row, 1988.

> A journalistic overview of the major impact Hispanics are having in the United States.

## *Periodicals*

Journals devoted exclusively to the Hispanic experience are *Aztlán* (1969) and *Hispanic Journal of Behavioral Sciences* (1979). The *Social Science Quarterly* devoted its March 1973 and June 1984 issues to Chicanos. *Latina* is among the popular periodicals oriented to the Hispanic audience.

*Chapter Ten*

# CHICANOS: THE NATION'S LARGEST ETHNIC GROUP

*Chapter Outline*

**Legacy of the Nineteenth Century**
**The Immigrant Experience**
Repatriation
Los Braceros Program
Operation Wetback
**Organizations Within the Chicano Community**
Chicanismo
Political Organizations
The Church
**Education**

Social Isolation
Higher Education
**Family Life**
The "Culture of Poverty"
Machismo and Marianismo
Familism
**Health Care**
**Prejudice and Discrimination**
**Glancing Back and Looking Ahead**
**Key Terms**
**For Further Information**

## ✳ HIGHLIGHTS ✳

Chicanos make up over 60 percent of the largely Spanish-speaking Hispanic population. The history of Chicanos is closely tied to immigration, which has been encouraged (*Los Braceros* program) when Mexican labor is in demand, or discouraged (*repatriation* and *Operation Wetback*) when Mexican workers are unwanted. Chicanos find themselves on the periphery of formal education, facing a curriculum unsuited to their needs and colleges ill-prepared to receive them. As is true of other subordinate groups, the strength of Chicanos rests in their organizations—political groups, the church, and the family. The continuing gap between Chicanos and Anglos has given birth to an awakened consciousness and contributed to the popularity of such charismatic leaders as César Chávez and Reies Tijerina.

Chicanos, Americans of Mexican origin, are the largest ethnic group in the country. Numbering more than 12 million, they are part of a still larger group, Hispanics. Chicanos have a long history in the United States, stretching back before the nation was even formed to the early days of European exploration. Santa Fe, New Mexico, was founded more than a decade before the Pilgrims landed at Plymouth. The Chicano people trace their ancestry back to the merging of Spanish settlers with the Native Americans of Central America. This ancestry reaches back to the brilliant Mayan and Aztec civilizations, which attained their height about A.D. 700 and 1500, respectively. Roots in the land do not guarantee a group dominance over it. The Spaniards conquered the land and merged with the Native Americans over several centuries to form the Mexican people. In 1821 Mexico obtained it independence, but this independence was short lived, for domination from the north began less than a generation later (Meier and Rivera, 1972, pp. 3–37).

Today the Southwest, once a part of Mexico, is dominated by the descendants of Europeans, although heavily populated by Chicanos. The Chicano people are a varied group, differing in their retention of Spanish heritage, in history, and in culture. Even the term Chicano is not universally adopted, because many wish to be called "Mexican American," "Hispanic," "Mexican," "Spanish American," or "Latin American." Regardless, most see themselves as a distinctive group and not merely as assimilated Americans (Grebler et al., 1970, p. 386; Moore and Pachon, 1976, p. 8; F. Padilla, 1984).

Assimilation may be the key word in the history of many immigrant groups, but for Chicanos the key term is *La Raza*. *La Raza* literally means *the people* but among contemporary Chicanos the term connotes pride in a pluralistic Spanish, American Indian, and Mexican heritage. Chicanos cherish their legacy, and as we shall see, strive to regain some of the economic and social glory that once was theirs. Compared to Anglos, and to even Hispanics as a group, Chicanos are more likely to be unemployed and poor, as shown in Table 10.1. We will explore the historical factors that have led to this subordinate status in the United States.

## LEGACY OF THE NINETEENTH CENTURY

Many Chicanos trace their ancestors as far back as the sixteenth century in land that is today the United States. The Spanish and Mexican heritage therefore lives on in people, not just in place names like San Francisco, the Pecos River, or the San Joaquin Valley. Approximately 1.3 million Chicanos today descend from Mexicans residing in the Southwest as far back as 1848 (L.Hernandez, 1969).

These people first became Mexican Americans with the conclusion of the Mexican-American War. The Treaty of Guadalupe Hidalgo, signed February 2, 1848, acknowledged the annexation of Texas to the United States and ceded California and most of Arizona and New Mexico to the United States for $15 million. In exchange, the United States granted citizenship to the 75,000 Mexican nationals who still remained in the annexed land after one year. With citizenship, the United States was to guarantee religious freedom, property rights, and cultural integrity—that is, the right to continue Mexican and Spanish cultural traditions and to use the Spanish language.

The descendants of these Mexican nationals are today called Hispanos. Though often placed in the same category as Chicanos, the Hispanos' ancestry in North America is similar to that of the earliest European settlers on the East Coast. For this reason, some of the estimated 850,000 Hispanos repudiate the

---

**TABLE 10.1**  Selected Social and Economic Characteristics: Chicanos, 1990

Compared both to Hispanics as a group and to Anglos, several government indicators show Chicanos are doing poorly.

| Characteristic | Total Anglo | Total Hispanic | Chicanos |
|---|---|---|---|
| Median age | 33.5 | 26.0 | 24.1 |
| Percent completing college | | | |
| 25 to 34 years | 25.5 | 9.0 | 5.3 |
| 35 years and over | 22.2 | 9.2 | 5.4 |
| Percent unemployed | | | |
| Male | 5.7 | 8.0 | 8.6 |
| Female | 4.9 | 8.5 | 9.8 |
| Percent living below poverty level | 11.6 | 26.2 | 28.4 |
| Income | | | |
| Male | $22,081 | 14,047 | 12,527 |
| Female | 11,885 | 9,861 | 8,874 |

*Source:* Bureau of the Census, 1991f, pp. 6–11.

label of "Chicano" or "Mexican American" (Cortés, 1980, p. 697; Moquin and Van Doren, 1971, pp. 241–249; Moore and Pachon, 1985, p. 23; Quintana, 1980).

The beginnings of the Chicano experience were as varied as the Chicano people themselves. Some Chicanos were affluent, with large landholdings. Others were poor peasants barely able to survive. Along such rivers as the Rio Grande, commercial towns grew up around the growing river traffic. In New Mexico and Arizona, many Chicano people welcomed the protection Americans offered against several Native-American tribes. In California, life was quickly dominated by the gold miners, and Anglos controlled the newfound wealth. One generalization can be made about the many segments of the Chicanos in the nineteenth century. They were regarded as conquered people. In fact, even before the war, Whites who traveled into the West brought feelings against people of mixed blood (in this instance, against Mexicans). Whenever Chicano and Anglo interests conflicted, Anglo interests won out (Servin, 1974).

Although a pattern of second-class treatment for Chicanos emerged well before the twentieth century, it was not pursued consistently. Gradually the Anglo system of property ownership replaced the American Indian and Hispanic systems. Chicanos inheriting land proved no match for Anglo lawyers. Court battles provided protection for poor, Spanish-speaking landowners. Unscrupulous lawyers occasionally defended Chicanos successfully, only to demand half the land as their fee. Anglo cattlemen gradually pushed out Chicano ranchers. By 1892, the federal government granted grazing privileges on public grasslands and forests to anyone but Chicanos.

In California, laws passed to drive the Chinese out of mine work except as menial laborers likewise banned Chicanos. Prior to 1860, Californios (that is, Chicanos in California) owned all parcels of land valued at more than $10,000. By the 1870s, they owned only a quarter of this land. Anglos saw an end of landowning among Californios and the transfer of their fortunes to Whites as a price the Californios ought to pay for injustices that some Mexican governors committed against the American Indians. This explanation was accepted widely, yet few thought that Anglos should suffer for abusing both the American Indians and Chicanos. Chicanos did not respond to such obvious violations of the 1848 treaty with passive acceptance. Chicanos frequently resorted to violence and formed vigilante groups to protect what they saw as their rights. These efforts, however, were only met with greater retaliatory force and mob hysteria, culminating in countless lynchings (McWilliams, 1968, pp. 102–111; R. Padilla, 1973; Pitt, 1966, pp. 248, 277; Stoddard, 1973, pp. 10–12).

The Mexican-American War ended with the Mexicans losing much more than they gained. By the end of the nineteenth century, the Chicanos had lost more than they had gained with American citizenship. Wayne Moquin and Charles Van Doren called this the period of Anglo-American conquest, when the Chicanos "became outsiders in their own homeland" (1971, p. 251). In retrospect, the Anglos' land grab left the Chicanos as unable to escape it as the American Indians had been. The expansion of cattle and sheep industries, farming, and mining was financed by Anglos who profited from Chicano labor and experience. The ground was laid for the social structure of the Southwest in the twentieth century, an area of growing productivity in which minority groups have increased in size but remained subordinate.

## THE IMMIGRANT EXPERIENCE

Official immigration from Mexico has totalled nearly two million, but the figure must be regarded with extreme caution because of the large number of illegal border crossings. Nowhere else in the world do two countries with such different standards of living and wage scales share a relatively open border. Immigration from Mexico is unique in several respects. First, it has been a continuous large-scale movement for most of this century. The United States did not restrict immigration from Mexico through legislation until 1965. Therefore the flow of new immigrants has been continuous. Second, the proximity of Mexico encourages past immigrants to maintain strong cultural and language ties with the homeland through friends and relatives. Return visits to the old country are only one- or two-day bus rides for Chicanos, not once-in-a-lifetime voyages as they have been for Europeans. The third point of uniqueness is the aura of illegality that has surrounded the Mexican migrant. Throughout the twentieth century the suspicion in which Anglos have held Chicanos has contributed to mutual distrust between the two groups.

The years preceding World War I brought large numbers of Mexicans into the expanding agricultural industry of the Southwest. The Mexican revolution of 1909–1922 thrust even more refugees into the United States, and World War I curtailed the flow of people from Europe, leaving the labor market open to the Chicanos. After the war, continued political turmoil in Mexico and more prosperity in the Southwest brought still more Mexicans across the border.

Simultaneously, American corporations, led by agribusinesses, invested in Mexico in such a way as to maximize their profits but minimize the amount of money remaining in Mexico to provide needed employment. Conflict theorists view this as a part of a continuing process in which American businesses have used Mexican people when it has been in corporate leaders' best interests (first, as we shall see, as braceros, then as cheap laborers either in their own country or as undocumented workers here) or dismissed them when they are no longer judged to be useful (first during a program called repatriation and sporadically now during crackdowns on "illegal" immigration). During the 1920s, nearly a half million Mexicans emigrated. The Southwest welcomed the laborers onto the bottom rungs of the social and economic ladders of Anglo-dominated society (Acuña, 1981; Burbach and Flynn, 1980).

### Repatriation

The influx of Mexicans slowed markedly after 1929 as the Great Depression gripped the United States. Unemployed city workers flocked to agriculture, but the dust bowl decreased the need for farm labor. More Mexicans were not needed by Anglo businesses, and those already here were seen as a burden.

Government officials developed a quick way to reduce welfare rolls and eliminate people seeking jobs: ship Mexicans back to Mexico. This program of deporting Mexicans during the 1930s was referred to as *repatriation*. As officially stated, the program was constitutional, for only illegal aliens were to be repatriated. Actually it was much more complex. Border records were incomplete because before 1930 the United States had shown little interest in whether Mexicans entered with all the proper credentials. Also, many Mexicans who could be classified as illegal aliens had resided in the United States for decades. Because they had children who were citizens by birth, they therefore could not legally be deported. The legal process of fighting a deportation order was overwhelming, however, especially to a poor, Spanish-speaking family. The Anglo community virtually ignored this outrage against the civil rights of those deported, nor did it show interest in assisting repatriates to ease the transition (Meier and Rivera, 1972, pp. 159–163).

Approximately half a million people were deported to Mexico. The majority were Chicanos, that is, American citizens, who were unable to prove their citizenship and therefore were assumed to be illegal aliens. The largest number of repatriates came from Texas and California. The program was not limited to the Southwest, however. The third largest number came from Illinois and Indiana, from which half of the Hispanics were repatriated. Essentially, the United States government and its people had welcomed Mexicans when they were needed to increase Anglo profits and, after paying them subsistence wages, sent them back destitute when their labor was no longer useful (Meier and Rivera, 1972, pp. 164–165; Moquin and Van Doren, 1971, p. 383). Even while repatriation was still taking place, some Los Angeles industrialists smugly predicted that the Mexican laborer could be lured back "whenever we need him." Mexico was regarded merely as a surplus labor depot for the United States (McWilliams, 1968).

For those Chicanos and Mexicans who were allowed to remain, the 1930s were not good times. Many Chicano landholders lost their real estate because they were unable to pay taxes. They flocked to the growing concentrations of Chicanos living in segregated areas, called *barrios*, of the urban Southwest. Meanwhile many in the cities lost their jobs and left for rural areas that were merely less densely populated poverty areas. The Roosevelt administration's efforts to alleviate the Depression were helpful to Chicanos, but many were disqualified from participation by local or state requirements (Meier and Rivera, 1972, pp. 153–159).

## Los Braceros Program

When the Depression ended, Mexican laborers again became attractive to industry. In 1942, the United States and Mexico agreed to a program allowing migration across the border by contracted laborers, or *braceros*. Within a year of the initiation of Los Braceros program, more than 80,000 Mexican nationals had been brought in; they made up one-eleventh of the farm workers on the Pacific Coast. The program continued with some interruptions until 1964. It was devised to recruit labor from Mexican poverty areas to American farms. In a program that was supposed to be jointly supervised by Mexico and the United States, minimum standards were to be maintained for the transportation, housing, wages, and health care of the braceros. Ironically, these safeguards placed the braceros in a better economic situation than Chicanos, who often worked alongside the protected Mexican nationals. The Mexicans were still regarded as good only when useful, and the Chicano people were merely tolerated (Galarza, 1964; Scott, 1974; Stoddard, 1973, pp. 24–25).

World War II created new opportunities for Chicanos as they replaced Anglos in skilled trades and served in the armed forces. But incidents during the war emphasized the deep hatred that Anglos felt for the Chicano community. In California, and especially in Los Angeles and San Diego, public fears about wartime juvenile delinquency grew.

In the minds of Anglos, Chicano youth was synonymous with delinquency. McWilliams wrote, "Los Angeles had revised the old saying that 'boys will be boys' to read 'boys, if Mexican, will be gangsters!' " (1968, p. 239). Newspapers minimized Anglo violence and focused on Chicano gangs and boys who dressed in bizarre "drapes" or "zoot suits" (broad hats, long coats, and baggy

*The play* Zoot Suit *by Luis Valdez vividly brought to the stage and later to the screen the injustices of the* Sleepy Lagoon *trials.*

trousers with tight-fitting cuffs). In June 1943, tension ran high following a sensational murder case. Servicemen roamed the streets of Los Angeles for a week, attacking those they thought were *zoot-suiters*. An undeclared war developed against all Chicanos, with law enforcement officials arresting the Chicano victims of the attack, not the Anglo attackers. Similar outbreaks followed in several California towns. At this time, the riots were blamed entirely on the Chicanos. The sailors and soldiers were said to be acting in self-defense. Later reports completely reversed this assessment (Adler, 1974; McWilliams, 1968, pp. 239–258; Meier and Rivera, 1972, pp. 192–195; Mills, 1943).

## Operation Wetback

Another crackdown on illegal aliens was to be the third step in dealing with "the Mexican problem." Variously called Operation Wetback and Special Force Operation, it was fully inaugurated by 1954. The term *wetbacks*, or *mojados*, the derisive slang for Mexicans who enter illegally, refers to those who secretly swim across the Rio Grande. As with other roundups, this effort did not stop the illegal flow of workers. For several years some Mexicans were brought in under the bracero program, while other Mexicans were being deported. With the end of the bracero program in 1964 and stricter immigration quotas on Mexico, illegal border crossings increased because legal crossings became more difficult (W. Gordon, 1975; Stoddard, 1973, 25–26, 1976a, 1976b).

Although Operation Wetback was formally phased out by 1956, the deportations have continued to the present. As we discussed in Chapter 4, illegal immigration remains controversial. Illegal aliens take jobs from Americans, but generally they get only least desirable ones. César Chávez, organizer of migrant farm workers, has repeatedly expressed concern that illegal aliens are used as strikebreakers (Severo, 1974).

More dramatic than the negative influence continued immigration has had on employment conditions in the Southwest is the effect on the Mexican and Chicano people themselves. Routinely the rights of Mexicans, even the rights to which they are entitled as illegal aliens, are ignored. Of those illegal immigrants deported, less than 2 percent were expelled through formal proceedings. The remaining 98 to 99 percent left for Mexico under threat of legal action, frequently taking their children who were born in the United States. These children, of course, are American citizens. The Mexican American Legal Defense and Education Fund (MALDEF) has repeatedly expressed concern over the government's handling of illegal aliens. The organization argues that Mexican nationals do not waive their rights by crossing the border (V. Briggs, 1975; Bustamante, 1972; Martinez, 1976; Meier and Rivera, 1972; Rosen, 1974).

Despite passage of the Immigration Reform and Control Act of 1986, the apprehension of illegal aliens is not likely to end. Chicanos will continue to be more closely scrutinized by law enforcement officials because their Mexican descent makes them more suspect as potential illegal aliens. But officials have been restrained from acting overzealously. Indiscriminate raids on Hispanic neighborhoods in 1974 led to a lawsuit to block "sweeps" aimed at migrant workers and other Hispanics. In October 1975, in response to a court decision, the Immigration and Naturalization Service announced it would discontinue mass raids and that before entering a home or business its agents would require probable cause.

The Mexican border created in 1848 is not an impenetrable barrier. Many employers in the Southwest wish the laborers of Mexico to be readily available and try to keep wages for manual labor low. The Mexicans themselves are eager to earn higher wages. They view employment in the United States as a means to move upward socially and economically. Foreign wage labor has become a regular feature in the economy of many Mexican households. By the mid-twentieth century, a certain momentum was established through bonds of friendship and kinship which meant migrants were not so much pioneers as merely reuniting with familiar people.

In the United States, Chicanos have mixed feelings toward the illegal Mexican immigrants. Many are their kin and Chicanos realize that entry into the United States brings Mexicans better economic opportunities. Massive deportations, however, only perpetuate the Anglo stereotype of Mexican and Chicano alike as surplus labor. Chicanos, largely the product of past immigration, find that the continued controversy over illegal immigration places them in an ambivalent role of citizen and relative. Chicano organizations opposing illegal immigration must confront people to whom they are closely linked by culture and kinship, and cooperate with government agencies they deeply distrust (Massey, 1986; Massey et al., *Return*, 1987; Portes, 1974).

As the Chicano population has increased, organizations of Chicanos have grown. These groups, as we will see in the next section, have used different tactics to meet many goals, as Chicanos grew from 382,000 in 1910 to more than 13 million in 1990.

## ORGANIZATIONS WITHIN THE CHICANO COMMUNITY

The earliest Chicano community organizations were similar to those created by other immigrant groups. These organizations provided mutual aid as the Mexican immigrants pooled their meager resources. An exception to these was the Order of the Sons of America (*La Orden de los Hijos de América*), organized in San Antonio, Texas, in 1921. The order restricted its membership to Chicanos who were citizens of the United States. This limitation permitted the group to work for the election of public officials who would better represent the needs of Chicanos. In 1929, because of a disagreement over the speed with which the group was moving, some members split away to form the League of United Latin American Citizens (LULAC). From the beginning, LULAC was committed to total assimilation and asked its members to be the "most perfect type of a true and loyal citizen of the United States of America." Today local LULAC councils are found in 43 states and Puerto Rico. It has gradually changed from a conservative, middle-class organization to showing concern for the residents of the barrios and rural areas (Cortés, 1980; Galvan, 1982; Tirado, 1970, pp. 54–60).

Immediately after World War II, two organizations were founded in the Chicano community. Both the Community Service Organization (CSO) and the GI Forum responded to the needs of younger, generally less affluent Chicanos. The CSO was founded in 1947 in Los Angeles to address the social problems and the need for educational reform in that city's barrio. It quickly became apparent that the group's aims could be accomplished only by more responsive public officials. In 1949, the CSO finally succeeded in electing the first Chicano to the city council since 1881. Eventually the CSO became less involved with promoting political leaders and developed mutual benefit programs such as resource centers and credit unions. From the CSO have come such Chicano leaders as Congressman Edward Roybal and activist César Chávez (Tirado, 1970, pp. 62–66).

## Chicanismo

The social protests that characterized much of the political activity in the America of the mid-1960s touched the Chicano community as well. In southern California in 1966, young Chicanos in college were attracted to the ideology of *Chicanismo* (or *Chicanozaje*) and joined what is popularly called the Chicano movement. Like Black power, Chicanismo has taken on a variety of meanings, but all definitions stress a positive self-image and place little reliance on conventional forms of political activity. Followers of Chicanismo, unlike the more assimilation-oriented older generations, have been less likely to accept the standard claim that the United States is equally just to all.

The origin of the word *Chicano* is not clear, but until the 1960s it was a derogatory term Anglos used for Mexican Americans. Now the word Chicano has taken on a new, positive meaning (Cuellar, 1970; Gutiérrez and Hirsch, 1970; J. Vigil, 1980, p. 202).

Besides a positive self-image, Chicanismo and the movement of La Raza include renewed awareness of the plight of Chicanos at the hands of Anglos. Chicanos are a colonial minority, as Joan Moore (1970) describes, because their relationship with Anglos was involuntary, Mexican culture was either transformed or destroyed by Anglos, and the Chicano people themselves have been victims of racism (see also Barrera et al., 1972; Moore and Pachon, 1976, pp. 99–100). The colonial model points out the ways in which societal institutions have failed Chicanos and perpetuated their problems. Militant Chicanos refer to assimilationists, whom they say would sell out to the White people, as *vendidos*, or traitors. The ultimate insult is the term *Malinche*, the name of the American Indian woman who became the mistress of the Spanish conqueror, Cortez. Many in the Chicano movement believe that if one does not work actively for the struggle one is working against it.

The best known of the urban Chicano leaders has been Rodolfo ("Corky") Gonzales of Denver. Gonzales is the author of an epic poem entitled *Yo Soy*

*Joaquin,* written in 1976, which is a statement of the Chicanos' unconquerable quest for freedom (Gonzales, 1972). Gonzales took up his organizing work in 1966, when he left behind brief careers as a professional boxer and in the War on Poverty, and organized the Crusade for Justice. The Crusade for Justice is a civil rights organization that strives to reform the police and the courts, improve housing and education for Chicanos, and diversify employment opportunities. Police-Chicano relations have continued to be a source of tension. Many Chicanos still fear the Texas Rangers and the border patrol, nor is it a coincidence that the two landmark Supreme Court decisions limiting police interrogation *(Escobedo* v. *Illinois* and *Miranda* v. *Arizona)* involved Chicano suspects (Acuña, 1981; *Time,* 1969).

***Tijerina and Land Rights.*** Reies López Tijerina, perhaps as well as any recent Chicano, captures the spirit of Chicanismo. In fact Tijerina in New Mexico, along with César Chávez (head of the United Farm Workers) in California, Gonzales (leader of the Crusade for Justice) in Colorado, and José Gutiérrez (head of *La Raza Unida Partido*) in Texas, share responsibility for popularizing Chicanismo. Born in a cotton field worked by migrant farmers, Tijerina became a pentecostal preacher and in the late 1950s took an interest in old Spanish land grants. From research in Mexico, Spain, and the Southwest, he concluded that the Chicanos, more specifically the Hispanos, had lost significant tracts of land through quasi legal chicanery and other questionable practices.

In 1963, he formed the *Alianza Federal de Mercedes* (Federal Alliance of Land Grants) whose purpose is to recover the lost land. To publicize his purpose when few Anglos would pay attention, he seized part of the Kit Carson National Forest in New Mexico. Arrested for trespassing, Tijerina spent the next few years either in jail or awaiting trial. Tijerina's quest for restoration of land rights has been at times violent. During one trial in 1967, Tijerina sympathizers became involved in a gun battle at the Tierra Amarilla courthouse, which ended with two law enforcement officials shot. The land dispute was partially resolved in 1975 when more than a thousand acres of the National Forest were transferred to 75 Hispanic families. For his participation in the protest, Tijerina was sentenced to two years in prison, but was paroled in 1971 on condition that he hold no official position in the *Alianza.* By 1987, Tijerina was leading an isolated existence outside a small town in New Mexico (Blawis, 1971; Callanan, 1987; Nabokov, 1970).

Tijerina and the *Alianza* were not as active in the 1980s as they were in the late 1960s, but they had not been forgotten. Even as individuals like Corky Gonzales and Reies Tijerina passed from center stage, their presence was still felt. The problems they fought have continued to exist and Chicanos still press for solutions. Chicanos who were in college from 1965 to about 1972 are those most aware of Chicanismo; they have been unlikely to forget its significance to them as individuals and as Chicanos. They continue to carry on the fight for their rights. As they do, an action foremost in their memory has been the struggle by César Chávez on behalf of migrant farm workers in southern California.

*Chávez and Farm Laborers.* The best-known Chicano leader is César Chávez, who crusaded to organize migrant farm workers. Those laborers had never won collective bargaining rights, partly because their mobility made it difficult for them to organize into a unified group. Efforts to organize agricultural laborers date back to the turn of the century, but Chávez was the first to succeed.

In 1962, Chávez, 35 years old, resigned from leadership in the Community Service Organization to form the National Farm Workers Association (NFWA), later to become the United Farm Workers Union (UFW). Organizing migrant farm workers was not easy, for they had no savings to pay for organizing or to live on while striking. Growers could rely on a virtually limitless supply of Mexican laborers to replace the Chicanos and Filipinos who struck for higher wages and better working conditions. Chávez's first success was the grape boycott launched in 1965, which carried the struggle into the kitchens of families throughout the country. "Listen to Their Voices," reproduces the "Boycott Day Proclamation" issued by the grape workers on May 10, 1969. It took five years before the grape growers signed three-year contracts with Chávez's union, which had affiliated with the AFL-CIO. This victory signaled a new era in labor relations and made Chávez a national folk hero (Levy, 1975).

Despite their success, Chávez and the United Farm Workers were plagued with problems.

1. Increased mechanization of agriculture reduced the need for migrant farm workers.
2. Chicanos in urban areas did not offer mass support.
3. The UFW has been increasingly dependent for money and guidance on the AFL-CIO, with which it is affiliated.
4. Chávez has been criticized for his refusal to take a broader leadership role in the Chicano movement.
5. The union leaders lack administrative experience.

The worst problem in the early years was competition from the Teamsters Union. The Teamsters challenged the UFW in the signing of new contracts from 1972 to 1977. Chávez charged that the Teamsters offered growers "sweetheart contracts," which brought raises to the farm workers but were not as good for them as the agreements backed by the UFW. The long, bitter, and sometimes violent struggle between the unions ended in March 1977. At that time a five-year agreement was signed, giving the field hands to the UFW and the canners, packers, and farm-truck drivers to the Teamsters Union.

Problems resurfaced in the 1980s as California's governor and lawmakers became less supportive of Chávez. This came about at a time when UFW was also trying to heighten the public consciousness about the pesticides in fields worked by laborers. Research into the long-term effects of pesticides has only begun. Although Chávez's 1988 fast to bring attention to this issue was widely publicized, the grape boycotts of the 1980s, also directed at this problem, have had little public appeal (Weisskopf, 1988; D. Wilson, 1988). A 1985 survey, for example, found Californians split on whether to support a boycott of grapes to exert pressure on the state's grape growers to abide more vigorously by state farm labor laws.

These problems are likely to make it difficult for Chávez to fulfill all his objectives. In addition membership has dwindled from a high of 50,000 to 20,000 in 1989. Nevertheless, what he and the UFW have accomplished to date is considerable. First, they have succeeded in making federal and state governments more aware of the exploitation of migrant laborers. Second, the migrant workers, or at least those organized in California, have developed a sense of their own power and worth that will make it extremely difficult for growers to abuse them in the future as they have in the past. Third, working conditions have improved. California agricultural workers were paid an average of less than $2 an hour in the mid-1960s. By 1987, they were paid an average of about $5.85 an hour. Workers covered by UFW contracts averaged nearly $7 an hour three years earlier.

Migrant workers still face a very harsh life. Under pressure to reduce government spending in general, the federal government in the 1980s reduced enforcement of migrant-worker laws. Only two Labor Department officers ride herd over North Carolina's 1,000 migrant worker camps. Tuberculosis, alcoholism, and malnutrition are common among migrant farm workers. The agenda for Chávez and his successors remains full (Chaze, 1982b; DeParle, 1991a; Erlich, 1987; W. King, 1981; Lindsey, 1984; Majka, 1981, pp. 541–544; Moore and Pachon, 1976, p. 110; A. Navarro, 1974; Nordheimer, 1988; Taylor and John, 1985).

*César Chávez achieved unprecedented success in organizing migrant farm workers in California.*

---

### ❖ *LISTEN TO THEIR VOICES* ❖

*1969 Proclamation of the
Delano Grape Workers*

*César Chávez*

*For four years, Chávez and his fellow or-
ganizers had asked consumers throughout
the nation to support their cause by refusing to buy or eat table grapes. In 1969,
they issued the following statement at a
time when it was apparent to major
wholesalers that grape consumption had
indeed dropped due to the efforts of the
United Farm Workers.*

We, the striking grape workers of California, join on this International Boycott Day with the consumers across
the continent in planning the steps
that lie ahead on the road to our liberation. As we plan, we recall the foot-
steps that brought us to this day and
the events of this day. The historic
road of our pilgrimage to Sacramento
later branched out, spreading like the
unpruned vines in struck fields, until
it led us to willing exile in cities across
this land. There, far from the earth we
tilled for generations, we have culti-
vated the strange soil of public understanding, sowing the seed of our truth
and our cause in the minds and hearts
of men.

We have been farm workers for
hundreds of years and pioneers for
seven. Mexicans, Filipinos, Africans
and others, our ancestors were among
those who founded this land and
tamed its natural wilderness. But we
are still pilgrims on this land, and we
are pioneers who blaze a trail out of
the wilderness of hunger and deprivation that we have suffered even as our
ancestors did. We are conscious today
of the significance of our present
quest. If this road we chart leads to the
rights and reforms we demand, if it
leads to just wages, humane working
conditions, protection from the mis-
use of pesticides, and to the fundamental right of collective bargaining,
if it changes the social order that relegates us to the bottom reaches of society, then in our wake will follow
thousands of American farm workers.
Our example will make them free. But
if our road does not bring us to victory and social change, it will not be
because our direction is mistaken or
our resolve too weak, but only because our bodies are mortal and our
journey hard. For we are in the midst
of a great social movement, and we
will not stop struggling 'til we die, or
win!

We have been farm workers for
hundreds of years and strikers for
four. It was four years ago that we
threw down our plowshares and
pruning hooks. These Biblical symbols of peace and tranquility to us represent too many lifetimes of unpro-
testing submission to a degrading
social system that allows us no dig-

nity, no comfort, no peace. We mean to have our peace, and to win it without violence, for it is violence we would overcome—the subtle spiritual and mental violence of oppression, the violence subhuman toil does to the human body. So we went and stood tall outside the vineyards where we had stooped for years. But the tailors of national labor legislation had left us naked. Thus exposed, our picket lines were crippled by injunctions and harassed by growers; our strike was broken by imported scabs; our overtures to our employers were ignored. Yet we knew the day must come when they would talk to us, *as equals.*

We have been farm workers for hundreds of years and boycotters for two. We did not choose the grape boycott, but we *had* chosen to leave our peonage, poverty and despair behind. Though our first bid for freedom, the strike, was weakened, we would not turn back. The boycott was the only way forward the growers left to us. We called upon our fellow men and were answered by consumers who said—as all men of conscience must—that they would no longer allow their tables to be subsidized by our sweat and our sorrow: They shunned the grapes, fruit of our affliction.

We marched alone at the beginning, but today we count men of all creeds, nationalities, and occupations in our number. Between us and the justice we seek now stand the large and powerful grocers who, in continuing to buy table grapes, betray the boycott their own customers have built. These stores treat their patrons' demands to remove the grapes the same way the growers treat our demands for union recognition—by ignoring them. The consumers who rally behind our cause are responding as we do to such treatment—with a boycott! They pledge to withhold their patronage from stores that handle grapes during the boycott, just as we withhold our labor from the growers until our dispute is resolved.

Grapes must remain an unenjoyed luxury for all as long as the barest human needs and basic human rights are still luxuries for farm workers. The grapes grow sweet and heavy on the vines, but they will have to wait while we reach out first for our freedom. The time is ripe for our liberation.

From Wayne Moquin and Charles Van Doren, eds. *A Documentary History of the Mexican Americans*, pp. 472–473, 1971.

## Political Organizations

More directly involved with effective political representation than the organizations just described is the Mexican American Political Association (MAPA), founded in 1958 in California. Although primarily middle class in membership, it has sought to promote political organization among lower-class Chicanos. MAPA conducts political education efforts and voter registration drives. It strives to be nonpartisan, but most of its support usually comes from Democrats; it in turn endorses Democratic political candidates. In the early 1960s, concern that other Hispanics were excluded from MAPA led to creation of PASSO

(Political Association of Spanish-Speaking Organizations). PASSO's success in California has been less dramatic than in Texas. PASSO was the first Hispanic political coalition in Texas during the twentieth century that succeeded without the consent of the local Democratic party. In 1963, PASSO successfully elected a completely Chicano slate to the Crystal City, Texas, city council. Two years later, Anglos and conservative Chicanos voted them out of office, however (Juarez, 1972; Tirado, 1970, pp. 66–68).

Political activity varies widely among Chicanos in the Southwest. Chicanos have had the greatest political representation in New Mexico, both when it was a territory and since being granted statehood in 1912. Unlike California, where the Hispanics were driven out, or Texas, which was the site of a full-scale war between Anglos and Hispanics, New Mexico had a continuous heritage of leadership from the Hispanos or descendants of the colonized Mexicans. This role was barely interrupted by Anglo settlements. The state constitution provides that individuals who speak only Spanish may vote and hold office. Not too surprisingly, a third of New Mexico's state legislators are Hispano and that state has been the location of the only mass movement among Hispanos, Tijerina's *Alianza*. Although New Mexico's Chicanos play a pivotal political role within the Democratic party, Hispanics in other states are less fortunate. Despite MAPA and PASSO, they have been less successful in California. In Texas, however, until recently the outlook for Chicanos in politics has been bleakest. As we have seen, PASSO marked increasing politicization among Chicanos in Texas. But Chicanos received no help from regular party organizations and had to take an even more dramatic step, forming a new political party (Lindsey, 1978; Moore, 1970).

*La Raza Unida Partido* (LRU, United Peoples Party) is the latest stage of Chicano political organization. *La Raza Unida* has been a third party supporting candidates who offer alternatives to the Democratic and Republican parties. It was organized by José Angel Gutiérrez in Texas in 1970 and has had remarkable successes. The LRU candidate for governor captured 6 percent of the vote in 1972. Most notable has been the party's success in Crystal City, where Chicanos ran the community without forming any political coalition with Anglos. But Crystal City is not typical. It has fewer than 10,000 people and has had a very large Chicano majority for some time, which is unusual even for south Texas. Nonetheless, the Chicanos made changes that have been welcomed by some Anglos as well. By the mid-1970s, LRU fell into disarray. Disagreements within the party as well as delays by established state politicians in supplying federal money to Crystal City hastened its demise. Even more discouraging is that some of the reforms introduced, such as Chicano studies in high school, have been undone (Marquez, 1987; Pedersen, 1987).

Organized in 1967, the Mexican-American Legal Defense and Education Fund (MALDEF) has emerged as a potent force to protect Chicano's constitutional rights. While not endorsing candidates, it has made itself felt in the political arena much like NAACP has for African Americans. On the education side, it has addressed segregation, biased testing, inequities in school financing, and failure to address bilingualism. MALDEF has been involved in litigation involving employment practices, and immigration reform voting rights. It has emerged as the primary civil rights group on behalf of Chicanos (Vigil, 1990).

The politically successful movements have been increasingly drawn to conventional political parties, and the Democrats serve as standard bearer. Acknowledging the growing numbers of Chicanos, however, the Republicans also cater to Chicanos with some success. Some observers decry the *fiesta politics*, in which every four years presidential candidates make blatant overtures to the Chicano community although their special needs are forgotten between elections.

The growth of the Chicano population and especially of the number of registered Chicano voters can no longer be ignored or taken for granted. Chicanos are concentrated in the politically significant states of California and Texas. Similarly Puerto Ricans and Cuban Americans are a political force in New York and Florida respectively. Fiesta politics may continue, but more enduring efforts to attract Hispanics will develop as well. Redistricting following the 1980 census shows increased representation in Congress as well as local city councils. This should greatly accelerate the rise in Hispanic elected officials which grew 28 percent between 1984 and 1990. Overall political power is growing, but Chicanos have not achieved a political base appropriate to the size of the group (Acuña, 1981; Hirsch, 1982; Hume, 1984; Moore and Pachon, 1985, pp. 184–186; Mydans, 1991a; Tostado, 1985).

## The Church

The most important organization in the Chicano community is the church, specifically the Roman Catholic Church. In 1986, 85 percent of Hispanics were Roman Catholic, 83 percent of these considering religion very important in their lives. The strong identification of Chicanos and Mexican immigrants with Catholicism has reinforced the already formidable barriers between them and the predominantly Protestant Southwest. By virtue of its size, wealth, and widespread support, the Catholic Church has the potential to be a significant force in bringing about social justice for Chicano people (Berger, 1986a; Moore and Pachon, 1985).

The Church has only sporadically involved itself in the Chicano movement, and rarely have the upper levels of the church hierarchy supported Chicanismo. Many Chicanos have found this relative inactivity frustrating because two-thirds of the church's membership in the Southwest are Chicanos. Admittedly, by the church's standards, Chicanos are relatively inactive. They are highly spiritual in their religious beliefs, but relatively few go to church, seek penance, or receive communion. It remains to be seen if the Church can accept a form of participation in the faith that cares less about organizational matters dictated by the European heritage and more about celebrating the spirit in the Latin fashion (K. Briggs, 1983).

Leaders in the Hispanic community are outspoken in their views on the Roman Catholic Church. César Chávez, speaking as early as 1968, explained what Chicanos want the Roman Catholic Church to do:

We don't ask for more cathedrals. We don't ask for bigger churches or fine gifts. We ask for its presence with us, beside us, as Christ among us. We ask the Church to *sacrifice with the people* for social change, for justice, and for love of brother. We don't ask for words. We ask for deeds. We don't ask for paternalism. We ask for servanthood. (1973, p. 218)

In spite of this criticism, the Catholic Church is relevant to the Chicano movement (Acuña, 1981).

The Catholic Church has basically taken an assimilationist role whether with Mexican Catholics or with other minority Catholics. Because the Chicano movement rejects assimilation, the Catholic Church appears to be at odds with Chicanismo. Even Chicano priests, because of their middle-class training, support programs with long-range goals, whereas barrio residents seek instant results. The Church has in fact spoken out against high-school protests and against militants who embrace communism; it has defended itself against charges that its own parochial schools suppress Mexican culture. Nevertheless, efforts to give the Chicanos a bigger voice within the Church have been made. In 1969, a nationwide association of Chicano priests named PADRES (*Padres Asociados para Derechos Religiosos, Educativos y Sociales,* Priests United for Religious, Educational, and Social Rights) was formed to urge the Church to provide more assistance for social projects and adequate education in barrio parochial schools. At the local level the Catholic Church has supported aspects of the Chicano movement. Chávez has asked for, and usually received, approval for his UFW from priests throughout southern California.

The Roman Catholic Church, like the rest of the nation, has found it impossible to ignore the Chicano movement. Recognizing this, the United States bishops in 1987 issued the "National Pastoral Plan for Hispanic Ministry." It comes none too soon as survey data reveal that Hispanic Catholics have left the church at a rate of approximately 100,000 a year, joining fundamentalist or Baptist faiths with which they find it easier to identify (Acuña, 1981, pp. 405–408; Cortés, 1980; El Nasser, 1990; Greeley, 1988; McNamara, 1973; Mirandé, 1985; Suro, 1989).

Every indication is that the number of Chicanos leaving the Roman Catholic Church is growing. Given that the Southern Baptists claim 2,300 Hispanic pastors to the Catholics' fewer than 2,000 Hispanic priests it is little wonder. Clearly the Roman Catholic Church, with one-third of its membership Hispanic, can ill afford not to be responsive.

## EDUCATION

Although statistics on Chicanos and formal schooling seem positive at first glance, they become disturbing on closer examination. While the number of Hispanic college students has increased, their gains have not kept pace with the population increase. As apparent in Table 10.1, Chicanos fall well behind other Hispanics, and even further behind Anglos. While bilingual education is still endorsed in the United States, implementation of effective, quality programs has been difficult, as the previous chapter showed. Two other areas of concern in education are the increasing segregation of Chicano students and their absence from higher education.

## Social Isolation

While Black students have managed to hold to early gains in school desegregation, Hispanics, including Chicanos, have become increasingly isolated. In 1968, 54.8 percent of all Hispanics attended predominantly minority schools—that is, schools where at least half of the students were minorities. By 1984, this rate was 70.6 percent—a level of segregation higher than that for Black students. Significantly, certain states with large numbers of Hispanics such as Illinois, New York, and Texas are more segregated than the national averages. In a parallel development, between 1970 and 1985, the percent of Whites in the typical Chicano student's school in Los Angeles County dropped from 45 percent to 17 percent. The trend toward growing isolation of Hispanics is found in virtually all parts of the nation and since 1972 has prevailed in almost every period in which national data have been collected (Jaeger, 1987; Orfield and Monfort, 1988).

Three factors explain this increasingly social isolation of Chicanos from other students in school. First, Hispanics are increasingly concentrated in the largest cities where minorities dominate. Second, the numbers of Hispanics have increased dramatically since the 1970s when efforts to desegregate schools began to lose momentum. Third, schools once desegregated have become "resegregated" as numbers of school-age Chicanos in an area have increased and determination to maintain balance in schools, as noted, has lessened (Moore and Iadicola, 1981).

## Higher Education

Chicanos are missing from higher education—in all roles. Recent reports have documented the absence of Hispanics among college teachers and administrators. The situation is similar in this respect to that of Blacks; however, there are no Hispanic counterparts to historic Black colleges such as Tuskegee Institute to provide a source of leaders (Fiske, 1988a).

The problem of students seeing few teachers and administrators like themselves is perpetuated through what is often termed the *educational pipeline:* insufficient numbers of Hispanic university students have been prepared to serve as teachers and administrators. In 1990, only 44 percent of Chicanos aged 25 years or over completed high school, compared to 80 percent of non-Hispanics. Even these data are deceptively encouraging with respect to Hispanics. Chicanos who do choose to continue their education beyond high school are more likely to select a proprietary, or technical, school or community colleges to acquire work-related skills. The pipeline narrows still further as we reach the baccalaureate level (Bureau of the Census, 1991f, p. 6; Estrada, 1988).

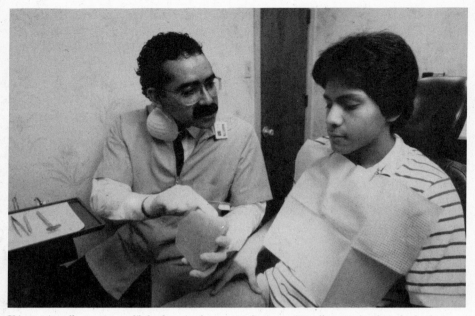

*Chicanos in college are more likely than Anglos to attend community colleges and technical schools.*

Chicanos face challenges similar to those Black students meet on predominantly White campuses. Chicanos are likely, given the social isolation of Hispanic high schools, to have to adjust for the first time to an educational environment almost totally populated by Anglos. They may experience racism for the first time, just as they are trying to accommodate to a heavier academic load. Chicanos at more selective universities report that classmates accuse them of having benefitted from affirmative action admissions policies and not really belonging (Fiske, 1988a, 1988b).

The plight of Hispanics sometimes leads to innovative responses. The University of Texas at El Paso, for example, has allowed Mexicans to commute over the border since 1989, and if they demonstrate financial need, to pay in-state tuition. In 1992, there were 927 Mexican students, of whom 84 percent qualified for the lower tuition rate. Since many of the commuters are not fluent in English, the University provides an array of support services for non-English-speaking students (Manigan, 1992).

The next section will consider family life among Chicanos and look at how close family ties can contribute to and support educational achievement. Yet college recruiters report that some Chicanos are hesitant to leave home to attend a residential college. Data show that Hispanics who drop out of college, more than other minorities and Blacks, are likely to report that they did so to provide financial assistance for their families—another sign of the close-knit character of many Chicano households. Stress over family-related issues is frequently cited by college counselors working with Chicano students. This is all not surprising given Table 10.1's report of the high proportion of Chicano families below the poverty level. Stress is particularly noticeable for Chicanas, that is Chicano women, who are often the first of their gender in their families to enter college (Fields, 1988; Fiske, 1988b; Muñoz, 1986; Vasquez, 1982).

## FAMILY LIFE

In 1987 San Antonio mayor Henry Cisneros, the first Hispanic ever to serve as chief executive of a major United States city, announced that he would drop out of the governor's race. He was regarded as a popular frontrunner, but his reasons were not political. His new son was ailing from birth defects and he chose his family role over staying in the political landscape. Many people saw Cisneros's choice of family first as typical of many other Chicanos who value the family.

The most important organization or institution among Chicanos, or for that matter any group, is the family. The structure of the Chicano family differs little from the families of other Americans, a statement remarkable in itself given the impoverishment of Chicanos. In 1985, most American families (80 percent) and most Chicano families (76 percent) were headed by both a husband and a wife. Only 5.7 percent of Chicanos are divorced, compared to 7.9 percent of the population generally. Chicano households do tend to be larger, one-third of them having five or more persons, compared to 10 percent for the nation's households (Bureau of the Census, 1991f, pp. 6, 12).

Much writing on the Chicano family, as well as on the family in Mexico, has repeated the error of describing it as homogeneous. It is often characterized as a simple peasant family surviving upward mobility. Even the concept of the peasant family has received little qualification. Good and bad traits, but usually the latter, have been assigned to Chicano families regardless of the truth. We shall briefly examine the characteristics of "the culture of poverty," machismo and marianismo, and familism to determine their usefulness in descriptions of the Chicano family (Stoddard, 1973, pp. 38–43).

### The "Culture of Poverty"

As with the Black American family described in Chapter 8, Chicano families are labeled as having traits that, in fact, describe poor families rather than specifically Chicano families. Indeed a 1980 report of the Commission on Civil Rights (1980d, p. 8) states that the two most prevalent stereotypic themes appearing in works on Hispanics show them as (1) exclusively poor, and (2) prone to commit violence. Similarly, movies from *Tony the Greaser* in 1911 to *Fort Apache, The Bronx* in 1981 do little to change this image (Woll, 1981).

Social scientists have also relied excessively on the traits of the poor to describe a minority group like Chicanos. Anthropologist Oscar Lewis (1959, 1965,

1966), in several publications based on research conducted among Mexicans and Puerto Ricans, identified "the culture of poverty." The *culture of poverty* embraces a deviant way of life according to its theorists, which involves no future planning, no enduring commitment to marriage, and absence of the work ethic. This culture supposedly follows the poor, even when they move out of the slums or the barrio. Hispanic groups protested the remarks of a Housing and Urban Development official who showed little concern over overcrowding because, he said, it was "a cultural preference" for families to double up (*New York Daily News*, 1984; Penalosa, 1968).

The culture of poverty view is another way of "blaming the victim" (Ryan, 1976)—the affluent are not responsible for social inequality, nor are the policy makers; it is the poor who are to be blamed. This allows government and society to blame the failure of anti-poverty and welfare programs on Chicanos and other poor people, rather than on the programs themselves. These are programs designed and largely staffed by middle class, Anglo, English-speaking professionals (Shannon, 1979). Conflict theorists join Ryan in saying that it is unfair to blame the poor for their lack of money, low education, poor health, and low-paying jobs.

Lewis's hypothesis about the culture of poverty, whether exaggerated or not, came to be indiscriminately applied to explain continued poverty. Critics argue that Lewis sought out exotic, pathological behavior, ignoring the fact that even among the poor most people live fairly conventionally and strive to achieve goals similar to those of the middle class. A second criticism challenges use of the term "culture of poverty" to describe an entire ethnic group. This refutation is similar to the debate over the Moynihan Report and its oversimplified look at the Black family. Because Lewis's data were on poor people, social scientists have increasingly stressed that his conclusions may be correct as far as the data permit, but the data cannot be generalized to all Hispanics because the sample was not a representative cross-section drawn from different economic and educational levels (Burma, 1970, pp. 17–28; Casavantes, 1970; Moore and Pachon, 1985, pp. 98–99; Valentine, 1968, pp. 48–77).

Social science research has since been conducted that, unlike Lewis's, does sample Chicano families across a broad range of socioeconomic levels. This research shows that when Anglo and Chicano families of the same social class are compared, they differ little in family organization and attitudes toward child-rearing. In addition, comparisons of work ethics find no significant differences between Chicanos and Anglos. Poverty is present among Chicanos; there is no doubt about that. However that does not mean there is a *culture of poverty* or a permanent underclass. Institutions such as the family and the church seem viable, although schools are in disrepair and the picture on businesses is mixed. To question the label of "culture of poverty" does not deny the poor life chances facing many Chicanos (Aponte, 1991; Caine, 1972; Irelan et al., 1969; Isonio and Garza, 1987; E. Martinez, 1988; Moore, 1989; Winkler, 1990b).

## Machismo and Marianismo

Chicanos, like other people are expected to fulfill certain roles as men and women. Among Chicanos and other Hispanics, there are particular versions of masculinity and femininity. Hispanic men are expected to take great pride in their maleness, and women in being females.

For men, the sense of virility, of personal worth in one's own eyes and in those of peers, is called *machismo*. The idea of male dominance and superiority is probably the characteristic emphasized in most descriptions of both Chicano and Mexican families. Machismo is often misrepresented or exaggerated. First, it may be demonstrated differently by different men. For some it may entail resorting to weapons or fighting, but for others it may mean being irresistible to women. Generally the machismo of a man is more imagined than real; that is, it consists of claiming achievements never accomplished.

*Marianismo* describes the qualities of femininity that are complementary to those of machismo in men. A good woman accepts the dominance of men and consistently places the needs of the family first. The few research studies that have focused on machismo and marianismo have limited sample sizes. Yet there is little evidence to date that male-dominated or patriarchal households are typical of Chicanos and other Hispanics. Research data collected in Los Angeles, New York City, and San Antonio suggest that common notions of machismo are disappearing, or perhaps were never very prevalent after all. More recent research has found no important differences between Anglos and Chicanos on wives' labor-force participation and male versus female dominance in family decision making (Alvirez and Bean, 1976, pp. 277–278; Burma, 1970, pp. 23–24; Anne Campbell, 1987, pp. 461–463; Erlanger, 1976; Mirandé, 1985, pp. 165–181; Vega et al., 1986, p. 858).

Several factors contribute to the decline of machismo. The feminist movement in both the United States and Latin America has changed the way in which men and women react toward one another. Feminists argue that male Chicanos have falsely glorified machismo, giving this aspect of Mexican culture more attention than it deserves. Urbanization, upward mobility, and assimilation are all combining to make machismo more of a historical footnote with each passing generation of Chicanos (Moore and Pachon, 1985; Stevens, 1973; Winkler, 1990a).

## Familism

Chicanos are described as laudably more familistic than other people in the United States. By *familism* is meant pride and closeness in the family, which results in family obligation and loyalty coming before individual needs (Wallace, 1984). The family, therefore, is the primary source of both social interaction and caregiving.

Familism has been viewed as both a positive and negative influence on individual Chicanos. It may have the negative effect of discouraging youths with a bright future from taking advantage of opportunities that would remove them from the family. Familism is generally regarded as good, however, because an extended family provides emotional strength at times of family crisis. Close family ties maintain the mental and social well-being of the elderly. The family, therefore, is seen as a norm and as a nurturing unit that provides support throughout the individual's lifetime. The many significant aspects of familism include: (1) importance of *compadrazgo* (godparent-godchild relationship); (2) benefits of financial dependency of kin; (3) availability of relatives as a source of advice; and (4) active involvement of the elderly within the family.

Familism and machismo are two traits associated with the traditional Mexican family. These traditional values, whether judged good or bad, are expected to decline in importance with urbanization, industrialization, and acquisition of middle-class status. Characteristics that marked differences between Chicano and Anglo family life were sharper in the past. Even among past generations, differences were of degree, not of kind—that is, Chicano families tended to exhibit some traits more than Anglos, not different traits altogether. A comparison between similar Anglo and Chicano families in San Diego found no significant differences in family life between the two groups. Variations that did appear as the result of statistical analysis tended to be of degree rather than kind. Some of these differences are disappearing; the "culture of poverty" is a somewhat different matter because of sharp disagreement over whether it exists, let alone whether it is vanishing. The Chicano family, in summary, displays all the variety of American families in general. Unlike Anglos, however, Chicanos are subject to prejudice and discrimination (Vega et al., 1986; see also Gratton, 1987; Grebler et al., 1970, pp. 350–377; Mirandé, 1985; Rosaldo, 1985; Sabogal et al., 1987; Vega, 1990; Wallace, 1984; Wallace and Facio, 1986).

## HEALTH CARE

Earlier, in Chapter 5, we were introduced to the concept of *life chances*, which refers to people's opportunities to provide themselves with material goods, positive living conditions, and favorable life experiences. We have consistently seen Chicanos and other Hispanic groups as having more limited life chances. Perhaps in no other area does this apply so literally as in the health care system.

Hispanics as a group are locked out of the health care system more often than any other racial or ethnic group. A third have no health insurance (or other coverage such as Medicaid) compared to 13 percent of Whites and 20 percent of Blacks. Chicanos are especially vulnerable, with 37 percent uncovered compared to 16 percent of Puerto Ricans and 20 percent of Cuban Americans. Predictably the uninsured are less likely to have a regular source of medical care. This means waiting for a crisis before seeking care. Fewer are immunized and rates of preventable diseases like lead poisoning are higher. Noncoverage is increasing, which may reflect a further breakdown in health care delivery or it may be a result of continuing immigration (Chavez, 1989; Mendoza et al., 1991; *New York Times,* 1992).

The health care dilemma facing Chicanos and other Hispanic groups is complicated by the lack of Hispanic health professionals. They account for 7 percent or less of dentists, nurses, and pharmacists and 5 percent of the physicians, yet are approaching 10 percent of the population. Less than 5 percent of students in medical school are Hispanic, so the situation will not soon change. Obviously one does not need to be administered health care by one's same ethnic group, but the paucity of Hispanic professionals increases the likelihood the group will be underserved (Bureau of the Census, 1991a, p. 395; Council on Scientific Affairs, 1991; Ginzberg, 1991).

Given the circumstances of the high proportion of uninsured individuals and low number of Hispanic health care personnel, it is not surprising to learn of the poor status of Hispanics' health care as a group. They are at increased risk for certain medical conditions, including diabetes, hypertension, tuberculosis,

*Migrant farm workers, many of whom are Chicano or from other minority groups, continue to experience harsh working conditions.*

AIDS, alcoholism, and specific cancers. The situation begins to deteriorate at the start of life. Only about 60 percent of Chicanos and Puerto Ricans initiate prenatal care in the first trimester compared to 80 percent of Whites. Yet infant mortality rates are generally lower for Chicano children than for Whites. Experts suggest that familism may account for the surprising advantage in infant health in that they receive more help even if it is not "professional." However this is less true of Hispanics born in the United States to parents who show signs of assimilating, unfortunately, to some U.S. habits such as poor diet and smoking. Women's health has not received sufficient attention and this is especially true of minority women. The American Medical Association acknowledges, for example, that not enough is known as to why Hispanic women are especially vulnerable to cervical cancer and AIDS. There is a challenge to develop a health care system that can respond to these needs (Becerra et al., 1991; Council on Scientific Affairs, 1991; Kleinhuizen, 1991a; Novello et al., 1991).

Some Chicanos and many other Hispanics have cultural beliefs that inhibit the use of the medical system. They may interpret their illnesses according to folk practices or *curanderismo*—Hispanic folk medicine—a form of holistic health care and healing. This orientation influences how one approaches health care and even how one defines illness. The use of folk healers, or *curanderos*, is probably infrequent, but perhaps 20 percent rely on home remedies. While these are not necessarily without value, especially if a dual system of folk and establishment medicine is followed, reliance on natural beliefs may be counterproductive. Another aspect of folk beliefs is the identification of folk-defined illnesses such as *susto* (or fright sickness) and *atague* (or fighting attack). While these complaints, alien to Anglos, often have biological bases, they need to be dealt with carefully by sensitive medical professionals to diagnose and treat illnesses accurately (Council on Scientific Affairs, 1991; Rivera, 1988).

## PREJUDICE AND DISCRIMINATION

The term *taco circuit* has an unpleasant meaning for FBI agents. It refers to the dead-end jobs in dreary Southwest cities that have too often been the lot of the bureau's Hispanic agents. In 1988, a federal judge ruled that the FBI had systematically discriminated against its Hispanic agents by assigning them to the least rewarding or, in some cases, the most hazardous assignments. In all, 311 plaintiffs, more than three-fourths of all the bureau's Hispanic agents, successfully charged that they had been harassed by their superiors in the nation's most prestigious law enforcement agency (Isikoff, 1988).

Discrimination is not limited to the "taco circuit" for Chicanos. They, like other racial and ethnic groups, continue to be victims of prejudice and discrimination. Movies and advertisements that perpetuate stereotypes continue to reinforce prejudice. The stereotypical Mexican village in movies or advertisements have residents who are either sleeping around a fountain or walking around in bored laziness. In the late 1960s, several Chicano groups protested against portrayals of Mexicans as either bandits or lazy peasants. The mass media and advertisers mostly have responded by avoiding such negative stereotyping. The result is that Chicanos are now all together absent from advertisements and films, with the exception of taco advertisements (T. Martinez, 1973; Moore and Pachon, 1985).

The prevailing poverty of Chicanos affects the quality of their life. They are more likely to live in overcrowded, substandard housing than are Anglos, and in the Southwest they fall far behind Blacks as well. The urban Chicano finds barrio life depressing because it lacks city services and opportunities for employment. Disease, death, and mental illness are more likely in the Chicano household. Not only are crime rates higher among Chicanos than among Whites, but they are more likely to be the victims of assault or theft. Whether approached through statistics or in-depth descriptive studies, the conclusion remains that the standard of living of Chicanos falls far short of the minimal standards American society has set. The life of the urban poor in the barrio has been graphically described by several Chicano authors (Acosta, 1972; Galarza, 1971; Gonzales, 1972).

Language proficiency serves as a barrier to upward mobility for Chicanos more than for Anglos. Sometimes, however, language difference is merely an excuse for discrimination. Speaking English is used as a job requirement either unnecessarily or artificially, placing standards of proficiency higher than needed for the employment sought (Moore and Pachon, 1985, p. 73).

Data indicate that on most measures of socioeconomic status, Chicano's lives are improving. Figure 10.1 shows that the median family increase increased from $10,300 to $21,400 from 1976 to 1990. Chicano have even begun heading firms in significant numbers. By 1982, Hispanics owned 2.1 percent of the firms and accounted for 1.5 percent of business revenues. About 58 percent of these firms were owned by Mexican Americans. The largest number of Hispanic firms were in the Los Angeles metropolitan area, followed by Miami and New York (Bureau of the Census, 1986c; Dunn, 1986a). Yet the gains of minority groups have been matched by the increased economic prosperity of the dominant group. In 1970, Chicano family income was 70 percent of White family income. In 1990, it was 73 percent; the gap in income has changed very little (see Figure 10.1).

## GLANCING BACK AND LOOKING AHEAD

David Gomez (1971) described Chicanos as "strangers in their own land." The Chicano people were native to the Southwest long before the expansion westward of European immigrants and the redrawing of the United States' boundaries. Possession of the land did not guarantee dominance, however. In fact, title to the land was soon lost, and today many individuals, following the lead of Reies Tijerina, have attempted to reclaim the land on behalf of the Chicano people.

**FIGURE 10.1**    Median Family Income of Whites and Chicanos

Chicanos' family income has increased since 1976, but not as rapidly as White income.

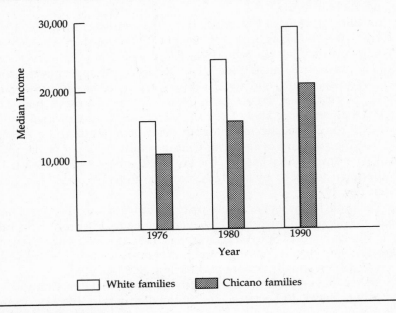

Note: 1990 data is for households.
Source: Bureau of the Census, 1991f, p. 12.

Not all Chicanos are descended from the Mexicans who lived in the territory ceded to the United States following the Mexican-American War. Many are descendants of Mexican immigrants, like the *braceros* and *mojados*, or are themselves immigrants. Nearly half of the Chicanos feel most comfortable communicating in Spanish. Consequently, Chicanos have been poorly educated and have had difficulty being elected to public office. Only recently has the United States begun to recognize this bilingual heritage. The culture of the Chicanos is a rich one that is receiving renewed attention in the contemporary Chicano movement.

The Chicano movement has made itself known in several ways. Individuals like Corky Gonzales, Tijerina, César Chávez, and José Gutiérrez have questioned why Anglos dominate Chicanos as if they were a conquered minority. This second-class treatment is found in accounts of Chicano life that have described the culture of poverty as typical of the life of most Chicanos.

Puerto Ricans share many of the same characteristics of Chicanos—they also face the language barrier, are victims of prejudice and discrimination, and have poor political representation. It would be an oversimplification, however, to assume that Puerto Ricans are indistinguishable from Chicanos. Chapter 11 describes the unique history and contemporary status of Puerto Ricans.

## KEY TERMS

**barrios**   Segregated urban slums populated by Chicanos, Puerto Ricans, or other Hispanic group.

**bracero**   Contracted Mexican laborers brought to the United States during World War II.

**Chicanismo**   An ideology emphasizing pride and positive identity among Chicanos.

**culture of poverty**   According to its proponents, a way of life that involves no future planning, no enduring commitment to marriage, no work ethic; this culture follows the poor even when they move out of the slums or the barrio.

**curanderismo**   Hispanic folk medicine.

**education pipeline**   The process that begins when pupils pass through formal schooling and travel in an ever-narrowing funnel, attaining professional degrees at the end.

**familism**   Pride and closeness in the family that result in placing family obligation and loyalty before individual needs.

**fiesta politics**   Blatant overtures by presidential candidates to Chicanos for their support.

**life chances**   People's opportunities to provide themselves with material goods, positive living conditions, and favorable life experiences.

**machismo**   A male's sense of virility, of personal worth, in his own eyes and in those of his peers.

**marianismo**   A female's acceptance of man's dominance, and placing of family needs first.

**mojados**   "Wetbacks," derisive slang for Mexicans who enter illegally, supposedly by swimming the Rio Grande.

**Raza**   "The People"—a term referring to the rich heritage of Chicanos, and hence used to designate a sense of pride among Chicanos today.

**repatriation**   The program of deporting Mexicans during the 1930s.

**zoot-suiters**   Chicano youth during the mid-1940s in southern California; a derisive term.

## FOR FURTHER INFORMATION

Rodolfo Acuña. *Occupied America: A History of Chicanos*, 2nd ed. New York: Harper and Row, 1981.

> The author reexamines conventional accounts of the Chicano experience and argues that they are biased. Acuña feels that exploitation of Chicanos is comparable to that of a colonized people.

Irene I. Blea. *Toward A Chicano Social Science*. New York: Praeger, 1988.

> An overview of the Chicano experience, with an emphasis on seeing it from an ethnic perspective.

Charles L. Briggs and John R. Van Ness, eds. *Land, Water, and Culture*. Albuquerque: University of New Mexico Press.

> Explores the social, ecological, political, and legal roots of land grants to many Hispanic and Pueblo Indian communities.

Leo R. Chavez. *Shadowed Lives: Undocumented Immigrants in American Society*. Fort Worth, TX: Harcourt Brace Javonovich, 1992.

An anthropological study of illegal Mexican immigrants, ranging from temporary farmworkers to skilled craftspersonnel.

Rodolfo O. de la Garza, Frank D. Bean, Charles M. Bonjean, Ricardo Romo, and Rodolfo Alvarez. *The Mexican American Experience: An Interdisciplinary Anthology*. Austin: University of Texas Press, 1985.

This collection of 45 articles has many selections previously published in Social Science Quarterly.

Gilbert G. Gonzalez. *Chicano Education in the Era of Segregation*. Philadelphia: The Balch Institute Press, 1990.

An overview of Chicano education in the U.S. Southwest.

Z. Anthony Kruszewski, Richard L. Hough, and Jacob Ornstein-Galicia. *Politics and Society in the Southwest: Ethnicity and Chicano Pluralism*. Boulder, CO: Westview Press, 1982.

This anthology covers such topics as language, identity, social class, and politics as they affect Chicanos in the Southwest.

Alfredo Mirandé. *The Chicano Experience: An Alternative Perspective*. Notre Dame, Ind.: University of Notre Dame Press, 1985.

A very insightful look at sociology's treatment of the Chicano experience, with special emphasis on education, crime, and family life.

Wayne Moquin and Charles Van Doren, eds. *A Documentary History of the Mexican Americans*. New York: Praeger, 1971.

There are very few collections of historical documents about Chicanos and Mexico's relations with the United States. This, undoubtedly the best, covers from the planting of Spanish settlements in the Southwest in 1536 to militant pleas on behalf of the Chicano movement in 1970.

John Shockley. *Chicano Revolt in a Texas Town*. Notre Dame, IN: University of Notre Dame Press, 1974.

Shockley describes the rise of La Raza Unida in Crystal City, Texas, in 1969, one of the few successful contemporary grass-roots political movements of Chicanos.

## Chapter Eleven

# PUERTO RICANS: DIVIDED BETWEEN ISLAND AND MAINLAND

*Chapter Outline*

**The Island of Puerto Rico**
Issues of Statehood and Self-Rule
Economic Development
**Bridge Between Island and Mainland**
**Race in Puerto Rico and on the Mainland**
**El Barrio**
Education

Employment and Income
Family Life
Religious Life
Political Organizations
**Glancing Back and Looking Ahead**
**Key Terms**
**For Further Information**

---

**✴ HIGHLIGHTS ✴**

The Puerto Rican people are divided between those who live on the island commonwealth and those who live on the mainland itself. Although citizens, Puerto Ricans on the island do not have the same responsibilities and privileges as non-Puerto Ricans. Self-rule is the major political issue, overshadowed only by the dire poverty of the island. Those who migrate to the mainland most often come in search of better jobs and housing. Because Puerto Rico is so poor, living in the United States does provide opportunity for advancement, but most Puerto Ricans on the mainland are confined to the lower class and the *barrio*.

---

Puerto Ricans share the major problems of their fellow American citizens, especially those who belong to subordinate groups. Nearly 6 million Puerto Ricans face prejudice and discrimination. More than 2 million of them who live on the mainland are seen by many as outsiders, occupying an unenviable social and economic position (see Table 11.1). For the more than 3 million residents of the island commonwealth of Puerto Rico, citizenship carries different responsibilities and privileges. For no other minority group in the United States is citizenship so ambiguous. Even American Indians, who are subject to some unique laws and are exempt from others because of past treaties, have a future firmly

---

**TABLE 11.1**　Selected Social and Economic Characteristics: Puerto Ricans, 1990

The urban-based Puerto Ricans, like other Hispanics, have less formal schooling, experience more unemployment, and have high levels of poverty.

|  | Total Anglo | Total Hispanic | Puerto Rican |
|---|---|---|---|
| Median age | 33.5 | 26.0 | 27.0 |
| Percent completing college |  |  |  |
| 　25 to 34 years | 25.5 | 9.0 | 11.8 |
| 　35 years and over | 22.2 | 9.2 | 9.7 |
| Percent unemployed |  |  |  |
| 　Male | 5.7 | 8.0 | 8.2 |
| 　Female | 4.9 | 8.5 | 9.1 |
| Percent living below poverty level | 11.6 | 26.2 | 33.0 |
| Income |  |  |  |
| 　Male | $22,081 | 14,047 | 18,222 |
| 　Female | 11,885 | 9,861 | 12,812 |

*Source:* Bureau of the Census, 1991f, pp. 6–11.

dominated by the United States. This description does not necessarily fit Puerto Ricans. They and their island home are the last major United States colonial remnant, and, for that matter, one of the few such areas remaining in the world. Before assessing, as one author wrote, "the evidence for success or survival" of Puerto Ricans on the mainland, we will assess the relationship of the United States to Puerto Rico (Bureau of the Census, 1985b; Cunningham and Molina, 1976, p. 207).

## THE ISLAND OF PUERTO RICO

Puerto Rico, located about a thousand miles from Miami, has never been the same since it was discovered by Columbus in 1493 (see Figure 11.1). The original inhabitants of the island were wiped out in a couple of generations by disease, tribal warfare, hard labor, unsuccessful rebellions against the Spanish, and fusion with their conquerors. Among the institutions imported to Puerto Rico by Spain was slavery. Although slavery in Puerto Rico was not as harsh as in the southern United States, the legacy of the transfer of Africans is present in the appearance of Puerto Ricans today, many of whom are seen by people on the mainland as Black.

During the four centuries of Spanish rule, life for most Puerto Ricans was

**FIGURE 11.1**   Puerto Rico

Puerto Rico is a bit smaller than Connecticut and lies twice as far from Florida as it does from Venezuela.

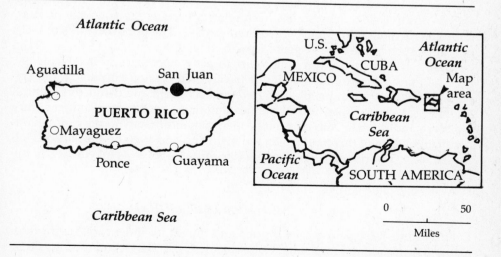

difficult. A few rich landowners and multitudes of poor workers labored in a country still underdeveloped when the United States seized the island in 1898 during the Spanish-American War. Spain relinquished control of it in the Treaty of Paris. The value of Puerto Rico for the United States, as it had been for Spain, was mainly its strategic location, which was advantageous for maritime trade.

The beginnings of American rule quickly destroyed any hope that Puerto Ricans had for self-rule. All power was given to officials appointed by the President and any act of the island's legislature could be overruled by Congress. Even the spelling changed briefly to Porto Rico to suit North American pronunciation. English, previously unknown on the island, became the only language permitted in the school systems. The people were colonized—politically, then culturally, and finally economically (Aran et al., 1973; Christopulos, 1974; EPICA, 1976).

Citizenship was extended to Puerto Ricans by the Jones Act of 1917, but Puerto Rico remained a colony. This political dependence altered in 1948 when Puerto Rico elected its own governor and became a commonwealth, rather than a colony. This status, officially *Estado Libre Asociado,* or Associated Free State, extends to Puerto Rico and its people privileges and rights different from those of people on the mainland. Although Puerto Ricans are U.S. citizens and elect their own governor, they may not vote in presidential elections and have no voting representation in Congress. They are subject to military service, selective service registration, and all federal laws. Courts on the island are patterned after those in the United States and appeals may be made to the Supreme Court. The proceedings on the island, however, are conducted in Spanish, except in San Juan, where English is used. Puerto Ricans pay a local income tax but no federal income tax. Most federal grants-in-aid, however, are significantly lower in Puerto Rico than those on the mainland.

The commonwealth period has been a most significant one for Puerto Rico. Change has been dramatic, though whether it has all been progress is debatable. On the positive side, Spanish has been reintroduced as the language of classroom instruction, with English a required elective. The popularity in the 1980s of groups such as the rock singers Menudo show that even Puerto Rican young people wish to maintain ties with their ethnicity. Such success is a challenge, because Puerto Rican music is almost never aired on non-Hispanic radio stations. The Puerto Rican people also have had a vibrant and distinctive cultural tradition, as clearly seen in folk heroes, holidays, sports, and contemporary literature and drama. Dominance by American culture may in the future hamper maintenance of this heritage on the mainland and even on the island (Holzapfel, 1976; Rodriquez, 1989; Senior, 1965, pp. 84–86; Wagenheim, 1975, pp. 219–263).

## Issues of Statehood and Self-Rule

Puerto Ricans have periodically argued and fought for independence for most of the five hundred years since Columbus landed. They continued to do so through the 1980s. The contemporary commonwealth arrangement is popular with many Puerto Ricans, but others prefer complete independence from the United States.

Since 1948, the *Partido Popular Democratico* (PPD), or Popular Democratic Party, has dominated the island's politics. The party has consistently favored commonwealth status. Both in 1968, when the PPD split, and in 1976, when the island's economy was hard pressed, however, the PPD lost the governorship to the *Partido Nuevo Progresista* (PNP), or New Progressive Party, which favors statehood. It is difficult to determine the true feelings of all Puerto Ricans toward independence, statehood, or continuation of commonwealth status. A 1967 referendum resulted in a 60 percent preference for the commonwealth relationship, 39 percent favoring statehood, and less than 1 percent choosing independence. These results are misleading, however, because many nationalists, as they are called, boycotted the vote, for the results were not binding on the United States. At present, a plebiscite is more likely to be held on the issue of statehood, not independence.

Some of the supporters of independence have been vocal and even militant. In 1950, nationalists attempted to assassinate President Truman, killing a White House guard in doing so. Four years later, another band of nationalists opened fire in the gallery of the United States House of Representatives, wounding five congressmen. Beginning in 1974, a group calling itself the Armed Forces of National Liberation (FALN, for *Fuerzas Armadas de Liberación Nacional*) took

*Militant Puerto Ricans led by FALN have protested against the mainland's economic exploitation of Puerto Rico by bombings such as this one on New York's Wall Street in 1982.*

responsibility for more than 100 explosions, including bombings of New York and Chicago headquarters of banks and corporations with investments in Puerto Rico. Even the arrest and conviction of 11 of the leaders in 1980 did not prevent the bombings, which continued through 1987. FALN is not alone, for at least four other militant groups advocating independence have been identified at work in the 1980s. The island itself is occasionally beset by violent demonstrations, often reacting to United States military installations there (Breasted, 1977; Kleiman, 1977; McFadden, 1983; Suarez, 1985).

The issue of Puerto Rico's political destiny is in part ideological. Independence is the easiest way for the island to retain and strengthen a sense of cultural as well as political identity. Some nationalists express the desire that autonomous Puerto Rico develop close political ties with communist Cuba. The crucial arguments for independence are probably economic. An independent Puerto Rico would no longer be required to use American shipping lines, which are more expensive than those of foreign competitors. An independent Puerto Rico, however, might be faced by a tariff wall when trading with its largest current customer, the United States. Also, Puerto Rican migration to the mainland could be restricted. Perhaps we can begin to understand the fervor of those militantly in support of independence from Oscar López-Rivera in "Listen to Their Voices."

Puerto Rico's future status heated up again in 1989 when President George Bush called for an island-wide election on self-determination. "Personally, I favor statehood," Bush said, "But I ask the Congress to take the necessary steps to let the people decide." Eventually Congress authorized a nonbinding referendum to occur in 1993 or 1994. Governor Rafael Hernandez Colon favors commonwealth status but his predecessor and leader of the opposition, Carlos Romero Barcelo, favors statehood. Polls show the nearly 4 million people in Puerto Rico evenly divided between statehood and commonwealth status with fewer than 10 percent favoring independence (M. Navarro, 1990; Phillips, 1991; Walters, 1990).

## Economic Development

Depending on what the Puerto Rican economy is compared to and what part of it is being studied, the United States's influence either has been very progressive or it has stagnated the island's economy. The major economic initiative has been Operation Bootstrap, begun in 1947, which exempted industries locating in Puerto Rico from taxes on profits for at least ten years. This incentive, combined with the absence of minimum wage laws, unquestionably made Puerto Rico attractive to American corporations. Skeptics point out that as a result the island's agriculture has been virtually ignored. Furthermore, economic benefits are limited. Businesses have spent their profits on the mainland (Angle, 1976; Aran et al., 1973).

Puerto Rico's economy is already in severe trouble. Its unemployment rate has always been at least double that of the mainland. By 1983, unemployment islandwide exceeded 22 percent—three times the average on the mainland. In addition the per capita income was less than half that of the United States. Efforts to raise the wages of Puerto Rican workers only make the island less attractive to "labor-intensive" businesses, that is, those employing larger numbers of unskilled people. "Capital-intensive" companies like petrochemical industries have recently found Puerto Rico attractive, but they did not create jobs for the semi-skilled. In 1983 there were fewer manufacturing jobs than ten years earlier (*Business Week,* 1983; Commonwealth of Puerto Rico, 1976; EPICA, 1976; Stuart, 1983; Suarez, 1985).

Another major sector of Puerto Rico's economy is tourism. Government subsidies have encouraged the construction of luxury hotels. After American travel to Cuba was closed in 1962, tourists discovered Puerto Rico's beaches and climate. Critics complain that the major economic beneficiaries of tourism are foreigners, primarily American investors, and that high prices prevent the less affluent from visiting, thus unnecessarily restricting tourism. The irony of the tourist boom was seen by historian Mary Vaughan: "The vegetables on the table at the Puerto Rican Sheraton have been picked in New Jersey by Puerto Rican migrant workers whose fathers once worked the now uncultivated land of Puerto Rico" (1974, p. 281). As has been true of other aspects of the island's economic development, the tourist boom has had little positive effect on most Puerto Ricans (Morley, 1974; Wagenheim, 1975).

*Some success occurred in attracting to Puerto Rico selected industries such as the oil refinery pictured here. Such enterprises, however, employ few semiskilled or unskilled workers.*

❖ *LISTEN TO THEIR VOICES* ❖

## Who is the Terrorist? The Making of a Puerto Rican Freedom Fighter

Oscar López-Rivera

*López-Rivera, a FALN member, wrote from the federal penitentiary in Marion, Illinois in 1989. He was originally sentenced to 55 years imprisonment following a 1981 arrest for "seditious conspiracy." While in prison he was found guilty of plotting his own escape and that of an African American activist. An additional 40 years was added to his original sentence.*

I am writing from within the labyrinth of this Gulag known as U.S.P.-Marion. According to the U.S. government, I am in this concentration camp because I am a "terrorist," an "incorrigible and notorious criminal." There are those who argue that one person's terrorist is another's freedom fighter. My position is that I am a freedom fighter and a prisoner of war.

Why do I not consider myself a terrorist? Because I was born a colonized subject, and as such I have an inalienable right to fight for my nation's self-determination, for its natural drive towards democracy and justice, its search for freedom and truth, and for the human rights of the Puerto Rican people. The fact that I was born a colonized subject was an accidental matter, because I, like all other human beings, was not given the choice of selecting my birthplace. But the fact that my place of birth was accidental does not exempt me from my responsibilities to fulfill my patriotic duties and obligations. And one of those du-

ties is to fight, by any means necessary, for the liberation of Puerto Rico, so that, as a nation, my people can exercise their right to self-determination and national sovereignty. Ninety-one years of colonial domination has denied my people that right.

Had I chosen to ignore the fact that Puerto Rico is a militarily occupied colony of the United States, and accepted the life that Uncle Sam imposed on me, my masters would have considered me a "good" Puerto Rican. Had I chosen such a path of ease and "least resistance," my conscious would have grown limp; I would have become a pariah and thus become something less than a human being. It would have meant a negation of any possibility to achieve self-realization. Had I accepted the kind of life that had been dictated to me by my colonizer, I would have only aped, emulated, and internalized his behavior and way of life. I would have become, in other words, a "good" slave. But I'm a "bad" slave. I chose to fight for the freedom of my nation. And it is that choice which has brought me to Marion, where I am forced to live in a state of helplessness. But my conscience and my will to fight and resist are as strong as the *guayacon*, that tree of the tropical forest known for its hard and longlasting wood. . . .

I manage to survive this Gulag called Marion with the comforting thought that the American authorities can imprison my body but they cannot imprison the spirit of Puerto Rican nationalism. In the words of a Chilean freedom song, "They can cut the flowers, but they cannot stop the spring." The revolutionary love of my compatriots has not abandoned me. While in prison, Ho Chi Minh wrote a poem about sowing a peach seed and observing it grow into a fully developed tree. Each generation of Puerto Rican patriots has sown a seed to keep our ideas and ideals alive. I can only hope that the newer generation of Puerto Ricans will not fail to sow another seed for the generations yet to come.

From Oscar López-Rivera with Bernard Headley, *Social Justice* 16 (Winter), pp. 163–164, 174. Reprinted by permission of the author.

For years, especially in the 1950s, migration to the mainland was a safety valve for Puerto Rico's population, which has annually grown at a rate of 50 percent faster than that of the United States. Typically, migrants from Puerto Rico are more likely to be laborers and semi-skilled workers than are the people of the island as a whole. Yet the most recent studies found that 69 percent of migrants leaving Puerto Rico had been unemployed. In 1987, two-thirds of the people on the island were receiving some form of federal assistance, with half collecting food stamps, and estimates of unemployment ranged up to 25 percent. In virtually all social areas, such as housing, health care, and education, Puerto Rico compares favorably to its Caribbean neighbors, but it stills falls disastrously short of minimal standards acceptable on the mainland (Barrett, 1976; Carrion, 1986; Chaze, 1982a; Christopulos, 1974; Fitzpatrick, 1987, p. 35; Morley, 1974; Nordheimer, 1984; Ortiz, 1986; Rodriquez, 1989).

## BRIDGE BETWEEN ISLAND AND MAINLAND

In Chapter 10 we pointed out that the proximity of Mexico accounts for the stronger cultural distinctiveness of Chicanos than one finds among Whites of European descent. This is even more true of Puerto Ricans, because as American citizens they may go to and from the mainland without legal restriction. Citizenship does not mean that they can move without meeting difficulties, however. Despite their citizenship, Puerto Ricans are occasionally challenged by immigration officials. Because other Latin Americans may attempt to enter the country posing as Puerto Ricans, Puerto Ricans find their papers more closely scrutinized than do other United States citizens.

Puerto Ricans came in relatively small numbers during the first half of the century, often encouraged by farm labor contracts similar to those extended to Mexican *braceros*. During World War II the government recruited hundreds of Puerto Ricans to work in railroads, food manufacturing plants, and copper mines on the mainland. But migration has been largely a post-World War II phenomenon. The 1940 census showed fewer than 70,000 on the mainland, or 10,000 fewer than were in Massachusetts alone in 1970. Among the factors that have contributed to migration are (1) the economic pull away from the under-developed island, (2) the absence of legal restrictions against travel, and (3) the growth of relatively cheap air transportation. As the migration continued, the United States offered the added attraction of a large Puerto Rican community in New York City, which makes adjustment easier for new arrivals.

New York City still has a formidable population of Puerto Ricans compared to metropolitan San Juan's, but Puerto Ricans are now more dispersed through-out the mainland's cities, with sizable numbers in New Jersey, Illinois, Florida, California, Pennsylvania, and Connecticut.

The Puerto Ricans who have moved out of the large ethnic communities in cities like New York City, Chicago, and Philadelphia are a group more familiar with American culture and the English language. This movement from the major settlements has been hastened as well by the loss of manufacturing jobs in these cities, a loss that hits Puerto Rican men especially hard. Figure 11.2 illustrates this dispersal of Puerto Ricans on the mainland out of New York (Allen and Turner, 1988, pp. 160–161).

---

**FIGURE 11.2**    U.S.-born Puerto Rican Origin Population

---

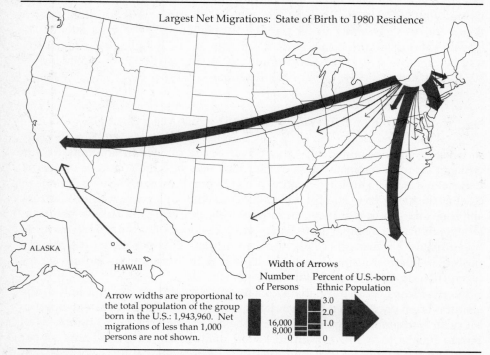

Largest Net Migrations:  State of Birth to 1980 Residence

ALASKA

HAWAII

Width of Arrows

Number      Percent of U.S.-born
of Persons      Ethnic Population

Arrow widths are proportional to the total population of the group born in the U.S.: 1,943,960.  Net migrations of less than 1,000 persons are not shown.

16,000
8,000
0

3.0
2.0
1.0
0

---

As the U.S. economy underwent recession in the 1970s and 1980s, unemployment among mainland Puerto Ricans, always high, increased dramatically. This shows in migration. In the 1950s, Puerto Ricans were half of the Hispanic arrivals. By the 1970s they accounted for only 3 percent. Indeed, in some years during the last decade more Puerto Ricans went from mainland to island than left for the mainland. Yet overall, the net migration from 1980 through 1986 was 207,000 from Puerto Rico out of that island. This amounts to a net loss of 16 percent of the population.

Puerto Ricans returning to the island have become a significant force. Indeed they have come to be given the name *Neoricans* (or *Nuyoricans*)—a term the islanders also use for Puerto Ricans in New York. Long-time islanders direct a modest amount of hostility toward these *Neoricans*. They return from the mainland usually with more formal schooling, more money, and a better command of English than native Puerto Ricans. Not too surprisingly, *Neoricans* compete very well with the islanders for jobs and land. The situation is further exacerbated by an apparent "brain drain" similar to that described in Chapter 4. A 1982 estimate indicated that from one-fourth to one-half of the University of Puerto Rico's graduates head north for employment. Although employment possibilities for these top graduates may appear to be better in the United States, the graduates have to adjust to mainland definitions of race (Bureau of the Census, 1987; Davis et al., 1983; Fitzpatrick, 1987, pp. 179–194; Maldonado-Denis, 1980; Stockton, 1978; Velez, 1984; Wagenheim, 1983; Wright, 1982).

## RACE IN PUERTO RICO AND ON THE MAINLAND

As the balance of this chapter will discuss, Puerto Rican migrants to the mainland must make adjustments in language, housing, and employment. These changes are required of most immigrants, but Puerto Ricans must also adapt to new racial identities. Racism does exist in Puerto Rico. People are arbitrarily denied opportunities merely because of their skin color. The racism, however, is not the same as on the mainland. Slavery was not as significant on the island as it was in the American South, and Puerto Rico has a long history of accepting interracial marriages. Puerto Rico did not experience the mainland practices of segregation, antimiscegenation laws, and Jim Crow. More recently, however, Puerto Rico has started to resemble the mainland in taking on rigid racial attitudes (Fitzpatrick, 1987; Flores, 1985, pp. 9–10; Rodriquez, 1989).

The most significant difference between the meaning of race on Puerto Rico and in the United States is that Puerto Rico, like so many other Caribbean societies, has a color gradient. The phrase *color gradient* describes distinctions based on skin color made on a continuum, rather than by sharp categorical separations. Rather than being either "black" or "white," people are judged in such societies as "lighter" or "darker" than others. Puerto Rico has such a color gradient. The presence of a color gradient rather than two or three racial categories does not necessarily mean that prejudice is less. Generally, however, societies with a color gradient permit more flexibility and therefore are less likely to impose specific sanctions against a group of people based on skin color alone.

Although Puerto Rico has not suffered from interracial conflict or violence, its people are conscious of the different racial heritages. Rather than seeing people as either black or white in skin color, they perceive people as ranging from pale white to very black. Puerto Ricans are more sensitive to degrees of difference and make less effort to pigeonhole a person into one of two categories. Studies disagree on the amount of prejudice in Puerto Rico, but all concur that race is not as clear-cut an issue on the island as it is on the mainland.

Racial identification in Puerto Rico depends a great deal on the attitude of the individual making the judgment. If one thinks highly of a person, he or she may be seen as a member of a more acceptable racial group. A variety of terms are used in the color gradient to describe people racially—*blanco* (white), *triqueño* (almost white or black), *prieto, moreno,* or *de color* (dark-skinned), and *negro* (black) are a few of these. Factors such as social class and social position determine race, but in the United States race is more likely to determine social class. This situation may puzzle people from the States, but racial etiquette on the mainland may be just as difficult to comprehend and accept for Puerto Ricans (Egerton, 1971; Rodriguez, 1989; Tumin and Feldman, 1961).

The Puerto Rican in the United States finds a new identity thrust upon him or her by dominant society. On the island, distinctions are by social class, but on the mainland people are preoccupied with color. Many, taken for Blacks, are forced to emphasize that they are Puerto Rican. Still others are mistaken sometimes for Blacks and accepted other times as Puerto Rican, which also makes adjustment difficult. In fact, evidence indicates that those Puerto Ricans whose skin color is intermediate, between Black and White, have the most difficulty adapting to or being accepted by American society. A study of Puerto Rican college students in New York found most considered themselves to be "White" or "Tan" and less than 7 percent viewed themselves as "Black." Yet when asked how Anglos saw them, they dropped any reference to an intermediate category like "Tan": 58 percent said "White" and 42 percent indicated "Black" (A. Martinez, 1988). Mainland-born Puerto Ricans feel the challenge of defining a racial identity less acutely than do migrants. We will see in the sections that follow that most other problems faced by new arrivals from the island, however, are shared by their children born on the mainland (Cunningham and Molina, 1976, pp. 204–205; Fitzpatrick, 1980, pp. 864–865; Glazer and Moynihan, 1970, pp. 133–136; Mills et al., 1950, pp. 151–152; Padilla, 1958; Stockton, 1978, p. 91; P. Thomas, 1967; Westfried, 1981, p 146).

## EL BARRIO

Whether outsiders referred to is as East Harlem or Spanish Harlem or El Barrio, a section of upper Manhattan was the most important Puerto Rican neighborhood in the United States during the 1950s and much of the 1960s. It is less significant now because Puerto Ricans no longer migrate only to New York City, and even those who do are more likely to live outside El Barrio. By 1970, more Puerto Ricans lived in either the Bronx or Brooklyn than in this section of Manhattan. As with other minority groups, Puerto Ricans are generally concentrated in certain neighborhoods. They are segregated by both their social class and their darker skin. The latter factor clearly matters, because Puerto Ricans are more segregated from Whites than are Chicanos in such cities as Los Angeles. Puerto Ricans coming of age in the barrio are challenged simply to survive, let alone succeed (Fitzpatrick, 1987; Glazer and Moynihan, 1970, pp. 107–108; N. Kantrowitz, 1973; Massey and Bitterman, 1985).

The Puerto Rican neighborhoods need tremendous improvement in housing quality. The Bronx and Brooklyn, the two New York City boroughs where most Puerto Ricans live, accounted for more than 80 percent of the net loss of housing units in the entire nation between 1970 and 1980. Even more specific, the South Bronx—the densest and largest Puerto Rican settlement in the United States— has suffered such devastation that its very name has come to mean urban blight. With the vanished housing went social networks, ethnic stores, and dance clubs. Such changes underscore that the Puerto Rican neighborhoods have little of the charm conveyed in *West Side Story*. All social institutions—political, educational, familial, and religious—suffer as a result (Lemann, 1991; Rodriguez, 1989; Young and Devaney, 1982).

As revolving door migration between island and mainland has become more common, Puerto Rican organizations have gone through a transition. The home-town clubs on the mainland, where ties to one of the island's 72 municipalities were central to social life, have withered with no clear successor group. The militancy of the 1960s, reflected in the Young Lords Party, organized along lines similar to the Black Panther Party, has also faded as a basis of social organization. As the second—and third—generation population of Puerto Ricans on the mainland grows, political action groups working in and on behalf of Puerto Rican communities in the United States may well grow stronger and more numerous. As the twentieth century draws to a close, however, this promise has yet to be fulfilled (Jennings and Rivera, 1984; Stevens–Arroyo and Diaz-Ramirez, 1982).

The problems of South Bronx and other urban Puerto Rican settlements raise again thoughts of "underclass" and "culture of poverty." The high proportion of low income households is certainly present. The unemployment that creates the poverty has certainly been exacerbated if not triggered by the loss of hundreds of thousands of jobs from the central city. Studies of labor force participation document the declining opportunities of the early 1980s especially in the "Rustbelt" where mainland Puerto Ricans reside compared to the "Sunbelt" home of Chicanos and Cubans. Whether Puerto Ricans are moving out of the labor market permanently or can begin to return to gainful employment remains to be seen (Lemann, 1991; Tienda, 1989a).

**FIGURE 11.3**   Median Family Income of Whites and Puerto Ricans

Puerto Ricans family income has increased in the last ten years, but has fallen behind gains made by Whites.

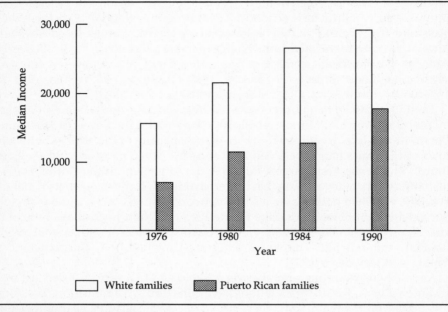

Note: 1990 data are for households.
Source: Bureau of the Census, 1991f.

## Education

Puerto Ricans confront several problems in education that are similar to those faced by Chicanos. Relative to Whites, both groups have lower educational attainment and are more likely to complete the same amount of schooling at an older age than Whites. In addition, Puerto Ricans have an even higher dropout rate than Chicanos. In 1990, 56 percent of Puerto Ricans aged 25 and older had completed high school, compared to 80 percent of non-Hispanics. Approximately 12 percent of Puerto Ricans have college degrees, in contrast to 21 percent of non-Hispanics (Bureau of the Census, 1991f; Ortiz, 1986, p. 35).

The challenge of being a Puerto Rican in a society dominated by Anglos is evident in the public schools. Part of the difficulty, as we have seen with other Hispanics, is the language barrier. Puerto Ricans on the island applying to colleges often take special standardized admissions tests in addition to such exams as the SAT and ACT. Studies document that regardless of high aptitude on the Spanish test, proficiency in English is almost as important a factor as aptitude, for achievement on the conventional examinations in English. These findings are especially important since Puerto Ricans taking SATs are even more likely than Chicanos to indicate that English is not their best language (Pennock-Román, 1986, pp. 193–198).

These problems with standardized examinations are compounded by *tracking*. Tracking is the practice of placing students in specific classes or curriculum groups on the basis of test scores and other criteria. Tracking begins very early in the classroom, often in reading groups during first grade. These tracks can reinforce the disadvantages of Puerto Rican children from less affluent families and non-English-speaking households who have not been exposed to English reading materials in their homes during early childhood (Rodriguez, 1989; Schaefer and Lamm, 1992).

The usual problems of low-income youth are compounded for Puerto Ricans by the disruptive transfer of public school children between Puerto Rico and the mainland. The New York City Board of Education records that from 1964 to 1973, 108,000 children transferred to New York City and another 106,000 transferred to the island. In New York City, Puerto Rican parents have shown interest in their children's education. Some of this interest erupted into an emotional battle during the 1968–69 school strike over decentralization. The parents favored substantial local control, but the teachers' union, which supported more centralized control, was stronger, and only a moderately decentralized program was eventually adopted. The benefits to Puerto Ricans that giving local school boards in New York City autonomy from the central board would have had is not completely clear. Modest gains in the number of Puerto Rican teachers and administrators have recently been made, but parental involvement in important school decisions remains marginal (Commission on Civil Rights, 1976c, pp. 92–118; Fitzpatrick, 1987, pp. 139–168; Steiner, 1974, pp. 392–396).

## Employment and Income

The broad comparisons in Chapter 9 between Hispanics and the rest of the population document the poor economic situation of Puerto Ricans. The position relative to that of Whites has grown worse over the years; it has not even remained the same, as it has with Blacks. In 1959, Puerto Rican family earnings were 71 percent of the national average. As Figure 11.3 indicates, Puerto Rican income dropped to 64 percent that of Whites by 1990.

Whatever economic measure is used, the conclusion is the same: Puerto Ricans fall desperately short of parity with Whites. A staggering 30 percent of Puerto Rican families lived below the poverty level in 1989. This figure compares to 26 percent of Chicanos and 9 percent for the nation's non-Hispanic families. Nationally in 1989, 8.6 percent of Puerto Ricans were unemployed, compared to the national figure of 5.3 percent. Economic downturns are especially hard on Puerto Ricans because they are concentrated in low-paying jobs that are subject to frequent layoffs and seasonal unemployment (Bureau of the Census, 1991f).

Several barriers keep Puerto Ricans from receiving a fair share of better-paying jobs. First is the language barrier, an obstacle described in detail in Chapter 9. Puerto Ricans who are not fluent in English falter in schools that lack effective bilingual programs. They are also placed in jobs that do not require language skills or training. These jobs are low paying and do not lead to advancement up the occupational ladder. A second factor is the lack of work experience. Rural migrants do not have the skills sought by employers in the cities of the Northeast and Midwest, where most Puerto Ricans reside. Without the necessary job experience, Puerto Ricans have difficulty obtaining better-paying jobs.

Another factor that has kept Puerto Ricans in a depressed economic position is the timing of their immigration. These cities, particularly New York, have not only stopped growing, but have seen a decline in employment opportunities for newcomers. During New York City's financial crisis, which became especially acute in 1975 and 1976, nearly half the Puerto Ricans holding civil service appointments lost their jobs in cutbacks. Even when the New York City economy rebounded, the new jobs required skills that neither the local Puerto Ricans or those migrating from the island were likely to have. In addition, jobs had moved out into the metropolitan area away from the Puerto Rican communities. These hindrances to the Puerto Rican workforce in New York City continued into the 1990s and have been repeated in other cities with significant Puerto Rican populations. Industrial Bridgeport, Connecticut, has a growing Puerto Rican community, but as their numbers increased, their economic situation worsened, as factories and the jobs that went with them left the city for suburbs and small towns (Fitzpatrick, 1989; Leebaw and Heyman, 1976; Rodriquez, 1989).

The Commission on Civil Rights concluded in 1976 that even after taking into account factors like language and job experience, "the evidence is compelling that racial, ethnic, and sex discrimination are barriers to job opportunities for Puerto Ricans" (1976c, p. 61). Arbitrary job requirements disqualify Puerto Ricans. Height standards used by law enforcement agencies are gradually being revised, but while in effect they eliminate short-statured Puerto Ricans from consideration. Even when they do have work experience that should qualify them for a position, Puerto Ricans may be denied employment because they lack a high school diploma. A 1985 survey of Hispanics in Chicago found that 51 percent of Puerto Ricans felt that Anglos discriminated against them. This proportion perceiving mistreatment was even larger than that among foreign-born Hispanics (Ogletree and Ujlaki, 1985, p. 33).

The courts and various government agencies have sought to eliminate the barriers to effective participation by Puerto Ricans in the labor force. The inequities remain, however, and Puerto Ricans are underrepresented even in agencies that service Puerto Ricans. As might be expected, given their low incomes, a large number of Puerto Rican families receive public assistance or welfare. Many other immigrant groups have depended on social services, but the earlier arrivals from Europe were aided by settlement houses that manifested deeper concern for the individual. Today's welfare bureaucracy primarily coordinates paper forms and people, seeming to see the two as interchangeable. Consequently, today more than ever, public aid workers must be responsive to their clients (Commission on Civil Rights, 1976c, pp. 51, 62; Glazer and Moynihan, 1970, p. 121; Mizio, 1972).

## Family Life

Education in the public schools can support or detract from the maintenance of traditional values. Schooling introduces ethnic children, whether Puerto Ricans or from any other immigrant group, to the traditions of the host society. This exposure usually puts the school in conflict with ethnic traditions and also weakens parental authority during the crucial period of adolescence. In this way, the Puerto Rican family resembles the families of European immigrants in the past and Chicanos today. Like the former, the Puerto Rican migrant family has experienced the cultural shock of adjusting to a new society. Even though they are citizens of the United States, island-born migrants find life different on the mainland. Many Puerto Rican migrants hold some childrearing and self-image values in common with Chicanos.

Some traditional values are likely to fade as the second generation takes on the cultural values of Anglo society. The extended family is likely to take on a less important role in what can be a detrimental change, but the fading of machismo and marianismo is probably a move for the better. As familism declines and the extended family weakens, Puerto Ricans are forced to turn to impersonal bureaucratic agencies for the services that used to be provided by their kinfolk. One manifestation of the decline already taking place in machismo is the fact that women on the mainland are more likely to work than they are on the island. It remains to be seen whether such positive attributes found among many Puerto Ricans as zest for life, sociability, sense of pride, and emotional warmth will be maintained as Puerto Ricans become residents as well as citizens (Fitzpatrick, 1987, pp. 68–91; Francis, 1976, p. 231; Preble, 1968).

As is so often the case with subordinate groups, poverty takes its toll on family life. In 1989, in 57 percent of Puerto Rican families no man was present while by comparison 80 percent of non-Hispanic families had both husband and wife present. Puerto Rican female-headed families, even after considering government transfer payments like public assistance and Social Security, are the poorest segment in the United States (Bureau of the Census, 1991f; Darrity and Myers, 1987).

## Religious Life

The church has been an important element of immigrant family life. Religion, for Puerto Ricans however, has not played a major unifying role. About four-fifths of Puerto Ricans are Roman Catholic, reflecting the Spanish colonial period. The balance of the population is Protestant, the legacy of missionaries who came shortly after the American acquisition of the island.

The number of Protestants is growing on the island as evangelicals and pentecostals step up recruiting. *Evangelical faiths* are Christian religions that emphasize a personal relationship between the individual and God. Evangelicals believe that each adherent must spread the faith and bear personal witness. Adherents to *pentecostal faiths* have beliefs similar to evangelicals, but in addition believe in the infusion of the Holy Spirit into services and in religious experiences such as faith healing. Puerto Rican Catholics, even more than other Hispanics, do not have their own clergy and consequently lack the strong support that ethnic parishes provided for the Irish and Poles. The Catholic Church might have been a stabilizing factor, but the American presence in Puerto Rico has reduced its positive influence. Until 1961, the Church on the island was under the leadership of American bishops. Even as recently as 1984, fewer than 15 percent of the priests were born on Puerto Rico.

With this background, the traditional sense of religious identity that might have developed was weakened, as the typical Puerto Rican was forced to choose between loyalty to the Americanized Catholic Church and identity as a Puerto Rican. Even on the mainland, Catholic parishes populated by Puerto Ricans have usually been under the direction of Anglos or Chicanos. Consequently, the Puerto Ricans who migrate have not found the Church as useful in assisting them in their adjustment as other immigrants have. By contrast the pentecostal congregation has provided a warmth and a more emotional form of worship that more closely mirrors the culture of the island (EPICA, 1976, pp. 73–75; Fayer, 1985; Fitzpatrick, 1980, p. 861, 1987, pp. 117–138; Glazer and Moynihan, 1970, pp. 103–104; Stuart, 1984).

## Political Organizations

As it does among other groups, political activity among Puerto Ricans takes two forms. First is the work to elect individuals to office, and second is organizing into political action groups, which are sometimes scrutinized by law enforcement agencies because of their activities.

As a group Puerto Ricans do not play a decisive role in electoral politics and have less influence than Black Americans. On the whole, the Puerto Rican population is much smaller than the Black population, but even in New York City, where, coupled with other Hispanics, they comprise 20 percent of the population, their effect has been slight. Steps, such as providing election information in Spanish and registration drives, may encourage greater Puerto Rican participation. Despite legal remedies, voter turnout will likely continue to be modest.

Puerto Rican voters are often alienated from the political process because (1) they frequently move due to job layoffs, (2) they find life in cities impersonal when contrasted to Puerto Rico's small towns, (3) district boundaries are drawn in some instances to divide Hispanic communities, effectively diluting the power base, and (4) some may assume that their stay in the United States is temporary. Puerto Ricans may also have little desire to participate actively in a

*Beginning in 1987, committees were organized to register Puerto Rican voters in New York City.*

political system that appears to be retreating from its earlier commitment to special social and economic programs for minorities (V. Irwin, 1987; Nelson, 1980).

There are some encouraging signs. A Puerto Rican has been consistently elected from the South Bronx to the United States House of Representatives, first Herman Badillo, later succeeded by Robert Garcia. Miami became the first city to elect a Puerto Rican mayor. The relatively new National Puerto Rican Coalition has been established to increase Puerto Rican political strength. A 1987 registration drive *Atrévete* ("I dare you"), backed by private and commonwealth of Puerto Rico money, signed up voters in New York City. Puerto Rican Governor Hernández Colón participated in the drive, telling mainland Puerto Ricans that they have a responsibility to vote as long as they are on the mainland. Puerto Ricans in New York City tend to be more active in political protests, signing petitions, and contacting public officials than are Anglos. Yet Puerto Rican political strength is weakened by the presence of other Hispanics in their communities. Congressman Garcia has been heavily involved in promoting development in the Dominican Republic because of the many Dominicans in his district (Fitzpatrick, 1987, pp. 42–45; V. Irwin, 1987; Levy and Kramer, 1972, pp. 88–93; Moore and Pachon, 1985; Wagenheim, 1983, p. 17).

Not all organizations in the Puerto Rican community are concerned with electoral politics. Founded in 1961, *Aspira* (Spanish for "strive" or "aspire") encourages Puerto Rican youths to undertake higher education and enter professional schools. A number of groups representing special interests such as merchants, fraternal social organizations, and various occupational groups have also formed (Fitzpatrick, 1987; Glazer and Moynihan, 1970, p. 101; Marden and Meyer, 1978, pp. 277–278).

## GLANCING BACK AND LOOKING AHEAD

The Puerto Rican people share many problems with other subordinate groups— poor housing, inadequate health care, weak political representation, and low incomes. Like Chicanos, they have a language and cultural tradition at variance with that of Anglo society. The dominant society is belatedly removing some barriers to achievement by Spanish-speaking people in the United States and slowly making education a constructive experience through bilingual and bicultural programs. Chicanos and Puerto Ricans are poorly represented among key decision makers in both corporate offices and governmental agencies. Both Chicanos and Puerto Ricans, however, are close to or actually in their home country, a situation that facilitates maintaining a rich cultural tradition. Hispanics' ability to maintain their original identity and solidarity means they have not been as compelled as European immigrants to assimilate White American customs and values.

The situation of Puerto Ricans is unique. Those on the island must resolve the issues of its political relationship to the mainland and set the proper pace and emphasis for economic development. Those migrating to the mainland must adapt to a social definition of race different from that on the island and adjust to a system that leaves some Puerto Ricans in an ambiguous social position.

The problems of Puerto Rican barrios throughout the United States are not just cold statistics or symptoms subject to the latest government program. Their real, human meaning has frequently been brought out by civil disturbances as in Chicago in 1966, New York City in 1967, and Newark in 1974, when Puerto Ricans participated in desperate riots. A survey conducted in Chicago shortly after that disorder rated police relations and unemployment as the major problems (Forni, 1971). Puerto Rican respondents seemed to turn more eagerly to individual solutions (getting more education and other forms of self-improvement) than to work through public agencies. In part, this reflects public agencies' ineffectiveness in dealing with the problems facing Puerto Ricans. Once again Myrdal's observation, in *An American Dilemma*, that the problems of a subordinate group are actually the problems of the dominant group, seems apt.

The Puerto Rican mainland population is also distinct. Many first-generation immigrants have endured poverty in the past; in this respect the Puerto Rican migrant is not unique. The Commission on Civil Rights, however, more than 15 years ago concluded its report on Puerto Ricans this way:

The United States has never before had a large migration of citizens from offshore, distinct in culture and language and also facing the problem of color prejudice. After 30 years of significant migration, contrary to conventional wisdom that once Puerto Ricans learned the language the second generation would move into the mainstream of American society, the future of this distinct community in the United States is still to be determined. (1976c, p. 145)

Puerto Ricans are still among the groups who find themselves economically on the outside despite Hispanics' long history of immigration to the United States. Another group with such a history has met problems of racial prejudice and economic discrimination: Asian Americans.

## KEY TERMS

**color gradient**    Placement of people on a continuum from light to dark skin color, rather than in distinct racial groupings by skin color.

**evangelical faiths**    Christian faiths that place great emphasis on a personal relationship between the individual and God and believe that each adherent must spread the faith and bear personal witness by openly declaring the religion to nonbelievers.

**Neoricans**    Puerto Ricans who return to the island to settle after living on the mainland of the United States (also *nuyoricans*).

**pentecostal faiths**    Religious groups similar in many respects to evangelical faiths which, in addition, believe in the infusion of the Holy Spirit into services and in religious experiences such as faith healing.

**tracking**    The practice of placing students in specific curriculum groups on the basis of test scores and other criteria.

## FOR FURTHER INFORMATION

Edna Acosta-Belén, ed. *The Puerto Rican Woman: Perspectives on Culture, History, and Society*, 2nd ed. New York: Praeger, 1986.

This collection of 11 articles deals with Puerto Rican woman both on the island and the mainland.

Joseph P. Fitzpatrick. *Puerto Rican Americans: The Meaning of Migration to the Mainland*, 2nd ed. Englewood Cliffs, NJ: Prentice-Hall, 1987

A good sociological treatment of Puerto Ricans, this book emphasizes the degree to which they have been assimilated into Anglo society. Chapters are devoted to education, welfare, mental illness, drug abuse, religion, and the differing definitions of race on the island and the mainland.

James Jennings and Monte Rivera, eds. *Puerto Rican Politics in Urban America*. Westport, Conn.: Greenwood Press, 1984.

This reader provides a historical look as well as contemporary political developments in Boston, Chicago, and New York City.

Alfredo Lopez. *Dona Licha's Island: Modern Colonialism in Puerto Rico*. Boston: South End Press, 1987.

A critical look at the plight of Puerto Ricans in Puerto Rico, that concludes that independence is the only acceptable solution for the island.

Manuel Maldonado-Denis. *Puerto Rico: A Socio-Historic Interpretation*. New York: Random-House, 1972.

A well-produced account of Puerto Rico's history, beginning with European contact and written from a pro-independence perspective.

Edward Rivera. *Family Installments: Memories of Growing Up Hispanic*. New York: William Morrow, 1982.

English professor Rivera was born in Puerto Rico and draws upon his own experience of growing up in El Barrio.

Clara E. Rodriquez. *Puerto Ricans: Born in the U.S.A.* Boston: Unwin Hyman, 1989.

This authoritative book concentrates on Puerto Ricans in New York City with special emphasis on education and housing. It includes a look at the impact of the pop group Menudo.

Piri Thomas. *Down These Mean Streets*. New York: Signet, 1967.

In an autobiographical account of life in El Barrio, Thomas discusses the especially difficult existence of a dark-skinned Puerto Rican.

Kal Wagenheim. *Puerto Ricans in the U.S.* New York: Minority Rights Group, 1983.

This brief (20-page) booklet reviews the island's history, describes the migration to the mainland, and summarizes the status of Puerto Ricans in the United States.

Alex Huxley Westfried. *Ethnic Leadership in a New England Community: Three Puerto Rican Families*. Cambridge, MA: Schenkman, 1981.

Westfried traces three college-educated, professional Puerto Rican families and their involvement in the Spanish Community Center, where they have difficulty relating to working-class Hispanics.

# Chapter Twelve

# ASIAN AMERICANS: GROWTH AND DIVERSITY

## Chapter Outline

**Korean Americans**
Historical Background
The Present Picture
**Filipino Americans**
Immigration Patterns
The Present Picture
**Indochinese Americans**
The Refugees
The Present Picture
**Hawaii and Its People**
Historical Background

The Present Picture
**The "Model Minority" Image Explored**
Education
The Work Force
Income
The Door Half Open
**Asian American Identity**
**Glancing Back and Looking Ahead**
**Key Terms**
**For Further Information**

---

## ❋ HIGHLIGHTS ❋

Asian Americans are a diverse group that is one of the fastest-growing segments of the population. Immigration is the primary source of growth among Koreans, Filipinos, and refugees from Indochina. All Asian groups, along with Blacks and Whites (or *Haoles*, as they are known) coexist in Hawaii. Asian Americans are often viewed as a "model minority" that has successfully overcome discrimination. This image disguises lingering maltreatment and denies them the opportunities afforded other racial minorities.

---

Two characteristics of the group of Americans of Asian descent are growth and diversity. Asian Americans in 1990 number 7.2 million, up from 1.5 million in 1970 (see Table 12.1). Although they are just 3 percent of the United States population, they are the third largest racial or ethnic minority after Blacks and Hispanics.

Asia is a vast region with more than half the world's population. The successive waves of immigrants to the United States from that continent constitute a vast array of nationalities and cultures. Besides the eight groups listed in Table 12.1, the Census Bureau enumerates the Bangladeshi, Bhutanese, Bornean, Burmese, Celebesian, Cernan, Indochinese, Iwo-Jiman, Japanese, Malayan, Maldinean, Nepali, Okinawan, Sikkimese, Singaporean, and Sri Lankan. Knowing this variety among Asian people, we can apply to Asian Americans several

---

**TABLE 12.1**  Asian American Population

The Asian American population doubled in the 1970s and doubled again during the 1980s.

| | Population (in thousands) | | | Change (percentage) | |
|---|---|---|---|---|---|
| Group | 1970 | 1980 | 1990 | 1970–1980 | 1980–1990 |
| Chinese Americans | 453 | 806 | 1,640 | 85 | 104 |
| Filipino Americans | 343 | 775 | 1,407 | 126 | 82 |
| Japanese Americans | 591 | 701 | 848 | 19 | 21 |
| Asian Indians | — | 362 | 815 | — | 125 |
| Korean Americans | 69 | 355 | 799 | 413 | 116 |
| Vietnamese | — | 262 | 615 | — | 135 |
| Laotian | — | 48 | 149 | — | 210 |
| Cambodian | — | 16 | 147 | — | 819 |
| All other | 80* | 176 | 854 | — | 485 |
| Total | 1,539 | 3,501 | 7,274 | 127 | 108 |

*Includes Asian Indians, Vietnamese, Laotian, and Cambodian.
*Source:* Bureau of Census data reported in Ng, 1991.

generalizations made earlier about American Indians. Both groups are a collection of diverse peoples with distinct linguistic, social, and geographic backgrounds (Odo, 1973, p. 372). The stereotyped portrait of Asians as expressionless people with their heads bowed is just as useless as the stereotype of the cigar-store Indian. It is easy to lump together all people of the same color, but doing so ignores the sharp differences among them. Any examination of Asian Americans quickly reveals their diversity.

As is true of all minority groups discussed so far, to be accepted, Asians in the United States have been pressured to assimilate. The effects of this pressure vary. For recent refugees from Asia, assimilation is a new experience, whereas the grandchildren of Japanese immigrants may be culturally indistinguishable from Whites. As is evident in Table 12.2, many Asian Americans cluster on the West Coast and in Hawaii, but significant settlements of most Asian-American groups can be found in a number of the larger cities. Figure 12.1 shows how Asian Americans combine with other groups to form the diversity typical of an American metropolitan area such as Los Angeles.

This chapter will examine Asian Americans in general and three of the larger groups—Koreans, Filipinos, and refugees from Indochina—in greater depth. The chapter concludes with an examination of the coexistence of a uniquely mixed group of peoples—Hawaiians—among whom Asian Americans form the numerical majority. Chapters 13 and 14 will concentrate on the Chinese and Japanese, the two Asian groups with the largest historical tradition in the United States.

## KOREAN AMERICANS

The population of Korean Americans is now nearly as large as that of Japanese Americans. Yet Korean Americans are often overlooked in favor of the larger groups from Asia.

### *Historical Background*

Today's Korean-American community is the result of three waves of immigration. The initial wave, of a little more than 7,000 immigrants, came to the United States between 1903 and 1910, when laborers migrated to Hawaii. Under Japanese colonial rule (1910–1945), Korean migration was halted except for a few hundred "picture brides" allowed to join their prospective husbands.

The second wave followed the end of the Korean War, accounting for about 14,000 immigrants from 1951 through 1964. Most of these immigrants were wives of American serviceman and war orphans. Relatively little research has been done on these first two periods of immigration.

The passage of the 1965 Immigration Act greatly facilitated movement from Korea. For the four years prior to the act, Koreans accounted for only 7 out of every 1,000 immigrants. In the first four years after the act, Koreans were 38 out

**TABLE 12.2**   Largest Asian American Populations, by States, 1990

Asian Americans have settled mostly in a few states, particularly California and Hawaii. Five states account for anywhere from 55 percent (Korean Americans) to 74 percent (Japanese Americans) of these four groups.

| Rank | Population | Percentage of Group |
|---|---|---|
| *Chinese Americans* | | |
| 1. California | 704,850 | 43 |
| 2. New York | 284,144 | 17 |
| 3. Hawaii | 68,804 | 4 |
| 4. Texas | 63,232 | 4 |
| 5. Massachusetts | 53,792 | 3 |
| 6. Other states | 470,650 | 29 |
| Total | 1,645,472 | 100 |
| *Filipino Americans* | | |
| 1. California | 731,685 | 52 |
| 2. Hawaii | 168,682 | 12 |
| 3. Illinois | 64,224 | 5 |
| 4. New York | 62,259 | 4 |
| 5. New Jersey | 53,146 | 4 |
| 6. Other states | 326,774 | 23 |
| Total | 1,406,770 | 100 |
| *Japanese Americans* | | |
| 1. California | 312,989 | 37 |
| 2. Hawaii | 247,486 | 29 |
| 3. New York | 35,281 | 4 |
| 4. Washington | 34,366 | 4 |
| 5. Illinois | 21,831 | 3 |
| 6. Other states | 195,609 | 23 |
| Total | 847,562 | 100 |
| *Korean Americans* | | |
| 1. California | 259,941 | 33 |
| 2. New York | 95,648 | 12 |
| 3. Illinois | 41,506 | 5 |
| 4. New Jersey | 38,540 | 5 |
| 5. Texas | 31,775 | 4 |
| 6. Other states | 331,439 | 41 |
| Total | 798,849 | 100 |

*Source:* Bureau of the Census data reported in Ng, 1991.

of every 1,000 immigrants to the United States. This third wave, continuing to the present, has reflected the admission priorities set up in the 1965 immigration law. These immigrants have been well educated, and have arrived in the United States with professional skills.

Many of the immigrants, though, must settle at least initially for positions of lower responsibility than those they held in Korea and must suffer through a

**FIGURE 12.1** Ethnic Diversity in Los Angeles

The diversity of life in the United States' second-largest city reflects migration from Mexico (the barrio), Korean (Koreatown), China and Hong Kong (Chinatown), Taiwan (Monterey Park), and Japan (Little Tokyo). Also noted on the map are the location of the 1965 riots (Watts) and 1992 riots (South-Central).

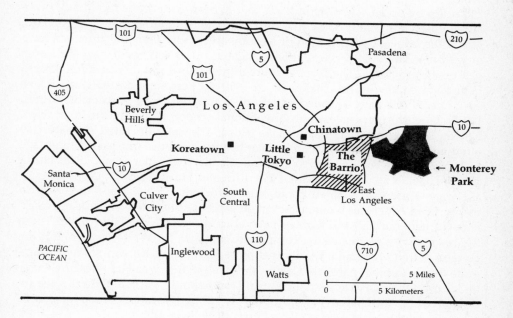

period of "exigency" or disenchantment, as described in Chapter 2. The problems that have been documented such as stress, loneliness, alcoholism, family strife, and mental disorders reflect the pain of adjustment. They have also been termed the *ilchomose* or "1.5 generation," the Korean American immigrants who accompanied their parents to the United States when they are young occupy. They are today middle-aged, remain bilingual and bicultural, and tend to form the professional class in the Korean American community (Hurh, 1990; Hurh and Kim, 1984, 1987, 1988; Shin, 1971).

## The Present Picture

Today's young Korean Americans face many of the cultural conflicts common to any first generation born in a new country. The parents may speak the native tongue, but the road to opportunity is paved with American culture and the English language. It is very difficult to maintain a sense of Korean culture in the United States; the host society is not particularly helpful. Although the United

States fought a war there and American troops remain in South Korea, Korean culture is very foreign to contemporary Americans. The few studies of attitudes toward Korean Americans show Americans responding with vague, negative attitudes or simply lumping Korean Americans with other Asian groups (Hurh, 1977b; Hurh and Kim, 1982, 1984; Kitano and Matsushima, 1981; Rodriquez, 1982).

Studies by social scientists indicate that Korean Americans face many problems typical for immigrants, like difficulties with language. In Los Angeles, where the largest concentration of Koreans live, more than 100 churches have only Korean language services and local television stations feature several hours of Korean programs. The Korean immigrants' high level of education should help them cope with the challenge. In 1980, 40 percent of Korean Americans 20–24 years old were enrolled in school, compared to 24 percent of Whites. While Korean Americans stress conventional schooling as a means to success, Korean schools have begun in major cities. Typically operated on Saturday afternoons, they offer classes on Korean history, customs, music, and language to help students maintain their cultural identity (Gardner et al., 1985; Hurh, 1977a; Hurh et al., 1978; H. Kim, 1980; Kim and Hurh, 1983; D. Lee, 1992).

Korean American women commonly participate in the labor force, as do many Asian American women. About 60 percent of native-born Korean-American women and half the women born abroad work in the labor force. These figures may not seem striking compared with data for White women, but the cultural differences make the figures more significant. Korean women immigrate from a family system that establishes well-defined marital roles: the woman is expected to serve as homemaker and mother only. Although these roles are carried over to the United States, women are pressed, because of their husband's struggles to establish themselves, to support their families.

Many Korean American men begin small service or retail businesses and gradually involve their wives in the business. Wages do not matter as the household mobilizes to make a profitable enterprise out of a marginal business. The situation is made more difficult by the hostility Korean-American-run businesses often encounter from their prospective customers. Under economic pressure, Korean-American women must move away from traditional cultural roles. The move, however, is only partial; studies show that despite the high rate of participation in the labor force by Korean immigrant wives, first-generation immigrant couples continue in sharply divided sex roles in other aspects of daily living (Kim and Hurh, 1984, 1985a, 1985b).

Korean American businesses should not be regarded as major operations—most are relatively small. They do benefit from a special form of development capital (or cash) used to subsidize businesses called a *kye* (pronounced KAY). Korean Americans pool their money through the *kye*—an association that grants members money on a rotating basis to gain access to even more additional capital. Rotating credit associations are not unique to Korean Americans; they have, for example, been used by West Indians. Not all Korean business entrepreneurs use the kye, but a 1984 Chicago survey revealed that 34 percent did rely on such associations (Goozner, 1987; I. Kim, 1988; Light and Bonacich, 1988, pp. 243–272).

In the early 1990s, nationwide attention was given to the apparent friction between Korean Americans and another subordinate group, African Americans. In New York City, Los Angeles, and Chicago, the scene was replayed where a Korean-American merchant confronted a Black allegedly threatening or robbing him. The Black neighborhood responded with hostility to what they perceived as the disrespect and arrogance of the Korean American entrepreneur. Such friction is not new; earlier generations of Jewish, Italian, and even Arab merchants encountered similar hostility from what to outsiders seems an unlikely source—another oppressed minority. The contemporary conflict was even dramatized in Spike Lee's 1989 movie *Do the Right Thing* in which African Americans and Korean Americans clashed. The situation stems from Korean Americans' being the latest immigrant group prepared to cater to the needs of the inner city abandoned by those who moved up the economic ladder (Commission on Civil Rights, 1992; El Nasser, 1991a; Goodstein, 1990).

The tension that can arise between subordinate groups gained national attention during the 1992 South-Central Los Angeles riots. In that city's poor areas, the only shops in which to buy groceries or liquor or gasoline are owned by Korean immigrants. They have largely replaced the White business people who left the ghetto area after the 1965 Watts riot. African Americans were well aware of the dominant role Korean Americans play in their local retail market. Some Blacks expressed resentment that had previously been fueled by the 1991 fatal shooting of a 15-year-old Black girl by a Korean grocer in a dispute over pay-

*Police protect a Korean-American merchant in Brooklyn fearing retaliation after a Black woman said that she was roughed up by a store employee who accused her of stealing.*

ment for orange juice. The resentment grew when the grocer, convicted of manslaughter, had her prison sentence waived by a judge in favor of a 5-year probation period.

The 1992 riots focused in part on retailers in South-Central Los Angeles, and therefore on Korean Americans. During the unrest, 1,000 Korean businesses valued at $300 million were destroyed. In a post-riot survey of those African Americans arrested, 80 percent felt that Korean Americans were disrespectful, compared to 56 percent who felt similarly about Whites. The desire to succeed by Korean Americans led them to the inner city where they did not face competition from Whites. But it also meant that they have to deal on a daily basis with the frustration of another minority group (Commission on Civil Rights, 1992, pp. 32–39; McIntosh, 1992; Mydans, 1992).

Among Korean Americans the most visible organization holding the group together is the church. Half the immigrants were affiliated with Christian churches prior to immigrating. One study of Koreans in Chicago and Los Angeles found that 70 percent were affiliated with Korean ethnic churches, mostly Presbyterian, with small numbers of Roman Catholics and Methodists. Korean ethnic churches are the fastest growing segment of the Presbyterian and Methodist faiths. The church performs an important function, apart from the manifest religious one, giving Korean Americans a sense of attachment and a practical way to meet other Korean Americans. The churches are much more than simple sites for religious services; they assume multiple, secular roles for the Korean community. The fellowship Korean Americans participate in is both spiritual and ethnic (Hurh and Kim, 1984, 1989, 1990b; I. Kim, 1981, pp. 187–207).

## FILIPINO AMERICANS

Relatively little has been written about the Filipinos (also spelled *Pilipinos*) although they are the second largest Asian American group in the United States, now at more than a million. Social science literature considers them as Asians for geographical reasons, but physically and culturally they are very different, reflecting centuries of Spanish rule.

### Immigration Patterns

The earliest Filipino immigrants came as American nationals, when, in 1899, the United States gained possession of the Philippine Islands at the conclusion of the Spanish-American War. In 1934, the islands gained commonwealth status. Yet despite the close ties, immigration was sharply restricted to only 50 to 100 persons annually until the 1965 Immigration Act lifted these quota limitations. Before the restrictions were removed, pineapple growers in Hawaii successfully lobbied to import workers to the islands. Another exception was the U.S. Navy, which put Filipino citizens to work in kitchens aboard ship; as recently as 1970, 14,000 Filipinos were employed as mess stewards. Many of them later settled on the mainland of the United States (Gardner et al., 1985, p. 5; Melendy, 1980; Takaki, 1989, pp. 315–354).

Sociologist Harry Kitano divides Filipino immigration into four historical periods:

1. The first generation, immigrating in the 1920s, was mostly male and employed in agricultural labor. Acculturation has been slow.
2. The second and third generations, although more assimilated, face job discrimination and social exclusion. Born in America, they have very little if any contact with their native land and culture.
3. The post-World War II arrivals include many war veterans.
4. The newest immigrants, who include many professionals (physicians, nurses, and others), arrived under the 1965 Immigration Act. (Kitano, 1991, pp. 238–239; Pido, 1986).

Just as with other Asian groups, the people are diverse. Besides these stages of immigration, the Filipinos can also be defined by different states of immigration—different languages, regions of origin, and religions—differences that sharply separate the people in their homeland as well. In the Philippines and among Filipino immigrants to the United States, 8 distinct languages with 200 dialects are spoken (Pido, 1986, p. 17).

## The Present Picture

As shown in Table 12.1, the Filipino population increased dramatically when restrictions on immigration were eased in 1965. More than two-thirds of the new arrivals qualified for entry as professional and technical workers, but, like Koreans, they have often worked at jobs below those they left behind in the Philippines. Surprisingly, American-born Filipinos often have less formal schooling and lower job status (see Figure 12.3). They come from poorer families unable to afford higher education and have been relegated to unskilled work, including migrant farm workers. Their relatively poor economic background means they have little startup capital for businesses. Therefore, unlike other Asian American groups, Filipinos have not developed small-business bases such as retail or service outlets capitalizing on their ethnic culture. The volume of Philippine exports to the United States is low—less than one-third of Korean exports. The Filipino exports are mostly agricultural, and so their volume and the content of the products do not provide an opening for small businesses. Filipinos, therefore, have been absorbed into primarily low-wage, private-sector jobs. Prospects for immediate economic advancement for Filipino Americans as a group seem dim (Min, 1987; Nee and Sanders, 1985).

Despite their numbers, no significant Filipino social organization has formed, for several reasons. First, Filipino's strong loyalty to family and church, particularly Roman Catholicism, works against time-consuming efforts at creating organizations. Second, the people's diversity makes forming ties here difficult. Third, though Filipinos have organized many groups, these tend to be clublike or fraternal. They do not seek to represent the general Filipino population, and therefore remain invisible to Anglos. Fourth, although Filipinos have initially stayed close to events in their homeland, especially about the political developments of the late 1980s, they show every sign of seeking involvement in broader non-Filipino organizations and avoiding group exclusiveness (Kim and Condon, 1975; Kitano and Matsushima, 1981; Melendy, 1980; Morales, 1976; Nakanishi, 1986; Rabaya, 1971; Yu, 1980).

## INDOCHINESE AMERICANS

The people of Indochina—the Vietnamese, Cambodians (Kampucheans), and Laotians—were part of the former French Indochinese Union. *Indochinese* is only a term of convenience, for the peoples of these areas are ethnically and linguistically diverse. The ethnic Laotians constitute only half of the Laotian people, for example; a significant number of Mon-Khmer, Yao, and Hmong form minorities (Kitano and Daniels, 1988, pp. 135–158; M. B. Wright, 1980).

### The Refugees

The problem of American involvement in Indochina did not end when all American personnel were withdrawn from South Vietnam in 1975. The final tragedy was the reluctant welcome given to the refugees from Vietnam, Cambodia (Kampuchea), and Laos by Americans and people of other nations. One week after the evacuation of Vietnam in April 1975, a Gallup poll reported that 54 percent of Americans were against giving sanctuary to the Asian refugees, with 36 percent in favor and 12 percent undecided. The primary objection to Vietnamese immigration was that it would further increase unemployment (Schaefer and Schaefer, 1975).

Many Americans offered to house refugees in their homes, but others declared that the United States had too many Asians already and were in danger of losing our "national character." This attitude toward the Indochinese has been characteristic of the feeling that Harvard sociologist David Riesman named the *gook syndrome. Gook* is a derogatory term for Asians, and the syndrome refers to the tendency to stereotype these people in the very worst of lights. Riesman believed that the American news media created an unflattering image of the South Vietnamese and their government, leading the American people to believe they were not worth saving (Luce, 1975, p. E19).

The initial 135,000 Vietnamese refugees who fled in 1975 were joined by more than a million running from later fighting and religious persecution that plagued Indochina. The United States accepted about half of the refugees, some of them the so-called boat people, who took to the ocean in overcrowded vessels, hoping that some ship would pick them up and offer sanctuary. Hundreds of thousands were placed in other nations or remain in overcrowded refugee camps administered by the United Nations.

As immigration to the United States continued, so too did mixed feelings among Americans. Surveys in the 1980s show that although few Americans regarded the Indochinese as undesirable, 30 to 50 percent still worried that the Indochinese would be an economic drain. Furthermore, some critics argued that the movement which began as a genuine refugee flow had clearly shifted to a migratory flow composed of some refugees, a growing number of people seeking family reunification, and an even larger economic migrant component (Gwetzman, 1985; Starr and Roberts, 1981).

## *The Present Picture*

As has been so of other immigrants, the Indochinese refugees face a difficult adjustment. Few expect to return to their country for visits and fewer still hope to ever return to their homeland permanently. Therefore, many look to the United States as their future home and the home of their children. They may still, however, have to accept jobs well below their occupational positions in southeast Asia; geographic mobility has been accompanied by downward social mobility. For example, of those who had been employed as managers in Vietnam, only 5 percent were employed in similar positions in the United States. Available data, including a 1982 survey, indicate that Indochinese refugees have increased their earnings at a relatively fast rate, often by working long hours. Partly because the Indochinese people comprise significantly different subgroups, assimilation as well as acceptance are not likely to occur at the same rate for all (Bach and Bach, 1980; Kelly, 1986).

Even though most Indochinese children spoke no English upon arrival here, they have done extremely well in school. One study of 350 refugee children showed 27 percent scoring in the 90th percentile on national standardized tests of math achievement—almost three times better than the national average. More than a quarter earn top marks in their English courses.

The picture for young Indochinese in the United States is not completely pleasant. Crime is not unknown, of course, but some fear that it has two very ugly sides. Some of this crime may represent reprisals for the war—militant nationalists who dream of toppling the communist government of Vietnam may strike out at their fellows in the United States who do not take such a stance. Also, it has been charged that gangs have organized intending to link communities into an organization. The allegations continue, but no strong evidence has surfaced to support them. By contrast, violent episodes directed at Indochinese by Whites and others expressing resentment over their employment or even their mere presence have been clearly documented (Butterfield, 1985; Kelly, 1986; Sandza, 1984).

In contrast with its action with earlier immigrant groups, the federal government conspicuously involved itself in locating homes for Indochinese refugees. Pressured by many communities afraid of being overwhelmed by Indochinese immigrants, these agencies attempted to disperse the refugees throughout the nation. Such efforts failed, though, mostly because the refugees, like European

*Vietnamese businesses form a Little Saigon mall in Westminster, California.*

immigrants before them, sought out their compatriots. As a result, Indochinese communities and neighborhoods have begun to be visible, especially in California and Texas. In such areas of the nation where refugees from Asia have reestablished some cultural practices from their homeland, a more pluralistic solution to their adjustment seems a possible alternative to complete assimilation.

## HAWAII AND ITS PEOPLE

Social relationships among racial groups in Hawaii are very different form conditions on the mainland; assumptions that might be valid elsewhere are not valid in Hawaii. That Hawaii has no Japantown or Little Tokyo of the sort in which one-third of Japanese Americans on the mainland reside is no indication that local Japanese Americans are not interested in Japanese culture. On the contrary, the entire state reinforces cultural diversity. It has six television stations broadcasting in Japanese, along with many Japanese-run retail establishments (Research Committee, 1986). Nevertheless, prejudice, discrimination, and pressure to assimilate are present in Hawaii because life on the island is much closer to that in the rest of the country than to the ideal of a pluralistic society. Hawaii's population is unquestionably diverse, as shown in Table 12.3. To grasp contemporary social relationships we must first understand the historical context that brought races together on the islands—the various Asian peoples plus the *Haoles* (pronounced "hah-oh-lehs"), the term frequently used to refer to Whites in Hawaii.

## Historical Background

Geographically remote, Hawaii was initially populated by Polynesian people who had their first contact with Europeans in 1778 when English explorer Captain James Cook arrived. The Hawaiians were rather tolerant of the subsequent arrival of plantation operators and missionaries. Fortunately, the Hawaiian people were united under a monarchy and received respect from the European immigrants, a respect that developed into a spirit of goodwill. Slavery was never introduced, even during the colonial period, as it was in so many areas of the Western Hemisphere. Nevertheless, the effect of the White arrival on the Hawaiians themselves was disastrous. Civil warfare and disease reduced the number of full-blooded descendants to fewer than 30,000 by 1900 and is probably well under 6,000 now. Meanwhile large sugarcane plantations imported laborers from China, Portugal, Japan, and, in the early 1900s, from the Philippines, Korea, and Puerto Rico.

In 1893, a revolution encouraged by foreign commercial interests overthrew the monarchy. During the revolution the United States landed troops, and five years later Hawaii was annexed as a territory to the United States. The 1900 Organic Act guaranteed racial equality, but foreign rule dealt a devastating

---

**TABLE 12.3**    Hawaii: Racial Composition, 1950 and 1990

Since 1950, the relative proportion of Hawaii's people who are of Japanese, Hawaiian, or Chinese ancestry has declined.

| | 1950 | | 1990 | |
|---|---|---|---|---|
| *Racial group* | *Percent* | *Total* | *Percent* | *Total* |
| White | 23.0 | 114,793 | 33.4 | 369,616 |
| Japanese | 36.9 | 184,598 | 22.3 | 247,486 |
| Filipino | 12.2 | 61,062 | 15.2 | 168,682 |
| Hawaiian | 17.2 | 86,090 | 11.7 | 129,663 |
| Chinese | 6.5 | 32,376 | 6.2 | 68,804 |
| Black | .5 | 2,651 | 2.4 | 27,195 |
| Korean | 1.4 | 7,030 | 2.2 | 24,454 |
| All other | 2.2 | 11,169 | 6.6 | 72,329 |
| Total | 99.9 | 499,769 | 100.0 | 1,108,229 |

*Sources:* Lind, 1969, p. 47; Bureau of the Census, 1991; Ng, 1991. Hawaiian 1990 count are author's estimates.

psychological blow to the proud Hawaiian people. American rule had mixed effects on relations among races. Citizenship laws granted civil rights to all those born on the islands, not just the wealthy *Haoles*. But the anti-Asian laws still applied, excluding the Chinese and Japanese from political participation.

The twentieth century has witnessed Hawaii's transition from a plantation frontier to the fiftieth state and an integral part of the economy. During that transition Hawaii became a strategic military outpost, although that role has had only a limited effect on race relations. Even the attack on Pearl Harbor had relatively little influence on Japanese Americans in Hawaii.

## The Present Picture

Hawaii's racial mixture was not always admired. Congressional opposition to statehood was based chiefly on opposition to admitting so many non-Whites. But Hawaii has now achieved some fame for its good race relations. In fact, tourists, who are predominantly White, have come from the mainland and seen and generally accepted the racial harmony. Admittedly Waikiki Beach, where most tourists congregate, is atypical of the islands, but even there the tourist cannot ignore the difference in intergroup relations. One clear indication is the degree of exogamy on the islands. The rate of out-group marriage varies by group from a high of 90 percent for Hawaiians in 1984 to a low of 19 percent for *Haoles*. Interracial marriage steadily increased in the previous 40 years, but the increase leveled off after the late 1970s, to 33 percent in 1985 (C. Cheng, 1951; Hawaii, 1986, p. 58; Hormann, 1982; Kanahele, 1982; Labor and Jacobs, 1986).

A closer look shows that equality among the people is not absolute, let alone among the races as groups. The pineapple and sugarcane plantation legacy persists. A 1972 estimate placed 97 percent of Hawaiian workers in the employ of 40 landholders. One estate alone owned nearly one-tenth of the state's territory. Native Hawaiians tend to be least well off, working land they do not own. The economy is dominated by Japanese Americans and *Haoles*. The *AJAs* (Americans of Japanese Ancestry, as they are called in Hawaii) are especially important in education, where they account for nearly 58 percent of teachers, and in politics, where they dominate. Political activity of the AJAs certainly contrasts to that of mainland Japanese Americans. In 1976, Hawaii's governor, both representatives in the United States House, one senator, and the majority of the state legislators were AJAs. Chinese Americans have been successful business people in Hawaii, but top positions are almost all filled by *Haoles*. Recent immigrants from Asia and, more significant, even long-term residents of Filipino and Hawaiian descent, show little evidence of sharing in Hawaii's overall picture of affluence (Kaser, 1977; Kitano, 1976, pp. 73–79; *Time*, 1975; W. Turner, 1972; Wright and Gardner, 1983).

Prejudice and discrimination are not alien to Hawaii. Attitudinal surveys show definite racial preferences and sensitivity to color differences. Housing surveys taken prior to passage of civil rights legislation showed commitment to nondiscrimination, but racial preferences were still present. Residential neighborhoods are sometimes dominated by certain groups, but there are no racial ghettos. As shown in Figure 12.2, the various racial groups are not uniformly distributed among the islands, but they are clustered rather than segregated. All civilian census tracts in Honolulu have residents of the five largest groups—*Haoles*, Japanese, Chinese, Hawaiian, and Filipino.

Discrimination by exclusive social clubs exists but is diminishing. Groups like the Rotary and Lions' clubs opened their doors to Asians in Hawaii before they did on the mainland. Undoubtedly, Hawaii has gradually absorbed the mainland's racial consciousness, but a contrast between the islands and the rest of the nation remains. Evidence of racial harmony is much more abundant. Hawaii has never known forced school segregation, Jim Crow laws, slavery, or laws prohibiting racial intermarriage (Ball and Yamamura, 1960; Hormann, 1972, 1982; Lind, 1969; Rapson, 1980; Samuels, 1969, 1970).

---

**FIGURE 12.2**   Racial Distribution in the Hawaiian Islands

There are few racial enclaves in Hawaii. The best known is Niihau, a privately owned island populated entirely by Hawaiians.

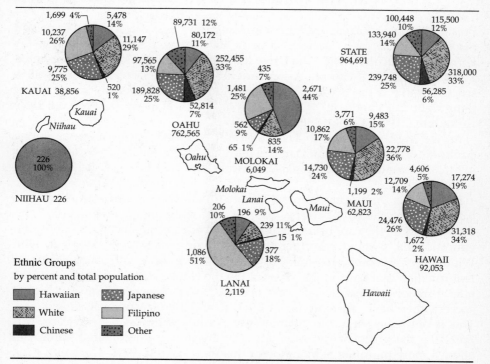

*Source:* Department of Geography, University of Hawaii, *Atlas of Hawaii*, 2nd Ed., p. 113.

The multiracial character of the islands will not change quickly. Although the culture has gradually come to resemble that of the mainland, cultural differences remain strong. Revivals of traditional culture are evident among the Hawaiians, Chinese, and Japanese. Several groups are working on behalf of the Hawaiians to settle claims for land illegally seized in the 1898 annexation. In 1978, Hawaiian was made the co-official state language, and the teaching of native history, language, and culture was made mandatory in public schools (Commission on Civil Rights, 1980b; A. Howard, 1980; Kealoha, 1976, p. 417; McGregor-Alegado, 1980; *The New York Time,* 1973).

In an absolute sense, Hawaii is not a racial paradise. Certain occupations and even social classes tend to be dominated by a single racial group. Hawaii is not immune to intolerance, and there is little reason not to expect that the people will totally resist prejudice as the island's isolation is reduced. By the same token, newcomers to the islands set aside some of their old stereotypes and prejudices (Adams, 1969). The future of race relations in Hawaii is uncertain, but relative to the mainland and much of the world, Hawaii's race relations more closely resemble harmony than bigotry.

## THE "MODEL MINORITY" IMAGE EXPLORED

President Ronald Reagan called Asian Americans "our exemplars of hope and inspiration." *Time* and *Newsweek* articles have featured headlines such as "A Formula for Success" and "The Drive to Excel." CBS's "60 Minutes" presented a glowing report. "Why are Asian Americans doing so exceptionally well in school?" Mike Wallace asked, and quickly added, "They must be doing something right. Let's bottle it." (Commission on Civil Rights, 1980c; McLeod, 1986; A. Ramirez, 1986; Takaki, 1989, p. 474).

As we learn in "Listen to Their Voices," Asian Americans even as young adults are acutely aware of this model minority image and the price they pay for it. Making friends with non-Asian Americans is not always easy, as Jeanne Park shows us.

Many other Americans also see Asian American groups as constituting a *model* or *ideal minority,* because, despite past sufferings from prejudice and discrimination, they are believed to have succeeded economically, socially, and educationally without resorting to political or violent confrontations with Whites. Some observers point to the existence of a model minority as reaffirmation that anyone can get ahead in the United States. Proponents of the model minority view declare that because Asian Americans have achieved success, they have ceased to be a minority, and are no longer disadvantaged. This is only a variation of "blaming the victim"; with Asian Americans, it is "praising the victim." An examination of areas of socioeconomic status will allow a more thorough exploration of this view (Gould, 1988; Hurh and Kim, 1989; E. Wong, 1985).

### ❖ LISTEN TO THEIR VOICES ❖

#### Eggs, Twinkies and Ethnic Stereotypes

#### Jeanne Park

*As a New York City high school junior, Asian American Jeanne Park writes about what it is like to "come of age" as a member of a model minority.*

Who am I?

For Asian-American students, the answer is a diligent, hard-working and intelligent young person. But living up to this reputation has secretly haunted me.

The labeling starts in elementary school. It's not uncommon for a teacher to remark, "You're Asian, you're supposed to do well in math." The underlying message is, "You're Asian and you're supposed to be smarter."

Not to say being labeled intelligent isn't flattering, because it is, or not to deny that basking in the limelight of being top of my class isn't ego-boosting, because frankly it is. But at a certain point, the pressure became crushing. I felt as if doing poorly on my next spelling quiz would stain the exalted reputation of all Asian students forever. . . .

The problem of social segregation still exists in the schools. With few exceptions, each race socializes only with its "own kind." Students see one another in the classroom, but outside the classroom there remains distinct segregation.

Racist lingo abounds. An Asian student who socializes only with other Asians is believed to be an Asian Supremacist or, at the very least, arrogant and closed off. Yet an Asian student who socializes only with whites is called a "twinkie," one who is yellow on the outside but white on the inside.

A white teen-ager who socializes only with whites is thought of as prejudiced, yet one who socializes with Asians is considered an "egg," white on the outside and yellow on the inside.

These culinary classifications go on endlessly, needless to say, leaving many confused, and leaving many more fearful than ever of social experimentation. Because the stereotypes are accepted almost unanimously, they are rarely challenged. Many develop harmful stereotypes of entire races. We label people before we even know them. . . .

It may be too late for our parents' generation to accept that each person can only be judged for the characteristics that set him or her apart as an individual. We, however, can do better.

## Education

There is some truth to the belief that Asian Americans have succeeded. As shown in Table 12.4, every Asian-American group has impressive school enrollment rates in relation to Whites as well as to Black and Hispanic minorities. Although these data do include Asians who come to the United States in order to study, enrollment rates for native-born Asian Americans are also generally higher than for Whites of the same age.

Asian-American youths are also more likely to be at work as well as in school, as is evident from the very low *inactivity rate* for Asian Americans. The inactivity rate is the proportion of people neither in school nor in the labor force. In 1980, 8 percent of Whites aged 16–19 were inactive, compared to 3 percent for Korean Americans. The pattern was similar for other groups. Only recently arrived Vietnamese-born youths had inactivity rates higher than those of Whites (Gardner et al., 1985, p. 32; Hirschman and Wong, 1986).

This encouraging picture does carry some qualifications for the optimistic model-minority view. Asian Americans maintain that at some universities they must have better records than other applicants to gain admission, and even when they have such records, they are turned down. Some observers therefore claim that some institutions adopt unofficial quotas to reduce Asian Americans' disproportionately high representation among college students. At the very least, many colleges fail to even consider that some Asian Americans deserve some of the same consideration given to talented members of other minorities (D. A. Bell, 1985, pp. 28–29; Biemiller, 1986; Butterfield, 1986; Lindsey, 1987; Salholz, 1987; Sue et al., 1985; Wang, 1988).

By 1990, there were growing charges that well-known universities were using unofficial quotas (similar to those historically used against Jewish applicants) to

**TABLE 12.4**   Asian American School Enrollment, 1980

Compared to White, Black, and Hispanic American youths, Asian Americans display high levels of enrollment in high school and college.

| | Percentage Enrolled in School | |
|---|---|---|
| *Population* | *Aged 16–17* | *Aged 20–24* |
| White | 89.0 | 23.9 |
| Black | 87.9 | 21.1 |
| Hispanic | 80.2 | 18.2 |
| Japanese | 96.2 | 48.0 |
| Chinese | 96.0 | 59.8 |
| Filipino | 92.8 | 27.1 |
| Korean | 94.9 | 40.1 |
| Asian Indian | 92.2 | 44.5 |
| Vietnamese | 90.2 | 41.8 |

*Source:* Gardner et al., 1985, p. 27.

*Are college admissions biased? A 1987 Stanford University subcommittee concluded that "unconscious biases" might be responsible for lower admission rates for Asian Americans (Salholz, 1987).*

restrict the percentage of Asian American students. In 1989, several selective universities announced plans to revise their admissions policies substantially to correct what was termed "possible unintentional discrimination" against Asian American students. However, in 1990, the Department of Education charged that the mathematics department of the University of California at Los Angeles (UCLA) had been guilty of racial discrimination in denying admission to five Asian American applicants. In addition, incidents of racial harassment on college campuses have begun to receive public attention (Commission on Civil Rights, 1992, pp. 41–44; Jaschik, 1990).

Even the positive stereotype of Asian American students as "academic stars" can be dysfunctional. Asian Americans who do only modestly well in school may face criticism from parents or teachers for their failure to conform to the "whiz kid" image, as Jeanne Park told us in "Listen to Their Voices." In fact, despite the model minority label, the high school dropout rate for Asian Americans is increasing rapidly. California's special program for low-income, academically disadvantaged students has a 30 percent Asian American clientele, and the proportion of Asian students in the programs is on the rise (F. Lee, 1991; Tachibana, 1990).

## The Work Force

The fact that Asian Americans as a group work in the same occupations as Whites suggests that they have been successful, but the pattern shows some differences (see Figure 12.3). Asian immigrants, like other minorities and immigrants before them, are found disproportionately in the low-paying service occupations. Even among these immigrants, though, substantial proportions are also concentrated at the top in professional, managerial, and executive positions. Yet, as we'll see, they rarely get to be at the very top. Among engineers, for example, they form a large minority of about 6 percent overall and almost 20 percent of engineers with doctorates. However they hit the "glass ceiling" (or some others say, "climb a broken ladder") before they reach management.

A comparison in Figure 12.3 of the occupational profiles of Asian American groups with those of Whites, Blacks, and Hispanics, shows that the middle or "other" category is smaller for most Asian American groups, particularly the Chinese Americans. Wen Lang Li describes the *bipolar occupational structure* of Chinese Americans (which also applies to other Asian American groups), referring to the clustering of workers in both high-paying professional occupations and low-paying service jobs with relatively few in between (1982, pp. 318–319; also see Sung, 1976, pp. 66–89). Figure 12.3 shows the bipolarity for native-born Chinese Americans, 45 percent of whom are employed in these extreme categories. The large numbers of service workers reflect the type of employment Asian Americans were restricted to in the past. The strong representation at the other end of the occupational ladder partly results from upward mobility but also from selective immigration. Many Asian Americans still find themselves in service occupations, just as their ancestors did.

The absence of Asian American executives from firms, too, indicates that success is not complete. Asian Americans have become middlemen in the economy, doing well in small businesses and modest agricultural ventures. While self-employed and managing their own businesses, Asian Americans' operations have been of very modest size. Because of the long hours, income from such a business may be below prevailing wage standards, so even when they are "business-owners," they may well still constitute cheap labor. Chinese restaurants, Korean American cleaning businesses and fruit and vegetable stores, and motels, gasoline stations, and newspaper-vending businesses operated by Asian Indians fall into this category.

Asian Americans are therefore typical of what sociologists refer to as *middlemen minorities*—groups that occupy middle positions rather than positions at the bottom of the social scale, where racial and ethnic minorities are typically located. Asian Americans involved in small businesses tend to maintain closer ties with the other Asian Americans than do individuals who join larger corporations. These ethnic owners generally hire other ethnics who are paid low wages in exchange for paternalistic benefits such as on-the-job training or even

**FIGURE 12.3** Occupational Status of Asian Americans Compared to Whites, Blacks, and Hispanics

Asian Americans are more likely to be found at either the top or bottom occupationally, compared with Whites and other minorities.

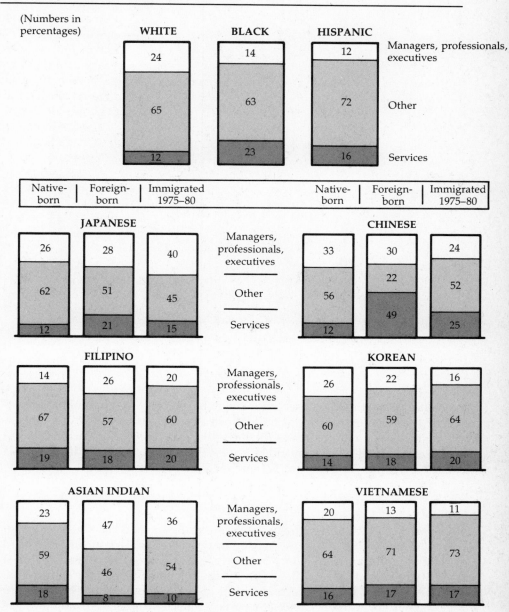

*Source:* Robert W. Gardner, Bryant Robey, and Peter C. Smith, "Asian Americans: Growth, Change, and Diversity," *Population Bulletin,* 40, Oct. (Washington, DC: Population Reference Bureau, Inc. 1985).

*Asian Americans are called middlemen minorities because they occupy middle positions, as does this Korean woman, pictured with a worker, who owns a garment shop in Portland, Oregon.*

assistance in creating their own middleman businesses. The present disproportionality of Asian Americans as middlemen, however, is the result of exclusion from other work, not of success (Blalock, 1967, pp. 79–84; Bonacich, 1988; Bonacich and Modell, 1981; Kim and Hurh, 1983; Kim et al., 1988; Model, 1992; Sue et al., 1985; Tang, 1991; for a different view, see E. Wong, 1985).

### Income

Wide publicity was given to the 1980 census figure of $23,600—the median family income of the six largest Asian American groups. This income exceeded the comparable figure for Whites by nearly $3,000. Once again, the model racial minority appeared successful. Yet these family income figures are misleading. Asian Americans live almost exclusively in urban areas, where incomes are higher. They are also concentrated in parts of the nation where prevailing wages are higher. For example, in the high-wage area of New York City, Asian Americans do have high incomes, yet a 1989 study found 30 percent living in poverty compared to 25 percent of non-Asians (Howe, 1989). Furthermore, several workers are more likely to contribute to that family income. As we have also seen Asian Americans are better educated than Whites, a situation which adds to their earning power.

Asian American family income approaches parity with Whites because of their greater achievement compared to Whites in formal schooling. However, this is because Asian Americans have more education as a group. Looking at specific educational levels, Whites earn more than their Asian counterparts of the same age. In 1990, Asian Americans' average earnings increased $2,300 each additional year, while Whites gained almost $3,000 (Commission on Civil Rights, 1988, pp. 110–113; O'Hare and Felt, 1991, p. 8).

Even more than income, Asian Americans differ from Whites in the way they mobilize their households. In 1980, 63 percent of Asian American families had two or more paid workers, compared to 55 percent for Whites. Rates per worker show earning power comparable to that of Whites. While figures for recent arrivals show low incomes, these reflect only paid labor, and a significant number of Asian Americans operate family businesses (the proportion of Korean Americans is three times that of Whites), in which all family members contribute long hours to make them a success. Moreover, the talk of "model minority" ignores the diversity among Asian Americans. There are rich and poor Japanese, rich and poor Filipinos, and rich and poor among all other Asian immigrants (D. A. Bell, 1985, pp. 28, 39; Gardner et al., 1985, pp. 33–35, 38–39).

## The Door Half Open

On June 19, 1982 in a Detroit lounge, two White males began arguing with a Chinese American, Vincent Chin. Believing him to be of Japanese descent, they blamed Chin for the dire straits of the American automobile industry. They chased Chin into the parking lot, where they repeatedly beat him with a baseball bat. He died four days later. Through plea-bargaining, the two laid-off automobile workers were found guilty of manslaughter. Much to the shock of the Asian American community, the accused killers of Vincent Chin were sentenced to three years' probation and fined $3,700 each. Subsequently they were tried in federal courts for interfering with Chin's civil rights. The one not directly involved in beating Chin was acquitted, and the other was sentenced to 25 years in prison (Commission on Civil Rights, 1986).

The Chin case is an extreme example of ways Asian Americans have been made to feel unwelcome in U.S. society, but it was not the most recent. In 1989 a Chinese American was killed in Raleigh, North Carolina by Whites mistaking him for a Vietnamese and wishing to avenge the war in South Asia. Organized hate groups killed an Asian Indian in New Jersey in 1987 and a Vietnamese boy in Houston, Texas in 1990. Most dramatically, a man with intense racial hatred, and for no other reason, entered a Stockton, California, elementary school in

1989 and killed four Indochinese children with an assault rifle. Asian Americans are certainly being victimized throughout the United States (Commission on Civil Rights, 1992, pp. 22–30).

The major problem with the model minority image is that social acceptance by the dominant group has been incomplete: their fellow citizens consider them still Asian, not quite 100 percent American. That a model minority has a positive stereotype does not necessarily indicate either that the group is assimilated into American society or that cultural pluralism will henceforth be tolerated. Racial slurs, job tension, and sporadic acts of violence continue. In 1984 and again in 1992, the United States Commission on Civil Rights investigated the growing acts of violence, particularly those directed at refugees. These have occurred in urban areas. Violence attracts the headlines, but subtler ways of reminding Asian Americans of their "place" persist, such as asking a fourth-generation American of Asian descent how he or she "learned to speak English so well" (Butterfield, 1985; Commission on Civil Rights, 1986, 1992).

An all-too-common incident shows how easily both prejudice and discrimination can surface. In northern Nevada the army arranged with a civilian contractor to handle the tricky business of clearing a 743-acre dump site, which for

*Despite the popular image of their success, Asian Americans still encounter prejudice and discrimination. Unwelcomed by their neighbors, Cambodians are left to survey their burned-out home in Revere, Massachusetts.*

30 years had received defective or leftover bombs. A Vietnam War veteran got the contract but could find no one locally to do the hot and sometimes dangerous work. Drawing upon his experiences with Indochinese he had known during the war, the contractor brought in 19 strong young Vietnamese and Laotians. Trouble soon began and escalated when some of the youths tried to attend a dance. Fights and attacks by Whites on their homes forced many of the Asian Americans to leave. Still faced with a job to be done, the contractor completed the project with a few remaining Asian Americans supplemented by Blacks and American Indians (Stanley, 1986).

At first glance, one might be puzzled to see a positive generalization such as "model minority" criticized. Why should the stereotype of adjusting without problems be a disservice to Asian Americans? This incorrect view serves to exclude Asian Americans from social programs and conceals unemployment and other social ills. When representatives of their groups do seek assistance for those in need, they are resented by those who are convinced of the model minority view. If a minority group is viewed as successful, it is unlikely that its members will be included in programs designed to alleviate problems they encounter as minorities. We have seen how important small businesses are in Asian Americans' economic life. Yet laws to support the development of small businesses often fail to include Asian Americans as an eligible minority. The stereotype means that the special needs of recent immigrants may be ignored. Although few foreign-born Asian Americans have yet succeeded, the positive stereotype reaffirms the American system of mobility: other minorities ought to achieve more merely by working the system. Viewed from the conflict perspective outlined in Chapter 1, this becomes yet another instance of "blaming the victims," for Blacks and Hispanics must be irresponsible if Asian Americans have succeeded (Commission on Civil Rights, 1980c; Hurh and Kim, 1986; Ichiyama, 1991; Ryan, 1976; Wong, 1991).

## ASIAN AMERICAN IDENTITY

Despite the diversity among groups of Asian Americans, they have spent generations being treated as a monolithic group. Out of similar experiences have come panethnic identities in which people share a self-image, as among African Americans or Whites of European descent.

Are Asian Americans finding a panethnic identity? It is true that in the United States extremely different Asian nationalities have been lumped together in past discrimination and present stereotyping. Asian Americans can be seen as having called upon unifying principles that are clearly products of contact with Whites. After centuries of animosity between ethnic groups in Asia, any feelings of community among Asian Americans must develop anew here; none are brought with them. We find some structural signs of a unitary identity: the development of Asian studies programs in various colleges and the growth organizations meant to represent all Asian Americans, such as the Asian Law Collective in Los Angeles (Greene, 1987; Trottier, 1981).

Despite these signs of a panethnic identity, compelling evidence shows that Americans of Asian descent define their identity by their status as a racial minority, their ancestry, and their participation in American society as contributing members. Asian American minorities immigrated at very different stages in United States history, so that their patterns of work, settlement, and family life have varied greatly. Even though all have been subjected to many of the same policies and laws, the ones that denied cultural differences have not been in effect for at least 30 years. Most Asian Americans can rejuvenate their ethnic culture because the traditions live on in the home countries—China, Japan, Korea, and the Philippines. Although the people of Indochina in the United States have trouble keeping in close contact with homelands, continuing immigration revives distinctive traditions that separate rather than unite Asian American groups.

## GLANCING BACK AND LOOKING AHEAD

Asian Americans seem to some people to be a cohesive, easy to understand group; but like other subordinate groups, Americans of Asian descent represent varied ways of life. They immigrated to the United States at different times, leaving behind a bewildering array of cultural experiences. Yet they have been expected to assimilate rather than preserve elements of this rich cultural heritage.

Asian Americans are a rapidly growing group, of well over 7 million. Despite striking differences among them, they are frequently viewed as if they came from one culture, all at once. They are characterized, too, as being a successful or model minority. Individual cases of success and some impressive group data do not imply, though, that the diverse group of peoples who make up the Asian American community are uniformly successful. Indeed, despite significantly high levels of formal schooling, Asian Americans earn far less than Whites with comparable education and continue to be victims of discriminatory employment practices (Commission on Civil Rights, 1980c, p. 24).

Who are the Asian Americans? This chapter has begun to answer that question by focusing on three of the larger groups—the Korean Americans, the Filipino Americans, and the Indochinese Americans. The ties of the United States to all three groups came out of warfare, but today these groups' descendants work to succeed in civilian society. Hawaii is a useful model because its relatively harmonious social relationships cross racial lines. Though not an interracial paradise, Hawaii does illustrate that, given proper historical and economic conditions, continuing conflict is not inevitable. Chinese and Japanese Americans, the subjects of Chapters 13 and 14, have experienced problems in American society despite striving to achieve economic and social equality with the dominant majority.

# KEY TERMS

**AJAs**   Americans of Japanese ancestry in Hawaii.

**bipolar occupational structure**   Clustering at the higher- and lower-paying ends of the occupational scale, with relatively few in the middle—a situation in which Chinese Americans, and other Asian Americans, find themselves.

**gook syndrome**   David Riesman's phrase describing Americans' tendency to stereotype Asians and to regard them as all alike and undesirable.

**Haoles**   Hawaiian term for Caucasians.

**ilchomose**   The 1.5 generation of Korean Americans—those who immigrated to the United States as children.

**inactivity rate**   Proportion of a population neither in school nor in the labor force.

**kye**   Rotating credit system used by Korean Americans to subsidize the start of businesses.

**middlemen minorities**   Groups such as Japanese Americans who typically occupy middle positions in the social and occupational stratification system.

**model or ideal minority**   A group that, despite past prejudice and discrimination, succeeds economically, socially, and educationally without resorting to political or violent confrontations with Whites.

# FOR FURTHER INFORMATION

Fred Cordova. *Filipinos: Forgotten Asian Americans*. Dubuque, IA: Demonstration Project for Asian Americans, 1983.

> A 232-page pictorial essay developed for the Demonstration Project for Asian Americans, covering the earliest immigrants of the eighteenth century through the 1960s.

Robert W. Gardner, Bryant Robey, and Peter C. Smith. *Asian Americans: Growth, Change, and Diversity*. Washington, DC: Population Reference Bureau, 1985.

> A concise (44 pages) demographic and social picture of contemporary Asian Americans.

Won Moo Hurh and Kwang Chung Kim. *Korean Immigrants in America: A Structural Analysis of Ethnic Confinement and Adhesive Adaptation*. Rutherford, NJ: Fairleigh Dickinson University Press, 1984.

> Besides presenting the results of the author's empirical research in the Korean American communities in Chicago and Los Angeles, this book offers theoretical and historical insights into this fast-growing group.

Harry H. L. Kitano and Roger Daniels. *Asian Americans: Emerging Minorities*. Englewood Cliffs, NJ: Prentice-Hall, 1988.

> This book provides an overview of all the major Asian American groups, drawing upon the latest available sociological research.

John F. McDermott, Jr., Wen-Shing Tseng, and Thomas W. Maretzki, eds. *People and Cultures of Hawaii*. Honolulu: University of Hawaii Press, 1980.

> Twelve articles provide an in-depth look at the major racial groups forming contemporary Hawaiian society.

Linda S. Parker. *Native American Estate: The Struggle over Indian and Hawaiian Lands*. Honolulu: University of Hawaii Press, 1989.

Parker, an attorney and a Cherokee, provides the similarities and differences between land claims of native Hawaiians and the American Indians.

Antonio J. A. Pido. *The Filipinos in America*. New York: Center for Migration Studies, 1986.

Sociologist Pido offers the most detailed examination of this significant minority group.

Parmatma Saran. *The Asian Indian Experience in the United States*. Cambridge, MA: Schenkman, 1985.

A fine analysis of a growing minority in the United States, this book includes ten in-depth interviews with representatives of the Asian Indian community.

Stanley Sue and Nathaniel Wagner. *Asian-Americans: Psychological Perspectives*. Palo Alto, CA: Science and Behavior Books, 1973.

An excellent collection of 27 articles on Chinese, Japanese, and Filipino Americans covering ethnic identity, crime and juvenile delinquency, mental illness, and family life.

Amy Tachiki, Eddie Wong, Franklin Odo, and Buck Wong, eds. *Roots: An Asian American Reader*. Los Angeles: Asian American Studies Center, UCLA, 1971.

This is the most thorough and up to date compact source on Asian Americans. The anthology covers subjects historically and sociologically and reflects the various viewpoints (conservative to radical) found in Asian American groups.

Ronald Takaki. *Strangers from a Different: A History of Asian Americans*. Boston: Little, Brown, 1989.

An overview of the historical experiences of the diverse groups among Asian Americans.

## Periodicals

*Amerasia Journal* (1971) is an interdisciplinary journal focusing on Asian Americans. Also useful is the *P/AAWHRC Review* (1981) published by the Pacific/Asian American Mental Health Research Center and The Contemporary Pacific (1989) published by the Center for Pacific Islands Studies. The *Journal of Social Issues* (1973), the *Civil Rights Digest* (1976), *Change* (1989), and the *California Sociologist* (1980) have devoted special issues to Asian Americans. Periodicals presenting contemporary coverage of Asian Americans include *Asian American Review* (1972), *Bridge* (1971), and *Jade* (1974). The *Aloha Aina* is a newspaper that represents the interests of native Hawaiians. *Asian Week*, published in San Francisco, stresses concerns and events in the Chinese American, Japanese American, and Korean American communities.

## Chapter Thirteen

# CHINESE AMERICANS: CONTINUED EXCLUSION

*Chapter Outline*

**Legacy of the Yellow Peril**

**Chinatowns Today**

Organizational Life

Social Problems

Beyond Chinatown

**Industry and Occupations**

**Family and Religious Life**

**Politics**

**Militancy and Resistance**

**Remnants of Prejudice and Discrimination**

**Glancing Back and Looking Ahead**

**Key Terms**

**For Further Information**

---

### ✳ HIGHLIGHTS ✳

Present-day Chinese Americans are both descendants of pre-Exclusion Act immigrants and of post-World War II immigrants. Non-Chinese Americans associate Chinese Americans with Chinatown and its glitter of tourism. This glitter, however, is a façade hiding the poverty of the *fobs* (the newly arrived Chinese) and the discontent of the American-born *jooksings*. As the Chinese American population has stabilized, patterns have begun to develop in such social institutions as the family, religion, and politics.

---

China, the most populous country in the world, has been a source of immigrants for centuries. Many nations have a sizable Chinese population, whose history may be traced back more than five generations. The United States is such a nation. Even before the great migration from Europe began, more than 100,000 Chinese were in America. Today the Chinese in America number 1.6 million.

## LEGACY OF THE YELLOW PERIL

In the nineteenth century, Chinese immigration was welcome because it brought to these shores needed, hard-working laborers. It was also unwelcome because it brought an alien culture the European settlers were unwilling to tolerate. As detailed in Chapter 4, the anti-Chinese mood led to passage of the Exclusion Act in 1882, which was not repealed until 1943. Even then, the group that lobbied for repeal, the Citizens Committee to Repeal Chinese Exclusion, encountered the old racist arguments against Chinese immigration.

The early years of Chinese settlement were very difficult for the immigrants. Not only did they meet prejudice and discrimination, but Chinese Americans had to overcome the handicap of *mutilated marriages*. Commonly men emigrated, leaving behind their wives and families for many, many years. It is hard to image the adjustment demanded of these pioneers from China, isolated in a hostile social environment (Kitano and Matsushima, 1981, p. 169; Lyman, 1986).

Very gradually, the Chinese were permitted to enter the United States after 1943. Initially, only 105 a year were allowed, then several thousand wives of servicemen were admitted, and later, college students were allowed to remain after finishing their education. Also, in 1943 for the first time, foreign-born Chinese Americans were eligible to become citizens. American-born Chinese had become citizens at birth since an 1898 Supreme Court ruling. Not until after the 1965 Immigration Act did Chinese immigrants arrive again in large numbers, almost doubling the Chinese-American community (R. Lee, 1960; Melendy, 1972).

Explicit in all but the most recent immigration legislation has been the fear that the Chinese, by their very numbers, threaten the American mainland. This fear of the *yellow peril* has gradually given way to other images. In the movies the sinister Dr. Fu Manchu (1929) was replaced by the benevolent Charlie Chan (various movies from 1931 to 1981 show Chinese Americans as law enforcers instead of lawbreakers). During the 1930s, China's heroic resistance to Japan won favor in America. Later, as a wartime ally, China again gained esteem in the eyes of many White Americans (Cosford, 1981; Oehling, 1980; Paik, 1971; Wu, 1972, pp. 213–214). The rise of a Communist government in China and the wars in Korea and Vietnam undoubtedly took their toll on attitudes toward Chinese. Opinion polls conducted before and after President Richard Nixon's trip to China, however, showed that the trip fostered a far more favorable image of the Chinese.

These changes in White attitudes have affected Chinese Americans themselves. In one study, Chinese-American students acknowledged increased pride in being Chinese after this country established closer ties with China. Some of this enthusiasm was political and took the form of support for the teachings of Mao Tse-tung. Generally, the new spirit has meant greater interest in the rich cultural heritage of the Chinese people. One sign of this spirit is the growth and popularity of Asian-American studies on college campuses (Ching, 1973; Huang, 1975; Kagiwada and Fujimoto, 1973).

The character of the Chinese-American community is the result of past and present immigration. That the Chinese brought not only their culture but their institutions as well is most apparent in the Chinatowns scattered throughout the United States.

## CHINATOWNS TODAY

Chinatowns represent a paradox. The casual observer or tourist sees them as thriving areas of business and amusement, bright in color and lights, exotic in sounds and sight. They have, however, large poor populations and face the problems associated with slums. All Chinatowns are in older, deteriorating sections of cities. The problems of Chinatowns include the entire range of social ills that infest low-income areas, but here the difficulties are greater because the glitter sometimes conceals the problems from the outsider and even from social planners. A unique characteristic of Chinatowns, distinguishing them from other ethnic enclaves, is the variety of social organizations they encompass.

### Organizational Life

The Chinese have a rich history of organizational membership, much of it carried over from China. Chief among such associations are the clans, or *tsu;* the benevolent associations, or *hui kuan;* and the secret societies, or *tongs*.

The clans, or *tsu,* that operated in Chinatown have their origins in the Chinese practice that families with common ancestors unite. Immigrant Chinese con-

*In the 1890s, San Francisco's Chinatown provided the only housing and much of the employment available to the area's Chinese population. Everyday life was closely governed by Chinese tradition.*

tinued to affiliate themselves with those sharing a family name, even if a blood relationship was absent. Even today some families dominate in certain cities—Toms in New York, Moys and Chins in Chicago, and Lees in Philadelphia, for example. Social scientists agree that the influence of clans is declining as young Chinese become increasingly acculturated. The clans in the past provided mutual assistance, a function increasingly taken on by government agencies. The strength of clans, although less today, points to the extended family's important role for Chinese Americans. Social scientists have found parent-child relationships stronger and more harmonious than those among non-Chinese Americans. Just as the clans have become less significant, however, so has the family structure undergone change. The differences between Chinese and non-Chinese family life are narrowing with each new generation (Li, 1976, pp. 315–317; Lyman, 1986; Sung, 1967, pp. 151–186).

The benevolent associations, or *hui kuan,* assist their members in adjusting to a new life. But instead of being organized along kinship ties like the clans, *hui kuan* membership is based on the person's district of origin in China. Besides extending assistance, the *hui kuan* give loans and settle disputes among their members. They have thereby exercised wide control over members. The various *hui kuan* are traditionally in turn part of an unofficial supragovernment in each city called the Six Chinese Companies, or the Chinese Consolidated Benevolent Association (CCBA). The president of the CCBA is sometimes called the mayor of a Chinatown. The CCBA often protects newly arrived immigrants from racism. The organization actively works to promote political involvement among Chinese Americans and to support the democracy movement within the People's Republic of China. Some members of the Chinese community have resented, and still resent, the CCBA's authoritarian ways and its attempt to speak as the sole voice of Chinatown.

The Chinese have also organized in *tongs*, or secret societies. The secret societies' membership was not determined by family or locale but by interest. Some have been political, attempting to resolve the dispute over which China (People's Republic of China or the Republic of China) is the legitimate government, and others have protested exploitation of Chinese workers. Other *tongs* provide illegal services, like drugs, gambling, and prostitution. Because they are secret, it is difficult to determine accurately the power of *tongs* today. Most observers concur that their influence has dwindled over the last 50 years and that their functions, even the illegal ones, have been taken over by elements not so closely tied to Chinatown.

Some conclusions can be reached about these various social organizations. First, all followed patterns created in traditional China. Even the secret societies had antecedents, organizationally and historically, in China. Second, all three types performed similar functions, providing mutual assistance and representing their members' interests to a sometimes hostile dominant group. Third, because all these groups had similar purposes and operated in the same locale, conflict among them was inevitable. Such conflicts were very violent in the nineteenth century, but in the twentieth century have tended to be political. Fourth, the old associations have declined in significance notably in the last 20 years as new arrivals come from urban metropolises of Asia, with little respect for the old rural ways to which such organizations were important. Fifth, when communicating with dominant society, all these groups have downplayed the problems that afflict Chinatowns. Only recently has the magnitude of social problems become known (Kessner and Caroli, 1981, p. 249; Lai, 1980; Lyman, 1974, pp. 29–46, 1986; Sherry, 1992; Sung, 1967; Weiss, 1974, pp. 33–39).

## Social Problems

It is a myth that Chinese Americans and Chinatowns have no problems. This false impression grows out of our tendency to stereotype groups as being all one way or the other, as well as the Chinese people's tendency to hide the problems they face.

In the late 1960s, White society became aware that all was not right in Chinatown. The awareness grew not from suddenly deteriorating living conditions in Chinese American settlements. Rather, it was because the various community organizations could no longer maintain the facade that hid Chinatown's social ills. Despite Chinese American's remarkable achievements as a group, the inhabitants suffered by most socioeconomic measures. Poor health, high suicide rate, run-down housing, rising crime rate, poor working conditions, inadequate care for the elderly, and weak union representation of laborers were a few of the documented problems.

These problems have grown more critical as Chinese immigration has increased. For example, the population density of San Francisco's Chinatown in the late 1980s was ten times that in the city as a whole. The problems faced by elderly Chinese are also exacerbated by the immigration wave because the proportion of older Chinese immigrants is more than twice that of older people among immigrants in general (Ikels, 1984).

Life in Chinatown, now and in the past, is particularly dreary for Chinese American women. Often above a restaurant will be dozens of women laboring over sewing machines 10 hours a day. According to one recent estimate, 75 percent of Chinatown's women work under such conditions. While newly arrived Chinese men who settle in Chinatown seem to fare better economically than those who locate elsewhere, the same is not true for women. Their labor is poorly rewarded and there is little advancement in the stratification system (Lum and Kwong, 1989; Spector, 1990; Zhou and Logan, 1989).

Not only have Chinatown communities grown in population, but they have also become more diverse. Toysanese, as spoken in Kwangtung Province, is

*Chinese immigrant women often work long days for little pay as piece-work garment workers in Chinatowns.*

no longer the only dialect spoken throughout America's Chinatowns. Several dialects are now found, thus dividing somewhat an enclave that once was more cohesive. The diversity has also led new Chinese firms to appeal to more varied preferences in cuisine, reading material, and so forth. Although to outsiders Chinatowns may appear "untouched by time," they are not (B. Wong, 1982).

Language, regardless of dialect, insulates many Chinese Americans from the rest of society. A third of adults whose primary language is Chinese have difficulty with English. Even 11 percent of people under 18 who speak Chinese have yet to master the dominant tongue of the United States. Theirs is like the difficulty Spanish-speaking people have today, and makes Chinatown an attractive place to live and seek employment, despite the social problems (Bureau of the Census, 1982a).

The barrier that Chinese Americans created around their settlements may have protected them in the past, but it now denies them needed social services. No Chinatown was designated to receive funds under the Model Cities Program, even though 150 cities developed such programs (Light and Wong, 1975, p. 1355). Nevertheless, Chinatowns have undergone urban renewal, although it has sometimes threatened their existence. In Honolulu, Chicago, New York City, and Philadelphia, massive relocation of residents caused by renovation in the 1960s and 1970s required many to leave Chinatown altogether. Chinatowns are not disappearing, however. Their future is unclear, but it will not be a reenactment of the past (Commission on Civil Rights, 1980a; Light and Wong, 1975; Lyman, 1974, pp. 151–157; Quan, 1986; Rice, 1977; Sung, 1967, pp. 130–150; F. Williams, 1976; M. Yee, 1972b).

## Beyond Chinatown

Not all Chinese live in a Chinatown; most have escaped them or have never experienced their social ills. Only one out of six Chinese Americans in Chicago and one out of four in New York actually lives in Chinatown (Griggs, 1974; Weiss, 1973). Of course, Chinatown remains important for many of those who live outside its borders, but not as important as in the past. For many Chinese movement out of Chinatown is itself a sign of success. Upon moving out, however, they soon encounter discriminatory real estate practices and White parents' fears about their children playing with Chinese American youths.

Yuan (1963) traces four hypothetical stages of the development of a Chinatown. The first is *involuntary choice,* the result of discrimination and prejudice. The next two stages are *defensive insulation,* the need for mutual help, followed by *voluntary segregation.* Yuan identifies a number of reasons why ethnic groups continue these enclaves voluntarily. The reasons include relatives' desire to live together, language difficulties, and the desire to preserve customs including religious faiths (in this case Buddhism). The final stage is *gradual assimilation,* as Chinese move out of Chinatown and increase their contact with White Americans. The upwardly mobile, acculturated Chinese American has gone beyond the first stages of *involuntary choice* and *defensive insulation.* To remain in Chinatown would be *voluntary segregation,* and so most opt for *gradual assimilation* and movement out of Chinatown. For the newly arrived Chinese immigrant, however, Chinatowns perform almost the same functions they did for immigrants a century ago.

Another development has taken place which emends Yuan's formulation. In certain locales, Chinese Americans have assimilated but moved together into new, middle-class Chinese communities. While suburban Los Angeles community Monterey Park has a distinct presence of Chinese Americans, new arrivals from Taiwan have caused it to be referred to as "Little Taipei" (see Figure 12.1).

As recently as 1960, Monterey Park had been 85 percent white, 12 percent Spanish-surname, and only 3 percent Asian and other minorities. Ten years later, Japanese represented 9 percent and Chinese 4 percent of the city's 49,166 residents. Since then the Chinese have become the largest ethnic group, totaling over 50 percent of the 61,000 residents in 1988. During the early 1980s, the city elected its first Chinese American mayor, Lilly Chen. But not everyone has welcomed the new Chinese presence. In 1986 a sign at a gas station near the city limits, for example, displayed two slanted eyes with the declaration: "Will the last American to leave Monterey Park please bring the flag" (Takaki, 1989, p. 425).

The movement of Chinese Americans out of Chinatowns parallels the movement of White ethnics out of similar enclaves. It signals the upward mobility of Chinese Americans coupled with their growing acceptance by the rest of the population. This mobility and acceptance are especially evident in occupations.

## INDUSTRY AND OCCUPATIONS

Asian Americans are employed in all aspects of the economy, and the Chinese are no exception. Superficially they appear to do very well. They have lower unemployment rates and are better represented in professional occupations than the population as a whole (refer to Figure 12.3).

The background of the contemporary Chinese-American labor force lies in Chinatown. For generations Chinese Americans were virtually barred from working elsewhere. The Chinese Exclusion Act was only one example of discriminatory legislation. Many laws were passed that made it difficult or more expensive for Chinese Americans to enter certain occupations. Whites did not object to Chinese in domestic service occupations or in the laundry trade, for White males were uninterested in such menial, low-paying work. When given the chance to enter better jobs, as they were in wartime, Chinese Americans jumped at the opportunities. Without those opportunities, however, many Chinese sought the relative safety of Chinatown. The tourist industry and the restaurants dependent on it grew out of the need for employment of the growing numbers of idle workers in Chinatown (R. Lee, 1960; Light, 1973, 1974).

The new immigration has added to Chinatown's economic dependence on tourism. First, new immigrants have difficulty finding employment outside

*The Chinese-American architect I. M. Pei has risen to the top of his profession in the United States. Here he is outside one of his sites, the East Building of the National Gallery of Art in Washington, D.C.*

Chinatown. Potential employers who are not Asian Americans are reluctant to hire Chinese Americans because they believe that many Asians are illegal aliens. Instead they hire a White job applicant to avoid the issue. Second, because many new immigrants speak little English, they flock to Chinatowns, where they are frequently employed as restaurant workers. The tourist industry is a double-edged sword. It does provide needed jobs, even if some are at substandard wages. But it also forces Chinatown to keep its problems quiet and not seek outside assistance. Slums do not attract tourists. This dilemma is being resolved by events beyond Chinese Americans' control. The tourist industry has not kept pace with the population growth of Chinatowns caused by immigration. Increasingly, outside assistance has to be sought, regardless of its consequences for the lights and glitter of Chinatown. This parallel between Chinese Americans and American Indians finds both groups depending on the tourist industry even at the cost of hiding problems.

## FAMILY AND RELIGIOUS LIFE

For all immigrant groups, family life and religious worship are major forces shaping their experience in the United States. Generally, assimilation takes its toll on distinctiveness in cultural behavior. Family life and religious practices are no exceptions. For Chinese Americans, the latest immigration wave has helped preserve some of the old ways. But traditional cultural patterns have undergone change even in the People's Republic of China, and so the situation is most fluid.

The modern Chinese American family is often indistinguishable from its White counterpart except in that it is victimized by prejudice and discrimination. Immigration policy has imposed two points of difference. In the past, Chinese American families had to overcome immigration laws forbidding entry by other family members left outside the United States. The reuniting of families that European immigrants took for granted was not possible. Because nineteenth-century Chinese immigrant men came for economic reasons, a significant imbalance of men over women resulted. Statistical data are lacking, but it appears that even though the sex ratio for Chinese Americans as a whole is now balanced, the imbalance remains in Chinatowns.

Where acculturation has taken hold less strongly, the legacy of China remains. Parental authority, especially the father's, is more absolute, and the extended family is more important than is typical in middle-class families. Divorce is rare and attitudes about sexual behavior tend to be strict because the Chinese generally frown upon public expressions of emotion. We noted earlier that in Chinatown, Chinese immigrant women survive a harsh existence. A related problem that is beginning to surface is domestic violence. While available data do not indicate Asian American men are different from other groups, their wives as a rule are less willing to talk about their plight and seek help. The nation's first shelter for Asian women was established in Los Angeles in 1981, but increasingly the problem is being recognized in more cities (Commission on Civil Rights, 1992, pp. 174–176; Rubien, 1989).

Change in family life is one of the most difficult cultural changes to accept. The questioning of parental authority by children that most Americans grudgingly accept is a painful experience for tradition-oriented Chinese. The youthful rebellion among Chinese Americans of the 1960s, discussed in the next section, was seen by many elders not simply as a challenge to their authority as business leaders. The political protest also amounted to a challenge to their authority as parents (Huang, 1976).

As is true of the family and other social organizations, religious life has its antecedents in China, which has no single Chinese faith. In China, religious beliefs tend to be much more accommodating than Christian beliefs are: one can be a Confucian, Buddhist, and Taoist at the same time. Consequently, when they came to the United States immigrants found it easy to accept Christianity, even though doing so ultimately meant rejecting their old faiths. In the United States, a Christian cannot also be a Taoist. As a result, with each generation, Chinese Christians depart from traditional ways. About 20 percent of Chinese Americans are Christian, almost two-thirds of those are Protestant.

Although traditional Chinese temples are maintained in most Chinese American communities, many exist only as museums and few are places of worship with growing memberships. Religion is still a source of community attachment, but it is in the Protestant Chinese church, not in the temple (Hsu, 1971, pp. 52–65; Lai, 1980, p. 229; R. Lee, 1960, pp. 276–98; Lyman, 1974, pp. 46–48, 1986).

## *POLITICS*

In the past, Chinese Americans have mostly been interested in the events of their home—People's Republic of China, Republic of China (Taiwan), and Hong Kong. Party politics for many brings to mind the Communist party and a deep distrust for government. It has been proven difficult for some to make the transition to American political systems. However, as the number of United

*A polling place in Chicago's Chinatown area. While Chinese Americans have not been elected to office often, they remain a potential force in politics in many areas of the nation.*

States-born Chinese Americans has grown, the relative lack of interest in American politics has begun to change. The process has been gradual.

Since relatively few Chinese Americans have been politically active, their role in partisan politics is difficult to assess. Those who have long been in the United States appear more likely to follow Republican candidates, remembering that party's strong anti-People's Republic of China stand of the 1960s. More recent immigrants tend to be attracted to the Democratic Party's support of social welfare measures aimed at the poor and unemployed. In San Francisco, where there are proportionately more Chinese Americans (15 percent of the population) than in any other major city, they are split 60 percent Democrat and 40 percent Republican. Evidence suggests, however, that when a Chinese American is on the ticket, ethnic unity takes over and Chinese Americans will cross over to support their fellow citizen. Indeed, Chinese American candidates receive significant financial help from other Chinese Americans living outside the area they seek to represent. Delaware Lieutenant Governor S. B. Woo, who unsuccessfully ran for governor in 1988, raised 70 percent of his campaign funds from Chinese Americans outside his state.

Newly emerging politicians from the Chinese American community face tough scrutiny. Will they speak out on ethnic issues? If so, they may confront power interests within the minority community. For example, housing advocates want politicians to fight against zoning law changes and highrise developments that real estate interests support. Similarly, union activists want candidates who take policy positions against Chinese restaurant and factory owners to combat violations of labor laws and improve sweatshop-like conditions.

At least six factors have been identified that explain why Chinese Americans, and to a large extent Asian Americans in general, have not been more active in politics.

1. To become a candidate means to take risks, bring on criticism, be assertive, and willing to extol your virtues. These are traits alien to Chinese culture.
2. Older people remember when the discrimination was blatant and tell others to "be quiet" and not attract attention.
3. As noted earlier, many recent immigrants have no experience with democracy and arrive with a general distrust of government.
4. Like many new immigrant groups, Chinese Americans have concentrated on getting ahead economically and educating their children rather than thinking in terms of the larger community.
5. The careers pursued by the brightest tend to be in business and science, rather than law or public administration, and, therefore, provide poor preparation for politics.
6. Chinatowns notwithstanding, Chinese and other Asian American groups are dispersed and cannot control an election of even local candidates.

Yet Asian Americans are regarded as a future political force in the United States. Frustrated by conventional politics, whether headed by Chinese Americans or not, some Chinese Americans seek to change the status quo through more militant means (Gross, 1989).

## MILITANCY AND RESISTANCE

Younger Chinese Americans, unlike their elders, are not content to be grateful for what they have been given in exchange for their labor, but expect the full rights and privileges of citizenship. More than their parents, they refuse to tolerate continued discrimination in employment (Montgomery, 1974; Wu, 1972, pp. 213–269).

In the 1960s, Chinese American students and their peers started to speak out against injustice. The activity was first noticeable on college campuses in the western states but soon involved noncollege youths in Chinatowns. Some Chinese Americans created reform movements, like Leway, Inc., founded in 1967 in San Francisco. *Leway*, which stood for *legitimate way*, tried to improve opportunities for youths through self-help and community contributions. Local police and the Chinese Chamber of Commerce gave this innovative approach little chance to succeed. Disgruntled, radical Leway members left Leway in 1969 to form the Red Guards. They took their lead from the Red Guards in China, who were purging that country of outside influences. The Red Guards of San Francisco's Chinatown similarly wished to purify, by eliminating what they regarded as the excessive control Chinese elders and White outsiders

*The Chinese community in the United States demonstrated their anger over the People's Republic of China's crushing student protests at Tiananmen Square in Beijing in 1989.*

exercised over Chinatown. The traditional Chinese elders were called China-town's "Uncle Tongs." The Red Guard movement lasted only until 1971, and did not attract the active support of large numbers of youth (R. Chin, 1971; M. Yee, 1972b).

Another problem has been the rise in gang activity since the mid-1970s. Battles between opposing gangs have taken their toll, including the deaths of some innocent bystanders. Some trace the gangs to the *tongs* and thus are an aspect, admittedly destructive, of groups trying to maintain cultural tradition. However, a more realistic interpretation is that Chinese American youth from lower classes are not part of that "model minority." Upward mobility is not in their future. Alienated, angry, and with prospects of low-wage work in restaurants and laundries, they turn to gangs like Ghost Shadows and Flying Dragons, and force Chinese American shopkeepers to give them extortion money. Asked why he became involved in crime, one gang member replied, "To keep from being a waiter all my life" (Takaki, 1989, p. 431; also see Butterfield, 1985; *Seward World*, 1988).

Chinese American youths cannot be typed any more than the adolescent population of any minority group can. Two segments of the new generation stand out, however: those sometimes referred to as the *jook-sings* and those called the *fobs*. *Jook-sing* is the hollow part of a bamboo pole, the name implying that an individual is Chinese on the outside but hollow in cultural knowledge. The *jook-sings* are American-born youths who are acculturated and yet rejected because of a bigotry in wider society. They may either see their ethnicity as a handicap and reject it or have pride in their Chinese heritage in a society that tends to look down upon it. The *fobs*, for *fresh off the boat*, are the newly arrived immigrant youths. They adapt differently, of course, depending on whether they come from westernized Hong Kong or rural China. The less acculturated immigrants face the double barrier of racial prejudice and adjustment to an alien culture (Chan, 1986; Chen, 1970; Kuo and Lin, 1977; W. Miller, 1977; Nee and DeBary, 1973; Rice, 1977; Watanabe, 1973).

Some Chinese Americans wish to maintain their cultural identity, whereas others are eager to be as American as possible. But as a group Chinese Americans are not as silent a minority as they once were.

## REMNANTS OF PREJUDICE AND DISCRIMINATION

The Fu Manchu image may be gone, but the replacement is not much better. In the popular television series, "Kung Fu," the only Chinese American able to win fights was half-White, a Eurasian. In *Dr. No*, the title character, an Asian, threatened everyone's hero, James Bond. In the Oscar-nominated movie *Chinatown*, the Chinese played servants, and the leading character spoke derisively of Chinese sexual behavior (F. Chin, 1974). The 1980s continued with disturbing portrayals of Chinese Americans in movies such as *Sixteen Candles* and *Big Trouble in Little China*, which seemed to overshadow Japanese American Noriyuki "Pat" Morita's sensitive roles in the *Karate Kid* movies (Fong-Torres, 1986; Hwang, 1985).

Chinese Americans are ignored or misrepresented in history books. Even past mistakes are repeated. When the transcontinental railroad was completed in Utah in 1869, Chinese workers were barred from attending the ceremony. Their contribution is now well known, one of the stories of true heroism in the West. However, in 1969 when Secretary of Transportation John Volpe made a speech marking the hundredth anniversary of the event, he neglected to mention the Chinese contribution. He exclaimed, "Who else but Americans could drill tunnels in mountains 30 feet deep in snow? Who else but Americans could chisel through miles of solid granite? Who else but Americans could have laid 10 miles of track in 12 hours?" (P. Yee, 1973, p. 100). The Chinese contribution was once again forgotten (Hsu, 1971, p. 104; Huang, 1976).

Although they avoid obvious anti-Black slurs, Whites somehow continue to see anti-Chinese slurs as less harmful. Pekin High School in Illinois called its athletic teams the "Chinks" and featured a student dressed up as a "Chinaman" who paraded at halftime at football games and struck a gong when the team scored. Despite pressure in 1974 from the Organization of Chinese Americans and the Illinois Department of Human Relations and brief consideration of more neutral nicknames, the school retained the "Chinks" nickname until 1980, when they finally became the Dragons (Holmberg, 1974; Sloan, 1980).

Chinese Americans generally believe that prejudice and discrimination have decreased in the United States, but subtle reminders remain. Third-generation Chinese Americans feel insulted when they are told, "You speak English so well." Adopting new tactics, Chinese Americans have organized to fight racist and exclusionary practices. Organized in 1974, the Asian Americans for Fair Employment work for better job opportunities for Asian Americans, especially in the building trades. Discriminatory treatment causes Chinese Americans to take renewed interest in their cultural heritage (Lem, 1976). Chinese Americans are called to reaffirm their loyalty in ways Whites are not, as a bitter veteran recounts in "Listen to Their Voices."

Maintaining links with a tradition different from that of the dominant group is difficult. In 1971, a court-ordered busing plan caused Chinatown residents to be transported to other neighborhoods in San Francisco. Many parents expressed concern when programs tailored to their children's needs and cultural background were dropped. A subsequent Supreme Court decision in 1974 (*Lau* v. *Nichols*) ruled that San Francisco must provide special classes for non-English-speaking youth. But this decision did not affect the virtual elimination of special Chinese cultural classes. In response, some Chinese Americans created "freedom schools," which often took a decidedly anti-White approach. Educating Chinese American youth is another example of the difficulty of maintaining pluralism in an assimilationist society (T. Wolfe, 1969; M. Yee, 1972a, 1972b).

Marriage statistics also illustrate the problem. At one time 29 states prohibited or severely regulated marriages between Asians and non-Asians. Today intermarriage, though not typical, is certainly more common, and more than one-

## ❖ *LISTEN TO THEIR VOICES* ❖

### *Are Asian GIs Gooks?*

#### *Sam Choy*

*The following first-person account of one Asian's experiences in the army during the war in Vietnam, is told through an interview with a former GI, a 20-year-old New York City youth named Sam Choy. The interview appeared in* Getting Together, *the New York Chinatown-based youth publication, and was conducted by representatives of the youth group, I Wor Kuen.*

*Where were you stationed?*

Duk Foi, a small supply post. I don't even know where it was; they never told us. I was with a combat unit, up next to the front lines. I was a heavy-equipment operator. They didn't want me to be on the front lines; they didn't trust me.

*Were you the only Asian in the unit?*

Yes.

*What kind of treatment did you receive?*

Well, a couple of days after, the Viet Cong started shelling us. Then the other GIs started making comments about me looking like the Viet Cong.

*How did you react?*

I didn't do nothing. I was just doing a job. This went on and got worse. They asked me what I was doing on their side; I told them I was just doing a job. I didn't have any political awareness.

*When was this harassment the worst?*

Right after the GIs got back from patrol. They really gave it to me. They started asking me where I was born, where my parents were born, if I was a Communist. They even asked me

what I thought about China. They thought I could turn traitor any time.

*What kind of job did you have at the base?*

They made me the cook. The mess sergeant was mean. He made me do all these things and kept bossing me around. I couldn't take it any more. One day I got so mad I threw a knife on the floor after he called me a Chink. He ordered me to pick it up. I refused. He started yelling at me. He kept yelling all kinds of remarks, like "slant-eyed Chinaman," "gook," "Chink," and he went on and on. I just got madder. So he went to get the staff sergeant. I went to get my rifle. I waited for them to come back and when they did they started to sweet talk me to give my rifle up. I said, "If you come any closer, I'll shoot." I fired a warning shot and they froze. Then I left the tent and the corporal came after me. He tried to grab my rifle. I fired once and he froze; he was scared as hell. Then the MPs came and I shot at them, too. I had bad eyes so I missed. By this time I was near the perimeter of the base and was thinking of joining the Viet Cong; at least they would trust me. But the MPs sent for tanks and armored carriers to come after me, and I got caught.

They beat me up and sent me to the hospital for observation. They knew they were wrong but they put me up for court-martial.

*Did you have any friends to help you out?*

No, the only friends I had were the blacks. They couldn't do anything, though, they were just regular GIs and even if they did, they'd get in trouble. They used to protect me from the white GIs when they picked on me. Like, I took showers only with the blacks for protection and because they were my friends.

*How long was it before the court-martial?*

They sent me to Long Binh stockade first. That's where all the GI dissenters were.

*How was it?*

The place was bad. The conditions were unfit for animals. Everybody was in a cage. Most of the dissenters were black; they were there because they refused to fight any more. The place was so bad they had a riot. It lasted all night and into the morning. The black GIs were beating up the guards and smashing everything. They were getting back for all the treatment they had been given. The army had to surround the camp before it stopped.

*How long were you in Long Binh?*

Four months. They were preparing my case.

*Where did your court-martial take place?*

Pleiku, Vietnam.

*Who were the judges?*

They had a board of majors and colonels.

*How long was the court martial?*

Three hours.

*What was the charge?*

Aggravated assault and culpable negligence.

*Did anybody know what was happening to you?*

No, they censored all my mail. I couldn't even tell my parents.

*What happened next?*

The army sentenced me to eighteen months of hard labor at Fort Leavenworth. There was a maximum sentence of seven years but they made a deal with me. If I pleaded guilty then I would only get eighteen months.

*How was Leavenworth?*

Fort Leavenworth is the worst place in the world. They beat me up every day, like a time clock. It makes me mad and sick to think about it. Right now, I don't want to think about it any more.

*When did you get out?*

I only served nine months. I kept quiet, so they discharged me.

*Is there anything else?*

One thing: I want to tell all the Chinese kids that the army made me sick. They made me so sick that I can't stand it.

From Cheng-Tsu Wu, *Chink!* (New York: Meridian, 1972), pp. 267–269.

---

fourth of Chinese Americans under 24 marry someone not Chinese. Endogamy, marrying within the same group, has decreased and out-group marriage is no longer the rare exception. Among all three major groups of Asian Americans, the Chinese, Japanese, and Filipinos, youths are more likely to marry a member of another racial group than was true of the older generation, partly because a greater proportion of the older generation was foreign born and already married before arrival (Department of Health, Education, and Welfare, 1974b, p. 49; Huang, 1975, pp. 8–10; C. Lee, 1965, p. 135).

The increased intermarriage indicates growing White acceptance of Chinese Americans. It also suggests that Chinese cultural ties are weakening and that the traditionally strong authority of Chinese parents is shrinking. Dating attitudes and sex roles of each successive generation have become more Americanized. As happened with the ways of life of European immigrants, the traditional norms are being cast aside for those of the host society. In one sense, these changes make Chinese Americans more acceptable, less alien to Whites. Increased interaction with other Americans can also increase the likelihood that they will face hostility (Fong, 1965, 1973).

Acceptance is not complete. Chinese Americans are still excluded in an informal, extralegal fashion from several labor unions on the grounds that they are too short. One critic has pointed out the inappropriateness of this justification since the Chinese constructed the Great Wall in China and worked on the transcontinental railway in the West (Lyman, 1974, p. 139). Even American-educated professionals of Chinese ancestry are not welcomed by many non-Chinese. Some Chinese Americans have responded by arguing against accepting Anglo ways and by being more Chinese. Most continue to accept the American way of life, but speak out more militantly against the examples of racism that remain.

## GLANCING BACK AND LOOKING AHEAD

It would be simple to say that Asian Americans are one group, easy to understand. But like other minority groups, Americans of Asian descent represent a variety of ways of life. They differ in country of origin and length of residency in the United States. As will be further apparent in Chapter 14, Asian Americans share little except the part of the world from which their ancestors came and the subordinate role they have been forced into in this society.

The Chinese American experience illustrates the efforts to which a group will go to overcome second-class citizenship. Barred from most high-paying occupations, Chinese Americans sought to maximize what opportunities were left. Because Chinese Americans were faced with housing restrictions and bigotry, Chinatowns became havens of escape from anti-Chinese hostility. Social organizations like the clans and the benevolent associations provided valuable help to both the newly arrived immigrant and life-long resident of Chinese ancestry.

The future for the Chinese American community is uncertain. Reduced prejudice and an end to overt discrimination will mean a better life for individuals. As a group, Chinese Americans have undergone great changes. Chinatowns are now slowly shedding their glitter so that finally, perhaps too late, they will receive governmental assistance. The continued influx of Chinese immigrants brings a mixture of English-speaking professionals who head for suburbia and non-English-speaking laborers looking about for any kind of employment, however menial. The problems are complex and the prospects unclear. Although it seems that for at least the present this country is more willing than ever before to accept Chinese Americans as people and not as aliens, full acceptance has not taken place and is not necessarily inevitable.

## KEY TERMS

**defensive insulation** Social structures for mutual help as found in enclaves like Chinatowns.

**fobs** Recent immigrants from China, fresh off the boat.

**hui kuan** Chinese American benevolent associations organized on the basis of the district of the immigrant's origin in China.

**jook-sings** Chinese Americans who fail to carry on the cultural traditions of China or maintain a sense of identification with other Chinese Americans.

**mutilated marriages** The separations of early Chinese immigrants, most of whom were male and had to leave behind their wives and children.

**tongs** Chinese American secret associations.

**tsu** Clans established along family lines and forming a basis for social organization by Chinese Americans.

**yellow peril** Generalized prejudice toward people and customs of Asian background.

## FOR FURTHER INFORMATION

Frank Ching. *900 Years in the Life of a Chinese Family*. New York: William Morrow, 1988.

A journalist of *The Wall Street Journal* traces his ancestry through many generations, offering a biographical tour of Chinese history.

Roger Daniels. *Asian America: Chinese and Japanese in the United States since 1850*. Seattle: University of Washington Press, 1988.

A historical analysis of two of our largest Asian American minorities.

Francis L. K. Hsu. *The Challenge of the American Dream: The Chinese in the United States*. Belmont CA: Wadsworth, 1971.

This book is especially strong in its treatment of the Chinese backgrounds of the life of Chinese Americans.

Ivan H. Light. *Ethnic Enterprise in America: Business and Welfare Among Chinese, Japanese, and Blacks*. Berkeley: University of California Press, 1973.

Light gives an exhaustive account of the differences in entrepreneurship among Black, Chinese, and Japanese Americans. He also discusses the development and importance of a cohesive ethnic community.

Stanford M. Lyman. *Chinese Americans*. New York: Random House, 1974.

The best sociological study of Chinese Americans, this book deals not only with the Chinese backgrounds, but with the anti-Chinese movement, the Chinatown ghetto, and the rebelliousness among youths.

Stanford M. Lyman. *Chinatown and Little Tokyo*. Millwood, NY: Associated Faculty Press, 1986.

A useful comparison of Chinese and Japanese immigrants to the United States with emphasis on social organizations and kinship patterns.

Ruthanne Lum McCunn. *Chinese American Portraits*. San Francisco: Chronicle Books, 1988.

In this excellently illustrated book are profiled Chinese Americans who reflect their diversity, ranging from railroad baron to cowboy to immigrant.

Bernard P. Wong. *Chinatown: Economic Adaptation and Ethnic Identity of the Chinese*. New York: Holt, Rinehart and Winston, 1982.

Anthropologist Wong provides a detailed, systematic view of New York City's Chinatown, emphasizing its occupational and family structure.

Jade Snow Wong. *Fifth Chinese Daughter*. New York: Harper and Row, 1950.

In a vivid autobiographical account of growing up in San Francisco's Chinatown from the 1920s to 1940s, Wong underscores the difficulty of reconciling the conflicts between one's own culture and that of dominant society.

Cheng-Tsu Wu. *Chink!* New York: Meridian, 1972.

This documentary history of anti-Chinese prejudice has a fine concluding chapter outlining the extent of hostility.

## Chapter Fourteen

# JAPANESE AMERICANS: OVERCOMING EXCLUSION

*Chapter Outline*

**Early Immigration**

**The Anti-Japanese Movement**

**The Wartime Evacuation**

Executive Order 9066

The Concentration Camps

The Road Out

The Evacuation: What Does It Mean?

**Postwar Success**

**Assimilation Accomplished, Almost**

**Comparing Chinese and Japanese American Experiences**

**Glancing Back and Looking Ahead**

**Key Terms**

**For Further Information**

### ❋ HIGHLIGHTS ❋

Japanese Americans encountered discrimination and ill treatment during the early twentieth century. Like the Chinese, their employment opportunities were severely limited. The involuntary wartime evacuation of 113,000 Japanese Americans was the result of sentencing without charge or trial. Merely to be of Japanese ancestry was reason enough to be suspected of treason. For the *evacuees*, the economic effect of the evacuation camps was devastating and the psychological consequences were incalculable. A little more than a generation later, Japanese Americans have done very well, with high educational and occupational attainment. Assimilation is incomplete because Japanese Americans are still readily identified as Japanese Americans, not just Americans.

The Japanese American experience in the United States is a study of contrasts. Not once but twice has the government launched a conscious effort to exclude the Japanese from American society, first by not letting them enter the country and later by placing those already here in concentration camps. Both episodes occurred well after slavery was abolished and the American-Indian/cavalry wars were over, and they cannot be written off as caused by ignorance of people long ago.

The Japanese American story does not end with another account of oppression and hardship. Today Japanese Americans have achieved success by almost any standard. We must qualify, however, the progress that *Newsweek* (1971) once billed as their "Success Study: Outwhiting the Whites." First, it is easy to forget that the achievements made by several generations of Japanese Americans were accomplished by overcoming barriers American society created, not because Japanese Americans had been welcomed. Many, if not most, acculturated, successful Japanese Americans are still not wholeheartedly accepted into the dominant group's inner circle of social clubs and fraternal organizations, or into the family. Second, Japanese Americans today may represent a stronger indictment of society than economically oppressed Blacks, American Indians, and Hispanics. There are few excuses apart from racism that Whites can use to explain why they continue to look upon Japanese Americans as different, as "them."

## EARLY IMMIGRATION

The nineteenth century was a period of vast social change for Japan, the end of feudalism and the beginning of rapid urbanization and industrialization. Only a few pioneering Japanese came to the United States prior to 1885, for Japan prohibited emigration. After 1885 the numbers remained small relative to the great immigration from Europe at the time (see Table 14.1).

Japanese Americans sharply distinguish among themselves according to the number of generations an individual's family has been in the United States. Generally each succeeding generation is more acculturated; each is successively less likely to know any Japanese. The *Issei* (pronounced "EE-say") are the first generation, the immigrants born in Japan. Their children, the *Nisei* ("NEE-say") are American born. The third generation, the *Sansei* ("SAHN-say) must go back to their grandparents to reach their roots in Japan. The *Yonsei* ("YAWN-say") are the fourth generation. Because Japanese immigration is relatively recent, these four terms describe virtually the entire contemporary Japanese American population. Some *Nisei* were sent by their parents to Japan for schooling and to have marriages arranged. Such people, referred to as the *Kibei* ("KEE-boy") are expected to be less acculturated than other *Nisei*. These terms are sometimes used rather loosely, and occasionally *Nisei* is used to describe all Japanese Americans. But we will use them as they were intended, to differentiate the four groups.

## THE ANTI-JAPANESE MOVEMENT

The Japanese who immigrated to the United States in the 1890s took jobs as laborers at low wages with poor working conditions. Their industriousness in such circumstances made them popular with employers but unpopular with unions and other employees. The Japanese had the mixed blessing of arriving just as bigotry toward the Chinese had been dignified with legislation in the harsh Chinese Exclusion Act of 1882. For a time after the act, the *Issei* were

---

**TABLE 14.1**   Chinese American and Japanese American Population, 1860–1990

Although Chinese and Japanese patterns of immigration to the United States have been quite different, the two groups have reached relatively similar proportions of the United States population.

| Year | Chinese Americans | Japanese Americans |
|------|-------------------|--------------------|
| 1860 | 34,933 | — |
| 1880 | 105,465 | 148 |
| 1900 | 89,863 | 24,326 |
| 1930 | 74,954 | 138,834 |
| 1950 | 117,629 | 141,768 |
| 1960 | 198,958 | 260,059 |
| 1960* | 237,292 | 464,332 |
| 1970* | 435,062 | 591,290 |
| 1980* | 806,027 | 700,747 |
| 1990* | 1,640,000 | 848,000 |

*Includes Alaska and Hawaii
Source: Ng, 1991.

*Anti-Japanese sentiment began as the number of immigrants from Japan increased. About 120,000 Japanese Americans were in the United States during the 1920s (and about 80,000 of these in California) when these signs appeared on a Los Angeles house.*

welcomed by powerful business interests on the West Coast. They replaced the dwindling number of Chinese laborers in some industries, especially agriculture. In time, however, anti-Japanese feeling grew out of the anti-Chinese movement. The same Whites made the same charges about the yellow peril. Eventually a stereotype developed of Japanese Americans as lazy, dishonest, and untrustworthy.

The attack on Japanese Americans concentrated on limiting their ability to earn a living. In 1913, California enacted the Alien Land Act, amended to make it still stricter in 1920. The act prohibited anyone who was ineligible for citizenship from owning land and limited leases to three years. Initially, federal law had allowed only Whites to be citizens but was amended to include Blacks in 1870 and some Native Americans in 1887. What about Asians? They had not been mentioned in the amendments. The Supreme Court repeatedly saw this not as an oversight, but as a constitutional prohibition against citizenship for Asians. As Chapter 13 noted, this omission was finally remedied for the Chinese in 1943. Those born in Japan were excluded from citizenship until 1952.

The anti-Japanese laws permanently influenced the form Japanese American business enterprise was to take. In California, the land laws drove the *Issei* into cities. In the cities, however, government and union restrictions prevented large numbers from entering available jobs, leaving self-employment. Japanese, more than other groups, ran hotels, grocery stores, and other medium-sized businesses. Although this specialty limited their opportunities to advance, it did give the urban Japanese Americans a marginal position in the expanding economy of cities (Bonacich, 1972; Light, 1973, pp. 8–10; Lyman, 1986).

Three aspects of the anti-Japanese movement distinguish it from the anti-Chinese movement. First, and most obvious, is the difference in time. The anti-Chinese efforts preceded and provided the groundwork for the anti-Japanese movement. Second, Japanese Americans spoke out more vehemently against the racist legislation than their Chinese American counterparts. The *Issei* and *Nisei* constantly organized demonstrations, led boycotts to counter boycotts of Japanese products, published books, and enlisted the support of sympathetic Whites. Third, Japan took a more active interest in what was happening to its citizens in the United States than did China. The discriminatory legislation that the United States and especially California consistently passed later strengthened the hand of militarists in Japan who wished to attack the United States. Japan's attack on Pearl Harbor immediately made the Japanese Americans the most feared group of people (Chuman, 1976; Daniels, 1967, p. 23; Ichioka, 1988; Kimura, 1988; Mosley, 1966, p. 69; Yoneda, 1971).

## THE WARTIME EVACUATION

The decades following the end of immigration in 1924 were not easy for Japanese Americans. The *Issei* and their *Nisei* children adapted to a new way of life while preserving aspects of their ancestral home. Whether they lived in the "Little Tokyos" of the West Coast or on farms, the obligation they felt to help fellow Japanese Americans was strong. The Japanese Association was strictly an *Issei* organization, with the motto "Don's become too American too quickly." In 1930 the *Nisei* founded the Japanese American Citizens League (JACL), which is still influential among Japanese Americans today. The JACL tended to be more assimilationist than the Japanese Association, and grew in strength as the *Nisei* grew in numbers. Generally such groups represented a conscious effort to become acceptable to Whites. Few were under the delusion that this change could be completely accomplished. If they were, the wartime evacuation proved how wrong they were (Hosokawa, 1982a).

Japan's attack on Pearl Harbor on December 7, 1941, began World War II for the United States and a painful tragedy for the *Issei* and *Nisei*. Almost immediately public pressure mounted to "do something" about the Japanese Americans living on the West Coast. Many feared that if Japan attacked the mainland, Japanese Americans would fight on behalf of Japan, making a successful invasion a real possibility. Pearl Harbor was followed by successful invasions of one Pacific island after another. A Japanese submarine actually attacked a California oil tank complex early in 1943.

Rumors mixed with racist bigotry rather than facts explain the events that followed. Japanese Americans on Hawaii were alleged to have cooperated in the attack on Pearl Harbor by using signaling devices to assist the pilots from Japan.

Front-page attention was given to pronouncements by the secretary of the navy that Japanese Americans had the greatest responsibility for Pearl Harbor. Newspapers covered in detail FBI arrests of Japanese Americans allegedly engaging in sabotage by assisting the attackers. They were accused of poisoning drinking water, cutting sugar cane fields to form arrows directing enemy pilots to targets, and blocking traffic along highways to the harbor. None of these charges was substantiated, despite thorough investigations. It made no difference. In the 1940s, as it had been a generation earlier, the treachery of the Japanese Americans was a foregone conclusion regardless of evidence to the contrary (Kimura, 1988; Lind, 1946, pp. 43–46; ten Brock et al., 1954, pp. 68–96).

## Executive Order 9066

On February 13, 1942, President Franklin Roosevelt signed Executive Order 9066. It defined strategic military areas in the United States and authorized removal from those areas any people considered threats to national security. Subsequent congressional action, with bills often passed overwhelmingly by a voice vote, designated General John DeWitt to make the western portions of California, Washington, Oregon, and part of Arizona "militarily secure."

The events that followed were tragically simple. All people on the West Coast of at least one-eighth Japanese ancestry were taken to assembly centers for transfer to concentration camps. These camps are identified in Figure 14.1. This order covered 90 percent of the 126,000 Japanese Americans on the mainland. Of those evacuated, two-thirds were citizens and three-fourths were under 25. Ultimately 120,000 Japanese Americans were in the camps. Of mainland Japanese Americans, 113,000 were evacuated but to those were added 1,118 "evacuated" from Hawaii, 219 voluntary residents (Caucasian spouses, typically), and most poignantly of all, the 5,981 who were born in the camps (Weglyn, 1976). What must it have been like for a Japanese American in 1942? In "Listen to Their Voices," we hear of those memories.

The evacuation order did not arise from any court action. No trials took place. No indictments were issued. Merely having a Japanese great-grandparent was enough to mark an individual for involuntary confinement. The evacuation was carried out with little difficulty. For Japanese Americans to have fled or militantly defied the order would only have confirmed the suspicions of their fellow Americans. The JACL even decided not to arrange a court test of the evacuation order. They felt that cooperating with the military might lead to sympathetic consideration later when tensions subsided. From April to October 1942, the evacuees moved through hastily constructed assembly centers. One center, at Santa Anita Racetrack in Los Angeles, "housed" more than 18,000 people at one time. Those Japanese Americans who fled the West Coast and moved inland before the order took effect were greeted by towns that refused entry and gas station operators who refused to service their automobiles (Hosokawa, 1969, pp. 303–336; 1982).

**FIGURE 14.1** Evacuation Camps

Japanese Americans were first ordered to report to "assembly centers" from which, after a few weeks or months, they were resettled in "relocation centers."

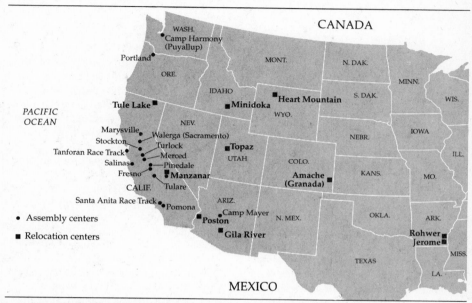

Source: Adapted from Michi Weglyn, *Years of Infamy: The Untold Story of America's Concentration Camps.* Copyright 1976 by Michi Nishura Weglyn. By permission of William Morrow and Company, Inc.

Even before reaching the camps the *evacuees,* as Japanese Americans being forced to resettle came officially to be called, paid a price for their ancestry. They were instructed to carry only personal items. No provision was made for shipping their household goods. The federal government took a few steps to safeguard the belongings they left behind, but the evacuees assumed all risks and agreed to turn over their property for an indeterminate length of time. These Japanese Americans were economically destroyed. Merchants, farmers, and business owners had to sell all their property at any price they could get. The short time and the large number of people liquidating possessions left the Japanese Americans in a difficult position. For example, one woman sold a 37-room hotel for $300. Precise figures of the loss in dollars are difficult to obtain, but after the war the Federal Reserve Bank estimated it to be $400 million. To place this amount in perspective, one estimate stated that in 1982 dollars the economic damages sustained, excluding personal income, would be in excess of $6 billion (Commission on Wartime Relocation and Internment of Civilians, 1982a, 1982b; Hosokawa, 1969, p. 440; Thomas and Nishimoto, 1946, pp. 14–17).

## ❖ LISTEN TO THEIR VOICES ❖

### Pearl Harbor and Japanese Americans

*Norman Mineta*

*In 1974, Norman Mineta became the first mainland Japanese American elected to the House of Representatives. But years earlier he was one of many interned in the relocation centers. On the occasion of the fiftieth anniversary of the attack on Pearl Harbor, he provides his recollections.*

We all knew that when the Japanese attacked Pearl Harbor they attacked every American, including Americans of Japanese ancestry. But the historical discrimination in the United States against Japanese Americans was too well-known to pretend that our lives would be unaffected after the attack. Federal exclusion laws had long prevented Asian immigrants from becoming citizens and California state laws had long prevented residents who were ineligible to become citizens from owning land. But, we wondered, would the attack on Pearl Harbor become an excuse for a new round of home-grown injustice directed against Japanese Americans?

There was no question that our community was loyal to the United States. I remember a young friend of mine—an American of Japanese ancestry—who climbed the roof of his house in Mountain View, pointed his BB-gun up at the sky and stood ready to defend his family against Japanese planes. But would that depth of patriotism, which ran through the entire community, protect us against injustice?

We didn't have to wait long for an answer.

That Sunday afternoon, I vividly recall my neighborhood friend Joyce Hirano running through the break in the hedge between our houses screaming, "They're taking my father away!" The "they" were the FBI. For the next two months, the Hiranos had no idea where he'd been taken.

Later toward the evening, after the initial shock in the neighborhood had died down, I remember seeing my father walk into this office, which was in a separate part of our house. He closed the office door, but not completely. I looked in at him through the doorway as he sat down at his desk. He looked through some papers, leaned back in his chair and started to cry. That shook me. The full weight of what had happened must have just hit him then, and that moment was when I began to understand that, even though I was only 10-year-old, my life had significantly changed.

Later that month, my father and mother sat us down as a family: my brother, two sisters and I. My father said that he did not know what would happen to him and my mother, since they were not citizens. But he did believe that because his children were

American-born and therefore American citizens that we would be safe.

He was wrong.

In February after President Roosevelt signed Executive Order 9066 and set the stage for the internment of Japanese Americans, I remember being struck for the first time by the stigma of disloyalty written into the notices that the Army had posted throughout the West Coast. The signs addressed us as "aliens and non-aliens." Imagine. Even though I was born a citizen in the United States, the only status my government would grant me was the rank of "non-alien."

When your own government disowns you—a 10-year-old child whose only alleged crime was his ancestry—the only hope you have are the rights endowed by our Constitution. But as Japanese Americans learned then, even our Constitution can be ignored by those who control access to the corridors of political power and influence. The result was the internment.

More than 120,000 Americans of Japanese ancestry were eventually interned. When my family was forcibly removed from San Jose on May 29, 1942, my father did not know if we'd ever see the valley again. Our train pulled out of the freight yards in downtown San Jose with its shades drawn, and with armed soldiers posted at every doorway. That was the second time I saw my father cry. We did not return to San Jose until after the war.

We fought for another 45 years to redress the injustices of the internment. In 1988 we finally achieved that victory. We achieved that victory because we educated the Congress, the President and our fellow Americans that the internment wasn't merely a Japanese American issue or an Asian American issue. It was, and is, an American issue.

But even with that victory, the anniversary of Pearl Harbor will never lose its sting for Americans of Japanese ancestry. For us, it was a multiple tragedy. That day, attackers from the land of our ancestry killed and maimed thousands of our fellow Americans. And on that same day, our rights and freedoms as Americans of Japanese ancestry began to fall victim to wartime hysteria, racism and weak political leadership.

Fifty years later, our prayer is that tragedies like these will never occur again.

From "Pearl Harbor and Japanese Americans" by Rep. Norman Mineta, *Asian Week,* 13 December 6, 1991, p. 14. Reprinted by permission of Asian Week.

## The Concentration Camps

Ten camps were established in seven states. Were they actually *concentration* camps? Obviously they were not concentration camps constructed for the murderous purposes of those in Nazi Germany, but such a comparison is no compliment to the United States. To refer to them by their official designation, relocation centers, ignores these facts: the Japanese Americans did not voluntarily come there, had been charged with no crime, and could not leave without official sanction.

Milton S. Eisenhower, brother of Dwight Eisenhower (military chief of staff, later to become president), headed the War Relocation Authority (WRA). He saw to it that the Japanese Americans would be able to work at wage labor. The maximum wage was set at $19 a month, which meant that camp work could not possibly recoup the losses incurred by evacuation. The evacuees had to depend on the government for food and shelter, a situation they had not experienced in prewar civilian life. More devastating than the economic damage of camp life was the psychological damage. Guilty of no crime, the Japanese American moved through a monotonous daily routine with no chance of changing the situation. Forced community life, with such shared activities as eating in mess halls, weakened strong family ties that Japanese Americans, especially the *Issei*, took so seriously (Kitsuse and Broom, 1956).

Amid the economic and psychological devastation, the concentration camps began to take on some semblance to American cities of similar size. High schools were established, complete with cheerleaders and yearbooks. Ironically, Fourth of July parades were held, with camp-organized Boy Scout and Girl Scout troops

*Hisako Hibi was a wife and the mother of two children when she painted this in Topaz Relocation Center, Utah, in 1943. Entitled "Mothers Bathing Children in Laundry Room," it poignantly reflects everyday life.* Source: *Reprinted with permission of the artist, in Gesensway and Roseman, 1987, p. 110.*

marching past proud parents. But the barbed wire remained and the Japanese Americans were asked to prove their loyalty.

The loyalty test came in 1943 on a form all had to fill out, the "Application for Leave Clearance." The Japanese Americans were undecided how to respond to two questions:

No. 27. Are you willing to serve in the armed forces of the United States on combat duty, wherever ordered?

No. 28. Will you swear to abide by the laws of the United States and to take no action which would in any way interfere with the war effort of the United States? (Daniels, 1972, p. 113)

Many felt that *no* votes were the only acceptable response, as a protest to the treatment received. Nevertheless, approximately 84 percent of the concentration camp residents given the questionnaire answered in the affirmative. Eventually the government used the responses to segregate the "disloyals" and ship them to a separate camp, Tule Lake in California. Predictably, Tule Lake became a trouble spot, where several serious beatings and one murder occurred (Thomas and Nishimoto, 1946, pp. 113–220).

Japanese Americans consistently showed loyalty to the government that had created the camps. In general, security in the camps was not a problem. Heart Mountain, Wyoming, with 10,000 evacuees, had only 3 officers and 124 enlisted men in the guard detail. The army, which oversaw removal of the Japanese Americans, recognized the value of the Japanese Americans as translators in the war ahead. About 6,000 *Nisei* were recruited to work as interpreters and translators, and by 1943 a special combat unit of 23,000 *Nisei* volunteers was created to fight in Europe. The predominantly *Nisei* unit was unmatched, and concluded the war as the most decorated of all American units.

Milton Eisenhower, as WRA head, had hoped initially to relocate some of the evacuees in western states nearer their homes, but when he met with western governors and attorneys general he saw that such a plan was unacceptable. Wyoming Governor Nels Smith warned that if Eisenhower's plan were attempted "there would be Japs hanging from every pine tree" (Zich, 1986, p. 528). Eventually, the WRA allowed some evacuees to leave the camps to attend college, and later allowed more to leave to work in wartime industry, but they always went to areas far from the West Coast (Daniels, 1972, p. 72; Girdner and Loftis, 1969, pp. 342–354; Hosokawa, 1969, pp. 393–422).

Japanese American behavior in the concentration camps can only be seen as reaffirming their loyalty. True, some refused to sign an oath, but that was hardly a treasonous act. More typical were the tens of thousands of evacuees who contributed to the American war effort.

## The Road Out

A few Japanese Americans resisted the evacuation and took their case to the courts. They received little support even from those segments of the White

*Ironically, one of the few ways in which the* Nisei *could leave the internment camps was to volunteer for military service. Pictured above is the Honor Guard of the all-Nisei 442nd Regimental Combat team in France in 1944.*

community usually sympathetic to minority causes. A 1942 survey of members of the American Civil Liberties Union in northern California showed overwhelming support for Executive Order 9066. Earl Warren, who later presided over the Supreme Court and wrote many of the Court's most progressive decisions, including *Brown* v. *Board of Education*, was Attorney General of California during the evacuation. Although a liberal, he supported the evacuation as firmly as if he had thought of it himself (Petersen, 1971, pp. 77–81).

Several cases arising out of the evacuation and the detention in concentration camps reached the Supreme Court during the war. Amazingly, the Court upheld lower court decisions on Japanese Americans without even raising the issue of the whole plan's constitutionality. Essentially the Court upheld the idea of the collective guilt of an entire race. Finally, after hearing *Mitsuye Endo* v. *United States*, the Supreme Court ruled on December 18, 1944 that the defendant (and presumably all evacuees) must be granted their freedom. Two weeks later Japanese Americans were allowed to return to their homes for the first time in three years. Some of the injustices committed by the Supreme Court were not overturned until 1986, when a Japanese American successfully appealed a 1943 conviction for failing to register for evacuation to a camp. The legacy of this chapter in American history lingers on (Hohri, 1988; ten Brock et al., 1954, pp. 211–223, 248–250).

The immediate postwar climate was not pro-Japanese American. Whites terrorized returning evacuees, in attacks similar to those against Blacks a generation earlier. Labor unions called for work stoppages when Japanese Americans reported for work. Portland refused to grant any business license to any *Issei*. Fortunately, the most blatant expression of anti-Japanese feeling disappeared rather quickly. Japan stopped being a threat as the atomic bomb blasts destroyed Nagasaki and Hiroshima. For the many evacuees who lost relatives and friends in the bombings, however, it must have been a high price to pay for marginal acceptance (Maykovich, 1972a, 1972b; Petersen, 1971, pp. 116–117).

## The Evacuation: What Does it Mean?

The wartime evacuation cost the American taxpayer a quarter of a billion dollars in construction, transportation, and military expenses. Japanese Americans, as already noted, effectively lost several billion dollars. These are only the tangible costs to the nation. The relocation was not justifiable on any security grounds. No verified act of espionage or sabotage by a Japanese American was recorded. How could it happen?

Racism cannot be ignored as an explanation. Japanese Americans were placed in camps, though German and Italian Americans were for the most part ignored. Many of those whose decisions brought about the evacuation were of German and Italian ancestry. The fact was that the Japanese were expendable. Placing them in camps posed no hardship for the rest of society, and in fact some profited by their misfortune. The secretary of California's Grower-Shipper Vegetable Association responded, "We do," to the charge that they wanted to get rid of the Japanese Americans for selfish reasons (F. Taylor, 1942, p. 66). That Japanese Americans were evacuated because they were seen as expendable is evident from the decision not to evacuate Hawaii's Japanese. In Hawaii, the Japanese were an integral part of the society; removing them would have economically destroyed the islands (Hosokawa, 1969, pp. 457–472; Kimura, 1988; Miyamoto, 1973).

Some argue that Japanese nonresistance made internment possible. Certainly this seems a weak effort to transfer guilt. Curiously, the *Sansei* and *Yonsei* are the quickest to show concern about the alleged timidity of their parents and grandparents when faced with evacuation orders. Probably many, if not most, evacuees did not really believe what was happening. "It just cannot be that bad," they thought. At worst the evacuees can be accused of being naive. But even if their reactions were realistic, what alternatives were open? None (Haak, 1970; Kitano, 1976, pp. 84–86).

As the *Endo* case shows, legal recognition that the evacuation was a crime was very slow in coming. No action granting compensation to the evacuees for property lost was taken until the 1948 Japanese American Evacuation Claims

Act, which was passed at the insistence of the JACL. Two years after its passage only 73 people had received any money. Eventually 23,000 claims were made, and the government paid $38 million, less than one-tenth of the Federal Reserve Bank estimate of the cost to Japanese Americans. All claims were settled with no interest paid and no consideration of increase in land values. No payments were made for "death or personal injury, personal inconvenience, physical hardship, or mental suffering." The settlements were so delayed that when the final payments were made in 1967, many of the claimants were dead (Hosokawa, 1982a, pp. 288–292; Petersen, 1971, pp. 104–107).

The year 1952 marked a watershed in the civil rights of Japanese Americans. As we have seen, in that year the *Issei* could finally become citizens. Japanese immigration was again legal, and relatives of Japanese Americans were given preference. The California Supreme Court finally declared the 40-year-old Alien Land Act unconstitutional. The civil rights enjoyed by Whites had finally been extended to Japanese Americans (Daniels, 1972, pp. 168–170).

Could it happen again? It is too easy to minimize the evacuation and the concentration camp experience. After all, some say, the Japanese Americans survived the camps to move into the economic upper ranks of society. Yet, even in the *Endo* case, the Supreme Court did not actually rule out the possibility of forced evacuation to camps in time of war. Justice William O. Douglas concluded in another case that "we cannot sit in judgment on the military requirements of that hour." Several of the camps, although entirely populated by Japanese Americans, were maintained under a variety of congressionally approved measures "for the detention of persons who there are reasonable grounds to believe will commit or conspire to commit espionage or sabotage" (Daniels, 1975, p. 57). On September 25, 1971, Senator Daniel Inouye of Hawaii successfully pushed through Congress a measure that led to the dismantling of the camps. Inouye himself had served in the all-*Nisei* military unit and had learned from fellow *Nisei* the indignity that the camps represented.

The absence of legislative or even constitutional authority does not preclude the possibility of another evacuation, relocation, or detention: such authority was absent in 1942. It could still happen again to some powerless group singled out by the overwhelming majority for imprisonment. A sobering prospect is provided by a 1967 survey of Californians which found 48 percent believing the wartime evacuation to be a proper action. A 1981 Oregon survey found only 33 percent favored the move; 63 percent in that survey, however, opposed further compensation (Keene, 1982; Levine and Montero, 1973).

After lobbying efforts by the JACL, President Carter created the Commission on Wartime Relocation and Internment of Civilians. In 1981 the Commission held hearings on whether additional reparations should be paid to evacuees or their heirs. The final Commission recommendation in 1983 was for a formal apology from the government and $20,000 tax-free to each of the approximately 66,000 surviving internees. Congress began hearings in 1986 on the bill authorizing these steps and President Ronald Reagan signed the Civil Liberties Act of 1988 which authorized the payments. The payments, however, were slow in being authorized because other federal expenditures had higher priorities. Yet the aging internees were dying at a rate of 200 a month. In 1990 the first checks were finally issued accompanied by President Bush's letter of apology. Many Japanese Americans were disappointed and critical with the begrudging nature of compensation and the length of time it took to receive compensation (Commission on Wartime Relocation and Internment of Civilians, 1982a, 1982b; Squitieri, 1989).

## POSTWAR SUCCESS

Aside from the legacy of the camps, the Japanese American community of the 1950s was very different from that of the 1930s. Japanese Americans were more widely scattered. In 1940, 89 percent lived on the West Coast. By 1950, only 58 percent of the population had returned to the West Coast. Another difference was that a smaller proportion than before were *Issei*. The *Nisei* or even later generations accounted for 63 percent of the Japanese population.

More dramatic than these demographic changes was the upward mobility that Japanese Americans collectively and individually accomplished. Occupationally and academically, two indicators of success, Japanese Americans are doing very well. The educational attainment of Japanese Americans as a group, as well as their family earnings, are higher than those of Whites, but caution should be used in interpreting such group data. Obviously, large numbers of Asian Americans, as well as Whites, have little formal schooling and are employed in poor jobs. Furthermore, Japanese Americans are concentrated in areas of the United States such as Hawaii, California, Washington, New York, and Illinois, where wages as well as the cost of living are far above the national average. Also, the proportion of Japanese American families with multiple wage earners is higher than that of Whites. Nevertheless, the overall picture for Japanese Americans is remarkable, especially for a racial minority and their having been discriminated against (Inoue, 1989; Kitano, 1980; Woodrum, 1981).

After the war leadership changed among Japanese Americans. The *Issei* had dominated through loosely coordinated relationships and Buddhist religious organizations. Gradually during the war the *Nisei*, through the JACL, gained prominence. The shift was not simply a progression of generations. The policy of dispersing the evacuees throughout the country made community-based groups more difficult to maintain. During the evacuation, community-based organizing was threatened because the JACL cooperated with the WRA, in a position not supported by all *Nisei*. Although the JACL is the primary organization of its type today, it still does not enjoy uncontested leadership. Politically, individual Japanese Americans have achieved success. Several have been elected to Congress, and in Hawaii, a Japanese American became governor. As a group, Japanese Americans show virtually no evidence of the political organization of many other racial or ethnic groups (Burma, 1953; Hosokawa, 1982b; Kitano, 1976, pp. 66–68, 191–192; Nakanishi, 1987; Powers, 1976).

*The emergence of anti-Japan feelings in the 1990s was, for this illustrator, reminiscent of the internment camps of the 1940s.*
Jim Bergman, Cincinnati Enquirer, © 1992.

The contemporary Japanese-American family seems to continue the success story. The divorce rate has been low, although it is probably rising. Similar conclusions apply to crime, delinquency, and mental illness. Data on all types of social disorganization show Japanese Americans with a lower incidence of such behavior than all other minorities; it is also lower than that of Whites. Japanese Americans find it possible simultaneously to be good Japanese as well as good Americans. Japanese culture demands high in-group unity, politeness, respect for authority, and duty to community, all traits highly acceptable to middle-class Americans. Basically, psychological research has concluded that Japanese Americans share the high achievement orientation held by many middle-class White Americans. One might expect, however, that as Japanese Americans continue to acculturate, the breakdown in Japanese-oriented behavior will be accompanied by a rise in social deviance (Caudill, 1952; Caudill and DeVos, 1956; Kitano, 1976, pp. 143–163; Kitano and Kikumura, 1976; Nagata, 1991a; Nakamaru, 1979; Petersen, 1971, pp. 131–151; for a different view see Lindsey, 1985).

## *ASSIMILATION ACCOMPLISHED, ALMOST*

In comparison to other racial and ethnic groups, younger Japanese Americans have made relatively little effort to preserve or resurrect cultural ties to the past.

*Sansei* youth indicate they would like to learn Japanese. It is questionable whether many will. The very success of Japanese Americans seems to argue that they will not maintain a unique cultural tradition. In fact, their success has been in part the result of Japanese Americans assimilating, forsaking the cultural heritage of Japan. Emphasis on college education and advanced training makes it likely that Japanese Americans will scatter throughout the country. Dispersal will make cultural ties difficult to maintain. Little Tokyos do exist, but even in some major cities such a basic symbol of ethnic solidarity is absent (Garrison, 1974; Kitano, 1971; Levine and Montero, 1973; F. Williams, 1976).

The results of the UCLA Japanese American Research Project, begun in 1963, emphasize the degree of acculturation that had taken place already with the *Nisei*, especially among the well educated. Half of the high-school educated were Buddhists and spoke Japanese fluently. On the other hand, only about 10 percent of the college graduates had similar cultural ties to Japan. In summary, it appears that the *Nisei* have acquired knowledge, habits, and attitudes that more closely resemble those of the United States than those of Japan. Although the *Issei* may have successfully merged Japanese culture with American, the *Nisei* have adapted themselves to American culture. Further research into the third generation, the *Sansei*, indicates that assimilation has continued. There is little evidence of Marcus Hansen's principle of third-generation interest in the homeland's culture, as described in Chapter 5. Yet many of the *Sanseis'* lives have been shaped by the internment experience as they choose careers intended to finish the unfulfilled dreams of their previously-interned relatives (Montero, 1973, 1981; Nagata, 1991b).

In addition to geographical mobility, the degree of outmarriage by Japanese Americans indicates further assimilation. Census data show a higher rate of exogamy among younger Japanese Americans than that of their parents' generation. Several studies corroborate the census data. Obviously if such trends continue, it will be increasingly difficult to make a sense of cultural continuity last beyond the present generation. Not only has outmarriage increased, but it appears to have become more egalitarian. No longer are most intermarriages characterized by dominant American servicemen in patriarchal unions with Japanese women. Marriages between Japanese Americans and Whites more and more follow the pattern of marriages that are not interracial (Kikumura and Kitano, 1973; Kitano, 1976; Levine and Rhodes, 1981; Tinker, 1973).

It would be incorrect to interpret assimilation as an absence of protest. Because militancy characterized the attitudes of a sizable segment of the college youth of the 1960s and early 1970s, it was to be expected that some Japanese Americans, especially the *Sansei*, would be militant. The *Sansei* are more heterogeneous than their *Nisei* and *Issei* ancestors. Recently they have expressed activism through Hiroshima Day ceremonies, marking the anniversary of the detonation in World War II of the first atomic bomb over the major Japanese city. Also, each February a group of Japanese American youths makes a pilgrimage to the site of the Tule Lake evacuation camp in a "lest we forget" observance. Such protests are mild compared even to those associated with Chinese Americans, but they are a militant departure from the almost passive role played by the *Nisei* (Maykovich, 1972a, 1973, 1974).

Is assimilation complete? By the definition of assimilation used in Chapter 1, it is clear that, even for the *Sansei* or *Yonsei*, assimilation is incomplete. Although the ties to Japanese culture may be weakened, or even completely broken, Japanese Americans are still readily identified as *Japanese* Americans, not as Americans. Indeed, the 1990s saw a re-emergence of anti-Japanese feeling in the United States. The growing trade competition between Japan and the United States brought strong feelings that Japan was somehow not "playing fair" as the only explanation of why we are suffering a trade imbalance. Each time a Japanese company bought a U.S. company, the media gave it tremendous attention, yet similar actions by Australian, British, or German investors were relatively unnoticed. The fiftieth anniversary of the attack on Pearl Harbor rekindled feelings that people from Japan cannot be trusted. Sporadic vandalism of symbols of Japanese American presence occurred at the time. In this light, we are probably not surprised to learn that 44 percent of *Sansei* recently surveyed who had both parents interned during World War II agreed that Japanese Americans would again be held captive if the United States and Japan were at war (El Naser, 1991b; Foderaro, 1990; Cose, 1989; Muto, 1991; Nagata, 1990).

Is pluralism developing? Japanese Americans give little evidence of wanting to maintain a distinctive way of life. Japanese values that have endured are attitudes, beliefs, and goals shared by and rewarded by middle-class America. The Japanese American is caught in the middle. He or she is culturally a part of a society that is dominated by a group that excludes him or her because of racial distinctions (Hosokawa, 1982b; Kitano, 1974; Montero, 1977; Okimoto, 1971; Padilla et al., 1985; Yamamoto, 1968).

Sociologist Minako Maykovich has distinguished among the three generations by the "three *y's*" and the "three *b's.*" Specifically, they are: (1) *Issei*—

Even cartoons showed anti-Japanese sentiment in the 1990s amidst growing concerns of Japan's economic power. "Kudzu" by 1988 Pulitzer Prize winning cartoonist Doug Marlette satirized the takeover of a small town by a Japanese corporation (Sayonara Inc.). The series was criticized for the use of stereotypes and Japan-bashing. Marlette, who was asked to respond, defended his work and said that his critics don't have a sense of humor and are trying to impose their beliefs on him. "My experience is that there are two kinds of racial groups—one has a sense of humor, the other doesn't," he is quoted as saying.

yellow peril and bamboo; (2) *Nisei*—yellow pansy and banana; (3) *Sansei*—yellow power and bee (1972a, pp. 78–79). The first Japanese Americans, the *Issei*, were attacked by the yellow peril stereotype but did not accept this image. Like bamboo, the *Issei* easily bent in whatever direction the wind blew, only to eventually spring back straight and proud. Their children became quiet and wishy-washy, hence the name yellow pansy. They were bananas, yellow on the outside but white inside. Their children, the *Sansei*, were less accommodating. It is in this generation that yellow power emerged. The bee, active and with a sting that hurts, is a more suitable image. Maykovich acknowledges the oversimplification. Not all *Sansei* would identify with the bee, for example. Although the labels may be misleading, they do underscore once again that Japanese American experience has not been one long success story. Nor has the story been uniform throughout the country. The conclusions on the assimilation of Japanese Americans apply most accurately to the mainland. Hawaii's acceptance of Japanese Americans, as well as other Asians and for Whites, has been different (see Chapter 12).

## COMPARING CHINESE AND JAPANESE AMERICAN EXPERIENCES

Most White adults are confident of their ability to distinguish Asians from Europeans. Unfortunately, though, White Americans frequently cannot tell Asians apart but are not disturbed about their confusion. There are, however, definite differences in the experience of the Chinese and Japanese, several of which should now be obvious. The Chinese arrived in large numbers before the Japanese, although movements to discriminate predictably followed the same pattern. Japanese American immigrants, mostly male, began sending back to Japan for brides soon after their arrival. As a result, the preponderance of males did not last as long as it did with urban Chinese Americans.

There are also obvious differences in the degree of assimilation. The Chinese have maintained their ethnic enclaves more than the Japanese. Chinatowns live on, but Little Tokyos are few because of the cultures the immigrants left behind. China was almost untouched by European influence, but even in the early 1900s Japan had been influenced by the West. Relatively speaking, then, the Japanese arrived somewhat more assimilated than their Chinese counterparts. The continued migration of Chinese in recent years has also meant that Chinese Americans as a group have been less assimilated than Japanese Americans (Beach, 1934; Lyman, 1974, pp. 57–63; 1986).

Both groups have achieved some success, but only to a degree. For Chinese Americans, a notable exception to success is the prevalence of Chinatowns, which behind the tourist front are just other poverty areas in American cities. Neither Chinese nor Japanese Americans have figured prominently in the executive offices of the nation's large corporations and financial institutions. Compared to other racial and ethnic groups, their political activity and militancy have had relatively little impact.

## GLANCING BACK AND LOOKING AHEAD

Japanese Americans encompass a success story better than the rags-to-riches saga of some enterprising inventor. Here is a group that in little more than a generation went from total rejection by society to success, at least by middle-class standards.

The success, however, is that of the Japanese Americans, not that of society. First, they have been considered a success only because they conform to dominant societies' expectations. The acceptance of Japanese Americans as a group does not indicate that the United States is moving toward pluralism. Second, the ability of the *Nisei* to recover from the camps cannot be taken as a precedent for other racial minorities. The Japanese Americans left the camps a skilled group, ambitious to overcome their adversity, and placing a cultural emphasis on formal education. They entered a booming economy in which Whites and others could not afford to discriminate even if they wished to. Blacks after slavery and Hispanic immigrants have entered the economy without skills at a time when the demand for manual labor was limited. Many of them have been forced to remain in a marginal economy, whether that of the ghetto, the barrio, or subsistence agriculture. For Japanese Americans the post-World War II period marked the fortunate coincidence of their having assets and ambition when they could be used to full advantage. Third, some Whites, though not many, use the success of the Japanese Americans to prop up their own prejudice. Japanese-American success is twisted by bigoted individuals to show that racism cannot possibly play a part in another group's subordination. If the Japanese can do it, why can't the Blacks, the illogical reasoning goes. Or more directly, and even less frequently, Japanese Americans's success serves as an excuse for another's failure ("they advanced at my expense") or as a sign that they are clannish or too ambitious. Regardless of what a group does, to a prejudiced eye the group can do no right.

The final evaluation has to be with Asian Americans. As with other racial and ethnic minorities, assimilation seems to be the path most likely to lead to tolerance but not necessarily to acceptance. But assimilation has a price that is well captured in the Chinese phrase *Zhancao zhugen*—to eliminate the weeds, one must pull out their roots. To work for acceptance means to uproot all traces of your cultural heritage and your former identity (Wang, 1991, p. 197).

## KEY TERMS

**evacuees** Japanese Americans interned in camps for the duration of World War II.

*Issei* First-generation immigrants from Japan to the United States.

***Kibei*** Americans of the *Nisei* generation sent back to Japan for schooling and to have marriages arranged.

***Nisei*** Children born of immigrants from Japan.

***Sansei*** The children of the *Nisei;* that is, the grandchildren of the original immigrants from Japan.

***Yonsei*** The fourth generation of Japanese Americans in the United States, the children of the *Sansei.*

# FOR FURTHER INFORMATION

Masie Conrat and Richard Conrat. *Executive Order 9066.* Los Angeles: California Historical Society, 1972.

> The Conrats have constructed a very moving photographic essay of the relocation and internment of the Japanese Americans.

Roger Daniels. *Asian America: Chinese and Japanese in the United States since 1850.* Seattle: University of Washington Press, 1988.

> A balanced, authoritative look at two race minorities who have experienced success and continued bigotry.

Roger Daniels. *Concentration Camps U.S.A.: Japanese Americans and World War II.* New York: Holt, Rinehart and Winston, 1972.

> Daniels gives a detailed account of the evacuation, the camps, and the post-World War II period.

Deborah Gesensway and Mindy Roseman, eds. *Beyond Words: Images From America's Concentration Camps.* Ithaca: Cornell University Press, 1987.

> The editors have gathered a vivid collection of paintings by internees.

Audrie Girdner and Anne Loftis. *The Great Betrayal: The Evacuation of the Japanese-Americans During World War II.* New York: Macmillan, 1969.

> This book is the most detailed single-volume account of the evacuation. The authors very briefly examine the pre- and post-World War II life of Japanese Americans.

William Minoru Hohri. *Repairing America: An Account of the Movement for Japanese-American Redress.* Pullum: Washington State University Press, 1988.

> A summary of the testimony that led to the presidential apology and payment of $20,000 to each surviving evacuee.

Bill Hosokowa *JACL in Quest of Justice.* New York: William Morrow, 1982.

> A well-illustrated, detailed account of the Japanese American Citizens League (JACL) from its founding through its efforts to gain reparations in the 1980s.

Japanese American Evacuation and Resettlement Study.

> This six-year study (1942–1948) based at the University of California, produced the most detailed report on the camps and was published in three volumes by the University of California Press. They are: *The Spoilage,* by Dorothy S. Thomas and Richard S. Nishimoto (1946), *The Salvage,* by Thomas (1952), and *Prejudice, War, and the Constitution,* by Jacobus ten Brock, Edward N. Barnhart, and Floyd W. Matson (1954).

Harry H. L. Kitano. *Japanese Americans: The Evolution of a Subculture,* 2nd ed. Englewood Cliffs, NJ: Prentice-Hall, 1976.

> Kitano gives a thorough review of Japanese Americans with unusually detailed coverage of such aspects of contemporary life as family, cultural beliefs, mental illness, and crime. A chapter is

devoted to Japanese in Hawaii. The author graduated from high school while in the Topaz evacuation camp.

Tule Lake Committee. *Kinenhi: Reflections on Tule Lake*. San Francisco: Tule Lake Committee, 1980.

A richly illustrated paperback that provides not only historical views of the controversial camp but also a glimpse of Japanese Americans returning to the site today.

Yoshiko Uchida. *Desert Exile*. Seattle: University of Washington Press, 1982.

A chronicle of life in an evacuation camp written by someone who experienced the hardships of the camps and the recovery that followed.

## *Government Documents*

The federal government carefully recorded the relocation from beginning to end. Documents can be consulted that were issued by these now-defunct agencies: War Agency Liquidation Unit, War Relocation Authority (both of the Department of the Interior), the Western Defense Command (Army), and the Select Committee Investigating National Defense Migration (House of Representatives, 1942). Still another source is the Commission on Wartime Relocation and Internment of Civilians, which met in the 1980s.

*Chapter Fifteen*

# JEWISH AMERICANS: QUEST TO MAINTAIN IDENTITY

*Chapter Outline*

The Jewish People: Race or Religion or Ethnic Group?

Migration of Jews to the United States

Anti-Semitism Past and Present

Origins

American Anti-Semitism: Past

Contemporary Anti-Semitism

Position of Jewish Americans

Employment and Income

Education

Organizational Activity

Political Activity

Religious Life

Jewish Identity

Role of the Family

Role of Religion

Role of Cultural Heritage

Glancing Back and Looking Ahead

Key Terms

For Further Information

### ❋ HIGHLIGHTS ❋

Jewish identity does not rest on the presence of physical traits or religious devoutness but on a sense of belonging that is tied to Jewish ancestry. The history of *anti-Semitism* is as ancient as the Jewish people themselves. American Jews have experienced less discrimination than had earlier generations in Europe, but some opportunities are still denied them. Contemporary Jews figure prominently in the professions and as a group exhibit a strong commitment to education. Many Jews share a concern about either the lack of religious devotion of some or the division within American Judaism over the degree of orthodoxy. Paradoxically, the growing acceptance of Jews by Gentiles has made the previously strong identity of Jews weaker with each succeeding generation.

The United States has the largest Jewish population in the world. This nation's 5.5 million Jews account for 44 percent of the world's Jewish population. Jewish Americans are not only a significant group in the United States but also play a prominent role in the worldwide Jewish community. The nation with the second largest Jewish population, Israel, is the only one in which Jews are in the majority, accounting for 84 percent of that nation's population, compared to less than 3 percent in the United States. Figure 15.1 depicts the worldwide distribution of Jews (Kosmin et al., 1991; Ritterband, 1986).

The Jewish people form a contrast to the other minority groups we have studied. It has been at least 1,500 years since Jews were the dominant group in any nation. Israel, created in 1948, would be the exception, but even there Jews are in competition for power. American Jews superficially resemble Asian Americans in their relative freedom from poverty compared to Chicanos or Puerto Ricans. Unlike any of these groups, however, the Jewish cultural heritage is not nationalistic in origin. Perhaps the most striking difference is that the history of anti-Jewish prejudice and discrimination (usually referred to as anti-Semitism) is nearly as old as relations between Jews and Gentiles (non-Jews).

Statistical data on Jewish Americans are unreliable. Because the Bureau of the Census no longer asks people their religions, the kinds of statistical information on other minority groups, who are identified in the census, are lacking. The last count the Bureau of the Census made, in 1957, placed the Jewish population over age 14 at nearly 4 million. Estimates for 1990 placed the Jewish population at about 5.5 million. The Jewish birthrate remains well below that of the national population, and so growth of the Jewish population during the 1980s did not keep pace with that of the nation as a whole. Indeed, the proportion of the U.S. population that is Jewish has been estimated to be the lowest since the first decade of the century.

The most distinctive aspect of the Jewish population is its concentration in urban areas and in the Northeast. The most recent estimates (for 1990) place 53

**FIGURE 15.1** Worldwide Distribution of Jews

While the United States, Israel, and the former Soviet Union have the largest numbers of Jews, significant Jewish populations can also be found in France, Great Britain, Canada, and Argentina.

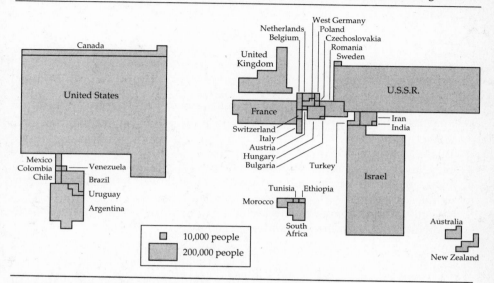

Source: *Atlas of the World Today* by Neil Grant and Nick Middleton, 1987. Copyright © by Itex Publishers. Reprinted by permission of Harper & Row, Publishers, Inc.

percent of the Jewish population in the Northeast (see Table 15.1). The special 1957 census of religion showed 96 percent of Jews living in urban areas, compared to 64 percent for the whole population. Although these data are old, they probably still reflect accurately the distribution of Jews today.

Jews are especially concentrated in New York City. Two-thirds of the nation's Jewish population in 1957 lived in New York City and neighboring cities in New York and New Jersey. There are more Jews in this area than in Israel's largest city, Tel Aviv. Although some portion of the Jewish population has left New York City in the last 35 years, New York remains the focus of the Jewish community (Berger, 1986b; Bureau of the Census, 1958; Goldscheider, 1986, p. 3; Goldstein, 1971; L. Shapiro, 1971).

## THE JEWISH PEOPLE: RACE OR RELIGION OR ETHNIC GROUP?

Jews are a minority group. They fulfill all the criteria set forth in Chapter 1.

1. Jews have characteristics that distinguish them from the dominant group.
2. Jews do not choose to be Jewish in the same way that Whites do not choose to be White or Chicanos to be Chicano.

**TABLE 15.1**    Jewish Population Distribution in the United States (percentages)

| Region | 1900 | | 1990 | |
| --- | --- | --- | --- | --- |
| | Jewish | Total | Jewish | Total |
| Northeast | 56.6 | 27.7 | 40.1 | 26.4 |
| Midwest | 23.7 | 34.6 | 12.7 | 24.0 |
| South | 14.2 | 32.2 | 23.7 | 34.4 |
| West | 5.5 | 5.4 | 23.6 | 21.2 |

Note: Percentages may not add up to 100 because of rounding.
Source: S. Goldstein, 1971, 1981, p. 63; Kosmin et al., 1991. Data reproduced with the permission of the American Jewish Committee and the Council of Jewish Federation.

3. Jews have a strong sense of group solidarity.
4. Jewish men and women tend to marry one another rather than marrying Gentiles.
5. Jewish Americans experience unequal treatment from non-Jews in the form of prejudice, discrimination, and segregation.

The first criterion for classification as a minority group on this list requires special attention. What are the distinguishing traits? Are they physical features, thus making Jews a racial group? Are they characteristics that are matters of faith, suggesting that Jews are best considered as a religious minority? Or are they cultural and social, making Jews an ethnic group? Answering these questions, requires an approach to the ancient and perennial question: What is a Jew?

The question of what is a Jew is not only a scholarly question, for in Israel it is a matter of policy. Following the 1988 general election, Israeli Prime Minister Yitshak Shamir was under great pressure by tradition-minded Jews in both his own country and the United States to redefine Israel's Law of Return. This law defines and extends Israeli citizenship to all Jews. Currently, the law recognizes all converts to the faith but pressure has grown recently to limit citizenship to those whose conversions were performed by more orthodox rabbis. While the change would have had little practical impact, symbolically it showed the tension and lack of consensus even among Jews over who is a Jew (Watson, 1988).

The definition of race used here is fairly explicit. The Jewish people are not physically differentiated from non-Jews. True, many people believe they can tell a Jew from a non-Jew, but actual distinguishing physical traits are absent. Jews today come from all areas of the world and carry a variety of physical features. Most Jewish Americans are descended from Northern and Eastern Europeans and have the appearance of Nordic and Alpine people. Many others carry Mediterranean traits, making them indistinguishable from Spanish or Italian Catholics. Many Jews reside in North Africa and, although they are not significantly represented in the United States, many would consider them Black.

The wide range of variation among Jews makes it inaccurate to speak of a Jewish race in a physical sense (Gittler, 1981, pp. 1–29; Montagu, 1972, pp. 51–57).

To define Jews by religion would seem the obvious answer, because there are Judaic religious beliefs, holidays, and rituals. But these beliefs and practices do not distinguish Jews from non-Jews. To be a Jewish American does not mean that one is affiliated with one of the three religious groups: the Orthodox, the Reform, and the Conservative. A large segment of Jewish Americans, more than a third, do not participate as adults in religious services or even belong, however tenuously, to a temple or synagogue. They are not converting to Christianity nor do they cease to think of themselves as Jews. This is not to say that Jewish religious beliefs and the history of religious practices are not significant legacies for all Jews today, however secularized their everyday behavior.

The trend for some time, especially in the United States, has been toward a condition that Herbert J. Gans (1956) calls *Judaization,* the lessening importance of Judaism as a religion and the substitution of cultural traditions as the tie that binds Jews. Depending on one's definition, Judaization has caused some Jews to become so assimilated in the United States that more traditional Jews would cease to consider them acceptable spouses. Estimates of the proportion of "problematic" Jews by the year 2000 range from 4 to 20 percent (American Jewish Committee, 1987).

Jewish identity is ethnic. Jews share cultural traits, not physical features or religious beliefs. The level of this cultural identity differs for the individual Jew. Just as some Apaches may be more acculturated than others, the degree of assimilation varies for Jewish people. Judaization as defined by Gans may base identity on such things as traditional Jewish foods, Jewish jokes, and the Star of David. For others this cultural identity may be a sense of a common history of centuries of persecution. For still others it may be a relatively unimportant identification. They say, "I am a Jew," just as they say, "I am a resident of California."

The question of what constitutes Jewish identity is not easily resolved, except that it is not based on physical features or religiosity. In "Listen to Their Voices," one Jewish American reflects on ethnic identity, which for him has revolved around the decision whether he should wear the *yarmulka*—a skullcap. The most appropriate explanation of Jewish identity may be the simplest. A Jew in contemporary America is an individual who thinks of himself or herself as a Jew (Himmelfarb, 1982).

## MIGRATION OF JEWS TO THE UNITED STATES

As every schoolchild knows, 1492 was the year in which Christopher Columbus reached the Western Hemisphere, exploring on behalf of Spain. That year also marked the expulsion of all Jews from Spain. The exodus the expulsion caused was not the first migration of Jews, nor was it the last. One of the most significant movements among Jews is the one that created history's largest concentration of

### ❖ *LISTEN TO THEIR VOICES* ❖

#### *The Agony of the* Yarmulka—*A Confession*

*Julian Ungar-Sargon*

*In a poignant, somewhat humorous manner, Ungar-Sargon shows how the simple act of wearing the* yarmulka *or* kippah, *a skullcap, comes to symbolize his identity as a Jew and his affinity with his father and grandfather. The author is an instructor in neurology at the Harvard Medical School.*

We are told by the Code of Jewish Law that covering the head is in deference to the presence of the Almighty and that one should not walk for more than four paces without a head covering. An act of deference, it is well known in the East, where people cover their heads out of respect, in contrast to the West where one usually bares one's head in deference to the Holy (church) or even the upper class (the squire, a "lady" or "gentleman").

Yet, for me, growing up as an observant Jew in a secular world, no single observance has caused me greater sacrifice and more grief than this one. I can easily tolerate the embarrass-ment and excuses of early Fridays, holidays, and even dietary restrictions, but the *yarmulka* again and again challenges my deepest commitment. To remove it would plunge me into a longed-for world of anonymity, which I crave, not having constantly to "stand out in a crowd." It's not even the people you work with that are the problem; they soon recognize you to be as mortal as they, with similar human inadequacies and failings. They rightly learn to accept you despite your "little beanie." It's the constant meeting with strangers, where you are sized up by your dress and categorized as friend or foe, fiend or fanatic, normal or eccentric, of similar class and background or "extremist sectarian." To stand separately, as a Jew is supposed to, is one thing, but the relentless self-awareness soon turns into the very thing that it was designed to do, i.e., to prevent social intercourse with people of different persuasions. Yet that is precisely what my father had brought me up to reject: not to be a Jew in the ghetto, protected and shielded, but to be a "*Yisroel mensch,*" a Jew out in the secular world interacting with the enlightened. He and his father had rejected that isolation in Vienna at the turn of the century, when its gates were opened to the Jews of the *sheva kehillos* (the seven communities surrounding the city) for the first time in four hundred years. This flush of excitement and the wondrous involvement in a new world that was open to him was,

I suppose, genetically transmitted to me. . . .

Coming to the United States changed everything initially. In New York, the *yarmulka* was commonplace, and immediately I felt unconscious of its ubiquitous presence on my head, but, then, also, I felt a general devaluation of the currency of many *mizvot* [commandments or religious duties], as the social and cultural milieu of living among millions of Jews seemed to distract me in its vitality and dynamism. Maybe halakhah [Jewish law] has less meaning if one is culturally involved in things Jewish and Yiddish. This same question was even more poignant when I visited Israel. Was Zionism and living a life in Israel a fair substitute for the ritual that kept Jews distinct in the *Golah* [Exile], and was ritual now redundant? I wanted ever so much to disassociate myself from the politics of orthodoxy there. I felt a much greater kindred to those who were constructively "building the land," as Rav Kook put it, than with those with a *yarmulka* similar to mine who engaged in "other" activities.

On moving to Boston, however, much of the European embarrassment returned and the flushed face before a weekly audience at Harvard now gives me a nostalgia for my days at the London hospital. Once again, it has reluctantly become for me a focal point that represents all that separates me from a modern secular professional class that I yearn to be part of, but never can. Earlier, I had thought it was entirely due to my self-imposed isolation because of the *yarmulka;*

however, slowly I am beginning to realize that, even without the *yarmulka,* the isolation continues and that I probably could still not be part of that world.

It must mean something. However, I'm not sure I yet understand and a deep ancestral sigh down inside me keeps telling me that it is more important than I think. As I get older and the enthusiasm and innocence of my youth wane, and as I compromise morals and principles more and more, I feel that possibly I should not be privileged to wear the *kippah* [or yarmulka]. Maybe one's personal standards need to merit this level of external observance. Indeed, it was my father who always told me that those who wish to compromise themselves in public should not wear the *yarmulka* during visits to a nightclub, etc. He also felt that the *yarmulka* itself can propel a person to maintaining standards by, in a sense, preventing that person from misconduct by its very presence. So, ever so slowly, I begin to feel that maybe it is the *yarmulka* that is "keeping me" and even paying me back for those years of agony. Slowly, ever so slowly, I'm finally making my peace with this most difficult of *mizvot.*

An addendum . . . my sons came home with new *yarmulkas* this week. Painted on them were figures of Superman and He-man—fate has, indeed, a divine sense of humor!

From "The Agony of the Yarmulka—A Confession" by Julian Ungar-Sargon, *Judaism* Vol. 36, (pp. 320–322), 1987. Reprinted by permission.

Jews—the migration to the United States. The first Jews arrived in 1654 and were of Sephardic origin, meaning that they were from Spain and Portugal. These immigrants came looking for refuge after they were expelled from European countries.

When the United States gained its independence from Great Britain, there were only 2,500 Jews in the population. By 1870, the Jewish population climbed to about 200,000, supplemented mostly by Jews of German origin (referred to, along with Eastern European Jews, as Ashkenazi Jews). They did not immediately merge into the older Jewish American settlements any more than the German Catholics fused immediately with native Catholics. Years passed before the two groups' common identity as Jews overcame nationality differences (Birmingham, 1971; Gager, 1983; Goren, 1980, pp. 572–579; Herberg, 1983).

The greatest migration of Jews to the United States occurred around the turn of the century, simultaneous with the great European migration described in Chapter 4. This similarity in timing does not mean that the movement of Gentiles and of Jews was identical in all respects. One significant difference was that Jews were much more likely to stay in the United States—few returned to Europe. Although between 1908 and 1937, one-third of immigrants returned to Europe, only 5 percent of Jewish immigrants did. The legal status of Jews in Europe at the turn of the century had improved since medieval times, but their rights were still revoked from time to time (Sherman, 1974).

Despite the legacy of anti-Semitism in Europe, past and present, most of the Jews who migrated to the United States up to the early twentieth century came voluntarily. Sociologist Marshall Sklare writes, "the immigration of the European Jew was basically elective rather than enforced" through expulsions (1971, p. 16). These immigrants tended to be the less pious, less observant of Judaic religious customs than those who remained in Europe. As late as 1917, there were only five small day schools, as Jewish parochial schools were called, in the entire nation. Although the earliest Jewish immigration did not come directly in response to fear, the United States had special meaning for the Jewish arrival. The United States had no history of anti-Semitism like that of Europe. Many Jews must have felt a new sense of freedom, and many clearly demonstrated their commitment to their new nation by becoming citizens at a rate unparalleled in other ethnic groups (Herberg, 1983).

The immigration acts of the 1920s sharply reduced the influx of Jews, as it did those of other European groups. Beginning in about 1933, the Jews arriving in the United States were not merely immigrants; they were also refugees. The tyranny of the Third Reich began to take its toll well before World War II. German and Austrian Jews fled Europe as the impending doom became more evident. Many of the refugees from Nazism in Poland, Hungary, and the Ukraine tended to be more religiously orthodox and adapted slowly to the ways of earlier Jewish immigrants, if they adapted at all. The concentration camps, the speeches of Hitler, the atrocities, the war trials, and the capture of Nazi leaders undoubtedly made all American Jews—natives and refugees, the secular and orthodox—acutely aware of their Jewishness and the price one may be required to pay for ethnicity alone.

Because the Immigration and Naturalization Service does not identify an immigrant's religion, precise data are lacking for the number of people of Jewish background migrating recently to the United States. Estimates of 500,000 have been given, however, for the number of Jews who made the United States their home during the 1960s and 1970s. The majority came from Israel, but 75,000 came from the Soviet Union and another 20,000 from Iran, escaping persecution in those two nations. As the treatment of Jews in the Soviet Union improved in the late 1980s, the United States immigration officials began to scrutinize requests for entry to see if refugee status still needed to be granted. While some Soviet Jews had difficulty demonstrating that they had a "well-founded fear of persecution," the United States admitted over 13,600 in 1988 through Rome alone. The situation grew more complicated with the collapse of the Soviet Union in 1991. Throughout the period, the immigrants' arrival brought about a growth in the United States Jewish community.

The large number of Jews immigrating to the United States from Israel has obvious significance for that small nation, and those who leave for North America or Europe are often regarded as "traitors" by those left behind in the besieged land of Israel. Some of the emigrants, and especially those from the Soviet Union, are referred to pejoratively as *noshrim*, or dropouts, in terms of faith and

Most Orthodox Jews, and many Conservative and Reformed Jews, attend religious schools such as this one in Baltimore to increase their understanding of Jewish culture.

Jewish organizations. The Iranian Jews who have tended to cluster in Los Angeles are more traditional but also linked to a culture alien to that of most American Jews (S. Gold, 1988; Kass and Lipset, 1980, 1982; Shipler, 1981; Simon and Simon, 1982).

## ANTI-SEMITISM PAST AND PRESENT

The historical tradition of the Jewish people has included the struggle to overcome centuries of hatred. Several religious observances, like Passover, Hanukkah, and Purim, commemorate the past sacrifices or conflicts Jews have experienced. Anti-Jewish hostility or *anti-Semitism* has followed the struggle of the Jewish people from the beginning of the Christian faith to the present.

### Origins

Many anti-Semites justify their beliefs by pointing to the role of some Jews in the crucifixion of Jesus Christ, who was a Jew. For nearly 2,000 years various Christians have argued that all Jews share in the responsibility of those Jewish elders. Much anti-Semitism over the ages bears little direct relationship to the crucifixion, however, and has more to do with the persisting stereotype that sees Jews as behaving treacherously to members of the larger society in which they live. As Chapter 2 showed, people may continue to be familiar with a stereotype, whether or not they accept it as true. Table 2.1 shows the change in the stereotype of Jews from 1932 to 1982. Although negative aspects were cited less frequently, many still saw Jews in a less-than-positive light. Studies such as the one shown in Table 2.1 and that of Bruno Bettelheim and Morris Janowitz (1964) confirm that many Gentiles believe that Jews use underhanded methods in business and finance and that Jewish people tend to be clannish (Glassman, 1975; Wuthnow, 1982).

What truth is there in such stereotypes? Even prominent political leaders have publicly expressed stereotyped opinions about Jews. In 1974, the chairman of the Joint Chiefs of Staff of the United States armed forces declared that Jews "own, you know, the banks in this country" (*Time*, 1974b). Yet the facts show that Jewish Americans are dramatically underrepresented in management positions in the nation's leading banks. Even in New York City—where Jews account for half the college graduates—Jewish Americans represent only 4 percent of that city's senior banking officials (Slavin and Pradt, 1979, 1982). Similarly, sociologists Richard Alba and Gwen Moore (1982), using national data for the period 1972 to 1980, concluded that Jews account for 8.9 percent of college-educated men but only 6.9 percent of the business elite.

If the stereotype of being money-minded is false, how did it originate? Social psychologist Gordon Allport, among others, advances the *fringe-of-values* theory (1958, pp. 120–121). Throughout history, Jews have occupied positions economically different from those of Gentiles often because laws forbade them to farm or practice trades. For centuries the Christian church prohibited the taking of interest in the repayment of loans, calling it the sin of usury. Most Jews were not moneylenders, and most of those who were did not charge interest. In fact, many usurers were Christians, but because they worked in secret, it was only the reputation of the Jews that was damaged. In the minds of Europeans the sinful practice of moneylending was equated with the Jew. To make matters worse, the nobles of some European countries used Jews to collect taxes, which only increased the ill feeling. To the Gentile, such business practices by the Jews constituted behavior on the *fringes* of proper conduct, hence this theory for the perpetuation of anti-Semitism is called *fringe of values* (American Jewish Committee, 1965, 1966a, 1966b; De Fleur et al., 1976, p. 268; *Time,* 1974a).

A similar explanation is given for such other stereotypes as the assertion that Jews are clannish, that they stay among themselves and do not associate with others. In the ancient world, Jews in the Near East area were frequently under attack from neighboring peoples. This experience naturally led them to unify and rely on themselves rather than others. In more recent times, the stereotype that Jews are clannish gained support in that Jews have been more likely to interact with Jews than Gentiles. But this behavior is reciprocal, for Gentiles have tended to stay among their own kind too. It is another example of *in-group virtues* becoming *out-group vices.* Sociologist Robert Merton describes how proper behavior by one's own group becomes unacceptable when practiced by outsiders (1968, pp. 480–488). For Christians to take their faith seriously is commendable; for Jews to withstand secularization is a sign of backwardness. For Gentiles to prefer Gentiles as friends is understandable; for Jews to choose other Jews as friends suggests clannishness. The assertion that Jews are clannish is an exaggeration and ignores the fact that the dominant group shares the same tendency. It also fails to consider to what extent anti-Semitism has logically encouraged, indeed forced, Jews to seek out other Jews as friends and fellow workers (Allport, 1958, pp. 122–123).

This has been only the beginning of an exploration of the alleged Jewish traits, their origin, and the limited value such stereotypes have in accurately describing several million Jewish people. Stereotypes are only one aspect of anti-Semitism—another has been discrimination against Jews. In A.D. 313, Christianity became the official religion of Rome. Within another two centuries, Jews were forbidden to marry or try to convert Christians. Because Christians shared with Jews both the Old Testament and the origin of Jesus, they felt ambivalently toward the Jewish people. Gentiles attempted to purge themselves of their doubts about the Jews by projecting exaggerated hostility onto the Jews. The expulsion of Jews from Spain in 1942 is but one example. Spain was merely one on a list of countries, which included England and France, from which the Jews were thrown out. During the middle of the fourteenth century, the bubonic plague wiped out a third of Europe's population. Because of their social conditions and some of their religious prohibitions, Jews were less likely to die from the plague. Anti-Semites pointed to this as evidence that the Jews were in league with the devil and had poisoned the wells of non-Jews. Consequently from 1348 to 1349, 350 Jewish communities were exterminated, not by the plague, but by Gentiles.

The injustices to the Jewish people continued for centuries. It would, however, be a mistake to say that all Gentiles were anti-Semitic. History, plays, and literature do record daily, presumably friendly, interaction between Jew and Gentile. At particular times and places anti-Semitism was an official government policy. In other situations it was the product of a few bigoted individuals and sporadically became mass movements. Anti-Semitism was a part of Jewish life, something Jews were forced to contend with. By 1870, most legal restrictions aimed at Jews were abolished in Western Europe. Since then, however, Jews have again been used as scapegoats by opportunists who blame them for a nation's problems. The most tragic example of such an opportunist was Adolf Hitler, whose "final solution" to Germany's problems led to the Holocaust, the extermination of 6 million Jewish civilians during World War II. Two-thirds of Europe's total Jewish population was killed; in Poland, Germany, and Austria

*European Jews resisted the Nazi genocide through such rebellions as the Warsaw ghetto uprising of 1943. Other Jews resisted by preserving the spirit of human dignity and creativity despite the horrors of the death camps. The artists of Terezin (Theresienstadt), a concentration camp in Czechoslovakia, fought the Nazis with their art by capturing the Holocaust in drawings and paintings—which had to be done secretly and smuggled out of the camp or buried for posterity. Shown here is* Execution, *by Leo Haas, which depicts the public hanging of a concentration camp inmate by the Nazis.*

90 percent were murdered (Dawidowicz, 1967, pp. 68–81, 1975, p. 403; Hertzler, 1942).

With the collapse of Communism and the Soviet Union in 1991, there has emerged a concern that the absence of authoritarian states will allow old hatreds to resurface. The fear is that with freedom of speech, bigotry, which was dysfunctional to a centralized form of government, is beginning to be expressed openly. Anti-Semitic literature has been distributed, and expressions of alarm over Jews migrating from the former Soviet Union to Europe are not uncommon. Yet even a half-century after Nazi Germany mounted its war on the Jews of Eastern Europe, the Jewish population is relatively small. Hungary has the most with about 60,000, but many of the 1.5 million Jews in the countries formerly controlled by Moscow are expected to leave. The future of the Jewish community in Europe even without the threat of Communist repression, like many other aspects of life, is uncertain (T. Mathews, 1990).

## American Anti-Semitism: Past

Compared to the brutalities of Europe from the time of the early Christian church to the rule of Hitler, the United States cannot be described as a nation with a history of severe anti-Semitism. The United States has also had its outbreaks of anti-Semitism, however, though none have reached the scope of Western Europe's. An examination of the status of Jewish Americans today will determine the extent of discrimination against Jews that remains. Contemporary anti-Semitism, however, must be seen in relation to past injustices.

In 1654, the year Jews arrived in colonial America, Peter Stuyvesant, governor of New Amsterdam (the Dutch city later named New York) attempted to expel them from the city. Stuyvesant's efforts failed, but they began an unending effort to separate Jews from the rest of the population. Because the pre-1880 immigration of Jews was relatively small, anti-Semitism was little noticed except, of course, by Jews. Most nineteenth-century movements against minorities were targeted at Catholics and Blacks and ignored Jews. In fact, Jews occasionally joined in such movements. By the 1870s, however, signs of a pattern of social discrimination against Jews appeared. Colleges limited the number of Jews or excluded them altogether. The first Jewish fraternity was founded in 1898 to compensate for the barring of Jews from campus social organizations. As Jews began to compete for white-collar jobs early in the twentieth century, job discrimination became the rule, rather than the exception (Higham, 1966; Selzer, 1972, pp. 9–11).

The 1920s and the 1930s were the period of the most virulent and most overt anti-Semitism. During these decades the myth of an internationally organized Jewry took shape. According to a forged document entitled the *Protocols of the Elders of Zion*, Jews throughout the world planned to conquer all governments, and the major vehicle for this rise to power was communism, said by anti-Semites to be a Jewish movement. Absurd though this argument was, some respected Americans accepted the thesis of an international Jewish conspiracy and believed in the authenticity of the *Protocols*. Henry Ford, founder of the automobile company that bears his name, was responsible for publication of the *Protocols. The Dearborn Independent*, a weekly newspaper owned by Ford, published anti-Semitic material for seven years. Finally, in 1927, faced with several million dollars' worth of civil suits for slandering well-known Jewish Americans, he published a halfhearted apology. In his later years Ford expressed regret for his espousal of anti-Semitic causes, but the damage was done; he had lent an air of respectability to the most exaggerated charges against Jewish people.

It is not clear why Henry Ford was, even for only a short period of his life, so willing to accept anti-Semitism. But Ford was not alone. Groups like the Ku Klux Klan and the German-American Bund, as well as radio personalities like the Catholic priest Charles E. Coughlin, preached about the Jewish conspiracy as if it were fact. By the 1930s, those who held such sentiments usually expressed fondness for Hitler and showed little concern for Germany's actions against Jews. Even the famed aviator Charles Lindbergh made speeches to gatherings claiming that Jews were forcing the United States into a war so that Jewish people could profit by wartime production. When the barbarous treatment of the Jews by Nazi Germany was exposed, most Americans were horrified at such events, and individuals like Lindbergh were as puzzled as anyone about how some Americans could have been so swept up by the pre-World War II wave of anti-Semitism (Meyers, 1943; Selzer, 1972, pp. 144–156).

The next section examines anti-Semitic feelings in contemporary America. But first, consider several crucial differences between anti-Semitism in Europe and in the United States. First, and most important, the United States government has never promoted anti-Semitism. Unlike its European counterparts, the U.S. government has never embarked on an anti-Semitic program of expulsion or extermination. Second, because anti-Semitism was never institutionalized in the United States as it has sometimes been in Europe, American Jews have not needed to develop a defensive ideology to ensure survival of their people. A Jewish American can make a largely personal decision about how much to assimilate or how secular to become. For Jewish Europeans, on the other hand, the major question of life has more often been how to survive, not whether to assimilate (Halpern, 1974).

## Contemporary Anti-Semitism

Next to social research on anti-Black attitudes and behavior of Whites, anti-Semitism has been the major focus of study of prejudice by sociologists and psychologists. Most of the conclusions described in Chapter 2 apply equally to the data collected on anti-Semitism. Relatively little concern was expressed by Jews in the United States about anti-Semitism immediately after World War II. From the latter 1960s through the 1980s, however, anti-Semitism appeared to be a threat again in many parts of the world. For example, the infamous *Protocols*, used earlier to promote the notion of an international conspiracy of Jews, resur-

*Mike Jenkins. © 1988* The Montgomery *(County, Maryland)* Journal.

faced in the Soviet Union in the 1970s and in Japan in the 1980s (D. Harris, 1987; G. Johnson, 1987).

Anti-Semitic incidents in the United States ranging from desecration to murder occur annually. In recent years a rash of anti-Semitism and of "JAP-baiting" has been impossible to ignore on several college campuses. *JAP* is an acronym for *Jewish-American Princess,* a stereotyped presentation of young Jewish women as materialistic and obnoxious. "JAP-baiting" went beyond joke-telling and manifested itself as chanting and group harassment at public events such as athletic games (Chayat, 1987; Dinnerstein, 1988; L. Shapiro, 1988; Spencer, 1987).

The Anti-Defamation League (ADL) of B'nai B'rith, founded in 1913, makes an annual survey of anti-Semitic incidents. Although the number has fluctuated, the 1991 tabulation reached the highest level in the 12 years the ADL has been recording such incidents. Also a record number of 23 college campuses reported more than one anti-Semitic episode.

A series of anti-Semitic events occurred at Indiana's Ball State University in 1991 when a professor of theater instructed the mostly non-Jewish cast of *The Ghetto* to wear yellow Stars of David to better understand the stigma Jews experienced under the Nazi regime. This exercise in sensitivity provoked hostility, obscene name-calling, receipt of neo-Nazi literature, and refusal to cooperate in other classes. In one incident, a driver motioned for a cast member to cross the street, then gunned his car forward, with the student narrowly escap-

*Vandalism or desecration of Jewish cemeteries, businesses, schools, and, as shown here, synagogues is not uncommon in the United States, but usually represents isolated incidents rather than organized efforts.*

ing injury. The play proceeded with sell-out crowds but the events in Muncie showed the persistence of anti-Semitism (ADL, 1992, pp. 7–8).

On the other side of the scale, Gallup Polls show that favorable opinions of Jews have increased. Yet a 1984 survey revealed that Jews by a two-to-one ratio deny that positions of influence in the United States are open to them without regard to their being Jewish. Such seemingly contradictory findings prompted Rabbi Alexander Schindler, president of the American Jewish Congress in New York City, to conclude that "the number of those prone to anti-Semitism has not increased, but those who are prone are more daring, more willing to commit those acts" (Elson, 1982, p. 4; see also *Public Opinion,* 1987; T. Smith, 1991).

Acts of anti-Semitic violence along with the continuing Middle East conflict and advocacy of an anti-Semitic theme by some militant Black Americans has prompted renewed national attention to anti-Semitism.

*American Jews and Israel.* When the Middle East became a major hot spot in international affairs in the 1960s, what many Jews considered a revival of 1930s anti-Semitism was rekindled. Many Jewish Americans expressed concern that because Jews are freer in the United States than they have been in perhaps any other country in their history they will ignore the struggle of other Jews. Israel's precarious status has proved to be a strong source of identity for Jewish Americans. Major wars in the Middle East in 1967, 1973, and 1991 reminded the world of Israel's vulnerability. Palestinian uprisings in the Occupied Territories and international recognition of the Palestine Liberation Organization (PLO) in 1988 eroded the strong pro-Israeli front among western powers. A few Jewish Americans have shown their commitment to the Israeli cause by actually immigrating to Israel. Although not all American Jews agree with Israel's actions, many Jews express support for Israel's struggles by contributing money through the United Jewish Appeal and by trying to influence American opinion and policy to be more favorable to Israel.

The Anti-Defamation League (ADL) has carefully watched for any trends in disfavor for Israel. The 1973 oil embargo by the Arab states and the subsequent rise in American gasoline prices led to what some leaders of the ADL identified as an "oil backlash" of Americans holding Jews responsible for empty gas tanks. The ADL saw the oil embargo as signaling an end to "the golden age of Jewish life in America" when anti-Jewish feelings were minimal. Arab nations pressured American corporations not to invest in Israel and even not to place Jews in high management positions. The U.S. army acknowledged in 1975 that it did not send Jewish soldiers to Saudi Arabia because of that government's pressure. Such stipulations ended during the massive build-up for the 1991 Persian Gulf War. Nevertheless, national surveys from 1984 through 1987 showed that a quarter of the public believed Jews were more loyal to Israel than to the United States (*Public Opinion*, 1987).

In the year after the oil embargo, 1974, the United Nations General Assembly ignored American and Israeli objections and passed a resolution declaring that "Zionism is a form of racism and racial discrimination." *Zionism*, which initially referred to the old Jewish religious yearning to return to the biblical homeland, in the twentieth century has been expressed in the movement to create a Jewish state in Palestine. Ever since the *diaspora*, the exile of Jews from Palestine several centuries before Christianity began, many Jews have seen the destiny of their people only as establishment of a Jewish state in the Holy Land. The Zionism resolution, finally repealed in 1991, had no lasting influence and did not change any nation's foreign policy. It did, however, increase Jewish fears of reawakened anti-Semitism thinly disguised as attacks on Zionist beliefs (Carroll, 1975; Heilman, 1982, pp. 147–148; Lichtenstein and Denenberg, 19785; Sheinberg and Schulman, 1977; Spiegel, 1973a, 1973b; Stark and Steinberg, 1967; Stember, 1966, pp. 171–196; Strober, 1974, pp. 7–11).

*American Jews and African Americans.* An aspect of contemporary anti-Semitism that has been a subject of special concern is anti-Semitism by African Americans. There is no reason why anti-Semites should be exclusively White, but Jews have been especially troubled by Blacks expressing ethnic prejudices. Jewish Americans have been active in civil rights causes and have contributed generously to legal defense funds. Jewish neighborhoods and employers have also been quicker to accept Blacks than their Gentile counterparts. For these reasons some Jews find it especially difficult to understand why another group experiencing prejudice and discrimination should express anti-Semitic sentiments.

Surveys (Simpson and Yinger, 1985, pp. 131–133) generally conclude that Blacks as a group are no more anti-Semitic than Whites, but in the last few years events have occurred that bring attention to alleged Black anti-Semitism. Beginning in the 1960s, some African American activists and the Black Panther party supported the Arabs to the Middle East Conflict and called on Israel to surrender. The issue of Black–Jew relations was inflamed during the 1984 campaign by the Reverend Jesse Jackson for the Democratic nomination for president. His off-the-record reference to Jews as "Hymies" and the publicly broadcast anti-Semitic remarks by one of his supporters, the Black Muslim minister Louis Farrakhan, gave rise to new tensions between Blacks and Jews. During the 1988 campaign, Jackson distanced himself from anti-Semitic rhetoric, stating, "The sons and the daughters of the Holocaust and the sons and the daughters of slavery must find common ground again" (W. Schmidt, 1988; also see M. Coleman, 1984; Silberman, 1985, p. 339).

In the 1990s unrelated events again seemed to draw attention to the relationship between Jews and African Americans. On several college campuses invited Black speakers made anti-Israeli statements, inflaming Jewish students in attendance. Jewish Americans were faced with explaining Israel's close economic ties with South Africa, even in the heat of the worldwide anti-Apartheid movement. In a 1991 incident, a Hasidic Jew ran a red light, killing a Black child and the ambulance that regularly served the Hasidic community did not pick up the child. In the emotional climate that resulted, an Australian Jewish researcher was stabbed to death and several days of rioting in the Brooklyn, New York neighborhood of Crown Heights followed (Jackson, 1991; Leatherman, 1990; Marty, 1992; Raab, 1991).

Black resentment, in many situations attracting notoriety, was rarely anti-Jewish as such, but rather was opposed to White institutions. As author James Baldwin said, Blacks "are anti-Semitic because they're anti-White" (1967, p. 114). That racial prejudice is deep in the United States is shown by the fact that two groups suffering discrimination, groups that might unite in opposition to dominant society, instead fight each other.

An old Yiddish saying, *Schwer zu sein a Yid*, means "It is tough to be a Jew." Anti-Semitism past and present is related. The old hostilities seem never to die. The atrocities of Nazi Germany have not been forgotten, nor should they be. Racial and ethnic hostility, whatever group is the victim, unifies the group against its attackers, and Jewish Americans are no exception. The Jewish people of the United States have come together, regardless of nationality, to form a minority group with a high degree of group identity.

## POSITION OF JEWISH AMERICANS

Jewish Americans have an important role in contemporary America. They are active participants in the fight for civil rights and work on behalf of Israel. These efforts are important, but for most of America's 5 to 6 million Jews they do not involve full-time participation. For a better perspective of Jewish people in the United States, a summary follows of the present situation of Jews with respect to (1) employment and income, (2) education, (3) organizational activity, and (4) political activity.

## Employment and Income

Discrimination conditions all facets of a subordinate group's life. Jews have experienced, and to a limited extent still experience, differential treatment in the American job market. As recently as 1956, a survey of employers in San Francisco found one out of four acknowledging that it either barred Jews altogether or limited their employment to a predetermined level. Civil rights acts and Supreme Court decisions have made it illegal to discriminate in employment. Through perseverance and emphasis on education, Jewish Americans as a group have overcome barriers to full employment and as a group now enjoy high incomes. Survey data indicate that Jews are the wealthiest group of White Americans (Greeley, 1976, p. 71; also see Steinberg, 1977).

This high income level does not mean that Jews find it as easy to enter all occupations as Gentiles do. Jewish Americans are conspicuously absent from banks, savings and loan institutions, utilities, insurance companies, and major industrial occupations. The legal profession is attractive to Jews, but few enter the prestigious private law firms. Many Jewish professionals find it easiest to work for Jewish law firms or to affiliate with Jewish hospitals (American Jewish Committee, 1965, 1966a, 1966b; De Fleur et al., 1976, p. 268; Porter, 1981; Sklare, 1971, p. 65; Slavin and Pradt, 1982; Zweigenhaft and Domhoff, 1982).

Social science studies using a variety of techniques have shown declining evidence of discrimination against Jews in the business world. Most recently, sociologist Samuel Klausner interviewed business school graduates, comparing Jews with Protestants and Roman Catholics who graduated from the same university in the same year. Klausner (1988, p. 33) concludes that: "(1) Jewish MBAs are winning positions in the same industries as their Catholic and Protestant classmates; (2) they are rising *more* rapidly in corporate hierarchies than their Catholic and Protestant colleagues; (3) they are achieving *higher* salaries than their Catholic and Protestant colleagues." Klausner adds that researchers tested seven indicators of discrimination and, in each case, *failed* to find evidence of discrimination against Jewish executives. Interestingly, however, this same study detected substantial discrimination against African Americans and women.

The economic success of the Jewish people as a group does obscure the poverty of many individual Jewish families. We reached a similar conclusion in Chapter 12 with income data on Asian Americans and their image as a "model minority." Sociologists largely agree that Jews in 1930 were as likely to be poverty stricken and to be living in slums as any minority group today. Most have escaped poverty, but there remains what Ann Wolfe (1972) calls "the invisible Jewish poor," invisible to the rest of society. Like Chinese Americans, the Jewish poor were not well served by the Economic Opportunity Act and other federal experiments of the 1960s and 1970s to eradicate poverty. Although the proportion of the poor among the Jews is not as substantial as among Blacks or Hispanics, it does remind us that affluence and the life-style of all Jewish families are not the same (M. Gold, 1965; Lavender, 1977; Levine and Hochbaum, 1974).

## Education

Jews are unique among ethnic groups in their emphasis on education. This desire for formal schooling stems, it is argued, from the Judaic religion, which places the rabbi, or teacher, at the center of religious life. In the United States today, all Jewish congregations emphasize religious instruction more than is typically found among Protestants. The more religiously orthodox require instruction on Sundays as well as on weekday afternoons following attendance at public schools. Eighty-four percent of young men (15 to 19 years) and 72 percent of young women received some Jewish education (Goren, 1980, p. 596). Jews have created summer camps in which Hebrew is the only language spoken. Theological seminaries provide rabbinic training. The Jewish-sponsored component of higher education, however, is not limited to strict religious instruction. Beginning in 1947, Jews founded graduate schools of medicine, education, social work, and mathematics, along with Brandeis University, which offers both undergraduate and graduate degrees. These institutions are nonsectarian (that is, admission is not limited to Jews) and are conceived as a Jewish-sponsored contribution to higher education (Greenberg, 1970; Waxman, 1983, pp. 68–70).

The religiously-based tradition of lifelong study left as a legacy a value system that stressed education. The poverty of Jewish immigrants kept them from devoting years to secular schooling, but they were determined that their children should do better. Exact data are lacking on how successful the second and successive generations have been in fulfilling the hopes of their immigrant ancestors. Samples in New York City (Elinson et al., 1967) indicate that Jews' level of educational mobility is much greater than among any other minority group or among non-Jewish Whites. (Educational mobility is the increase in the years of schooling of the child over that of his or her father.) Andrew Greeley (1976), relying on nationwide surveys conducted between 1963 and 1974, found that Jewish adults had an average of 14 years of education, compared to 12.5 for Irish Catholics, 12.4 for British Protestants, and 11.4 for Scandinavian Protestants. All available data indicate that, based on years of schooling, Jews have succeeded by dominant society standards (Goldstein and Goldscheider, 1968, p. 64).

Despite their high levels of educational attainment, some members of the Jewish community express concern about Jewish education. They express disappointment over its highly secularized nature—not just that religious teaching has been limited, but that the Jewish sociocultural experience has been avoided altogether. A group of sociologists (Glock et al., 1975; I. Spiegel, 1975), after uncovering anti-Semitism among a sample of grade school and high school children, recommended that public schools should not ignore the history of Judaism or sidestep anti-Semitism. There is no evidence that American public schools have changed curriculum materials to consider the Jewish experience as they have the role of Black Americans. With this secularization of Jewish children, the survival of Jewish identity may be threatened. Secularization may, however, be compensated by the high level of organizational activity among Jews of all ages.

## Organizational Activity

The American Jewish community has encompassed a variety of organizations from the beginning. These groups serve many purposes—some are religious, others are charitable, political, or educational. No organization, secular or religious, represents all American Jews, but there are more than 300 nationwide organizations. Among the most significant are the United Jewish Appeal (UJA), the American Jewish Committee, the American Jewish Congress, and the B'nai B'rith. The UJA was founded in 1939 and serves as a fund-raising organization for humanitarian causes. Recently Israel has received the largest share of funds collected. The American Jewish Committee (founded in 1906) and Congress (1918) work toward the similar purpose of improving Jewish-Gentile relations. B'nai B'rith (Sons of the Covenant) was founded in 1843 and claims 500,000 members in 40 nations. It promotes cultural and social programs, and through its Anti-Defamation League, fights anti-Semitism.

Besides those on the national level, there are many community-based organizations. Some local organizations, such as social and business clubs, were founded because existing groups barred Jews from membership. The Supreme Court has consistently ruled that private social organizations like country clubs and business clubs may discriminate against Jews or any ethnic or racial group. Jewish community centers are also prominent local organizations. To Gentiles the synagogue is the most visible symbol of the Jewish presence at the community level. The Jewish community center, however, serves as an important focus of local activity. In many Jewish neighborhoods throughout the United States it is the focus of secular activity. Hospitals, nurseries, homes for the elderly, and child care agencies are only a few of the community-level activities sponsored by Jewish Americans (Rabinove, 1970; Sklare, 1971, pp. 135–143).

## Political Activity

American Jews play a prominent role in politics both as voters and elected officials. Jews as a group are not typical in that they are more likely than the general population to label themselves liberal. Although upper-middle-class voters tend to vote Republican, Jewish voters have been steadfastly Democratic. In the 12 presidential elections beginning in 1940, Jews have voted at least 82 percent Democratic 7 times and have always given the Democrats more of their votes than Republicans. Jewish suburban voters, unlike those in central cities, tend to be more supportive of Republican candidates, but are still more Democratic than their Gentile neighbors. Jews have long been successful in being elected to office, but it was not until 1988 that an Orthodox Jew was elected to the United States Senate from Connecticut. Joseph Lieberman refrained from campaigning on the Sabbath each week; his religious views were not an issue.

As with all subordinate groups, the political activity of Jewish Americans has not been limited to conventional electoral politics. Radical Jewish politics have been dominated by college students. At the height of their involvement in the late 1960s, Jewish youths were active with Gentiles in the New Left movement as well as working alone for causes unique to Jews, like support of Israel. Jack Nusan Porter (1970) presents factors accounting for the rise of radicalism among young Jews in the last half of the 1960s.

1. The spread of racial and ethnic pride.
2. The 1967 Israeli-Arab War, which reminded the younger generation of Israel's vulnerability.
3. The influence of the New Left and general student unrest.
4. Growing abhorrence of middle-class suburban Jewishness to the younger generation.
5. Anti-Zionist and anti-Semitic postures of the New Left and Black Power movement.

The last factor explains why many Jewish activists began to feel uncomfortable in the leftist organizations.

Most conspicuous among militant Jewish responses was the formation of the Jewish Defense League (JDL). Meir Kahane, the New York rabbi who founded the JDL, advanced a "Jewish is beautiful" theme. The JDL also, however, decried Black anti-Semitism, the Soviet government's persecution of Jews, and Arabs and leaders of Arab states. National Jewish organizations denounced the JDL's harassment tactics. The Jewish Defense League had a short, stormy history. By 1973, the JDL's activities had fallen off, in part due to Kahane's moving to Israel where he was successfully elected to the Knesset, their legislature, in 1984. His radicalism led to his being ousted in 1988 and returning to the United States. In 1990 he was assassinated while speaking to a small audience. Prominent Jews, while stressing that they did not agree with Kahane's militancy, found many of his specific concerns to their liking. Despite its excesses and short life, the JDL aroused a new sense of Jewishness and drew attention to the mixed success that the old-line organizations were having in meeting the new challenges (*Facts on File*, 1990; Flacks, 1967; C. Liebman, 1973, pp. 160–173; Strober, 1974, pp. 143–177).

## RELIGIOUS LIFE

Jewish identity and participation in the Jewish religion are not the same. Many Americans consider themselves to be Jewish and are considered by others to be

Jewish even though they have never participated in Jewish religious life. Available data suggest that about 60 to 70 percent of American Jews are affiliated with a synagogue, but only 20 to 30 percent attend services more than once a month. Even in Israel, only 30 percent of Jews are religiously observant. Nevertheless, the presence of a religious tradition is an important tie among Jews, even secular Jews (Kleinman, 1983; Watson, 1988).

The unitary Jewish tradition developed in the United States into three sects beginning in the middle of the nineteenth century. The differences among Orthodox, Conservative, and Reformed Judaism are based on acceptance of traditional rituals. The differences developed out of a desire by some Jews to be less distinguishable from other Americans. Another significant factor in explaining the development of different groups is the absence of a religious elite and bureaucratic hierarchy. This facilitated the breakdown in traditional practices. All three sects embrace a philosophy based on the Torah, the first five books of the Bible. Orthodox Jewish life is very demanding, especially in a basically Christian society like the United States. Almost all conduct is defined by rituals that require an Orthodox Jew to reaffirm his or her religious conviction constantly. Most Americans are familiar with *kashrut*, the laws pertaining to per-

*Some Orthodox Jews seek to convince other Jews of the value of following more traditional beliefs. Pictured here at a Jewish Peoplehood Festival in New York City, a rabbi offers services designed to introduce the rewards of Orthodox observance.*

missible and forbidden foods. When strictly adhered to, *kashrut* governs not only what foods may be eaten (*kosher*), but how the food is prepared and the manner in which it is served and eaten (Shenker, 1979). Besides day-to-day practices, Orthodox Jews have weekly and annual observances. Marshall Sklare summarizes the contrast between the Jewish faith and that of dominant society: "the thrust of Jewish religious culture is sacramental . . . [while] the thrust of American religious culture is moralistic" (1971, p. 111).

Orthodox Jews differ in degree of adherence to traditional practices. Among the ultraorthodox are the Hasidic Jews, or *Hasidim,* who reside chiefly in several neighborhoods in Brooklyn. These neighborhoods and their residents are like another world. To the Hasidim, following the multitude of *mitzvahs,* or commandments of behavior, is as important in the 1980s as it was in the time of Moses. They wear no garments that mix linen and wool. Men wear a *yarmulka,* or skullcap, constantly, even while sleeping. Attending a secular college is frowned upon. Instead, men undertake a lifetime of study of the Torah and the accompanying rabbinical literature of the Talmud. Women's education consists of instruction on how to run the home in keeping with Orthodox tradition.

Orthodox children attend special schools so as to meet minimal New York State educational requirements. The devotion to religious study is reflected in this comment by a Hasidic Jew: "Look at Freud, Marx, Einstein—all Jews who made their mark on the non-Jewish world. To me, however, they would have been much better off studying in a *yeshivah* [a Jewish school]. What a waste of three fine Talmudic minds" (Arden, 1975, p. 294). Although devoted to their religion, the Hasidim participate in local elections, politics, and employment in outside occupations. All such activities are influenced by their orthodoxy and a self-reliance rarely duplicated elsewhere in the United States (Arden, 1975; Danzger, 1989; Liebman, 1973; Schoenfeld, 1976, pp. 338–339; R. Schultz, 1974; *Time,* 1972b).

Reformed Jews, though deeply committed to the religious faith, have altered many of the rituals. Women and men usually sit together in Reformed congregations, and some congregations have introduced organ music and choirs. A few have even experimented with observing the Sabbath on Sunday. Circumcision is not mandatory for males. Civil divorce decrees are sufficient and recognized, so that a divorce granted by a three-man rabbinic court is not required prior to remarriage. All these practices would be unacceptable to the Orthodox Jew. Conservative Judaism is a compromise between the rigidity of the Orthodox and the extreme modification of the Reformed. In Table 15.2 are displayed some results from the National Jewish Population Survey. The three sects include here *both* members *and* nonmembers of local congregations. Reformed Jews are least likely of the three groups to have had Jewish education, participate in religious events, be involved in the Jewish community, or participate in predominantly Jewish organizations.

The one exception in their relative low levels of participation is on issues confronting world Jewry such as Israel or treatment of Jews in such nations as the former Soviet Union and Iran. For the Orthodox Jew these issues are less

**TABLE 15.2**   Jewish Identification by Group (percentages)

Orthodox Jews are the strictest in ritual. The denominations do not differ on concern about worldwide Jewry. The data are based on a national survey in 1970–1971 of Jewish adults.

| Indices | Orthodox | Conservative | Reformed |
|---|---|---|---|
| Jewish education | 63 | 44 | 26 |
| Religious observances | 72 | 44 | 15 |
| Ethnic community involvement | 69 | 48 | 19 |
| Involvement in Jewish organizations | 44 | 35 | 24 |
| Concerns about world Jewry | 30 | 31 | 28 |
| Number of respondents | 530 | 1,631 | 1,190 |

*Source:* Lazerwitz, 1983. Used by permission of the authors. Copyright © 1983 by Bernard Lazerwitz and Michael Harrison.

important than those strictly related to the observance of the faith (Harrison and Lazerwitz, 1982; Lazerwitz and Harrison, 1979). Although no nationwide organized movement advocates this, in recent years Reformed Jews seem to have reclaimed traditions they once rejected. Yet a survey reported in 1982 that Reformed temples record that anywhere from 7 to 22 percent of the membership is made up of non-Jews (National Jewish Family Center, 1982, p. 3).

Unlike most faiths in the United States, Jews historically have not embarked on recruitment or evangelistic programs to attract new members. Beginning in the late 1970s, Jews, especially Reformed Jews, debated the possibility of outreach programs. Least objectionable to Jewish congregations were efforts begun in 1978 aimed at non-Jewish partners and children in mixed marriages. In 1981, the program was broadened to invite conversions by Americans who expressed no religious connection, but these modest recruitment drives are still far from resembling those carried out by Protestant denominations for decades (K. Briggs, 1978; *New York Times*, 1982).

The Judaic faith embraces a number of factions or denominations that are similar in their roots but marked by sharp distinctions. No precise data reveal the relative numbers of the three groups. Part of the problem is the difficulty of placing individuals in the proper group. It is common, for example, for a Jew to be a member of an Orthodox congregation but consider himself or herself Conservative. The following levels of affiliation are based on the 1990 National Jewish Population Study (Kosmin et al., 1991) and show ranges depending upon whether one considers only those born Jewish or also those who converted: Orthodox: 6–7 percent; Conservative: 31–38 percent; Reformed: 42–49 percent; other: 13–14 percent. As with denominations among Protestants, Jewish denominations carry social class, nationality, and other social differences. The Reformed Jews are the wealthiest and best formally educated of the group, the Orthodox the poorest and least educated in years of formal secular schooling, and the Conservatives occupy a position between the two, as shown in Table

15.3 A fourth branch of American Judaism, Reconstructionism, an offshoot of the Conservative movement has only recently developed an autonomous institutional structure. Many of the ritual and other differences among the three branches shown in the table may be rooted in social class. Religious identification is also associated with generation: immigrants tend to be Orthodox and their grandchildren are more likely to be Reformed (Cohen, 1988; Goldstein and Goldscheider, 1968, pp. 175–181; Liebman, 1973, p. 84).

## JEWISH IDENTITY

Ethnic and racial identification can be positive or negative. Awareness of ethnic identity can contribute to an individual's self-esteem and give him or her a sense of group solidarity with similar people. When experienced only as a basis for discrimination or insults, the individual may want to shed his or her identity in favor of one more acceptable to society. Unfavorable differential treatment can also encourage closer ties among members of the community being discriminated against, as it has for Jews. Louis Wirth, in his study of Jewish American slum life, *The Ghetto*, wrote:

> What has held the Jewish community together . . . is . . . the fact that the Jewish community is treated as a community by the world at large. The treatment which the Jews receive at the hands of the press and the general public imposes collective responsibility from without. (1928, p. 270)

Most would judge the diminishing of out-group hostility and the ability of Jews to leave the ghetto as a positive development (G. Friedman, 1967, pp. 262–283).

The improvement in Jewish-Gentile relations also creates a problem in Jewish social identity not present before. It has become possible for Jews to shed their "Jewishness" or *Yiddishkait*. Many retain their *Yiddishkait* even in suburbia, but it is more difficult there than in the ghetto. In the end, however, Jews cannot lose their identity entirely. Jews are still denied total assimilation in the United States

---

**TABLE 15.3**   Social Characteristics of Group (percentages)

For every social characteristic there are significant differences among the three groups, as shown in these data from the 1970–1971 National Jewish Population Survey.

| Characteristics | Orthodox | Conservative | Reformed |
|---|---|---|---|
| Age: 60 or over | 33 | 30 | 21 |
| Foreign-born | 45 | 23 | 8 |
| Parents U.S.-born | 5 | 14 | 24 |
| College graduates | 24 | 30 | 37 |
| Income: $20,000+ | 15 | 19 | 31 |

*Source:* Lazerwitz, 1983. Used by permission of the authors. Copyright © 1983 by Bernard Lazerwitz and Michael Harrison.

no matter how much the individual ceases to think of himself or herself as Jewish. Social clubs will still refuse membership and prospective in-laws will still deny their child's hand in marriage. Events in the world also remind the most assimilated Jew of the heritage left behind. A few such reminders in the past generation include: Nazi Germany, founding of Israel in 1948, Six-Day War of 1967, Soviet interference with Jewish life and migration, the terrorist attack at the 1972 Munich Olympics, the Yom Kippur War of 1973, the 1973 oil embargo, the 1974 anti-Zionism vote, and the Scud attacks during the 1991 Gulf War.

Three factors contribute to Jewish identity: family, religion, and cultural heritage (Dashefsky and Shapiro, 1974, pp. 1–9, 128–130; Gans, 1956; Herberg, 1983; Porter, 1985; Rosenthal, 1960).

## *Role of the Family*

The Jewish family has been the subject of more novels than that of probably any other ethnic group. A common theme is the child's struggle to free himself or herself from the mother's domination. Unfortunately, no wealth of social science studies matches the fictional literature. In general, the family performs the functions of childhood socialization and adult management of sexual desires, but for religious Jews it also fulfills a religious commandment. In the past this compulsion was so strong that the *shadchan* (the marriage broker or matchmaker) fulfilled an important function in the Jewish community by ensuring marriage for all eligible people. The emergence of romantic love in modern society made the *shadchan* less acceptable to young Jews, but recent statistics show Jews more likely to marry than any other group.

Jews have traditionally remained in extended families, intensifying the transmission of Jewish identity. Numerous observers have argued that the Jewish family today no longer maintains its role in identity-transmission and that consequently the family is contributing to assimilation. The American Jewish Committee (Conver, 1976) released a report in 1976 identifying ten problems that are endangering "the family as the main transmission agent of Jewish values, identity, and continuity." The following issues are still relevant to Jews nearly two decades later.

1. More Jews marry later than members of other groups.
2. Most organizations of single Jews no longer operate solely for the purpose of matching. These groups are now supportive of singles and the single way of life.
3. The divorce rate is rising; there is no presumption of the permanence of marriage and no stigma attached to its failure.
4. The birthrate is falling and childlessness has become socially acceptable.
5. Financial success has taken precedence over childraising in importance and for many has become the major goal of the family.
6. Intensity of family interaction has decreased, although it continues to be higher than in most other religious and ethnic groups.

7. There is less socializing across generational lines, partly as a result of geographical mobility.
8. The sense of responsibility of family members to other family members has declined.
9. The role of Jewishness is no longer central to the lives of Jews.
10. Intermarriage has lessened involvement of the Jewish partner in Jewish life and emphasis on Jewish aspects of family life.

Data and sample surveys have verified these trends. To use a term introduced in Chapter 10 with the Chicano family, Jewish Americans still have a higher than typical degree of *familism*. Jews are more likely than other ethnic or religious groups to be members of a household that interacts regularly with kinfolks. Nonetheless, the trend is away from familism, which could further erode Jewish identity (Farber et al., 1976, pp. 355–372; Rosenblatt, 1977; Sklare, 1971, pp. 73–102; I. Spiegel, 1974; Winch et al., 1967).

Without question, of the ten problems cited by the American Jewish Committee, intermarriage has received the greatest attention from Jewish leaders. Since Christianity's influence grew, a persistent fear among Jews has been that their children or grandchildren would grow up to be *amhaaretz*, ignorant of the Torah. Even worse, a descendant might become *apikoros*, an unbeliever who engages in intellectual speculation about the relevance of Judaism. Intermarriage, of course, makes a decrease in the American Jewish community more likely. As tolerance of mixed marriages rises in the United States, so too does Jewish leaders' concern over it especially since the decrease in cultural differences between Jews and Gentiles makes such marriages a greater possibility (Bell, 1961; Dinnerstein, 1988, p. 6; Farber et al., 1976, pp. 360–362; Goldscheider, 1986, p. 11; Mayer, 1983; Volsky, 1985). The results of the 1990 National Jewish Population Study document a high degree of outmarriage. Since 1985, 52 percent of all marriages involving Jews have been interfaith compared to only 9 percent a generation earlier. This means that American Jews today are just as likely to marry a Gentile as a Jew. Three-quarters of the children of the Jewish-Gentile marriage are not raised as Jews (Kosmin et al., 1991).

Intermarriage, however, need not mean a decline in the number of faithful. Non-Jewish spouses could convert to Judaism and raise children in the faith. For example 60 percent of intermarried Jews still participate in Passover rituals. However, some more traditional Jews question the integrity of these occasional ventures into the faith and see it as further evidence of *Judaization*. Yet many Jewish leaders respond that intermarriage is inevitable and that the Jewish community must build on whatever links the intermarried couple may still have with their ethnic culture (K. Woodward, 1991).

## Role of Religion

Devotion to Judaism appears to be the clear way to preserve ethnic identity. Jews are divided as to how they practice their faith. Many of the Orthodox see Reformed Jews as little better than nonbelievers. Even among the Orthodox, some sects like the Lubavitchers try to awaken less observant Orthodox to their spiritual obligation.

The religious question facing Jews is not so much one of ideology as of observing the commandments of traditional Jewish law. The religious variations among the nearly 6 million Jewish Americans are a product of attempts to accommodate traditional rituals and precepts to life in the dominant society. It is in adhering to such rituals that Jews are most likely to be at odds with the Christian theme advanced in public schools, even if it appears only in holiday parties. In Chapter 1, we introduced the term *marginality* to describe the status of living in two distinct cultures simultaneously. Walter Gerson's (1969) study of Jews at Christmastime was cited as an example of individuals accommodating themselves to two cultures. For all but the most Orthodox, this acceptance means disobeying commandments or even accepting non-Jewish traditions by singing Christmas carols or exchanging greeting cards (M. Gordon, 1964, pp. 192–193).

In Chapter 5, we discussed the third-generation principle advanced by Marcus Hansen (1952). He maintained that ethnic interest and awareness that decreased among the children of immigrants would increase in the third generation—"what the son wishes to forget the grandson wishes to remember." A writer, Paul Cowan, for example, whose father, a CBS executive, changed his name from Cohen, and whose mother had been raised a Christian Scientist, a faith to which her parents converted in 1910, in middle age embraced Judaism. Cowan's wife, a Protestant, converted as well (Silberman, 1985).

Is there a widespread pattern among Jewish Americans of reviving the "old ways"? Some Jews, especially those secure in their position, have taken up renewed orthodoxy. It is difficult to say whether the rise of traditionalism among Jews is a significant force, rather than a fringe movement as it was viewed in the 1960s. Generally, the assimilation of each successive generation has been accompanied by relaxing traditional rituals and accepting more secular practices within a Jewish context. For some Jews, however, and perhaps a growing proportion, elements of the tradition are being revived and reaffirmed (Gittleson, 1984).

## Role of Cultural Heritage

For many Jews, religious observance is a very small aspect of their Jewishness. Rather, they express their identity in a variety of political, cultural, and social activities. For them, acts of worship, fasting, eating permitted foods, and the study of the Torah and Talmud are irrelevant to being Jewish. Religious Jews, of course, find such a position impossible to accept (Liebman, 1973, pp. 196–197).

Many Gentiles, mistakenly suppose that a measure of Jewishness is the ability to speak Yiddish. Few people have spoken as many languages as the Jews through their long history. Yiddish is but one, and it developed in Jewish communities in Eastern Europe between the tenth and twelfth centuries. Fluency in Yiddish in the United States has been associated with the immigrant generation and the Orthodox. Sidney Goldstein and Calvin Goldscheider report that evidence overwhelmingly supports the conclusion that linguistic assimilation among Jews is almost complete by the third generation (1968, p. 227; see also Shenker, 1974). The 1960s and 1970s, however, brought a slight increase in the use of Hebrew. This change was probably due to increased pride in Israel and greater interaction between that nation and the United States.

Overall, the differences between Jews and Gentiles have declined in the United States. To a large extent this reduction is a product of generational changes typical of all ethnic groups. The first-generation Mexican American poses sharp contrasts with the middle-class White living in suburban Boston. The convergence in culture and identity is much greater between the fourth generation Chicano and his or her White counterpart. A similar convergence is occurring among Jews. This change does not mean the eventual demise of the Jewish identity. Moreover, Jewish identity is not a single identity, as we can see from the heterogeneity in religious observance, dedication to Jewish and Israeli causes, and participation in Jewish organizations.

Being Jewish comes from the family, the faith, and the culture, but it does not require any one criterion. Jewishness transcends nation, religion, or culture. A sense of *peoplehood* is present that neither anti-Semitic bigotry or even an ideal state of fellowship would destroy. American life may have drastically modified Jewish life in the direction of dominant society values, but it has not eliminated it. Milton Gordon refers to peoplehood as a group with a shared feeling (1964, pp. 23–24). For Jews this sense of identity originates from a variety of sources, past and present, both within and without (Heilman, 1982; Himmelfarb, 1982; Liebman, 1973, pp. 196–197).

## GLANCING BACK AND LOOKING AHEAD

Jewish Americans are the product of three waves of immigration originating from three different Jewish communities—the Sephardic, the Western European, and the Eastern European. They brought different languages and, to some extent, different levels of religious orthodoxy. Today they have assimilated to form an ethnic group that transcends the initial differences in nationality. Not that Jews are a homogeneous group. Among them are the Reformed, the Conservative, and Orthodox denominations, listed in ascending order of adherence to traditional rituals.

Nonreligious Jews make up another group, probably as large as any one segment, and still look upon themselves as Jewish.

Jewish identity is reaffirmed from within and outside the Jewish community; however, both sources of affirmation are less strong today. Identity is strengthened by the family, religion, and the vast network of national and community-based organizations. Anti-Semitism outside the Jewish community strengthens the in-group feeling and the perception that survival as a people is threatened.

Today American Jews face a new challenge: they must maintain their identity in an overwhelmingly Christian society in which discrimination is fading and outbreaks of prejudice are sporadic. *Yiddishkait* may not so much have decreased as changed. Elements of the Jewish tradition have been shed in part because of modernization and social change. Some of this social change—decline in anti-Semitic violence and restrictions—is certainly welcomed. While *kashrut* observance has declined, the vast majority of Jews care deeply about Israel and many engage in pro-Israel activities. Commitment has changed with the times but it has not disappeared (Cohen, 1988, pp. 24–26).

Some members of the Jewish community view the apparent assimilation with alarm and warn against the grave likelihood of the total disappearance of a sizable and identifiable Jewish community in the United States. Others see the changes not as erosion but as an accommodation to a pluralistic environment. We are witness to a progressive change in the substance and style of the Jewish life. According to this view, Jewish identity has shed some, the Orthodox and Conservative traditions notwithstanding, of its traditional characteristics but acquired others. The strength of this view comes with the knowledge that doomsayers have been present in the American Jewish community for at least two generations. Only the passage of time will divulge the nature of Jewish life in the United States (Finestein, 1988; Glazer, 1990).

Although discrimination against the Jews has gone on for centuries, far more ancient than anti-Semitism and the experience of the diaspora is the subordinate role of women. Women were perhaps the first to be relegated to an inferior role and may be the last to work collectively to struggle for equal rights. Studying women as a minority group will reaffirm the themes in our study of racial and ethnic minorities.

## KEY TERMS

**anti-Semitism**   Anti-Jewish prejudice or discrimination.

**fringe-of-values theory**   Behavior which is on the border of conduct that a society regards as proper and which is often carried out by subordinate groups, subjecting those groups to negative sanctions.

**in-group virtues**   Proper behavior by one's own group ("in-group virtues") becomes unacceptable when practiced by outsiders ("out-group vices").

**Judaization**   The lessening importance of Judaism as a religion and the substitution of cultural traditions as the tie that binds Jews.

**kashrut**   Laws pertaining to permissible (*Kosher*) and forbidden foods and their preparation.

**noshrim**   Immigrants who have discarded all traces of Jewish religious faith and commitment to the larger Jewish community.

**out-group vices**   See "in-group virtues," above.

**peoplehood**   Milton Gordon's term for a group with a shared feeling.

**Yiddishkait**   Jewishness.

**Zionism**    Traditional Jewish religious yearning to return to the biblical homeland, now used to refer to support for the state of Israel.

## FOR FURTHER INFORMATION

*American Jewish Yearbook.* Philadelphia: Jewish Publication Society.

> Published annually since 1899, this is the best available reference book on Jewish Americans. Each edition contains different articles in addition to updated biographies and bibliographies.

Steven M. Cohen. *American Assimilation or Jewish Revival?* Bloomington: Indiana University Press, 1988.

> The author views cautiously, but optimistically, the response of the American Jewish community to the "threat" of assimilation.

M. Herbert Danzger. *Returning to Tradition.* New Haven: Yale University Press, 1989.

> A study of nonobservant Jewish families who have chosen to become practicing Orthodox Jews.

Calvin Goldscheider. *Jewish Continuity and Change: Emerging Patterns in America.* Bloomington: Indiana University Press, 1986.

> Two surveys of the Boston Jewish community are placed in the context of issues on Jewish identity and group cohesion.

Irving Howe. *World of Our Fathers.* New York: Harcourt Brace Jovanovich, 1976.

> This substantial volume (714 pages) is a narrative of two generations of "bedraggled and inspired" Jewish immigrants on New York City's Lower East Side.

Jonathan Kaufman. *Broken Alliance.* New York: Scribners, 1988.

> A look at Black-Jewish animosity as seen through the lives of a handful of Blacks and Jews such as Paul Parks, a Black American who, as a soldier, rescued Holocaust survivors and who later became an aide to Martin Luther King, Jr.

Abraham D. Lavender, ed. *A Coat of Many Colors: Jewish Subcommunities in the United States.* Westport, CT: Greenwood Press, 1977.

> The author has compiled 32 articles dealing with segments of the Jewish community routinely overlooked: small-town Jews, Southern Jews, poor Jews, Hasidic Jews, Black Jews, Jewish women, and Sephardic Jews.

Charles S. Liebman and Steven M. Cohen. *Two Worlds of Judaism: The Israeli and American Experiences.* New Haven: Yale University Press, 1990.

> The authors explore how Israeli and American Jews differ in the ways they conceptualize their Judaism.

Egon Mayer. *Love and Tradition: Marriage Between Jews and Christians.* New York: Plenum, 1985.

> Sociologist Mayer presents this descriptive and empirical study on Jewish intermarriage.

Marshall Sklare, ed. *Understanding American Jewry.* New Brunswick, NJ: Transaction Books, 1982.

> This fine collection of articles focuses on such topics as demography, Jewish identity, religion, and family structure.

Stephen L. Slavin and Mary A. Pradt. *The Einstein Syndrome: Corporate Anti-Semitism in America Today.* Washington, DC: University Press of America, 1982.

> The authors assess the presence of Jewish Americans in financial institutions and big corpora-

tions. They also offer a thorough analysis of recruitment practices that may contribute to the underrepresentation of Jews in executive suites.

Herbert A. Strauss and Werner Bergmann, eds. Current Research on Antisemitism. Hawthorne, NY: Walter de Gruyter, 1987–1990.

This series of five volumes will eventually deal with the causes, forms, and consequences of anti-Semitism. Published so far are Helen Fein, ed., *The Persisting Question: Sociological Perspectives and Social Contexts of Modern Antisemitism,* and Werner Bergmann, ed., *Error Without Trial: Psychological Research on Antisemitism.*

## *Periodicals*

The Jewish community is served by many newspapers and periodicals, of which the weekly *Commentary* (1946), published by the American Jewish Congress, is perhaps the most authoritative. Journals include *Judaism* (1952), *The Jewish Journal of Sociology* (1958), the *Jewish Review* (1946), *Contemporary Jewry* (1975), and *Jewish Social Studies* (1938).

## Part Four

# OTHER PATTERNS OF DOMINANCE

## Chapter Sixteen

# WOMEN: THE OPPRESSED MAJORITY

*Chapter Outline*

**Gender Roles and Gender Identity**

**Sociological Perspectives**

**The Feminist Movement**

The Suffrage Movement

The Women's Liberation Movement

**The Position of American Women**

Employment

Education

Family Life

Politics

**Double Jeopardy: Minority Women**

**Glancing Back and Looking Ahead**

**Key Terms**

**For Further Information**

---

### ✳ HIGHLIGHTS ✳

Minority group status means confinement to subordinate roles not justified by an individual's abilities. Society is increasingly aware that women are a subordinate group. There are biological differences between males and females even if not among races and nationalities; however, one must separate differences of gender from those produced by *sexism,* distinctions that results from socialization. The *feminist movement* did not begin with the *women's liberation* *movement* but has a long history, and like protest efforts by other minority groups has not been warmly received by society. A comparison of the socioeconomic position of men and women leaves little doubt that opportunities are unequal in employment and political power. Minority women occupy an especially difficult position, in that they experience subordinate status by virtue of their race or ethnicity and their gender.

---

Women are an oppressed group; they are a social minority in the United States and throughout Western society. Men dominate in influence, prestige, and wealth. Women do occupy positions of power, but those who do are the exception, as evidenced by newspaper accounts that declare "she is the first woman" or "she is the only female."

Many people, men and women, find it difficult to conceptualize women as a subordinate group. After all, women do not live in ghettos. They no longer have to attend inferior schools. They freely interact and live with their alleged oppressors, men. How then are they a minority? Let us reexamine the five properties of a minority group introduced in Chapter 1.

1. Women have physical and cultural characteristics that distinguish them from the dominant group (men).
2. Women do experience unequal treatment. Although they are not residentially segregated, they are victims of prejudice and discrimination.
3. Membership in the subordinate group is involuntary.
4. Through the rise of contemporary feminism, women have become increasingly aware of their subordinate status and have developed a greater sense of group solidarity.
5. Women are not forced to marry within the group, yet many women feel that their subordinate status is most irrevocably defined within marriage.

In this chapter the similarities between women and the other minority groups will be apparent (R. Dworkin, 1982; Hochschild, 1973, pp. 118–120).

The most common analogy among minorities used in the social sciences is the similarity between the status of Blacks and that of women. Blacks are obviously a minority group, but, one asks, how can women of all groups be so similar in condition? An entire generation has observed and participated in both the civil rights movement and the women's liberation movement. Suffrage campaigns, demonstrations, sit-ins, lengthy court battles, and self-help groups are common to the movement for equal rights for both women and Blacks. But similarities were recognized long before the recent protests against inequality. Gunnar Myrdal in *An American Dilemma*—the famous study of race described in Chapter 1—observed that a parallel to the Black's role in society was found with women (1944, pp. 1073–1078). Others, like Helen Mayer Hacker (1951, 1974) later elaborated on the similarities.

What do these groups have in common besides being recent protest movements? The negative stereotypes directed at the two groups are quite similar—both have been considered emotional, irresponsible, weak, or inferior. Their status is even rationalized—"women's place is in the home" and the myth of the "contented Negro." Both are thought to fight subtly against the system—women allegedly try to outwit men by feminine wiles, as Blacks allegedly outwit Whites by pretending to be deferential or respectful. To these must be added another similarity—neither women nor Blacks can be expected to accept a subordinate role in society any longer.

Nearly all Whites give lip service to, even if they do not wholeheartedly believe, the contention that Blacks are innately equal to Whites. They are inherently the same. But men and women are not the same, and they vary most dramatically in their roles in reproduction. Biological differences have contributed to sexism. *Sexism* refers to the ideology that one sex is superior to the other. Quite different is the view that there are few differences between the sexes. Such an idea is expressed in the concept of *androgyny*. An androgynous model of behavior permits people to see that persons can be both aggressive *and* expressive, depending upon requirements of the situation. People do not have to be locked into the labels "masculine" and "feminine." In the United States, people disagree widely as to what implications, if any, the biological differences between the sexes have for social roles. We will begin our discussion of women as a minority group by treating this topic.

## GENDER ROLES AND GENDER IDENTITY

Males and females are not biologically the same, nor are the sociocultural expectations and opportunities for men and women. How much do the biological differences of men and women contribute to the cultural differences of the sexes?

Distinctions a culture makes, whether about who is primarily responsible for teaching children or who leads a battalion into war, reflect cultural assumptions about sex differences. The term *gender identity* refers to the individual's self-concept of him- or herself as male or female. Gender identity is one of the first identities that a human being acquires; it is shaped by the particular values of

**SMITH, YOU TAKE THAT HILL .... DAVIS, YOU TAKE THAT MACHINE-GUN NEST.... JONES, YOU TAKE DICTATION ....**

*The 1991 Desert Storm maneuver brought attention again to the large proportion of women in the military who are denied most combat roles—a key to upward mobility within the command structure.*
*By Peters for the Dayton Daily News, Ohio.*

a culture. As this chapter will show, not all cultures assign qualities to each sex in the same way.

The social consequences of gender identity are reflected in *gender roles,* sometimes called *sex roles.* Gender roles refer to expectations regarding the proper behavior, attitudes, and activities of males and females. "Toughness" has been traditionally seen in the United States as masculine—and desirable only in men—while "tenderness" has been viewed as feminine. A society may require that one sex or the other take primary responsibility for socialization of the children, economic support of the family, or religious leadership. Gender identity, implemented through sex roles, can reinforce the structure of a society that sharply differentiates between the positions of women and men.

Gender roles vary from society to society. Surveys of cultures past and present find the degree of male dominance ranging from total to minimal (M. Whyte, 1978). The differences arise out of socialization patterns. We are conditioned to conform to the prevailing norms of what men and women are supposed to be like. In the United States, boys have been channeled into competitive sports and woodworking, and girls traditionally have been led to dolls and the kitchen. Men have been expected to be the breadwinners and women have been obligated to prepare the food.

It may be obvious now how males and females are conditioned to assume men's and women's roles, but the origin of gender roles as we know them is less clear. Many studies have been made using laboratory animals, injecting monkeys and rats with doses of male and female hormones. Primates in their natural surroundings have been closely observed for the presence and nature of gender roles. Animal studies do not point to instinctual gender differences similar to what humans are familiar with as masculinity and femininity. Historically, women's work came to be defined as a consequence of the birth process. Men, free of child-care responsibilities, generally became the hunters and foragers for food. Even though women must bear children, men could have cared for the young. Exactly why women were assigned that role in some societies is not known. Women's role did not turn out to be the same cross-culturally. Furthermore, we know that definitions of masculinity and femininity change in a society. The men in the royal courts of Europe in the late 1700s fulfilled present-day stereotypes of feminine behavior in their display of ornamental dress and personal vanity rather than resembling men of a century later. The social roles of the sexes have no constants in time or space (Bernard, 1975, p. 15; Kessler, 1976, p. 14; Martin and Voorhies, 1975, pp. 144–177).

## SOCIOLOGICAL PERSPECTIVES

Through socialization, people are labeled by virtue of their sex. Certain activities and behaviors are associated with men and others with women. Besides the labeling perspective, we can also employ functionalist and conflict perspectives to grasp more firmly how gender roles develop.

Functionalists maintain that sex differentiation has contributed to overall social stability. Sociologists Talcott Parsons and Robert Bales (1955, pp. 13–15; 22–26) argued that to function most efficiently, the family requires adults who will specialize in particular roles. They believed that the arrangement of gender roles with which they were familiar arose because marital partners needed a division of labor.

The functionalist view is initially persuasive in explaining the way in which women and men are typically brought up in American society. It would lead us, however, to expect girls and women with no interest in children to become babysitters and mothers. Similarly, males with a caring feeling for children might be "programmed" into careers in the business world. Clearly, such differentiation between the sexes can have harmful consequences for the individual who does not fit into prescribed roles, while depriving society of the optimal use of many talented individuals who are confined by sexual labeling. Consequently, the conflict perspective is increasingly convincing in its analysis of development of gender roles.

Conflict theorists do not deny the presence of a differentiation by sex. In fact, they contend that the relationship between females and males has been one of unequal power, with men dominant over women. Men may have become powerful in preindustrial times because their size, physical strength, and freedom from childbearing duties allowed them to dominate women physically. In contemporary societies, such considerations are not as important, yet cultural beliefs about the sexes are now long established.

Both functionalists and conflict theorists acknowledge that it is not possible to change gender roles drastically without dramatic revisions in a culture's social structure. Functionalists see potential social disorder, or at least unknown social consequences, if all aspects of traditional sex differentiation are disturbed. Yet, for conflict theorists, no social structure is ultimately desirable if it has to be maintained by oppressing a majority of its citizens (Miller and Garrison, 1982; Schaefer and Lamm, 1992, pp. 326–333).

The labeling approach emphasizes how the media, even in the present, display traditional gender-role patterns. For example, the portrayal of women and men on television has tended to reinforce conventional gender roles. A cross-cultural content analysis of television advertising in the United States, Mexico, and Australia found sexual stereotyping common in all three countries. Australia was found to have the lowest level of stereotyping, but even in that country, feminist groups were working to eliminate the "use of the woman's body to sell products" (Courtney and Whipple, 1982, p. 183; Gilly, 1988).

In the United States, women have traditionally been presented on primetime television as homemakers, nurses, and household workers—positions that reflect stereotyped notions of women's work. However, by the late 1980s, women had achieved a better image on primetime programs. A 1987 study found that 75 percent of the women portrayed on these shows were employed outside the home; only about 8 percent were full-time homemakers. Indeed, television seemed to be presenting an overly favorable picture of the types of jobs women hold. In 1987, more than half of women characters on primetime shows had professional careers, while only 25 percent worked in clerical or service jobs. Researchers noted that the real-life portrait was "almost exactly reversed;" 47 percent of women held clerical or service jobs while only 24 percent worked in professional or managerial jobs (Cabrera, 1989; Waters and Huck, 1989, p. 50).

Knowledge about the similarity of sexes and establishment of equal opportunity for men and women are not the same. Feminists, both male and female, have struggled to allow the sexes to have the same options. It has not been an easy struggle, as documented in the next section.

## THE FEMINIST MOVEMENT

Women's struggle for equality, like the struggles of other subordinate groups, has been long and multifaceted. From the very beginning, women activists and sympathetic men who spoke of equal rights were ridiculed and scorned.

In a formal sense, the American feminist movement was born in upstate New York, in a town called Seneca Falls, in the summer of 1848. On July 19, the first women's rights convention began, attended by Elizabeth Cady Stanton, Lucretia Mott, and other pioneers in the struggle for women's rights. This first wave of *feminists,* as they are currently known, battled ridicule and scorn as they fought for legal and political equality for women. They were not afraid to risk controversy on behalf of their cause. In 1872, for example, Susan B. Anthony was arrested for attempting to vote in that year's presidential election.

All social movements, and feminism is no exception, have been marked by factionalism and personality conflicts. The civil rights movement and pan-Indianism have been hurt repeatedly by conflicts over what tactics to use and which reforms to push for first, not to mention personality conflicts. Despite similar divisiveness, the women's movement struggled on toward its major goal—to gain the right to vote (Sochen, 1982).

## The Suffrage Movement

The *suffragists* worked for years to get women the right to vote. From the beginning this reform was judged to be crucial. If women voted, it was felt, other reforms would quickly follow. The struggle took so long that many of the initial advocates of women's suffrage died before victory was reached. In 1879, an amendment to the Constitution was introduced that would have given women the right to vote. Not until 1919 was it finally passed, and not until the next year was it ratified as the Nineteenth Amendment to the Constitution.

The opposition to women voting came from all directions. Liquor interests and brewers correctly feared that women would assist in passing laws restricting or prohibiting sale of their products. The South feared the influence more Black voters (that is, Black women) might have. Southerners had also not forgotten the pivotal role women had played in the abolitionist movement. Despite the opposition, the suffrage movement succeeded in gaining women the right to vote, a truly remarkable achievement, because it had to rely on male legislators to do so (Henslin, 1975, pp. 357–358; Sochen, 1982).

The Nineteenth Amendment did not automatically lead to other feminist reforms. Women did not vote as a bloc and have not themselves been elected to office in proportion to their numbers. The singleminded goal of suffrage was, in several respects, harmful to the cause of feminism. Many suffragists thought that any changes more drastic than granting the vote would destroy the home. They rarely questioned the subordinate role assigned to women. For the most part agitation for equal rights ended when suffrage was gained. In the 1920s and 1930s, large numbers of college-educated women entered professions, but these individual achievements did little to enhance the rights of women as a group. The feminist movement as an organized effort that gained national attention faded, to regain prominence only in the 1960s (Freeman, 1975, pp. 18–19; O'Neill, 1969, pp. 264–294; Rossi, 1964, pp. 609–614).

Nevertheless, the women's movement did not die out completely in the first half of the century. Many women carried on the struggle in new areas. Margaret Sanger fought for legalized birth control. She opened birth control clinics because the medical profession refused to distribute such information. Sanger and Katherine Houghton Hepburn (mother of the actress Katharine Hepburn) lobbied Congress for reform throughout the 1920s and 1930s. Sanger's early clinics were closed by police. Not until 1937 were nationwide restrictions on birth control devices listed, and some state bans remained in force until 1965.

## The Women's Liberation Movement

Ideologically, the women's liberation movement has its roots in the continuing feminist movement that began with the first subordination of women in Western society, whenever that was. Psychologically, it took form in America's kitchens, as women felt unfulfilled and did not know why, and in the labor force, where women were made to feel guilty and saw no reason to. Demographically, by the 1960s women had greater control over their reproductive capability by contraception and, hence, the size of the population (Heer and Grossbard-Shectman, 1981).

Sociologically, several events combined in the mid-1960s. The civil rights movement and the antiwar movement were slow to embrace women's rights. The New Left seemed as sexist as the rest of society. Groups protesting the draft and demonstrating on college campuses generally rejected women as leaders and assigned them to prepare refreshments and publish organization newsletters. The core of early feminists often knew each other from participating in other protest or reform groups that were initially unwilling to accept women's

*Discrimination in the workplace is being fought in many other countries besides the United States. Here new railway employees in Japan are being welcomed. The presence of women reflects a 1985 equal opportunity law.*

rights as a legitimate goal. Beginning in about 1967, as Chapter 7 showed, the movement for Black equality was no longer as willing to accept help from sympathetic Whites. White men moved on to protest the draft, a cause not as crucial to women's lives. While somewhat involved in the anti-war movement, many White women moved on to struggle for their own rights, although at first they had to fight alone. Existing groups of women in nontraditional roles, like the 180,000-member Federation of Business and Professional Women, explicitly avoided embracing the feminist cause. Eventually civil rights groups, the New Left, and most established women's groups endorsed the feminist movement with the zeal of new converts, but initially they resisted the concerns of the growing number of feminists (Freeman, 1973, 1983).

A focal point of the feminist movement during the 1970s and early 1980s was passage of the Equal Rights Amendment. First proposed to Congress in 1923, it was finally passed in 1972. The amendment as proposed declares that "Equality of rights under the law shall not be denied or abridged by the United States or by any State on account of sex." The ERA, like other constitutional amendments, requires approval of three-fourths, or 38, of the stage legislatures. Ten years later it had failed to meet this number by only three states. Clearly, the failure of the ERA effort was discouraging to the movement and its leaders. In many states they had been outspent by their opponents, and in some states they were out-organized by effective anti-ERA groups and insurance companies, which feared that their sex-differentiated insurance and pension plan payments would be threatened by the passage of an ERA. Ironically, these insurance practices were overturned in the courts in 1983 (Langer, 1976; O'Reilly, 1982).

The movement has also brought about reexamination of men's roles. Supporters of "male liberation" wished to free men from the constraints of the masculine value system. There is as much a masculine mystique as a feminine one. Boys are socialized to think they should be invulnerable, fearless, decisive, and even emotionless in some situations. Men are expected to achieve physically and occupationally at some cost to their own values, not to mention those of others. Men are regarded as breadwinners and are supposed to view women as sex objects. Failure to take up these roles and attitudes can mean that a man will be considered less than a man. Male liberation is the logical counterpart of female liberation. If women are to redefine their gender role successfully, men must redefine theirs as worker, husband, and father (Cicone and Ruble, 1978; Farrell, 1974; Richardson, 1981; Sawyer, 1972; Schaefer and Lamm, 1992).

The thinking in the feminist movement has undergone significant change. Betty Friedan, a founder of the National Organization for Women (NOW), argued in the early 1960s that women had to recognize *the feminine mystique,* which lulled them into being content as mother and wife. Later in the 1980s, though not denying that women deserved to have the same options in life as men, she called for restructuring the "institution of home and wife." Friedan and others recognize that many young women are now frustrated when they are unable to do it all—career, motherhood, and marriage. Difficult issues remain, leading to discussions among feminists. Activists on behalf of women's rights are divided about laws requiring leave for pregnancy. Some argue that the provisions are necessary, but other feminists balk at any privilege extended to one sex, even if it is to women. These discussions make plain the challenge of creating fairness amidst inequality (Friedan, 1963, 1981, 1991).

## THE POSITION OF AMERICAN WOMEN

Americans are constantly reminded of women's subordinate role. The Commission on Civil Rights concluded that the passage in the Declaration of Independence proclaiming that all men are created equal has been taken too literally for too long (1976b, p. 1). Besides recognizing disparities in political and employment rights, the commission concluded that women are discriminated against in every facet of American society. The following section will assess the position of women in: (1) employment, (2) education, (3) family life, and (4) political activity. The appropriateness of studying women as a social minority will become apparent in this evaluation of their status relative to men in these four areas.

### Employment

Women experience all the problems in employment associated with other minority groups and several that are especially acute for women. Women's subordinate role in the occupational structure is largely the result of institutional discrimination, rather than individual discrimination. Women, more than any other group, are confined to certain occupations. Some sex-typed jobs for women pay well above minimum wages and carry moderate prestige, like nursing and elementary teaching. Nevertheless, they are far lower in pay and prestige than such stereotyped male positions as physician, college president, or university professor. When they do enter nontraditional positions, women as a group receive lower wages or salary.

What about women aspiring to crack the "glass ceiling"? In 1989, a controversy erupted concerning the role of women in corporate America. The debate followed a view about the management styles of men and women. Felice Schwartz, the president and founder of Catalyst, a women's business research group, made her case in the respected *Harvard Business Review*. Schwartz argues that women managers *are* different because many eventually have children and leave work, or cut back on their work commitments, while their children are young. Without a strategy for handling these women, she says, companies pay a high price. Businesses, according to Schwartz, do not receive a full return on their investment in training some women for top jobs if the women quit or are unable to put in long hours after they become mothers.

In suggesting ways to reduce these costs, Schwartz proposes an idea quite unacceptable to many feminists. She says that executives should think of female managers as fitting into two broad categories. "Career primary" women who put work first would be identified early and groomed for top-level positions alongside ambitious men. But executives would also recognize that "career and family" women can be valuable assets. To allow them to spend more time at home, companies would offer more options like flexible hours and part-time jobs. Schwartz herself did not use the term *mommy track*, but it quickly became the buzzword to describe her "career and family" track. Even if it is desirable, there is little evidence that companies are willing to be that flexible.

Women find a very cool reception for ideas that accommodate family commitments. Another common objection to Schwartz's position is that it may only reinforce corporate and social prejudices about women. "My fear is that if only women take this option, they won't move up the career ladder, and they have a guaranteed position as the primary parent," says University of Texas psychologist Lucia A. Gilbert. "We'll be back where we were in the '60s" (B. Kantrowitz, 1989; A. Miller, 1991).

*Labor Force.* The data in Table 16.1 present an overall view of how males dominate high-paying occupations. Among the representative occupations chosen, men unquestionably dominate in high-paying professions and managerial occupations. Women dominate as secretaries, seamstresses, health service workers, and household workers. Trends show the proportions of women increasing slightly in the professions, indicating that women have advanced into better-paying positions, but these gains have not changed the overall picture.

How pervasive is sex-typing of occupations? In studying this question, sociologists William Bielby and James Baron (1986) drew upon data provided by 290

**TABLE 16.1**   Employment of Women in Selected Occupations, 1950 and 1989

Most occupations are routinely filled by members of one sex.

| | Women as Percentage of All Workers in the Occupation | |
| --- | --- | --- |
| *Occupation* | *1950* | *1989* |
| Professional workers | 40 | 50 |
| Engineers | 1 | 8 |
| Lawyers and judges | 4 | 22 |
| Physicians | 7 | 18 |
| Registered nurses | 98 | 94 |
| College teachers | 23 | 39 |
| Other teachers | 75 | 73 |
| Managers | 14 | 40 |
| Sales workers | 35 | 49 |
| Clerical workers | 62 | 82 |
| Machine operators | 34 | 41 |
| Transport operatives | 1 | 9 |
| Service workers | 57 | 60 |

*Sources:* Bureau of the Census, 1991a, pp. 395–397; Department of Labor, 1980, pp. 10–11.

economic establishments in California. The researchers reviewed the 10,000 job titles held by some 51,000 workers. They found complete occupational segregation by gender in jobs employing 17 percent of California's workers. That is, these jobs are held either only by women or only by men. Social scientists have traditionally argued that the psychological and social effects of tokenism become evident when a dominant group constitutes 80 percent or more of those fulfilling a role (Kanter, 1977; Pettigrew, 1985). Using this criterion, 63 percent of the California workers studied by Bielby and Baron are in occupations where gender balance is severely skewed.

In another study, researchers compiled a "segregation index" to estimate the percentage of women who would have to change their jobs to make the distribution of men and women in each occupation mirror the relative percentage of each sex in the adult working population. This study showed that 58 percent of women workers would need to switch jobs in order to create a labor force without sex segregation (Jacobs, 1990; Reskin and Blau, 1990).

While sex-typing of occupations continues, women have increased participation in the labor force. A greater proportion of women seek and obtain paid employment than ever before in United States history. In 1890 fewer than one is seven workers were women, compared to almost one in two in 1992. The most dramatic rise in the female work force has been among married women. In 1991, 58 percent of married women worked, compared to fewer than 5 percent in 1890. In 1991, 58 percent of women in the United States were working or seeking work, compared to 77 percent of men. By the year 2000 these proportions are projected to be 63 percent for women and 76 percent for men (Bureau of the Census, 1991a, p. 384). The proportions remain close to half regardless of whether the woman is single or married or a mother. More than half of married mothers with children under six are working (see Table 16.2).

It is logical to assume that these proportions would be even higher if day care in the United States received more support. A number of European nations, including France, the Netherlands, Sweden, and the former Soviet Union, provide pre-school care at minimal or no cost. However, in the United States, these costs are generally borne by the working parent. Recently, some employers have recognized the benefits of offering care and have begun to provide or subsidize this care, but this is the exception not the rule.

Women's work for wages is not a recent change, as is popularly assumed. It is a phenomenon that has increased steadily throughout this century, although especially noticeable gains have been made in recent years among mothers. Nearly half—48 percent—of women who gave birth in 1985 were back at work within 12 months. The proportion was 31 percent in 1976. This increase is especially remarkable given the general lack of high-quality, reasonably-priced child care available to working mothers (J. Dworkin, 1982; Schaefer and Lamm, 1992).

A primary goal of many feminists is to eliminate sex discrimination in the labor force and to equalize job opportunities for women. Without question, women earn less than men. Tables 3.1 and 3.2 show that women earn less than

**TABLE 16.2**   Labor Force Participation by Marital Status, 1950 and 1991

A growing number of women—married and single, with children and childless—participate in the nation's paid labor force.

| | Percentage in Labor Force | |
| --- | --- | --- |
| Sex and Marital Status | 1950 | 1991 |
| Total | | |
| Women | 33.9 | 58.0 |
| Men | 86.8 | 77.0 |
| Married persons with spouse present | | |
| Women | 23.8 | 58.6 |
| Men | 91.6 | 81.5 |
| Married women with spouse present | | |
| No children under 18 years old | 30.3 | 51.0 |
| Children 6–17 years old only | 28.3 | 73.7 |
| Children under 6 years old | 11.9 | 58.7 |
| Women working with spouse absent* | | |
| Children 6–17 years old only | 63.6 | 79.0 |
| Children under 6 years old | 41.4 | 64.0 |

*Includes divorced and separated. 1950 data also include widowed.
Sources: Bureau of the Census, pp. 27–32, 40; 1976; 1991a, pp. 384, 391; Department of Labor, 1991; and author's estimate.

men even when race and education are held constant; that is, college-educated women working full time make less than comparably educated men. Even when additional controls are introduced, like previous work experience, a substantial earnings gap remains (Suter and Miller, 1973).

*Sources of Discrimination.* Returning to the definition of discrimination cited above, are not men better able to perform some tasks than women, and vice versa? If ability means performance, there certainly are differences. The typical woman can sew better than the typical man, but the latter can toss a ball farther than the former. These are group differences. Certainly many women outthrow many men and many men outsew many women, but society expects women to excel at sewing and men to excel at throwing. The differences in those abilities are due to cultural conditioning. Women are usually taught to sew but men are less likely to learn such a skill. Men are encouraged to participate in sports requiring the ability to throw a ball much more than are women. True, as a group males have greater potential for the muscular development required to throw a ball, but American society encourages men to realize their potential in this area more than it encourages women to pursue athletic skills.

Today's labor market involves much more than throwing a ball and using a needle and thread, but the analogy to these two skills is repeated time and again. Robert Tsuchigane and Norton Dodge identify three components of male-female earning differentials (1974, pp. 97–99).

1. *Market discrimination.* Qualified women are underpaid or underemployed. This condition can be eliminated in a relatively short time by changes in hiring and promotion practices.
2. *Social and cultural conditioning.* There are not enough qualified women for certain high-paying, high-status jobs. This shortage could take longer to eliminate completely because it requires training women who are genuinely interested in pursuing what are now judged to be male careers.
3. *Physiological differences in capabilities.* Women suffer lost job experience and pay due to childbirth. Many feminists argue that employers should grant time for such absences and grant paid maternity leave.

Removing barriers to equal opportunity would eliminate market discrimination and social and cultural conditioning. Theoretically, men and women would sew and perhaps even throw a ball with the same ability. We say theoretically because cultural conditioning would take generations to change. In some formerly male jobs, like being a gas station attendant, society seems quite willing to accept women. In other occupations (being president) it will take longer, and many years may pass before full acceptance can be expected in other fields (professional contact sports).

Many efforts have been taken to eliminate what Tsuchigane and Dodge refer to as market discrimination. The 1964 Civil Rights Act and its enforcement arm, the Equal Employment Opportunity Commission, address cases of sex discrimination. As we saw in Chapter 3, the inclusion of sex bias along with prejudice based on race, color, creed, and national origin was an unexpected last-minute change in the provisions of the landmark 1964 Act. Federal legislation has not removed all discrimination against women in employment. The same explanations presented in Chapter 3 for the lag between the laws and reality with race discrimination apply to sex discrimination: (1) lack of money, (2) weak enforcement powers, (3) occasionally weak commitment to using the laws available, and (4) most important, institutional and structural forces that perpetuate inequality. A fifth factor affects sex discrimination: the courts and enforcement agencies have been slower to mandate equal rights for women than they have been for African Americans and other racial minorities.

*Sexual Harassment.* A particularly damaging form of on-the-job discrimination experienced primarily by women is *sexual harassment,* which has been defined as "the unwarranted imposition of sexual requirements in the context of a relationship of unequal power" (MacKinnon, 1979, p. 1). The most blatant example in the office or factory is the boss who tells a subordinate: "Put out or get out." As a federal advisory council said, however, sexual harassment can take a number of forms, including use of crude or suggestive remarks directed at a person, solicitations of sexual activity by promising a reward, sexual coercion by threat of punishment, and sexual crimes and misdemeanors (*Ms.,* 1981).

Although estimates and definitions vary, a study of the federal workplace released in 1988 found that 42 percent of the women had experienced some form of sexual harassment during the preceding two years. These figures remained

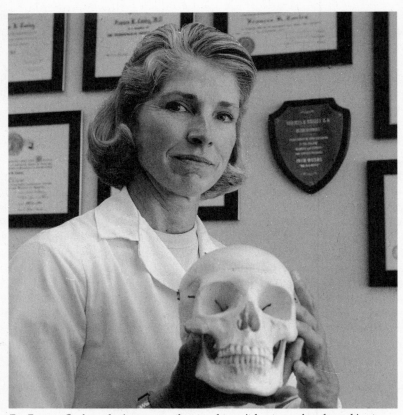

*Dr. Frances Conley, a brain surgeon, threatened to quit her tenured professorship at Stanford Medical School in 1992 after 25 years there, citing sexism and saying that she was the long-time object of demeaning comments and unwelcome advances.*

constant during the 1980s. Not only is such harassment humiliating, but it is costly. A 1992 estimate states that the problem cost $282 per employee per year in paying sick leave to employees who missed work, in replacing employees who left their jobs, and in reduced productivity (Webb, 1992).

In 1986, the Supreme Court in a unanimous decision (*Meritor Savings Bank* v. *Vinson*) declared that sexual harassment by a supervisor violates the federal law against sex discrimination in the workplace as outlined in the 1964 Civil Rights Act. Harassment if sufficiently severe is a violation even if the unwelcomed sexual demands are not linked to concrete employment benefits such as a raise or promotion. Women's groups hailed the court's decisiveness in identifying harassment as a form of discrimination. In the Fall of 1991, national attention was given to sexual harassment as Supreme Court nominee Clarence Thomas was accused by a former co-worker, law professor Anita Hill, of repeatedly harassing her over a period of years. While Thomas was eventually confirmed, the televised hearings encouraged women to come forward. A survey at the time found that 21 percent had been harassed at work and 42 percent said they knew someone who had been harassed (B. Kantrowitz, 1991).

*Pay Equity*. What should be done to close the gap between the earnings of women and men? During the 1980s, *pay equity* or *comparable worth* was a controversial solution presented to alleviate the second-class status of working women. It directly attempted to secure equal pay when sex-typing of occupations was particularly pervasive. *Pay equity* calls for equal pay for different types of work that are judged to be comparable by measuring such factors as employee knowledge, skills, effort, responsibility, and working conditions.

Theoretically, this doctrine sounds straightforward, but it is not so simple to put into operation. How exactly does one determine the comparability of jobs in order to identify comparable worth? Should a zookeeper be paid more than a child care worker? Does our society pay zookeepers more because we value caretaking for children less than caretaking for animals? Or do zookeepers earn more than child care workers because the former tend to be male but the latter are generally female?

In American society, women's work is undervalued and underpaid. Efforts to address the problem of wage discrimination have resulted in legislation and increased public awareness, yet women's salaries remain far lower than those of men. The federal Equal Pay Act of 1963, which mandates equal pay for equal work, applies to a relatively small proportion of female workers—those who perform the same job under the same roof as a male worker. Although these women's wages have increased as a result of the Equal Pay Act, most female workers, as we have seen, remain segregated in a few occupations in which no male workers do the same jobs, so these underpaid women cannot compare themselves to males.

In some instances, the lack of pay equity is difficult to defend. In Arlington County, Virginia, entry-level gardeners working for the county must have a high school diploma and one year's experience before being hires. They earn $13,927 per year to start. By contrast, the position of entry-level Library Assistant I requires two years of college or two years of library experience, yet the pay is only $12,598 per year. Of the entry-level librarians, 93.4 percent are female, while 87.5 percent of the gardeners are male. Such data are cited by advocates of comparable worth, who insist that we need a more equitable way of evaluating jobs to determine their value.

Although sex discrimination is one obvious explanation for the lack of pay equity, other explanations are possible. Employers commonly cite the influence of labor market supply and demand on wages in various occupations. "You can't measure productivity on jobs or the intrinsic worth of a job," argues Owen Johnson of Continental Bank. "Women are disproportionately found in relatively few jobs in our society, and there is an oversupply of women in certain occupations. This oversupply typically results in low wages" (National Commission on Working Women, 1984). Johnson's comment, however, appears questionable because of a labor-market phenomenon evident in the nursing profession. Thousands of nurses have left the field because of low pay; yet, in response to this shortage, wages have not increased. Instead, a general reduction in nursing services has followed, and some institutions have hired nurses from outside the United States who will accept lower wages.

What are potential solutions to the problem of wage discrimination? The courts have generally been reluctant to address this issue or to find wage discrimination in female-dominated occupations that pay less than male-dominated occupations requiring the same or fewer job skills. Many public employers, including the states of New York and New Jersey, have developed voluntary plans to put pay equity policies into effect. According to the National Committee on Pay Equity, by 1988 more than 1,500 local governments and school districts in 24 states had taken steps to address the issue of pay equity. During the 1980s, more than $450 million was allocated by state and local governments to upgrade employees' pay in such traditional "women's jobs" as clerk, typist, librarian, and nurse—with the goal of bringing their salaries up to the level of those of maintenance workers, gardeners, and other government workers in male-dominated classifications (Lewin, 1989, p. 8; Saetre, 1989).

Pay equity is only now beginning to receive public attention. A 1986 national survey showed that only a quarter of the respondents felt they had heard "a fair amount" or "a great deal" about pay equity or comparable worth. Yet most Americans feel that men and women should be paid equally for jobs of comparable worth. Two-thirds agree that it is too difficult and therefore not fair to compare and evaluate jobs that are quite different, such as that of secretary and electrician, to see if they deserve similar compensation. Now that 40 states have started collecting data on pay equity, 34 have established task forces or commissions to study it, 24 are preparing job evaluation studies, and 13 have already implemented pay equity plans at some level, the public will be hearing much more about this concept (*Public Opinion*, 1986; for a different view see Gimenez, 1987).

*Feminization of Poverty.* Since World War II, an increasing proportion of America's poor have been female—many of them divorced or never-married mothers. Currently, two out of three adults classified as poor by the federal government are women (Ehrenreich and Stallard, 1982). In 1959, female heads of household accounted for 26 percent of the nation's poor; by 1989, that figure had doubled to 52 percent. This alarming trend has come to be known as the *feminization of poverty.*

About half of American women in poverty are "in transition," coping with an economic crisis caused by the departure, disability, or death of a husband. The other half tend to be locked into the welfare system or economically dependent on friends or relatives living nearby. A major study of poverty by sociologist Greg J. Duncan (1984, pp. 79–82) pointed to women's role among welfare recipients. Female households were overrepresented (67 percent) among persistent welfare recipients and were an even larger share (78 percent) of recipients continually dependent on welfare sources for more than half their income.

According to economist Isabel Sawhill of the Urban Institute, the feminization of poverty accounts for almost all of the 53 percent increase in the nation's poverty rolls since 1970. Consequently, the President's National Advisory Council on Economic Opportunity has warned that if this trend continues, the "poverty population would be composed solely of women and their children before the year 2000" (Reese, 1982, pp. 21–22). The life chances of these low-income families are of course far from ideal. Children whose mothers live in poverty run an increased risk of birth defects and malnutrition. They are more likely to fare poorly in elementary school and to drop out of high school than are children from other types of families. Low-income single mothers suffer higher levels of stress than other Americans and are much less likely to receive adequate medical care.

Poor women share many social characteristics with poor men: low educational attainment, lack of market-relevant job skills, and residence in economically deteriorating areas. Conflict theorists, however, feel that the higher rates of poverty among women can be traced to two distinct causes. Because of sex discrimination on the job and sexual harassment, women are at a clear disadvantage for vertical social mobility. As mentioned in Chapter 3, year-round White female workers made only $20,840 in 1990, compared with $30,186 for a comparable White male worker.

The burden of supporting a family is especially difficult for single mothers not only because of low salaries but because of inadequate child support as well. According to studies by the Bureau of the Census (1990), the average payment for child support in 1987 was a mere $2,710 per year, or about $52 per week. This level of support is clearly insufficient for rearing a child in the 1990s. Moreover, of the 5.6 million American women scheduled to receive child support payments from their former husbands in 1987, only 51 percent actually received all the money they were scheduled to get, while 25 percent received some of the money due and 24 percent did not receive any of the scheduled payments. In light of these data, federal and state officials have intensified efforts to track down delinquent parents and ensure payment of child support. Policy makers acknowledge that such enforcement efforts have led to substantial reductions in welfare expenditures (Hinds, 1989).

Welfare payments to single mothers remain far from adequate. About 4 million women receive Aid to Families with Dependent Children (AFDC) benefits for themselves and their 7 million dependent children. However, in 1989, the average monthly AFDC payment for a family was only $383. In the view of the Children's Defense Fund, AFDC benefits in most states are "intolerably low, failing to provide even a minimum level of decency" (Bureau of the Census, 1991a, p. 373).

What is the daily life of these women like? According to a study by the University of Michigan's Institute for Social Research (1984) that focused on 300 Michigan families whose AFDC grants had been completely cut off, nearly half had run out of food. In addition, 42 percent were behind in their bills by two months or more; 16 percent had experienced shutoffs of utilities. How, then, did these women and their families survive? One-fifth of the respondents reported that they earned extra money by collecting bottles and cans for refunds; nearly half obtained old produce from grocery stores.

Many feminists feel that continuing dominance of the political system by men contributes to government indifference to the problem of poor women. Patricia B. Reuss, a lobbyist for the Women's Equity Action League, has challenged male politicians who merely pay lip service to this issue. "I'm critical of the leaders of both parties who failed to take hold of the equity act and push the whole thing through," she states. "The things that have gotten through are nice beginnings, rather than real remedies" (S. Roberts, 1984, p. A18). As more and more women fall below the official poverty line, policymakers will face growing pressure to combat the feminization of poverty.

## Education

The experience of women in education has been similar to that in the labor force—a long history of contribution but in traditionally defined terms. In 1833, Oberlin College became the first institution of higher learning to admit women, years after the first men's college began in this country. In 1837, Wellesley became the first women's college. But it would be a mistake to believe these early experiments brought about equality for women in education: at Oberlin, the women were forbidden to speak in public. Furthermore,

> Washing the men's clothes, caring for their rooms, serving them at table, listening to their orations, but themselves remaining respectfully silent in public assemblages, the Oberlin "co-eds" were being prepared for intelligent motherhood and a properly subservient wifehood. (Flexner, 1959, p. 30)

The early graduates of these schools, despite the emphasis in the curriculum on traditional roles, became the founders of the feminist movement.

Today, research confirms that boys and girls are treated differently in school: teachers give boys more attention. In teaching students the values and customs of the larger society, American schools have traditionally socialized children into conventional gender roles. Professors of Education Myra Sadker and David Sadker (1985, p. 54) note that "although many believe that classroom sexism disappeared in the early '70s, it hasn't." They headed a three-year study in which field researchers observed students in more than 100 fourth-, sixth-, and eighth-grade classes in four states and the District of Columbia. The researchers found that teachers commonly engage in differential treatment of students based on gender. Teachers praise boys more than girls and offer boys more academic assistance. In addition, they reward boys for academic assertiveness (for example, calling out answers without raising their hands) while reprimanding girls for similar behavior.

Besides receiving less attention, females are more likely to be encouraged to take courses that will lead them to enter lower-paying fields of employment. This has been the experience of girls who are exposed to courses that prepare them for a role as housewives and who, even when showing the aptitude for "men's work," will be advised to pursue "women's work." Researchers have documented sexism in education in the books used, the vocational counseling provided, and even the content of educational television programs. Perhaps the most apparent result of sexist practices and gender-role conditioning in education is staffing patterns. Administrators and university professors are male and public school teachers are female. Thus, at the college level where women make up half the student body, they are one-third of the faculty. School systems grew more aware of sexism in the 1970s, just as they became suddenly aware of their racism during the 1960s (Bienen et al., 1975; Chow, 1976; Dohrmann, 1975; Dullea, 1975; Ladd and Lipset, 1975; Rossi and Calderwood, 1973; Wikler, 1976).

At all levels of schooling, congressional amendments to the Education Act of 1972 and Department of Health, Education, and Welfare guidelines developed in 1974 and 1975 can be expected to make tremendous changes. Collectively referred to as *Title IX* provisions, the regulations are designed to eliminate sexist practices from almost all school systems. Schools must make these changes or risk loss of all federal assistance.

1. Schools must eliminate all sex-segregated classes and extracurricular activities. This means an end to all-girl home economics and all-boy shop classes, although single-sex hygiene and physical education classes are permitted.
2. Schools cannot discriminate by sex in admissions or financial aid and cannot inquire into whether an applicant is married, pregnant, or a parent. Single-sex schools are exempted.
3. Schools must end sexist hiring and promotion practices among faculty members.
4. Although women do not have to be permitted to play on all-men's athletic teams, schools must provide more opportunities for women's sports, intramurally and extramurally. (*Federal Register*, June 4, 1975).

Title IX is one of the most controversial steps ever taken by the federal government to promote and ensure equality. Not surprisingly, the federal government has been attacked for going too far. Conflict theorists maintain that such criticism reflects an underlying desire to protect the privileged positions of males rather than genuine feeling about federal control and education. Feminists opposed the government moves to soften some Title IX regulations, especially because Title IX fails to affect sex stereotyping in textbooks and curricula and exempts elementary schools and the military academies.

Its supporters feel that Title IX has played a major role in the growing involvement of American women and girls in athletics, however, financial support has not kept pace. By 1992, one out of three athletic scholarships went to a female, yet women comprise half of the students. Similarly, in overall budgets, women's athletics grew from 2 percent in 1972 to 23 percent in 1992. Even when football is eliminated, however, there are significant gaps in men's and women's athletics at almost all colleges (de Varona, 1984, p. 25; Lederman, 1992; *Time*, 1974c).

*The Title IX provisions are designed to eliminate sexist practices from almost all school systems. This legislation played a major role in the growing involvement of women and girls in athletics.*

## *Family Life*

"Does your mother work?" "No, she's a housewife."

This familiar exchange suggests that a woman is married to both a husband and a house and that homemaking does not constitute work. There is some truth to it. Our society generally equates work with wages and holds work not done for pay in low esteem. Women, through household chores and volunteer work, do just such work and are given little status in our society. Furthermore, the demands traditionally placed on a mother and homemaker are so extensive as to make pursuing a career next to impossible. For women, the family is, sociologists Lewis Coser and Rose Laub Coser (1974) say, a "greedy institution." They observed the overwhelming burden of the multiple social roles associated with being a mother and working outside the home.

*Child Care.* A man, boy, or girl can act as a homemaker and caretaker for children, but in the United States these roles are customarily performed by women. Rebelsky and Hanks (1973) examined interactions between fathers and babies and found that the longest time any father in the sample devoted to his infant was 10 minutes 26 seconds. The average period of verbal interaction between father and baby was only 38 *seconds* a day. More recently, psychologist Wade Mackey (1987) conducted a cross-cultural study of 17 societies—including Morocco, Hong Kong, Ireland, and Mexico—and found that the limited father-child interactions in the United States were typical of all the societies surveyed.

American fathers currently find little time for the basic tasks of child rearing. Some men have reworked their job commitments to maximize the amount of time they can spend with their children. For example, a Connecticut salesman comes home for lunch so that he can play with his 7-month-old daughter. On weekends, he rises at 6:00 A.M. so that he can spend time alone with her. Yet, while Bell Telephone has offered men the option of six-month paternity leave since 1969, there have been few takers. It remains difficult for men in two-parent households to deviate from their traditional occupational roles in order to become more involved in child rearing (Langway, 1981).

*Housework.* If child rearing is still primarily women's work, even with most mothers in the labor force, what about housework?

The division of household and child care duties is far from trivial in defining power relations within the family. Heidi Hartmann (1981, p. 377) argues that "time spent on housework, as well as other indicators of household labor, can be fruitfully used as a measure of power relationships in the home." Hartmann points out that as women spend more hours per week working for wages, the amount of time they devote to housework decreases, yet their overall "work-week" increases. However, men in dual-career marriages do not spend more time on housework chores than do husbands of full-time homemakers.

Data from a 1989 national survey suggest that men and women hold somewhat differing perceptions of who does the housework. When asked whether housework was shared equally, 59 percent of women but only 45 percent of men responded that the woman in the couple does more housework. Forty-six percent of men but only 35 percent of women stated that housework is shared equally between male and female partners. Overall, the survey underscored the common sex segregation evident in the performance of household tasks (see Figure 16.1). For example, 78 percent of women report that they do all or most of their families' meal preparation, and 72 percent say they provide all or most of the child care. By contrast, 74 percent of men indicate that they do all or most of the minor home repairs and 63 percent state that they do all or most of the yard work (DeStefano and Colasanto, 1990, pp. 28–29, 31).

Given that housework is still considered most appropriate for women even in the 1990s, perhaps the findings of a Canadian study are not surprising. Sociologist Susan Shaw (1988) found that men and women view housework and child care differently. Specifically, men were more likely to define both as "leisure" and less likely to view them as work than were their wives. The reason for this gender difference is closely associated with such work's being viewed as "women's work." Men perceive themselves as having more freedom of choice in engaging in housework and child care and are more likely to report that cooking, home chores, shopping, household obligations, and child care are, in fact,

**FIGURE 16.1** Household Tasks by Gender

In a national survey conducted in 1989, men and women indicated whom they felt did all or most of a variety of household tasks. Segregation of housework and child care was evident, and other studies indicate that women spend more than twice as much time on housework as men—even when child care is not included.

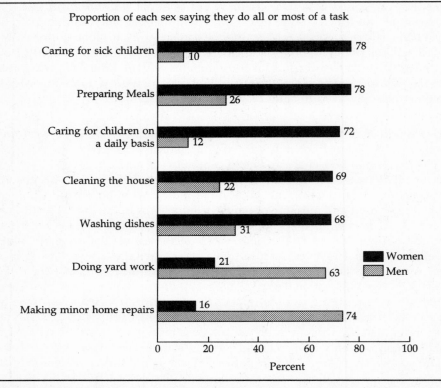

Proportion of each sex saying they do all or most of a task

*Note:* Questions regarding child care were asked only of respondents with children living at home.
*Source:* From "Unlike 1975, Today Most Americans Think Men Have It Better" by Linda DeStefano and Dr. Diane Colasanto from *The Gallup Poll Monthly*, February 1990. Reprinted by permission of The Gallup Poll.

leisure. Confirming early sociological research, Shaw found employment status of women to have no affect on this difference. The growth of women's participation in the labor force has had little effect on men's and women's participation in and perception of housework and child care.

Sociologist Arlie Hochschild (1989, 1990) has used the term *second shift* to describe the double burden—work outside the home followed by child care and housework—that many women face and few men share equitably. On the basis of interviews with and observations of 52 couples over an 8-year period, Hochschild reports that the wives (and not their husbands) drive home from the office while planning domestic schedules and play dates for children—and then begin their second shift. Drawing on national studies, she concludes that women spend 15 fewer hours in leisure activities each week than do their husbands. In a year, these women work an extra month of 24-hour days because of the second shift phenomenon. Over a dozen years, they work an extra year of 24-hour days.

Hochschild found that the married couples she studied were fraying at the edges, and so were their careers and their marriages. The women she spoke with hardly resembled the beautiful young businesswomen pictures in magazine advertisements, dressed in power suits but with frilled blouses, holding brief-cases in one hand and happy young children in the other. Instead, many of Hochschild's female subjects talked about being overtired and emotionally drained by the demands of their multiple roles. They were much more intensely torn by the conflicting demands of work outside the home and family life than their husbands were. Hochschild (1990, p. 73) concludes that "if we as a culture come to see the urgent need of meeting the new problems posed by the second shift, and if society and government begin to shape new policies that allow working parents more flexibility, then we will be making some progress toward happier times at home and at work." This view is shared by many feminists.

*Abortion.* A particularly controversial subject affecting family life in the United States has been the call for women to have greater control over their bodies, espe-cially their reproductive lives, through contraceptive devices and increased availability of abortions. Abortion law reform was one of the demands NOW made in 1967, and the controversy continues despite many court rulings and passage of laws at every level of government. Initially, NOW attempted to work for state-by-state reform that would allow women to obtain abortions on de-mand, which generally means a woman's right to terminate a pregnancy without needing permission from parents, the father, or a panel of physicians and psy-chiatrists.

On January 22, 1973, the feminist movement received unexpected assistance from Supreme Court decisions in *Doe* v. *Bolton* and *Roe* v. *Wade*. In these cases the Court held by a seven-to-two margin that "the right to privacy . . . founded in the Fourteenth Amendment's concept of personal liberty . . . is broad enough to encompass a woman's decision whether or not to terminate her pregnancy." The Court ruled that during the first three months, or first trimester, of preg-nancy the decision to have an abortion must be left solely to the woman and her licensed physician. During the second trimester, only regulations "reasonably related to maternal health" are permitted. During the third trimester the fetus may be capable of life, and therefore a state can restrict abortions in the final three months to instances in which the abortion is required in order to preserve the mother's life, physical health, or mental health.

In the first 12 years after the 1973 Supreme Court decision, over 16 million legal abortions were obtained. In 1976, at the urging of a growing antiabortion movement, Congress passed the Hyde Amendment prohibiting use of federal medical funds to pay for abortions, except when the woman's life was in danger or when she was the victim of rape or incest. The effects of the Hyde Amend-ment were dramatic: federally funded abortions were reduced by 99 percent (Bureau of the Census, 1988F, p. 70; Kramer, 1981, pp. 14–15; T. Schultz, 1977).

The 1989 Supreme Court case *Webster* v. *Reproductive Health Services* will have much more dramatic impact than the Hyde Amendment. In this five-to-four decision the Court upheld a Missouri law that forces physicians to conduct tests to determine whether a fetus is viable if the mother's pregnancy is 20 or more weeks. Furthermore, it approved a state's right to prohibit abortions from being performed in state hospitals or other publicly owned or leased facilities. While the Supreme Court stopped short of overturning the *Roe* and *Doe* decisions, it indicates that a majority of the Court no longer considers abortion to be a fundamental constitutional right. *Webster* sets the stage for each state's passing its own restrictions subject to judicial review. These restrictions could include notice to parents that a minor child is considering abortion, provisions that the procedure must be performed in a hospital and not a clinic, and mandated counseling aside from that provided by abortion clinics. It will leave a pregnant woman, especially one who is either too sick or too poor, with fewer choices (Greenhouse, 1989).

In their attack on parental notification and consent requirements, pro-choice activists frequently discuss the death of Becky Bell. In the summer of 1988, this 17-year-old pregnant high school junior went to a Planned Parenthood clinic in Indianapolis to examine her options. She decided to have an abortion but was afraid to hurt her parents with the news that she had become pregnant. Since state law in Indiana required that she seek the consent of one parent, Bell planned to travel to Kentucky for an abortion. But she became desperate, attempted to abort herself, and died. Becky Bell's grieving father has become an outspoken opponent of the parental consent laws that he believes contributed to his daughter's death. "I am not against laws governing abortion," says William Bell. "What I am against is that legislators said my daughter had to come to me. Therefore she was denied the right to make a safe choice" (Salholz, 1990, p. 32).

In 1992, the Supreme Court ruled in *Planned Parenthood* v. *Casey* that a Pennsylvania law was constitutional when it required teenagers to have the consent of one parent or a judge and imposed waiting periods unless subsequent time shows them to be unfair. However, it struck down a provision requiring a married woman to tell her husband of her intent to have an abortion. While a mixed decision, the Supreme Court no longer seemed to regard abortion as "a fundamental right" but rather, wishes to guard against "undue burdens" for a woman who has decided to terminate a pregnancy.

As of 1990, the American people appeared to support the right to legal abortion in principle, but were ambivalent concerning certain applications of that right. In a national survey, 71 percent of respondents stated that a woman should be allowed to have an abortion if she and her doctor agree to it. However, when asked if a "woman should be able to get an abortion if she wants one no matter what the reason" only 43 percent of respondents agreed with the statement (*American Enterprise*, 1990).

## Politics

Women in the United States constitute 53 percent of the voting population and 45 percent of the labor force, but only 8 percent of high government position

holders. In 1992, Congress included only 28 women (out of 435 members) in the House of Representatives and only 2 women (out of 100 members) in the Senate. As shown in Table 16.3, while the number of women in state legislatures in 1992 was more than four times larger than it was 20 years ago, only three states had women governors. As of 1992, women held no more than 18 percent of the available positions at any level of public office (Center for the American Woman and Politics, 1992).

Sexism has been the most serious barrier to women interested in holding office. Female candidates have had to overcome the prejudices of both men and women regarding women's fitness for leadership. Not until 1955 did a majority of Americans state that they would vote for a qualified woman for president. Moreover, women often encounter prejudice, discrimination, and abuse after they are elected. In 1979 a questionnaire was circulated among male Oregon legislators asking them to "categorize the lady legislators" with such labels as "mouth, face, chest, dress, and so forth" (Shreve and Clemans, 1980, p. 105).

The low representation of women office-holders is not the result of women's not being active in politics. About the same proportion of eligible women vote in presidential elections as men. The League of Women Voters, founded in 1920, performs a valuable function in educating the electorate of both sexes, publishing newsletters describing candidates' positions and holding debates between

**TABLE 16.3**    Women in Elected Office

Women have overcome tremendous barriers over the last few decades to make inroads on the male world of elective office.

|  | *1969* | *1975* | *1981* | *1987* | *1992* |
|---|---|---|---|---|---|
| House | 10 | 19 | 21 | 23 | 28 |
| Senate | 1 | 0 | 2 | 2 | 2 |
| Governors | 0 | 1 | 1 | 2 | 3 |
| State Legislatures | 301 | 604 | 908 | 1,170 | 1,375 |

*Source:* Center for the American Woman and Politics, 1992.

candidates. Perhaps women's most visible role in politics is as unpaid workers for male candidates—doorbell ringers, telephone callers, newsletter printers, and petition carriers. In addition, wives of elected male politicians play significant supportive roles and increasingly have spoken out in their own right (Bledsoe and Herring, 1990).

Women have worked actively in the two political parties, and more recently in the National Women's Political Caucus (NWPC), to get more women elected. The NWPC was founded in 1971 by Betty Friedan, Gloria Steinem (founder of *Ms.* magazine), Bella Abzug, and Shirley Chisholm (the last two have both been Congresswomen from New York City). The NWPC oversees state caucuses that rally support for women's issues and works for the election of women. The caucus finds it difficult to represent all politically active women, because women encompass the whole range of ideologies and includes women who are unmistakable antifeminists (Freeman, 1975, pp. 160–162).

## DOUBLE JEOPARDY: MINORITY WOMEN

We have seen the historical oppression of women that limits them by tradition and law to specific roles. Many women experience differential treatment not only because of sex but because of race and ethnicity as well. These citizens face a *double jeopardy*—that of subordinate status twice defined. A disproportionate share of this low status group also are impoverished, so that the double jeopardy becomes a triple jeopardy. The litany of social ills continues for many as we add old age, ill-health, disabilities, and the like.

Feminists have addressed themselves to the needs of minority women, but overshadowing the oppression of these women because of their sex is the subordinate status imposed by both White men and women, because of their race or ethnicity. The question for the Chicana (Chicano woman), Black woman, Native American woman, and so on appears to be whether she should unify with her brothers against racism or challenge them for their sexism. The answer is that society cannot afford to let up on the effort to eradicate both sexism and racism (Sutherland, 1970; E. Vasquez, 1970).

The discussion of gender roles among Blacks has always provoked controversy. In Chapter 8, we discussed debates about the vitality of family life. There is a similar division of opinion over the relevance of the women's movement to Black women. Advocates of Black nationalism contend that feminism only takes women away from the Black struggle. Fostering feminist groups among Blacks, they feel, is a divide-and-conquer strategy that will serve the dominant group. Black feminists like Florynce Kennedy, on the other hand, have seen little to be gained by adopting or maintaining the gender roles of dominant society that place women in a subservient position. In 1973, the National Black Feminist Organization was formed, based on the belief that liberation for less than half a race is not real liberation. Black people need all their resources and cannot afford to commit more than half their people to household chores and child care. Black women do actively participate in the labor market—in fact, they do so at higher levels than White women. In 1989, 59 percent of Black women were in the labor force, compared to 57 percent of White women. Historically, Black women are more likely not only to be working but also to suffer from higher unemployment rates. Clearly, Black women stand to gain from increased opportunities (A. Davis, 1981; Giddings, 1984; H. Hacker, 1974, 1975; Ladner, 1971, 1986; G. Lerner, 1972; Lewis, 1977; Steinem, 1973).

The plight of Chicanas is usually considered part of either the Chicano or women's liberation movements, ignoring the particular experience of Chicanas. In the past they have been excluded from decision making in the two institutions that most affect their daily lives, the family and the Church. The family, especially in the lower class, feels the pervasive tradition of male domination called *machismo* discussed in Chapter 10. The Roman Catholic church relegates women to supportive roles while reserving for men the leadership positions (Burciaga et al., 1977: Rosaldo, 1985, p. 415).

Activists among minority women do not agree on whether priority should be given to equalizing the sexes or eliminating inequality among racial and ethnic groups. It is not solely a question of priorities, for, as Helen Hacker says there are "conflicting interests of the beneficiaries of these movements" (1975, p. 171). White women encouraged to enter all occupations may compete with minority males who are less educated and will be at a disadvantage in hiring that is free of sexism. Joyce Ladner in "Listen to Their Voices" wrote in 1971 of the double oppression faced by Black women, which she saw not fully understood by those who concentrate on ending sexism alone.

Chicana feminist Enriqueta Longauex y Vasquez, while acknowledging the importance of the Chicano movement, believes in stressing sexual equality. "When a man can look upon a woman as human, then, and only then, can he feel the true meaning of liberation and equality" (Vasquez et al., 1970, p. 384).

Perhaps it would be most accurate to conclude that both components of inequality cannot be ignored. Helen Mayer Hacker, who pioneered research on the role of being both Black and female, stated before the American Sociological

## ❖ LISTEN TO THEIR VOICES ❖

*Tomorrow's Tomorrow:*
*The Black Woman*

*Joyce A. Ladner*

The Black woman suffers from the twin burden of being *Black* and *female.* Her life is shaped by the subjugated statuses which are assigned to being a woman and being Black, both of which carry with them a double jeopardy. On the surface this would imply that Black women should be at the forefront of the Women's Liberation movement. Yet the problems to which members of Women's Liberation groups are addressing themselves are far less relevant to Black women. The movement is led largely by white middle-class women whose problems are basically different from those of Black women, regardless of class. The protective shelters which the society has imposed on white women have never been problematic to Black women because the society has refused to offer them the same protectiveness. One of the most blatant symbols of institutional racism has historically been the society's refusal to allow Black men to protect their women. As a result, Black women have always been "liberated."

Another major difference is that the "battle between the sexes" which characterizes the Women's Liberation groups—struggles over equalization of power in interpersonal relations—is the kind of luxury which Black people as a race can ill afford. Black women do not perceive their enemy to be Black men, but rather the enemy is considered to be the oppressive forces in the larger society which subjugate Black *men, women and children.* A preoccupation with the equalization of roles between Black men and women is almost irrelevant when one places it within the context of total priorities related to the survival of the race. All of the energies and resources of males and females are necessary to obliterate institutional racism.

Association that: "As a partisan observer it is my fervent hope that in fighting the twin battles of sexism and racism Black women and Black men together will [create] the outlines of the good society for all Americans" (1973, p. 11). The recent history of the rights movements of women and racial minorities indicates some dispute over priorities, accompanied by a genuine recognition that social equality among all people is the ultimate goal.

## GLANCING BACK AND LOOKING AHEAD

Women and men are expected to perform, or at least to prefer to perform, specific tasks in society. The appropriateness to a sex for all but a very few of these tasks cannot be justified by the biological differences between females and males, any more than can differential treatment based on race. Psychologists Sandra Bem and Daryl Bem make this analogy:

> Suppose that a white, male college student decided to room with a black, male friend. The typical white student would not blithely assume that his room-mate was better suited to handle all domestic chores. Nor should his conscience allow him to do so even in the unlikely event that his roommate would say, "No, that's okay. I like doing housework. I'd be happy to do it." We would suspect that the white student would still feel uncomfortable about taking advantage of the fact that his roommate has simply been socialized to be "happy with such an arrangement." But change this hypothetical black roommate to a female marriage partner and the student's conscience goes to sleep. (1970, p. 99)

The feminist movement has awakened women *and* men to the assumptions based on sex and gender. New opportunities followed by new results for the sexes require the same commitment from individuals and the government as it does to achieve equality among racial and ethnic groups.

Socially defined roles for men and women are not limited to the United States. The United Nations declared 1975 International Women's Year (IWY), wishing to support women's rights in activities throughout the world that would culminate in an international woman's conference in Mexico City. Little changed directly as the result of the IWY, but the year did stress that women's subordinate status is worldwide. Chapter 17 will concentrate on the inequality of racial and ethnic groups in societies other than the United States. Just as sexism is not unique to this nation, neither is racism nor religious intolerance.

## KEY TERMS

**androgyny** The state of being both masculine and feminine, aggressive and gentle.

**double jeopardy** The subordinate status twice defined as experienced by women of color.

**feminine mystique** The ideology in which a woman thinks of herself only as her children's mother and her husband's wife.

**feminization of poverty** The trend since 1970 that has women accounting for a growing proportion of those below the poverty line.

**gender identity** The self-concept of an individual as male or female.

**gender roles** Expectations regarding the proper behavior, attitudes, and activities of males and females.

**market discrimination** The underpayment or underemployment of qualified women.

**mommy track** The problematic corporate career track for women who want to divide their attention between work and family.

**pay equity** Same wages for different types of work that are judged to be comparable by such measures as employee knowledge, skills, effort, responsibility, and working conditions; also called *comparable worth*.

**second shift** The double burden—work outside the home followed by child care and housework—faced by many women, which few men share equitably.

**sexism** The ideology that one sex is superior to the other.

**sexual harassment** The unwanted imposition of sexual requirements in the context of unequal power.

**suffragists** Women and men who worked successfully to gain women the right to vote.

## FOR FURTHER INFORMATION

Nijole V. Benokraitis, and Joe R. Feagan. *Modern Sexism: Blatant, Subtle, and Covert Discrimination*. Englewood Cliffs, NJ: Prentice-Hall, 1986.

Sociologists analyze how sex discrimination occurs on many different levels.

Jane Condon. *A Half Step Behind: Japanese Women of the '80s*. New York: Dodd, Mead, 1985.

Condon examines women's role in Japanese society within the family, in the educational system, and in the work force.

Paula England and George Farkas. *Households, Employment, and Gender*. New York: Aldine, 1986.

The authors integrate the study of the household with research on paid employment.

Susan Faludi. *Backlash: The Undeclared War Against American Women*. New York: Crown Publishing Group, 1991.

A Pulitzer Prize-winning journalist reviews the counterattack against the women's movement.

Jo Freeman. *The Politics of Women's Liberation*. New York: David McKay, 1975.

Freeman analyzes women's liberation as a social movement. Her coverage of the origins of the movement and of NOW is especially effective.

Betty Friedan. *The Feminine Mystique*. New York: Dell, 1963.

Friedan explodes the myth that women's true fulfillment can come only through the home and motherhood. Still a classic despite the author's changed views in *The Second Stage*, published in 1981.

Paula Giddings. *When and Where I Enter*. New York: William Morrow, 1984.

Giddings, an editor at Howard University Press, has written a superb historical account of Black women in the United States.

Beth B. Hess and Myra Marx Ferree, eds. *Analyzing Gender: A Handbook of Social Science Research.* Newbury Park, CA: Sage, 1987.

Included in this anthology are treatments of popular culture, female sexuality, family roles, religion, and the women's health movement.

Arlie Russell Hochschild with Anne Machung. *The Second Shift: Working Parents and the Revolution at Home.* New York: Viking Penguin, 1989.

A critical look at housework in dual-career couples.

Cheris Kramarae and Paul Treichler. *A Feminist Dictionary.* Boston: Pandora Press, 1985.

A unique sourcebook of nearly 600 pages that places women at the center of the English language.

Robin Morgan, ed. *Sisterhood Is Powerful.* New York: Vintage Books, 1970.

This is the most complete collection of writings from the beginning of the contemporary women's liberation movement. It covers women in the professions, sexuality, sexism in advertising, lesbians, minority women, and much more.

Laurel Walum Richardson. *The Dynamics of Sex and Gender: A Sociological Perspective,* 2nd ed. Boston: Houghton Mifflin, 1981.

An overview of gender roles in a sociological context, Richardson's book is unique in its coverage of men's roles as well as women's.

Harrell R. Rodgers, Jr. *Poor Women, Poor Families.* Armonk, NY: M. E. Sharpe, 1987.

This book analyzes data on the changing profile of low-income families over the last 35 years and provides a clear view of poverty among women.

Alice S. Rossi, ed. *The Feminist Papers: From Adams to de Beauvoir.* New York: Columbia University Press, 1973.

An excellent anthology of source material on the feminist movement that stresses the roots of the struggle, as indicated by the 400 pages devoted to the period before the 1848 Seneca Falls convention.

Virginia Sapiro. *Women in American Society.* Palo Alto, CA: Mayfield, 1986.

Intended as a text for women's studies classes, this book provides an overview of the position of women in our society.

## Statistical Data

Almost all government collected data (census, health statistics, crime data, labor figures, and so on) are broken down by sex.

## Periodicals

*Ms.* (1972) is a monthly mass-market publication that presents the feminist point of view. Other publications taking strong positions are quarterly *Lilith* (1976), monthly *Off Our Backs* (1970), and monthly *Working Woman* (1976). The more traditional women's magazines have increasingly confronted the issues raised by the women's liberation movement. Journals devoted to women as a social group are the quarterly *Gender and Society* (1987), the bimonthly *Sex Roles: A Journal of Research* (1975), the quarterly *Signs: Journal of Women in Culture and Society* (1972), quarterly *Women's Studies* (1972), and *Feminist Studies* (1972) published three times a year.

## Chapter Seventeen

# BEYOND THE UNITED STATES: THE COMPARATIVE PERSPECTIVE

*Chapter Outline*

**Brazil: Not a Racial Paradise**
Legacy of Slavery
"Mulatto Escape Hatch" Illusion
Brazilian Dilemma
**Great Britain: Former Colonial Subjects Not Welcomed**
Legacy of Immigration
British Approach to Racial Injustice
British Dilemma
**Northern Ireland**
Partition
Civil Rights Movement
Search for Solutions

**Israel and the Occupied Territories**
Creation of a Jewish Homeland
Arab-Israeli Conflicts
The Intifada
**Republic of South Africa**
Legacy of Colonialism
Apartheid
South Africa in the World Community
The South African Dilemma
**Glancing Back and Looking Ahead**
**Key Terms**
**For Further Information**

---

**❋ HIGHLIGHTS ❋**

---

Subordinating people because of race, nationality, or religion is not a uniquely American phenomenon, but occurs throughout the world. This chapter will first explore patterns of domination in Brazil, where the descendants of slavery are still bound by second-class status. Great Britain, with its long history as a colonizer, is adjusting to a non-White minority comprising former colonial subjects and their children. Northern Ireland is a modern nation torn by religious strife. In Israel, Jews and Palestinians compete for territory. The final example is the Republic of South Africa—where race dominates all aspects of life.

---

Ironically, modernization, by bringing more and more diverse groups of people into contact, has increased the opportunities for confrontation, both peaceful and violent, among culturally and physically different people. Throughout the world, groups defined by race or ethnicity confront other groups so defined. These confrontations, as Chapter 1 showed, can lead to extermination, expulsion, secession, segregation, fusion, assimilation, or pluralism. Whatever the outcome, confrontations among racial and ethnic groups have escalated in frequency and intensity in the twentieth century.

As is true of intergroup relations in the United States, violent encounters have received the largest share of attention: the overturning of colonial regimes in developing countries, tribal warfare in Africa, and Christian-Muslim clashes in Lebanon. These conflicts remind us that the processes operating in the United States to deny minority groups their rights and opportunities are at work throughout the world. The dissolution of the Union of Soviet Socialist Republics in 1991, for example, was along lines defined by ethnicity and language.

The sociological perspective on relations between dominant and subordinate groups treats race and ethnicity as social categories. As *social* concepts they can be understood only in the context of the shared meanings attached to them by societies and their members. Dominant and subordinate group relationships vary greatly. Although these majority-minority pairings vary, there are similarities across societies. Racial and ethnic hostilities arise out of the economic needs and demands of people. These needs and demands may not always be realistic—that is, a group might seek out enemies where none exist or where victory will yield no rewards. Racial and ethnic conflicts are both the results and the precipitators of change in the economic and political sectors (Barclay et al., 1976, pp. 3–8; Coser, 1956, pp. 48–55).

Relations between dominant and subordinate groups differ from society to society, as this chapter will show. Conflict among racial, religious, and ethnic groups is not the same in Brazil, Great Britain, Northern Ireland, Israel, and South Africa. Differences such as the presence or absence of a history of slavery and the degree of central control on the movement of people within the country are evident. Study of these five societies, coupled with knowledge of subordinate groups in the United States, will provide the background with which to draw some conclusions about patterns of race and ethnic relations.

## BRAZIL: NOT A RACIAL PARADISE

To someone knowledgeable of race and ethnic relations in the United States, Brazil seems familiar in a number of respects. Like the United States, Brazil was colonized by Europeans who overwhelmed the native people. Like the United States, Brazil imported Black Africans as slaves to meet the demand for laborers. Even today Brazil is second to the United States in the number of people of African descent, excluding nations on the African continent. Although the focus here is on Black and White people in Brazil, another continuing concern is the treatment of Brazil's native peoples, as this developing nation continues to modernize.

### Legacy of Slavery

The present nature of Brazilian race relations is influenced by the legacy of slavery, as is true of Black-White relations in the United States. It is not necessary to repeat here the discussion of the brutality of the slave trade and slavery itself, or of the influence of slavery on the survival of African cultures and family life. Scholars agree that slavery was not the same in Brazil as it was in the United States, but disagree on how different it was and how significant these differences are (Elkins, 1959; Tannenbaum, 1946).

Brazil depended much more than the United States on the slave trade. Franklin Knight estimated the total number of slaves imported to Brazil at 3.5 million, eight times the number brought to the United States (1974, p. 46). At the height of slavery, however, both nations had approximately the same slave population, 4 to 4.5 million. Brazil's reliance on African-born slaves meant that typical Brazilian slaves had closer ties to Africa than did their U.S. counterparts. Revolts and escapes were more common among slaves in Brazil. The most dramatic example was the slave *quilombo* (or hideaway) of Palmores, whose 20,000 inhabitants repeatedly fought off Portuguese assaults until 1698. It is easier to recognize the continuity of African cultures among Brazil's Blacks than among Black Americans. The contributions of the African people to Brazil's history have been kept alive by the attention given them in the schools. Whereas American schools have just recently taught about the Black role in history, the Brazilian schoolchild has typically become acquainted with the historical role of the Africans and their descendants. As in the United States, however, the surviving African culture is overwhelmed by dominant European traditions (Andrews, 1991; Degler, 1971, pp. 7–8, 47–52; Frazier, 1942, 1943; Herskovits, 1941, 1943; Stan, 1985).

The most significant difference between slavery in the southern United States and in Brazil was the amount of *manumission*, the freeing of slaves. For every 1,000 slaves, 100 were freed annually in Brazil, compared to four a year in the American South. It would be hasty to assume, however, as some have, that Brazilian masters were more benevolent. Quite the contrary, Brazil's slave economy was poorer than that of the South and so slaveowners in Brazil freed slaves into poverty whenever they became crippled, sick, or old. But this custom does not completely explain the presence of the many freed slaves in Brazil. Again unlike in the United States, the majority of Brazil's population was composed of Africans and their descendants throughout the nineteenth century. Africans were needed as craftsworkers, shopkeepers, and boatmen, not just as agricultural workers. Freed slaves filled these needs.

In Brazil, race was not seen as a measure of innate inferiority, as it was in the United States. Rather, even during the period of slavery, Brazilians saw free Blacks as contributing to society, which was not the view of White U.S. Southerners. In Brazil you were inferior if you were a slave. In the United States you were inferior if you were Black. Not that Brazilians were more enlightened than Americans; quite the contrary, Brazil belonged to the European tradition of a hierarchical society that did not conceive of all people as equal. Unlike the English, who emphasized individual freedom, however, the Brazilian slaveowner had no need to develop a racist defense of slavery. These distinctions help explain why Whites in the United States felt compelled to dominate and simultaneously fear both the slave and the Black man and woman. Brazilians did not have these fears of free Blacks and thus felt it unnecessary to restrict manumission (D. Davis, 1966; Degler, 1971; M. Harris, 1964; Marger, 1985, pp. 221–224; Mason, 1970a, pp. 316–317; O. Patterson, 1982, p. 273; R. S. Rose, 1988; Skidmore, 1972; Sundiata, 1987).

## *"Mulatto Escape Hatch" Illusion*

Carl Degler (1971) identifies the *mulatto escape hatch* as the key to the differences in Brazilian and American race relations. In Brazil, the mulatto is recognized as a group separate from either *brancos* (Whites) or *prêtos* (Blacks), whereas in the United States mulattos are classed with Blacks. Yet this escape hatch is an illusion because economically mulattos fare only marginally better than Blacks. In addition, mulattos do not escape in the sense of mobility into the income and status enjoyed by White Brazilians. Labor market analyses demonstrate that Blacks with the highest levels of education and occupation experience the most discrimination in terms of jobs, mobility and income (Fiola, 1989; Winant, 1989).

Today the presence of approximately 40 racial groups along the lines of a color gradient (see Chapter 10) is obvious in Brazil, because, unlike in the United States, mulattos are viewed as an identifiable social group. The 1980 census in Brazil classified 55 percent White, 38 percent mulatto, 6 percent Black, and 1 percent other. Over the past 50 years, the mulatto group has grown and the proportions of both Whites and Blacks declined (Brazil, 1981).

The presence of mulattos does not mean that color is irrelevant in society or that miscegenation occurs randomly. The incidence of mixed marriages is greatest among the poor and among those similar in color. Marriages between partners from opposite ends of the color gradient are rare. The absence of direct racial confrontation and the presence of mixed marriages lead some writers to conclude that Brazil is a "racial paradise." The lack of racial tension does not, however, mean prejudice does not exist, or that Blacks are fully accepted. For example, residential segregation is present in Brazil's urban areas.

In Brazil, today as in the past, light skin color enhances status but the impact is often exaggerated. When Degler advanced the idea of "mulatto escape hatch," he implied that it was a means to success. The most recent income data do show that mulattos earn 42 percent more than Blacks. Given mulattos' more extensive formal schooling, this difference is not particularly remarkable. Yet Whites earn another 98 percent more than mulattos. Clearly the major distinction is between Whites and all "people of color" rather than between mulattos and Blacks (Dzidzienyo, 1987; N. Silva, 1985; Telles, 1992).

## Brazilian Dilemma

The most startling phenomenon in Brazilian race relations since World War II has been the recognition that racial prejudice and discrimination exist. During the twentieth century, Brazil changed from a nation that prided itself on its freedom from racial intolerance to a country legally attacking discrimination against people of color. In 1951, the Afonso Arinos law was unanimously adopted, prohibiting racial discrimination in public places. Opinion is divided over the effectiveness of the law, which has been of no use in overturning subtle forms of discrimination. Even from the start certain civilian careers such as the diplomatic and military officers ranks were virtually closed to Blacks. Curiously, the push for the law came from the United States, after a Black American dancer, Katherine Dunham, was denied a room at a São Paulo luxury hotel. Yet employers may still specify "Spanish" or "Portuguese" applicants only, which means *branco* or White.

Brazilians today are surprisingly inactive in civil rights work. The best and strongest rights movement, the *Frente Negra Brasileira,* or Brazilian Black Front, lasted only a few years in the 1930s and claimed at most only 2,000 followers. New groups have surfaced in recent years—one called the Unified Black Movement (MNV, or Movimento Negro Unificado) was organized in 1978 as a reaction to incidents of police violence and private club discrimination. The MNV holds an annual congress and is currently the largest Black organization in Brazil, attracting several thousand to their major meetings (Andrews, 1991; Covin, 1990; Fiola, 1989).

In 1988, Brazil marked as a national holiday the hundredth anniversary of the abolition of slavery, but for 40 to 50 percent of the Brazilian people of color there was little rejoicing. Zézé Motta, Brazil's leading Black actress and a longtime campaigner for Black advancement, observed, "We have gone from the hold of the ship to the basements of society." Of the 559 members of Congress, only 7 are Black. Whites are 7 times more likely to be college graduates. Job advertisements still appear seeking individuals of "good appearance," a euphemism for light skin. Even Black professionals such as physicians, teachers, and engineers earn 20 to 25 percent less than their White counterparts. (Robinson, 1989; Simons, 1988; Webster and Dwyer, 1988).

Similar to the situation in other multiracial societies, women of color fare particularly poorly in Brazil. White men, of course, have the highest incomes while Black men have earning levels comparable to White women. Black women are furthest behind with 68 percent earning less than the minimum salary compared to 24 percent for White men (Fiola, 1989).

Gradually groups have organized among Blacks to address the many grievances. The alleged escape hatch does not necessarily work for the darker people on the skin-color gradient. For Blacks, even professional status can achieve only so much for one's social standing. An individual's blackness does not suddenly become invisible simply because he or she has acquired some social standing. The fame achieved by the Black Brazilian soccer player Pelé is a token exception and does not mean that Blacks have it easy or even have a readily available "escape hatch" through professional sports (Dzidzienyo, 1979).

Is Brazilian society becoming more polarized, or are Brazilians as tolerant as they seem always to have been? There is no easy answer because Brazil has not

*Pelé, the retired soccer star, is by far the best-known Brazilian Black man and is probably among the richest. He has been criticized by younger Blacks, who feel he should speak out against racism in Brazilian society.*

been the subject of the intensive research and opinion polling that the United States has. Several scholars of Brazilian society believe that race has become more important. This does not mean that belief in racial inferiority and the practice of de facto segregation will become common in Brazil. Brazil does not have, nor is it likely to have, a Black middle-class society separate from White middle-class society. By suggesting that Brazil is becoming more conscious of race, these scholars mean that coming generations will have a heightened awareness of race in Brazil, similar to that witnessed in the United States in the 1960s, although not of the same magnitude.

Continued denial that racial inequality exists in Brazil means that there is little pressure to assist poor Blacks, because their subordinate status is perceived to reflect class, not differential racial treatment. As Philip Mason summarized it, Brazil's great asset is public commitment to the idea that racial discrimination is wrong; its great weakness is reluctance to admit that it does take place (1970b, p. 123). Even more than in the United States, class prejudice reinforces racial prejudice to the point of obscuring it. Lower-class Whites and Blacks do experience limited opportunities because of life-long poverty. For some Brazilians, though, skin color is an added disability, and even in Brazil race makes a difference in a person's opportunities and way of life (Freyre, 1946, 1959, 1963; Webster and Dwyer, 1988).

## GREAT BRITAIN: FORMER COLONIAL SUBJECTS NOT WELCOMED

Unlike Brazil, Great Britain was not colonized but was a colonizer. For several centuries, White British citizens had experience with non-Whites, but only recently have many non-Whites been native English citizens rather than colonial subjects. Despite the long tradition of empire, as recently as 1950 there were probably no more than 100,000 non-White people in Great Britain in a population of 48 million. This disparity changed dramatically in the 1960s, when relatively inexpensive commercial transportation and perceived job opportunities in Britain brought an ever-increasing number of non-White subjects of the Crown to the mother country.

### Legacy of Immigration

Britain had slaves and a vast colonial empire, but it did not have a large internal non-White population for a long time, so majority-minority relations were not institutionalized as they were in the United States. Like Brazil, the British did not develop a popular theory of racial inferiority like that of the American South. They did, however, have a racist tradition. The colonial heritage emphasized gold, glory, and gospel, and the British looked upon their subjects as barely human beings, scarcely equal to themselves. Despite the empire, a 1951 national survey revealed that half of the British had never even met a non-White. Many

White contacts with non-Whites were made overseas, and apparently few British Whites formed any real acquaintanceships in Great Britain with non-Whites (S. Allen, 1971, pp. 166–173; K. Little, 1947; S. Patterson, 1969, p. 1).

As in the great migration to the United States described in Chapter 4, the primary push-and-pull factors in migration to England were economic. Immigrants were pulled by perceived job opportunities and pushed by high unemployment. Britain had a policy of unrestricted entry privileges for all immigrants from the former colonies of the commonwealth. The commonwealth immigrants came primarily from India, Pakistan (including Bangladesh), and the West Indies, particularly Jamaica. Britain's open-door policy for commonwealth immigrants went into effect in July 1962. Supporters of restrictive legislation worried that there were not enough jobs for the newcomers, but racist feelings were also apparent, as some suggested barring entry to the "new commonwealth" immigrants (meaning Black and Brown residents of former colonies in Africa, Asia, and the Caribbean) while permitting entry from the "old commonwealth" nations (meaning White Canadians, Australians, and New Zealanders). The immigrants became both scapegoats for Britain's social ills and victims of discrimination and prejudice (Barclay et al., 1976, pp. 138–139; E. Rose, 1969, pp. 639–656; Schaefer and Schaefer, 1975).

## British Approach to Racial Injustice

Many observers saw British race relations enter a new phase with a 1968 speech delivered by Enoch Powell, a member of Parliament. A few days before his Conservative Party announced opposition to an anti-discrimination measure, Powell declared:

> We must be mad, literally, as a nation to be permitting the annual inflow of some 50,000 dependents who are for the most part the material of the future growth of the immigrant-descended population. It is like watching a nation busily engaged in heaping up its own funeral pyre. (1968, p. 99)

His speech marked an end to the long tradition of keeping race problems out of partisan political debate. Except for newspaper editorials, which generally denounced him, Powell received dramatic popular support, which worried those sympathetic to the plight of the immigrants. Beginning in 1970 and again in a well-publicized speech in 1976, Powell suggested that the government pay immigrants to return home. After this last speech, 58 percent of a nationally representative sample said that they thought that in the country as a whole feelings were deteriorating between Whites and the immigrant minorities (Butt, 1968; Foot, 1969; Little and Kohler, 1977; Spearman, 1968a, 1968b; Studler, 1974, 1975).

Prejudice was not the only problem confronting the immigrants. One-third of all employers in a 1991 study would hire Whites over equally qualified Blacks without even giving the Black applicant an interview. In a move analogous to the passage of the civil rights acts of the United States, Britain enacted race relations acts in 1965, 1968, and 1976, which are enforced by the Commission for Racial Equality. The earlier race relations acts had little effect on minority employment. Part of the problem was the unwieldy, ineffective way of handling complaints about discrimination. The Community Relation Commission, created by these acts, could assist a person pursuing discrimination complaints through an industrial tribunal panel with a top award of only $17,000 as of 1991. Unlike the United States, there are no provisions for class-action suits or contract compliance measures such as set asides to motivate employers to hire minorities (Rule, 1991).

Still another stage was entered beginning with the Brixton civil disorders in 1981. An encounter between police and a Black youth touched off three days of rioting. Brixton, a neighborhood of inner London, is about one-third Black. A series of events following the precipitating incident escalated into more civilian violence and increasing response by the metropolitan police. Although no deaths occurred, the injuring of 279 police, countless civilians, and the destruction of 28 buildings was previously unknown in recent British history. Unlike riots in the United States, a small number of White youths were among the participants. Nonetheless, attention was focused on problems experienced by the new generation of British-born Blacks. The Brixton riot was not an isolated incident. Indeed, Bristol (see Figure 17.1 for location) had been marked by disorders the year before; in the same year that Brixton, Liverpool, Manchester, and 17 other cities were racked by violence. Riots again struck British cities in 1985 (Killian, 1982; R. Knight, 1985; Riot Not To Work Collective, 1982; Scarman Report, 1982).

## British Dilemma

A little more than 4 percent of the current population was born in new commonwealth countries or have parents who were. Unlike minorities in America, Britain's non-Whites are relatively evenly distributed throughout the country, although they tend to be concentrated in the inner-city areas of England's larger cities (see Figure 17.1). In sheer numbers, Britain appears to have an easier task than the United States in amicably resolving tensions between dominant and subordinate groups, but to date that solution appears out of reach (Schaefer, 1973b, 1973c, 1974a, 1974b, 1975, 1976a).

The non-White minority is not a uniform group in Britain, any more than it is in the United States. The Asians include Hindus and Muslims from India, Muslims from Pakistan and Bangladesh, and Indians (and a few Pakistanis) from Kenya and Uganda. The West Indians raised in an English-language culture were generally unprepared for what awaited them in the British Isles. Because they had lived in a British-dominated culture, they expected to adjust quickly. Instead, Blacks who had skilled occupations in the West Indies were employed in England as unskilled laborers. The Asians as a group were better organized and have apparently been more successful in transporting their institutions (religious centers, recreational activities, and worker groups) than the

**FIGURE 17.1** United Kingdom

*Source:* U.S. Department of State, *Background Notes*, July 1981.

West Indians. In addition to the groups mentioned, non-White immigrants have come from Africa, Cyprus, and Sri Lanka (Ceylon), adding to the diversity of peoples (S. Allen, 1971, pp. 86–102; Schaefer, 1976b).

Accounts indicate that British race relations are following the American pattern, although not identically. Charges of police brutality and insensitivity are common, and commissions, especially following the 1980–1982 disorders and the rioting in 1985, have been formed to make recommendations. Publicly supported schools have been overwhelmed by the challenge of educating youths who speak foreign languages and were socialized in alien cultures.

Except for those professionals who immigrated, non-Whites, especially West Indian youths, suffer higher unemployment rates. Militancy among immigrants has grown, in a trend reminiscent of American Black nationalism. Anti-immigrant groups are flourishing as well (Hiro, 1973, pp. 85–95, 173–181; Humphrey, 1972; Lambert, 1974; Nugent, 1976; Scarman Report, 1982).

The balance sheet in Britain is certainly tipped in favor of Whites. The Black and Asian unemployment rate is twice that of Whites. Those non-Whites who are employed earn only 85 percent of the dominant group. A recent survey shows that one in four minority members are victimized by verbal or physical assaults in a given year. The Blacks and Asians who do succeed and who graduate from college are less likely to find employment. For non-Whites gains are evident, but even so, only three Blacks and one Asian sit in the 650-member House of Commons and there is not a single person of color in the top echelons of the British government, judiciary, police, or civil service (Commission for Racial Equality, 1987; DeYoung, 1988; Monroe, 1988; Rule, 1991).

*Racism is both subtle and overt in Great Britain. This youth sports his "Anti-Pakki League" teeshirt.*

For the first time in its long history Britain is experiencing the growth of a non-White population born in England. These youths do not know any other home but Great Britain. Will they fare better than their parents? The American experience suggests that the answer is a qualified yes. Successive generations are likely to be more thoroughly assimilated and thus more acceptable to White Britons. Assimilation is not easy, however, and the conflict between Asian and West Indian parents and their British-born offspring is already apparent.

Many Blacks born in Britain find that White Britons continue to classify them as immigrants. Asians, even if they speak fluent English, are still automatically expected to have language problems. Thirty years ago, British intolerance was depicted as the result of alien newcomers adjusting to a new society. As the newcomers adjust, however, White Britons' demands that they be repatriated to the former colonies continue. There is little reason to expect that the children or even the grandchildren of the new commonwealth immigrants will be fully accepted into British society. The peoples of India, Pakistan, and the West Indies are in the unenviable position of having been dominated first by English colonists and then forced to occupy a subordinate role in Britain as well (S. Allen, 1971, pp. 21–24; Schaefer, 1976a, p. 2).

## NORTHERN IRELAND

Armed conflict between Protestants and Catholics is difficult for many people in the United States to understand. Our recent history in racial and ethnic relations makes it relatively easy for us to appreciate that societies may be torn apart by differences based on skin color or even language. But atrocities among compatriots who share the bond of the Christian faith, even if in name only, can strike Americans as incredible. Yet newspapers and television news regularly recount the horrors from Northern Ireland—a very troubled land of fewer than 2 million people.

### Partition

The roots of today's violence are in the invasion of Ireland by the English (then the Anglo-Normans) in the twelfth century. England, however, preoccupied with European enemies and hampered by resistance from the Irish, never gained complete control of the island. The northernmost area, called Ulster, received a heavy influx of Protestant settlers from Scotland and England in the seventeenth century following Cromwell's defeat of the Irish supporters of Britain's Catholic monarch (refer to Figure 17.1).

Ireland was united with Great Britain (England, Scotland, and Wales) in 1801 to form the United Kingdom. Despite this union, Ireland still was governed as a colony, and most of the people of Ireland found it difficult to accept union and did not consider the government in London theirs. In secret, the native Irish continued to speak Irish (or Gaelic) and worship as Catholics in defiance of the

Church of England. Protestant settlers continued to speak English and pay homage to the British monarch. Unhappy with their colonial status, the Irish, as they had done for the previous seven centuries, again pushed for independence or at least *home rule* with a local Irish parliament. Protestants in Ireland and most people in Britain objected to such demands, derisively referring to them as "Rome rule." During the latter 1800s, as home rule bills were introduced, Irish Catholics marched in support, only to be confronted by angry Protestants.

A very limited home rule bill was passed in 1914, only to have its implementation delayed by World War I. Tired of waiting, a small group of militant Irish nationalists declared they would accept no compromises and no more delays. What could have been an isolated incident, unsupported by the majority of Catholic and Protestant Irish alike, aroused an extremist reaction from England and escalated the Easter Rebellion of 1916 into the Anglo-Irish War of 1919–1921. In 1921 a treaty was signed that provided for establishing an independent sovereign nation in the south, which evolved into today's Republic of Ireland. The United Kingdom retained its sovereignty over the counties of Ulster—today's Northern Ireland, as Britain officially refers to it. The Republic was a nation of 95 percent Roman Catholic, but Northern Ireland with its population two thirds Protestant, one-third Catholic, was still a land divided. The partition had been completed, but peace was not established (D. Schmitt, 1974, pp. 2–4).

## Civil Rights Movement

The immediate post-partition period was fairly peaceful, with fewer than 20 deaths through the late 1960s related to the Protestant-Catholic conflict that had divided the island for centuries. Britain was relatively indifferent to Northern Ireland governance and looked the other way as the Protestants capitalized upon their majority. Political districts were created that minimized the voting strength of Catholics in sending representatives to Stormont, Northern Ireland's Parliament, while Protestant areas were divided to maximize electoral power. In some local elections the abuses were more blatant, tying voting to home ownership and thereby disenfranchising large numbers of Catholics, who were more likely to be renters or to be living with kin (Terchek, 1977).

These political problems faced by Roman Catholics were compounded by other social problems. Because they had historically worked for Protestant factory owners, the Catholics are more likely to be poor, live in substandard housing, and suffer from more and longer periods of unemployment. Residential segregation and separate schools further isolated the two groups from one another (Boal and Douglas, 1982; Conroy, 1981; Whyte, 1986).

The civil rights movement of Northern Ireland began with a march in Londonderry (see Figure 17.1) in 1968, with Catholics joined by some sympathetic Protestants, protesting the social ills described here. Marching in defiance of a police order, demonstrators soon confronted the police, and violence broke out, leaving civilians injured. A year later, Belfast protests led to an escalation of violence, and ten demonstrators were killed. British troops were ordered into Northern Ireland the next day. Within two years a well-organized guerilla movement, the Provisional wing of the Irish Republican Army (IRA), rose on behalf of militant Catholics. Simultaneously, terrorist paramilitary Protestant groups surfaced. The violence continued to escalate amid futile efforts by civil rights workers to have the issues discussed. In 1971, Britain initiated the policy of internment, allowing Britain to hold suspected terrorists, mostly Roman Catholics, without making charges against them. In the next year British paratroopers killed 13 demonstrators on the day that has come to be called Bloody Sunday. Britain also suspended Stormont and instituted direct rule from London. In the period from 1969 through 1987 there were over 10,000 attacks by both sides with property damage over $1.7 billion (Hewitt, 1988).

A peace movement was founded in 1976, based on the assumption that Catholics and Protestants had more in common than that which divided them. It gathered wide initial support, but when concrete moves toward solving the violence were not forthcoming, the admirable effort failed to retain that support. In 1985, amid much publicity, Britain agreed, in the Anglo-Irish Accord, to give the Republic of Ireland a voice in resolving sectarian violence. In return for this role in the north, Ireland formally recognized British sovereignty over the six northern counties which its own constitution had claimed as belonging to the Republic of Ireland. While sporadic talks continue into the 1990s, the violence also endures. Perhaps the only significant change is that bombs claimed by the IRA are now occurring at museums, government offices, and transportation centers in London, rather than in Northern Ireland alone (DeYoung, 1988; Prokesch, 1991; Tercheck, 1977).

## Search for Solutions

A survey held in 1968 and probably still valid today found that three-quarters of the Catholics thought of themselves as "Irish." Protestants clearly rejected such a term and preferred "British" (39 percent) or "Ulster" (32 percent) as the appropriate labels. This mutually exclusive identification, coupled with violence, has not lent itself to a simple solution. Beyond continued hostilities with varying degrees of military and police control directed from London, what are the possible solutions? Any of them would be unpleasant or extremely difficult to achieve or both (R. Rose, 1971).

***Maintaining the British Connection.*** The first solution, maintaining all ties with the United Kingdom, would restore, or some would say continue, dominance by the Protestants. Although London would deny that this interpretation is necessarily true, the Catholics of Northern Ireland would believe that Protestant rule had been solidified if political rule were left in either the hands of the British or the government of Northern Ireland.

***Federation with the South.*** The second alternative is the opposite of the first—that is, unification of Ulster with the Republic of Ireland. Naturally, Protestants would be distressed by becoming a minority. Objectively, the 5 percent of the Republic of Ireland's population that is Protestant seem to suffer little, yet the Protestants of the north are unlikely to surrender what they regard as their inalienable right to be a part of the United Kingdom. It is also reasonable to assume that even the Catholics of the south would not warmly welcome such a unification. Although they applaud such a move on patriotic and ideological grounds, they certainly would worry about taking on the economic devastation and deep-seated mistrust of any government of the people of Northern Ireland. Because the United Kingdom finances a program of social services much more extensive than that found in the south, the Republic of Ireland would be faced with the dilemma of increasing taxes by as much as 50 percent to maintain the program or slashing the services granted—neither of which would be popular moves even in a unified Ireland (Buckley, 1984; Hunt and Walker, 1979, p. 73; J. Thompson, 1983).

*Repartition.* A third possibility is a further partition that would continue the "solution" first attempted in the 1920s. Boundaries would be redrawn between Northern Ireland (that is, the United Kingdom) and the Republic of Ireland. This repartition, coupled with a large-scale population migration could lead to a Northern Ireland without a Roman Catholic minority. To move people, especially people like the Catholics of the north who are tied to their land as farmers, would not be easy. Further, repartition would seem to end for Irish nationalists any prospects of a unified Ireland.

*Independence.* A fourth alternative, which a 1981 survey showed more English favor than any other, would be to make Northern Ireland an independent nation. Obviously this solution is attractive to the English, for it would absolve the United Kingdom of future responsibility and bring the soldiers back home. A survey taken at the same time in Northern Ireland found relative support for some of the alternatives along predictable lines—Protestants favored full integration with London, Catholics favored unification with the Republic of Ireland. Only 22 percent of the Roman Catholics and 9 percent of Protestants favored repartitioning of the nation (Lipsey, 1981; Terchek, 1982).

Viewing all these alternatives, it is difficult to be optimistic. And the people of Northern Ireland are not. Surveys show that they expect the situation to deteriorate further. The young are especially pessimistic. It is difficult to imagine the violence these people have come to live with for the past 25 years. Through 1992, about 3,000 people had been killed and over 200,000 injured since 1968. Translated proportionately to the United States it would be as if almost 4 million people had been killed or wounded. People are leaving, but perhaps not as many as one might expect—about 10 percent have fled Northern Ireland since the civil rights protests began and the violence broke out. Protestants and Catholics share at least one value: commitment to live in the territory they regard as their own (A. Lee, 1983; Lipsey, 1981; Spuitieri, 1992; J. Thomas, 1985; Whitney, 1988).

# ISRAEL AND THE OCCUPIED TERRITORIES

In 1991 when the Gulf War ended, hopes were high in many parts of the world to hammer out a comprehensive Middle East peace plan. The key element in any such plan was to resolve the conflict between Israel and its Arab neighbors. While the issues are debated in the political arena, the origins of the conflict can be found in race, ethnicity, and religion.

## Creation of a Jewish Homeland

Nearly 2,000 years ago Jews were exiled from Palestine and, in the *diaspora*, settled throughout Europe and elsewhere in the Middle East. There they often encountered the hostile anti-Semitism described in Chapter 15. With the conversion of the Roman Empire to Christianity, Palestine became the site of many pilgrimages. Beginning in the seventh century, Palestine gradually fell under the Moslem influence of Arabs, except for ill-fated efforts such as the Crusades to recover the area for Europe. By the beginning of this century tourism became established, with some Jews migrating from Russia and establishing settlements that were tolerated by the Ottoman Empire, which then controlled Palestine.

Great Britain expanded its colonial control from Egypt into Palestine during World War I, driving out the Turks. Britain ruled the land while simultaneously endorsing the eventual establishment of a Jewish national homeland in Palestine. Even at that time, the spirit of *Zionism*, the yearning to restore Jewish national existence to the biblical homeland, was already a generation old. From the Arab perspective Zionism meant the subjugation, if not the elimination, of the Palestinians. Thousands of Jews came to settle from throughout the world, even though in the 1920s Palestine was only about 15 percent Jewish. Ethnic tension grew as the Arabs of Palestine were threatened by the Zionist fervor. Rioting grew to the point that in 1939 Britain yielded to Palestinian demands that Jewish immigration be stopped. This occurred at the same time as large numbers of Jews were fleeing the growth of Naziism. Following World War II, Jews resumed their demand for a homeland despite Arab objections. Britain turned to the newly-formed United Nations to settle the dispute. In May 1948, the British mandate over Palestine ended and the state of Israel was founded (Lesch, 1983; Said et al., 1988).

## Arab-Israeli Conflicts

No sooner had Israel been recognized than the Arab nations, particularly Egypt, Jordan, Iraq, Syria, and Lebanon, announced their intentions to restore control to the Palestinian Arabs, by force if necessary. As hostilities broke out, the Israeli military stepped in to preserve the borders, which no Arab nation agreed to recognize. Some 60 percent of the 1.3 million Arabs fled or were expelled from the Israeli territory, becoming refugees in neighboring countries. An uneasy peace followed as Israel attempted to encourage massive new Jewish immigration. Israel also extended the same services such as education and health care to the 750,000 Palestinians as were available to Jews. The new Jewish population continued to grow under the country's Law of Return which gave every Jew in the world the right to settle permanently as citizens. The question of Jerusalem remained unsettled, with the city divided into two separate sections—Israeli Jewish and Jordanian Arab—a division both sides refused to regard as permanent (Lesch, 1983).

In 1967, Egypt, followed by Syria, responded to Israel's military actions in what has come to be called the Six-Day War. In the course of defeating the Arab state militaries, Israel occupied the Gaza Strip, the West Bank, the Golan Heights, and the entire Sinai of Egypt (see Figure 17.2). The defeat was all the more bitter for the Arabs as Israeli-held territory expanded.

The October 1973 war (called the Yom Kippur War by Jews, the Ramadan War by Arabs), launched against Israel by Egypt and Syria, did not change any boundaries but it did lead to huge oil price rises as Arab and other oil-rich nations retaliated for the European and U.S. backing of Israel. In 1979, Egypt, through the mediation of President Carter, recognized Israel's right to exist, for which Israel returned the Sinai, but there was no suggestion the other occupied territories would be returned to neighboring Arab states. This recognition by Egypt, following several unsuccessful Arab military attacks, signaled to the Palestinians that they were alone in their struggle against Israel (Seale, 1980).

While our primary attention here is to the Palestinians and Jews, there is another significant ethnic issue present in Israel. The Law of Return has brought to Israel Jews of varying cultural backgrounds. European Jews have been the dominant force, but significant migration of the so-called "Oriental" Jews from North Africa and other parts of the Middle East has created what sociologist Ernest Krausz (1973) termed "the two nations." While the Oriental and European Jews are culturally diverse, there are also significant socioeconomic differences, with the Europeans generally being more prosperous, better represented in the Knesset (Israel's parliament), and better educated. The Oriental Jews are well aware of their subordinate status and even today are suspicious about efforts to ease the absorption of Russian Jews while their own problems seem to be unaddressed (Ben-Rafael and Sharot, 1991; Friendly and Silver, 1981).

## The Intifada

The Occupied Territories were regarded initially by Israel as a security zone between it and its belligerent neighbors. By the 1980s, however, it was clear that they were also serving as the location for new settlements for Jews migrating to Israel, especially from Russia. Palestinians, while having the political and monetary support of Arab nations, saw little likelihood for yet another successful military effort to eliminate Israel. Therefore in December 1987 they began the *intifada,* the uprising against Israel by the Palestinians in the occupied territories through attacks against soldiers, boycott of Israeli goods, general strikes, resistance, and noncooperation with Israeli authorities. An important precipitat-

**FIGURE 17.2** Israeli Settlements

Scattered throughout the Gaza Strip, West Bank, and the Golan Heights are settlements built for Jews in areas that Israel captured in 1967 from Jordan, Egypt, and Syria.

ing factor for the outbreak of the intifada was Palestinian frustration over an Arab summit meeting where the Palestinian issue was given low priority and the PLO's (Palestine Liberation Organization) leader, Yassar Arafat, was not received with the same recognition as heads of state. The real target of the intifada has been the Israelis. It should be realized that for several years of the intifada has been a grass roots, popular movement whose growth in support was as much a surprise to the PLO and Arab nations as it was to Israel and its

*Israelis demonstrate what they feel is their right to settle in the occupied territories. Palestinians, on the other hand, fear losing their land forever in future diplomatic negotiations.*

supporters. The broad range of participants in the intifada—students, workers, union members, professionals, and business leaders—showed the unambiguous Palestinian opposition to occupation. By June 1991, Israeli troops and civilians had killed 781 Palestinians, Palestinian activists had killed 319 Arabs suspected of being Israeli collaborators, and 69 Jews had lost their lives.

Despite condemnation from the United Nations and the United States, Israel continues to expel suspected activists from the territories into neighboring Arab states. The intifada began out of the frustration of the Palestinians within Israel but the confrontations are now encouraged by the PLO, an umbrella organization for several Palestinian factions varying in their militancy.

Palestinians now number 4-5 million with about 40 percent living under Israeli control. Of the Israeli Palestinians about one-third are regarded as residents, with the rest being in the occupied territories. The diaspora of Jews that the creation of Israel was to remedy has led to the displacement of the Palestinian Arabs (refer back to refugee data in Table 4.2). From the Israeli perspective the continued possession of these lands is vital, as evidenced by Iraq's firing of 39 Scud missiles into Israel during the 1991 Gulf War. The land is also justified as homes for Jewish immigrants. Israel, a nation of little more than 4 million, is expected to receive one million Jews during the 1989–1995 period (Aronson, 1990; Doherty, 1992; Galtung, 1989; NBC News, 1992; Said et al., 1988; Schiff and Ya'ari, 1990).

Almost an entire generation of Israelis and Palestinians have been born since the 1967 Six-Day War. Time, if not force, has given Israel its maximum territorial control, with a declining number of people personally recalling the time when the Jews did not have a homeland. Israel proclaims its interest in improving the socioeconomic status of Palestinians under its control to a standard of living higher than that of Arabs in Arab states. Peace talks are underway involving Israel, Palestinian representatives, and Arab nations, leading some Israelis to feel that acceptance of a Jewish state is possible. To accomplish this peacefully, it probably will not be possible to maintain the occupation of the Palestinian territories, but given the region's history of violence, Israel would be understandably suspicious of any "land for peace" overtures (Diehl, 1992).

# REPUBLIC OF SOUTH AFRICA

In every nation in the world, some racial, ethnic, or religious groups enjoy advantages denied other groups. Nations differ in the extent of this denial and whether it is supported by law or custom. In no other industrial society has the denial been so entrenched in law as in the Republic of South Africa.

The Republic of South Africa is different from the rest of Africa, because the original African peoples of the area are no longer present. Today the country is multiracial, as shown in Table 17.1. The largest group is the Black Africans, or *Bantus,* who migrated from the north in the eighteenth century. *Cape Coloureds,* the product of mixed-race, and *Asians* comprise the remaining non-Whites. The small White community is made up of the *English* and the *Afrikaners,* the latter descended from Dutch and other European settlers. Colin Legum, himself a South African, has correctly stated that "color is the sole determinant of power in South Africa," and this fact distinguishes the nation from all other contemporary societies (1967, p. 483). Not only is race the sole determinant of power, but it is the vastly outnumbered Whites who rule with little consideration for the other 80 percent of the people. It would be incorrect, however, to

---

**TABLE 17.1**   Racial Groups in the Republic of South Africa (percentages)

Whites in South Africa are outnumbered by more than four to one, and their proportion of the population is declining, yet they clearly represent the dominant economic and political force in this troubled nation.

|  | Whites | All non-Whites | Black Africans | Coloureds | Asians |
|---|---|---|---|---|---|
| 1904 | 22 | 78 | 67 | 9 | 2 |
| 1936 | 21 | 79 | 69 | 8 | 2 |
| 1951 | 21 | 79 | 68 | 9 | 3 |
| 1990 | 14 | 86 | 75 | 9 | 3 |
| 2010 (est.) | 10 | 90 | 81 | 7 | 2 |

*Notes:* Data for 1990 and 2010 include the Black homelands/"nations." Percentages do not add up to 100 because of rounding.
*Sources:* South African Institute of Race Relations, 1992, pp. 2, 3; van den Berghe, 1978, p. 102.

assume that White South Africans are a particularly perverse people or that their actions are unique. The racist South African society can be understood only as the product of a historical tradition firmly rooted in colonialism.

## Legacy of Colonialism

Permanent settlement of South Africa by Europeans began in 1652 when the Dutch East India Company established a colony in Cape Town as a port of call for shipping vessels bound for India. The area was sparsely populated and the original inhabitants of the Cape of Good Hope, the Hottentots and Bushmen, were pushed inland like the indigenous people of the New World. To fill the need for laborers, the Dutch imported slaves from areas of Africa farther north. Slavery was mostly confined to areas near towns and involved more limited numbers than in either the United States or Brazil. The *Boers*, seminomads descended from the Dutch, did not remain on the coast but trekked inland to establish vast sheep and cattle ranches. The *trekkers,* as they were known, regularly fought off the Black inhabitants of the interior regions. Sexual relations between Dutch men and slave and Hottentot women were quite common, giving rise to a mulatto group referred to today as Cape Coloureds.

The British entered the scene by acquiring South Africa in 1814, at the end of the Napoleonic Wars. The British introduced workers from India as indentured servants on sugar plantations. They also freed the slaves by 1834, with little compensation to the Dutch slave owners, and gave the Blacks virtually all political and civil rights. The Boers were not happy with these developments and spent most of the nineteenth century in a violent struggle with the growing number of English colonists. In 1902 the British finally overwhelmed the Boers, leaving bitter memories on both sides. The British were victorious due to a successful alliance with the Black Africans. Once in control, however, they recognized that the superior numbers of the non-Whites were a potential threat to their power, as they had been to the power of the Afrikaners.

The growing non-White population consisted of the Coloureds, or mixed population, and the Black tribal groups, collectively referred to as Bantus. The British gave both groups the vote but restricted the franchise with property qualifications. *Pass laws* were introduced, placing curfews on the Bantus and limiting their geographic movement. These laws, enforced through "reference books" until 1986, were intended to prevent urban areas from being overcrowded with job-seeking Africans, a familiar occurrence in colonial Africa (Barclay et al., 1976, pp. 249–251; Fredrickson, 1981; Treen, 1983; van den Berghe, 1965, pp. 13–37; W. Wilson, 1973, pp. 162–171).

## Apartheid

In 1948 South Africa was granted its independence, and the National Party dominated by the Afrikaners assumed control of the government. Under the leadership of this party, the rule of White supremacy, already well under way in the colonial period as custom, became more and more formalized into law. To deal with the multiracial population, the Whites devised a policy called *apartheid* to ensure their dominance. Apartheid (in Afrikaans, the language of the Afrikaners, it means "separation" or "apartness") has come to mean a policy of separate development, euphemistically now called *multinational development* by the government.

Multinational development reached its full evolution during the 1980s. Officially, multinational development calls for "economic co-operation between Blacks and Whites coupled with the highest possible degree of political freedom" (South African Department of Foreign Affairs and Information, 1983, p. 195). Beginning in 1976, the most developed Bantustan area, the Transkei, was awarded "independence." Because of the close control that White South Africa exercises over the people of the Transkei, no other nation recognized this new state as having independent status.

The ruling class is not homogeneous. The English and Afrikaners belong to different political parties, live apart, speak different languages, and worship separately, but they share the belief that some form of apartheid is necessary. Apartheid can perhaps best be understood as a twentieth-century effort to reestablish the paternalistic form of race relations typified by the master-slave relationship (Burns, 1978; Butler, 1974; W. Wilson, 1973, pp. 167–168).

Four independent republics and six "self-governing" states were identified by the Republic of South Africa through 1992 (see Figure 17.3), which for simplicity we will refer to as *homelands* or *Bantustans*. These changes were regarded outside South Africa and by most Black South Africans as cosmetic. Blacks and most foreign governments felt the changes were going too slowly. However, within White South Africa, the government encountered opposition from Whites who felt even the most modest changes, such as desegregating beaches and parks, were too radical. Demonstrations by Blacks grew and in 1986 a national state of emergency was declared by the government leading to massive arrests and worldwide condemnation.

A significant turn of events came in 1990 when Prime Minister F. W. De Klerk legalized 60 banned Black organizations and freed Nelson Mandela, leader of the African National Congress, after 27 years of imprisonment. Mandela's triumphant remarks following his release appear in "Listen to Their Voices." The following year, De Klerk and Black leaders signed a National Peace Accord, pledging themselves to the establishment of a multi-party democracy and an end to violence. Following a series of political defeats, De Klerk called for a referendum in 1992 to allow Whites to vote on ending apartheid. If he failed to receive popular support, he vowed to resign. A record high turnout gave a solid 68.6 percent vote favoring the continued dismantling of legal apartheid and the creation of a new constitution through negotiation. While the Whites are centralized behind the government, the non-White community is fragmented. Besides the Asians and Coloureds with their particular interests, the Black South African majority has many groups. Mandela's ANC is the oldest and appears to be most powerful. However, Chief Buthelezi of the Zulu tribe leads the Inkatha,

**FIGURE 17.3** African Homelands of South Africa

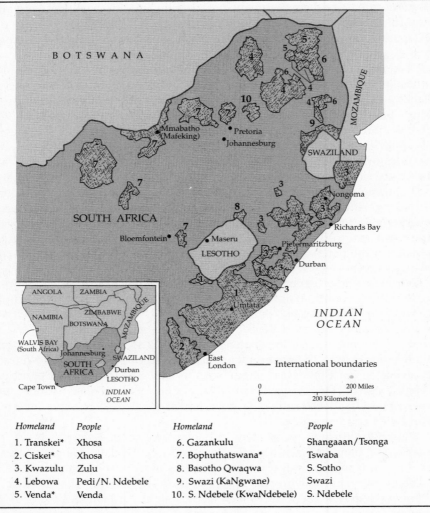

| Homeland | People | Homeland | People |
|----------|--------|----------|--------|
| 1. Transkei* | Xhosa | 6. Gazankulu | Shangaaan/Tsonga |
| 2. Ciskei* | Xhosa | 7. Bophuthatswana* | Tswaba |
| 3. Kwazulu | Zulu | 8. Basotho Qwaqwa | S. Sotho |
| 4. Lebowa | Pedi/N. Ndebele | 9. Swazi (KaNgwane) | Swazi |
| 5. Venda* | Venda | 10. S. Ndebele (KwaNdebele) | S. Ndebele |

*Indicates homelands declared to be independent by South Africa.
*Source:* From Roger J. Southall, *South Africa's Transkei.* Copyright © 1983 by Roger Southall. Reprinted by permission of Monthly Review Foundation.

Inkatha, a political party that tends to be less militant than the ANC. For example, the ANC favors mass mobilization techniques such as consumer boycotts, protest marches, and rent boycotts, which the Inkatha regard as too provocative. Fighting among Black civilians with allegiance to different groups began in the 1980s and continues to the present (Jeffery, 1991; Ottaway and Taylor, 1992).

Because of economic considerations, South Africa is not totally isolated. Western nations, principally Great Britain (which receives 12 percent of South Africa's exports), Japan (14 percent), and the United States (14 percent), trade with the country. What should be the United States' role in economic ties with South Africa? in 1975, acting at the request of Black leaders in South Africa, the Rev. Leon Sullivan of Philadelphia began to devise a code of conduct for General Motors, on whose board he sits, and for other American corporations doing business in South Africa. When first announced in 1977, the *Sullivan Principles* were adopted by a dozen companies and within three years the list of signatories had grown to 137, including most of the major American firms operating in South Africa. This code calls for desegregation of all eating and work areas in factories, equal and fair employment practices, including support for eliminating discrimination. In 1984, the principles were further strengthened, requiring efforts to see that Blacks live and work where they choose; and lobbying to end all apartheid laws.

Progress in the businesses subscribing to the Sullivan Principles has been significant and by local South African standards considered enlightened. This step is not enough for some, though. Even Sullivan himself in 1987 called on all American companies operating in South Africa to sell their investments there and to end all commercial ties with that country within nine months. Despite their notable record, Sullivan felt that the companies upholding the principles had failed to undermine apartheid. He also called for a trade embargo and for

*Key figures in South Africa: African National Congress's Nelson Mandela, Prime Minister F. W. De Klerk, and Inkatha's (Zulu political party) Mangosuthu Buthelezi.*

### ❖ LISTEN TO THEIR VOICES ❖

### "Africa, It Is Ours"

*Nelson Mandela*

*The following excerpts are from 71-year old Black nationalist leader Nelson Mandela's speech, delivered in front of the Cape Town City Hall following his being released from a 27-year imprisonment on February 12, 1990.*

Amandla! Amandla! i-Afrika, mayi-buye! [Power! Power! Africa it is ours!]

My friends, comrades and fellow South Africans, I greet you all in the name of peace, democracy and freedom for all. I stand here before you not as a prophet but as a humble servant of you, the people.

Your tireless and heroic sacrifices have made it possible for me to be here today. I therefore place the remaining years of my life in your hands.

On this day of my release, I extend my sincere and warmest gratitude to the millions of my compatriots and those in every corner of the globe who have campaigned tirelessly for my release.

Negotiations on the dismantling of apartheid will have to address the overwhelming demand of our people for a democratic nonracial and unitary South Africa. There must be an end to white monopoly on political power.

And a fundamental restructuring of our political and economic systems to insure that the inequalities of apartheid are addressed and our society thoroughly democratized. . . .

Our struggle has reached a decisive moment. We call on our people to seize this moment so that the process toward democracy is rapid and uninterrupted. We have waited too long for our freedom. We can no longer wait. Now is the time to intensify the struggle on all fronts.

To relax our efforts now would be a mistake which generations to come will not be able to forgive. The sight of freedom looming on the horizon should encourage us to redouble our efforts. It is only through disciplined mass action that our victory can be assured.

We call on our white compatriots to join us in the shaping of a new South Africa. The freedom movement is the political home for you, too. We call on the international community to continue the campaign to isolate the apartheid regime.

To lift sanctions now would be to run the risk of aborting the process toward the complete eradication of apartheid. Our march to freedom is irreversible. We must not allow fear to stand in our way.

Universal suffrage on a common voters roll in a united democratic and nonracial South Africa is the only way to peace and racial harmony.

In conclusion, I wish to go to my own words during my trial in 1964. They are as true today as they were then. I wrote: I have fought against white domination, and I have fought against black domination. I have cherished the idea of a democratic and free society in which all persons live together in harmony and with equal opportunities.

It is an ideal which I hope to live for and to achieve. But if needs be, it is an ideal for which I am prepared to die.

had failed to undermine apartheid. He also called for a trade embargo and for the United States to break off diplomatic relations (Feder, 1987).

Pressure intensified in the United States throughout the 1980s for withdrawing investment in the racially divided nation of South Africa. From college campuses and politicians came increasing demands to support *divestment*, the broad effort to end all economic relations with South Africa. Under the divestment movement, companies are encouraged by apartheid opponents to stop dealing with South African companies. Universities, pension funds, and insurance companies have been the objects of petitions, rallies, and protests seeking cooperation in not investing in American businesses that continue to operate in South Africa.

Following the removal of some aspects of apartheid and the release of Mandela, President George Bush in 1991 lifted the sanctions that had been imposed by the Comprehensive Anti-Apartheid Act of 1986. Some observers felt that the administration had moved prematurely since political prisoners were still being held and many localities had passed laws forbidding Blacks' moving into "White areas." Rev. Sullivan reiterated that sanctions should remain, but as the most flagrant aspects of apartheid faded the divestment movement also lost momentum (Carrington, 1991; Guy, 1991; Mufson, 1990; Sullivan, 1985, 1986).

## The South African Dilemma

Compared to a decade ago, the political position of Black South Africans is significantly better. After years of oppression, their leaders are free and recognized by the White ruling class.

Apartheid has changed, but significant aspects remain. Black South Africans have no vote in national affairs. Only Whites are subject to compulsory military service. White retirees receive larger government pensions than their Black counterparts. Racially segregated city councils persist and de facto segregation remains. The vast inequality continues. The dramatic income differences as in health care between the dominant White and subordinate Blacks. More than 80 percent of Black homes have no electricity. For every $8 spent on the education of White children, $1 is spent on Blacks. While Blacks and other non-Whites may now go where they like and do what they wish, the economic imbalance built up by decades of apartheid ensures that Whites continue to enjoy the nation's rights and privileges to the exclusion of Black South Africans' sharing in that country's wealth (Andersson and Marks, 1988; Benedetto, 1991; C. Wren, 1991).

South Africa remains a nation where color is the determinant of power. It is also a nation not at peace. While organizations from the United Nations to the International Olympic Committee have welcomed the White South African government, the political, social, and economic inequalities remain. Annually, 1,000 civilians die in civil disorders. Many casualties occur in clashes between the Inkatha and the ANC and other Black groups. There has also been a marked increase in White vigilante groups as they seek to maintain the separatism now fading with the dismantling of apartheid. Nelson Mandela proclaimed in December of 1991 that "the process of moving towards democracy is unstoppable." While this may be true, the barriers remaining are still significant (*South African Review*, 1992, p. 4; see also South African Institute of Race Relations, 1990).

---

**FIGURE 17.4**   Per Capita Income by Population Group, South Africa

The significant income inequality is apparent as we see White incomes continue to rise. Of the remaining groups, only the Asians have finally matched the 1917 levels of their White counterparts.

---

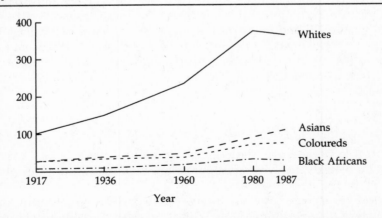

*Key:* 100 represents 4,100 Rand, the per capita income of White South Africans in 1917.
*Source:* Based on data appearing in South Africa Institute of Race Relations, *Race Relations Survey 1988/89*, p. 423.

# GLANCING BACK AND LOOKING AHEAD

Intergroup relations in Brazil, Great Britain, Northern Ireland, Israel, and South Africa are striking in their similarities and contrasts. The colonial experience has played a part in three cases. In Brazil and South Africa, where a multiracial society has existed much longer than in Britain, mixed-race sexual relations have been widespread but with different results. Mulattos in Brazil occupy a middle racial group and experience reduced tension, whereas in South Africa the Cape Coloureds have freedoms almost as limited as those of the Bantus. South Africa enforces de jure segregation; British communities seem to have de facto segregation; and Brazilian relations resemble a pattern of integration. Israel's and South Africa's intergroup conflicts are complicated by the involvement of the world community. Complete assimilation is absent in all five societies and unlikely in the near future; the legal and informal barriers to assimilation and pluralism vary for those subordinate people choosing either option.

If we add the United States to these societies, the comparison becomes even more significant. The problems of racial and ethnic adjustment in the United States have dominated our attention, but they parallel past and present experiences in other societies with racial, ethnic, or religious heterogeneity. The United States government has been involved in providing educational, financial, and legal support for programs intended to help particular racial or ethnic groups, and it continues to avoid interfering with religious freedom. Bilingual, bicultural programs in schools, autonomy for Native Americans on reservations, and increased participation in decision making by residents of ghettos and barrios are all viewed as acceptable goals, although not pursued to the extent many subordinate group people would like. While it promotes racial, ethnic, and religious diversity, the United States strives to impose universal criteria on employers, educators, and realtors, so that minority people can participate fully in the larger society. In some instances, in order to bring about equality of results, not just equality of opportunity, programs have been developed to give competitive advantages to women and minority men. This latest answer to inequality has provoked much controversy over how to achieve the admirable goal of a multiracial, multiethnic society, undifferentiated in opportunity and rewards.

Relations among racial, ethnic, or religious groups take two broad forms; as situations characterized by either consensus or conflict. Consensus prevails where assimilation or fusion among groups has been completed. Consensus also prevails in a pluralistic society in the sense that members have agreed to respect differences among groups and not demand conformity. Pluralism tolerates disagreement, but relations among groups are harmonious. By eliminating the contending group, extermination and expulsion also lead to a consensus society. In the study of intergroup relations, it is often easy to ignore conflict where there is high degree of consensus because it is assumed that an orderly society has no problems. In some instances, however, this condition can be misleading.

Through long periods of history, misery inflicted upon a racial, ethnic, or religious group was judged to be appropriate, if not actually divinely inspired (Grove, 1974; Horton, 1966; Schermerhorn, 1970, pp. 20–64).

In recent history, harmonious relations among all racial, ethnic, and religious groups has been widely accepted as a worthy goal. The struggle against oppression and inequality is not new. It dates back at least to the revolutions in England, France, and the American colonies in the seventeenth and eighteenth centuries. The twentieth century is unique in the extension of equality to the less privileged classes, generally racial and ethnic minorities. Conflict along racial and ethnic lines is especially bitter now because it evokes memories of slavery, colonial oppression, and overt discrimination. Today's African Americans are much more aware of slavery than contemporary poor people are of seventeenth-century debtors' prisons (Mason, 1970a, p. 163).

Racial and ethnic equality implies the right of the individual to choose his or her own way of life. As Hunt and Walker observed, however, individual rights may conflict with the group consensus (1979). This conflict makes the situation exceedingly complex; even if a society allows a group to select its own destiny, individual members of the group may then be unable to pursue freely their own course of action. If American Indians as a group choose to emphasize their cultural distinctiveness, those individuals who wish to integrate into White society may be looked upon by their peers as traitors to their tribe.

Unquestionably, the struggle for justice among racial and ethnic groups has not completely met its goals. Many people are still committed to repression, although they may see it only as benign neglect of those less privileged. Such repression leads only to the dehumanization of both the subordinated individual and the oppressor. Growth in equal rights movements and self-determination for Third-World countries largely populated by non-White people has moved the world onto a course that seems irreversible. Philip Mason acknowledges that people are more willing to reject stability if preserving it means inequality (1970b, p. 339). Self-determination, whether for groups or individuals, is often impossible in societies as they are currently structured. Bringing about social equality will therefore require significant change in existing institutions. Because such change is not likely to come about with everyone's willing cooperation, the social costs will be quite high. If there is a trend in racial and ethnic relations in the world today, however, it is the growing belief that the social costs, however high, must be paid to achieve self-determination.

It is naive to foresee a world of societies in which one person equals one vote and is accepted without regard to race, ethnicity, religion, or sex. It is equally unlikely to expect to see a society, let alone a world, that is without a privileged class or prestigious job-holders. Contact between different peoples, as we have seen numerous times, precedes conflict. Contact also may initiate mutual understanding and appreciation. What may well emerge out of contemporary and future unrest is the recognition by human beings that people are fundamentally alike and share the same abilities, weaknesses, and dreams.

# KEY TERMS

**apartheid** The policy of the South African government intended to maintain separation of Blacks, Coloureds, and Asians from the dominant Whites.

**diaspora** The exile of Jews from Palestine several centuries before Christianity began.

**divestment** The withdrawal of investments, referring to the general effort to end economic investment in South Africa.

**home rule** Britain's grant of a local parliament to Ireland.

**intifada** The Palestinian uprising against Israeli authorities in the occupied territories.

**manumission** Freeing of slaves by a master.

**mulatto escape hatch** In Brazil, social movement into a higher class based on gradation of skin color.

**multinational development** South African government program promoting the creation of so-called homelands or Bantustans in desolate areas.

**pass laws** Laws that control internal movement by non-Whites in South Africa, now called reference-book laws.

**quilombo** Hideaway used by Brazilian slaves in the nineteenth century.

**Sullivan Principles** Code of behavior promoting an end to apartheid in United States corporations doing business in South Africa.

**Zionism** Traditional Jewish religious yearning to return to the biblical homeland, now used to refer to support for the State of Israel.

# FOR FURTHER INFORMATION

Pierre-Michel Fontaine, ed. *Race, Class, and Power in Brazil.* Los Angeles: UCLA Center for Afro-American Studies, 1986.

A collection of essays examining the various aspects of Black Brazilians' changing situation.

Chester L. Hunt and Lewis Walker. *Ethnic Dynamics: Patterns of Intergroup Relations in Various Societies,* 2nd ed. Holmes Beach, FL: Learning Publications, 1979.

This is a comprehensive and very readable account of race relations in many societies, including South Africa, Britain, Northern Ireland, Soviet Union, Philippines, Kenya, Mexico, Nigeria, France, and Yugoslavia.

Alfred McClung Lee. *Terrorism in Northern Ireland.* Bayside, NY: General Hall, 1983.

A sociohistorical analysis of the problems besetting the people of Northern Ireland.

Joseph Lelyveld. *Move Your Shadow: South Africa, Black and White.* New York: New York Times Books, 1985.

An effective account of the present situation by a respected *New York Times* journalist.

Alan Paton. *Cry, the Beloved Country.* New York: Scribner, 1948.

Paton's widely acclaimed novel about an old Zulu parson who discovers his sister is a prostitute and his son the murderer of a White industrialist.

E. J. B. Rose in association with Nicholas Deakin, et al. *Colour and Citizenship: A Report on British Race Relations.* London: Oxford University Press, 1969.

Still the most detailed coverage of race relations in Britain, this book discusses immigration patterns, life in Britain, census data, results of a nationwide survey of prejudice, and responses by immigrants. It also offers 70 pages of conclusions and recommendations.

Thomas Skidmore. *Black into White.* New York: Oxford University Press, 1974.

A perceptive analysis of the myth and reality of the "whitening" of Black people in Brazil.

Pierre L. van den Berghe. *Race and Racism: A Comparative Perspective,* 2nd ed. New York: Wiley, 1978.

Besides presenting his typology of paternalistic and competitive race relations, van den Berghe incisively analyzes the patterns of race relations in Mexico, Gret Britain, South Africa, and the United States.

William J. Wilson. *Power, Racism, and Privilege: Race Relations in Theoretical and Socio-historical Perspective.* New York: Macmillan, 1973.

Wilson concentrates on relations between Blacks and Whites in South Africa and the United States, stressing the historical development of racial stratification and the emergence of institutional racism. The author revised some of his conclusions about the United States in his 1980 book, *The Declining Significance of Race.*

## *Periodicals*

Journals that cover race and ethnic relations from a cross-national perspective include *Ethnic and Racial Studies* (1978), *Race and Class* (1959), and *Race Today* (1968). A special issue on Blacks in Brazil appeared in *The Journal of Black Studies* (December 1980) and several articles on civil disorders in Britain appeared in *The Political Quarterly* (April–June 1982). Other journals relevant to this chapter include *Israel Social Science Research* (1983), *Israeli Studies* (1981), *Journal of South African Studies* (1974), and *Palestine Refugees Today* (1960).

# Glossary

Parenthetical numbers refer to the pages where the term was first used.

**abolitionists** Whites and free Blacks who favored the end of slavery. (190)

**absolute deprivation** The minimum level of subsistence below which families or individuals should not be expected to exist. (68)

**affirmative action** Positive efforts to recruit minority group members or women for jobs, promotions, and educational opportunities. (83)

**Afrocentric perspective** View that African cultures have penetrated the history, culture, and behavior of Blacks in the United States and throughout the world. (33, 212)

**AJAs** Americans of Japanese ancestry in Hawaii. (338)

**amalgamation** The process by which a dominant group and a subordinate group combine through intermarriage to form a new group. (27)

**androgyny** The state of being both masculine and feminine, aggressive and gentle. (432)

**anti-Semitism** Anti-Jewish prejudice or discrimination. (404)

**apartheid** The policy of the South African government intended to maintain separation of Blacks, Coloureds, and Asians from the dominant Whites. (483)

**assimilation** The process by which an individual forsakes his or her own cultural tradition to become part of a different culture. (28)

**asylee** A person already in the United States who fears persecution if forced to return to his or her homeland. (112)

**authoritarian personality** A psychological construct of a personality type likely to be prejudiced and to use others as scapegoats. (45)

**barrios** Segregated urban slums populated by Chicanos, Puerto Ricans, or other Hispanic group. (278)

**bilingual education** A program designed to allow students to learn academic concepts in their native language while they learn a second language. (257)

**bilingualism** The use of two or more languages in places of work or in educational facilities, with each language treated as equally legitimate. (256)

**biological race** A genetically isolated group characterized by a high degree of inbreeding, leading to distinctive gene frequencies. (10)

**bipolar occupational structure** Clustering at the higher- and lower-paying ends of the occupational scale, with relatively few in the middle—a situation in which Chinese Americans, and other Asian Americans, find themselves. (344)

**Black nationalism** The philosophy that encourages Blacks to see themselves in a positive light as Black people and carriers of a distinctive cultural tradition. (210)

**bracero** Contracted Mexican laborers imported to the United States during World War II. (278)

**brain drain** Immigration to the United States of skilled workers, professionals, and technicians who are desperately needed by their home countries. (103, 269)

**caste approach** An approach that views race and social class as synonymous, with disadvantaged minorities occupying the lowest social class and having little, if any, opportunity to improve their social position. (43)

**Chicanismo** An ideology emphasizing pride and positive identity among Chicanos. (282)

**civil disobedience** Tactic promoted by Martin Luther King, Jr., based on the belief that individuals have the right to disobey unjust laws under certain circumstances. (201)

**civil religion** The religious dimension in American life in which the state merges with sacred beliefs. (135)

**class** As defined by Max Weber, persons who share similar levels of wealth. (14, 234)

**colonialism** The maintenance of political, social, economic, and cultural dominance over a people by a foreign power for an extended period. (21)

**color gradient** Placement of people on a continuum from light to dark skin color rather than in distinct racial groupings by skin color. (268, 313, 465)

**comparable worth** See pay equity.

**conflict perspective** A sociological approach that assumes that social behavior is best understood in terms of conflict or tension among competing groups. (16)

**contact hypothesis** An interactionist perspective stating that interracial contact between people with equal status in noncompetitive circumstances will reduce prejudice. (63)

**creationists** People who support a literal interpretation of the Biblical book of Genesis on the origins of the universe and argue that evolution should not be presented as established scientific thought. (141)

**crossover effect** An effect that appears as previously high-scoring American-Indian children become "below average" in intelligence when tests are given in English rather than their native languages. (170)

**culture of poverty** According to its proponents, a way of life that involves no future planning, no enduring commitment to marriage, no work ethic; this culture follows the poor even when they move out of the slums or the barrio. (294)

**curanderismo** Hispanic folk medicine (298)

**de facto segregation** Segregation that results from residential patterns, such as use of neighborhood schools in communities in which there is residential segregation. (221)

**defensive insulation** Social structures for mutual help, as found in enclaves like Chinatowns. (359)

**de jure segregation** Segregation that results from assignment of children to schools specifically to maintain racial separation in schools. (198)

**denomination** A large organized religion not officially linked with the state or government. (118)

**diaspora** The exile of Jews from Palestine several centuries before Christianity began. (411)

**discrimination** The denial of opportunities and equal rights to individuals and groups because of prejudice or other arbitrary reasons. (39)

**divestment** The withdrawal of investments, referring to the general effort to end economic investment in South Africa. (487)

**double jeopardy** The subordinate status twice defined as experienced by women of color. (456)

**dual labor market** Division of the economy into two areas of employment, the secondary one of which is populated primarily by minorities working at menial jobs. (71)

**dysfunction** Elements of society that may disrupt a social system or lead to a decrease in its stability. (15)

**education pipeline**   The process of students passing through formal schooling and traveling in an ever-narrowing funnel attaining professional degrees at the end. (291)

**emigration**   Leaving a country to settle in another. (19)

**English immersion**   Teaching English by teachers who know the students' native language, but use it only when students do not understand the lessons. (258)

**ethclass**   Merged ethnicity and class in a person's status. (134)

**ethnic group**   A group set apart from others because of its national origin or distinctive cultural patterns. (7)

**ethnocentrism**   The tendency to assume that one's culture and way of life are superior to all others. (38)

**ethnophaulism**   Ethnic or racial slurs, including derisive nicknames. (39)

**evacuees**   Japanese Americans interned in camps for the duration of World War II. (379)

**evangelical faiths**   Christian faiths that place great emphasis on a personal relationship between the individual and God and believe that each adherent must spread the faith and bear personal witness by openly declaring the religion to nonbelievers. (320)

**exploitation theory**   A Marxist theory that views racial subordination in the United States as a manifestation of the class system inherent in capitalism. (43)

**familism**   Pride and closeness in the family that result in placing family obligation and loyalty before individual needs. (295)

**feminine mystique**   The ideology in which a woman thinks of herself only as her children's mother and her husband's wife. (438)

**feminization of poverty**   The trend since 1970 that has women accounting for a growing proportion of those below the poverty line. (446)

**fiesta politics**   Blatant overtures by presidential candidates to Chicanos for their support. (289)

**fish-ins**   Tribal protests over government interference with their traditional rights to fish as they would like. (174)

**fobs**   Recent immigrants from China, fresh off the boat. (366)

**fringe-of-values theory**   Behavior that is on the border of conduct that a society regards as proper and that is often carried out by subordinate groups, subjecting those groups to negative sanctions. (404)

**functionalist perspective**   A sociological approach emphasizing the way in which parts of a society are structured in the interest of maintaining the system as a whole. (15)

**gender identity**   The self-concept of an individual as male or female. (432)

**gender roles**   Expectations regarding the proper behavior, attitudes, and activities of males and females. (433)

**genocide**   The deliberate, systematic killing of an entire people or nation. (23)

**gook syndrome**   David Riesman's phrase describing Americans' tendency to stereotype Asians and to regard them as all alike and undesirable. (334)

**Haoles**   Hawaiian term for Caucasians. (337)

**home rule**   Britain's grant of a local parliament to Ireland. (474)

**hui kuan**   Chinese American benevolent associations organized on the basis of the district of the immigrant's origin in China. (355)

**ilchomose**   The 1.5 generation of Korean Americans—who immigrated to the United States as children. (329)

**immigration** Coming into a new country as a permanent resident. (19)

**inactivity rate** Proportion of a population neither in school nor in the labor force. (342)

**in-group virtues** Proper behavior by one's own group ("in-group virtues") becomes unacceptable when practiced by outsiders ("out-group vices"). (405)

**institutional discrimination** A denial of opportunities and equal rights to individuals or groups resulting from the normal operations of a society. (69)

**intelligence quotient (IQ)** The ratio of an individual's mental age (as computed by an IQ test) divided by his or her chronological age. (11)

**interactive effect** Pettigrew's view that race and class act together to place an individual in a stratification system. (14)

**intifada** The Palestinian uprising against Israeli authorities in the occupied territories. (478)

**irregular economy** Transfer of money, goods, or services that are not reported to the government. Common in inner-city neighborhoods and poverty-stricken rural areas. (71)

**Issei** First-generation immigrants from Japan to the United States. (375)

**Jim Crow** Southern laws passed during the latter part of the nineteenth century that kept Blacks in their subordinate position. (191)

**jook-sings** Chinese Americans who fail to carry on the cultural traditions of China or maintain a sense of identification with other Chinese Americans. (366)

**Judaization** The lessening importance of Judaism as a religion and substitution of cultural traditions as the tie that binds Jews. (422)

**kashrut** Laws pertaining to permissible *(kosher)* and forbidden foods and their preparation. (418)

**Kibei** Japanese Americans of the *Nisei* generation sent back to Japan for schooling and to have marriages arranged. (375)

**kickouts or pushouts** American-Indian school dropouts, who leave behind an unhealthy academic environment. (170)

**kye** Rotating credit system used by Korean Americans to subsidize the start of businesses. (330)

**labeling theory** An approach introduced by Howard Becker that attempts to explain why certain people are viewed as deviants and others engaging in the same behavior are not. (16)

**life chances** People's opportunities to provide themselves with material goods, positive living conditions, and favorable life experiences. (133)

**machismo** A male's sense of virility, of personal worth, in his own eyes and in those of his peers. (295)

**manumission** The granting of freedom to a slave. (465)

**marginality** Status of being between two cultures at the same time, such as might describe a Jewish immigrant to the United States. (29)

**marianismo** A female's acceptance of man's dominance, and placing of family needs first. (295)

**Marielitos** People who arrived from Cuba, in the fourth wave of Cuban immigration, most specifically those forcibly deported via Mariel Harbor. The term is generally reserved for those refugees seen as especially undesirable. (263)

**market discrimination** The underpayment or underemployment of qualified women. (443)

**melting pot** Diverse racial or ethnic groups or both forming a new creation, a new cultural entity. (27)

**middlemen minorities** Groups such as Japanese Americans who typically occupy middle positions in the social and occupational stratification system. (344)

**migration** General term to describe any transfer of population. (19)

**millenarian movements** Movements, such as the Ghost Dance, that prophesize a cataclysm in the immediate future, followed by collective salvation. (153)

**minority group** A subordinate group whose members have significantly less control or power over their own lives than that held by the members of a dominant or majority group. (5)

**model or ideal minority** A group that, despite past prejudice and discrimination, succeeds economically, socially, and educationally without resorting to political or violent confrontations with Whites. (340)

**mojados** "Wetbacks," derisive slang for Mexicans who enter illegally, supposedly by swimming the Rio Grande. (280)

**mommy track** The problematic corporate career track for women who want to divide their attention between work and family. (440)

**mulatto escape hatch** In Brazil, social movement into a higher class based on gradation of skin color. (465)

**multinational development** South African government program promoting creation of so-called homelands or Bantustans in desolate areas. (483)

**mutilated marriages** The separations of early Chinese immigrants, most of whom were male and had to leave behind their wives and children. (354)

**nativism** Beliefs and policies favoring native-born citizens over immigrants. (95)

**neocolonialism** Continuing domination of former colonies by foreign countries. (23)

**Neoricans** Puerto Ricans who return to the island to settle after living on the mainland of the United States (also *nuyoricans*). (313)

**Nisei** Children born of immigrants from Japan. (375)

**noshrim** Immigrants who have discarded all traces of Jewish religious faith and commitment to the larger Jewish community. (403)

**out-group vices** See "in-group virtues." (405)

**padrone** Labor contractor who would find work and sometimes homes for the new Italian immigrants. (130)

**pan-Indianism** Intertribal social movements in which several tribes, joined by culture but not by kinship, unite, usually to confront an enemy—such as the federal government. (173)

**pass laws** Laws that control internal movement by non-Whites in South Africa, now called reference-book laws. (482)

**pay equity** Same wages for different types of work that are judged to be comparable by such measures as employee knowledge, skills, effort, responsibility, and working conditions, also called *comparable worth*. (445)

**pentecostal faiths** Religious groups similar in many respects to evangelical faiths which, in addition, believe in the infusion of the Holy Spirit into services and in religious experiences such as faith healing. (320)

**peoplehood** Milton Gordon's term for a group with a shared feeling. (424)

**pluralism** Mutual respect between the various groups in a society for one another's cultures, allowing minorities to express their own culture without experiencing prejudice or hostility. (31)

**politically correct** Efforts on behalf of racial, ethnic, and religious minorities as well as women. Phrase is often used in criticism of such measures. (5)

**prejudice** A negative attitude toward an entire category of people, such as a racial, or ethnic minority. (39)

**quilombo** Hideaway used by Brazilian slaves in the nineteenth century. (464)

**racial group** A group that is socially set apart from others because of obvious physical differences. (7)

**racism** A doctrine that one race is superior. (12)

**Raza** "The People"—a term referring to the rich heritage of Chicanos, and hence used to designate a sense of pride among Chicanos today. (274)

**redlining** Practice of financial lenders refusing to grant home and commercial loans in minority and racially changing neighborhoods. (238)

**relative deprivation** The conscious feeling of a negative discrepancy between legitimate expectations and present actualities. (50, 67, 206)

**repatriation** The program of deporting Mexicans during the 1930s. (278)

**respectable bigotry** Michael Lerner's term for the social acceptance of prejudice against White ethnics, when intolerance toward non-White minorities is regarded as unacceptable. (126)

**restrictive covenants** Private contracts or agreements that discourage or prevent minority group members from purchasing housing in a neighborhood. (197)

**riff-raff theory** Also called the rotten-apple theory; the belief that the riots of the 1960s were caused by discontented youths, rather than by social and economic problems facing all African Americans. (205)

**sanctuary movement** A movement of loosely connected organizations that offer asylum, often in churches, to those who seek refugee status but are regarded by the Immigration and Naturalization Service as illegal aliens. (111, 268)

**Sansei** The children of the *Nisei;* that is, the grandchildren of the original immigrants from Japan. (375)

**scapegoat** A person or group blamed irrationally for another person's or group's problems or difficulties. (44)

**secessionist minority** Groups such as the Hutterites, who reject assimilation as well as coexistence. (140)

**second shift** The double burden—work outside the home followed by child care and housework—faced by many women which few men share equitably. (452)

**segregation** The act of physically separating two groups; often imposed on a subordinate group by the dominant group. (25)

**self-fulfilling prophecy** The tendency of individuals to respond to and act on the basis of stereotypes, a predisposition that can lead to validation of false definitions. (17)

**set asides** Programs stipulating a minimum proportion of government contracts that must be awarded to minority-owned businesses. (228)

**setoffs** Deductions from U.S. money due in settlements to Indians equal to the cost of federal services provided to the tribe. (159)

**sexism** The ideology that one sex is superior to the other. (432)

**sexual harassment** The unwanted imposition of sexual requirements in the context of unequal power. (443)

**slave codes** Laws that delineated the low position held by enslaved Blacks in the United States. (187)

**Social Darwinism** The belief that societies and races are engaged in a struggle for existence in which the fit survive. (12)

**states' rights** The principle reinvoked in the 1950s, which holds that each state is sovereign and has the right to order its own affairs without interference from the federal government. (81)

**stereotypes** Unreliable generalizations

about all members of a group that do not take into account individual differences within the group. (17)

**strain-reducing mechanisms** Techniques used to reduce the conflict created by marginality. (29)

**stratification** A structured ranking of entire groups of people that perpetuates unequal rewards and power in a society. (14)

**structural approach** The view that prejudice is influenced by societal norms and situations that serve to encourage or discourage tolerance of minorities. (45)

**suffragists** Women and men who worked successfully to gain women the right to vote. (436)

**Sullivan Principles** Code of behavior promoting an end to apartheid in United States corporations doing business in South Africa. (485)

**symbolic ethnicity** Herbert Gans's term to describe emphasis on ethnic food and ethnically associated political issues rather than deeper ties to one's heritage. (125)

**third-generation interest principle** Marcus Hansen's contention that ethnic interest and awareness increase in the third generation, among the grandchildren of immigrants. (123)

**tongs** Chinese American secret associations. (355)

**total discrimination** The combination of current discrimination with past discrimination created by poor schools and menial jobs. (68)

**tracking** The practice of placing students in specific curriculum groups on the basis of test scores and other criteria. (317)

**tsu** Clans established along family lines and forming a basis for social organization by Chinese Americans. (355)

**underclass** Lower-class members not a part of the regular economy whose situa-

tion is not changed by conventional assistance programs. (72)

**underemployment** Work at a job for which the worker is overqualified; involuntary part-time employment instead of full-time; intermittent employment. (226)

**victimization surveys** Annual attempt to measure crime rates by interviewing ordinary citizens who may or may not have been crime victims. (241)

**White backlash** White resistance to further improvement in the status of Black people. (53)

**White primary** Legal provisions forbidding Black voting in election primaries, which in one-party areas of the South effectively denied Blacks their right to select elected officials. (192)

**xenophobia** The fear or hatred of strangers or foreigners. (95)

**yellow peril** Generalized prejudice toward people and customs of Asian background. (355)

**Yiddishkait** Jewishness. (420)

**Yonsei** The fourth generation of Japanese Americans in the United States, the children of the *Sansei*. (375)

**Zionism** Traditional Jewish religious yearning to return to the biblical homeland now used to refer to support for the state of Israel. (411, 477)

**zoning laws** Legal provisions stipulating land use and architectural design of housing, often employed to keep racial minorities and low-income persons out of suburban areas. (240)

**zoot-suiters** Chicano youth during the mid-1940s in southern California; a derisive term. (279)

# References

Aaron, Henry J.
1972   *Shelter and Subsidies: Who Benefits from Federal Housing Subsidies?* Washington, DC: Brookings Institution.

Aberbach, Joel D., and Walker, Jack L.
1970   The Meanings of Black Power: A Comparison of White and Black Interpretations of a Political Slogan. *American Political Science Review* 64 (June), pp. 367–388.
1973   *Race in the City.* Boston: Little, Brown.

Abraham, Henry J.
1965   *The Judiciary: The Supreme Court in the Governmental Process.* Boston: Allyn and Bacon.

Abramson, Harold J.
1973   *Ethnic Diversity in Catholic America.* New York: Wiley.

Abron, JoNina M.
1986   The Legacy of the Black Panther Party. *The Black Scholar* 17 (November–December), pp. 33–37.

Acosta, Oscar Zeta
1972   *The Autobiography of a Brown Buffalo.* San Francisco: Straight Arrow Books.

Acosta-Belén, Edna, ed.
1986   *The Puerto Rican Women: Perspectives on Culture, History, and Society,* 2nd ed. New York: Praeger.

Acuña, Rodolfo
1981   *Occupied America: A History of Chicanos,* 2nd ed. New York: Harper and Row.

Adamic, Louis
1931   *Dynamite: The Story of Class Violence in America.* 1960; rpt. Gloucester, MA: Peter Smith.

Adams, David Wallace
1988   Fundamental Considerations: The Deep Meaning of Native American Schooling, 1880–1900. *Harvard Educational Review* 58 (February), pp. 1–28.

Adler, Patricia Rae
1974   The 1943 Zoot-Suit Riots: Brief Episode in a Long Conflict. In Manuel P. Servin, ed., *An Awakened Minority: The Mexican Americans,* 2nd ed., pp. 142–158. Beverly Hills, CA: Glencoe Press.

Adorno, T. W.; Frenkel-Brunswik, Else; Levinson, Daniel J.; and Sanford R. Nevitt
1950   *The Authoritarian Personality.* New York: Wiley.

*Akwesasne Notes*
1972a  Columbus a Trader in Indian Slaves. 4 (Early Autumn), p. 22.
1972b  Navajo Testimony Reveals Treatment at Hands of Traders. 4 (Early Autumn), p. 5.
1974a  Alaskaland Settlement: Boon or Doom. 6 (Early Spring), pp. 22–23.
1974b  Pine Ridge Election: Was It a Fair Fight? 6 (Early Spring), pp. 8–9.
1974c  White House Replies to Oglala 15 Questions. 6 (Early Spring), pp. 10–11.
1977   The Deaths at Pine Ridge in the Reign of Terror, 1973–1976. 8 (Midwinter), p. 9.
1986   Native Unemployment Remains Critically High. 18 (Autumn), pp. 11–13.
1988   Competing Sovereignties in North America and the Right-Wing and Anti-Indian Movement. 20 (Early Spring), pp. 12–13.

Alba, Richard D.
1976   Social Assimilation Among American Catholic National-Origin Groups. *American Sociological Review* 41 (December), pp. 1030–1046.
1985   *Italian Americans: Into the Twilight of Ethnicity.* Englewood Cliffs, NJ: Prentice-Hall.

1990    *Ethnic Identity: The Transformation of White America.* New Haven, Yale University Press.

Alba, Richard D., ed.
1988    *Ethnicity and Race in the U.S.A.* New York: Routledge.

Alba, Richard D., and Moore, Gwen
1982    Ethnicity in the American Elite. *American Sociological Review* 47 (June), pp. 373–383.

Allen, James Paul, and Turner, Eugene James
1988    *We the People: At Atlas of America's Ethnic Diversity.* New York: Macmillan.

Allen, Sheila
1971    *New Minorities, Old Conflicts: Asian and West Indian Migrants in Britain.* New York: Random House.

Allen, Walter R., Epps, Edgar G., and Haniff, Nesha Z.
1991    *College in Black and White.* Albany: State University of New York Press.

Allen, Walter R., and Reynolds, Farley
1986    The Shifting Social and Economic Tides of Black America, 1950–1980. In *Annual Review of Sociology, 1986,* pp. 277–306. Palo Alto, CA: Annual Review of Sociology.

Allport, Gordon W.
1962    Prejudice: Is It Societal or Personal? *Journal of Social Issues* 18 (April), pp. 120–134.
1979    *The Nature of Prejudice,* 25th Anniversary Edition. Reading, MA: Addison-Wesley.

Alvirez, David, and Bean, Frank D.
1976    The Mexican American Family. In Charles H. Mindel and Robert W. Habenstein, eds., *Ethnic Families in America: Patterns and Variations,* pp. 271–292. New York: Elsevier.

*American Enterprise*
1990    "Is Abortion a 'Women's Issue'?" 1 (July/August) (No. 4), pp. 102–104.

American Indian Policy Review Commission.
1976a   *Indian Law Revision, Consolidation and Codification.* Task Force #9. Washington, DC: U.S. Government Printing Office.

1976b   *Task Force on Alaskan Natural Issues.* Washington, DC: U.S. Government Printing Office.
1976c   *Urban and Rural Non-Reservation Indians.* Task Force #8. Washington, DC: U.S. Government Printing Office.

American Jewish Committee
1965    *Mutual Savings Banks of New York City.* New York: American Jewish Committee.
1966a   *Mutual Savings Banks: A Follow-up Report.* New York: American Jewish Committee.
1966b   *Patterns of Exclusion from the Executive Suite: Corporate Banking.* New York: American Jewish Committee.
1987    Family Issues and Jewish Unity. *Newsletter* 6 (Fall), pp. 1–3.

Anderson, Charles H.
1970    *White Protestant Americans: From National Origins to Religious Group.* Englewood Cliffs, NJ: Prentice-Hall.

Anderson, David Earle
1985    Which Way Civil Rights? *Present Tense* 13 (August), pp. 25–30.

Andersson, Neil, and Marks, Sheila
1988    Apartheid and Health in the 1980s. *Social Science and Medicine* 27 (No. 7), pp. 667–681.

Andersson-Brolin, Lillemor
1988    Ethnic Residential Segregation: The Case of Sweden. *Scandinavian Journal of Development Alternatives* 7 (March), pp. 33–45.

Andrews, George Reid
1991    *Blacks and Whites in São Paulo, Brazil, 1888–1988.* Madison: University of Wisconsin Press.

Angle, John
1976    Mainland Control of Manufacturing and Reward for Bilingualism in Puerto Rico. *American Sociological Review* 41 (April), pp. 289–307.

Anti-Defamation League of B'nai B'rith
1992    *Audit of Anti-Semitic Incidents.* New York: Anti-Defamation League.

Aponte, Robert
1991    Urban Hispanic Poverty: Disaggregations and Explanations. *Social Problems* 38 (November), pp. 516–528.

Apple, R. W., Jr.
1975    Toward the Bilingual Election. *New York Times* (July 27), p. E5.

Aran, Kenneth; Arthur, Herman; Colon, Ramon; and Goldenberg, Harvey
1973    *Puerto Rican History and Culture: A Study Guide and Curriculum Outline.* New York: United Federation of Teachers.

Arden, Harvey
1975    The Pious Ones. *National Geographic* (August), pp. 276–298.

Arocha, Zita
1988    A Wave of Immigration to Match the Turn of the Century's. *Washington Post National Weekly Edition* 5 (August 1–7), pp. 31–32.

Aronson, Geoffrey
1990    *Israel, Palestinians and the Intifada.* London: Kegan Paul.

Asante, Molefi Kete
1987    *The Afrocentric Idea.* Philadelphia: Temple University Press.
1991    Putting Africa at the Center. *Newsweek* 118 (September 23), p. 46.

Asante, Molefi Kete, and Mattson, Mark T.
1991    *The Historical and Cultural Atlas of African Americans:* New York: Macmillan.

Ashe, Arthur R. Jr., with Branch, Kip; Chalk, Ocania; and Harris, Francis
1989    *A Hard Road to Glory: A History of the African-American Athlete.* New York: Amistad Books.

Aspy, David N.
1970    Groping or Grouping for Teachability. *Contemporary Education* 41 (May), pp. 306–310.

Ayres, Ian
1991    Fair Driving: Gender and Race Discrimination in Retail Car Negotiations. *Harvard Law Review* 104 (February), pp. 817–872.

Bach, Robert L., and Bach, Jennifer B.
1980    Employment Patterns of Southeast Asian Refugees. *Monthly Labor Review* 103 (October), pp. 31–38.

Bacon, John
1987    Court Ruling Hasn't Quieted School Prayer. *USA Today* (April 3), p. 3A.

Bagley, Christopher
1970    *Social Structure and Prejudice in Five English Boroughs.* London: Institute of Race Relations.

Bahr, Howard M.
1972    An End to Invisibility. In Howard M. Bahr, Bruce A. Chadwick, and Robert C. Day, eds., *Native Americans Today: Sociological Perspectives,* pp. 404–412. New York: Harper and Row.

Bahr, Howard M.; Chadwick, Bruce A.; and Stauss, Joseph H.
1972    Discrimination Against Urban Indians in Seattle. *Indian Historian* 5 (Winter), pp. 4–11.

Baldus, David C.; Pulaski, Charles A. Jr., and Woodworth, George
1986    Arbitrariness and Discrimination in the Administration of the Death Penalty: A Challenge to State Supreme Courts. *Stetson Law Review* 15 (Spring), pp. 133–261.

Baldwin, James
1967    Negroes Are Anti-Semitic Because They're Anti-White. *New York Times* (May 21), p. 114.

Ball, Harry V., and Yamamura, Douglas S.
1960    Ethnic Discrimination and the Market Place. *American Sociological Review* 25 (October), pp. 687–694.

Ball-Rokeach, Sandra J.; Rokeach, Milton; and Grulse, Joel W.
1984    *The Great American Values Test: Influencing Behavior and Belief Through Television.* New York: Free Press.

Banfield, Edward
1974    *The Unheavenly City Revisited.* Boston: Little, Brown.

Banton, Michael
1967    *Race Relations.* London: Tavistock Publications.

Banton, Michael, and Harwood, Jonathan
1975    *The Race Concept.* New York: Praeger.

Barbaro, Fred
1974    Ethnic Resentment, *Society* 11 (March–April), pp. 67–75.

Barclay, William; Kumar, Krishna; and Simms, Ruth P.
1976    *Racial Conflict, Discrimination, and Power: Historical and Contemporary*

*Studies.* New York: AMS Press.

Baron, Harold B.
1968    Black Powerlessness in Chicago.
        *Transaction* 6 (November), pp. 27–
        33.
1975    Postscript—1974. In Norman R.
        Yetman and C. Roy Steele, eds.,
        *Majority and Minority: The Dynamics
        of Racial and Ethnic Relations,* 2nd
        ed., pp. 388–389. Boston: Allyn and
        Bacon.

Barrera, Mario
1988    *Beyond Aztlan: Ethnic Autonomy in
        Comparative Perspective.* New York:
        Praeger.

Barrera, Mario; Muñoz, Carlos; and Ornelas,
Charles
1972    The Barrio as an Internal Colony.
        In Harlan Mahlan, ed., *People and
        Politics in Urban Society,* pp. 465–
        499. Beverly Hills, CA: Sage Pub-
        lications.

Barrett, Laurence I.
1976    Trying to Make It Without Mira-
        cles. *Time* 107 (February 16), pp.
        15–16. 21.

Barrett, Wayne, and Cooper, Andrew
1981    Koch's 99 Attacks Against the Oth-
        er New York. *Village Voice* 26 (April
        15–21), pp. 22–31.

Barta, Russell
1974    *The Representation of Poles, Italians,
        Latins and Blacks in the Executive
        Suites of Chicago's Largest Corpora-
        tions.* Chicago: Institute of Urban
        Life.

Bash, Harry M.
1979    *Sociology, Race and Ethnicity.* New
        York: Gordon & Breach.

Baskin, Jane A.; Hartweg, Joyce K.; Lewis,
Ralph G.; and McCullough, Lester W., Jr.
1971    *Race Related Civil Disorders; 1967–
        1969.* Waltham, MA: Lemberg Cen-
        ter for the Study of Violence, Bran-
        deis University.

Baskin, Jane A.; Lewis, Ralph G.; Mannis,
Joyce Hartweg; and McCullough, Lester W.,
Jr.
1972    The Long, Hot Summer, *Justice
        Magazine* 1 (February), p. 8.

Bataille, Gretchen, and Sands, Kathleen
1984    *American Indian Women Telling Their*

*Lives.* Lincoln: University of Nebraska Press.

Bauer, Raymond A., and Bauer, Alice H.
1942    Day to Day Resistance to Slavery.
        *Journal of Negro History* 27 (Octo-
        ber), pp. 388–419.

Bauman, David
1985    English-Only Drive Gaining Steam.
        *USA Today* (April 1), p. A3.

Baumann, Marty
1992    Agreement on King. *USA Today*
        (May 11), p. 4A.

Beach, Walter G.
1934    Some Considerations in Regard to
        Race Segregation in California. *So-
        ciology and Social Research* 18
        (March), pp. 340–350.

Bean, Frank D.; Edmonston, Barry; and Passel, Jeffrey S.
1990    *Undocumented Migration to the
        United States.* Santa Monica, CA:
        Rand Institute.

Bearak, Barry
1982    Many "Marielitos" Still Find U.S.
        Life Hard After 2 Years. *Los Angeles
        Times* (April 19), pp. 1, 10.

Becerra, José E., et al.
1991    Infant Mortality Among Hispanics:
        A Portrait of Heterogeneity. *Journal
        of the American Medical Association*
        265 (January 9), pp. 217–221.

Becker, Gary S.
1971    *The Economics of Discrimination,* 2nd
        ed. Chicago: University of Chicago
        Press.

Belair, Felix, Jr.
1970    1965 Law Changes Ethnic Patterns
        of Immigration. *New York Times*
        (August 31), pp. 1, 37.

Bell, Daniel
1953    Crime as an American Way of Life.
        *Antioch Review* 13 (Summer), pp.
        131–154.
1961    Reflections on Jewish Identity. *Com-
        mentary* 31 (June), pp. 471–478.

Bell, David A.
1985    The Triumph of Asian-Americans.
        *The New Republic* 193 (July 15), pp.
        24–26, 28–31.

Bell, Wendell
1974    Comparative Research on Ethnicity:
        A Conference Report. *Items* 28 (De-

cember), pp. 61–64.
1981    Neocolonialism. In *Encyclopedia of Sociology*, p. 193. Guilford, CT: DPG Publishing.

Bellah, Robert
1967    Civil Religion in America. *Daedalus* 96 (Winter), pp. 1–21.
1968    Response to Commentaries on "Civil Religion in America." In Donald R. Cutler, ed., *The Religious Situation: 1968*, pp. 388–393. Boston: Beacon Press.
1970    *Beyond Belief: Essays on Religion in a Post-Traditional World.* New York: Harper and Row.
1989    Comment to Mathisen. *Sociological Analysis* 50 (Summer), p. 147.

Bem, Sandra L., and Bem, Daryl J.
1970    Case Study of a Nonconscious Ideology: Training the Woman to Know Her Place. In Daryl J. Bem, ed. *Beliefs, Attitudes, and Human Affairs*, pp. 89–99. Belmont, CA: Brooks/Cole.

Benedetto, Richard
1991    "Pillars of Apartheid" Gone. *USA Today* (July 11), p. 1A.

Bennett, Lerone, Jr.
1965    *Confrontation: Black and White.* Chicago: Johnson.
1966    *Before the Mayflower,* rev. ed. Baltimore: Penguin.

Benokraitis, Nijole, and Feagin, Joe R.
1977    Institutional Racism: A Critical Assessment of Literature and Suggestions for Extending the Perspective. In Charles V. Willie, ed., *Black/Brown/White Relations,* pp. 121–143. New Brunswick, NJ: Transaction Books.

Ben-Rafael, Eliezer, and Sharot, Stephen
1991    *Ethnicity, Religion and Class in Israeli Society.* Cambridge: Cambridge University Press.

Berg, Bruce
1988    The Chanukah Bush: Chanukah and Christmas Celebration among Jews. *Free Inquiry in Creative Sociology* (November).

Berg, Philip L.
1975    "Racism and the Puritan Mind." *Phylon* 26 (Spring), pp. 1–7.

Berger, Joseph

1986a   Hispanic Catholics Found to Hew to Tradition. *New York Times* (February 9), p. 14.
1986b   Split Widens on a Basic Issue: What Is a Jew? *New York Times* (February 28), pp. 1, 18.
1986c   Speakers Discern a Decline in U.S. Anti-Semitism. *New York Times* (March 23), p. 23.

Bernard, Jessie
1975    *Women, Wives, Mothers: Values and Options.* Chicago: Aldine.

Berndt, Ronald M., and Berndt, Catherine
1951    *From Black to White in South Australia.* Melbourne: F. W. Chesire.

Bernstein, Richard
1990    In U.S. Schools A War of Words. *New York Times Magazine* (October 14), pp. 34–38, 48, 50, 52.

Berreman, Gerald D.
1960    Caste in India and the United States. *American Journal of Sociology* 66 (September), pp. 120–127.
1973    *Caste in the Modern World.* Morristown, NJ: General Learning Press.

Besharov, Douglas J.; Quin, Alison; and Zinsmeister, Karl
1987    A Portrait in Black and White: Out-of-Wedlock Births. *Public Opinion* (May–June), pp. 43–45.

Bettelheim, Bruno, and Janowitz, Morris
1950    Prejudice. *Scientific American* 183 (October), pp. 3–8.
1964    *Social Change and Prejudice.* New York: Free Press.

Bielby, William T., and James N. Baron
1986    Men and Women at Work: Sex Segregation and Statistical Discrimination. *American Journal of Sociology* 91 (January), pp. 759–799.

Biemiller, Lawrence
1986    Asian Students Fear Top Colleges Use Quota Systems. *The Chronicle of Higher Education* 23 (November 19), pp. 1, 34–35, 37.

Bienen, Leigh; Ostriker, Alicia; and Ostriker, J. P.
1975    Sex Discrimination in the Universities: Faculty Problems and No Solution. *Women's Rights Law Reporter* 2 (March), pp. 3–12.

Billard, Jules B.

1974　*The World of the American Indian.*
　　　Washington, DC: National Geo-
　　　graphic Society.

Billingsley, Andrew
1987　Black Families in a Changing Soci-
　　　ety. In Janet Dewart, ed., *The State
　　　of Black America,* pp. 97–111. New
　　　York: National Urban League.

Billington, Ray Allen
1938　*The Protestant Crusade, 1800–1860.*
　　　1963 rpt. Gloucester, MA: Peter
　　　Smith.

Billson, Janet Mancini
1988　No Owner of Soil: The Concept of
　　　Marginality Revisited on Its Six-
　　　tieth Birthday. *International Review
　　　of Modern Sociology* 18 (Autumn),
　　　pp. 183–204.

Birmingham, Stephen
1971　*The Grandees: America's Sephardic
　　　Elite.* New York: Harper and Row.

Blackstock, Nelson
1976　*COINTELPRO: The FBI's Secret War
　　　on Political Freedom.* New York: Vin-
　　　tage Press.

Blackwell, James E.
1976　The Power Basis of Ethnic Conflict
　　　in American Society. In Lewis A.
　　　Coser and Otto N. Larsen, eds., *The
　　　Uses of Controversy in Sociology,* pp.
　　　179–196. New York: Free Press.

Blackwell, James E., and Janowitz, Morris,
eds.
1974　*Black Sociologists: Historical and Con-
　　　temporary Perspectives.* Chicago: Uni-
　　　versity of Chicago Press.

Blake, Robert R., and Mouton, Jane S.
1962　The Inter-group Dynamics of Win-
　　　Lose Conflict and Problem-Solving
　　　Collaboration in Union-
　　　Management Relations. In Musafer
　　　Sherif, ed., *Inter-group Relations and
　　　Leadership,* pp. 94–100. New York:
　　　Wiley.

Blalock, Hubert M., Jr.
1967　*Toward a Theory of Minority-Group
　　　Relations.* New York: Capricorn
　　　Books.

Bland, Dorothy, and De Quinne, Jeanne
1987　New Drives Mounted for Official
　　　Languages, *USA Today* (August 12),
　　　p. 6A.

Blau, Peter M., and Duncan, Otis Dudley
1967　*The American Occupational Structure.*
　　　New York: Wiley.

Blauner, Robert
1972　*Racial Oppression in America.* New
　　　York: Harper and Row.

Blawis, Patricia Bell
1971　*Tijerina and the Land Grants: Mexican
　　　Americans in Struggle for Their Heri-
　　　tage.* New York: International Pub-
　　　lishers.

Blea, Irene I.
1988　*Toward A Chicano Social Science.*
　　　New York: Praeger.

Bledsoe, Timothy, and Herring, Mary
1990　Victims of Circumstances: Women
　　　in Pursuit of Political Office. *Amer-
　　　ican Political Science Review* 84
　　　(March), pp. 213–224.

Blendon, Robert J., et al.
1989　Access to Medical Care for Black
　　　and White Americans. *Journal of the
　　　American Medical Association* 261
　　　(January 13), pp. 278–281.

Block, A. G.
1986　March Fong Eu: A Political Career
　　　Stalled Near the Top? *California
　　　Journal* (November), pp. 547–550.

Bloom, Leonard
1971　*The Social Psychology of Race Rela-
　　　tions.* Cambridge, MA: Schenkman.

Boal, Frederick W., and Douglas, J. Neville
H.
1982　*Integration and Division: Geographical
　　　Perspectives on the Northern Ireland
　　　Problems.* New York: Academic
　　　Press.

Boas, Franz
1966　*Introduction to Handbook of American
　　　Indian Languages.* Lincoln: Uni-
　　　versity of Nebraska Press.

Bobo, Lawrence, and Kluegel, James R.
1991　Modern American Prejudice: Ste-
　　　reotypes, Social Distance, and Per-
　　　ceptions of Discrimination Toward
　　　Blacks, Hispanics, and Asians. Pa-
　　　per presented at the annual meet-
　　　ing of the American Sociological
　　　Association, Cincinnati.

Bogardus, Emory
1925　Measuring Social Distance. *Journal
　　　of Applied Sociology* 9 (March–April),

pp. 299–308.

1928 *Immigration and Race Attitudes*. Boston: Heath.

1933 A Social Distance Scale. *Sociology and Social Research* 17 (January–February), pp. 265–271.

1959 *Social Distance*. Yellow Springs, OH: Antioch Press.

1968 Comparing Racial Distance in Ethiopia, South Africa, and the United States. *Sociology and Social Research* 52 (January), pp. 149–156.

Bohland, James R.

1982 Indian Residential Segregation in the Urban Southwest: 1970 and 1980. *Social Science Quarterly* 63 (December), pp. 749–761.

Bonacich, Edna

1972 A Theory of Ethnic Antagonism: The Split Labor Market. *American Sociological Review* 37 (October), pp. 547–559.

1976 Advanced Capitalism and Black/White Race Relations in the United States: A Split Labor Market Interpretation. *American Sociological Review* 41 (February), pp. 34–51.

1988 The Social Costs of Immigrant Entrepreneurship. *Amerasia* 14 (Spring), pp. 119–128.

1989 Inequality in America: The Failure of the American System for People of Color. *Sociological Spectrum* 9 (No. 1), pp. 77–101.

Bonacich, Edna, and Modell, John

1981 *The Economic Basis of Ethnic Solidarity*. Berkeley: University of California Press.

Bonilla, Frank, and Campos, Ricardo

1981 A Wealth of Poor: Puerto Ricans in the New Economic Order. *Daedalus* 110 (Spring), pp. 133–176.

Bonson, John

1966 Interview with New SNCC Chairman. *Militant* 30 (May 23), p. 8.

Bordua, David J.

1970 Police-Community Relations. In Philip Meranto, ed., *The Kerner Report Revisited*, pp. 59–86. Urbana: Institute of Government and Public Affairs, University of Illinois.

Boswell, Thomas D., and Curtis, James R.

1984 *The Cuban-American Experience*. To-

towa, NJ: Rowman and Allanheld.

Bourne, Richard

1974 The Cubans of Miami. *New Society* 29 (August 8), pp. 347–350.

Bouvier, Leon F., and Davis, Cary B.

1982 *The Future Racial Composition of the United States*. Washington, DC: Demographic Information Services Center of the Population Reference Bureau.

Bouvier, Leon F., and Gardner, Robert W.

1986 Immigration to the U.S.: The Unfinished Story. *Population Bulletin* 41 (November).

Bracey, John H.; Meier, August; and Rudwick, Elliott, eds.

1970 *Black Nationalism in America*. Indianapolis: Bobbs-Merrill.

Braden, Charles Samuel

1949 *These Also Believe: A Study of Modern American Cults*. New York: Macmillan.

Brazil

1981 *IX Recenseamento Geral do Brasil— 1980, 1, P+. 1*. Rio de Janeiro: Secretaria de Planejamento da Presidencia da República, Fundacão Instituto Brasilerio de Geografia e Estatistica.

Breasted, Mary

1977 3-Year Inquiry Threads Together Evidence on F.A.L.N. Terrorism. *New York Times* (April 17), pp. 1, 49.

Brewer, Marilynn B., and Kramer, Roderick M.

1985 The Psychology of Intergroup Attitudes and Behavior. In Mark R. Rosenzweig and Lyman W. Porter, eds., *Annual Review of Psychology*, pp. 219–243. Palo Alto, CA: Annual Reviews.

Bridges, George S., and Crutchfield, Robert D.

1988 Law, Social Standing and Racial Disparities in Imprisonment. *Social Forces* 66 (March), pp. 699–724.

Briggs, Kenneth A.

1976 Churches Found Still Largely Segregated. *New York Times* (November 14), p. 26.

1978 Jewish Leader Urges a Program to

Convert "Seekers" to Judaism. *New York Times* (December 3), pp. 1, 37.

1983 Among Hispanic Catholics, Another Pattern of Practice. *New York Times* (January 9), p. E10.

Briggs, Vernon M., Jr.
1975 Illegal Aliens: The Need for a More Restrictive Border Policy. *Social Science Quarterly* 56 (December), pp. 477–484.

Brigham, John C.
1973 Ethnic Stereotypes and Attitudes: A Different Mode of Analysis. *Journal of Personality* 41 (June), pp. 206–223.

Brigham, John C., and Weissbach, Theodore, eds.
1972 *Racial Attitudes in America: Analyses and Findings of Social Psychology.* New York: Harper and Row.

Broder, David A.
1986 A Hispanic for the GOP. *Washington Post National Weekly Edition* 3 (January 27), p. 4.

Broderick, Francis
1959 *W. E. B. Du Bois: Negro Leader in a Time of Crisis.* Stanford, CA: Stanford University Press.

Brooks, Andree
1987 Women in the Clergy: Struggle to Succeed. *New York Times* (February 16), p. 15.

Broom, Leonard
1965 *The Transformation of the American Negro.* New York: Harper and Row.

Brown, Christopher
1990 Discrimination and Immigration Law. *Focus* 18 (August), pp. 3–4, 8.

Brown, Dee
1964 *Showdown at Little Big Horn.* Berkeley, CA: Berkeley Medallion.
1971 *Bury My Heart at Wounded Knee.* New York: Holt, Rinehart and Winston.

Brown, H. Rap
1969 *Die Nigger Die!* New York: Dial Press.

Brozan, Nadine
1973 Jews at Christmastime—Is It Proper to Join in the Holiday? *New York Times* (December 21), p. 24

Bryce-Laporte, Roy Simon
1975 Review of "Time on the Cross."

*Contemporary Sociology* 4 (July), pp. 353–361.

Buckley, Anthony D.
1984 Walls Within Walls: Religion and Rough Behavior in an Ulster Community. *Sociology* 18 (February), pp. 19–32.

Bufalino, William E.
1971 Housing and Ethnicity. In Otto Feinstein, ed., *Ethnic Groups in the City,* pp. 277–279. Lexington, MA: Heath.

Bunzel, John H., and Au, Jeffrey, K. D.
1987 Diversity or Discrimination? Asian Americans in College. *The Public Interest* 87 (Spring), pp. 49–62.

Burbach, Roger, and Flynn, Patricia
1980 *Agribusiness in the Americas.* New York: Monthly Review Press.

Burciaga, Cecilia Preciado de; Gonzales, Viola; and Hepburn, Ruth A.
1977 The Chicana as Feminist. In Alice G. Sargent, ed., *Beyond Sex Roles,* pp. 266–273. St. Paul: West.

Bureau of the Census
1958 Religion Reported by the Civilian Population of the United States, 1957. Current Population Reports Series P–20, No. 79. Washington, DC: U.S. Government Printing Office.
1960 *Historical Statistics of the United States, Colonial Times to 1957.* Washington, DC: U.S. Government Printing Office.
1975 The Social and Economic Status of the Black Population in the United States, 1974. Current Population Reports Series P–23, No. 54. Washington, DC: U.S. Government Printing Office.
1976 *A Statistical Portrait of Women in the United States.* Current Population Reports Series P–23, No. 60. Washington, DC: U.S. Government Printing Office.
1980a *Statistical Abstract, 1980.* Washington, DC: U.S. Government Printing Office.
1980b Statistical Portrait of Women in the United States, 1978. Current Population Reports, Series P–23, No. 100. Washington, DC: U.S. Govern-

ment Printing Office.

1982a Ancestry and Language in the United States: November 1979. Current Population Reports Series P–23, No. 116. Washington, DC: U.S. Government Printing Office.

1982b *Statistical Abstract, 1982.* Washington, DC: U.S. Government Printing Office.

1983 General Social and Economic Characteristics. Series PC80–1–C1. Washington, DC: U.S. Government Printing Office.

1985a The Hispanic Population in the United States: March 1985. Current Population Reports Series P–20, No. 422. Washington, DC: U.S. Government Printing Office.

1985b Estimates of the Population of Puerto Rico Municipio and Metropolitan Areas. Current Population Reports Series P–26, No. 84–51–C. Washington, DC: U.S. Government Printing Office.

1986a Fertility of American Women: June 1985. Series P–20, No. 406. Washington, DC: U.S. Government Printing Office.

1986b Projections of the Hispanic Population of the United States: 1983 to 2080. Series P–25, No. 995. Washington, DC: U.S. Government Printing Office.

1986c *Statistical Abstract, 1987.* Washington, DC: U.S. Government Printing Office.

1987 Populations of U.S. Pacific and Caribbean Islands Have Grown Rapidly Since 1980, Census Bureau Reports. News release. Washington, DC: U.S. Government Printing Office.

1988a Money Income and Poverty Status in the United States: 1987. Advanced Data Reports Series P–60, No. 161. Washington, DC: U.S. Government Printing Office.

1988b *Statistical Abstract, 1989.* Washington, DC: U.S. Government Printing Office.

1989a Money Income of Households, Families, and Persons in the United States, 1987. Current Population Reports Series P–20, No. 162.

Washington, DC: U.S. Government Printing Office.

1989b Voting and Registration in the Election of November 1988 (Advance Report). Current Population Reports Series P–20, No. 435. Washington, DC: U.S. Government Printing Office.

1990 *Child Support and Alimony, 1987,* Series P–23, No. 167. Washington, DC: U.S. Government Printing Office.

1991a *Statistical Abstract of the United States, 1991.* Washington, DC: U.S. Government Printing Office.

1991b *1990 Census Counts on Specific Racial Groups.* News Release June 12. Washington, DC: United States Department of Commerce.

1991c *Money Income of Households, Families, and Persons in the United States: 1990. Current Population Reports,* Series P–20. Washington, DC: U.S. Government Printing Office.

1991d Poverty in the United States: 1990. Current Population Reports, Series P–60, No. 175. Washington, DC: U.S. Government Printing Office.

1991e *Census Bureau 1990 Census Counts on Hispanic Population Groups.* News Release. Washington, DC: U.S. Government Printing Office.

1991f The Hispanic Population in the United States: March 1990. Current Population Reports, Series P–20, No. 449. Washington, DC: U.S. Government Printing Office.

1991g The Black Population in the United States: March 1990 and 1989. Current Population Reports, Series P–20, No. 448. Washington, DC: U.S. Government Printing Office.

1991h Child Support and Alimony, 1987. Current Population Reports, Series P. 29, No. 167. Washington, DC: U.S. Government Printing Office.

1991i *Hawaii First State to Receive Additional 1990 Census Population and Housing Information.* Washington, DC: U.S. Government Printing Office.

Bureau of Indian Affairs

1970 *Answers to Your Questions About Indians.* Washington, DC: U.S. Gov-

*dians*. Washington, DC: U.S. Government Printing Office.

1973   *Estimates of Resident Indian Population and Labor Force Status, by State and Reservation*. Washington, DC: U.S. Government Printing Office.

1974   *American Indians: Answers to 101 Questions*. Washington, DC: U.S. Government Printing Office.

1975   *Menominee Indian Tribes of Wisconsin: Inventory of Resources and Annotated Bibliography*. Washington, DC: U.S. Government Printing Office.

1976   *Statistical Data for Planning, Menominee Reservation*. Washington, DC: U.S. Government Printing Office.

1981   *BIA Profile: The Bureau of Indian Affairs and American Indians*. Washington, DC: U.S. Government Printing Office.

1986   *American Indians Today: Answers to Your Questions*. Washington, DC: U.S. Government Printing Office.

1988   *Report of BIA Education: Excellence in Indian Education Through the Effective School Process*. Washington, DC: U.S. Government Printing Office.

Bureau of Labor Statistics

1986   *Employment and Earnings Characteristics of Families: Third Quarter, 1986*. Washington, DC: U.S. Government Printing Office.

1988   *Employment in Perspective: Minority Workers: Fourth Quarter, 1988*. Washington, DC: U.S. Government Printing Office.

1991   *Employment in Perspective: Minority Workers, Fourth Quarter, 1991*. Washington, DC: U.S. Government Printing Office.

Burkholz, Herbert

1980   The Latinization of Miami. *New York Times Magazine* (September 21), pp. 44–47, 84, 86, 88, 98, 100.

Burma, John H.

1953   Current Leadership Problems Among Japanese-Americans. *Sociology and Social Research* 37 (January–February), pp. 157–163.

1970   *Mexican Americans in the United States*. Cambridge, MA: Schenkman.

Burnette, Robert, and Koster, John

1974   *The Road to Wounded Knee*. New York: Bantam.

Burns, John F.

1978   How Rules of "Petty Apartheid" Are Whittled Away. *New York Times* (June 4), pp. 1–14.

Bursma, Bruce, and Houston, Jack

1985   Leader Dissolves Black Muslim Sect. *Chicago Tribune* (May 3), Sect. 1, p. 7.

*Business Week*

1971   How the Immigrants Made It in Miami. (May 1), pp. 88–89.

1983   Why Puerto Rico's Economy Is Still Adrift. (October 3), pp. 139–140.

Bustamante, Jorge A.

1972   The "Wetback" as Deviant: An Application of Labeling Theory. *American Journal of Sociology* 77 (January), pp. 706–718.

Butler, Jeffrey E.

1974   Social Status, Ethnic Divisions and Political Conflict in New Nations: Afrikaners and Englishmen in South Africa. In Wendell Bell and Walter E. Freeman, eds., *Ethnicity and Nation-Building: Comparative, International and Historical Perspectives*, pp. 147–169. Beverly Hills, CA: Sage Publications.

Butt, Ronald

1968   The Politics of Race. *London Times* (February 18), p. 12.

Butterfield, Fox

1985   Chinese Organized Crime Said to Rise in U.S. *New York Times* (January 13), pp. 1, 10.

1986   Bostonians Debating Drive to Carve Out a Black City. *New York Times* (October 12), p. 26.

Cabrera, Denise

1989   Women on TV: More Than Just a Pretty Sight. *New York Post* (December 15), p. 113.

Cain, Bruce E., and Kiewiet, D. Roderick

1985   Latinos and the 1984 Election: A Comparative Perspective. Unpublished paper.

Caine, T. Allen

1972   Comparative Life-Styles of Anglos and Mexican-Americans. In Arnold M. Rose and Caroline B. Rose, eds.,

*Minority Problems,* 2nd ed., pp. 290–306. New York: Harper and Row.

Callanan, Tuss
1987    Coyote: A Town Without Pity. *Chicago Tribune* (April 12), Sect. 10, pp. 8–11, 13–20, 27.

Campbell, Angus
1971    *White Attitudes Toward Black People.* Ann Arbor, MI: Institute for Social Research; and Washington, DC: U.S. Government Printing Office.

Campbell, Angus, and Schuman, Howard
1968    *Racial Attitudes in Fifteen American Cities.* Institute for Social Research.

Campbell, Anne
1987    Self Definition by Rejection: The Case of Gang Girls. *Social Problems* 34 (December): 451–466.

Campbell, Gregory R.
1989    The Changing Dimension of Native American Health: A Critical Understanding of Contemporary Native American Health Issues. *American Indian Culture and Research Journal* 13 (Nos. 3–4), pp. 1–20.

Caplan, Nathan
1985    Working Toward Self-Sufficiency. *ISR Newsletter* (Spring/Summer), pp. 4, 5, 7.

Carey, Joseph
1984    Women of the Cloth: How They're Faring. *U.S. News and World Report* 97 (December 3), pp. 76–77.

Carlson, James M., and Iovini, Joseph
1985    The Transmission of Racial Attitudes from Fathers to Sons: A Study of Blacks and Whites. *Adolescence* 20 (Spring), pp. 233–237.

Carmichael, Stokely, and Hamilton, Charles V.
1967    *Black Power: The Politics of Liberation in America.* New York: Random House.

Carnegie Foundation for the Advancement of Teaching
1990    Native Americans and Higher Education: New Mood of Optimism. *Change* (January/February), pp. 27–30.

Carr, Robert K.; Bernstein, Marvin H.; Murphy, Walter F.; and Danielson, Michael N.
1971    *American Democracy,* 6th ed. New York: Holt, Rinehart and Winston.

Carrington, Walter C.
1991    Were Sanctions Lifted Too Soon? *Focus* 19 (August/September), pp. 6–8.

Carrion, Juan Manuel
1986    Changes in the Class Structure of Puerto Rico: 1940–1980. Paper presented at the annual meeting of the American Sociological Association, New York City.

Carroll, Raymond
1975    An "Infamous Act" at the U.N. *Newsweek* 8 (November 24), pp. 51–54.

Carson, Clayborne, et al.
1991    *The Eyes on the Prize Civil Rights Reader.* New York: Penguin Books.

Carter, Deborah J., and Wilson, Reginald
1991    *Minorities in Higher Education.* Washington, DC: American Council on Education.

Carter, Fred M., Jr., and Schaefer, Richard T.
1976a    Race in the College Classroom: An Exploratory Study. *Integrated Education* 14 (September–October), pp. 41–42.

1976b    Racial Consciousness in the College Classroom. *Integrated Education* 14 (May–June), pp. 41–44.

Carter, Hodding, III
1959    *The South Strikes Back.* Garden City, NY: Doubleday.

Carter, Stephen
1991    *Reflections of an Affirmative Action Baby.* New York: Basic Books.

Casavantes, Edward
1970    Pride and Prejudice: A Mexican American Dilemma. *Civil Rights Digest* 3 (Winter), pp. 22–27.

Case, Charles E.; Greeley, Andrew M.; and Fuchs, Stephen
1989    Social Determinants of Racial Prejudice. *Sociological Perspectives* 32 (Winter), pp. 469–483.

Caudill, William
1952    Japanese-American Personality and Acculturation. *Genetic Psychology Monograph* 45 (February): 3–102.

Caudill, William, and De Vos, George
1956    Achievement, Culture, and Personality: The Case of Japanese Amer-

icans. *American Anthropologist* 58 (December), pp. 1102–1126.

Center for the American Woman in Politics.
1992 *Women in Elective Office, 1992.* New Brunswick, NJ: Center for the American Woman in Politics.

Chalfant, H. Paul; Beckley, Robert E.; and Palmer, C. Eddie
1987 *Religion and Contemporary Society,* 2nd ed. Palo Alto, CA: Mayfield.

Chan, Mei-Mei
1986 For Chinese in USA, All is Not Happy. *USA Today* (February 7), p. A1.

Chávez, César E.
1973 The Mexican-American and the Church. In O. I. Ramano, ed., *Readings from El Grito,* pp. 215–228. Berkeley, CA: Quinto Sol Publications.

Chavez, Leo R.
1992 *Shadowed Lives: Undocumented Immigrants in American Society.* Fort Worth, TX: Harcourt Brace Javonovich.

Chavez, Linda
1989 Tequila Sunrise. *Policy Review* 48 (Spring), pp. 64–67.

Chayat, Sherry
1987 JAP-Baiting on the College Scene. *Lilith* (Fall), pp. 6–7.

Chaze, William L.
1982a Once Again, Puerto Rico Is a Problem Child. *U.S. News and World Report* (July 19), pp. 61–62.
1982b Migrant Farm Workers Still Face a Harsh Life. *U.S. News and World Report* (August 9), pp. 36–37.

Chen, Pei-ngor
1970 The Chinese Community in Los Angeles. *Social Casework* 51 (December), pp. 591–598.

Cheng, Ch'eng-k'un
1951 Assimilation in Hawaii and the Bid for Statehood. *Social Forces* 30 (1951), pp. 16–29.

Cheng, Nien
1987 *Life and Death in Shanghai.* New York: Grove Press.

Cherry, Robert
1989 *Discrimination.* Lexington, MA: Lexington Books.

Chin, Frank
1974 "Kung Fu" Is Unfair to Chinese. *New York Times* (March 24), p. D19.

Chin, Rocky
1971 New York Chinatown Today: Community in Crisis. In Amy Tachiki, Eddie Wong, Franklin Odo, and Buck Wong, eds., *Roots: An Asian American Reader,* pp. 282–295. Los Angeles: Asian American Studies Center, UCLA.

Ching, Frank
1973 Expansion of Asian-American Studies on U.S. Campuses Reflects Growth of Ethnic Consciousness. *New York Times* (July 26), p. 18.

Chow, Ester Ngan-ling
1976 Sex-Role Images of Children's Picture Books: China, France, and the United States. Paper presented at the annual meeting of the American Sociological Association, New York.

Christensen, Harold T., and Cannon, Kenneth L.
1978 The Fundamentalist Emphasis at Brigham Young University: 1935–1973. *Journal for the Scientific Study of Religion* 17 (March), pp. 53–57.

Christopulos, Diana
1974 Puerto Rico in the Twentieth Century: A Historical Survey. In Adalberto Lopez and James Petras, eds., *Puerto Rico and Puerto Ricans: Studies in History and Society,* pp. 123–163. New York: Wiley.

Chuman, Frank F.
1976 *The Bamboo People: The Law and Japanese-Americans.* Del Mar, CA: Publishers, Inc.

Cicone, Michael V., and Ruble, Diane N.
1978 Beliefs about Males. *Journal of Social Issues* 34 (Winter), pp. 5–16.

Cinel, Dean
1969 Ethnicity: A Neglected Dimension of American History. *International Migration Review* 3 (Summer), pp. 58–63.

Clark, Juan M.
1970 Selected Types of Cuban Exiles Used as a Sample of the Cuban Population. Paper presented at the meeting of the Rural Sociological

Society, Washington, DC.

Clark, Kenneth B., and Clark, Mamie P.
1947    Racial Identification and Prefer-
        ences in Negro Children. In Theo-
        dore M. Newcomb and Eugene L.
        Hartley, eds., *Readings in Social Psy-
        chology*, pp. 169–178. New York:
        Holt, Rinehart and Winston.

Clark, M. L.
1985    Social Stereotypes and Self-Concept
        in Black and White College Stu-
        dents. *Journal of Social Psychology*
        125 (December), pp. 753–760.

Clark, W. A. V.
1987    School Desegregation and White
        Flight: A Reexamination and Case
        Study. *Social Science Research* 16
        (September), pp. 211–228.

Clarke, John Henrik, ed.
1969    *Malcolm X: The Man and His Times.*
        New York: Collier.

Cleaver, Kathleen
1982    How TV Wrecked the Black Pan-
        thers. *Channels* (November–
        December), pp. 98–99.

Clem, Ralph S.
1980    The Ethnic Dimension of the Soviet
        Union. In Jerry G. Parkhurst and
        Michael P. Sacks, *Contemporary So-
        viet Society*, pp. 11–62. New York:
        Praeger.

Clymer, Adam
1986    Poll in South Africa Shows a Rise
        in Whites' Distaste for Apartheid.
        *New York Times* (August 3), pp. 1,
        12.

Coddington, Ron
1991    Native American Health Crisis.
        *USA Today* (November 12), p. 1A.

Cohen, Steven M.
1988    *American Assimilation or Jewish Re-
        vival?* Bloomington: Indiana Uni-
        versity Press.

Cohn, Bob
1991    The Q-Word Charade. *Newsweek*
        117 (June 3), pp. 16–18.

Colasanto, Diane
1989    Public Wants Civil Rights Widened
        for Some Groups, Not for Others.
        *Gallup Poll Monthly* 291 (December),
        pp. 13–22.

Coleman, James S.; Campbell, Ernest Q.;

Hobson, Carol J.; McPartland, James; Mood,
Alexander M.; Weinfold, Frederic D.; and
Link, Robert L.
1966a   *Equality of Educational Opportunity.*
        Washington, DC: U.S. Office of
        Education.
1966b   *Equality of Educational Opportunity:
        A Summary.* Washington, DC: U.S.
        Office of Education
1966c   *Supplemental Appendix to the Survey.*
        Washington, DC: U.S. Office of
        Education

Coleman, Milton
1984    18 Words, Seven Weeks Later.
        *Washington Post* (April 8), Sec. C, p.
        8.

Coles, Robert, and Erikson, Jon
1971    *The Middle Americans: Proud and
        Uncertain.* Boston: Little, Brown.

Commission on Civil Rights, United States
1963    *Freedom to the Free.* Washington,
        DC: U.S. Government Printing
        Office.
1970    The Relation of Literacy Tests to
        Voting in the North and West. *Civil
        Rights Digest* 3 (Winter), pp. 1–7.
1971a   The Puerto Ricans. *Civil Rights Di-
        gest* 4 (December), pp. 17–21.
1971b   *The Unfinished Education: Outcomes
        for Minorities in the Five South-
        western States.* Washington, DC:
        U.S. Government Printing Office.
1972    *The Excluded Student: Educational
        Practices Affecting Mexican Amer-
        icans in the Southwest.* Washington,
        DC: U.S. Government Printing
        Office.
1973    *Teachers and Students.* Washington,
        DC: U.S. Government Printing
        Office.
1974a   *Counting the Forgotten: The 1970
        Census Count of Persons of Spanish
        Speaking Background in the United
        States.* Washington, DC: U.S. Gov-
        ernment Printing Office.
1974b   *Toward Quality Education for Mex-
        ican Americans.* Washington, DC:
        U.S. Government Printing Office.
1974c   *Twenty Years After Brown: The Shad-
        ows of the Past.* Washington, DC:
        U.S. Government Printing Office.
1975    *Twenty Years After Brown: Equality
        of Economic Opportunity.* Wash-
        ington, DC: U.S. Government Print-

ing Office.

1976a  *Fulfilling the Letter and Spirit of the Law: Desegregation of the Nation's Public Schools.* Washington, DC: U.S. Government Printing Office.

1976b  *A Guide to Federal Laws and Regulations Prohibiting Sex Discrimination.* Washington, DC: U.S. Government Printing Office.

1976c  *Puerto Ricans in the Continental United States: An Uncertain Future.* Washington, DC: U.S. Government Printing Office.

1976d  *Using the Voting Rights Act.* Washington, DC: U.S. Government Printing Office.

1977a  *Statement on Metropolitan School Desegregation.* Washington, DC: U.S. Government Printing Office.

1977b  *Window Dressing on the Set: Women and Minorities in Television.* Washington, DC: U.S. Government Printing Office.

1979  *Window Dressing on the Set: An Update.* Washington, DC: U.S. Government Printing Office.

1980a  *Asian Americans: An Agenda for Action.* Washington, DC: U.S. Government Printing Office.

1980b  *Breach of Trust? Native Hawaiian Homelands.* Washington, DC: U.S. Government Printing Office

1980c  *Success of Asian Americans: Fact or Fiction?* Washington, DC: U.S. Government Printing Office.

1980d  *Characters in Textbooks: A Review of the Literature.* Washington, DC: U.S. Government Printing Office.

1981  *Affirmative Action in the 1980s: Dismantling the Process of Discrimination.* Washington, DC: U.S. Government Printing Office.

1986  *Recent Activity Against Citizens and Residents of Asian Descent.* Washington, DC: U.S. Government Printing Office.

1988  *The Economic Status of Americans of Asian Descent: An Exploratory Investigation.* Washington, DC: U.S. Government Printing Office.

1992  *Civil Rights Issues Facing Asian Americans in the 1990s.* Washington, DC: U.S. Government Printing Office.

Commission on Racial Equality

1987  *Living in Terror.* London: Commission on Racial Equality.

Commission on Wartime Relocation and Internment of Civilians

1982a  *Report.* Washington, DC: U.S. Government Printing Office.

1982b  *Recommendations.* Washington, DC: U.S. Government Printing Office.

Commonwealth of Puerto Rico

1976  *Socioeconomic Statistics of Puerto Rico, 1940 to 1975.* San Juan: Puerto Rico Planning Board.

Condon, Jane

1985  *A Half-Step Behind, Japanese Women of the '80s.* New York: Dodd, Mead.

Conforti, Joseph M.

1974  WASP in the Woodpile: Inequalities and Injustices of Ethnic Ecology. Paper presented at the annual meeting of the American Sociological Association, Montreal.

*Congressional Quarterly*

1984  Democratic Party Rules, Mondale Delegate Lead. 42 (June 23), pp. 1504–1505.

Conot, Robert

1967  *Rivers of Blood, Years of Darkness.* New York: Bantam.

Conover, Ted

1986  *Coyotes.* New York: Vintage.

Conrat, Masie, and Conrat, Richard

1972  *Executive Order 9066.* Los Angeles: California Historical Society.

Conroy, John

1981  Ulster's Lost Generation. *New York Times Magazine* (August 2), pp. 16–21, 70–72, 74–75.

Conver, Bill

1976  Group Chairman Lists Problems Endangering Jewish Family. *Peoria [IL] Journal Star* (December 4), p. A2.

Conyers, James E., and Wallace, Walter L.

1976  *Black Elected Officials: A Study of Black Americans Holding Governmental Office.* New York: Russell Sage Foundation.

Cornell, Stephen

1984  Crisis and Response in Indian-White Relations: 1960–1984. *Social Problems* 32 (October), pp. 44–59.

1987    American Indians, American Dreams, and the Meaning of Success. Paper presented at the Annual Meeting of the Eastern Sociological Society, Boston.

1991    Politics, Culture, and American Indian Economic Development. Paper presented at the annual meeting of the American Sociological Association, Cincinnati.

Cornell, Stephen, and Kalt, Joseph P.
1990    Pathways from Poverty: Economic Development and Institution-Building on American Indian Reservations. *American Indian Culture and Research Journal* 14 (No. 1), pp. 89–125.

Cortés, Carlos E.
1980    Mexicans. In Stephen Thornstrom, ed., *Harvard Encyclopedia of American Ethnic Groups*, pp. 697–719. Cambridge, MA: Harvard University Press.

Cortese, Charles F.; Falk, R. Frank; and Cohen, Jack K.
1976a    Further Considerations on the Methodological Analysis of Segregation Indices. *American Sociological Review* 41 (August), pp. 630–637.

1976b    Reply to Taeuber and Taeuber. *American Sociological Review* 41 (October), pp. 889–893.

Corzine, Jay, and Dabrowski, Irene
1975    The Ethnic Factor and Neighborhood Stability in St. Louis: The Czechs in Soulard and South St. Louis. Paper presented at the annual meeting of the Midwest Sociological Society, Chicago.

Cose, Ellis
1989    Yellow-Peril Journalism. *Time* 139 (November 27), p. 79.

Coser, Lewis A.
1956    *The Functions of Social Conflict.* New York: Free Press.

Coser, Lewis, and Coser, Rose Laub
1974    *Greedy Institutions.* New York: Free Press.

Cosford, Bill
1981    Charlie Chan Wit: Some High Proof. *The Miami Herald* (March 1), pt. L, pp. 1–2.

COSSA
1988    Clearinghouse Provides Information on Language Pluralism Issue. *COSSA Washington Update* 7 (May 27), pp. 2–3.

Couch, Arthur, and Keniston, Kenneth
1960    Yeasayers and Naysayers: Agreeing Response Set as a Personality Variable. *Journal of Abnormal and Social Psychology* 60 (March), pp. 151–175.

Council of Energy Resource Tribes
1986    Corporate Capability Statement. Denver: Council of Energy Resource Tribes.

1991    *15 Years.* Denver: Council of Energy Resource Tribes.

Council on Scientific Affairs
1991    Hispanic Health in the United States. *Journal of the American Medical Association* 265 (January 9), pp. 248–252.

Courtney, Alice W., and Whipple, Thomas W.
1983    *Sex Stereotyping in Advertising.* Lexington, MA: Lexington Books.

Covin, David
1990    Afrocentricity in *O Movimento Negro Unificado. Journal of Black Studies* 21 (December), pp. 126–144.

Cowgill, Donald O.
1968    Social Distance in Thailand. *Sociology and Social Research* 52 (July), pp. 363–376.

Cowley, Geoffrey
1989    The Plunder of the Past. *Newsweek* 113 (June 26), pp. 58–60.

Cowley, Susan Cheever, and Lisle, Laurie
1976    Jewish Feminists. *Newsweek* (May 31), pp. 67–69.

Cox, Oliver C.
1942    The Modern Caste School of Race Relations. *Social Forces* 21 (December), pp. 218–226.

1948    *Caste, Class, and Race: A Study in Social Dynamics.* New York: Modern Reader Paperbacks.

Crain, Robert L., and Mahard, Rita E.
1983    The Effect of Research Methodology on Desegregation-Achievement Studies: A Meta-Analysis. *American Journal of Sociology* 88 (March), pp. 839–854.

Crispino, James A.
  1980   *The Assimilation of Ethnic Groups:
          The Italian Case.* Staten Island, NY:
          Center for Migration Studies.
Cross, William E., Jr.
  1973   The Negro-to-Black Conversion Ex-
          perience. In Joyce A. Ladner, ed.,
          *The Death of White Sociology*, pp.
          267–286. New York: Random
          House.
  1991   *Shades of Black: Diversity in African-
          American Identity.* Philadelphia:
          Temple University Press.
Crossette, Barbara
  1992   U.S. Starts Return of Haiti Refugees
          after Justices Act. *New York Times*
          (February 2), pp. 1, 10.
Crull, Sue R., and Bruton, Brent T.
  1985   Possible Decline in Tolerance To-
          ward Minorities: Social Distance on
          a Midwest Campus. *Sociology and
          Social Research* 70 (October), pp. 57–
          62.
Cuellar, Alfredo
  1970   Perspective on Politics. In Joan W.
          Moore and Alfredo Cuellar, eds.,
          *Mexican Americans*, pp. 137–158.
          Englewood Cliffs, NJ: Prentice-Hall.
Cummings, Judith
  1973   Ethnic Fetes Tete-a-Tete. *New York
          Times* (September 17), p. 18.
  1983   Breakup of Black Family Imperils
          Gains of Decades. *New York Times*
          (November 20), pp. 1, 36.
Cunningham, Ineke, and Molina, Anibal
  1976   Puerto Rican Americans: A Study
          in Diversity. In Anthony Gary
          Dworkin and Rosalind J. Dworkin,
          *The Minority Report: An Introduction
          to Racial, Ethnic, and Gender Rela-
          tions*, pp. 190–220. New York: Prae-
          ger.
Curran, Thomas J.
  1966   Assimilation and Nativism. *Interna-
          tional Migration Digest* 3 (Spring),
          pp. 15–25.
Curry, George E.
  1986   Society Might Not Duck Fallout of
          the Black Family. *Chicago Tribune*
          (August 3), Sect. 6, pp. 8–9.
Daniel, William W.
  1968   *Racial Discrimination in England:
          Based on the PEP Report.* Ham-

mondsworth, G.B.: Penguin.
Daniels, Roger
  1967   *The Politics of Prejudice: The Anti-
          Japanese Movement in California and
          the Struggle for Japanese Exclusion.*
          New York: Atheneum.
  1972   *Concentration Camps, USA: Japanese
          Americans and World War II.* New
          York: Holt, Rinehart and Winston.
  1975   *The Decision to Relocate the Japanese
          Americans.* Philadelphia: Lippincott.
  1988   *Asian America: Chinese and Japanese
          in the United States since 1850.* Seat-
          tle: University of Washington Press.
  1990a  *Coming to America.* New York: Har-
          perCollins.
  1990b  *A History of Immigration and Ethnic-
          ity in American Life.* New York: Har-
          per Perennial.
Danzger, M. Herbert
  1989   *Returning to Tradition.* New Haven:
          Yale University Press.
Darrity, William, and Myers, Samuel
  1987   *Transfer Programs and the Economic
          Well-Being of Minorities.* Madison,
          WI: Institute for Research on Pov-
          erty.
Darwin, Charles
  1859   *Origin of Species.* Beckenham, Kent.
          Rpt. Cambridge, MA: Harvard Uni-
          versity Press, 1964.
  1874   *The Descent of Man, and Selection in
          Relation to Sex.* New York: A. L.
          Fowle.
Dashefsky, Arnold, and Shapiro, Howard M.
  1974   *Ethnic Identification among American
          Jews.* Lexington, MA: Heath.
Davis, Allison; Gardner, Burleigh B.; and
Gardner, Mary R.
  1965   *Deep South: A Social Anthropological
          Study of Caste and Class,* abr. ed.
          Chicago: University of Chicago
          Press.
Davis, Angela
  1981   *Women, Race, and Class.* New York:
          Random House.
Davis, Cary; Haub, Carl; and Willette, Jo
Anne
  1983   U.S. Hispanics: Changing the Face
          of America. *Population Bulletin* 38
          (June).
Davis, David Brion
  1966   *The Problem of Slavery in Western*

*Culture.* Ithaca, NY: Cornell University Press.

Davis, E.
1977    The Undermining of Unity and the Chain of Command. In E. Davis, ed., *Anthology on Institutional Discrimination,* pp. 66–70. Patrick A.F.B.: Defense Race Relations Institute.

Dawidowicz, Lucy S.
1967    *The Golden Tradition: Jewish Life and Thought in Eastern Europe.* New York: Holt, Rinehart and Winston.
1975    *The War Against the Jews, 1933–1945.* New York: Holt, Rinehart and Winston.

Day, Robert C.
1972    The Emergence of Activism as a Social Movement. In Howard M. Bahr, Bruce A. Chadwick, and Robert C. Day, eds., *Native Americans Today: Sociological Perspectives,* pp. 506–532. New York: Harper and Row.

De Fleur, Melvin; D'Antonio, William; and De Fleur, Lois
1976    *Sociology: Human Society,* 2nd ed. Glenview, IL: Scott, Foresman.

DeFleur, Melvin L., and Westie, Franklin R.
1958    Verbal Attitudes and Overt Acts. *American Sociological Review* 23 (December), pp. 667–673.

Degler, Carl N.
1969    The Negro in America—Where Myrdal Went Wrong. *New York Times Magazine* (December 7), p. 64.
1971    *Neither Black nor White: Slavery and Race Relations in Brazil and the United States.* New York: Macmillan.
1976    Prejudice and Slavery. *New York Review of Books* (January 22), p. 53.

de la Garza, Rodolfo O.
1984    "And then there were some. . . . " Chicanos as National Political Actors, 1967–1980. *Aztlan* 15 (September), p. 309.

de la Garza, Rodolfo O.; Bean, Frank D.; Bonjean, Charles M.; Romo, Ricardo; and Alvarez, Rodolfo
1985    *The Mexican American Experience: An Interdisciplinary Anthology.* Austin: University of Texas Press.

Deloria, Vine, Jr.
1969    *Custer Died for Your Sins: An Indian Manifesto.* New York: Avon.
1970    *We Talk, You Listen.* New York: Dell.
1971    *Of Utmost Good Faith.* New York: Bantam.
1973    *God Is Red.* New York: Grossett and Dunlap.
1974    *Behind the Trail of Broken Treaties: An Indian Declaration of Independence.* New York: Delta Book.

Deloria, Vine, Jr., and Lytle, Clifford M.
1983    *American Indians, American Justice.* Austin: University of Texas Press.

Denton, John
1985    The Underground Economy and Social Stratification. *Sociological Spectrum* 5 (Nos. 1–2), pp. 31–42.

DePalma, Anthony
1991    Separate Ethnic Worlds Grow on Campus. *New York Times* (May 18), pp. 1, 7.

DeParle, Jason
1991a   New Rows to Hoe in the 'Harvest of Shame.' *New York Times* (July 28), p. E3.
1991b   What to Call the Poorest Poor? *New York Times* (August 26), p. E4.

Department of Education
1988    *Trends in Minority Enrollment in Higher Education, Fall 1976–Fall 1986.* Washington, DC: U.S. Government Printing Office.

Department of Health, Education, and Welfare
1974    *A Study of Selected Socio-Economic Characteristics of Ethnic Minorities Based on the 1970 Census. Volume 2: Asian Americans.* Washington, DC: U.S. Government Printing Office.

Department of Health and Human Services
1987    Unpublished data for *Quarterly Public Assistance Statistics.*

Department of Justice
1980    *Prevention and Control of Urban Disorders: Issues for the 1980s.* Washington, DC: U.S. Government Printing Office.

Department of Labor
1965    *The Negro Family: The Case for National Action.* Washington, DC: U.S. Government Printing Office.

1980 *Perspectives on Working Women: A Databook.* Washington, DC: U.S. Government Printing Office.

1991 *Employment in Perspective: Women in the Labor Force, Fourth Quarter 1991.* Washington, DC: U.S. Government Printing Office.

De Pillis, Mario S.
1978 Mormons Get Revelations Often, But Not Like This. *New York Times* (June 11), p. E10.

DeQuinne, Jeanne
1986 Hispanic Miami May Mirror Future. *USA Today* (November 26), p. 9A.

Derbyshire, Robert, and Brody, Eugene
1964 Social Distance and Identity Conflict in Negro College Students. *Sociology and Social Research* 48 (April), pp. 301–314.

De Stefano, Linda, and Colasanto, Diane
1990 Unlike 1975, Today Most Americans Think Men Have It Better. *Gallup Poll Monthly* 293 (February), pp. 25–36.

Deutscher, Irwin
1973 *What We Say/What We Do: Sentiments and Acts.* Glenview, IL: Scott, Foresman.

de Varona, Donna
1984 Women's Fight for Sports Equality Beings Again. *New York Times* (March 18), p. 25.

DeYoung, Karen
1988 The Struggle of Being Black in Britain. *Washington Post National Weekly Edition* 5 (July 18), pp. 17–18.

Diehl, Jackson
1992 A Common Ground of Uncertainty for Israel. *Washington Post National Weekly Edition* (January 5), pp. 18–19.

Dinnerstein, Leonard
1988 Antisemitism in the United States Today. *Patterns of Prejudice* 22 (Autumn), pp. 3–14.

Dinnerstein, Leonard; Nichols, Roger; and Reimers, David M.
1990 *Natives and Strangers,* 2nd ed. New York: Oxford University Press.

Dinnerstein, Leonard, and Reimers, David M.

1975 *Ethnic Americans: A History of Immigration and Assimilation.* New York: Harper and Row.

Dionne, E. J., Jr.
1988 Jackson Share of Votes by Whites Triples in '88. *New York Times* (June 13), p. B7.

Doherty, Carroll J.
1992 Question of Ability to Repay Loans Shadows Israel's Guarantee Request. *Congressional Quarterly Weekly Report* (January 18), pp. 120–121.

Dohrmann, Rita
1975 Male and Female Role Models on Children's Television Programming. Paper presented at the annual meeting of the Midwest Sociological Society, Chicago.

Doi, Ayako
1985 It's Getting Uncomfortable Again to Be a Japanese in America. *The Washington Post National Weekly Edition* 2 (July 29), 23–24.

Domestic Council Committee on Illegal Aliens
1976 *Preliminary Report of the Domestic Council.* Washington, DC: Immigration and Naturalization Service, Department of Justice.

Donahue, Thomas S.
1985 U.S. English: Its Life and Works. *International Journal of the Sociology of Language* 56, pp. 99–112.

Doran, Terry, ed.
1988 *A Road Well Traveled: Three Generations of Cuban American Women.* Fort Wayne, IN: Latin American Educational Center.

Dorris, Michael A.
1981 The Grass Still Grows, the Rivers Still Flow: Contemporary Native Americans. *Daedalus* 110 (Spring), pp. 43–69.

1988 For the Indians, No Thanksgiving. *New York Times* (November 24), p. A23.

Dorsey, Valerie Lynn
1991 Native Americans Say Teams Turn People into Mascots. *USA Today* (October 23), p. 6C.

Draeger, Harlan
1975 "Quiet Indian" Turns-in Rage at

Abbey. *Chicago Daily News* (January 13), pp. 1, 16.

Driedger, Leo, and Clifton, Rodney A.
1984    Ethnic Stereotypes: Images of Ethnocentrism, Reciprocity or Dissimilarity? *Canadian Review of Sociology and Anthropology* 21 (August), pp. 288–301.

Du Bois, W. E. B.
1903    The Talented Tenth. In Booker T. Washington et al., *The Negro Problem: A Series of Articles by Representative American Negroes of Today*, pp. 31–76. New York: James Pott.
1939    *Black Folk: Then and Now.* New York: Holt, Rinehart and Winston.
1952    *Battle for Peace: The Story of My 83rd Birthday.* New York: Masses and Mainstream.
1961    *The Souls of Black Folk.* New York: Fawcett.
1967    *The Philadelphia Negro: A Social Study.* New York: Schocken.
1968    *Dusk of Dawn.* New York: Schocken.
1969a   *The Suppression of the African Slave-Trade to the United States of America, 1638–1870.* New York: Schocken.
1969b   *An ABC of Color.* New York: International Publications.
1970    *The Negro American Family.* Cambridge, MA: MIT Press.

Duff, John B.
1971    *The Irish in the United States.* Belmont, CA: Wadsworth.

Dullea, Georgia
1975    Women in Classrooms, Not the Principal's Office. *New York Times* (July 13), p. E7.

Duncan, Beverly, and Duncan, Otis Dudley
1968    Minorities and the Process of Stratification. *American Sociological Review* 33 (June), pp. 356–364.

Duncan, Greg J.
1984    *Years of Poverty, Years of Plenty.* Ann Arbor, MI: Institute for Social Research.

Duncan, Otis Dudley; Featherman, David; and Duncan, Beverly
1972    *Socioeconomic Background and Achievement.* New York: Seminar Press.

Dunn, Marvin, and Porter, Bruce
1981    Miami, 1980: A Different Kind of Riot. New York: Preliminary Report to the Ford Foundation.

Dunn, William
1986    Hispanic Americans: Taking Care of Business. *USA Today* (November 5), p. 13A.

Dunn, William, and Johnson, Kevin
1991    Integration Not as Easy as Moving In. *USA Today* (March 12), pp. 1A–2A.

Duran, Richard P.
1986    Prediction of Hispanics' College Achievement. In Michael A. Olivas, ed., *Latino College Students*, pp. 221–245. New York: Teachers College Press.

Durant, Thomas J., Jr., and Louden, Joyce S.
1986    The Black Middle Class in America: Historical and Contemporary Perspectives. *Phylon* 47 (December): 253–263.

Dworkin, Anthony Gary
1965    Stereotypes and Self-Images Held by Native-Born and Foreign-Born Mexican Americans. *Sociology and Social Research* 49 (January), pp. 214–224.

Dworkin, Rosalind J.
1982    A Woman's Report: Numbers Are Not Enough. In Anthony Dworkin and Rosalind Dworkin, eds., *The Minority Report*, 2nd ed., pp. 375–400. New York: Holt, Rinehart and Winston.

Dyer, James
1989    Social Distance Among Racial and Ethnic Groups in Texas: Some Demographic Correlates. *Social Science Quarterly* 70 (September), pp. 607–616.

Dzidzienyo, Anani
1987    Brazil. In Jay A. Sigler, ed., *International Handbook on Race and Race Relations.* New York: Greenwood Press.

Dzidzienyo, Anani, with Casai, Lourdes
1979    *The Position of Blacks in Brazilian and Cuban Society.* New York: Minority Rights Group.

Edwards, Harry

1970 *Black Students.* New York: Free Press.

Egerton, John
1971 Racism Differs in Puerto Rico. *Race Relations Reporter* 2 (July 6), pp. 6–7.
1973 How to Eradicate an Indian Tribe. *Race Relations Reporter* 4 (November), pp. 26–30.

Ehrenreich, Barbara, and Stallard, Karin
1982 The Nouveau Poor. *MS.* 11 (July–August), pp. 217–224.

Elder, Rob
1976 Exiles Growing Years Apart. *Miami Herald* (January 26), p. 1.

Elinson, Jack; Haberman, Paul W.; and Gell, Cyrelle
1967 *Ethnic and Educational Data on Adults in New York City, 1963–1964.* New York: School of Public Health and Administrative Medicine, Columbia University.

Elkins, Stanley
1959 *Slavery: A Problem in American Institutional and Intellectual Life.* Chicago: University of Chicago Press.

Ellis, Richard N.
1972 *The Western American Indian: Case Studies in Tribal History.* Lincoln: University of Nebraska Press.

El Nasser, Haya
1990 Catholics Reach Out to Shrinking Hispanic Flock. *USA Today* (April 4), p. 3A.
1991a Melting Pot of Blacks, Koreans Boils Over. *USA Today* (September 18), p. 7A.
1991b Japanese-Americans Face Prejudice. *USA Today* (December 6), p. 8A.

Elsasser, Glen
1987 Bias No Bar to Death Penalty. *Chicago Tribune* (April 23), pp. 1, 8.

Elson, Mary
1982 '80s anti-Semitism: Is It Old Bigotry or New Ignorance? *Chicago Tribune* (July 25), sect. 12, pp. 1, 4.

Emerson, Rupert
1968 *Colonialism: Political Aspects.* In David L. Sills, ed., *International Encyclopedia of the Social Sciences,* vol. 3, pp. 1–5. New York: Macmillan.

England, Paula, and Norris, Bahar
1985 Comparable Worth: A New Doctrine of Sex Discrimination. *Social Science Quarterly* 66 (September), pp. 629–643.

EPIC (Ecumenical Program for Intra-American Communication and Action)
1976 *Puerto Rico: A People Challenging Colonialism.* Washington, DC: EPICA Task Force.

Epstein, Joseph
1972 Blue Collars in Cicero. *Dissent* 19 (Winter), pp. 118–127.

Erlanger, Howard S., with Persily, Fred
1976 Estrangement, Machismo, and Gang Violence. Unpublished discussion paper. Madison, WI: Institute for Research on Poverty.

Erlich, Reese
1987 Latino Food Workers Strike a Double Blow. *The Christian Science Monitor* (March 16), p. 7.

Espenshade, Thomas J.
1990 A Short History of U.S. Policy Toward Illegal Immigration. *Population Today* 18 (February), pp. 6–9.

Espinosa, Dula
1987 The Impact of Affirmative Action Policy on Ethnic and Gender Employment Inequality. Paper presented at the annual meeting of the American Sociological Association, Chicago.

Essed, Philomena
1991 *Understanding Everyday Racism.* Newbury Park, CA: Sage.

Estrada, Leobardo F.
1988 Anticipating the Demographic Future. *Change* (May/June), pp. 14–19.

Exter, Thomas
1987 How Many Hispanics? *American Demographics* 9 (May), pp. 36–39, 67.

Facts on File
1990 *Israeli Extremist Kahane Assassinated in New York.* New York: Facts on File, p. 831.

Faludi, Susan
1991 *Backlash: The Undeclared War Against American Women.* New York: Crown Publishing Group.

Fanon, Frantz
1968 *The Wretched of the Earth.* New York: Grove Press.

Farber, Bernard; Mindel, Charles H.; and Lazerwitz, Bernard
   1976   The Jewish American Family. In
          Charles H. Mindel and Robert W.
          Habenstein, eds., *Ethnic Families in
          America: Patterns and Variations*, pp.
          347–378. New York: Elsevier.

Farber M. A.
   1975   Immigration Service Inquiry End-
          ing; Results in Dispute. *New York
          Times* (April 27), p. 47.

Farley, Reynolds
   1984   *Blacks and Whites: Narrowing the
          Gap?* Cambridge, MA: Harvard
          University Press.

Farley, Reynolds, and Allen, Walter R.
   1987   *The Color Line and the Quality of Life
          in America.* New York: Russell Sage
          Foundation.

Farrel, Walter C., and Jones, Cloyzell K.
   1988   Recent Racial Incidents in Higher
          Education: A Preliminary Perspec-
          tive. *Urban Review* 20 (Fall), pp.
          221–226.

Farrell, Charles S.
   1992   Black Colleges Still Carrying Their
          Load—And Then Some. *Black Issues
          in Higher Education* 9 (May 7), pp.
          10, 12–13.

Farrell, Warren T.
   1974   *The Liberated Man.* New York: Ran-
          dom House.

Farrell, William E., and Weaver, Warren, Jr.
   1984   A Preference for English. *New York
          Times* (March 13), p. B6.

Fayer, Joan M.
   1985   Puerto Rican Identity: Themes That
          Unite and Divide. *Journal of Amer-
          ican Culture* 8 (Winter), pp. 83–91.

Feagin, Joe R.
   1991   The Continuing Significance of
          Race: The Black Middle-Class Ex-
          perience. Paper presented at the an-
          nual meeting of the American So-
          ciological Association, Cincinnati.

Feagin, Joe R., and Eckberg, Douglas Lee
   1980   Discrimination: Motivation, Action,
          Effects, and Context. In Alex Ink-
          eles, ed., *Annual Review of Sociology,
          1980*, pp. 1–20. Palo Alto, CA: An-
          nual Reviews, Inc.

Feder, Barnaby J.

   1987   Sullivan Asks End of Business
          Links with South Africa. *New York
          Times* (June 4), pp. 1, 28.

Federal Trade Commission
   1973   *The Trading Post System on the Na-
          vajo Reservation.* Washington, DC:
          U.S. Government Printing Office.

Feliuce, Lawrence G.
   1977   The Effects of Busing and School
          Segregation on Majority and Mi-
          nority Student Dropout Rates: An
          Evaluation of School Socio-
          Economic Composition and Teach-
          er's Expectations. Paper presented
          at the annual meeting of the Amer-
          ican Sociological Association, Chi-
          cago.

Feng, Shih Tree
   1988   Chinese Immigrants in the United
          States. Unpublished paper, Ma-
          comb: Western Illinois University.

Ferman, Patricia R., and Ferman, Louis A.
   1973   The Structural Underpinnings of
          the Irregular Economy. *Poverty and
          Human Resources Abstracts* 8
          (March), pp. 3–17.

Fermi, Laura
   1971   *Illustrious Immigrants,* rev. ed. Chi-
          cago: University of Chicago Press.

Ferrell, Tom, and Adams, Virginia
   1977   Judaism's New Book of Daily Pray-
          er. *New York Times* (March 13), p.
          E9.

Feshbach, Seymour, and Singer, Robert
   1957   The Effects of Personal and Shared
          Threats upon Social Prejudice. *Jour-
          nal of Abnormal and Social Psychology*
          54 (May), pp. 411–416.

Fialka, John J.
   1978   The Indians, the Royalties, and the
          BIA: Window Rock, Arizona. *Civil
          Rights Digest* 10 (Winter), pp. 14–19.

Fields, Cheryl
   1988   The Hispanic Pipeline. *Change*
          (May/June), pp. 20–27.

Finestein, Israel
   1988   The Future of American Jewry. *The
          Jewish Journal of Sociology* 30 (De-
          cember), pp. 121–125.

Fiola, Jan
   1989   Race Relations in Brazil: A Reas-
          sessment of the "Racial Democ-

racy" Thesis. Paper presented at the annual meeting of the Midwest Sociological Society, St. Louis.

Fishman, Joshua A.
1966 Language Maintenance in a Supra-Ethnic Age: Summary and Conclusions. In Joshua A. Fishman, ed., *Language Loyalty in the United States*, pp. 392–411. London and The Hague: Mouton.

Fishman, Joshua A., ed.
1985 *The Rise and Fall of the Ethnic Revival*. Berlin: Mouton.

Fishman, Joshua A.; Hayden, Robert G.; and Warshaver, Mary E.
1966 The Non-English and the Ethnic Group Press, 1910–1960. In Joshua A. Fishman (ed.), *Language Loyalty in the United States*, pp. 51–74. London and The Hague: Mouton.

Fiske, Edward B.
1988a Colleges Are Seeking to Remedy Lag in Their Hispanic Enrollment. *New York Times* (March 20), pp. 1, 16.
1988b The Undergraduate Hispanic Experience. *Change* (May/June), pp. 28–33.

Fitzhugh, George
1857 *Cannibals All! or Slaves Without Masters*. Richmond, VA: A. Morris.

Fitzpatrick, Joseph P.
1980 Puerto Ricans. In Stephen Thernstrom, ed., *Harvard Encyclopedia of American Ethnic Groups*, pp. 858–867. Cambridge, MA: Belknap Press of Harvard University Press.
1987 *Puerto Rican Americans: The Meaning of Migration to the Mainland*, 2nd ed. Englewood Cliffs, NJ: Prentice-Hall.
1989 Puerto Ricans as a Social Minority on the Mainland. *International Journal of Group Tensions* 19 (Fall), pp. 195–208.

Fix, Michael, and Passel, Jeffrey S.
1991 *The Door Remains Open: Recent Immigration to the United States and a Preliminary Analysis of the Immigration Act of 1990*. Washington, DC: The Urban Institute.

Fixico, Donald L.
1988 The Federal Policy of Termination and Relocation, 1945–1960. In Phil-

ip Weeks, ed., *The American Indian Experience*, pp. 260–277. Arlington Heights, IL: Forum Press.

Flacks, Richard
1967 The Liberated Generation: An Exploration of the Roots of Student Protest. *Journal of Social Issues* 23 (July), pp. 52–75.

Flexner, Eleanor
1959 *Century of Struggle: The Women's Rights Movement in the United States*. Cambridge, MA: Harvard University Press.

Flores, Juan
1985 Que Assimilated, Brother, Yo Soy Assimilado: The Structuring of Puerto Rican Identity in the U.S. *Journal of Ethnic Studies* 13 (Fall), pp. 1–16.

Foderaro, Lisa W.
1990 Japanese in New York Area Feel Sting of Prejudice. *New York Times* (July 22), p. 20.

Fong, Stanley L. M.
1965 Assimilation of Chinese in America: Changes in Orientation and Perception. *American Journal of Sociology* 71 (November), pp. 265–273.
1973 Assimilation and Changing Social Roles of Chinese Americans. *Journal of Social Issues* 29 (No. 2), pp. 115–127.

Fong-Torres, Ben
1986 The China Syndrome. *Moviegoer* 5 (July), pp. 6–7.

Fontaine, Pierre-Michel
1986 *Race, Class, and Power in Brazil*. Los Angeles: Center for Afro-American Studies, UCLA.

Foot, Paul
1969 *Immigration and Race in British Politics*. Harmondsworth, G.B.: Penguin Books.

Ford, W. Scott
1986 Favorable Intergroup Contact May Not Reduce Prejudice: Inconclusive Journal Evidence, 1960–1984. *Sociology and Social Research* 70 (July), pp. 256–258.

Forni, Floreal
1971 *The Situation of the Puerto Rican Population in Chicago and Its Viewpoints*

*about Racial Relations.* Chicago: Community and Family Study Center, University of Chicago.

Fortney, Judith
1972    Immigrant Professionals: A Brief Historical Survey. *International Migration Review* 6 (Spring), pp. 50–62.

Francis, Emerich K.
1976    *Interethnic Relations: An Essay in Sociological Theory.* New York: Elsevier.

Franklin, John Hope, and Moss, Alfred A., Jr.
1988    *From Slavery to Freedom: A History of Negro Americans.* 6th ed. New York: Alfred A. Knopf.

Fratoe, Frank A.
1986    A Sociological Analysis of Minority Business. *Review of Black Political Economy* 15 (Autumn), pp. 5–30.

Frazier, E. Franklin
1942    The Negro Family in Bahia, Brazil. *American Sociological Review* 7 (August), pp. 465–478.
1943    Rejoinder: The Negro in Bahia, Brazil. *American Sociological Review* 8 (August), pp. 402–404.
1957    *Black Bourgeoise: The Rise of a New Middle Class.* New York: Free Press.
1964    *The Negro Church in America.* New York: Schocken.

Fredrickson, George M.
1981    *White Supremacy: A Comparative Study in American and South African History.* New York: Oxford University Press.

Freeman, Jo
1973    The Origins of the Women's Liberation Movement. *American Journal of Sociology* 78 (January), pp. 792–811.
1975    *The Politics of Women's Liberation.* New York: David McKay.
1983    On the Origins of Social Movements. In Jo Freeman, ed., *Social Movements of the Sixties and Seventies,* pp. 1–30. New York: Longman.

Freyre, Gilberto
1946    *The Masters and the Slaves: A Study in the Development of Brazilian Civilization.* New York: Alfred A. Knopf.
1959    *New World in the Tropics.* New York: Alfred A. Knopf.

1963    *The Mansions and the Shanties: The Making of Modern Brazil.* New York: Alfred A. Knopf.

Friedan, Betty
1963    *The Feminine Mystique.* New York: Dell.
1981    *The Second Stage.* New York: Summit Books.
1991    Back to the Feminine Mystique? *The Humanist* 51 (January/February), pp. 26–27.

Friedman, Georges
1967    *The End of the Jewish People?* Garden City, NY: Doubleday.

Friendly, Alfred, and Silver, Eric
1981    *Israel's Oriental Immigrants and Druzes.* London: Minority Rights Group.

Fuchs, Estelle, and Havighurst, Robert J.
1972    *To Live on This Earth: American Indian Education.* New York: Doubleday.

Fusfeld, Daniel R.
1973    *The Basic Economics of the Urban Racial Crisis.* New York: Holt, Rinehart and Winston.

Gager, John G.
1983    *The Origins of Anti-Semitism.* New York: Oxford University Press.

Galarza, Ernesto
1964    *Merchants of Labor: The Mexican Bracero Story.* Santa Barbara, CA: McNally and Loften.
1971    *Barrio Boy.* Notre Dame, IN: University of Notre Dame Press.

Gallo, Patrick J.
1974    *Ethnic Alienation: The Italian Americans.* Rutherford, NJ: Fairleigh Dickinson University Press.

Gallup, George H.
1972    *The Gallup Poll, Public Opinion 1935–1971.* New York: Random House.

Gallup Opinion Index
1987    *Religion in America, 1987.* 259 (April).

Galtung, Johan
1989    *Nonviolence and Israel/Palestine.* Honolulu: University of Hawaii Institute for Peace.

Galvan, Manuel
1982    On the National Scene, Two Who Are Making Their Mark. *Chicago*

*Tribune* (June 20), sect. 2, p. 2.

Gambino, Richard
1974a  *Blood of My Blood.* New York: Doubleday.
1974b  The Italian-Americans. *Chicago Tribune Magazine* (May 5), pp. 56–58.

Gans, Herbert J.
1956  American Jewry: Present and Future. *Commentary* 21 (May), pp. 424–425.
1979  Symbolic Ethnicity: The Future of Ethnic Groups and Cultures in America. *Ethnic and Racial Studies* 2 (January), pp. 1–20.

Garbarino, Merwyn S.
1971  Life in the City: Chicago. In Jack O. Waddell and O. Michael Watson, eds., *The American Indian in Urban Society,* pp. 168–205. Boston: Little, Brown.

Gardner, R. C.; Lalonde, R. N.; Nero, A. M.; and M. Y. Young
1988  Ethnic Stereotype: Implications of Measurement Strategy. *Social Cognition* 6 (1), pp. 40–60.

Gardner, Robert W.; Robey, Bryant; and Smith, Peter C.
1985  Asian Americans: Growth, Change, and Diversity. *Population Bulletin* 40 (October).

Garfinkel, Herbert
1959  *When Negroes March.* New York: Atheneum.

Garitty, Michael
1986  Trouble in Paradise: Apartheid Arizona Style. *Akwesasne Notes* 18 (Summer), pp. 10–15, 18–19.

Garrison, Troy
1974  Another Oriental Treat from San Francisco. *Chicago Tribune* (February 3), pp. IV, 6–7.

Gary, Lawrence E.; Beatty, Lula A.; Berry, Greta L.; and Price, Mary D.
1983  *Stable Black Families Final Report.* Washington, DC: Institute for Urban Affairs and Research, Howard University.

Gates, Henry Louis, Jr.
1989  TV's Black World Turns—But Stays Unreal. *New York Times* (November 12), pp. H1, H40.

Gates, Mireille Grangenois

1986  Poll: Blacks Less Worried About Civil Rights. *USA Today* (October 15), p. 3A.

Gellis, Audrey
1974  The View from the Back of the Shul. *Ms.* 2 (July), pp. 79–82.

General Mills
1977  *The American Family Report.* Conducted by Yankelovich, Skelly, and White, Inc. Minneapolis: General Mills.

Genovese, Eugene D.
1974  *Roll, Jordan, Roll: The World the Slaves Made.* New York: Pantheon.

Gerson, Walter
1969  Jews at Christmas Time: Role-Strain and Strain Reducing Mechanisms. In Walter Gerson, ed., *Social Problems in a Changing World,* pp. 65–76. New York: Crowell.

Gerth, H. H., and Mills, C. Wright
1958  *From Max Weber: Essays in Sociology.* New York: Galaxy Books.

Geschwender, James A.
1964  Social Structure and the Negro Revolt: An Examination of Some Hypotheses. *Social Forces* 43 (December), pp. 248–256.

Gesensway, Deborah, and Roseman, Mindy, eds.
1987  *Beyond Words: Images from America's Concentration Camps.* Ithaca: Cornell University Press.

Gibbons, Tom
1985  Justice Not Equal for Poor Here. *Chicago Sun-Times* (February 24), pp. 1, 18.

Giddings, Paula
1984  *When and Where I Enter.* New York: William Morrow.

Gilbert, Gilber M.
1951  Stereotype Persistence and Change Among College Students. *Journal of Abnormal and Social Psychology* 46 (April), pp. 245–254.

Giles, Michael W.; Gatlin, Douglas S.; and Cataldo, Everett F.
1976  Racial and Class Prejudice: Their Relative Effects on Protest Against School Desegregation. *American Sociological Review* 41 (April), pp. 280–288.

Gilliam, Franklin D., Jr.
1986    Black America: Divided by Class? *Public Opinion* 9 (February/March), pp. 53–57.
1989    Race, Class, and Attitudes Toward Social Welfare Spending. An Ethclass Interpretation. *Social Science Quarterly* 70 (March), pp. 88–100.

Gilly, M. C.
1988    Sex Roles in Advertising: A Comparison of Television Advertisements in Australia, Mexico, and the United States. *Journal of Marketing* 52 (April), pp. 75–85.

Gimenez, Martha E.
1987    The Feminization of Poverty: Myth or Reality. *Insurgent Sociologist* 14 (Fall), pp. 5–30.

Ginorio, Angela B.
1986    Puerto Rican Ethnicity and Conflict. In Jerry O. Boucher, Dan Landis, and Karen Arnold, eds., *Ethnic Conflict*, pp. 182–206. Newbury Park, CA: Sage.

Ginzberg, Eli
1991    Access to Health Care for Hispanics. *Journal of the American Medical Association* 265 (January 9), pp. 238–241.

Girdner, Audrie, and Loftis, Anne
1969    *The Great Betrayal: The Evacuation of the Japanese Americans During World War II.* New York: Macmillan.

Gittler, Joseph B., ed.
1981    *Jewish Life in the United States: Perspectives from the Social Sciences.* New York: New York University Press.

Gittleson, Natalie
1984    American Jews Rediscover Orthodoxy. *New York Times Magazine* (September 30), pp. 40–41, 60–61, 63–65, 71.

Glasgow, Douglas G.
1980    *The Black Underclass: Poverty, Unemployment, and Entrapment of Ghetto Youth.* San Francisco: Jossey-Bass.

Glassman, Bernard
1975    *Anti-Semitic Stereotypes Without Jews: Images of the Jews in England, 1290–1700.* Detroit: Wayne State University Press.

Glazer, Nathan
1971    The Issue of Cultural Pluralism in America Today. In *Pluralism Beyond Frontier: Report of the San Francisco Consultation on Ethnicity*, pp. 2–8. San Francisco: American Jewish Committee.
1990    American Jewry or American Judaism? *Society* 28 (November/December), pp. 14–20.

Glazer, Nathan, and Moynihan, Daniel Patrick
1963    *Beyond the Melting Pot: The Negroes, Puerto Ricans, Jews, Italians, and Irish of New York City.* Cambridge, MA: MIT Press.
1970    *Beyond the Melting Pot: The Negroes, Puerto Ricans, Jews, Italians, and Irish of New York City*, 2nd ed. Cambridge, MA: MIT Press.

Glock, Charles Y.; Selznick, Gertrude; and Spaeth, Joe L.
1966    *The Apathetic Majority.* New York: Harper and Row.

Glock, Charles Y., and Stark, Rodney
1965a   Is There an American Protestantism? *Transaction* 3 (November–December), pp. 8–13, 48–49.
1965b   *Religion and Society in Tension.* Chicago: Rand McNally.

Glock, Charles Y.; Wuthnow, Robert; Piliavin, Jane Allyn; and Spencer, Metta
1975    *Adolescent Prejudice.* New York: Harper and Row.

Goering, John M.
1971    The Emergence of Ethnic Interests: A Case of Serendipity. *Social Forces* 48 (March), pp. 379–384.

Gold, Michael
1965    *Jews Without Money.* New York: Avon.

Gold, Steven J.
1988    New Immigrant Organizations and Old Country Links: The Case of Soviet Jews in the U.S. Paper presented at the Annual Meeting of the American Sociological Association, Atlanta.

Goldberg, Philip A.; Gottesdiener, Marc; and Abramson, Paul R.
1975    Another Put-Down of Women? Perceived Attractiveness as a Function of Support for the Feminist

Movement. *Journal of Personality and Social Psychology* 32 (July), pp. 113–115.

Goldman, Ari L.
1986   As Call Comes, More Women Answer. *New York Times* (October 19), p. E6.

Goldman, Peter
1974   *The Death and Life of Malcolm X.* New York: Harper and Row.

Goldscheider, Calvin
1986   *Jewish Continuity and Change: Emerging Patterns in America.* Bloomington: Indiana University Press.

Goldstein, Henry
1971   The White Ethnics and the Minorities: Churches in Conflict. *City* (May–June), pp. 34–37.

Goldstein, Sidney
1971   American Jewry, 1970, A Demographic Profile. In *American Jewish Yearbook, 1971,* pp. 3–88. New York: American Jewish Committee.
1981   Jews in the United States: Perspectives from Demography. In Joseph B. Gittler, ed., *Jewish Life in the United States,* pp. 31–102. New York: New York University Press.

Goldstein, Sidney, and Goldscheider, Calvin
1968   *Jewish Americans: Three Generations in a Jewish Community.* Englewood Cliffs, NJ: Prentice-Hall.

Goleman, Daniel
1990   Anger over Racism is Seen as a Cause of Blacks' High Blood Pressure. *New York Times* (April 24), p. C3.

Gomez, David F.
1971   Chicanos: Strangers in Their Own Land. *America* 124 (June 26), pp. 649–652.

Gompers, Samuel, and Gustadt, Herman
1908   *Meat vs. Rice: American Manhood Against Asiatic Coolieism: Which Shall Survive?* San Francisco: Asiatic Exclusion League.

Gonzales, Rodolfo
1972   *Yo Soy Joaquin (I Am Joaquin).* New York: Bantam Books.

Goodstein, Laurie
1990   New York's Racial Tinderbox. *Washington Post National Weekly Edi-* tion 7 (May 21), p. 9.

Goozner, Merrill
1987   Age-old Tradition Bankrolls Koreans. *Chicago Tribune* (July 19), sect. 7, pp. 1–2.

Gordon, Leonard
1973   The Fragmentization of Literary Stereotypes of Jews and Negroes Among College Students. *Pacific Sociological Review* 16 (October), pp. 411–425.
1985   Racial and Ethnic Stereotypes of American College Students Over a Half Century. Paper presented at the Annual Meeting of the Society for the Study of Social Problems, Washington, DC.
1986   College Student Stereotypes of Blacks and Jews on Two Campuses: Four Studies Spanning 50 Years. *Sociology and Social Research* 70 (April), pp. 200–201.

Gordon, Milton M.
1964   *Assimilation in American Life: The Role of Race, Religion, and National Origins.* New York: Oxford University Press.
1975   Toward a General Theory of Racial and Ethnic Group Relations. In Nathan Glazer and Daniel P. Moynihan, eds., *Ethnicity: Theory and Experience,* pp. 84–110. Cambridge, MA: Harvard University Press.
1978   *Human Nature, Class, and Ethnicity.* New York: Oxford University Press.

Gordon, Wendell
1975   A Case for a Less Restrictive Border Policy. *Social Science Quarterly* 56 (December), pp. 485–491.

Goren, Arthur A.
1980   Jews. In Stephen Thernstrom, ed., *Harvard Encyclopedia of American Ethnic Groups,* pp. 571–598. Cambridge, MA: Belknap Press of Harvard University Press.

Gould, Ketayun H.
1988   Asian and Pacific Islanders Myth and Reality. *Social Work* 33 (March–April), pp. 142–147.

Gouldner, Alvin
1970   *The Coming Crisis in Western Sociology.* New York: Basic Books.

Graham, Jory
  1975    Coping with Christmas. *Chicago*
          (December), pp. 204–205.

Gratton, Brian
  1987    Familialism among the Black and
          Mexican American Elderly: Myth
          or Reality. *Journal of Aging Studies* 1
          (Spring), pp. 19–32.

Grebler, Leo; Moore, Joan W.; and Guzman,
Ralph C.
  1970    *The Mexican American People: The
          Nation's Second Largest People.* New
          York: Free Press.

Greeley, Andrew M.
  1972    *The Most Distressful Nation: The
          Taming of the American Irish.* Chica-
          go: Quadrangle Books.
  1974a   *Ethnicity in the United States: A Pre-
          liminary Reconnaissance.* New York:
          John Wiley and Sons.
  1974b   Political Participation Among Eth-
          nic Groups in the United States: A
          Preliminary Reconnaissance. *Amer-
          ican Journal of Sociology* 80 (July),
          pp. 170–204.
  1975    TV's Italian Cops—Trapped in Old
          Stereotypes. *New York Times* (July
          27), p. 1.
  1976    *Ethnicity, Denomination and Inequal-
          ity.* Research paper No. 4. Beverly
          Hills, CA: Sage Publications.
  1977    *The American Catholic.* New York:
          Basic Books.
  1988    Defection Among Hispanics. *Amer-
          ica* 159 (July 30), pp. 61–62.
  1989    *Religious Change in America.* Cam-
          bridge, MA: Harvard University
          Press.

Greeley, Andrew M., and Sheatsley, Paul B.
  1971    Attitudes Toward Racial Integra-
          tion. *Scientific American* 225 (De-
          cember 1971), pp. 13–19.

Greenberg, Bradley S., and Mazingo, Sherrie
L.
  1976    Racial Issues in Mass Media In-
          stitutions. In Phyllis A. Katz, ed.,
          *Towards the Elimination of Racism,*
          pp. 309–339. New York: Pergamon
          Press.

Greenberg, Simon
  1970    Jewish Educational Institutions. In
          Louis Finkelstein, ed., *The Jews:
          Their Religion and Culture,* 4th ed.,

          vol. 2, pp. 380–412. New York:
          Schocken.

Greenblatt, Susan L.
  1983    A Major Step Forward in Deseg-
          regation Research. *Contemporary So-
          ciology* 12 (November), pp. 650–663.

Greene, Elizabeth
  1987    Asian-Americans Find U.S. Col-
          leges Insensitive, Form Campus Or-
          ganizations to Fight Bias. *Chronicle
          of Higher Education* 34 (November
          18), pp. A1, A38–A40.

Greene, Victor R.
  1968    *The Slavic Community on Strike.*
          Notre Dame, IN: University of
          Notre Dame Press.

Greenhouse, Linda
  1989    Supreme Court, 5–4, Narrowing
          Roe v. Wade, Upholds Sharp State
          Limits on Abortions. *New York
          Times* (July 4), pp. 1, 8.
  1990    Use of Illegal Drugs as Part of Reli-
          gion Can Be Prosecuted, High
          Court Says. *New York Times* (April
          18), p. A10.

Gremley, William
  1952    Social Control in Cicero. *British
          Journal of Sociology* 3 (December),
          pp. 322–338.

Griggs, Anthony
  1974    Chicago Gets a Third Chinatown.
          *Race Relations Reporter* 5 (March 25),
          pp. 6–7.

Grimshaw, Allen D., ed.
  1969    *Racial Violence in the United States.*
          Chicago: Aldine.

Gross, Jane
  1989    Diversity Hinders Asians' Power in
          U.S. *New York Times* (June 25), p.
          A22.

Grove, David John
  1974    *The Race vs. Ethnic Debate: A Cross-
          National Analysis of Two Theoretical
          Approaches.* Denver: University of
          Denver Press.

Guest, Avery M., and Weed, James A.
  1976    Ethnic Residential Segregation: Pat-
          terns of Change. *American Journal of
          Sociology* 81 (March), pp. 1008–1011.

Guthrie, James W.; Kleindorfer, George B.;
Levin, Henry M.; and Stout, Robert T.
  1971    *Schools and Inequality.* Cambridge,

MA: MIT Press.

Gutiérrez, Armando, and Hirsch, Herbert
1970    The Militant Challenge to the American Ethos: "Chicanos" and "Mexican Americans." *Social Science Quarterly* 53 (March), pp. 830–845.

Gutman, Herbert G.
1976    *The Black Family in Slavery and Freedom, 1750 to 1925.* New York: Pantheon.

Guy, Pat
1991    Sullivan: Sanctions Should Remain. *USA Today* (July 11), p. 9A.

Gwertzman, Bernard
1985    The Debt to the Indochinese Is Becoming a Fiscal Drain. *New York Times* (March 3), p. E3.

Haak, Gerald O.
1970    Co-opting the Oppressors: The Case of the Japanese-Americans. *Society* 7 (October), pp. 23–31.

Hacker, Andrew
1992    *Two Nations: Black and White, Separate, Hostile, Unequal.* New York: Charles Scribner's Sons.

Hacker, Helen Mayer
1951    Women as a Minority Group. *Social Forces* 30 (October), pp. 60–69.
1973    Sex Roles in Black Society: Caste Versus Caste. Paper presented at the annual meeting of the American Sociological Association, New York.
1974    Women as a Minority Group: Twenty Years Later. In Florence Denmark, ed., *Who Discriminates Against Women,* pp. 124–134. Beverly Hills, CA: Sage Publications.
1975    Class and Race Differences in Gender Roles. In Lucile Duberman, ed., *Gender and Sex in Society,* pp. 134–184. New York: Praeger.

Hadden, Jeffrey K.
1967    A Protestant Paradox—Divided They Merge. *Transaction* 4 (July–August), pp. 63–69.
1969    *The Gathering Storm in the Churches.* Garden City, NY: Doubleday.
1971    *Religion in Radical Transition.* Chicago: Aldine.

Hagan, William T.
1961    *American Indians.* Chicago: University of Chicago Press.

Hakuta, Kenji, and Garcia, Eugene E.
1989    Bilingualism and Education. *American Psychologist* 44 (February), pp. 374–379.

Haley, Alex
1976    *Roots: The Saga of an American Family.* Garden City, NY: Doubleday.

Halpern, Ben
1974    America Is Different. In Marshall Sklare, ed., *The Jew in American Society,* pp. 67–89. New York: Behrman House.

Handlin, Oscar
1951    *The Uprooted: The Epic Story of the Great Migrations That Made the American People.* New York: Grossett and Dunlap.
1957    *Race and Nationality in American Life.* Boston: Little, Brown.

Hansen, Marcus Lee
1937    Who Shall Inherit America? Speech delivered at the National Conference of Social Work, Indianapolis.
1952    The Third Generation in America. *Commentary* 14 (November 1952), pp. 493–500.
1987    *The Problem of the Third Generation Immigrant,* with introductions by Peter Kwisto and Oscar Handlin. Rock Island, IL: Swenson Swedish Immigration Research Center.

Harjo, Suzan Shown
1991    I Won't Be Celebrating Columbus Day. *Newsweek* (October), p. 32.

Harlan, Louis R.
1970    Booker T. Washington in Biographical Perspective. *American Historical Review* 75 (October), pp. 1581–1599.
1971    The Secret Life of Booker T. Washington. *Journal of Southern History* 37 (August), pp. 393–416.
1972    *Booker T. Washington: The Making of a Black Leader.* New York: Oxford University Press.

Harrell-Bond, Barbara E.
1988    The Sociology of Involuntary Migration. *Current Sociology* 36 (Summer), pp. 1–6.

Harris, David A.
1987    Japan and the Jews. *Morning Freiheit* (November 8), pp. 1, 3.

Harris, Lou
1987 *Inside America*. New York: Vintage.
Harris, Marvin
1964 *Patterns of Race in the Americas*. New York: Norton.
Harrison, Michael I., and Lazerwitz, Bernard
1982 Do Denominations Matter? *American Journal of Sociology* 88 (September), pp. 356–377.
Hartley, Eugene L.
1946 *Problems in Prejudice*. New York: Kings Crown Press.
Hartmann, Heidi I.
1981 The Family as the Locus of Gender, Class, and Political Struggle: The Example of Housework. *Signs* 6 (Spring), pp. 366–394.
Hatchett, Shirley, J.
1991 Women and Men. In James S. Jackson, ed., *Life in Black America*, pp. 46–83. Newbury Park, CA: Sage Publications.
Hatchett, Shirley J.; Cochran, Donna L.; and Jackson, James S.
1991 Family Life. In James S. Jackson, ed., *Life in Black America*, pp. 46–83. Newbury Park, CA: Sage Publications.
Hawaii
1986 *Statistical Report, 1984*. Honolulu: Department of Health.
Hawkins, Hugh
1962 *Booker T. Washington and His Critics: The Problem of Negro Leadership*. Boston: Heath.
Hayakawa, S. I.
1988 USA Needs to Have an "Official" Language. *USA Today* (November 11), p. 12A.
Hechinger, Fred M.
1987 Bilingual Programs. *New York Times* (April 7), p. C10.
Heer, David M., and Grossbard-Shectman, Amyra
1981 The Impact of the Female Marriage Squeeze and the Contraceptive Revolution on Sex Roles and the Women's Liberation Movement in the United States, 1960 to 1975. *Journal of Marriage and the Family* 43 (February), pp. 49–76.
Heilman, Samuel C.

1982 The Sociology of American Jewry: The Last Ten Years. In Ralph H. Turner, ed., *Annual Review of Sociology, 1982*, pp. 135–160. Palo Alto, CA: Annual Reviews.
Hensley, Rebecca
1989 Social Distance Between Black Africans and Black Americans and the Attitudes of White Americans Toward Both Groups. Unpublished M.A. thesis, Western Illinois University.
Henslin, James M.
1975 *Introducing Sociology*. New York: Free Press.
Herberg, Will
1983 *Protestant-Catholic-Jew: An Essay in American Religious Sociology*, rev. ed. Chicago: University of Chicago Press.
Herbers, John
1981 Census Finds More Blacks Living in Suburbs of Nation's Large Cities. *New York Times* (May 31), pp. 1, 16.
Herman, Edith
1973 Ethnics Share Need for Education. *Chicago Tribune* (July 8), p. 11.
Hérnandez, Beatriz Johnston
1988 The Sanctuary Movement: Churches Aid Undocumented Workers. *Village Voice* 33 (December 6), pp. 17–18.
Hernandez, Luis F.
1969 *A Forgotten American: A Resource Unit for Teachers on the Mexican American*. New York: Anti-Defamation League of B'nai B'rith.
Herskovits, Melville J.
1930 *The Anthropometry of the American Negro*. New York: Columbia University Press.
1941 *The Myth of the Negro Past*. New York: Harper and Brothers.
1943 The Negro in Bahia, Brazil: A Problem in Method. *American Sociological Review* 8 (August), pp. 394–402.
Hertzler, J. O.
1942 The Sociology of Anti-Semitism Through History. In Isacque Graeber, ed., *Jews in a Gentile World*, pp. 62–100. New York: Macmillan.
Hess, Beth B., and Ferree, Myra Marx, eds.

1987    *Analyzing Gender: A Handbook of So-cial Science Research.* Newbury Park, CA: Sage.

Hewitt, Christopher
1988    The Costs of Terrorism: A Cross-National Study of Six Countries. *Terrorism* 11 (No. 3), pp. 169–180.

Higginbotham, Elizabeth, and Weber, Lynn
1991    Moving Up With Kin and Com-munity: Upward Social Mobility for Black and White Women. Paper presented at the annual meeting of the American Sociological Associa-tion, Cincinnati.

Higham, John
1966    American Anti-Semitism Histor-ically Reconsidered. In Charles Herbert Stember, ed., *Jews in the Mind of America*, pp. 237–258. New York: Basic Books.
1974    Integration vs. Pluralism: Another American Dilemma. *Center Maga-zine* 7 (July–August), pp. 67–73.

Hill, Herbert
1967    The Racial Practices of Organized Labor—The Age of Gompers and After. In Arthur M. Ross and Her-bert Hill, eds., *Employment, Race, and Poverty*, pp. 365–402. New York: Harcourt, Brace and World.

Hill, Robert B.
1972    *The Strengths of Black Families.* New York: Emerson Hall.
1987    The Future of Black Families. *Collo-qui* (Spring), pp. 22–28.

Hilts, Philip J.
1990    Life Expectancy for Blacks in U.S. Shows Sharp Drop. *New York Times* (November 29), p. A1, B27.

Himmelfarb, Harold S.
1982    Research on American Jewish Iden-tity and Identification: Progress, Pitfalls, and Prospects. In Marshall Sklare, ed., *Understanding American Jewry*, pp. 56–95. New Brunswick, NJ: Transaction Books.

Hinds, Michael de Courcy
1989    Better Traps Being Built for Delin-quent Parents. *New York Times* (De-cember 9), p. 11.

Hiro, Dilip
1973    *Black British, White British*, rev. ed. New York: Monthly Review Press.

Hirsch, Herbert
1982    Political Activation and the Social-ization of Support for a Third Party: Mexican-American Children and the Future of *La Raza Unida* Party. In Z. Anthony Kruszewski, et al., eds., *Politics and Society in the Southwest*, pp. 249–265. Boulder, CO: Westview Press.

Hirschman, Charles
1983    America's Melting Pot Recon-sidered. In Ralph H. Turner, ed., *Annual Review of Sociology*, pp. 397–423. Palo Alto, CA: Annual Review.

Hirschman, Charles, and Wong, Morrison G.
1986    The Extraordinary Educational At-tainment of Asian-Americans: A Search for Historical Evidence and Explanations. *Social Forces* 65 (Sep-tember), 1–27.

Hirsley, Michael
1991a    Women in Pulpit not Foreordained. *Chicago Tribune* (September 6), p. 8.
1991b    Religious Display Needs Firm Court. *Chicago Tribune* (December 20), Sect. 2, p. 10.

Hochschild, Arlie Russell
1973    A Review of Sex Role Research. *American Journal of Sociology* 78 (Jan-uary), pp. 1011–1029.

Hochschild, Arlie, with Anne Machung
1989    *The Second Shift: Working Parents and the Revolution at Home.* New York: Viking Penguin.
1990    The Second Shift: Employed Wom-en are Putting in Another Day of Work at Home. *Utne Reader* 38 (March/April), pp. 66–73.

Hockstader, Lee
1991    The Call of the Mainland Lures Cuba's Young and Restless. *Wash-ington Post National Weekly Edition* 8 (August 19), p. 15.

Hoebel, E. Adamson
1949    *Man in the Primitive World: An In-troduction to Anthropology.* New York: McGraw-Hill.

Hogan, Candace Lyle
1982    Revolutionizing School and Sports: Ten Years of Title IX. *Ms.* 10 (May), pp. 25–26, 29.

Hohri, William Minoru
1988    *Repairing America: An Account of the*

*Movement for Japanese-American Redress.* Pullum: Washington State University Press.

Holford, David M.
1975    The Subversion of the Indian Land Allotment System, 1887–1934. *Indian Historian* 8 (Spring), pp. 11–21.

Holmberg, David
1974    Pekin Isn't Ready to Give up "Chinks." *Chicago Tribune* (July 28), p. 24.

Holzapfel, Tamara
1976    The Theater of Rene Marques: In Search of Identity and Form. In Leon F. Lyday and George W. Woodyard, eds., *Dramatists in Revolt: The New Latin American Theater,* pp. 146–166. Austin: University of Texas Press.

Hormann, Bernhard L.
1972    Hawaii's Mixing People. In Noel P. Gist and Anthony Gary Dworkin, eds., *The Blending of Races,* pp. 213–236. New York: Wiley.
1982    The Mixing Process. *Social Process in Hawaii,* 29, pp. 116–129.

Hornsby, Alton, Jr.
1975    *The Black Almanac,* 2nd rev. ed. Woodbury, NY: Barron's Educational Series.

Hornung, Rick
1990    One Nation Under the Gun. *New York Times Magazine* (May 15), pp. 22–23.

Horton, John
1966    Order and Conflict Theories of Social Problems as Competing Ideologies. *American Journal of Sociology* 71 (May), pp. 701–713.

Hosokawa, Bill
1969    *Nisei: The Quiet Americans.* New York: William Morrow.
1982a    *JACL in Quest of Justice.* New York: William Morrow.
1982b    Accentuating the American in Japanese American. *Civil Rights Perspectives* 14 (Fall), pp. 40–44.

Hostetler, John A., and Huntington, Gertrude Enders
1971    *Children in Amish Society: Socialization and Community Education.* New York: Holt, Rinehart and Winston.

Howard, Alan
1980    Hawaiians. In Stephen Thernstrom, *Harvard Encyclopedia of American Ethnic Groups,* pp. 449–452. Cambridge, MA: Belknap Press of Harvard University Press.

Howard, John R.
1966    The Making of a Black Muslim. *Transaction* 4 (December), pp. 15–21.

Howe, Marvine
1989    Asians in New York Region: Poverty Amid High Ambition. *New York Times* (April 17), p. B4.

Hraba, Joseph, and Grant, Geoffrey
1970    Black Is Beautiful: A Reexamination of Racial Preference and Identification. *Journal of Personality and Social Psychology* 16 (November), pp. 398–402.

Hsu, Francis L. K.
1971    *The Challenge of the American Dream: The Chinese in the United States.* Belmont, CA: Wadsworth.

Huang, Lucy Jen
1975    The "Banana" Syndrome: Alienation of Chinese-Americans and the Yellow Power Movement. Paper presented at the annual meeting of the American Sociological Association, San Francisco.
1976    The Chinese American Family. In Charles H. Mindel and Robert W. Habenstein, eds., *Ethnic Families in America: Patterns and Variations,* pp. 124–147. New York: Elsevier.

Hufker, Brian, and Cavender, Gray
1990    From Freedom Flotilla to America's Burden: The Social Construction of the Mariel Immigrants. *Sociological Quarterly* 31 (No. 2), pp. 321–335.

Hughes, Michael, and Demo, David H.
1989    Self-Perceptions of Black Americans: Self-Esteem and Personal Efficacy. *American Journal of Sociology* 95 (July), pp. 132–159.

Huizinga, David, and Elliott, Delbert S.
1987    Juvenile Offenders: Prevalence, Offender Incidence, and Arrest Rates by Race. *Crime and Delinquency* 33 (April), pp. 206–223.

Hume, Ellen
1984    Reagan, Si? *Wall Street Journal* (Jan-

uary 6), pp. 1, 13.

Humphrey, Derek
1972 *Police Power and Black People.* London: Panther.

Hunt, Chester L., and Walker, Lewis
1979 *Ethnic Dynamics: Patterns of Intergroup Relations and Various Societies.* 2nd ed. Holmes Beach, FL: Learning Publications.

Hunter, Herbert M., and Abraham, Sameer Y., eds.
1987 *Race, Class, and the World System: The Sociology of Oliver C. Cox.* New York: Monthly Review Press.

Hurh, Won Moo
1977a *Assimilation of the Korean Minority in the United States.* Philip Jaisohn Memorial Papers, No. 1. Elkins Park, PA: Philip Jaisohn Memorial Foundation.
1977b *Comparative Study of Korean Immigrants in the United States: A Typological Approach.* San Francisco: R & E Research Associates.
1990 The "1.5 Generation": A Paragon of Korean American Pluralism. *Korean Culture* 4 (Spring), pp. 21–31.

Hurh, Won Moo; Kim, Hei C.; and Kim, Kwang C.
1978 *Assimilation Patterns of Immigrants in the United States.* Washington, DC: University Press of America.

Hurh, Won Moo, and Kim, Kwang Chung.
1982 Race Relations Paradigms and Korean American Research: A Sociology of Knowledge Perspective. In E. Yu, E. Phillips, and E. Yang, eds., *Koreans in Los Angeles,* pp. 219–255. Los Angeles: Center for Korean American and Korean Studies, California State University.
1984 *Korean Immigrants in America: A Structural Analysis of Ethnic Confinement and Adhesive Adaptation.* Rutherford, NJ: Fairleigh Dickinson University Press.
1986 The Success Image of Asian Americans: Its Validity, Practical and Theoretical Implications. Paper presented at the annual meeting of American Sociological Association, New York City.
1987 *Korean Immigrants in the Chicago*
*Area: A Sociological Study of Migration and Mental Health.* Interim Report to the National Institute of Mental Health
1988 *Uprooting and Adjustment: A Sociological Study of Korean Immigrants' Mental Health.* Final Report submitted to the National Institute of Mental Health. Macomb: Western Illinois University.
1989 The "Success" Image of Asian Americans: Its Validity, and its Practical and Theoretical Implications. *Ethnic and Racial Studies* 12 (October), pp. 512–538.
1990a Adaptation Stages and Mental Health of Korean Male Immigrants in the United States. *International Migration Review* 24 (Fall), pp. 456–479.
1990b Religious Participation of Korean Immigrants in the United States. *Journal for the Scientific Study of Religion* 29 (No. 1), pp. 19–34.

Husar, Jack
1976 Wolf "War": Angry Indians as Recreation Booms. *Chicago Tribune* (July 15), pp. iv, 1, 4.

Hwang, David
1985 Are Movies Ready for Real Orientals? *New York Times* (August 11), pp. H1, H21.

Hyman, Herbert H., and Sheatsley, Paul B.
1964 Attitudes Toward Desegregation. *Scientific American* (July), pp. 16–23.

Hyman, Paula
1974 Is It Kosher to Be Feminist? *Ms.* 2 (July), pp. 76–79.

Ichioka, Yuji
1988 *The Issei.* New York: Free Press.

Ichiyama, Michael A.
1991 Anti-Asian Sentiment and Activities in the United States: Contributing Factors. Paper presented at the annual meeting of the American Psychological Association, San Francisco.

Ikels, Charlotte
1984 Natural Helpers and the Adaptation of Elderly Chinese Immigrants. Paper presented at the annual meeting of the Society for the Study of Social Problems, San An-

tonio.

Imhoff, Gary, ed.
1990    *Learning in Two Languages.* New Brunswick, NJ: Transaction.

Immigration and Naturalization Service
1982    *1979 Statistical Yearbook of the Immigration and Naturalization Service.* Washington, DC: U.S. Government Printing Office.

Inoue, Miyako
1989    Japanese-Americans in St. Louis: From Internees to Professionals. *City and Society* 3 (December), pp. 142–152.

Institute for Social Research
1984    *Working Female-Headed Families.* Ann Arbor, MI: Center for Political Studies, Institute for Social Research.

Irelan, Lola M.; Moles, Oliver C.; and O'Shea, Robert M.
1969    Ethnicity, Poverty, and Selected Attitudes: A Test of the "Culture of Poverty" Hypothesis. *Social Forces* 47 (June), pp. 405–413.

Iris, Mark
1983    American Urban Riots Revisited. *American Behavioral Scientist* 26 (January–February), pp. 333–352.

Irwin, Richard
1972    Changing Patterns of American Immigration. *International Migration Review* 6 (Spring), pp. 18–31.

Irwin, Victoria
1987    Puerto Ricans Register Voters to Gain Voice on Capitol Hill. *Christian Science Monitor* (June 10), p. 7.

Isaacs, Harold
1963    *The New World of Negro Americans.* London: Phoenix House.

Isikoff, Michael
1988    Bitterness on the "Taco Circuit." *Washington Post National Weekly Edition* 6 (November 21–27), p. 11.

Isonio, Stevan A., and T. Garza
1987    Protestant Work Ethic Endorsement Among Anglo Americans, Chicanos, and Mexicans: A Comparison of Factor Structures. *Hispanic Journal of Behavioral Sciences* 9 (December), pp. 414–425.

Jackson, James S., ed.
1991    *Life in Black America.* Newbury Park, CA: Sage.

Jacobs, Jerry A.
1990    *Revolving Doors: Sex Segregation in Women's Careers.* Palo Alto, CA: Stanford University Press.

Jacoby, Susan
1974    Miami si, Cuba no. *New York Times Magazine* (September 29), p. 28.

Jacquet, Constant H. J., Jr.
1990    *Yearbook of American and Canadian Churches.* Nashville: Abingdon Press.

Jaeger, Christopher
1987    *Minority and Low Income High Schools: Evidence of Educational Inequality in Metro Los Angeles.* Chicago: Metropolitan Opportunity Project.

Jarvenpa, Robert
1985    The Political Economy and Political Ethnicity of American Indian Adaptations and Identities. *Ethnic and Racial Studies* 8 (January), pp. 29–48.

Jaschik, Scott
1990    U.S. Accuses UCLA of Bias Against Asian Americans. *The Chronicle of Higher Education* 37 (October), pp. A1, A26.

Jeffery, Anthea J.
1991    *Mass Mobilisation.* Johannesburg: South African Institution of Race Relations.

Jennings, James, and Rivera, Monte, eds.
1984    *Puerto Rican Politics in Urban America.* Westport, CT: Greenwood Press.

Jiobu, Robert M.
1988    Ethnic Hegemony and the Japanese of California. *American Sociological Review* 53 (June), pp. 353–367.

Johnson, Charles S.
1923    How Much Is the Migration a Flight from Persecution? *Opportunity: A Journal of Negro Life* 1 (September), pp. 272–274.
1939    Race Relations and Social Change. In Edgar T. Thompson, ed., *Race Relations and the Race Problem,* pp. 217–303. Durham, NC: Duke University Press.

Johnson, George
1987 The Infamous "Protocols of Zion" Endures. *New York Times* (July 26), p. E6.

Johnson, Helen W.
1969 *Rural Indian Americans in Poverty: Agricultural Economics Report.* Washington, DC: U.S. Department of Agriculture.

Johnson, Julie
1988 Reagan Vetoes Bill That Would Widen Federal Rights Law. *New York Times* (March 17), pp. 1, 14.

Johnson, Sharen Shaw
1991 Arab-Americans See Gap in Cultural Understanding. *USA Today* (February 7), p. 8A.

Jolidon, Laurence
1991 Battle Builds over Indians' Fishing Rights. *USA Today* (March 21), pp. A1, A2.

Jones, Faustine C.
1981 External Crosscurrents and Internal Diversity: An Assessment of Black Progress, 1960–1980. *Daedalus* 110 (Spring), pp. 71–101.

Jones, James H.
1981 *Bad Blood: The Tuskegee Syphilis Experiment.* New York: Free Press.

Jones, James M.
1972 *Prejudice and Racism.* Reading, MA: Addison-Wesley.

Jones, Le Roi
1963 *Blues People: Negro Music in White America.* New York: William Morrow.

Jorgenson, Joseph G.; Clemmer, Richard O.; Little, Ronald L.; Owens, Nancy J.; and Robbins, Lynn A.
1978 *Native Americans and Energy Development.* Cambridge, MA: Anthropology Resource Center.

Josephy, Alvin M., Jr.
1971 *Red Power: The American Indians' Fight for Freedom.* New York: McGraw-Hall.

Juarez, Alberto
1972 The Emergence of El Partido de La Raza Unida: California's New Chicano Party. *Aztlan* 3 (Fall), pp. 177–204.

Kagan, Jerome
1971 The Magical Aura of the IQ. *Saturday Review of Literature* 4 (December 4), pp. 92–93.

Kagiwada, George, and Fujimoto, Isao
1973 Asian American Studies: Implications for Education. *Personnel and Guidance Journal* 51 (January), pp. 400–405.

Kallen, Horace M.
1915a Democracy Versus the Melting Pot. *The Nation* 100 (February 18), pp. 190–194.
1915b Democracy Versus the Melting Pot. *The Nation* 100 (February 25), pp,. 217–221.
1924 *Culture and Democracy in the United States.* New York: Boni and Liveright.

Kalmijn, Matthijs
1991 Shifting Boundaries: Trends in Religious and Educational Homogamy. *American Sociological Review* 56 (December), pp. 786–800.

Kanahele, George S.
1982 The New Hawaiians. *Social Process in Hawaii* 19, pp. 21–31.

Kanamine, Linda
1991 Native Americans: Health Care Now Broken. *USA Today* (November 12), p. 5A.

Kanter, Rosabeth Moss
1977 *Men and Women of the Corporation.* New York: Basic Books.

Kantrowitz, Barbara
1987 The December Dilemma. *Newsweek* 110 (December 28), p. 56.
1989 Advocating a "Mommy Track." *Newsweek* 103 (March 13), p. 45.
1991 Striking a Nerve. *Newsweek* 118 (October 21), pp. 34–40.

Kantrowitz, Nathan
1973 *Ethnic and Racial Segregation in the New York Metropolis: Residential Patterns among White Ethnic Groups, Blacks, and Puerto Ricans.* New York: Praeger.

Kardiner, Abram, and Ovesey, Lionel
1962 *The Mark of Oppression.* New York: Meridian.

Karlins, Marvin; Coffman, Thomas; and Walters, Gary
1969 On the Fading of Social Stereo-

types: Studies in Three Generations of College Students. *Journal of Personality and Social Psychology* 13 (Sept.), pp. 1–16.

Kaser, Tom
1977     Hawaii's Schools: An Ethnic Survey. *Integrated Education* 15 (May–June), pp. 31–36.

Kass, Drora, and Lipset, Seymour Martin
1980     America's New Wave of Jewish Immigrants. *New York Times Magazine* (December 7), pp. 44–45, 100, 102, 110, 112, 114, 116–118.

1982     Jewish Immigration to the United States from 1967 to the Present: Israelis and Others. In Marshall Sklare, ed., *Understanding American Jewry*, pp. 272–294. New Brunswick, NJ: Transaction Books.

Katz, David, and Braly, Kenneth W.
1933     Racial Stereotypes of One Hundred College Students. *Journal of Abnormal Sociology and Psychology* 28 (October–December), pp. 280–290.

Katz, Wilbur G., and Southerland, Harold P.
1967     Religious Pluralism and the Supreme Court. *Daedalus* 96 (Winter), pp. 180–192.

Kealoha, Gard
1976     Aloha Dina: Native Hawaiians Fight for Survival. *Civil Rights Digest* 9 (Fall 1975), pp. 152–157.

Keen, Judy
1986     4M Would Get Amnesty. *USA Today* (October 17), p. 5A.

Keene, Karlyn
1982     Snapshots: Japanese Internment. *Public Opinion* 4 (December–January), p. 47.

Keil, Charles
1966     *Urban Blues.* Chicago: University of Chicago Press.

Kelly, Dennis
1991     A Call for Better Native Education. *USA Today* (December 3), p. 4D.

Kelly, Gail P.
1986     Coping with America: Refugees from Vietnam, Cambodia, and Laos in the 1970's and 1980's. *Annals* 487 (September), pp. 138–149.

Kennedy, John F.
1964     *A Nation of Immigrants.* New York:
Harper and Row.

Kephart, William M., and Zellner, William
1991     *Extraordinary Groups: The Sociology of Unconventional Life-Styles,* 4th ed. New York: St. Martin's Press.

Kessler, Evelyn S.
1976     *Women: An Anthropological View.* New York: Holt, Rinehart and Winston.

Kessner, Thomas, and Caroli, Betty Boyd
1981     *Today's Immigrants, Their Stories.* New York: Oxford University Press.

Kikumura, Akemi, and Kitano, Harry H. L.
1973     Interracial Marriage: A Picture of the Japanese Americans. *Journal of Social Issues* 29 (no. 2), pp. 67–81.

Killian, Lewis M.
1975     *The Impossible Revolution, Phase 2: Black Power and the American Dream.* New York: Random House.

1982     The Perils of "Race" and "Racism" as Variables. *New Community* 9 (Winter/Spring), pp. 378–380.

Kim, Bok-lim C., and Condon, Margaret E.
1975     *A Study of Asian Americans in Chicago: Their Socio-economic Characteristics, Problems and Service Needs. An Interim Report.* Washington, DC: National Institute of Mental Health.

Kim, Hyung-chan
1980     Koreans. In Stephen Thernstrom, ed., *Harvard Encyclopedia of American Ethnic Groups,* pp. 601–606. Cambridge, MA: Belknap Press of Harvard University Pres.

Kim, Illsoo
1981     *New Urban Immigrants: The Korean Community in New York.* Princeton, NJ: Princeton University Press.

1988     A New Theoretical Perspective on Asian Enterprises. *Amerasia* 14 (Spring), pp. xi–xiii.

Kim, Kwang Chung, and Hurh, Won Moo
1983     Korean Americans and the Success Image: A Critique. *Amerasia* 10 (No. 2), pp. 3–21.

1984     The Wives of Korean Small Businessmen in the U.S.: Business Involvement and Family Roles. Paper presented at the annual meeting of American Sociological Association, San Antonio.

1985a Immigration Experiences of Korean Wives in the U.S.: The Burden of Double Roles. Paper presented at the annual meeting of National Council on Family Relations, Dallas.

1985b The Wives of Korean Small Businessmen in the U.S.: Business Involvement and Family Roles. In Inn Sook Lee, ed., *Korean-American Women: Toward Self-Realization*, pp. 1–41. Mansfield, OH: Association of Korean Christian Scholars in North America.

Kim, Kwang Chung; Hurh, Won Moo; and Fernandez, Marilyn
1988 An Exploratory Analysis of Business Participation of Three Asian Immigrant Groups. *P/AAMHRC Review* 6 (June), pp. 19–22.

Kimmel, Michael S.
1986 Profile Thomas Pettigrew: A Prejudice Against Prejudice. *Psychology Today* 20 (December), pp. 46–48, 50–52.

Kimura, Yukiko
1988 *Issei: Japanese Immigrants in Hawaii.* Honolulu: University of Hawaii Press.

King, Martin Luther, Jr.
1958 *Stride Toward Freedom: The Montgomery Story.* New York: Harper and Brothers.
1963 *Why We Can't Wait.* New York: Mentor.
1967 *Where Do We Go from Here: Chaos or Community?* New York: Harper and Row.
1971 I Have a Dream. In August Meier, Elliott Rudwick, and Francis L. Broderick, eds., *Black Protest Thought in the Twentieth Century*, pp. 346–351. Indianapolis: Bobbs-Merrill.

King, Patricia
1989 When Desegregation Backfires. *Newsweek* (July 31), p. 56.

King, Wayne
1981 Chávez Faces Internal and External Struggles. *New York Times* (December 6), pp. 1, 40.

Kinloch, Graham C.
1973 Race, Socioeconomic Status and So-cial Distance in Hawaii. *Sociology and Social Research* 57 (January), pp. 156–167.
1974 *The Dynamics of Race Relations: A Sociological Analysis.* New York: McGraw-Hill.

Kinloch, Graham C., and Borders, J.
1972 Racial Stereotypes and Social Distance Among Elementary School Children in Hawaii. *Sociology and Social Research* 56 (April), pp. 368–377.

Kirscht, John P., and Dillehay, Ronald C.
1967 *Dimensions of Authoritarianism: A Review of Research and Theory.* Lexington: University of Kentucky Press.

Kitagawa, Evelyn
1972 Socioeconomic Differences in the United States and Some Implications for Population Policy. In Charles F. Westoff and Robert Parke, Jr., eds., *Demographic and Social Aspects of Population Growth*, pp. 87–110. Washington, DC: U.S. Government Printing Office.

Kitano, Harry H. L.
1971 An Interview. In Amy Tachiki, Eddie Wong, Franklin Odo, and Buck Wong, eds., *Roots: An Asian American Reader*, pp. 83–88. Los Angeles: Asian American Studies Center, UCLA.
1974 Japanese Americans: A Middleman Minority. *Pacific Historical Review* 43 (November), pp. 500–519.
1976 *Japanese Americans: The Evolution of a Subculture*, 2nd ed. Englewood Cliffs, NJ: Prentice-Hall.
1980 Japanese. In Stephen Thernstrom, ed., *Harvard Encyclopedia of American Ethnic Groups.* Cambridge, MA: Belknap Press of Harvard University Press.
1991 *Race Relations*, 4th ed. Englewood Cliffs, NJ: Prentice-Hall.

Kitano, Harry H. L., and Daniels, Roger
1988 *Asian Americans: Emerging Minorities.* Englewood Cliffs, NJ: Prentice-Hall.

Kitano, Harry H. L., and Kikumura, Akemi
1976 The Japanese American Family. In Charles H. Mindel and Robert W.

Habenstein, eds., *Ethnic Families in America: Patterns and Variations*, pp. 41–60. New York: Elsevier.

Kitano, Harry H. L.; and Matsushima, Noreen
1981   Counseling Asian Americans. In P. Pederson, J. Draguns, W. Lonner, and J. Trimble, eds., *Counseling Across Cultures*, rev. ed., pp. 163–180. Honolulu: University of Hawaii Press.

Kitsuse, John I., and Broom, Leonard
1956   *The Managed Casualty: The Japanese American Family in World War II.* Berkeley: University of California Press.

Klausner, Samuel Z.
1988   Anti-Semitism in the Executive Suite: Yesterday, Today and Tomorrow. *Moment* 13 (September), pp. 32–39, 55.

Klein, Stephen P.; Turner, Susan; and Petersilia, Joan
1988   *Racial Equity in Sentencing.* Santa Monica, CA: Rand.

Kleinhuizen, Jeff
1991a   Traditions Guard Hispanic Babies' Health. *USA Today* (February 4), p. 4D.
1991b   Tribal Colleges Combine Academics and Heritage. *USA Today* (May 7), p. 4D.

Kleinman, Dena
1977   The Potential for Urban Terror is Always There. *New York Times* (March 13), p. E3.
1983   Less Than 40% of Jews in Survey Observe Sabbath. *New York Times* (February 6), pp. 1, 19.

Knight, Franklin W.
1974   *The African Dimension in Latin American Societies.* New York: Macmillan.

Knight, Jerry
1991   Coloring the Chances of Getting a Mortgage. *Washington Post National Weekly Edition* 8 (October 28), p. 26.

Knight, Robin
1985   Racial Rioting Tests Thatcher and Law Itself. *U.S. News and World Report* 99 (October 21), p. 31.

Knowles, Louis L., and Prewitt, Kenneth
1969   *Institutional Racism in America.* Englewood Cliffs, NJ: Prentice-Hall.

Knudson, Thomas J.
1987   Zoning the Reservations for Enterprise. *New York Times* (January 25), p. E4.

Komives, Valerie, and Goodel, Blanche
1971   Language Survey: The Peoples of Detroit Project. In Otto Reinstein, ed., *Ethnic Groups in the City*, pp. 367–375. Lexington, MA: Heath.

Kornblum, William
1991   Who is the Underclass? *Dissent* 38 (Spring), pp. 202–211.

Kosmin, Barry A.
1991   *The National Survey of Religious Identification.* New York: The City University of New York.

Kosmin, Barry A., et al.
1991   *Highlights of the CJF 1990 National Jewish Population Survey.* New York: Council of Jewish Federations.

Kramer, Roz
1981   The Great Abortion Battle of 1981. *Village Voice* 26 (March 11–17), pp. 1, 14–16.

Krausz, Ernest
1973   Israel's New Citizens. In *1973 Britannica Book of the Year*, pp. 385–387. Chicago: Encyclopedia Britannica.

Krickus, Richard
1976   *Pursuing the American Dream: White Ethnics and the New Populism.* Garden City, NY: Doubleday.

Krug, Mark M.
1974   The Defamation of American Poles. *University of Chicago Magazine* 66 (Summer), pp. 29–32.

Kuo, Wen H., and Lin, Nan
1977   Assimilation of Chinese-Americans in Washington, D.C. *Social Forces* 18 (Summer), pp. 340–351.

Kutner, Bernard; Wilkins, Carol; and Yarrow, P. R.
1952   Verbal Attitudes and Overt Behavior Involving Racial Prejudice. *Journal of Abnormal and Social Psychology* 47 (July), pp. 649–652.

Labor, Teresa, and Jacobs, Jerry A.
1986   Intermarriage in Hawaii, 1950–1983. *Journal of Marriage and the Family* 48 (February), pp. 79–88.

Lacayo, Richard
1986   Placing a Lock on the Borders. *Time* 128 (December 29), p. 68.
1988   A Surging New Spirit. *Time* 132 (July 11), pp. 46–49.

Lacy, Dan
1972   *The White Use of Blacks in America.* New York: McGraw-Hill.

Ladd, Everett Carll, Jr., and Lipset, Seymour Martin
1975   Faculty Women: Little Gain in Status. *Chronicle of Higher Education* 11 (September 29), p. 2.

Ladner, Joyce
1967   What "Black Power" Means to Negroes in Mississippi. *Transaction* 5 (November), pp. 6–15.
1971   *Tomorrow's Tomorrow: The Black Woman.* Garden City, NY: Doubleday.
1986   Black Women Face the 21st Century: Major Issues and Problems. *Black Scholar* (September–October), pp. 12–19.

LaDuke, Winona
1980   C.E.R.T.—An Outsider's View. *Akwesasne Notes* 12 (Late Summer), pp. 19–23.

Lai, H. M.
1980   Chinese. In Stephen Thernstrom, ed., *Harvard Encyclopedia of American Ethnic Groups,* pp. 222–234. Cambridge, MA: Belknap Press of Harvard University Press.

Lambert, John, ed.
1974   Police and Community Relations. *New Community* 3 (Summer), entire issue.

Landry, Bart
1987   *The New Black Middle Class.* Berkeley: University of California Press.

Langdon, Steve J.
1982   Alaskan Native Land Claims and Limited Entry: The Dawes Act Revisited. Paper presented at the annual meeting of American Anthropology Association, Washington, DC.

Langer, Elinor
1976   Why Big Business Is Trying to Defeat the ERA. *Ms.* 4 (May), p. 64.

Langway, Lynn

1981   Women and the Executive Suite. *Time* (September 14), pp. 65–67.

LaPiere, Richard T.
1934   Attitudes vs. Actions. *Social Forces* 13 (October), pp. 230–237.
1969   Comment on Irwin Deutscher's Looking Backward. *American Sociologist* 4 (February), pp. 41–42.

Larrabee, John
1991   Connecticut Tribe Is on a Roll: *USA Today* (May 9), p. 9A.

Laumann, Edward O.
1969   The Social Structure of Religious and Ethnoreligious Groups in a Metropolitan Community. *American Sociological Review* 34 (April), pp. 182–197.

Laurenti, Luigi
1960   *Property Values and Race: Studies in Cities.* Berkeley: University of California Press.

Lavender, Abraham D., ed.
1977   *A Coat of Many Colors: Jewish Subcommunities in the United States.* Westport, CT: Greenwood Press.

Lawlor, Julia
1987   Bilingual Ed: The Word is Legislation. *USA Today* (April 21), A1, A2.

Lawson, Paul E., and C. Patrick Morris
1991   The Native American Church and the New Court: The "Smith" Case and Indian Religious Freedoms. *American Indian Culture and Research Journal* 15 (No. 1), pp. 79–91.

Lazarus, Edward
1991   *Black Hills White Justice.* New York: HarperCollins.

Lazerwitz, Bernard
1983   Correspondence to Richard T. Schaefer. Unpublished data from National Jewish Survey.

Lazerwitz, Bernard, and Harrison, Michael
1979   American Jewish Denominations: A Social and Religious Profile. *American Sociological Review* 44 (August), pp. 656–666.

Lazerwitz, Bernard, and Rowitz, Louis
1964   The Three-Generations Hypothesis. *American Journal of Sociology* 69 (March), pp. 529–538.

Leatherman, Courtney
1990   More Anti-Semitism is Being Re-

ported on Campuses, but Educators Disagree on How to Respond to It. *Chronicle of Higher Education* 36 (February 7), pp. A1, A40.

Lederman, Douglas
1992 Men Get 70% of Money Available for Athletic Scholarships at Colleges that Play Big-Time Sports, New Study Finds. *Chronicle of Higher Education* 38 (March 18), pp. A1, A45, A46.

Lee, Alfred McClung
1983 *Terrorism in Northern Ireland.* Bayside, NY: General Hall.

Lee, Calvin
1965 *Chinatown, U.S.A.* Garden City, NY: Doubleday.

Lee, Don
1992 A Sense of Identity. *Kansas City Star* (April 4), pp. E1, E7.

Lee, Felicia R.
1991 "Model Minority" Label Taxes Asian Youths. *New York Times* (March 30), pp. B1, B4.

Lee, Rose Hum
1960 *The Chinese in the United States of America.* Hong Kong: Hong Kong University Press.

Leebaw, Milton, and Heyman, Harriet
1976 Puerto Rico and Economics, *New York Times* (October 17), p. E5.

Legum, Colin
1967 Color and Power in the South African Situation. *Daedalus* 96 (Spring), pp. 483–495.

Lehman, Edward C., Jr.
1985 *Women Clergy: Breaking Through Gender Barriers.* New Brunswick, NJ: Transaction Books.

Lem, Kim
1976 Asian American Employment. *Civil Rights Digest* 9 (Fall), pp. 12–21.

Lemann, Nicholas
1986a The Origins of the Underclass. *The Atlantic Monthly* 258 (June), pp. 31–43, 47–55.

1986b The Origins of the Underclass. *The Atlantic Monthly* 258 (July), pp. 54–68.

1991 The Other Underclass. *The Atlantic Monthly* 286 (December), pp. 96–102, 104, 107–108, 110.

LeMoyne, James
1990 Most Who Left Mariel Sailed to New Life, a Few to Limbo. *New York Times* (April 15), pp. 1, 12.

Lenski, Gerhard
1961 *The Religious Factor.* Garden City, NY: Doubleday.

Lerner, Gerda, ed.
1972 *Black Women in White America: A Documentary History.* New York: Pantheon.

Lerner, Michael
1969 Respectable Bigotry. *American Scholar* 38 (August), pp. 606–617.

Lesch, Ann M.
1983 Palestine: Land and People. In Naseer H. Aruri, ed., *Occupation: Israel Over Palestine,* pp. 29–54. Belmont, MA: Association of Arab-American University Graduates.

Leslie, Connie
1991 Classrooms of Babel. *Newsweek* 117 (February 11), pp. 56–57.

Leslie, Gerald
1982 *The Family in Social Context,* 5th ed. New York: Oxford University Press.

Levin, Jack, and Levin, William C.
1982 *The Functions of Prejudice,* 2nd ed. New York: Harper and Row.

Levine, Gene N., and Montero, Darrel M.
1973 Socioeconomic Mobility Among Three Generations of Japanese Americans. *Journal of Social Issues* 29 (No. 2), pp. 33–48.

Levine, Gene N., and Rhodes, Colbert
1981 *The Japanese American Community.* New York: Praeger.

Levine, Irving M., and Herman, Judith
1972 The Life of White Ethnics. *Dissent* 19 (Winter), pp. 286–294.

Levine, Naomi, and Hochbaum, Martin, eds.
1974 *Poor Jews: An American Awakening.* New Brunswick, NJ: Transaction Books.

Levy, Jacques E.
1975 *César Chávez: Autobiography of La Causa.* New York: Norton.

Levy, Mark P., and Kramer, Michael
1972 *The Ethnic Factor: How America's Minorities Decide Elections.* New York: Simon and Schuster.

Lewin, Tamar
  1989   Pay Equity for Women's Jobs Finds
         Success Outside Courts. *New York
         Times* (October 7), pp. 1, 8.

Lewinson, Paul
  1965   *Race, Class, and Party: A History of
         Negro Suffrage and White Politics in
         the South.* New York: Universal Li-
         brary.

Lewis, Diane K.
  1977   A Response to Inequality: Black
         Women, Racism, and Sexism. *Signs*
         3 (Winter), pp. 339–361.

Lewis, Oscar
  1959   *Five Families: Mexican Case Studies in
         the Culture of Poverty.* New York:
         Basic Books.
  1965   *La Vida: A Puerto Rican Family in the
         Culture of Poverty—San Juan and
         New York.* New York: Random
         House.
  1966   The Culture of Poverty. *Scientific
         American* (October), pp. 19–25.

Li, Wen Lang
  1976   Chinese Americans: Exclusion from
         the Melting Pot. In Anthony and
         Rosalind Dworkin, eds., *Minority
         Report,* pp. 297–324. New York:
         Praeger.
  1982   Chinese Americans: Exclusion from
         the Melting Pot. In Anthony and
         Rosalind Dworkin, eds., *Minority
         Report,* 2nd ed., pp. 303–328. New
         York: Holt, Rinehart and Winston.

Lichtenstein, Eugene, and Denenberg, R. V.
  1975   The Army's Ethnic Policy. *New
         York Times* (July 20), p. E2.

Lichtenstein, Grace
  1981   The Wooing of Women Athletes.
         *New York Times Magazine* (February
         8), pp. 24, 30, 33, 50, 52, 54–55.

Lichter, Linda S.
  1985   Who Speaks for Black America.
         *Public Opinion* 8 (August–
         September), pp. 41–44, 58.

Lichter, S. Robert, and Lichter, Linda S.
  1988   *Television's Impact in Ethnic and Ra-
         cial Images.* New York: American
         Jewish Committee.

Lieberson, Stanley
  1962   Suburbs and Ethnic Residential Pat-
         terns. *American Journal of Sociology*
         67 (May), pp. 673–681.

  1963   *Ethnic Patterns in American Cities.*
         Glencoe, IL: Free Press.
  1982   Stereotypes: Their Consequences
         for Race and Ethnic Interaction. In
         Robert M. Hauser, et al., eds. *Social
         Structure and Behavior Essays in
         Honor of William Hamilton Sewell.*
         New York: Academic Press.

Liebman, Charles S.
  1973   *The Ambivalent American Jew.* Phil-
         adelphia: Jewish Publication Soci-
         ety of America.

Liebman, Charles S., and Cohen, Steven M.
  1990   *Two Worlds of Judaism: The Israeli
         and American Experience.* New Ha-
         ven: Yale University Press.

Liebow, Elliot
  1967   *Tally's Corner: A Study of Negro
         Streetcorner Men.* Boston: Little,
         Brown.

Light, Ivan H.
  1973   *Ethnic Enterprise in America: Busi-
         ness and Welfare Among Chinese, Jap-
         anese, and Blacks.* Berkeley: Uni-
         versity of California Press.
  1974   From Vice District to Tourist At-
         traction: The Moral Career of
         American Chinatowns. 1880–1940.
         *Pacific Historical Review* 43 (August),
         pp. 367–394.

Light, Ivan H., and Bonacich, Edna
  1988   *Immigrant Entrepreneurs: Koreans in
         Los Angeles 1965–1982.* Berkeley:
         University of California Press.

Light, Ivan H., and Wong, Charles Choy
  1975   Protest or Work: Dilemmas of the
         Tourist Industry in American Chi-
         natowns. *American Journal of Sociol-
         ogy* 80 (May), pp. 1342–1368.

Lincoln, C. Eric, and Mamiya, Lawrence H.
  1990   *The Black Church in the African
         American Experience.* Durham, NC:
         Duke University Press.

Lind, Andrew W.
  1946   *Hawaii's Japanese: An Experiment in
         Democracy.* Princeton, NJ: Princeton
         University Press.
  1969   *Hawaii: The Last of the Magic Isles.*
         London: Oxford University Press.

Lindsey, Robert
  1978   Latinos Have Numbers But Not Yet
         the Voters. *New York Times* (June 4),
         p. E5.

1979 Unions Move to Organize Illegal Aliens in the West. *New York Times* (June 3), pp. 1, 42.

1984 Glory Days Are Fading for Chávez and V.F.W. *New York Times* (December 23), p. E4.

1985 Signs of Old Japanese Crime Group Are Seen in U.S. *New York Times* (January 24), p. A16.

1986 In U.S., a Debate on Language. *International Herald Tribune* (July 22), p. 1.

1987 Colleges Accused of Bias to Stem Asians' Gains. *New York Times* (January 19), p. A10.

Lippmann, Walter
1922 *Public Opinion.* New York: Macmillan.

Lipset, Seymour Martin
1987 Blacks and Jews: How Much Bias? *Public Opinion* 10 (July/August), pp. 4–5, 57–58.

Lipsey, David
1981 What Should We Do About Northern Ireland? *New Society* (September 24), pp. 508–511.

Little, Alan, and Kohler, David
1947 *Negroes in Britain: A Study of Racial Relations in English Society.* London: Kegan Paul, Trench, Trubner and Co.

1977 Do We Hate Blacks? *New Society* 34 (January 27), pp. 184–185.

Lloyd, Sterling, and Miller, Russell L.
1989 Black Student Enrollment in U.S. Medical Schools. *Journal of the American Medical Association* 261 (January 13), pp. 272–274.

Loehlin, John C.; Lindzey, Gardner; and Spuhler, J. N.
1975 *Race Differences in Intelligence.* San Francisco: W. H. Freeman.

Logan, Rayford W.
1954 *The Negro in American Life and Thought: The Nadir, 1877–1901.* New York: Dial Press.

Lomax, Louis E.
1971 *The Negro Revolt,* rev. ed. New York: Harper and Row.

López-Rivera, Oscar, with Headley, Bernard
1989 Who is the Terrorist? The Making of a Puerto Rican Freedom Fighter. *Social Justice* 16 (Winter), pp. 162–

174.

Louw-Potgieter, J.
1988 The Authoritarian Personality: An Inadequate Explanation for Intergroup Conflict in South Africa. *Journal of Social Psychology* 128 (February), pp. 75–88.

Luce, Clare Booth
1975 Refugees and Guilt. *New York Times* (May 11), p. E19.

Luebben, Ralph A.
1964 Prejudice and Discrimination Against Navahos in a Mining Community. *The Kiva* 30 (October), pp. 1–17.

Lum, Joann, and Kwong, Peter
1989 Surviving in America: The Trials of a Chinese Immigrant Woman. *Village Voice* 34 (October 31), pp. 39–41.

Lurie, Nancy Oestreich
1971 The Contemporary American Indian Scene. In Eleanor Burke Leacock and Nancy Oestreich Lurie, eds., *North American Indians in Historical Perspective,* pp. 418–480. New York: Random House.

Lyman, Stanford M.
1973 *The Black American in Sociological Thought: New Perspectives on Black America.* New York: Capricorn Books.

1974 *Chinese Americans.* New York: Random House.

1986 *Chinatown and Little Tokyo.* Milwood, NY: Associated Faculty Press.

McBee, Susanna
1984 Are They Making the Grade? *U.S. News and World Report* 96 (April 2), pp. 41–43, 46–47.

McCarty, Teresa L.
1987 The Rough Rock Demonstration School—A Case History with Implications for Educational Evaluation. *Human Organization* 46 (Summer), pp. 103–113.

McCord, Colin, and Harold P. Freeman
1990 Excess Mortality in Harlem. *New England Journal of Medicine* 322 (January 18), pp. 173–177.

McCully, Bruce T.

1940   *English Education and Origins of In-dian Nationalism.* New York: Columbia University Press.

McCunn, Ruthanne Lum
1988   *Chinese American Portraits.* San Francisco: Chronicle Books.

McFadden, Robert D.
1983   F.A.L.N. Puerto Rican Terrorists Suspected in New Year Bombings. *New York Times* (January 2), pp. 1, 17.

McFate, Katherine
1987   Defining the Underclass. *Focus* 15 (June), pp. 8–12.

McGee, Kevin T.
1991   Casino Gives Minnesota Take a Needed Boost. *USA Today* (August 15), p. 6A.

McGregor-Alegado, Davianna
1980   Hawaiians: Organizing in the 1970s. *Amerasia* 7 (Fall/Winter), pp. 29–55.

Macias, Reynaldo Flores
1973   Developing a Bilingual Culturally-Relevant Educational Program For Chicanos. *Aztlan* 4 (Spring), pp. 61–77.

McIntosh, Shawn
1992   Survey of Those Arrested in the Riots. *USA Today* (May 11), p. 7A.

Mack, Raymond W.
1968   *Race, Class, and Power,* 2nd ed. New York: Van Nostrand.

Mackey, Wade C.
1987   A Cross-Cultural Perspective on Perceptions of Paternalistic Deficiencies in the United States: The Myth of the Derelict Daddy. *Sex Roles,* 12 (March), pp. 509–534.

MacKinnon, Catharine A.
1979   *Sexual Harassment of Working Women: A Case of Sex Discrimination.* New Haven: Yale University Press.

McLeod, Beverly
1986   The Oriental Express. *Psychology Today* 20 (July), pp. 48–52.

McManus, Ed
1985   The Death Penalty and the Race Factor. *Illinois Issues* 11 (March), p. 47.

McMillen, Liz
1991   American Indian College Fund Seeks Recognition and $10 Million for Tribal Institutions. *Chronicle of Higher Education* (May 1), p. A25.

McMillen, Neil R.
1971   *The Citizen's Council: Organized Resistance to the Second Reconstruction, 1954–1964.* Urbana: University of Illinois Press.

MacMurray, Val Dan, and Cummingham, Perry H.
1973   Mormons and Gentiles: A Study in Conflict and Persistence. In Donald E. Gelfand and Russell D. Lee, eds., *Ethnic Conflicts and Power: A Cross-Nation Perspective,* pp. 205–218. New York: Wiley.

McNamara, Patrick H.
1973   Catholicism, Assimilation, and the Chicano Movement: Los Angeles as a Case Study. In Rudolph O. de la Garza, A. Anthony Kruszewski, and Tomás Arciniega, eds., *Chicanos and Native Americans: The Territorial Minorities,* pp. 124–130. Englewood Cliffs, NJ: Prentice-Hall.

McNickle, D'Arcy
1973   *Native American Tribalism: Indian Survivals and Renewals.* New York: Oxford University Press.

McPhail, Thomas .
1981   *Electronic Colonialism: The Future of International Broadcasting and Communication.* Beverly Hills, CA: Sage.

McWilliams, Carey
1968   *North From Mexico: The Spanish-Speaking People of the United States.* New York: Greenwood Press.

Maeroff, Gene I.
1974   White Ethnic Groups in Nation Are Encouraging Heritage Programs in a Trend Toward Self-Awareness. *New York Times* (January 28), p. 11.

Maguire, Brendan, and Wozniak, John
1987   Racial and Ethnic Stereotypes in Professional Wrestling. *Social Science Journal* 24 (3), pp. 261–273.

Majka, Linda C.
1981   Labor Militancy Among Farm Workers and the Strategy of Protest: 1900–1979. *Social Problems* 28 (June), pp. 533–547.

Malcolm X

1964    *The Autobiography of Malcolm X.*
        New York: Grove Press.

Maldonado, Lionel, and Moore, Joan
1985    *Urban Ethnicity in the United States.*
        Beverly Hills, CA: Sage Publica-
        tions.

Maldonado-Denis, Manuel
1972    *Puerto Rico: A Socio-Historic Inter-
        pretation.* New York: Random
        House.
1980    *The Emigration Dialectic: Puerto Rico
        and the USA.* New York: Interna-
        tional Publishers.

Mallinckrodt, Brent
1988    Student Retention, Social Support,
        and Dropout Intention: Compa-
        rison of Black and White Students.
        *Journal of College Student Develop-
        ment* 29 (January), pp. 60–64.

Manigan, Katherine S.
1991    Mexican Students, Including Com-
        muters, Succeed at Texas Univer-
        sities. *Chronicle of Higher Education*
        38 (February 26), pp. A36–A37.

Mann, James
1983    One-Parent Family: The Troubles—
        And the Joys. *U.S. News and World
        Report* 95 (November 28), pp. 57–58,
        62.

Marable, Manning
1985    *Black American Politics: From the
        Washington Marches to Jesse Jackson.*
        London: Verso.

Marden, Charles F., and Meyer, Gladys
1978    *Minorities in American Society,* 5th
        ed. New York: Van Nostrand.

Marger, Martin
1978    A Reexamination of Gorden's Eth-
        class. *Sociological Focus* 11 (January),
        pp. 21–32.
1985    *Race and Ethnic Relations: American
        and Global Perspectives.* Belmont,
        CA: Wadsworth.

Margolis, Richard J.
1970    White Washing the Indians. *New
        Leader* 53 (December 28), pp. 13–14.
1972    Lost Chance for Desegregation. *Dis-
        sent* 19 (Spring), pp. 249–256.

Marini, Margaret Mooney
1989    Sex Differences in Earnings in the
        United States. In W. Richard Scott
        and Judith Plake, eds., *Annual Re-*

*view of Sociology, 1989,* pp. 343–380.
Palo Alto, CA: Annual Review of
Sociology.

Markham, James M.
1986    Bonn Takes Steps Against Ref-
        ugees. *New York Times* (August 28),
        p. A7.

Marquez, Benjamin
1987    The Politics of Race and Class: The
        League of United Latin American
        Citizens in the Post-World II Per-
        iod. *Social Science Quarterly* 68
        (March), pp. 84–101.

Marshall, Thurgood
1957    The Rise and Collapse of the
        "White Democratic Primary." *Jour-
        nal of Negro Education* 26 (Summer),
        pp. 249–254.

Martin, Douglas
1987    Indians Seek A New Life in New
        York. *New York Times* (March 22),
        p. 17.

Martin, M. Kay, and Voorhies, Barbara
1975    *Female of the Species.* New York:
        Columbia University Press.

Martinez, Angel R.
1988    The Effects of Acculturation and
        Racial Identity on Self-Esteem and
        Psychological Well-Being Among
        Young Puerto Ricans. Unpublished
        dissertation. City University of
        New York.

Martinez, Estella A.
1988    Child Behavior in Mexican Amer-
        ican/Chicano Families: Maternal
        Teaching and Child-Rearing Prac-
        tices. *Family Relations* 37 (July), pp.
        275–280.

Martinez, Rubén, and Dukes, Richard L.
1991    Ethnic and Gender Differences in
        Self-Esteem. *Youth and Society* 32
        (March), pp. 318–338.

Martinez, Thomas M.
1973    Advertising and Racism: The Case
        of the Mexican-American. In O. I.
        Romano, ed., *Voices: Readings from
        El Grito,* rev. ed., pp. 521–531.
        Berkeley, CA: Quinto Sol Publica-
        tions.

Martinez, Vilma S.
1976    Illegal Immigration and the Labor
        Force. *American Behavioral Scientist*

19 (January–February), pp. 335–350.

Marty, Martin E.
1976 *A Nation of Behavers.* Chicago: University of Chicago Press.
1983 Introduction to *Protestant–Catholic–Jew* by Will Herberg. Chicago: University of Chicago Press.
1985 Transpositions: American Religion in the 1980s. *Annals* 480 (July), pp. 11–23.
1992 Jewish-Christian Relations: An Update. In *Encyclopedia Britannica Book of the Year, 1992,* pp. 261–262. Chicago: Encyclopedia Britannica.

Marx, Gary T.
1969 *Protest and Prejudice: A Study of Belief in the Black Community.* New York: Harper and Row.

Marx, Karl, and Engels, Frederick
1955 *Selected Words in Two Volumes.* Moscow: Foreign Languages Publishing House.

Mason, Philip
1970a *Patterns of Dominance.* London: Oxford University Press.
1970b *Race Relations.* London: Oxford University Press.

Massey, Douglas S.
1986 The Social Organization of Mexican Migration to the United States. *Annals* No. 487 (September), pp. 102–113.

Massey, Douglas S., and Bitterman, Brooks
1985 Explaining the Paradox of Puerto Rican Segregation. *Social Forces* 64 (December), pp. 306–331.

Massey, Douglas S.; Condran, Gretchen A.; and Denton, Nancy A.
1987 The Effect of Residential Segregation on Black Social and Economic Well-Being. *Social Forces,* 66 (September), pp. 29–56.

Massey, Douglas S., and Denton, Nancy A.
1988 Suburbanization and Segregation in U.S. Metropolitan Areas. *American Journal of Sociology* 94 (November), pp. 592–626.
1989 Hypersegregation in U.S. Metropolitan Areas: Black and Hispanic Segregation Along Five Dimensions. *Demography* 26 (August), pp. 373–391.

Massey, Douglas S., et al.

1987 *Return to Aztlan.* Berkeley: University of California Press.

Masters, Stanley H.
1975 *Black-White Income Differentials.* New York: Academic Press.

Mathews, Jay, and John, Kenneth E.
1986 Jackson Is the Voice of Blacks. *The Washington Post National Weekly Edition* 3 (January 6), p. 37.

Mathews, Tom
1990 The Long Shadow. *Newsweek* 115 (May 7), pp. 34–44.

Mathisen, James A.
1989 Twenty Years After Bellah: Whatever Happened to American Civil Rights? *Sociological Analysis* 50 (Summer), pp. 129–146.

Matthiessen, Peter
1983 *In the Spirit of Crazy Horse.* New York: Viking Press.

Matza, David
1964 *Delinquency and Drift.* New York: Wiley.
1971 Poverty and Disrepute. In Robert K. Merton and Robert Nisbet, eds., *Contemporary Social Problems,* 3rd ed., pp. 601–656. New York: Harcourt, Brace and World.

Maxwell, Neil
1980 Civil Rights Groups Face Tough Challenge in Bid to Regain Power. *Wall Street Journal* (September 19), pp. 1, 17.

Mayer, Egon
1983 *Children of Intermarriage.* New York: American Jewish Committee.

Maykovich, Minako Kurokawa
1972a *Japanese American Identity Dilemma.* Tokyo: Waseda University Press.
1972b Reciprocity in Racial Stereotypes: White, Black and Yellow. *American Journal of Sociology* 77 (March), pp. 876–877.
1973 Political Activation of Japanese American Youth. *Journal of Social Issues* 29 (No. 2), pp. 167–185.
1974 Yellow Power in the U.S. *New Society* 28 (April 18), pp. 125–128.

Medicine, Beatrice
1973 The Native American. In Don Spiegel and Patricia Keith-Spiegel, eds., *Outsiders USA,* pp. 391–407. San

Francisco: Rinehart Press.

Meier, August
1957 Toward a Reinterpretation of Booker T. Washington. *Journal of Southern History* 23 (May), pp. 220–227.

Meier, August, and Rudwick, Elliott
1966 *From Plantation to Ghetto: An Interpretive History of American Negroes.* New York: Hill and Wang.

Meier, Matt S., and Rivera, Feliciano
1972 *The Chicanos: A History of Mexican Americans.* New York: Hill and Wang.

Melendy, Howard Brett
1972 *The Oriental Americans.* New York: Hippocreme.
1980 Filipinos. In Stephen Thernstorm, ed., *Harvard Encyclopedia of American Ethnic Groups,* pp. 354–362. Cambridge, MA: Belknap Press of Harvard University Press.

Memmi, Albert
1967 *The Colonizer and the Colonized.* Boston: Beacon Press.

Mencarelli, James, and Severin, Steve
1975 *Protest 3: Red, Black, Brown Experience in America.* Grand Rapids, MI: Wm. B. Eerdmans.

Mendoza, Fernando S., et al.
1991 Selected Measures of Health Status for Mexican-American, Mainland Puerto Rican, and Cuban-American Children. *Journal of the American Medical Association* 265 (January 9), pp. 227–232.

Merton, Robert K.
1949 Discrimination and the American Creed. In Robert M. MacIver, ed., *Discrimination and National Welfare,* pp. 99–126. New York: Harper and Row.
1968 *Social Theory and Social Structure.* New York: Free Press.
1976 *Sociological Ambivalence and Other Essays.* New York: Free Press.

Merton, Robert K., and Kitt, Alice S.
1950 Contributions of the Theory of Reference Group Behavior. In Robert K. Merton and Paul F. Lazerfeld, eds., *Continuities in Social Research: Studies in the Scope and Method of "The American Soldier,"* pp. 40–105. New York: Free Press.

Metzger, L. Paul
1971 American Sociology and Black Assimilation: Conflicting Perspectives. *American Journal of Sociology* 76 (January 1971), pp. 627–647.

Meyers, Gustavus
1943 *History of Bigotry in the United States.* Rev. by Henry M. Christman, 1960. New York: Capricorn Books.

Michalek, Laurence
1989 The Arab Image in American Film and Television. *Cineast* 17 (No. 1), pp. 3–9.

Middleton, Russell
1960 Ethnic Prejudice and Susceptibility to Persuasion. *American Sociological Review* 25 (October), pp. 679–686.
1976 Regional Differences in Prejudice. *American Sociological Review* 41 (February), pp. 94–117.

Miller, Annette
1991 Mommy Tracks. *Newsweek* 118 (November 25), pp. 48–49.

Miller, Arthur G., ed.
1982 *In the Eye of the Beholder: Contemporary Issues in Stereotyping.* New York: Praeger.

Miller, Joanne, and Garrison, Howard H.
1982 Sex Roles: The Division of Labor at Home and in the Workplace. In Ralph Turner, ed., *Annual Review of Sociology, 1982,* pp. 237–262. Palo Alto, CA: Annual Reviews.

Miller, Kelly
1903 Washington Policy. In August Meier and Elliott Rudwick, eds., *The Making of Black America,* vol. 2, pp. 119–124. New York: Atheneum, 1969.

Miller, Margaret I., and Linker, Helene
1974 Equal Rights Amendment Campaigns in California and Utah. *Society* 11 (May–June), pp. 40–53.

Miller, Norman
1987 Hazards in the Translocation of Research into Remedial Interventions. *Journal of Social Issues* 43 (1), pp. 119–126.

Miller, Randall M., ed.
1980 *The Kaleidoscopic Lens: How Hollywood Views Ethnic Groups.* Engle-

wood, NJ: Jerome S. Ozer.

Miller, Robert Stevens, Jr.
1967   Sex Discrimination and Title VII of the Civil Rights Act of 1964. *Minnesota Law Review* 51 (April), pp. 877–897.

Miller, Stuart Creighton
1969   *The Unwelcome Immigrant: The American Image of the Chinese, 1785–1882.* Berkeley: University of California Press.

Miller, Walter
1977   The Rumble This time. *Psychology Today* 10 (May), pp. 52–59, 88.

Mills, C. Wright
1943   The Sailor, Sex Market and Mexican: The New American Jitters. *The New Leader* (June 26), pp. 5–7.

Mills, C. Wright; Senior, Clarence; and Goldsen, Rose Kohn
1950   *The Puerto Rican Journey: New York's Newest Migrants.* New York: Harper and Row.

Min, Pyong Gap
1987   Filipino and Korean Immigrants in Small Business: A Comparative Analysis. *Amerasia* 13 (Spring), pp. 53–71.

Mincy, Ronald B.; Sawhill, Isabel; and Wolf, Douglas A.
1990   The Underclass: Definition and Measurement. *Science* 248 (April 27), pp. 405–453.

Mindel, Charles H.; Habenstein, Robert W.; and Wright, Roosevelt, Jr., eds.
1988   *Ethnic Families in America: Patterns and Variations.* 3rd ed. New York: Elsevier.

Mineta, Norman
1991   Pearl Harbor and Japanese Americans. *Asian Week* 13 (December 6), p. 14.

Miracle, Andrew W., Jr.
1981   Factors Affecting Interracial Cooperation: A Case Study of a High School Football Team. *Human Organization* 40 (No. 2), pp. 150–154.

Miranda, Lourdes
1974   Puertorriqueñas in the United States: The Impact of Double Discrimination. *Civil Rights Digest* 6 (Spring), pp. 20–27.

Mirandé, Alfredo
1985   *The Chicano Experience: An Alternative Perspective.* Notre Dame, IN: University of Notre Dame Press.

Miyamoto, S. Frank
1973   The Forced Evacuation of the Japanese Minority During World War II. *Journal of Social Issues* 29 (No. 2), pp. 11–31.

Mizio, Emelica
1972   Puerto Rican Social Workers and Racism. *Social Casework* 53 (May), pp. 267–272.

Model, Suzanne
1992   The Ethnic Economy: Cubans and Chinese Remembered. *Sociological Quarterly* 33 (No. 1), pp. 63–82.

Mohl, Raymond A.
1986   The Politics of Ethnicity in Contemporary Miami. *Migration World* 14 (No. 3), pp. 7–11.

Molotch, Harvey L.
1972   *Managed Integration: Dilemmas of Doing Good in the City.* Berkeley: University of California Press.

Monroe, Sylvester
1988   Behavior in Britain: Grim Lives, Grimmer Prospects. *Newsweek* 111 (January 4), pp. 32–33.

Montagu, Ashley
1972   *Statement on Race.* New York: Oxford University Press.

Montagu, Ashley, ed.
1975   *Race and IQ.* London: Oxford University Press.

Montero, Darrel M.
1973   Assimilation and Educational Achievement: The Case of the Second Generation Japanese American. Paper presented at the annual meeting of the American Sociological Association, New York.

1977   The Japanese American Community: A Study of Generational Changes in Ethnic Affiliation. Paper presented at the annual meeting of the American Sociological Association, Chicago.

1981   The Japanese Americans: Changing Patterns of Assimilation Over Three Generations. *American Sociological Review* 46 (December), pp. 829–839.

Montgomery, Paul L.
1974   Asians Picket Building Site, Charg-
       ing Bias. *New York Times* (June 1),
       p. 33.
Moore, Helen A., and Iadicola, Peter
1981   Resegregation Processes in Deseg-
       regated Schools and Status Rela-
       tionships For Hispanic Students.
       *Aztlan* 12 (September), pp. 39–58.
Moore, Joan W.
1970   Colonialism: The Case of the Mex-
       ican Americans. *Social Problems* 17
       (Spring), pp. 463–472.
1989   Is There a Hispanic Underclass? *So-
       cial Science Quarterly* 70 (June), pp.
       265–284.
Moore, Joan W., and Pachon, Harry
1976   *Mexican Americans*, 2nd ed. Engle-
       wood Cliffs, NJ: Prentice-Hall.
1985   *Hispanics in the United States*. Engle-
       wood Cliffs, NJ: Prentice-Hall.
Moquin, Wayne, and Van Doren, Charles,
eds.
1971   *A Documentary History of the Mex-
       ican Americans*. New York: Praeger.
Morales, Royal F.
1976   Philipino Americans: From Colony
       to Immigrant to Citizen. *Civil Rights
       Digest* 9 (Fall), pp. 30–32.
Morgan, Joan
1991   All-Black Male Classrooms Run
       into Resistance. *Black Issues in High-
       er Education* 7 (January 17), pp. 1,
       21–22.
Morgan, Richard E.
1974   The Establishment Clause and Sec-
       tarian Schools: A Final Installment.
       In Philip B. Kurland, ed., *1973, The
       Supreme Court Review*, pp. 57–97.
       Chicago: University of Chicago
       Press.
Morin, Richard
1983   What Miami Thinks. *Miami Herald*
       (December 18), pp. 7M–8M.
Morley, Morris
1974   Dependence and Development in
       Puerto Rico. In Adalberto Lopez
       and James Petra, eds., *Puerto Rico
       and Puerto Ricans: Studies in History
       and Society*, pp. 214–254. New York:
       Wiley.
Morris, Aldon

1984   *The Origins of the Civil Rights Move-
       ment: Black Communities Organizing
       for Change*. New York: Free Press.
Morris, Michael
1989   From the Culture of Poverty to the
       Underclass: An Analysis of a Shift
       in Public Language. *American So-
       ciologist* 20 (Summer), pp. 123–133.
Morrow, Victoria P., and Kuvlesky, William
P.
1982   Bilingual Patterns of Non-
       metropolitan Mexican-American
       Youth. In Z. Anthony Kruszewski
       et al., eds., *Politics and Society in the
       Southwest*, pp. 3–24. Boulder, CO:
       Westview Press.
Morse, Samuel F. B.
1835   *A Foreign Conspiracy Against the Lib-
       erties of United States*. New York:
       Leavitt, Lord.
Moskos, Charles C.
1966   Racial Integration in the Armed
       Forces. *American Journal of Sociology*
       72 (September), pp. 132–148.
1991   How Do They Do I? *The New Re-
       public* 205 (August 5), pp. 16–20.
Mosley, Leonard
1966   *Hirohito: Emperor of Japan*. Engle-
       wood Cliffs, NJ: Prentice-Hall.
Ms.
1981   Is Your Campus or Work Group
       Looking for a Good Definition of
       Sexual Harassment? 10 (July), p. 22.
Mufson, Steven
1990   The Long March from College
       Campuses to Corporate Board-
       rooms. *Washington Post National
       Weekly Edition* (February 19), p. 8.
Mullen, William
1975   Tribal Politics at Bottom of Take-
       over. *Chicago Tribune* (January 12),
       p. 8.
Mullins, Marcy E.
1991   USA's Changing Demographics.
       *USA Today* (August 26), p. 9A.
Muñoz, Daniel G.
1986   Identifying Areas of Stress for Chi-
       cano Undergraduates. In Michael
       A. Olivas, ed., *Latino College Stu-
       dents*, pp. 131–156. New York:
       Teachers College Press.
Muskrat, Joe

1972    Assimilate or Starve! *Civil Rights Digest* 8 (October), pp. 27–34.

Muto, Sheila
1991    Pearl Harbor Day Sparks Concern About Racism. *Asian Week* 13 (December 6), pp. 1, 14.

Mydans, Seth
1991a   California Expects Hispanic Votes to Transform Politics. *New York Times* (January 27), p. E4.
1991b   Foreign Millionaires in No Rush to Apply for Visas, U.S. Finds. *New York Times* (December 22), p. 10.
1992    A Target of Rioters, Koreatown Is Bitter, Armed, and Determined. *New York Times* (May 3), pp. 1, 16.

Myrdal, Gunnar
1944    *An American Dilemma: The Negro Problem and Modern Democracy.* With the assistance of Richard Steiner and Arnold Rose. New York: Harper.
1974    The Case Against Romantic Ethnicity. *Center Magazine* 7 (July–August), pp. 26–30.

NAACP
1989    *The Unfinished Agenda on Race in America.* New York: NAACP Legal Defense and Educational Fund.

Nabokov, Peter
1970    *Tijerina and the Courthouse Raid,* 2nd ed. Berkely, CA: The Ramparts Press.

Nagata, Donna K.
1990    The Japanese American Internment: Exploring the Transgenerational Consequences of Traumatic Stress. *Journal of Traumatic Stress* 3, pp. 47–69.
1991a   Evaluating the Effects of Ethnicity and Trauma Across Generations: The Japanese American Internment. Paper presented at the American Psychological Association, San Francisco.
1991b   The Impact of the World War II Internment Policies Upon the Present-Day Japanese American Community. Paper presented at the annual meeting of the American Psychological Association, San Francisco.

Nagel, Joane

1988    The Roots of Red Power: Demographic and Organizational Bases of American Indian Activism 1950–1990. Paper presented at the annual meeting of the American Sociological Association, Atlanta.
1989    American Indian Repertoires of Contention. Paper presented at the annual meeting of the American Sociological Association, San Francisco.

Nakamaru, Robert Tsunco
1979    The Assimilation of Japanese Americans: Regional and Generational Differences. Unpub. M.A. thesis, University of Wisconsin, Madison.
1986    Correspondence with R. Schaefer. September 26.

Nakanishi, Don T.
1986    Asian American Politics: An Agenda for Research. *Amerasia* 12 (Fall), pp. 1–27.
1987    Seeking Convergence in Race Relations Research. In Phyllis Katz and Dalmas Taylor, eds., *Eliminating Racism,* pp. 159–180. New York: Plenum Press.

Nash, Manning
1962    Race and the Ideology of Race. *Current Anthropology* 3 (June), pp. 258–288.

National Advisory Commission on Civil Disorders
1968    *Report.* With introduction by Tom Wicker. New York: Bantam.

National Clearinghouse for Bilingual Education
1983    Administration Proposes $95 Million for Fiscal Year 1984. *Forum* 6 (March/April), pp. 1, 2.
1985    President Proposes FY 1986 Budget. *Forum* 8 (April–May), pp. 1, 4.

National Commission on Population Growth and the American Future
1972    *Population and the American Future.* Washington, DC: U.S. Government Printing Office.

National Commission on Working Women
1984    *Women's Work: Undervalued, Underpaid.* Washington, DC: National Commission on Working Women.

National Jewish Family Center

1982    How the Family "Figures" in the 1980 Census. *Newsletter* 2 (Fall).

National Opinion Research Center
1991    *General Social Survey, 1972–1991, Cumulative Codebook.* Chicago: National Opinion Research Center.

Navarro, Armando
1974    The Evolution of Chicano Politics. *Aztlan* 5 (Spring and Fall), pp. 57–82.

Navarro, Mireya
1990    For 4 Puerto Rican Activists, Time Tempers Zeal. *New York Times* (October 21), p. 15.

NBC News
1992    *World Atlas and Almanac.* Chicago: Rand McNally.

Nee, Victor G., and DeBary, Brett, eds.
1973    *Longtime Californ': A Documentary Study of an American Chinatown.* New York: Pantheon.

Nelse, Johannes Michael
1988    Residential Segregation of Ethnic Groups in West Germany. *Cities* 5 (August), pp. 235–244.

Nelson, Candace, and Tienda, Marta
1985    The Structuring of Hispanic Ethnicity: Historical and Contemporary Perspectives. *Ethnic and Racial Studies* 8 (January), pp. 49–74.

Nelson, Dale C.
1980    The Political Behavior of New York Puerto Ricans: Assimilation or Survival? In Clara E. Rodriquez, Virginia Sanchez Karrol, and Jose Oscar Alers, eds., *The Puerto Rican Struggle,* pp. 90–110. Maplewood, NJ: Waterfront Press.

Newman, William M.
1973    *American Pluralism: A Study of Minority Groups and Social Theory.* New York: Harper and Row.

*Newsweek*
1979    A New Racial Poll. (February 26), pp. 48, 53.

*New York Daily News*
1984    Overcrowding? Hispanics "Prefer" It, HUD Aide Says (May 13), p. 19.

*New York Times*
1917a    The Immigration Bill Veto. (January 31), p. 210.
1917b    Illiteracy Is Not All Alike. (February 8), p. 12.
1973    Hawaiian Natives Seek Land Claims Bill. (November 11), p. 14.
1974a    Cuban Magazine Bombed in Miami. (May 14), p. 20.
1974b    Italian-Americans Here Unite to Fight Reverse Racial Bias (June 28), p. 29.
1979    Hispanic Pupils Held Hampered By Tests Tied to English Ability. (September 16), pp. 1, 66.
1980    National Survey Finds the Sexual Harassing of Students Is Rising. (October 12), p. 47.
1982    Converts to Judaism. (August 29), p. 23.
1984    House Adopts Bill on Bias Penalties. (June 28), p. A25.
1988a    Report Shows 12% Rise in Anti-Semitic Incidents. (January 27), p. A13.
1988b    Wide Harassment of Women Working for U.S. Is Reported. (July 1), p. B6.
1990    Health Data Show Wide Gap Between Whites and Blacks. (March 23), p. A17.
1992    Hispanic Residents Often Lack Health Coverage. (May 5), p. A23.

Ng, Johnny
1991    More Asian Children Living in Poverty. *Asian Week* 12 (June 14), pp. 1, 17.

Nichols, Bill
1991    Arrests Show Immigration Problem Worsens. *USA Today* (August 8), p. 5A.

Nickens, Herbert W.
1991    Minorities in Medicine: 3,000 by 2000? *Focus* 19 (June), pp. 3–4.

Nickerson, Steve
1971    Alaska Natives Criticize Bill. *Race Relations Reporter* 2 (November 15), pp. 7–10.

Nie, Norman H.; Currie, Barbara; and Greeley, Andrew M.
1974    Political Attitudes Among American Ethnics: A Study of Perceptual Distortion. *Ethnicity* 1 (December), pp. 317–343.

Niebuhr, H. Richard
1929    *The Social Sources of Denominationalism.* New York: Holt.

Noble, Kenneth B.
1989    The Black Ascent in Union Politics. *New York Times* (February 8), p. E3.

Noel, Donald L.
1972    *The Origins of American Slavery and Racism.* Columbus: Charles Merrill Publishing Co.

Nordheimer, Jon
1984    Gaining Self-Reliance: A Key for Puerto Rico. *New York Times* (November 18), p. 13.
1988    Older Migrants' Years of Toil in Sun End in Cold Twilight. *New York Times* (May 29), pp. 1, 9.

Norton, Eleanor Holmes
1985    Restoring the Traditional Black Family. *New York Times Magazine* (June 2), pp. 42–43, 79, 83, 96, 98–99.

Norwood, Janet L.
1984    *Working Women and Public Policy.* Washington, DC: U.S. Government Printing Office.

Novak, Michael
1973    *The Rise of the Unmeltable Ethnics: Politics and Culture in the Seventies.* New York: Collier.

Novello, Antonia C.; Wise, Paul H.; and Kleinman, Dushanka V.
1991    Hispanic Health: Time for Data, Time for Action. *Journal of the American Medical Association* 265 (January 9), pp. 253–257.

Nugent, Neill
1976    The Anti-Immigration Groups. *New Community* 5 (Autumn), pp. 302–310.

Oberschall, A.
1968    The Los Angeles Riot of August 1965. *Social Problems* 15 (Winter), pp. 322–341.

O'Dea, Thomas F.
1957    *The Mormons.* Chicago: University of Chicago Press.

Odo, Franklin S.
1973    The Asian American. In Don Spiegel and Patricia Keith-Spiegel, eds., *Outsiders, USA,* pp. 371–390. San Francisco: Rinehart Press.

O'Driscoll, Patrick
1985    But Still Not Moving Up the Church Ladder. *USA Today* (April 7), pp. 1A, 2A.

Oehling, Richard A.
1980    The Yellow Menace: Asian Images in American Film. In Randall M. Miller, ed., *The Kaleidoscopic Lens,* pp. 182–206, Englewood, NJ: Jerome S. Ozer.

Oelsner, Lesley
1975    Church-State Legal Conflicts Persist. *New York Times* (August 10), p. 1.

Ogletree, Earl J., and Ujlaki, Vilma E.
1985    American-Hispanics in a Pluralistic Society. *Migration Today* 13 (No. 3), pp. 30–34.

O'Hare, William P., and Curry-White, Brenda
1992    Is There a Rural Underclass? *Population Today* 20 (March), pp. 6–8.

O'Hare, William P., and Felt, Judy C.
1991    *Asian Americans: America's Fastest Growing Minority Group.* Washington, DC: Population Reference Bureau.

O'Hare, William P.; Pollard, Kelvin M.; Mann, Taynia L.; and Kent, Mary M.
1991    African Americans in the 1990s. *Population Bulletin* 46 (July).

O'Kane, James M.
1992    *The Crooked Ladder: Gangsters, Ethnicity, and the American Dream.* New Brunswick, NJ: Transaction.

Okimoto, Daniel
1971    The Intolerance of Success. In Amy Tachiki, Eddie Wong, Franklin Odo, and Buck Wong, eds., *Roots: An Asian American Reader,* pp. 14–19. Los Angeles: Asian American Studies Center, UCLA.

Olson, James C.
1965    *Red Cloud and the Sioux Problem.* Lincoln: University of Nebraska Press.

O'Neill, William
1969    *Everyone Was Brave: The Rise and Fall of Feminism in America.* Chicago: Quadrangle.

O'Reilly, Jane
1982    After the ERA: What Next? *Civil Rights Quarterly Perspectives* 14 (Fall), pp. 16–19.

Orfield, Gary

1972    Termination in Retrospect: The Menominee Experience. In Richard N. Ellis, ed., *The Western American Indian: Case Studies in Tribal History,* pp. 187–195. Lincoln: University of Nebraska Press.

1987    *School Segregation in the 1980's.* Chicago: National School Desegregative Report.

Orfield, Gary, and Monfort, Franklin
1988    *Change in the Racial Composition and Segregation of Large School Districts, 1967–1986.* Alexandria, VA: National School Boards Association.

Orlov, Ann, and Reed, Veda
1980    Central and South Americans. In Stephan Thernstrom, ed., *Harvard Encyclopedia of American Ethnic Groups,* pp. 210–217. Cambridge, MA: Belknap Press of Harvard University Press.

Ortiz, Vilma
1986    Changes in the Characteristics of Puerto Rican Migrants from 1955 to 1980. *International Migration Review,* 20 (Fall), pp. 612–628.

Oskamp, Stuart
1977    *Attitudes and Opinions.* Englewood Cliffs, NJ: Prentice-Hall.

Ostling, Richard N.
1987    John Paul's Feisty Flock. *Time* 130 (September 7), pp. 46–51.

Ottaway, David S., and Taylor, Paul
1992    A Minority Decides to Stand Aside for Majority Rule. *Washington Post National Weekly Edition* 9 (April 5), p. 17.

Owen, Carolyn A.; Eisner, Howard C.; and McFaul, Thomas R.
1981    A Half-Century of Social Distance Research: National Replication of the Bogardus Studies. *Sociology and Social Research* 66 (October 1981), pp. 80–97.

Padilla, Amado M.; Wagatsuma, Yuria; and Lindholm, Kathryn J.
1985    Acculturation and Personality as Predictors of Stress in Japanese and Japanese-Americans. *Journal of Social Psychology* 125 (June), pp. 295–306.

Padilla, Elena
1958    *Up from Puerto Rico.* New York:

Columbia University Press.

Padilla, Felix M.
1984    On the Nature of Latino Ethnicity. *Social Science Quarterly* 65 (June), pp. 651–664.

Padilla, Raymond V.
1973    A Critique of Pittian History. In O. I. Romano, ed., *Voices: Readings from El Grito,* rev. ed., pp. 65–106. Berkeley, CA: Quinto Sol Publications.

Paik, Irvin
1971    That Oriental Feeling: A Look at the Caricatures of the Asians as Sketched by American Movies. In Amy Tachiki, Eddie Wong, Franklin Odo, and Buck Wong, eds., *Roots: An Asian American Reader,* pp. 30–36. Los Angeles: Asian American Studies Center, UCLA.

Parenti, Michael
1967    Ethnic Politics and the Persistence of Ethnic Identification. *American Political Science Review* 61 (September), pp. 717–726.

1970    Assimilation and Counter-Assimilation. In Philip Green and Stanford Levinson, eds., *Power and Community: Dissenting Essays in Political Science,* pp. 173–194. New York: Vintage Books.

Park, Jeanne
1990    Eggs, Twinkies and Ethnic Stereotypes. *New York Times* (April 20), p. A33.

Park, Robert E.
1928    Human Migration and the Marginal Man. *American Journal of Sociology* 33 (May), pp. 881–893.

1950    *Race and Culture: Essays in the Sociology of Contemporary Man.* New York: Free Press.

Park, Robert E., and Burgess, Ernest W.
1921    *Introduction to the Science of Sociology.* Chicago: University of Chicago Press.

Parker, Linda S.
1989    *Native American Estate: The Struggle over Indian and Hawaiian Lands.* Honolulu: University of Hawaii Press.

Parsons, Talcott
1975    Some Theoretical Considerations on

the Nature and Trends of Change of Ethnicity. In Nathan Glazer and Daniel P. Moynihan, eds., *Ethnicity: Theory and Experience*, pp. 53–83. Cambridge, MA: Harvard University Press.

Parsons, Talcott, and Bales, Robert
1955    *Family, Socialization and Interaction Processes*. Glencoe, IL: Free Press.

Passell, Jeffrey S., and Berman, Patricia A.
1986    Quality of 1980 Census Data for American Indians. *Social Biology* 33 (Fall/Winter), pp. 163–182.

Patterson, Orlando
1977    Slavery. In Alex Inkeles, ed., *Annual Review of Sociology, 1977*, pp. 407–449. Palo Alto, CA: Annual Reviews.

1982    *Slavery and Social Death*. Cambridge, MA: Harvard University Press.

Patterson, Sheila
1969    *Immigration and Race Relations in Britain, 1960–1967*. London: Oxford University Press.

Pear, Robert
1982    Blacks Moving to Suburbs, But Significance Is Disputed. *New York Times* (August 15), p. 14.

1984    Federal Regulations Pare Requirements for Bilingual Ballots. *New York Times* (September 10), pp. A1, B9.

1987    Court Ruling May Open Way for More Political Refugees. *New York Times* (March 15), p. E3.

Pearce, Diana M.
1983    The Feminization of Ghetto Poverty. *Society* 21 (November–December), pp. 70–74.

Pedder, Sophie
1991    Social Isolation and the Labour Market: Black Americans in Chicago. Paper presented at the Chicago Urban Poverty and Family Life Conference, Chicago.

Pederson, Daniel
1987    All Thes Guys Owe Willie. *Newsweek 109 (March 16), pp. 30, 32.*

Penalosa, Fernando
1968    Mexican Family Roles. *Journal of Marriage and the Family 30 (November), pp. 680–689.*

Pennock-Román María
1986    New Directions for Research on Spanish-Language Tests and Test-Stem Bias. In Micheal A. Olivas, ed., *Latino College Students*, pp. 193–220.

Perez, Miguel
1976    Sociologist: Cuban Success Is a Myth. *Miami Herald* (October 17), pp. 1D, 2D.

Perlmutter, Philip
1991    *Divided We Fall: A History of Ethnic, Religious, and Racial Prejudice in America*. Ames: Iowa State University Press.

Peroff, Nicholas C.
1982    *Menominee Drums*. Norman: University of Oklahoma Press.

Peters, Victor
1965    *All Things Common: The Hutterian Way of Life*. New York: Harper and Row.

Petersen, William
1958    A General Typology of Migration. *American Sociological Review* 23 (June), pp. 256–266.

1962    Religious Statistics in the United States. *Journal for the Scientific Study of Religion* 1 (Spring), pp. 165–178.

1971    *Japanese Americans: Oppression and Success*. New York: Random House.

Petersen, William; Novak, Michael; and Gleason, Philip
1982    *Concepts of Ethnicity*. Cambridge, MA: Belknap Press of Harvard University Press.

Petersilia, Joan
1983    *Racial Disparities in the Criminal Justice System*. Santa Monica, CA: Rand.

Pettigrew, Thomas F.
1958    Personality and Socio-Cultural Factors in Intergroup Attitudes: A Cross-National Comparison. *Journal of Conflict Resolution* 2 (March), pp. 29–42.

1959    Regional Differences in Anti-Negro Prejudice. *Journal of Abnormal and Social Psychology* 59 (July), pp. 28–36.

1966    Parallel and Distinctive Changes in Anti-Semitic and Anti-Negro Attitudes. In Herbert Stember, ed., *Jews in the Mind of America*, pp. 377–403. New York: Basic Books

1971    *Racially Separate or Together?* New York: McGraw-Hill.

1981    Race and Class in the 1980's: An Interactive Brew. *Daedalus*, 110 (Spring), pp. 233–255.

1985    New Black-White Patterns: How Best to Conceptualize Them. In Ralph H. Turner, ed., *Annual Review of Sociology, 1985*, pp. 329–346. Palo Alto, CA: Annual Review.

Pettigrew, Thomas F.; Frederickson, George M.; Knobel, Dale T.; Glazer, Nathan; and Ueda, Reed

1982    *Prejudice*. Cambridge, MA: Belknap Press of Harvard University Press.

Pettigrew, Thomas F., and Martin, Joanne

1987    Shaping the Organizational Context for Black American Inclusion. *Journal of Social Issues* 43 (1), pp. 41–78.

Phillips, Leslie

1991    Puerto Ricans' Political Status in Limbo Again. *USA Today* (March 6), p. 7A.

Pido, Antonio J. A.

1986    *The Filipinos in America*. New York: Center for Migration Studies.

Pileggi, Nicolas

1971    Risorgimento: The Red, White, and Greening of New York. *New York Magazine* (June 7), pp. 26–36.

Pinkney, Alphonso

1970    Contemporary Black Nationalism. Paper presented at Douglass College, Rutgers University, New Brunswick, NJ.

1975    *Black Americans*, 2nd ed. Englewood Cliffs, NJ: Prentice-Hall.

1976    *Red, Black and Green: Black Nationalism in the United States*. Cambridge: Cambridge University Press.

1984    *The Myth of Black Progress*. New York: Cambridge University Press.

1987    *Black Americans*, 3rd ed. Englewood Cliffs, NJ: Prentice-Hall.

Pitt, Leonard

1966    *Decline of the Californios: A Social History of the Spanish-Speaking Californians, 1846–1890*. Berkeley: University of California Press.

Pitts, James P.

1972    The Study of Black Nationalism: Some Comments on New Directions. Paper presented at the annual meeting of the American Sociological Association, New Orleans.

Pleasant, William, ed.

1990    *Independent Black Leadership in America*. New York: Castillo International Publications.

Polzin, Theresita

1973    *The Polish Americans: Whence and Whither*. Pulaski, WI: Franciscan Publishers.

Porter, Jack Nusan

1970    Jewish Student Activism. *Jewish Currents* (May), pp. 28–34.

1981    *The Jew as Outsider*. Washington, DC: Washington University Press.

1985    Self-Hatred and Self-Esteem. *The Jewish Spectator* (Fall), pp. 51–55.

Porter, Jack Nusan, ed.

1982    *Genocide and Human Rights: A Global Anthology*. Lanham, MD: University Press of America.

Portes, Alejandro

1974    Return of the Wetback. *Society* 11 (March–April), pp. 40–46.

Portes, Alejandro, and Stepick, Alex

1985    Unwelcome Immigrants: The Labor Market Experiences of 1980 (Mariel) Cuban and Haitian Refugees in South Florida. *American Sociological Review* 50 (August), pp. 493–514.

Poussaint, Alvin F., and Comer, James

1975    *Black Child Care: How to Bring up a Healthy Black Child in America*. New York: Simon and Schuster.

Powell, Enoch

1968    Speech of 20 April 1968. *Race* 10 (July), pp. 94–100.

Powell, John Wesley

1966    *Indian Linguistic Families of America North of Mexico*. Lincoln: University of Nebraska Press.

Powell-Hopson, Darlene and Hopson, Derek

1988    Implications of Doll Color Preferences Among Black Preschool Children and White Preschool Children. *Journal of Black Psychology* 14 (February), pp. 57–63.

Powers, Charles H.

1976    Two Forms of Ethnicity: A Brief

Description of Japanese-American Organization. Paper presented at the annual meeting of the American Sociological Association, New York.

Preble, Edward
1968 The Puerto Rican-American Teenager in New York City. In Eugene B. Brody, ed., *Minority Group Adolescents in the United States*, pp. 48–72. Baltimore: Williams and Wilkins.

Presidential Commission on Indian Reservation Economics
1984 *Report and Recommendations to the President of the United States*. Washington, DC: U.S. Government Printing Office.

Price, John A.
1968 The Migration and Adaptation of Indians to Los Angeles. *Human Organization* 27 (Summer), pp. 168–175.

Princeton Religion Research Center
1984 4 in 10 Adults in U.S. Attended Church in Typical Week of 1984. *Emerging Trends* 6 (December), p. 1.
1986 Importance of God in Lives. *Emerging Trends* 8 (November–December), p. 5.
1988a Four in 10 Adults Attended Church in Typical Week of 1987. *Emerging Trends* 9 (September), p. 5.
1988b Trends in U.S. Religious Life Show Considerable Stability. *Emerging Trends* 10 (December), pp. 2–3.
1989 Little Change in Major Faiths. *Emerging Trends* 11 (February), p. 3.
1990a *Religion in America, 1990 Report*. Princeton, NJ.
1990b Church Attendance Unchanged as We Enter the 1990s. *Emerging Trends* 12 (June), p. 4.
1991 Life Cycle Changes are Leading to More Frequent Church Attendance. *Emerging Trends* 13 (June), pp. 1–3.
1992a Church Attendance Constant. *Emerging Trends* 14 (March), p. 4.
1992b Only One American in Nine Expresses No Religious Preference. *Emerging Trends* 14 (April), pp. 1–2.

Prokesch, Steven
1991 British Finding the Chances for

Ulster Political Talks Again Fading. *New York Times* (February 24), p. 13.

Public Opinion
1985 Americans Evaluate the Situation in South Africa. 8 (August–September), pp. 26–28, 40.
1986 Comparable Worth: Public Uninformed and Skeptical. 9 (September–October), pp. 34–35.
1987 Opinion Roundup: Jews. 10 (July/August), pp. 25–26.

Quan, Katie
1986 Chinese Garment Workers. *Migration World* 14 (No. 1/2), pp. 46–49.

Quinn, Bernard; Anderson, Herman; Bradley, Martin; Goetting, Paul; and Shriver, Peggy
1982 *Churches and Church Membership in the United States, 1980*. Atlanta: Glennary Research Center.

Quintana, Frances Leon
1980 Spanish. In Stephen Thernstrom, ed., *Harvard Encyclopedia of American Ethnic groups*, pp. 950–953. Cambridge, MA: Belknap Press of Harvard University Press.

Raab, Earl
1988 Intergroup Relations. In David Singer, ed., *American Jewish Yearbook, 1988*, pp. 143–159. New York: American Jewish Committee.
1991 Interracial Conflict and American Jews. *Patterns of Prejudice* 25 (Summer), pp. 46–61.

Rabaya, Violet
1971 Filipino Immigration: The Creation of a New Social Problem. In Amy Tachiki, Eddie Wong, Franklin Odo, and Buck Wong, eds., *Roots: An Asian American Reader*, pp. 188–200. Los Angeles: Asian American Studies Center, UCLA.

Rabinove, Samuel
1970 Private Club Discrimination and the Law. *Civil Rights Digest* 3 (Spring), pp. 28–33.

Rachlin, Carol
1970 Tight Shoe Night: Oklahoma Indians Today. In Stuart Levine and Nancy Oestreich Lurie, eds., *The American Indian Today*, pp. 160–183. Baltimore: Penguin.

Radelet, Michael L.
1989    Executions of Whites for Crimes Against Blacks: Exceptions to the Rule. *The Sociological Quarterly* 30 (No. 4), pp. 529–544.

Radzialowski, Thaddeus
1974    The View from a Polish Ghetto: Some Observations on the First One Hundred Years in Detroit. *Ethnicity* 1 (July), pp. 125–150.

Rainwater, Lee, and Yancey, William L., eds.
1967    *The Moynihan Report and the Politics of Controversy.* Cambridge, MA: MIT Press.

Ramirez, Anthony
1986    America's Super Minority. *Fortune* 114 (November 24), pp. 148–149, 152, 156, 160.

Ramirez, J. David; Yuen, Sandra D.; and Ramey, Dena R.
1991    *Final Report: Longitudinal Study of Structured English Immersion Strategy, Early-Exit and Late-Exit Transitional Bilingual Education Programs for Language-Minority Children.* San Mateo, CA: Aguirre International.

Randolph, A. Philip
1971    Calls for a March on Washington. In August Meier, Elliott Rudwick, and Francis Broderick, eds., *Black Protest Thought in the Twentieth Century,* 2nd ed., pp. 220–233. Indianapolis: Bobbs-Merrill.

Rapson, Richard L.
1980    *Fairly Lucky You Live Hawaii? Cultural Pluralism in the Fiftieth State.* Lanham, MD: University Press of America.

Raspberry, William
1991    Grim Reruns of the '60s. *Washington Post* (May 8), p. A3.

Rawick, George P.
1972    *From Sundown to Sunup: The Making of the Black Community.* Westport, CT: Greenwood Press.

Raybon, Patricia
1989    A Case for "Severe Bias." *Newsweek* 114 (October 2), p. 11

Raymer, Patricia
1974    Wisconsin's Menominees: Indians on a Seesaw. *National Geographic.* (August), pp. 228–251.

Raymond, Chris
1991    Cornell Scholar Attacks Key Psychological Studies Thought to Demonstrate Blacks' Self-Hatred. *Chronicle of Higher Education* 37 (May 8), pp. A5, A8, A11.

Reardon, Patrick T.
1991    The Other Chicago. *Chicago Tribune* (October 13), sec. 4, pp. 1, 4.

Rebelsky, Freda, and Hanks, Cheryl
1973    Fathers' Verbal Interaction with Infants in the First Three Months of Life. In Freda Rebelsky and Lyn Dorman, eds., *Child Development and Behavior,* 2nd ed., pp. 145–148. New York: Knopf.

Record, Wilson, and Record, Jane Cassels
1975    Review of "Time on the Cross." *Contemporary Sociology* 4 (July), pp. 361–366.

Reed, Adolph, Jr.
1985    What the Research Shows. *New York Times* (November 10), sect. 12, pp. 48–49.
1991    The Rise of Louis Farrakhan. *The Nation* 252 (January 21), pp. 1, 51, 52, 54–56.

Reese, Michael
1982    Life Below the Poverty Line. *Newsweek* 109 (April 5), pp. 20–22, 25–26, 28.

Reich, Peter
1975    History's Record of Refugees. *Chicago Tribune* (April 6), p. 7.

Reid, John
1986    Immigration and the Future U.S. Black Population. *Population Today* 14 (February), pp. 6–8.

Reimers, David M.
1983    An Unintended Reform: The 1965 Immigration Act and Third World Immigration to the United States. *Journal of American Ethnic History* 3 (Fall), pp. 9–28.

Research Committee on the Study of Honolulu Residents
1986    *The Third Attitudinal Survey of Honolulu Residents, 1983.* Honolulu: University of Hawaii Press.

Reskin, Barbara, and Blau, Francine
1990    *Job Queues, Gender Queues: Explaining Women's Inroads Into Male Occu-*

*pations.* Philadelphia: Temple University Press.

Rice, Berkeley
1977 The New Gangs of Chinatown. *American Sociological Review* 42 (May), pp. 60–69.

Richardson, Laurel Walum
1981 *The Dynamics of Sex and Gender: A Sociological Perspective,* 2nd ed. Boston: Houghton Mifflin.

Ridgeway, James
1986 Que Pasa, U.S. English? *Village Voice* 31 (December 2), pp. 32, 33.
1990 *Blood in the Face.* New York: Thunder's Mouth Press.

Riordan, Cornelius, and Ruggiero, Josephine
1980 Producing Equal Status Interracial Interaction: A Replication. *Social Psychology Quarterly* 43 (March), pp. 131–136.

Riot Not to Work Collective
1982 *We Want to Riot, Not to Work: The 1981 Brixton Uprisings.* London: A Distribution.

Ritterband, Paul
1986 The New Geography of Jews in North America, Occasional Papers No. 2. New York: Council of Jewish Federations.

Ritzer, George
1977 *Working: Conflict and Change,* 2nd ed. Englewood Cliffs, NJ: Prentice-Hall.

Rivera, George, Jr.
1988 Hispanic Folk Medicine Utilization in Urban Colorado. *Sociology and Social Research* 72 (July), pp. 237–241.

Roark, Anne C.
1977 Business Graduates Find It Helps to Be Female or Black or Both. *Chronicle of Higher Education* 14 (August 1), pp. 5, 6.

Roberts, D. F.
1955 The Dynamics of Racial Intermixture in the American Negro—Some Anthropological Considerations. *American Journal of Human Genetics* 7 (December), pp. 361–367.

Roberts, Steven B.
1984 Congress Stages a Pre-emptive Strike on the Gender Gap. *New York Times* (May 23), p. A18.

Robinson, Tracey
1989 African Heritage Pulses in Brazil's Salvador de Bahia. *Chicago Sun-Times* (April 23), p. D3.

Roche, John Patrick
1984 An Examination of the Resurgence of Ethnicity Literature. *Sociological Spectrum,* 4, pp. 169–186.

Rodriquez, Clara E.
1989 *Puerto Ricans: Born in the USA.* Boston: Unwin Hyman.

Rolle, Andrew F.
1972 *The Italian Americans: Their History and Culture.* Belmont, CA: Wadsworth.

Rollins, Bryant
1977 White Fear of Black Mayors: Unjustified But Persistent. *New York Times* (January 30), p. E7.

Roof, Wade Clark, and McKinney, William
1985 Denominational America and the New Religious Pluralism. *Annals* 480 (July), pp. 24–38.

Roos, Philip D.; Smith, Dowell H.; Langley, Stephen; and McDonald, James
1977 The Impact of the American Indian Movement on the Pine Ridge Indian Reservation. Paper presented at the annual meeting of the Society for the Study of Social Problems, Chicago.

Rosaldo, Renato
1985 Chicano Studies, 1970–1984. In Bernard J. Siegal, ed., *Annual Review of Anthropology, 1985,* pp. 405–427. Palo Alto, CA: Annual Reviews.

Rose, Arnold
1951 *The Roots of Prejudice.* Paris: UNESCO.

Rose, E. J. B., in association with Nicholas Deakin, et al.
1969 *Colour and Citizenship: A Report on British Race Relations.* London: Oxford University Press.

Rose, Peter I.
1981 *They and We,* 3rd ed. New York: Random House.

Rose, R. S.
1988 Slavery in Brazil: Does It Still Exist Today? Paper presented at the annual meeting of the American So-

ciological Association, Atlanta.

Rose, Richard
1971    *Governing Without Consensus.* Boston: Beacon Press.

Rosen, Sanford Jay
1974    Letter: When the Look Is Latin. *New York Times Magazine* (April 7), pp. 21, 102.

Rosenberg, Morris, and Simmons, Roberta G.
1971    *Black and White Self-Esteem: The Urban School Child.* Washington, DC: American Sociological Association.

Rosenblatt, Gary
1977    Intermarriage: A Dilemma for American Jews. *Chicago Tribune* (March 6), pp. 23–24.

Rosenhouse, Harry
1970    The Exodus and Success of Cubans. *Vision* 38 (March 13).

Rosenthal, Erich
1960    Acculturation Without Assimilation? The Jewish Community of Chicago, Ill. *American Journal of Sociology* 66 (November), pp. 275–288.

Rossell, Christine H.
1976    School Desegregation and White Flight. *Political Science Quarterly* 90 (Winter), pp. 675–695.
1988    Is It the Busing or the Blacks? *Urban Affairs Quarterly* 24 (September), pp.138–148.

Rossell, Christine H., and Crain, Robert L.
1973    *Evaluating School Desegregation Plans Statistically.* Baltimore: Center for Metropolitan Planning, Johns Hopkins University.

Rossi, Alice S.
1964    Equality Between the Sexes: An Immodest Proposal. *Daedalus* 93 (Spring), pp. 607–652.
1988    Growing Up and Older in Sociology 1940–1990. In M. W. Riley, ed., *Sociologial Lives,* pp. 43–64. Newbury Park, CA: Sage.

Rossi, Alice S., ed.
1973    *The Feminist Papers: From Adams to de Beauvoir.* New York: Columbia University Press.

Rossi, Alice S., and Calderwood, Ann
1973    *Academic Women on the Move.* New York: Russell Sage Foundation.

Rothman, Nancy Sacks
1990    Pluralism versus Assimilation: An Analysis of the Transformation of a Jewish Ritual in America. Paper presented at the annual meeting of the American Sociological Association, Washington, DC.

Royce, David D., and Turner, Gladys T.
1980    Strengths of Black Families: A Black Community Perspective. *Social Work* 25 (September), pp. 407–409.

Rubien, David
1989    For Asians in U.S., Hidden Strife. *New York Times* (January 11), p. C1.

Rudwick, Elliott
1957    The Niagara Movement. *Journal of Negro History* 42 (July), pp. 177–200.

Ruffini, Gene
1983    Employment Equity and Euro-Ethnics. *Perspectives* 15 (Summer), pp. 40–44.

Rule, Sheila
1991    Black Britons Describe a Motherland That has Long Held Them as Inferior. *New York Times* (March 31), p. 6.

Rustin, Bayard
1942    The Negro and Non-Violence. *Fellowship* 8 (October), pp. 166–167.

Ryan, William
1976    *Blaming the Victim,* rev. ed. New York: Random House.

Sabogal, Fabro, et al.
1987    Hispanic Families and Acculturation. What Changes and What Doesn't? *Hispanic Journal of Behavioral Sciences* 9 (December), pp. 397–412.

Sacks, Bracha
1974    Why I Choose Orthodoxy. *Ms.* (July), p. 82.

Sadker, Myra, and Sadker, David
1985    Sexism in the Schoolroom of the '80s. *Psychology Today* 19 (March), pp. 54–57.

Saetre, Sara
1989    Comparable Worth. *Utne Reader* 31 (January/February), pp. 14–15.

Said, Edward W., et al.
1988    A Profile of the Palestinian People. In Eward W. Said and Chris-

topher Hitchens, eds., *Blaming the Victims*, pp. 235–296. London: Verso.

Saito, Leland T.
1990 Japanese Americans and the New Chinese Immigrants: The Politics of Adaptation. Paper presented at the annual meeting of the American Sociological Association, Washington, DC.

Salholz, Eloise
1987 Do Colleges Set Asian Quotas? *Newsweek* 109 (February 9), p. 60.
1990 Teenagers and Abortion. *Newsweek* 115 (January 8), pp. 32–33, 36.

Samuels, Frederick
1969 Color Sensitivity Among Honolulu's Haoles and Japanese. *Race* 11 (October), pp. 203–212.
1970 *The Japanese and the Haoles of Honolulu: Durable Group Interaction.*New Haven, CT: College and University Press.

Sanchez, George I.
1934 Bilingualism and Mental Measures. *Journal of Applied Psychology 18* (December), pp.765–772.

Sanchez, Sandra
1991 Feelings of Frustration Boil Over. *USA Today* (May 8), p. 3A.

Sanders, Alvin J.
1986 Differentials in Marital Status Between Black and White Males. *Population Today* 14 (November), pp. 6–7.

Sanders, Irwin T., and Morawska, Ewa T.
1975 *Polish-American Community Life: A Survey of Research.* Boston: Community Sociology Training Program.

Sandza, Richard
1984 Refighting the Vietnam War. *Newsweek* 104 (November 26), p. 47.

Sargent, Edward D.
1986 The Plague of Blacks Killing Blacks. *The Washington Post National Weekly Edition* 3 (March 17), p. 7.

Sawyer, Jack
1972 On Male Liberation. *Civil Rights Digest* 5 (Winter), pp. 37–38.

Scanlan, John A.
1987 Why the McCarran-Walter Act Must Be Amended. *Academe* 73 (September–October), pp. 5–13.

Scarman Report
1982 *The Brixton Disorders: 10–12 April 1981.* London: Her Majesty's Stationery Office.

Schaefer, Richard T.
1969 The Ku Klux Klan: Continuity and Change. Working paper, No. 138. Chicago: Center for Social Organization Studies, University of Chicago.
1971 The Ku Klux Klan: Continuity and Change. *Phylon* 32 (Summer), pp. 143–157.
1973a Black Nationalism in the United States. In Richard T. Schaefer, ed., *Peoples and Prejudice: Minorities in the United States*, pp. 130–135. Lexington, MA: Xerox College Publishing.
1973b Contacts Between Immigrants and Englishmen: Road to Tolerance or Intolerance. *New Community* 2 (Autumn), pp. 355–371.
1973c Party Affiliation and Prejudice in Britain. *New Community* 2 (Summer), pp. 296–299.
1974a Correlates of Racial Prejudice. In Timothy Leggatt, ed., *Sociological Theory and Survey Research*, pp. 237–264. London: Sage Publications.
1974b The Dynamics of British Racial Prejudice. *Patterns of Prejudice* 8 (November–December), pp. 1–5.
1975 Regional Differences in Prejudice. *Regional Studies* 9 (March), pp. 1–14.
1976a *The Extent and Content of Racial Prejudice in Great Britain.* San Francisco: R & E Research Associates.
1976b Indians in Great Britain. *International Review of Modern Sociology* 6 (Autumn), pp. 305–327.
1980 The Management of Secrecy: The Ku Klux Klan's Successful Secret. In Stanton K. Tefft, ed., *Secrecy: A Cross-Cultural Perspective.* New York: Human Sciences Press.
1986 Racial Prejudice in a Capitalist State: What Has Happened to the American Creed? *Phylon* 47 (September).
1987 Social Distance of Black College Students at a Predominantly White

University. *Sociology and Social Research*, 72 (October), pp. 30–32.

1992    People of Color: The "Kaleidoscope" May Be a Better Way to Describe America Than "The Melting Pot." *Peoria Journal Star* (January 19), p. A7.

Schaefer, Richard T., and Lamm, Robert P.
1992    *Sociology*, 4th ed. New York: McGraw-Hill.

Schaefer, Richard T., and Schaefer, Sandra L.
1975    Reluctant Welcome: U.S. Responses to the South Vietnamese Refugees. *New Community* 4 (Autumn), pp. 366–370.

Schermerhorn, R. A.
1970    *Comparative Ethnic Relations: A Framework for Theory and Research.* New York: Random House.

Schiff, Ze'en, and Ya'air, Ehud
1990    *Intifada.* New York: Simon and Schuster.

Schay, Anne
1988    Banking Practices Contribute to Housing Ethnoviolence. *Forum* 3 (No. 4), pp. 3–4.

Schlozman, Kay Lehman
1977    Hard Hats and Ethnics Have Taken a Bum Rap: Public Opinion and Youth Dissent. *Ethnicity* 4 (March), pp. 71–89.

Schmidt, William E.
1982    Navajos Pose Challenge to Indian Energy Group. *New York Times* (November 21), p. 36.

1988    Religious Leaders Try to Heal Rift in Chicago. *New York Times* (November 27), p. 14.

Schmitt, David E.
1974    *Violence in Northern Ireland: Ethnic Conflict and Radicalization in an International Setting.* Morristown, NJ: General Learning Press.

Schoenfeld, Eugen
1976    Jewish Americans: A Religio-Ethnic Community. In Anthony Dworkin and Rosalind J. Dworkin, eds., *The Minority Report: An Introduction to Racial and Ethnic Minorities,* pp. 325–352. New York: Praeger.

Schramm, Wilbur; Nelson, Lyle M.; and Betham, Mere T.

1981    *Bold Experiment: The Story of Educational Television in American Samoa.* Stanford, CA: Stanford University Press.

Schrieke, Bertram J.
1936    *Alien Americans.* New York: Viking.

Schultz, Ray
1974    The Call of the Ghetto. *New York Times Magazine* (November 10), p. 34.

Schultz, Terri
1977    Though Legal, Abortions Are Not Always Available. *New York Times* (January 2), p. E8.

Schuman, Howard; Steeh, Charlotte; and Bobo, Lawrence
1985    *Racial Attitudes in America: Trends and Interpretations.* Cambridge, MA: Harvard University Press.

Schwartz, Barry N., and Disch, Robert
1970    *White Racism: Its History, Pathology and Practice.* New York: Dell.

Schwartz, Bernard
1986    *Swann's Way: The School Busing Case and the Supreme Court.* New York: Oxford University Press.

Schwartz, Felice
1989    Management Women and the New Facts of Life. *Harvard Business Review* 67 (January/February), pp. 65–76.

Schwartz, John
1988    The Return of "Redlining"! *Newsweek* 111 (May 16), p. 44.

Schwartz, Mildred A.
1967    *Trends in White Attitudes Toward Negroes.* Chicago: National Opinion Research Center.

Schwirian, Kent P.; Aguirre, Benigno E.; and LaGreca, Anthony J.
1976    The Residential Patterning of Latin American and Other Ethnic Populations in Metropolitan Miami. Paper presented at the annual meeting of the American Sociological Association, San Francisco.

Scott, Robin Fitzgerald
1974    Wartime Labor Problems and Mexican-Americans in the War. In Manuel Servin, ed., *An Awakened Minority: The Mexican Americans,* 2nd ed., pp. 134–142. Beverly Hills,

CA: Glencoe Press.

Seale, Patrick
1980   Two Peoples—One Land. In *1980 Britannica Book of the Year*, pp. 64–69. Chicago: Encyclopedia Britannica.

Sears, David O., and McConahay, J. B.
1969   Participation in the Los Angeles Riot. *Social Problems* 17 (Summer), pp. 3–20.
1970   Racial Socialization, Comparison Levels, and the Watts Riot. *Journal of Social Issues* 26 (Winter), pp. 121–140.
1973   *The Politics of Violence: The New Urban Blacks and the Watts Riots*. Boston: Houghton Mifflin.

Selzer, Michael
1972   *"Kike"—Anti-Semitism in America*. New York: Meridian.

Selznick, Gertrude J., and Steinberg, Stephen
1969   *The Tenacity of Prejudice*. New York: Harper and Row.

Senior, Clarence
1965   *The Puerto Ricans: Strangers—Then Neighbors*. Chicago: Quadrangle Books.

Servin, Manuel P.
1974   The Beginnings of California's Anti-Mexican Prejudice. In Manuel P. Servin, ed., *An Awakened Minority: The Mexican Americans*, 2nd ed., pp. 2–26. Beverly Hills, CA: Glencoe Press.

Severo, Richard
1970   New York's Italians: A Question of Identity. *New York Times* (November 9), pp. 43, 50.
1974   The Flight of the Wetbacks. *New York Times Magazine* (March 10), p. 17.

*Seward World*
1988   Gangs in Chinatown—Extortion, Prostitution, and Drugs. 31 (April), p. 2.

Shaheen, Jack G.
1984   Arabs—TV's Villains of Choice. *Channels of Communication* (March/April), pp. 52–53.

Shames, Deborah, ed.
1972   *Freedom With Reservation: The Menominee Struggle to Save Their Land and People*. Madison, WI: National Committee to Save The Menominee People and National Forests.

Shannon, Lyle W.
1979   The Changing World View of Minority Migrants in an Urban Setting. *Human Organizations* 38 (Spring), pp. 52–62.

Shapiro, Harry L.
1936   *The Heritage of the Bounty: The Story of Pitcairn Through Six Generations*. New York: Simon and Schuster.

Shapiro, Laura
1988   When Is a Joke Not a Joke? *Newsweek* (May 23), p. 79.

Shapiro, Leon
1971   World Jewish Population. In *American Jewish Year Book, 1971*, pp. 474–481. New York: American Jewish Committee.

Shapiro, Walter
1987   The Ghetto: From Bad to Worse. *Time* 130 (August 24), pp. 18–19.

Shaw, Susan M.
1988   Gender Differences in the Definition and Perception of Household Labor. *Family Relations* 37 (July), pp. 333–337.

Sheils, Merrill
1977   Teaching in English—Plus. *Newsweek* (February 7), pp. 64–65.

Sheinberg, Sheila, and Schulman, Sam
1977   Jewish Identity: Practices and Perceptions. Paper presented at the annual meeting of the American Sociological Association, Chicago.

Sheler, Jeffrey L.
1982   10 Million People Without Jobs—Who They Are. *U.S. News and World Report* 92 (March 15), pp. 71–74.

Shenker, Israel
1974   How Yiddish Survives at 2 New York City Schools. *New York Times* (January 16), p. 68.
1979   With Them, It's Always Strictly Kosher. *New York Times Magazine* (April 15), pp. 32, 33, 36–38, 40, 42.

Sherif, Muzafer, and Sherif, Carolyn
1969   *Social Psychology*. New York: Harper and Row.

Sherman, C. Bezalel

1974    Immigration and Emigration: The Jewish Case. In Marshall Sklare, ed., *The Jew in American Society*, pp. 51–55. New York: Behrman House.

Sherry, Linda
1992    New President at Chinese Six Co. *Asian Week* (January 10), p. 3.

Shin, Linda
1971    Koreans in America, 1903–1945. In Amy Tachiki, Eddie Wong, Franklin Odo, and Buck Wong, eds., *Roots: An Asian American Reader*, pp. 200–206. Los Angeles: Asian American Studies Center, UCLA.

Shipler, David K.
1981    Soviet Jews Choosing U.S., Put Israelis In a Quandary. *New York Times* (August 13), p. E5.

Shipp, E. R.
1984    Candidacy of Jackson Highlights Split Among Black Muslims. *New York Times* (February 27), p. A10.

Shreve, Anita, and Clemans, John
1980    The New Wave of Women Politicians. *New York Times Magazine* (October 19), pp. 28–31, 105–109.

Shribman, David
1981    Congress Finally Acts to Stem the Flood of Foreign Doctors. *New York Times* (December 20), p. E1.

Sigall, H., and Page, R.
1971    Current Stereotypes: A Little Fading, a Little Faking. *Journal of Personality and Social Psychology* 18 (May), pp. 247–255.

Silberman, Charles E.
1971    *Crisis in the Classroom: The Remaking of American Education*. New York: Random House.
1985    *A Certain People*. New York: Summit.

Silk, James
1986    *Despite a Generous Spirit: Denying Asylum in the United States*. Washington, DC: U.S. Committee for Refugees.

Silva, Helga
1985    *The Children of Mariel*. Miami: Cuban American National Foundation.

Silva, Nelson Do Valle
1985    Updating The Cost of Not Being White in Brazil. In Pierre-Michel Fontaine, ed., *Race, Class, and Power in Brazil*, pp. 42–55. Los Angeles: Center for Afro-American Studies, UCLA.

Simkus, Albert A.
1978    Residential Segregation by Occupation and Race in Ten Urbanized Areas, 1950–1970. *American Sociological Review* 43 (February), pp. 81–93.

Simmons, Jerry L.
1969    *Deviants*. Berkeley, CA: Glendessary Press.

Simon, Rita J., and Simon, Julian L.
1982    Some Aspects of the Socio-cultural Adjustment of Recent Soviet Immigrants to the United States. *Ethnic and Racial Studies* 5 (October), pp. 535–541.

Simons, Marlise
1988    Brazil's Blacks Feel Prejudice 100 Years After Slavery's End. *New York Times* (May 14), pp. 1, 6.

Simpson, George Eaton, and Yinger, J. Milton
1985    *Racial and Cultural Minorities: An Analysis of Prejudice and Discrimination*, 5th ed. New York: Plenum.

Singer, Audrey
1988    IRCA Aftermath. *Population Today* 16 (October), pp. 5, 9.

Singer, L.
1962    Ethnogenesis and Negro Americans Today. *Social Research* 29 (Winter), pp. 419–432.

Sites, Paul
1975    *Control and Constraint: An Introduction to Sociology*. New York: Macmillan.

Skidmore, Thomas E.
1972    Toward a Comparative Analysis of Race Relations Since Abolition in Brazil and the United States. *Journal of Latin American Studies* 4 (May), pp. 1–28.

Sklansky, Jeff
1989    Rock, Reservation and Prison: The Native American Occupation of Alcatraz Island. *American Indian Culture and Research Journal* 13 (No. 2), pp. 29–68.

Sklare, Marshall

1971    *America's Jews.* New York: Random House.

Skocpol, Theda
1988    An "Uppity Generation" and the Revitalization of Macroscopic Sociology. In M. W. Riley, ed., *Sociological Lives,* pp. 145–159. Newbury Park, CA: Sage.

Skolnick, Jerome
1969    *The Politics of Protest.* New York: Simon and Schuster.

Slagle, Alton
1973    A Trail of Bitter Truths Leads to Wounded Knee. *Chicago Tribune* (March 11), II, p. 1.

Slavin, Robert E.
1985    Cooperative Learning: Applying Contact Theory in Desegregated Schools. *Journal of Social Issues* 41 (No. 3), pp. 45–62.

Slavin, Stephen L., and Pradt, Mary A.
1979    Anti-Semitism in Banking. *Bankers Magazine* 162 (July–August), pp. 19–21.
1982    *The Einstein Syndrome: Corporate Anti-Semitism in America Today.* Washington, DC: University Press of America.

Sloan, George
1980    30 Pekin High School Students Walk Out of Classes. *Peoria Journal Star* (September 4), p. 4.

Smith, David J.
1974    *Racial Disadvantage in Employment.* London: Political and Economic Planning.

Smith, M. Estelli
1982    Tourism and Native Americans. *Cultural Survival Quarterly* 6 (Summer), pp. 10–12.

Smith, Tom W.
1984    America's Religious Mosaic. *American Demographics* 6 (June), pp. 19, 21, 23.
1991    *What Do Americans Think About Jews?* New York: American Jewish Committee.

Smith, Tom W., and Sheatsley, Paul B.
1984    American Attitudes Toward Race Relations. *Public Opinion* 7 (October/November), pp. 14–15, 50–53.

Snipp, C. Matthew

1980    Determinants of Employment in Wisconsin Native American Communities. *Growth and Change* 11 (No. 2), pp. 39–47.
1986a   The Changing Political and Economic Status of the American Indians: From Captive Nations to Internal Colonies. *American Journal of Economics and Sociology* 45 (April), pp. 145–157.
1986b   American Indians and Natural Resource Development: Indigenous People's Land, Now Sought After, Has Produced New Indian–White Problems. *American Journal of Economics and Sociology* 45 (October), pp. 457–474.
1989    *American Indians: The First of This Land.* New York: Russell Sage Foundation.

Snipp, C. Matthew, and Sandefur, Gary D.
1986    Earnings of American Indians and Alaskan Nations: The Effects of Residence and Migration. Madison, WI: Institute for Research on Poverty, Discussion Paper No. 813–86.

Snyder, Mark
1982    Self-Fulfilling Stereotypes. *Psychology Today* 16 (July), pp. 60, 65, 67–68.

Sochen, June
1982    *Herstory: A Woman's View of American History.* 2nd ed. Palo Alto, CA: Mayfield.

Son, In Soo; Model, Suzanne W.; and Fisher, Gene A.
1989    Polarization and Progress in the Black Community: Earnings and Status Gains for Young Black Males in the Era of Affirmative Action. *Sociological Forum* 4 (September), pp. 309–327.

Song, Tae-Hyon
1991    Social Contact and Ethnic Distance Between Koreans and the U.S. Whites in the United States. Unpublished paper, R. Schaefer's files.

Sorensen, Annemette; Taeuber, Karl E.; and Hollingsworth, Leslie J., Jr.
1975    Indexes of Racial Residential Segregation for 109 Cities in the United States, 1940 to 1970. *Sociological Focus* 8 (April), pp. 125–142.

Sorkin, Alan L.
1969   Some Aspects of American Indian
       Migration. *Social Forces* 48 (De-
       cember), pp. 243–250.

South African Department of Foreign Affairs
and Information
1983   *South Africa, 1983. Official Yearbook
       of the Republic of South Africa.* Jo-
       hannesburg: Republic of South Af-
       rica.

South African Institute of Race Relations
1989   *Race Relations Survey, 1988/89.* Jo-
       hannesburg: South African Institute
       of Race Relations.
1990   *Race Relations Survey, 1989/90.* Jo-
       hannesburg: South African Institute
       of Race Relations.
1992   *Race Relations Survey, 1991/92.* Jo-
       hannesburg: South African Institute
       of Race Relations.

South African Review
1992   Comments from Codesa. 4 (Jan-
       uary), p. 4.

Southall, Roger
1983   *South Africa's Transkei.* New York:
       Monthly Review Press.

Southern, David W.
1987   *Gunnar Myrdal and Black-White Rela-
       tions.* Baton Rouge: Louisiana State
       University.

Spearman, Diana
1968a  The Anti-Enoch Letters. *New Society*
       11 (June 27), p. 945.
1968b  Enoch Powell's Postbag. *New Soci-
       ety* 11 (May 9), pp. 667–669.

Spector, Michael
1990   In New York's Chinatown, the
       Newest Frontier. *Washington Post
       National Weekly Edition* 8 (December
       24), p. 22.

Spencer, Gary
1987   JAP-Baiting on a College Campus:
       An Example of Gender and Ethnic
       Stereotyping. Unpublished paper,
       Syracuse University.

Spencer, Samuel R.
1955   *Booker T. Washington and the Negro's
       Place in American Life.* Boston: Little,
       Brown.

Spicer, Edward
1980   American Indians. In Stephen
       Thernstrom, ed., *Harvard En-*

*cyclopedia of American Ethnic Groups*,
pp. 58–122. Cambridge, MA: Belknap Press of Harvard University
Press.

Spiegel, Don, and Keith-Spiegel, Patricia,
eds.
1973   *Outsiders, U.S.A.* San Francisco:
       Rinehart Press.

Spiegel, Irving
1973a  Jewish Official Fears a Backlash.
       *New York Times* (October 27), p. 9.
1973b  Jews Are Warned of Oil Backlash.
       *New York Times* (November 16), p.
       35.
1974   Rabbi Deplores Small Families.
       *New York Times* (January 24), p. 20.
1975   Educators Called Remiss About
       Bias. *New York Times* (November 9),
       p. 63.

Spindler, George, and Spindler, Louise
1984   *Dreamers with Power: The Menomi-
       nee.* Prospect Heights, IL: Waveland
       Press.

Spreitzer, Elmer, and Snyder, Eldon E.
1975   Patterns of Variation Within and
       Between Ethnoreligious Groupings.
       *Ethnicity* 2 (June), pp. 124–133.

Squitieri, Tom
1989   Many Await Restitution. *USA To-
       day* (September 13), p. 3A.
1992   For N. Ireland, No Celebration.
       *USA Today* (March 17), p. 4A.

Stampp, Kenneth M.
1956   *The Peculiar Institution: Slavery in the
       Ante-Bellum south.* New York: Ran-
       dom House.

Stan, Robert
1985   Samba, Candomble, Quilombo:
       Black Performance and Brazilian
       Cinema. *Journal of Ethnic Studies* 13
       (Fall), 55–84.

Stanfield, John M.
1988   Absurd Assumptions and False
       Optimism Mark the Social Science
       of Race Relations. *Chronicle of High-
       er Education* 35 (July 6), p. B2.

Stanley, Alessandra
1986   Scraphogs Invade Hawthorne. *Time*
       127 (June 30), p. 41

Staples, Brent
1987   Where Are the Black Fans? *New
       York Times Magazine* (May 17), Sect.

6, pp. 26–37, 56.

Staples, Robert E.
1986a The Political Economy of Black
Family Life. *Black Scholar* (Sep-
tember/October), pp. 2–11.
1986b *The Black Family: Essays and Studies,*
3rd ed. Belmont, CA: Wadsworth.

Stark, Rodney
1987 Correcting Church Membership
Rates: 1971 and 1980. *Review of Religious Research* 29 (September), pp.
69–77.

Stark, Rodney, and Bainbridge, William Sims
1985 *The Future of Religion.* Berkeley:
University of California Press.

Stark, Rodney, and Glock, Charles
1968 *American Piety: The Nature of Religious Commitment.* Berkeley: University of California Press.

Stark, Rodney, and Steinberg, Stephen
1967 It Did Happen Here. In Peter I.
Rose, ed., *The Ghetto and Beyond: Essays on Jewish Life in America,* pp.
357–383. New York: Random
House.

Starr, Paul, and Roberts, Alden
1981 Attitudes Toward Indochinese Refugees: An Empirical Study. *Journal
of Refugee Resettlement* 1 (August),
pp. 51–61.

Steinberg, Stephen
1977 *The Academic Melting Pot.* New
Brunswick, NJ: Transaction Books.
1989 The Underclass: A Case of Color
Blindness. *New Politics* 2 (Summer),
pp. 42–60.

Steinem, Gloria
1973 The Verbal Karate of Florynce B.
Kennedy, Esq. *Ms.* (March), p. 54.

Steiner, Stan
1968 *The New Indians.* New York: Harper
and Row.
1974 *The Islands: The Worlds of the Puerto
Ricans.* New York: Harper and
Row.
1976 *The Vanishing White Man.* New
York: Harper and Row.

Stember, Charles Herbert, ed.
1966 *Jews in the Mind of America.* New
York: Basic Books.

Sterba, James P.
1973 They're Trying Not to Vanish. *New
York Times* (November 11), p. E8.

Stevens, Evelyn P.
1973 Machismo and Marianismo. *Society*
10 (September–October), pp. 57–63.

Stevens-Arroyo, Antonio M., and Díaz-
Ramírez, Ana María
1982 Puerto Ricans in the States. In
Anthony Dworkin and Rosalind
Dworkin, eds., *The Minority Report,*
2nd ed., pp. 196–232. New York:
Holt, Rinehart and Winston.

Stewart, James H.
1979 Structural Pluralism and Urban Indians: A Research Strategy. Paper
presented at the annual meeting of
the Midwest Sociological Society.

Stockton, William
1978 Going Home: The Puerto Ricans'
New Migration. *New York Times
Magazine* (November 12), pp. 20–22,
87–93.

Stoddard, Ellyn R.
1973 *Mexican Americans.* New York: Random House.
1976a A Conceptual Analysis of the
"Alien Invasion": Institutionalized
Support of Illegal Mexican Aliens
in the U.S. *International Migration
Review* 10 (Summer), pp. 157–189.
1976b Illegal Mexican Labor in the Bor-
derlands: Institutionalized Support
of an Unlawful Practice. *Pacific Sociological Review* 19 (April), pp. 175–
210.

Stone, Andrea
1992 No Simple Answers to Rebuilding
a Community. *USA Today* (May 5),
p. 4A.

Stonequist, Everett V.
1937 *The Marginal Man: A Study in Personality and Culture Conflict.* New
York: Scribner.

Stouffer, Samuel A.
1955 *Communism, Conformity, and Civil
Liberties.* Garden City, NY: Doubleday.

Strober, Gerald S.
1974 *American Jews: Community in Crisis.*
Garden City, NY: Doubleday.

Stryker, Sheldon
1959 Social Structure and Prejudice. *Social Problems* 6 (Spring), pp. 340–

354.

Stuart, Reginald
1982    Judge Overturns Arkansas Law on Creationism. *New York Times* (January 6), pp. A1, B7–B8.
1983    Once a Showcase of Growth, Puerto Rico Battles a Slump. *New York Times* (July 24), pp. 1, 10.
1984    Protestants Stepping up Puerto Rico Conversion. *New York Times* (February 14), p. 13.

Studler, Donley
1974    British Public Opinion, Colour Issues, and Enoch Powell: A Longitudinal Analysis. *British Journal of Political Science* 4 (July), pp. 371–381.
1975    The Impact of the Colored Immigration Issue on British Electoral Politics, 1964–1970. Unpublished Ph.D. dissertation, Indiana University.

Stump, Roger W.
1986    Women Clergy in the United States: A Geographical Analysis of Religious Change. *Social Science Quarterly* 67 (June), pp. 337–352.

Suarez, Manuel
1985    F.B.I. Discerns Big Gain on Puerto Rico Terror. *New York Times* (August 8), p. 10.

Sue, Stanley; Zane, Nolan W. S.; and Sue, Derald
1985    Where Are the Asian American Leaders and Top Executives? *P/AAMHRC Review* 4 (January/April), pp. 13–15.

Sullivan, Cheryl
1986a    Seeking Self-sufficiency. *Christian Science Monitor* (June 26), pp. 16–17.
1986b    Indians in the City. *Christian Science Monitor* (June 26), pp. 16–17.

Sullivan, Leon H.
1985    Give the Sullivan Principles Two More Years. *Washington Post National Weekly Edition* 2 (June 10), p. 28.
1986    Going All-Out Against Apartheid. *New York Times* (July 27), sect. 3, p. 1.

Sumner, William G.
1906    *Folkways.* New York: Ginn.

Sundiata, Ibrahim K.

1987    Late Twentieth Century Patterns of Race Relations in Brazil and the United States. *Phylon* 48 (March), pp. 62–76.

Sung, Betty Lee
1967    *Mountains of Gold: The Story of the Chinese in America.* New York: Macmillan.
1976    *A Survey of Chinese-American Manpower and Employment.* New York: Praeger.

Suro, Roberto
1989    Switch by Hispanic Catholics Changes Face of U.S. Religion. *New York Times* (May 14), pp. 1, 14.

Sussman, Barry
1985    Loaded Questions, Faulty Data. *Washington Post National Weekly Edition* (October 14), p. 37.
1986    Black Men Know What They Need: Jobs and More Jobs. *Washington Post National Weekly Edition* 3 (March 3), p. 32.

Suter, Larry E., and Miller, Herman P.
1973    Income Differences Between Men and Career Women. *American Journal of Sociology* 78 (January), pp. 962–974.

Sutherland, Elizabeth
1970    Colonized Women: The Chicana. In Robin Morgan, ed., *Sisterhood Is Powerful,* pp. 376–379. New York: Random House.

Suttles, Gerald D.
1972    *The Social Construction of Communities.* Chicago: University of Chicago Press.

Svensson, Craig K.
1989    Representation of American Blacks in Clinical Trials of New Drugs. *Journal of the American Medical Association* 261 (January 13), pp. 263–265.

Sweet, Jill D.
1990    The Portals of Tradition: Tourism in the American Southwest. *Cultural Survival Quarterly* 14 (No. 2), pp. 6–8.

Swinton, David
1987    Economic Status of Blacks 1986. In Janet Dewart, ed., *The State of Black America,* pp. 49–73. New York: National Urban League.

Swoboda, Frank
1990 Workplace Discrimination? So What's New? *Washington Post National Weekly Edition* 7 (July 30), p. 37.

Tachibana, Judy
1986 California's Asians: Power from a Growing Population. *California Journal* (November), pp. 534–543.
1990 Model Minority Myth Presents Unrepresentative Portrait of Asian Americans, Many Educators Say. *Black Issues in Higher Education* 6 (March 1), pp. 1, 11.

Taeuber, Karl E.
1975 Racial Segregation: The Persisting Dilemma. *Annals of the American Academy of Political and Social Sciences* 442 (November), pp. 87–96.

Taeuber, Karl E., and Taeuber, Alma F.
1964 The Negro as an Immigrant Group: Recent Trends in Racial and Ethnic Segregation in Chicago. *American Journal of Sociology* 69 (January), pp. 374–382.
1969 *Negroes in Cities: Residential Segregation and Neighborhood Change.* New York: Atheneum.
1976 A Practitioner's Perspective on the Index of Dissimilarity. *American Sociological Review* 41 (October), pp. 884–889.

Takaki, Ronald
1989 *Strangers From a Different Shore: A History of Asian Americans.* Boston: Little, Brown.

Tang, Joyce
1991 Asian American Engineers: Earnings, Occupational Status, and Promotions. Paper presented at the annual meeting of the American Sociological Association, Cincinnati.

Tannenbaum, Frank
1946 *Slave and Citizen.* New York: Random House.

Taylor, Dalmas A.
1984 Toward the Promised Land. *Psychology Today* 18 (June), pp. 46–50.

Taylor, Frank J.
1942 The People Nobody Wants. *The Saturday Evening Post* 2,142 (May 9), pp. 24–25, 64, 66–67.

Taylor, Paul, and John, Kenneth

1985 Other Voices, *Washington Post National Weekly Edition* 2 (October 7), p. 38.

Taylor, Robert Joseph; Chatters, Linda M.; Tucker, M. Belinda; and Lewis, Edith
1990 Developments in Research on Black Families: A Decade Review. *Journal of Marriage and the Family* 52 (November), pp. 993–1014.

Taylor, Ronald A.
1982 Where Indian Tribes Fit into Reagan's Plan. *U.S. News and World Report* 92 (March 15), p. 68.

Taylor, Stuart, Jr.
1987a High Court Backs Basing Promotion on a Racial Quota. *New York Times* (February 26), pp. 1, 14.
1987b Supreme Court, 6–3, Extends Preferences in Employment for Women and Minorities. *New York Times* (March 26), pp. 1, 13.
1987c Court, 5–4, Rejects Racial Challenge to Death Penalty. *New York Times* (April 23), pp. A1, B13.
1988 Justices Back New York Law Ending Sex Bias by Big Clubs. *New York Times* (June 21), pp. A1, A18.

Taylor, Theodore W.
1972 *The States and Their Indian Citizens.* Washington, DC: U.S. Government Printing Office.

Telles, Edward E.
1992 Residential Segregation by Skin Color in Brazil. *American Sociological Review* 57 (April), pp. 186–197.

ten Brock, Jacobus; Barnhart, Edward N.; and Matson, Floyd W.
1954 *Prejudice, War and the Constitution.* Berkeley: University of California Press.

Terchek, Ronald J.
1977 Conflict and Cleavage in Northern Ireland. *The Annals* (September), pp. 47–59.
1982 Political Violence in Northern Ireland: Myths and Options. *USA Today* 3 (September), pp. 18–21.

Terry, Clifford
1975 Chicagoans—Pro Soccer. *Chicago Tribune Magazine* (May 5), p. 26.

Terry, Wallace
1984 *Bloods: An Oral History of the Vietnam War by Black Veterans.* New

York: Random House.

Thernstrom, Stephen, ed.
1980   *Harvard Encyclopedia of American Ethnic Groups.* Cambridge, MA: Belknap Press of Harvard University Press.

Thomas, Curlew O., and Thomas, Barbara Boston
1984   Blacks' Socioeconomic Status and the Civil Rights Movement's Decline, 1970–1979: An Examination of Some Hypotheses. *Phylon* 45 (March), pp. 40–51.

Thomas, Dorothy S., and Nishimoto, Richard S.
1946   *The Spoilage: Japanese-American Evacuation and Resettlement.* Berkeley: University of California Press.

Thomas, Jo
1985   Anglo-Irish Agreement Pits Both Ends Against the Middle. *New York Times* (November 24), p. E3.

Thomas, Melvin E., and Hughes, Michael
1986   The Continuing Significance of Race: A Study of Race, Class, and Quality of Life in America, 1972–1985. *American Sociological Review* 51 (December), pp. 830–841.

Thomas, Piri
1967   *Down These Mean Streets.* New York: Signet.

Thomas, Robert K.
1970   Pan-Indianism. In Stuart Levine and Nancy Oestreich Lurie, eds., *The American Indian Today*, pp. 128–140. Baltimore: Penguin.

Thomas, William Isaac
1923   *The Unadjusted Girl.* Boston: Little, Brown.

Thompson, John L. P.
1983   The Plural Society Approach to Class and Ethnic Political Mobilization. *Ethnic and Racial Studies* 6 (April), pp. 127–153.

Thompson, Morris S.
1990   New Face of U.S. to be More Global. *USA Today* (November 1), pp. A1–A2.

Thornton, Michael C., and Taylor, Robert J.
1988   Black American Perception of Black Africans. *Ethnic and Racial Studies* 2 (April), pp. 139–150.

Thornton, Russell
1981   Demographic Antecedents of the 1890 Ghost Dance. *American Sociological Review* 46 (February), pp. 88–96.
1991   North American Indians and the Demography of Contact. Paper presented at the annual meeting of the American Sociological Association, Cincinnati.

Thurow, Lester C.
1980   *The Zero-Sum Society: Distribution and the Possibilities for Economic Change.* New York: Basic Books.
1984   It's Not Just Demographics: The Disappearance of the Middle Class. *New York Times* (February 5), p. F3.

Tienda, Marta
1989a   Puerto Ricans and the Underclass Debate. *Annals* 501 (January), pp. 105–119.
1989b   Race, Ethnicity, and the Portrait of Inequality: Approaching the 1990s. *Sociological Spectrum* 9 (No. 1), pp. 23–52.

Tijerina, Kathryn Harris, and Biemer, Paul Philip
1988   The Dance of Indian Higher Education: One Step Forward, Two Steps Back. *Educational Record* 68 (Winter), pp. 86–91.

*Time*
1969   The Little Strike That Grew to LaCausa. (July 4): 16–22.
1970   Women at the Altar. (November 2), pp. 71, 79.
1972a   The Right to Be Different. (May 29), p. 67.
1972b   What It Means to Be Jewish. (April 10), pp. 54–64.
1974a   Are You a Jew? (September 2), pp. 56, 59.
1974b   Brown's Bomb. (November 25), pp. 16, 19.
1974c   The Women Gain. (July 1), p. 47.
1975   The A.J.A.'s Fast Rising Sons. (October 20), pp. 26, 31.
1979   Fuel Powwow. (August 20), p. 17.

Tinker, John N.
1973   Intermarriage and Ethnic Boundaries: The Japanese American Case. *Journal of Social Issues* 29 (No. 2), pp. 49–66.

Tirado, Miguel David
1970   Mexican American Community Political Organization. *Aztlan* 1 (Spring), pp. 53–78.

Tiryakian, Edward A.
1967   Sociological Realism: Partition for South Africa? *Social Forces* 46 (December), pp. 209–221.

Tomlinson, T. M.
1969   The Development of a Riot Ideology Among Urban Negroes. In Allen D. Grimshaw, ed., *Racial Violence in the United States*, pp. 226–235. Chicago: Aldine.

Toner, Robin
1987   Bible Is Being Translated Into a Southern Coastal Tongue Born of Slavery. *New York Times* (March 1), p. 18.

Tostado, Ricardo
1985   Political Participation. In Pastora San Juan Caffety and William C. McCready, eds., *Hispanics in the United States*, pp. 235–252. New Brunswick, NJ: Transaction Books.

Toth, Csanad
1972   The Media and the Ethnics. In Michael Wenk, S. M. Tomasi, and Geno Baroni, eds., *Pieces of a Dream: The Ethnic Worker's Crisis with America*, pp. 13–30. New York: Center for Migration Studies.

Treen, Joseph
1983   Apartheid's Harsh Grip. *Newsweek* (March 28), pp. 31–32, 37.

Trejo, Arnulfo, D., ed.
1979   *Chicanos: As We See Ourselves.* Tucson: University of Arizona Press.

Triandis, Harry C., and Triandis, Leigh M.
1960   Race, Social Class, Religion, and Nationality as Determinants of Social Distance. *Journal of Abnormal and Social Psychology* 61 (July), pp. 110–118.

Trillin, Calvin
1970   U.S. Journal: Provo, Utah. *New Yorker* (March 21), p. 120.

Trimble, Albert
1976   An Era of Great Change, A Single Decency Is Goal for Oglala Sioux. *Wassaja* 4 (May), p. 5.

Trotter, Robert J.

1985   Profile Muzafer Sherif: A Life of Conflict and Goals. *Psychology Today* 19 (September), pp. 54–59.

Trottier, Richard W.
1981   Charters of Panethnic Identity: Indigenous American Indians and Immigrant Asian-Americans. In Charles F. Keyes, ed., *Ethnic Change*, pp. 272–305. Seattle: University of Washington Press.

Tsuchigane, Robert, and Dodge, Norton
1974   *Economic Discrimination Against Women in the United States: Measures and Change.* Lexington, MA: Heath.

Tuch, Steven A.
1981   Analyzing Recent Trends in Prejudice Toward Blacks: Insights from Latent Class Models. *American Journal of Sociology* 87 (July), pp. 130–142.

Tule Lake Committee
1980   *Kinenhi: Reflections on Tule Lake.* San Francisco: Tule Lake Committee.

Tumin, Melvin M., with Feldman, Arnold
1961   *Social Class and Social Change in Puerto Rico.* Princeton, NJ: Princeton University Press.

Turner, James
1973   The Sociology of Black Nationalism. In Joyce A. Ladner, ed., *The Death of White Sociology*, pp. 234–252. New York: Random House.

Turner, Margery; Fix, Michael; and Struyck, Raymond J.
1991   *Opportunities Denied, Opportunities Diminished: Discrimination in Hiring.* Washington, DC: The Urban Institute.

Turner, Margery; Struyck, Raymond J.; and Yinger, John
1991   *Housing Discrimination Study: Synthesis.* Washington, DC: The Urban Institute.

Turner, Wallace
1972   New Hawaii Economy Stirs Minority Upset. *New York Times* (August 13), pp. 1, 46.

Twining, Mary Arnold
1985   Movement and Dance on the Sea Islands. *Journal of Black Studies* 15 (June), pp. 463–479.

Tyler, Gus

1972 White Worker/Blue Mood. *Dissent* 19 (Winter), pp. 190–196.

Tyler, S. Lyman
1973 *A History of Indian Policy.* Washington, DC: U.S. Government Printing Office.

Uchida, Yoshiko
1982 *Desert Exile.* Seattle: University of Washington Press.

*United Tribes News*
1974 Nixon in Retrospect. 1 (October 8), pp. 8–9.

*USA Today*
1985 4M Illegal Aliens Slip Over Border. (October 11), p. A1.
1991 By the Numbers, Tracking Segregation in 219 Metro Areas. (November 11), p. 3A.

U.S. Committee for Refugees
1990 *World Refugee Survey-1991.* Washington, DC: American Council for Nationalities Services.

Usdansky, Margaret L.
1991 USA at Home: Streets Still Isolate Race. *USA Today* (November 11), pp. 1A, 2A.

Valentine, Charles A.
1968 *Culture and Poverty: Critique and Counter-Proposals.* Chicago: University of Chicago Press.

van den Berghe, Pierre L.
1965 *South Africa: A Study in Conflict.* Middletown, CT: Wesleyan University Press.
1978 *Race and Racism: A Comparative Perspective,* 2nd ed. New York: Wiley.

Vander Zanden, James W.
1983 *American Minority Relations,* 4th ed. New York, Plenum.

Vanneman, Reene and Cannon, Lynn Weber
1987 *The American Perception of Class.* Philadelphia: Temple University Press.

Van Valey, Thomas L.; Roof, Wade Clark; and Wilcox, Jerome E.
1976 Trends in Residential Segregation: 1960–1970. *American Journal of Sociology* 83 (January), pp. 826–844.

Varner, Hazel S.
1981 Title IX: In Jeopardy. *Womannews* (November), pp. 4, 15.

Vasquez, Enriqueta Longauex y

1970 The Mexican-American Women. In Robin Morgan, ed., *Sisterhood Is Powerful,* pp. 379–384. New York: Random House.

Vasquez, Melba J. T.
1982 Confronting Barriers to the Participation of Mexican American Women in Higher Education. *Hispanic Journal of Behavioral Sciences* 4 (June), pp. 147–165.

Vass, Winifred Kellersberger
1979 *The Bantu-Speaking Heritage of the United States.* Los Angeles: Center for Afro-American Studies.

Vaughn, Mary K.
1974 Tourism in Puerto Rico. In Adalberto Lopez and James Petra, eds., *Puerto Rico and Puerto Ricans: Studies in History and Society,* pp. 271–295. New York: Wiley.

Vecoli, Rudolph J.
1970 Ethnicity: A Neglected Dimension of American History. In Herbert J. Bass, ed., *The State of American History,* pp. 70–88. Chicago: Quadrangle Books.
1987 Hansen's Classic Essay Revisited. Presentation at Ethnic Mosaic of the Quad Cities Conference, Rock Island, IL.

Vega, William A.
1990 Hispanic Families in the 1980s: A Decade of Research. *Journal of Marriage and the Family* 52 (November), pp. 1015–1024.

Vega, William A., et al.
1986 Cohesion and Adaptability in Mexican-American and Anglo Families. *Journal of Marriage and the Family* 48 (November), pp. 857–867.

Veidmanis, Juris
1963 Neglected Areas in the Sociology of Immigrants and Ethnic Groups in North America. *Sociological Quarterly* 4 (Autumn), pp. 325–333.

Velez, William
1984 Puerto Rico: Submerged or Emerging Nation. Paper presented at the Annual Meeting of the American Sociological Association, San Antonio.

Vidal, David
1977 Bilingual Instruction Is Thriving

But Criticized. *New York Times* (January 30), p. E19.

Vigil, James Diego
1980    *From Indians to Chicanos: A Sociocultural History.* St. Louis: Mosby Company.

Vigil, Maurilio
1990    The Ethnic Organization as an Instrument of Political and Social Change: MALDEF, a Case Study. *The Journal of Ethnic Studies* 18 (Spring), pp. 15–31.

Vobejda, Barbara
1991    The 1980s: Decade of the Immigrant. *Washington Post National Weekly Edition* 8 (January 7), p. 31.

Volsky, George
1976    U.S. Restudies Aid to Cuba Refugees. *New York Times* (August 8), p. 17.
1985    Jews Are Urged to Encourage Converts in Mixed Marriages. *New York Times* (November 10), p. 15.

Waddell, Jack O., and Watson, O. Michael
1973    *American Indian Urbanization.* Lafayette, IN: Purdue University Research Foundation.

Wagenheim, Kal
1975    *Puerto Rico: A Profile,* 2nd ed. New York: Praeger.
1983    *Puerto Ricans in the U.S.* New York: Minority Rights Group.

Wagley, Charles, and Harris, Marvin
1958    *Minorities in the New World: Six Case Studies.* New York: Columbia University Press.

Waite, Juan J.
1991    INS Too Stringent Some Critics Claim. *USA Today* (December 11), p. 10A.

Waitzkin, Howard
1986    *The Second Sickness: Contradictions of Capitalist Health Care.* Chicago: University of Chicago Press.

Wakabayashi, Ron
1987    After 45 Years, Attempting Amends. *USA Today* (September 16), p. 14A.

Walker, Kathryn E., and Woods, Margaret E.
1976    *Time Use: A Measure of Household Production of Family Goods and Services.* Washington, DC: American

Home Economics Association.

Wallace, Steven P.
1984    Macro and Micro Issues in Intergenerational Relationships Within the Latino Family and Community. Paper presented at the annual meeting of the Society for the Study of Social Problems, San Antonio.
1989    The New Urban Latinos: Central Americans in a Mexican Immigrant Environment. *Urban Affairs Quarterly* 25 (December), pp. 239–264.

Wallace, Steven P., and Facio, Elisa Linda
1986    Moving Beyond Familism: Potential Contributions of Gerontological Theory to Studies of Chicano/Latino Aging. Paper presented at the Annual Meeting of the Society for the Study of Social Problems, New York.

Wallerstein, Immanuel
1979    *Capitalist World-Economy.* Cambridge: Cambridge University Press.

Walters, Robert
1990    Puerto Rico Debates Its Future Again. *Macomb Journal* (May 18), p. 4.

Wang, L. Ling-Chi
1988    Meritocracy and Diversity in Higher Education: Discrimination Against Asian Americans in the Post-Bakke Era. *The Urban Review* 20 (Fall), pp. 189–209.
1991    Roots and Changing Identity of the Chinese in the United States. *Daedalus* 120 (Spring), pp. 181–206.

Warfield, Wallace
1987    Correspondence with R. Schaefer, March 24.

Warner, Sam Bass, Jr.
1968    *The Private City: Philadelphia in Three Periods of Its Growth.* Philadelphia: University of Pennsylvania Press.

Warner, W. Lloyd
1937    American Caste and Class. *American Journal of Sociology* 42 (September), 234–237.

Warner, W. Lloyd, and Srole, Leo
1945    *The Social Systems of American Ethnic Groups.* New Haven, CT: Yale University Press.

Washburn, Wilcomb E.
1984 A Fifty-Year Perspective on the Indian Reorganization Act. *American Anthropologist* 86 (June), pp. 279–289.

Washington, Booker T.
1900 *Up From Slavery: An Autobiography.* New York: A. L. Burt.

Watanabe, Colin
1973 Self-Expression and the Asian-American Experience. *Personnel and Guidance Journal* 51 (February), pp. 392–396.

Waters, Harry F.
1982 Life According to TV. *Newsweek* 100 (December 6), pp. 136–138, 140.

Waters, Harry F., and Huck, Janet
1989 Networking Women. *Newsweek* 103 (March 13), pp. 48–54.

Watson, Russell
1988 Your Jewishness Is Not Good Enough. *Newsweek* 112 (November 28), p. 51.

Waugh, Jack
1970 Indians Heartened by Grant of Sacred Lands. *Christian Science Monitor* (December 5), p. 9.

Wax, Murray L.
1968 The White Man's Burdensome "Business": A Review Essay on the Change and Constancy of Literature on the American Indians. *Social Problems* 16 (Summer), pp. 106–113.
1971 *Indian Americans: Unity and Diversity.* Englewood Cliffs, NJ: Prentice-Hall.

Wax, Murray L., and Buchanan, Robert W.
1975 *Solving "the Indian Problem": The White Man's Burdensome Business.* New York: New York Times Book Company.

Waxman, Chaim I.
1983 *America's Jews in Transition.* Philadelphia: Temple University Press.

Webb, Susan L.
1992 *Step Forward: Sexual Harassment in the Workplace.* New York: Master-Media.

Webster, Peggy Lovell, and Dwyer, Jeffrey W.
1988 The Cost of Being Nonwhite in Brazil. *Social Science Research* (January), pp. 136–142.

Weglyn, Michi
1976 *Years of Infamy.* New York: Quill Paperbacks.

Weicher, John C.
1988 Persistent Slums. *Public Opinion* 10 (January/February), pp. 52–54.

Weigel, Gustave
1961 *Churches in North America: An Introduction.* Baltimore: Helicon Press.

Weil, Frederick D.
1983 The Effects of Education on Anti-Semitism in the United States, West Germany, Austria, and France Since World War II. Paper presented at the annual meeting of the American Sociological Association, Detroit.

Weil, Thomas E.; Black, J.; Blutstein, H.; Johnston, K.; and McMorris, D.
1975 *Area Handbook for Brazil,* 3rd ed. Washington, DC: U.S. Government Printing Office.

Weinberg, Meyer
1977 *A Chance to Learn: A History of Race and Education in the United States.* Cambridge: Cambridge University Press.

Weinberg, Richard A.
1989 Intelligence and I.Q.: Landmark Issues and Great Debates. *American Psychologist* 44 (February), pp. 98–104.

Weisberger, Bernard A.
1971 *The American People.* New York: American Heritage.

Weisman, Steven R.
1984 President Signs a Bill to Permit School Worship. *New York Times* (August 11), pp. 1, 24.

Weiss, Melford S.
1973 *Valley City: A Chinese Community in America.* Cambridge, MA: Schenkman.

Weisskopf, Michael
1988 A Pesticide Peril in a Land of Plenty. *Washington Post National Weekly Edition* 5 (September 12–18), pp. 10–11.

Wells, Robert N., Jr.
1989 Native Americans' Needs Over-

looked by Colleges. Unpublished paper. Canton, NY: St. Lawrence University.

1991 Indian Education from the Tribal Perspective: A Survey of American Indian Tribal Leaders. Unpublished paper.

Wenneker, Mark B., and Epstein, Arnold M.
1989 Racial Inequalities in the Use of Procedures for Patients with Ischemic Heart Disease in Massachusetts. *Journal of the American Medical Association* 261 (January 31), pp. 253–257.

Weppner, Robert S.
1971 Urban Economic Opportunities. In Jack O. Waddell and O. Michael Watson, eds., *The American Indian in Urban Society*, pp. 244–273. Boston: Little, Brown.

Westfried, Alex Huxley
1981 *Ethnic Leadership in a New England Community: Three Puerto Rican Families.* Cambridge, MA: Schenkman.

Westie, Frank R.
1952 Negro-White Status Differentials and Social Distance. *American Sociological Review* 17 (October), pp. 550–558.

Westie, Frank R., and Howard, David H.
1954 Social Status Differentials and the Race Attitudes of Negroes. *American Sociological Review* 19 (October), pp. 584–591.

Weyr, Thomas
1988 *Hispanic U.S.A.* New York: Harper and Row.

White, O. Kendall, Jr., and White, Daryl
1980 Abandoning an Unpopular Policy: An Analysis of the Decision Granting the Mormon Priesthood to Blacks. *Sociological Analysis* 41 (Fall), pp. 231–245.

Whitman, Alden
1974 Male-Only Priesthoods Cite Chapter, If Not Verse. *New York Times* (August 4), p. E10.

Whitman, David
1987 For Latinos, a Growing Divide *U.S. News and World Report* (August 10), pp. 47–49.

Whitney, Craig R.

1988 Belfast: Strife-Wracked but No Beirut. *New York Times* (October 30), p. 10.

Whyte, John H.
1986 How Is the Boundary Maintained Between the Two Communities in Northern Ireland *Ethnic and Racial Studies* 9 (April), pp. 219–234.

Whyte, Martin King
1978 *The Status of Women in Preindustrial Societies.* Princeton, NJ: Princeton University Press.

Wikler, Norma Juliet
1976 Sexism in the Classroom. Paper presented at the annual meeting of the American Sociological Association, New York.

Wilkinson, Glen A.
1966 Indian Tribal Claims Before the Court of Claims. *Georgetown Law Journal* 55 (December 1966), pp. 511–528.

Willhelm, Sidney M.
1980 Can Marxism Explain America's Racism? *Social Problems* 28 (December), pp. 98–112.

Williams, Franklin H.
1976 The Forgotten Minority: A Review of Problems Confronting Asian Americans in New York City. Statement made as Chairperson of the New York State Advisory Committee to the United States Commission on Civil Rights. News release, May 27.

Williams, Jenny
1985 Redefining Institutional Racism. *Ethnic and Racial Studies* 8 (July), pp. 323–348.

Williams, Robin M., Jr.
1975 Race and Ethnic Relations. In Alex Inkeles, James Coleman, and Neil Smelser, eds., *Annual Review of Sociology*, pp. 125–164. Palo Alto, CA: Annual Reviews.

Willie, Charles V.
1978 The Inclining Significance of Race. *Society* 15 (July/August), pp. 10, 12–13.

1979 *The Caste and Class Controversy.* Bayside, NY: General Hall.

Willig, Ann C.

1985　A Meta-Analysis of Selected Studies on the Effectiveness of Bilingual Education. *Review of Educational Research,* 55 (3), pp. 269–317.

Wilson, David S.
1988　Grapes Are Selling Briskly Despite Farm Union Boycott. *New York Times* (November 27), p. 16.

Wilson, James Q., and Banfield, Edward C.
1964　Public Regardingness as a Value Premise in Voting Behavior. *American Political Science Review* 58 (December), pp. 876–887.

Wilson, John
1973　*Introduction to Social Movements.* New York: Basic Books.

Wilson, Thomas C.
1986　Interregional Migration and Racial Attitudes 65. *Social Forces* 65 (September), pp. 177–186.

Wilson, William J.
1973　*Power, Racism and Privilege: Race Relations in Theoretical and Sociohistorical Perspectives.* New York: Macmillan.
1978　The Declining Significance of Race: Revisited but Not Revised. *Society* 15 (July/August), pp. 11, 16–27.
1980　*The Declining Significance of Race: Blacks and Changing American Institutions,* 2nd ed. Chicago: University of Chicago Press.
1984　The Urban Underclass. In Leslie W. Dunbar, ed., *Minority Report,* pp. 75–117. New York: Pantheon.
1987a　*The Truly Disadvantaged: The Inner City, the Underclass, and Public Policy.* Chicago: University of Chicago Press.
1987b　The Ghetto Underclass and the Social Transformation of the Inner City. Paper presented at the Annual Meeting of the American Association for the Advancement of Science, Chicago.
1988　The Ghetto Underclass and the Social Transformation of the Inner City. *The Black Scholar* 19 (May–June), pp. 10–17.
1991　Poverty, Joblessness, and Family Structure in the Inner City: A Comparative Perspective. Paper presented at the Chicago Urban Poverty and Family Life Conference, Chicago.

Winant, Howard
1989　The Other Side of the Process: Racial Formation in Contemporary Brazil. Paper presented at the annual meeting of the American Sociological Association, San Francisco.

Winant, Howard, and Omi, Michael
1986　The Racial Formation Process: Constructing and Contesting the Meaning of Race in the United States. Paper presented at the annual meeting of the American Sociological Association, New York City.

Winch, Robert F.; Greer, Scott; and Blumburg, Rae Lesser
1967　Ethnicity and Extended Familism in an Upper-Middle Class Suburb. *American Sociological Review* 32 (April), pp. 265–272.

Winkler, Karen
1990a　Scholars Say Issues of Diversity Have "Revolutionized" Field of Chicano Studies. *Chronicle of Higher Education* 37 (September 26), pp. A1, A6, A8.
1990b　Researcher's Examination of California's Poor Latino Population Prompts Debate over the Traditional Definitions of the Underclass. *Chronicle of Higher Education* 37 (October 10), pp. A5, A8.

Winsberg, Morton D.
1983　Ethnic Competition for Residential Space in Miami, Florida, 1970–80. *American Journal of Economics and Sociology* 42 (July), pp. 305–314.

Wirth, Louis
1928　*The Ghetto.* Chicago: University of Chicago Press.
1945　The Problem of Minority Groups. In Ralph Linton, ed., *The Science of Man in the World Crisis,* pp. 347–372. New York: Columbia University Press.

Witt, Shirley Hill
1970　Nationalistic Trends Among American Indians. In Stuart Levine and Nancy Oestreich Lurie, eds., *The American Indian Today,* pp. 93–127. Baltimore: Penguin.

Wolf, Richard, and Benedetto, Richard
1992 Bush Moves "To Restore Hope."
*USA Today* (May 13), p. 4A.

Wolfe, Ann G.
1972 The Invisible Jewish Poor. *Journal of Jewish Communal Sciences* 48 (No. 3), pp. 259–265.

Wolfe, Tom
1969 The New Yellow Peril. *Esquire* (December), p. 190.

Woll, Allen
1981 How Hollywood Has Portrayed Hispanics. *New York Times* (March 1), pp. D17, D22.

Wong, Bernard P.
1982 *Chinatown.* New York: Holt, Rinehart and Winston.

Wong, Eugene F.
1985 Asian American Middleman Minority Theory: The Framework of an American Myth. *The Journal of Ethnic Studies* 13 (Spring), pp. 51–88.

Wong, Morrison G.
1991 Rise in Anti-Asian Activities in the United States. Paper presented at the annual meeting of the American Sociological Association, Cincinnati.

Wood, Robert C.
1959 *Suburbia, Its People and Their Politics.* Boston: Houghton Mifflin.

Woodrum, Eric
1981 An Assessment of Japanese American Assimilation, Pluralism, and Subordination. *American Journal of Sociology* 87 (July), pp. 157–169.

Woodson, Carter G.
1968 *The African Background Outlined.* New York: Negro Universities Press.

Woodward, C. Vann
1974 *The Strange Career of Jim Crow,* 3rd rev. ed. New York: Oxford University Press.

Woodward, Kenneth L.
1991 The Intermarrying Kind. *Newsweek* 118 (July 22), pp. 48–49.

Wren, Christopher
1991 South Africa Scraps Law Defining People by Color. *New York Times* (June 18), pp. A1, A8.

Wright, Mary Bowen

1980 Indochinese. In Stephen Thernstrom, ed., *Harvard Encyclopedia of American Ethnic Groups,* pp. 508–513. Cambridge, MA: Belknap Press of Harvard University Press.

Wright, Michael
1982 Stalled Economy Speeds Puerto Rico's Brain Drain. *New York Times.* (November 28).

Wright, Paul, and Gardner, Robert W.
1983 *Ethnicity, Birthplace, and Achievement: The Changing Hawaii Mosaic.* Honolulu: East-West Population Institute.

Wright, Susan
1992 Blaming the Victim, Blaming Society, or Blaming the Discipline: Fixing Responsibility for Homelessness. Presidential address presented at the annual meeting of the Midwest Sociological Society, Kansas City.

Wrong, Dennis H.
1972 How Important Is Social Class? *Dissent* 19 (Winter), pp. 278–285.

Wu, Cheng-Tsu
1972 *Chink!* New York: Meridian.

Wuthnow, Robert
1982 Anti-Semitism and Stereotyping. In Arthur G. Miller, ed., *In the Eye of the Beholder,* pp. 137–187. New York: Praeger.

Yamamoto, Joe
1968 Japanese American Identity Crisis. In Eugene B. Brody, ed., *Minority Group Adolescents in the United States,* pp. 135–156. Baltimore: Williams and Wilkins.

Yancey, William L.; Erickson, Eugene P.; and Juliani, Richard N.
1976 Emergent Ethnicity: A Review and Reformation. *American Sociological Review* 41 (June), pp. 391–403.

Yarrow, Marian Radke; Campbell, John D.; and Yarrow, Leon J.
1958 Acquisition of New Norms: A Study of Racial Desegregation. *Journal of Social Issues* 14 (No. 1), pp. 8–28.

Yates, Liz
1984 1984 Civil Rights Act Left to Die. *Off Our Backs* 14 (November), p. 14.

Yee, Albert H.

1973    Myopic Perceptions and Textbooks: Chinese Americans' Search for Identity. *Journal of Social Issues* 29 (No. 2), pp. 99–113.

Yee, Min S.
1972a    Busing Comes to Chinatown. *Race Relations Reporter* 3 (January), pp. 18–21.
1972b    Cracks in the Great Wall of Chinatown. *Ramparts* 7 (October), pp. 34–38.

Yetman, Norman R., and Steele, C. Hoy, eds.
1985    *Majority and Minority: The Dynamics of Race and Ethnicity in American Life,* 4th ed. Boston: Allyn and Bacon.

Yinger, J. Milton
1961    *Sociology Looks at Religion.* New York: Macmillan.
1976    Ethnicity in Complex Societies: Structural, Cultural, and Characterological Factors. In Lewis Coser and Otto Larsen, eds., *The Uses of Controversy in Sociology,* pp. 197–216. New York: Free Press.

Yinger, John
1978    The Black-White Price Differential in Housing: Some Further Evidence. *Land Economics* 54 (May), pp. 187–206.

Yoneda, Karl
1971    100 Years of Japanese Labor History in the USA. In Amy Tachiki, Eddie Wong, Franklin Odo, and Buck Wong, eds., *Roots: An Asian American Reader,* pp. 150–158. Los Angeles: Asian American Studies Center, UCLA.

Yong, Arthur, and Devaney, R. Hohn
1982    *Sheltering Americans: New Directions of Growth and Change.* Washington, DC: U.S. Government Printing Office.

Yu, Elena S. H.
1980    Filipino Migration and Community Organizations in the United States. *California Sociologist* 3 (Summer), pp. 76–102.

Yuan, D. Y.
1963    Voluntary Segregation: A Study of New York Chinatown. *Phylon* 24 (Fall), pp. 255–265.

Zhou, Min, and Logan, John R.
1989    Returns on Human Capital in Ethnic Enclaves. *American Sociological Review* 54 (October), pp. 809–833.

Zich, Arthur
1986    Japanese Americans, Home at Last. *National Geographic* 169 (April), pp. 512–539.

Zinsmeister, Karl
1988    Black Demographics. *Public Opinion* 10 (January/February), pp. 41–44.

Zweigenhaft, Richard L., and Domhoff, William G.
1982    *Jews in the Protestant Establishment.* New York: Praeger.

# Acknowledgments

2: © Morrow/Stock, Boston. 8: UPI/Bettmann Newsphotos. 13: NAACP photo file. 21: © USCG-SAPP/SABA. 24: H. Roger Viollet. 32: Michael Grecco/Picture Group. 37: © Richards/Picture Cube. 41: © Rohn Engh. 50: Kobal/SuperStock. 56: Mark Hirsch/NYT Photos. 66: Delevingne/Stock, Boston. 70: UPI/Bettmann Newsphotos. 72: © Marc PoKempner. 74: Courtesy Elliot Liebow. 79: © Gatewood/The Image Works. 87: Linda Sue Scott/NYT Pictures. 92: Bettmann Archives. 96: *Harper's Weekly*, September 30, 1871. 105: Dith Pran/NYT Photos. 107: Alon Reininger/Contact/Woodfin Camp & Assoc. 108: Hankin/Stock, Boston. 110: Cynthia Johnson/Gamma-Liaison. 116: © Velez/The Image Works. 123: Wide World. 132: Wide World. 136: Wide World. 139: Wide World. 142: UPI/Bettmann Newsphotos. 148: © Rowan/The Image Works. 151: "Trail of Tears" by Robert Lindneux, Woolaroc Museum, Bartlesville, Okla- homa. 161: Dayna Smith/*The Washington Post*. 168: © Lehman/SABA. 175: Michelle Vignes/Gamma-Liaison. 177: UPI/Bettmann Newsphotos. 180: Bill Sanders/*The Milwaukee Journal*. 185: © Buck/Picture Cube. 197: Reuters/Bettmann. 199: Carl Iwasaki, *Life* Magazine © Time Inc. 202: Wide World. 204: Wide World. 205: Reuters/Bettmann. 209: (top) Wide World. 209: (bottom) Stephen Shames/ Visions. 213: © Jeffrey Scales. 217: Grant/Picture Cube. 222: Dal Bayles/NYT Pictures. 223: Wide World. 230: © *The Des Moines Register*. 236: Courtesy William Julius Wilson, University of Chicago. 238: Doug Marlette/*The Atlanta Constitution*. 241: Gatewood/The Image Works. 250: © Daemmrich/The Image Works. 255: Herman J. Kokojan/Black Star. 257: Bart Bartholomew/ NYT Pictures. 261: Wide World. 263: Susan Greenwood/Gamma-Liaison. 267: © Hrynewych/Stock, Boston. 273: LeJeune/Stock, Boston. 279: © 1981 by Universal Pictures, a Division of Universal City Studios, Inc. Courtesy of MCA Publishing Rights, A Division of MCA Inc. 286: Wide World. 287: Paul Fusco/Magnum. 292: © Bob Daemmrich. 297: Fujihira/Monkmeyer Press Photo. 303: Franken/Stock, Boston. 307: Savulich/Gamma-Liaison. 309: Menzel/Stock, Boston. 321: Fred R. Conrad/NYT Pictures. 325: © Grant/ Picture Cube. 331: Asrin/Impact Visuals. 336: David Strick/NYT Pictures. 343: © Rick Browne. 346: © Maher/Stock, Boston. 348: Rick Friedman/NYT Pictures. 353: Kramer/Picture Cube. 356: Courtesy Bancroft Library, University of California at Berkeley. 358: Paul Calhoun. 361: Dennis Brack/Black Star. 363: © 1992, The Chicago Tribune Company, all rights reserved, used with permission. 365: Wide World. 373: © Kennard/Stock, Boston. 376: UPI/Bettmann Newsphotos. 380: Asian Week. 382: Courtesy Hisako Hibi. 384: UPI/Bettmann. 395: Aron/PhotoEdit. 400: Courtesy Julian Ungar-Sargon, M.D. 403:Fitzhugh/Stock, Boston. 406: From *The Artists of Terezin* by Gerald Greene. Photographs of illustrations copyright © 1969 by Hawthorn Books, Inc. Reproduced by permission of EP Dutton, a division of

NAL Penguin Inc. **410:** Ilene Perlman/The Picture Cube. **417:** Ricki Rosen/ Picture Group. **430:** © Shub/Picture Cube. **437:** Asahi Shimbun Photo. **444:** Wide World. **450:** © Malecki/PhotoEdit. **458:** Alex Gotfryd. **462:** © Hankin/ Stock, Boston. **467:** Eric Schweikardt/*Sports Illustrated*. **472:** Eliason/Impact Visuals. **480:** © Rosen/SABA. **485:** Reuters/Bettmann. **486:** Reuters/Bettman.

# Index

Aaron, Henry J., 239, 500
Aberbach, Joel D., 208, 500
abolitionists, 190, 213–214, 493
abortion, 453–454
Abraham, Sameer Y., 43, 530–531
Abramson, Harold J., 122, 135, 500
Abron, JoNina, 210, 500
absolute deprivation, 67–68, 89, 493
Acosta-Belén, Edna, 323, 500
Acuña, Rodolfo, 277, 283, 289–290, 301, 500
Adamic, Louis, 97, 500
Adler, Patricia Rae, 280, 500
Adorno, T. R., 45, 500
affirmative action, 83–89, 292, 493
Afonso Arinos law, 466
African Americans, 25, 47, 55–58, 73–78,
    87–88, 96, 113–114, 118–119, 124, 178,
    181–182, 185–249, 256, 260, 291, 331–332,
    411–412, 431–432, 456–459
African National Congress, 483–484, 488
Afrikaners, 481, 483
Afrocentric perspective, 33, 124, 212, 214, 493
Aid to Families with Dependent Children,
    447
AJA. See Americans of Japanese Ancestry
Alaska Native Settlement Act of 1971, 176
Alaskan Federation of Natives (AFN), 176
Alba, Richard D., 35, 76, 125, 127, 131, 135,
    145, 404, 500–501
Alcatraz occupation, 174–175
Alianza Federal de Mercedes, 283
Alien Act, 95
Alien Land Act, 376, 386
aliterate, 257
Allen, James Paul, 35, 268, 312, 501
Allen, Sheila, 469, 471, 473, 501
Allen, Walter R., 226, 247–248, 268, 312, 501,
    520
Allotment Act, 155–156
Allport, Gordon W., 18, 42, 44, 46, 59, 65,
    404–405, 501
amalgamation, 27, 34, 493
American Indian Movement (AIM), 173–174,
    177–178
American Indians, 23, 148–184, 361, 489
American Jewish Committee, 415, 421, 501
American Jewish Congress, 415, 501
Americans of Japanese Ancestry (AJAs), 338,
    351, 493
amhaaretz, 422

Amish, 140–141
amnesty, 106
Anderson, Charles H., 145, 501
Andersson, Neil, 488, 501
Andersson-Brolin, Lillemor, 26, 501
androgyny, 432, 459, 493
Angle, John, 308, 501
Anglo, 252
Anglo-Irish Accord, 475
annexation, 20, 275
Anti-Defamation League (ADL), 409–411, 415
anti-Semitism, 404–415, 425, 493
apartheid, 482–483, 487, 491, 493
Aponte, Robert, 294, 501
Apple, R. W., Jr., 257, 502
Arab Americans, 1, 60–61
Aran, Kenneth, 306, 502
Arden, Harvey, 418, 502
Asante, Molefi, 33, 212, 215, 502
Ashe, Arthur R., Jr., 215, 502
Ashkenazi Jews, 402
Asian Americans, 113–114, 325
Asian Indians, 326, 342, 345
Aspira, 321
Aspy, David N., 255, 502
assimilation, 28–31, 34, 122, 124, 131–133,
    136, 140, 156–157, 199, 208, 214, 247,
    269–270, 322, 327, 360–361, 388–391, 420,
    423, 425, 473, 489, 493
Associated Free State, 306
asylee, 112, 114, 493
asylum, 111–112, 269
Atrévete, 321
authoritarian personality, 44–45, 64, 493

Bach, Jennifer B., 335, 502
Bach, Robert L., 335, 502
Bagley, Christopher, 60, 502
Bahr, Howard M., 168, 502
Bainbridge, William Sims, 146, 562
*Bakke* v. *Regents of the University of California*,
    84–85
Baldus, David C., 243, 502
Baldwin, James, 412, 502
Bales, Robert F., 434, 550
Ball, Henry V., 339, 502
Ball-Rokeach, Sandra J., 60, 502
Banfield, Edward C., 58, 129, 502, 571
Banks, Dennis, 173, 178
Banton, Michael, 50, 502

Bantus, 481–482, 489
Bantustan, 483
Barbaro, Fred, 129, 502
Barclay, William, 463, 469, 482, 502
Baron, Harold, 76, 503
Baron, James, 440
Barrera, Mario, 257, 503
Barrett, Wayne, 259, 311
barrios, 278, 301, 314–315, 493
Barta, Russell, 77, 503
Bash, Harry M., 28, 503
Baskin, Jane A., 205, 503
Bataille, Gretchen, 183, 503
Bauer, Raymond A., 191, 503
Bauman, David, 260, 503
Baumann, Marty, 57, 503
Beach, Walter G., 391, 503
Bean, Frank D., 114, 302, 503
Bearak, Barry, 264, 503
Becerra, José E., 298, 503
Becker, Gary S., 89
Becker, Howard, 17
Belair, Felix, Jr., 102–103, 503
Bell, Daniel, 131, 503
Bell, David A., 342, 347, 503
Bell, Wendell, 124, 503–504
Bellah, Robert, 135, 504
Bellecourt, Clyde, 173
Bem, Daryl J., 459, 504
Bem, Sandra, 459, 504
Benedetto, Richard, 28, 488, 504
Bennett, Lerone, Jr., 191–192, 194, 196, 504
Benokraitis, Nijole V., 69, 460, 504
Berg, Bruce, 29, 504
Berg, Philip L., 187, 504
Berger, Joseph, 289, 504
Bernard, Jessie, 434, 504
Berndt, Catherine, 28, 504
Berndt, Ronald M., 28, 504
Bernstein, Richard, 260, 504
Berreman, Gerald D., 44, 504
Bettelheim, Bruno, 42, 44, 504
Bielby, William, 440, 504
Biemer, Paul Philip, 170, 566
Biemiller, Lawrence, 342, 504
Bienen, Leigh, 449, 504
bilingual education, 257–262, 266, 493
bilingualism, 256–262, 271, 493
Billard, Jules B., 150, 504–505
Billingsley, Andrew, 232, 505
Billington, Ray Allen, 95, 114, 505
Billson, Janet Mancini, 29, 505
biological race, 10–12, 34, 493
bipolar occupational structure, 344, 351, 493

Birmingham, Stephen, 402, 502
Bitterman, Brooks, 315, 543
Black Muslims. See Nation of Islam.
Black nationalism, 210–214, 493
Black Panther party, 208–210, 412
Black Power, 126, 207–210, 282
Blacks. See African Americans
Blackwell, James E., 35, 124, 248
Blalock, Hubert M., Jr., 35, 346, 505
blaming the victim, 16, 340, 349
Bland, Dorothy, 260, 500, 505
Blau, Peter, 127, 505
Blauner, Robert, 190, 204, 505
Blawis, Patricia Bell, 283, 505
Blea, Irene I., 301, 505
Bledsoe, Timothy, 456, 505
Bloom, Leonard, 58, 505
*Board of Education of Oklahoma City* v.
    *Dowell*,221
Boas, Franz, 150, 505
boat people, 334
Bobo, Lawrence, 55, 65, 505
bodegas, 270
Boers, 482
Bogardus, Emory, 49–51, 505–506
Bohland, James R., 164, 506
Bonacich, Edna, 71, 196, 331, 346, 506
Borders, J., 51, 535
Boswell, Thomas D., 264, 271, 506
Bouvier, Leon F., 101–102, 104, 112, 506
braceros, 278–280, 283, 300–301, 311, 493
Braden, Charles Samuel, 143, 506
brain drain, 103–104, 114, 269, 271, 493
Braly, Kenneth W., 46, 534
Brazil, 7, 268, 464–468, 489
Breasted, Mary, 308, 506
Brewer, Marilynn B., 48, 506
Briggs, Charles L., 301
Briggs, Kenneth A., 120, 411, 506–507
Briggs, Vernon M., Jr., 280, 507
Brigham, John C., 46, 49, 65, 507
Broder, David A., 260, 507
Broderick, Francis, 194, 507
Brody, Eugene, 51, 517
Brooks, Andree, 139, 507
Broom, Leonard, 28, 507
Brown, Christopher, 107, 507
Brown, Dee, 153, 183, 507
Brown, H. Rap, 210, 507
*Brown* v. *Board of Education*, 58, 81, 198–200,
    221, 384
Brozan, Nadine, 29, 507
Bruton, Brenton T., 51, 515
Buchanan, Robert W., 157, 162, 570

Buckley, Anthony, 476, 507
Bufalino, William E., 128, 507
Burbach, Roger, 277, 507
Burciaga, Cecilia Prediado de Gonzales, 457,
507
Bureau of Indian Affairs, 151, 156–157,
161–182
Burkholz, Herbert, 266, 509
Burma, John H., 294, 387, 509
Bursma, Bruce, 211, 509
Bush, George, 38, 88, 228, 270, 308, 387, 487
busing, 221–222
Bustamante, Jorge A., 280, 509
Buthelezi, Mangosuthu, 484
Butt, Ronald, 469, 509
Butterfield, Fox, 335, 342, 348, 366
"Buy Black" campaign, 227

Cabrera, Denise, 435, 509
Cain, Bruce E., 260, 509
Caine, T. Allen, 294, 509–510
Californios, 276
Callanan, Tuss, 283, 510
Cambodians, 326, 334–335
Campbell, Gregory R., 173, 510
Canada, 5
Cannon, Kenneth L., 144, 511
Cannon, Lynn Weber, 235, 568
Cape Coloureds, 481
capital punishment, 243
Capone, Al, 132
Carlson, James S., 51, 510
Carmichael, Stokely, 69, 208, 215, 510
Carr, Robert K., 81, 510
Carrington, Walter C., 487, 510
Carroll, Raymond, 411, 510
Carson, Clayborne, 215, 510
Carter, Fred M., Jr., 223, 510
Carter, Hodding, III, 200, 510
Carter, Jimmy, 118, 180, 263, 386, 478
Carter, Stephen, 90, 510
Casavantes, Edward, 294, 510
Case, Charles E., 60, 510
caste approach, 43, 64, 494
Catholics. See Roman Catholics
Caudill, William, 388, 510–511
Central Americans, 112, 267–270
Chalfant, H. Paul, 121, 145, 511
Chan, Mei-Mei, 366, 511
Chávez, César, 280, 282–290, 511
Chayat, Sherry, 409, 511
Chaze, William L., 287, 311
checklist approach, 46
Chen, Pei-ngor, 366, 511

Cheng, Ch'eng-K'un, 338, 511
Cheng, Nien, 108, 110, 511
Cherry, Robert, 90, 511
Chicanas, 293, 456
Chicanismo, 282, 301, 494
Chicanos, 48, 251–254, 270–271, 273–302,
315
Chin, Frank, 366, 511
Chin, Rocky, 366, 511
Chin, Vincent, 347
Chinatowns, 359, 391
Chinese Americans, 41–43, 97–99, 254, 262,
326, 328, 337, 342, 344–345, 350, 353–372
Chinese Consolidated Benevolent
Association (CCBA), 356
Chinese Exclusion Act, 99, 112, 354, 360,
375
Ching, Frank, 355, 371, 511
Chow, Ester Ngan-ling, 449, 511
Choy, Sam, 368–369
Christensen, Harold T., 144, 511
Christopulos, Diana, 306, 311, 511
Chuman, Frank F., 377, 511
Cicero, Illinois, 128
Cicone, Michael V., 438, 511
Cinel, Dean, 122, 511
Cisneros, Henry, 293
*Cisneros* v. *Corpus Christi Independent School
District*, 254
*City of Richmond* v. *Cronson Co.*, 85–86, 228
civil disobedience, 201, 214, 494
Civil Liberties Act of 1988, 386
civil religion, 135, 139, 145, 494
Civil Rights Act of 1964, 81, 443
civil rights movement, 198–203, 437
Civil Rights Restoration Act, 82
clans, 355–356, 371, 499
Clark, Juan M., 265, 511–512
Clark, Kenneth B., 58, 512
Clark, Mamie P., 48, 58, 512
Clarke, John Henrik, 212, 512
class, 14, 34, 134, 234, 248, 355, 494
Cleaver, Kathleen, 210, 512
Clemans, John, 455
Clifton, Rodney A., 48, 518
club membership, 82, 339, 415
Coddington, Ron, 172, 512
Cohen, Steven M., 420, 425–426, 512
Cohn, Bob, 88, 512
Colasanto, Diana, 85, 451–452, 512
Coleman, James S., 146, 170, 221, 244, 512
Coleman, Milton, 412, 512
Coleman Report, 221
Collier, John, 161

colonialism, 21–33, 34, 305–306, 464, 482, 490, 494
color gradient, 268, 271, 313–314, 323, 465, 467, 494
Columbian Coalition, 126
Columbians, 269–270
Commission for Racial Equality, 469–470
Commission on Civil Rights, 1, 254, 322, 348, 439
Commission on Wartime Relocation and Internment of Civilians, 379, 387
compadrazo, 296
comparable worth. See pay equity
Condon, Jane, 460, 513
Condon, Margaret E., 334, 534
conflict perspective, 16, 23, 34, 43, 72, 88, 98, 103–104, 143, 241–242, 258, 277, 294, 434–435, 494
Conforti, Joseph M., 130, 513
Congress of Racial Equality (CORE), 197–198, 208
Conot, Robert, 204, 513
Conover, Ted, 114, 513
Conroy, John, 474, 513
Conservative Jews, 417, 419–420, 424
contact hypothesis, 63–64, 494
Conver, Bill, 421, 513
Conyers, James E., 245, 513
Cooper, Andrew, 259, 503
Cornell, Stephen, 157, 169, 173, 513
Cortés, Carlos E., 276, 282, 290, 514
Cortese, Charles F., 239, 514
Cose, Ellis, 390, 514
Coser, Lewis A., 143, 450, 463, 514
Coser, Rose Laub, 450, 514
Cosford, Bill, 355, 514
Couch, Arthur, 45, 514
Council of Energy Resource Tribes (CERT), 180–182
Courtney, Alice W., 435, 514
Covin, David, 466, 514
Cowgill, Donald O., 50, 514
Cowley, Geoffrey, 179, 514
Cox, Oliver C., 43–44, 514
Crazy Horse, 152
creationists, 141, 145, 494
criminal justice, 70, 240–243, 388
Crispino, James A., 133, 515
Cross, William E., Jr., 210, 514
Crossette, Barbara, 111, 515
crossover effect, 170, 182, 494
Crull, Sue R., 51, 515
Cuban Americans, 111–112, 289, 296
Cuellar, Alfredo, 282, 515

culture of poverty, 293–295, 301, 315, 494
Cummings, Judith, 232, 515
Cunningham, Perry H., 143, 305, 314
curanderismo, 298, 301, 494
Curran, Thomas J., 97, 515
Curry, George E., 232, 515
Curry-White, Brenda, 73, 549
Curtis, James R., 264, 271, 506

Daniels, Roger, 115, 133, 334, 351, 371, 377, 383, 386, 393, 515
Danzger, M. Herbert, 418, 426, 515
Darrity, William, 319, 515
Darwin, Charles, 13, 141, 515
Davis, Allison, 43, 457, 515
Davis, Cary, 313, 515
Davis, David Brion, 465, 515–516
Davis, E., 69, 516
Dawes Act, 155–156
Dawidowicz, Lucy S., 407, 516
death penalty, 243
Deer, Ada, 163
de facto segregation, 200, 221, 248, 468, 487, 494
defensive insulation, 359, 371, 494
definition of the situation, 17
De Fleur, Melvin, 42, 405, 413, 516
Degler, Carl N., 204, 464–465, 516
de jure segregation, 198, 221, 248, 254, 494
Deloria, Vine, Jr., 151, 156–157, 159, 162–163, 183, 516
Demo, David H., 58, 530
Denenberg, R. V., 411, 539
denomination, 110, 145, 494
Denton, John, 71, 516
Denton, Nancy A., 26, 239, 516
DeParle, Jason, 73, 285, 516
Department of Justice, 219
De Pillis, Mario S., 144, 517
DeQuinne, Jeanne, 260, 265–266, 505, 517
Derbyshire, Robert, 51, 517
DeStefano, Linda, 451–452, 517
Deutscher, Irwin, 42, 517
De Varona, Donna, 449, 517
De Vos, George, 388, 510
DeYoung, Karen, 472, 478, 517
diaspora, 411, 477, 480, 491, 494
Diehl, Jackson, 481, 517
differential justice, 242–243
Dillehay, Ronald C., 45, 535
Dillingham Commission, 99
Dinnerstein, Leonard, 103, 183, 409, 422, 517
Dionne, E. J., Jr., 246, 517
disabled, 17

discrimination, 39–40, 64, 66–90, 107,
    127–128, 298–299, 338–339, 366–370, 377,
    387, 413, 442–443, 445–446, 468–469, 494
divestment, 487, 491, 494
Dodge, Norton, 442, 567
*Doe* v. *Bolton*, 453–454
Doherty, Carroll J., 480, 517
Dohrmann, Rita, 449, 517
Donahue, Thomas S., 260, 517
Doran, Terry, 272, 517
Dorris, Michael A., 182, 517
double jeopardy, 10, 456–459, 494
Douglass, Frederick, 193
Draeger, Harlan, 163, 517–518
*Dred Scott* v. *Sanford*, 81
Driedger, Leo, 48, 518
dropout, 169–170
DRUMS, 163
dual labor market, 71–72, 89, 270, 494
Du Bois, William E. B., 8–9, 188, 191–194,
    214–215, 228, 234, 518
Duff, John B., 96, 518
Duke, David, 1
Dullea, Georgia, 449, 518
Duncan, Beverly, 127, 518
Duncan, Greg J., 446, 518
Duncan, Otis Dudley, 127, 518
Dunn, Marvin, 219, 518
Dunn, William, 240, 518
Durant, Thomas J., Jr., 234, 518
Dworkin, Anthony Gary, 48, 437, 441, 518
Dwyer, Jeffrey, 467–468, 570
Dyer, James, 51, 518
dysfunction, 15, 34, 343, 494
Dzidzienyo, Anani, 466–467, 518

education, 78, 139–141, 169–172, 198–200,
    219–224, 290–293, 301, 316–317, 342–344,
    367, 387, 414–415, 419–420, 448–449
education pipeline, 291, 301, 495
educational mobility, 414
Edwards, Harry, 223, 518–519
Egerton, John, 163, 314, 519
Ehrenreich, Barbara, 446, 519
Elder, Rob, 266, 519
Elementary and Secondary Education Act
    (ESEA), 257–258
Elkins, Stanley, 188, 464, 519
Ellis, Richard N., 159, 519
El Nasser, Haya, 290, 331, 390, 519
El Salvadorians, 268–270
Elsasser, Glen, 243, 519
Elson, Mary, 410, 519
Emancipation Proclamation, 191

Emerson, Ralph Waldo, 95
Emerson, Rupert, 23, 519
emigration, 19, 34
employment, 166–169, 413–414, 439–448
Employment Assistance Program, 164–165
endogamy, 369
*Engel* v. *Vitale*, 140
Engels, Frederick, 68, 543
England, Paula, 460
English as a Second Language (ESL), 258
English immerson, 258–259, 271
enterprise zones, 228
Epstein, Joseph, 244, 519
Equal Employment Opportunity
    Commission (EEOC), 81–82, 443
Equal Pay Act of 1963, 445
Equal Rights Amendment, 14, 438
equal-status contact, 63
Erickson, Jon, 146, 512
Erlich, Reese, 285
*Escobedo* v. *Illinois*, 283
Espenshade, Thomas J., 105–106, 519
Espinosa, Dula, 86–87, 519
Essed, Philomena, 90, 519
Estrada, Leobardo F., 291, 519
ethclass, 134, 145, 234, 495
ethnic group, 7–8, 34, 117–118, 121–134, 398,
    400, 463, 495
ethnocentrism, 38, 64, 253, 258, 495
ethnophaulism, 39, 64, 495
evacuees, 379, 392, 495
evangelical faiths, 320, 323, 495
Exclusion act. See Chinese Exclusion Act
Executive Order 9066, 378, 381
Executive Order 9981, 80, 198
exploitation theory, 43–44, 64, 495
expulsion, 23–24
Exter, Thomas, 251, 519
extermination, 23

Fair Employment Practices Commission
    (FEPC), 80, 196
FALN, 307–308, 310
Faludi, Susan, 460, 519
familism, 295–296, 422, 495
family, 232–233, 293–296, 362, 388, 450–451
Farber, M. A., 106, 421–422, 520
Farkas, George, 460
Farley, Reynolds, 226, 247, 249, 501, 520
Farrakhan, Louis, 211, 412
Farrell, William E., 222, 260, 520
Farrell, William T., 430, 520
Fayer, Joan M., 320, 520
Feagin, Joe R., 69, 233, 460, 504, 520

Federal Fair Housing Law, 238
Federal Housing Administration, 239–239
Feldman, Arnold, 314, 567
feminine mystique, 438, 459, 495
feminist movement, 435–439
feminization of poverty, 446–447, 460, 495
Feng, Shih Tree, 93, 520
Ferman, Louis A., 72, 520
Ferman, Patricia R., 72, 520
Fermi, Laura, 100, 520
Ferraro, Geraldine, 131
Ferree, Myra Marx, 461
Fields, Cheryl, 293, 520
fiesta politics, 289, 301, 495
Filipino Americans, 326, 328, 332–334, 337,
    345–347
Fiola, Jan, 466–467, 520–521
fish-ins, 174, 183, 495
Fishman, Joshua A., 125, 136, 146, 521
Fiske, Edward B., 291, 293, 521
Fitzpatrick, Joseph P., 311, 313–315, 317, 323,
    521
Fix, Michael, 88, 108, 521
Flores, Juan, 313, 521
fobs, 366, 371, 495
Foderaro, Lisa W., 390, 521
Fong, Stanley L. M., 370, 521
Fong-Torres, Ben, 367, 521
Foot, Paul, 469, 521
Ford, Henry, 408
Ford, W. Scott, 64, 521
Fort Laramie Treaty, 161
Fortney, Judith, 103, 522
Francis, Emerich K., 319, 521–522
Franklin, John Hope, 188, 196, 203, 215,
    521–522
Frazier, E. Franklin, 234, 464, 522
Fredrickson, George M., 482, 522
freedom flotilla, 262–263
freedom schools, 200
Freeman, Harold P., 249, 540
Freeman, Jo, 436, 448, 456, 460, 522
Freyre, Gilberto, 468, 522
Friedan, Betty, 438–439, 460, 522
Friedman, Georges, 420, 522
fringe-of-values theory, 404–405, 425, 495
Fuchs, Estelle, 169–170, 172, 522
Fujimoto, Isao, 355, 533
functionalist perspective, 15–16, 34, 153, 343,
    434–435, 495
Fusfeld, Daniel R., 72, 90, 522
fusion, 26–27, 31

Gager, John G., 402, 522
Galarza, Ernesto, 279, 522

Gallo, Patrick J., 125, 522
Galtung, Johan, 480, 522
Galvan, Manuel, 282, 522–523
Gambino, Richard, 126–127, 132–133, 523
gambling on reservations, 167
Gans, Herbert J., 125, 399, 522–523
Garbarino, Merwyn S., 164, 523
Garcia, Eugene E., 258, 527
Gardner, R. C., 46, 523
Gardner, Robert W., 101–102, 104, 112, 333,
    338, 342, 345, 347, 351, 523, 573
Garfinkel, Herbert, 196, 523
Garitty, Michael, 160, 523
Garrison, Tony, 389, 435, 523
Gary, Lawrence E., 233, 523
Garza, T., 294, 532
Gates, Henry Louis, Jr., 61, 523
Gates, Mireille Grangenois, 57, 523
gender groups, 9–10
gender identity, 432–433, 460, 495
gender roles, 432–433, 457, 460, 495
General Allotment Act, 155–156
genocide, 23, 34, 495
Gentlemen's Agreement, 99
Germany, 5, 26
Gerson, Walter, 29, 423, 523
Gerth, H. H., 14, 133, 523
Geschwender, James A., 207
ghost dance, 152–153
Gibbons, Tom, 243, 523
Giddings, Paula, 457, 460, 523
GI Forum, 282
Gilbert, Gilber M., 46, 523
Giles, Michael W., 126, 523
Gilliam, Franklin D., Jr., 134, 235, 524
Gilly, M. C., 435, 523–524
Ginzberg, Eli, 297, 524
Girdner, Audrie, 383, 393, 524
Gittler, Joseph B., 399, 524
Gittleson, Natalie, 423, 524
Glasgow, Douglas, 90, 524
glass ceiling, 227, 229, 344, 439
Glassman, Bernard, 404, 524
Glazer, Nathan, 124, 127, 129, 134, 314–315,
    319–320, 425, 524
Glock, Charles Y., 60, 136, 414, 524, 562
Goering, John M., 123, 524
Gold, Michael, 414, 524
Gold, Steven J., 404, 524
Goldberg, Philip A., 49, 524–525
Goldman, Ari L., 139, 525
Goldman, Peter, 212, 525
Goldscheider, Calvin, 397, 414, 420, 422, 424,
    426, 525
Goldstein, Henry, 130, 414, 525

Goldstein, Sidney, 420, 424, 525
Gomez, David F., 299, 525
Gompers, Samuel, 98, 525
Gonzales, Rodolfo Corky, 282–283, 525
Goodstein, Laurie, 331, 525
gook syndrome, 334, 351, 368, 495
Goozner, Merrill, 331, 525
Gordon, Leonard, 46, 48, 525
Gordon, Milton M., 35, 125, 234, 423–424, 525
Gordon, Wendell, 280, 525
Goren, Arthur A., 402, 414, 525
Gould, Ketayun H., 340, 525
Gouldner, Alvin, 233, 525
Graham, Jory, 29, 526
Gratton, Brian, 296, 526
Great Britain, 42, 468–476, 489
Grebler, Leo, 274, 296, 526
greedy institution, 450
Greeley, Andrew M., 51, 53, 97, 121, 126, 128–129, 134, 136, 146, 290, 413–414, 510, 526
Greenberg, Simon, 414, 526
Greene, Elizabeth, 350, 526
Greene, Victor R., 97, 526
Greenhouse, Linda, 179, 526
Gremley, William, 128, 526
Griggs, Anthony, 359, 526
Grimshaw, Allen D., 196, 526
Gross, Jane, 364, 526
Grove, David John, 490, 526
*Grove City College* v. *Bell,* 82
Guest, Avery M., 128, 526
Gutiérrez, Armando, 282, 289, 527
Gutstadt, Herman, 98, 525
Guy, Pat, 487, 526–527
Gwetzman, Bernard, 335, 527

Haak, Gerald O., 385, 527
Hacker, Andrew, 231, 249, 527
Hacker, Helen Mayer, 31, 432, 457, 527
Hadden, Jeffrey K., 136, 527
Hagan, William T., 156, 527
Hakuta, Kenji, 258, 527
Haitians, 111
Haley, Alex, 212, 216, 527
Halpen, Ben, 408, 527
Hamilton, Charles V., 69, 208, 215, 510
Handlin, Oscar, 93, 122, 527
Haniff, Nesha Z., 248
Hanks, Chertl, 450, 554
Hansen, Marcus Lee, 123, 389, 527
Haoles, 337–338, 351, 495
Harjo, Suzan Shown, 153–155, 527
Harlan, Louis R., 193, 527

Harrell-Bond, Barbara E., 20, 527
Harris, David A., 409, 527
Harris, Lou, 85, 528
Harris, Marvin, 6, 465, 528, 568
Harrison, Michael I., 419–420, 528
Hartley, Eugene L., 51, 528
Hartmann, Heidi I., 450, 528
Hasidic Jews, 412, 418
Hatchett, Shirley J., 233–234, 528
Hate Crimes Statistics Act, 38–39
Havighurst, Robert, 169–170, 172, 522
Hawaii, 336–340, 378, 385, 391, 528
Hawaiian Americans, 336–340
Hawkins, Hugh, 193–194, 528
Hayakawa, S. I., 260–262, 528
health care, 172–173, 243–245, 296–298, 488
Heilman, Samuel C., 411, 424, 528
Henslin, James M., 436, 528
Herberg, Will, 123, 134–135, 146, 402, 528
Herman, Edith, 127, 528
Hernandez, Luis F., 275, 528
Herskovitis, Melville J., 464, 528
Hertzler, J. O., 407, 528
Hess, Beth B., 461, 528–529
Hewitt, Christopher, 475, 529
Heyman, Harriet, 318, 538
Higginbotham, Elizabeth, 234, 529
Higham, John, 31, 407, 529
Hill, Anita, 444
Hill, Robert B., 232, 529
Hilts, Philip J., 244, 529
Himmelfarb, Harold S., 399, 424, 529
Hinds, Michael de Courcy, 447
Hiro, Dilip, 472, 529
Hiroshima Day, 389
Hirsch, Herbert, 282, 289, 526, 529
Hirschman, Charles, 28, 342, 529
Hirsley, Michael, 139, 142, 529
Hispanics, 55, 57, 113–114, 136, 244, 250–324
Hispanos, 252, 275, 283
Hochschild, Arlie, 431, 432, 452–453, 461, 529
Hockstader, Lee, 264, 529
Hoebel, E. Adamson, 15, 529
Hohri, William Minoru, 385, 393, 529–530
Holford, David M., 156, 530
Holmberg, David, 367, 530
Holocaust, 23, 406, 412
Holzapfel, Tamara, 306, 530
homelands, 484–485
home rule, 474, 491
Hooks, Benjamin, 243
Hopi-Navajo land dispute, 159–160
Hormann, Bernard L., 338–339, 530
Hornsby, Aton, Jr., 198, 530
Hornung, Rick, 167, 530

Horton, John, 490, 530
Hosokawa, Bill, 378–379, 383, 386, 387, 390, 393, 530
Hostetler, John A., 141, 530
housing, 237–240
Houston, Jack, 211, 509
Howard, Alan, 340, 530
Howard, John R., 211, 530
Howe, Irving, 426
Howe, Marvin, 347, 530
Hsu, Francis L. K., 97, 363, 367, 371, 530
Huang, Lucy Jen, 355, 362, 367, 369, 530
Hufker, Brian, 264, 530
Hughes, Michael, 58, 235, 530
hui kuan, 355–358, 371, 495
Hume, Ellen, 289, 530–531
Humphrey, Derek, 472, 531
Hungarians, 111
Hunt, Chester L., 476, 490–491, 531
Hunter, Herbert M., 43, 531
Hurh, Won Moo, 28–31, 67, 329–330, 340, 349, 531, 534
Husar, Jack, 163, 531
Hwang, David, 367, 531
Hyde Amendment, 453

Ichioka, Yuji, 377, 531
Ichiyama, Michael A., 349, 531
Ikels, Charlotte, 358, 531–532
ilchomose, 329, 351, 495
Imhoff, Gary, 258, 532
immigration, 19, 34, 92–115, 277–281, 334–335, 362, 400–402, 468, 496
Immigration and Naturalization Act of 1965, 102–103, 327, 332, 354, 532
*Immigration and Naturalization Service* v. *Cardoza-Fonseca*, 112
Immigration Reform and Control Act of 1986, 102, 106–107, 112, 114, 280
inactivity rate, 342, 351, 496
indentured servants, 20
Indian Claims Commission, 157, 159–161
Indian Removal Act, 151
Indochinese Americans, 334–336
in-group, 6
in-group virtues, 405, 425, 496
Inkatha, 484
Inoue, Miyako, 387, 532
Inouye, Daniel, 386
institutional discrimination, 69–71, 83, 89, 187, 496
intelligence quotient, 10–11, 34, 170, 496
interactive effect, 14, 34, 496
intermarriage, 27, 367–368, 389, 422, 466–467

intifada, 479–480, 491, 496
Iovini, Joseph, 51, 510
IQ debate, 10–11, 70
Irelan, Lola M., 294, 532
Ireland, 95–97
Irish Americans, 95–97
Irish Republican Army, 475
irregular economy, 71–72, 89, 235, 270, 496
Irwin, Victoria, 321
Isaacs, Harold, 210
Isikoff, Michael, 298
Isonio, Stevan A., 294
Israel, 398, 410–411, 425, 477–481
Issei, 375–377, 382, 385, 387, 389–392, 496
Italian Americans, 48, 126–128, 130–133

Jackson, James S., 249, 532
Jackson, Jesse, 123, 211, 245–246
Jacobs, Jerry A., 338, 532, 536
Jacoby, Susan, 265, 267
Jaeger, Christopher, 291, 532
Janowitz, Morris, 35, 42, 44, 504
Japan, 5
Japanese American Citizens League (JACL), 377, 386, 387
Japanese American Evacuation Claims Act, 385–386
Japanese Americans, 43, 51–52, 80, 162, 326, 328–329, 337, 342, 345, 350, 373–394
"JAP-baiting," 409
Jarvenpa, Robert, 174, 532
Jaschik, Scott, 343, 532
Jaynes, Gerald David, 249
Jeffrey, Anthea J., 484, 530
Jennings, James, 315, 323, 532
Jewish Americans, 9, 29–30, 44, 47, 76, 137–138, 342, 395–427
Jewish Defense League (JDL), 416
Jim Crow, 191, 200, 214, 339, 496
Johnson, Charles S., 43, 196, 532
Johnson, George, 409, 533
Johnson, Helen W., 172, 533
Johnson, Lyndon B., 102, 175
Johnson, Sharen, 61, 533
Johnson-O'Malley Act, 169
Jolidon, Lawrence, 174
Jones, Faustine C., 226, 533
Jones, James H., 216, 533
Jones, Le Roi, 213, 533
Jones Act of 1917, 306, 533
*Jones* v. *Mayer*, 238
jook-sings, 366, 371, 496
Juarez, Alberto, 288, 533
Judaization, 422, 425, 496

Kagan, Jerome, 11, 533
Kagiwada, George, 355, 533
Kallen, Horace, 31–32, 533
Kalmijn, Mathijs, 27, 533
Kalt, Joseph P., 169, 514
Kanahele, George S., 338, 532
Kanamine, Linda, 172, 532
Karlins, Marvin, 46, 533–534
Kaser, Tom, 338, 534
kashrut, 417–418, 425, 495
Kass, Dora, 404, 534
Katz, David, 46, 534
Kaufman, Jonathan, 426
Kealoha, Gard, 340, 534
Keene, Karlyn, 386
Keil, Charles, 213, 534
Kelly, Gail P., 335, 534
Kennedy, John F., 83, 95, 175, 200–201, 238, 534
Kephart, William M., 140–141, 144, 146, 534
Kerner Commission. See National Advisory Commission on Civil Disorders
Kessler, Evelyn S., 434, 534
Kessner, Thomas, 357, 534
Kibei, 375, 393, 495
kickouts, 170, 183, 495
Kiewiet, D. Roderick, 260, 509
Kikumura, Akemi, 388–389, 534
Killian, Lewis, 200, 470
Kim, Bok-lim C., 334, 534
Kim, Hei C., 330, 531
Kim, Illsoo, 331, 534
Kim, Kwang C., 29–31, 67, 329–330, 340, 349, 531, 534–535
Kimmel, Michael S., 45, 535
Kimura, Yukiko, 377, 385, 535
King, Martin Luther, Jr., 118, 200–203, 205, 208, 212, 535
King, Patricia, 222, 535
King, Rodney, 1, 56, 218–219, 241
King, Wayne, 285, 535
Kinloch, Graham C., 45, 51, 535
Kirscht, John P., 45, 535
Kitano, Harry H. L., 330, 333–334, 338, 351, 354, 385, 387–390, 393, 535–536
Klausner, Samuel, 413, 536
Kleiman, Dena, 308, 536
Kleinhuizen, Jeff, 171, 298, 536
Kleinman, Dena, 417, 536
Kluegel, James R., 55, 505
Knight, Franklin W., 464, 536
Knight, Jerry, 239, 536
Knight, Robin, 470, 536
Knowles, Louis L., 69, 90, 536

Know-Nothings, 97
Knudson, Thomas J., 169, 536
Kohler, David, 469, 540
Korean Americans, 1, 326–332, 337, 341–342, 344–345, 347, 350
Kornblum, William, 73, 536
kosher, 418
Kosmin, Barry A., 121, 396, 398, 419, 422, 536
Kramarae, Cheru, 461
Kramer, Michael, 321, 538
Kramer, Roderick M., 48, 506
Krickus, Richard, 128, 536
Krug, Mark M., 126, 536
Ku Klux Klan, 60, 97, 408
Kuo, Wen H., 366, 536
Kutner, Bernard, 42, 536
Kwong, Peter, 358, 540
kye, 330–331, 351, 495

labeling theory, 16–18, 34, 48–49, 255, 434–435, 495
Labor, Teresa, 338, 536
Lacayo, Richard, 102, 537
Lacy, Dan, 192, 196, 537
Ladd, Everett Carll, Jr., 449, 537
Ladner, Joyce, 208, 232, 457–458, 537
Lai, H. M., 357, 363, 537
Lamm, Robert, 71, 73, 79, 221, 235, 317, 438, 441
Landry, Bart, 234, 249, 537
Langer, Elinor, 438, 537
language, 254–262, 271, 359
Laotians, 326, 333–336
LaPiere, Richard, 41–42, 537
Larrabee, John, 167, 537
Latinos. See Hispanics
*Lau* v. *Nichols*, 254, 262, 367
Laumann, Edward O., 135, 537
Laurenti, Luigi, 239, 537
Lavender, Abraham D., 414, 426, 537
Lawlor, Julia, 260, 537
Law of Return, 398, 478
Lazarus, Edward, 161, 183, 537
Lazarus, Emma, 99
Lazerwitz, Bernard, 123, 419–420, 527, 537
League of United Latin American Citizens, 281
League of Women Voters, 455
Leatherman, Courtney, 412
Lederman, Douglas, 449, 538
Lee, Alfred McClung, 476, 491, 538
Lee, Calvin, 369, 538
Lee, Don, 330, 538
Lee, Felicia R., 344, 538

Lee, Rose Hum, 354, 360, 363, 538
Lee, Spike, 27, 62, 331
Leebaw, Milton, 318, 538
*Lee* v. *Weisman*, 140
Legum, Colin, 481, 538
Lehman, Edward C., Jr., 139, 538
Lem, Kim, 367, 538
Lemann, Nicholas, 234, 315, 538
LeMoyne, James, 264, 538
Lenski, Gerhard, 123, 538
Lerner, Gerda, 457, 538
Lerner, Michael, 126, 144–145, 538
Lesch, Ann M., 477–478, 538
Leslie, Connie, 262, 538
Levin, Jack, 42, 538
Levin, William C., 42, 538
Levine, Gene N., 386, 389, 414
Levine, Irving M., 127, 538
Levy, Jacques E., 284, 538
Levy, Mark P., 321, 538
Leway, 365
Lewin, Tamar, 446, 539
Lewinson, Paul, 192, 538
Lewis, Diane K., 457, 538
Lewis, Oscar, 293–294, 538–539
Li, Wen Lang, 344, 356, 539
Lichtenstein, Eugene, 411, 539
Lichter, Linda S., 226, 245, 539
Lieberson, Stanley, 48, 125, 128, 539
Liebman, Charles, 416, 418, 420, 423, 424,
    426, 539
Liebow, Elliot, 73–75, 539
life chances, 133, 145, 301, 496
Light, Ivan H., 331, 360, 371, 539
Lin, Nan, 366, 536
Lincoln, Abraham, 191
Lincoln, C. Eric, 216, 539
Lind, Andrew W., 337–338, 539
Lindsey, Robert, 105, 257, 260, 285–288, 342,
    388, 539–540
Lippmann, Walter, 17, 539
Lipset, Seymour Martin, 404, 449, 533, 536,
    540
Lipsey, David, 476, 540
literacy test, 100
Little Havana, 265
Little, Alan, 469, 540
Logan, Rayford W., 193, 540
Lomax, Louis E., 212, 540
López-Rivera, Oscar, 308, 310–311, 540
Los Angeles, 1, 56–57, 218–219, 362
Louden, Joyce S., 234, 518
Louw-Potgieter, J., 46, 518
Luce, Clare Booth, 334, 540

Luebben, Ralph A., 168, 540
Lum, Joann, 358, 540
Lyman, Stanford M., 356–357, 359, 363,
    370–371, 391, 540

McCarran-Walter Act, 102
*McClesky* v. *Kemp,* 243
McConahay, J. B., 207, 558
McCord, Colin, 244, 540
McCully, Bruce T., 28, 540–541
McCunn, Ruthanne Lum, 372, 540
McFadden, Robert D., 308, 540
McGee, Kevin T., 167, 540
McGregor-Alegado, Davianna, 340, 541
machismo, 295, 301, 319, 457, 496
Macias, Reynoldo Flores, 254, 541
McIntosh, Shawn, 332, 541
Mack, Raymond W., 18, 541
McKinney, William, 136, 555
Mackinnon, Catherine A., 443, 541
*McLean* v. *Arkansas Board of Education,* 141
McLeod, Beverly, 340, 541
McManus, Ed, 243, 541
McMillen, Liz, 171, 541
McMillen, Neil R., 200, 541
MacMurray, Val Dan, 143, 541
McNamara, Patrick H., 290, 541
McNickle, D'Arcy, 152, 157, 163, 541
McPhail, Thomas, 23, 541
McWilliams, Carey, 276, 280, 541
Maguire, Brendan, 61, 541
Malcolm X, 211–212, 216, 541–542
Maldonado, Lionel, 146, 541
Maldonado-Denis, Manuel, 313, 323, 542
male liberation, 438
Malinche, 282
Mallinckrodt, Brent, 223, 542
Mandella, Nelson, 483, 486–488
Manigan, Katherine S., 292, 542
Mann, James, 230, 542
manumission, 465, 491, 496
March on Washington, 203
Marden, Charles F., 99, 542
Maretzki, Thomas W., 351
Marger, Nartin, 465, 542
marginality, 29, 34, 423, 496
Margolis, Richard J., 128, 542
marianismo, 295, 301, 496
Marielitos, 263, 271, 496
market discrimination, 443, 460, 496
Marks, Sheila, 488, 501
Marquez, Benjamin, 288, 542
Marshall, Thurgood, 198, 542
Martin, Douglas, 166, 542

Martin, Joanne, 60
Martin, M. Kay, 434, 542
Martinez, Angel B., 314, 542
Martinez, Estella A., 294, 542
Martinez, Thomas M., 299, 542
Martinez, Vilma S., 58, 280, 542–543
Marty, Martin E., 135, 412, 543
Marx, Gary T., 55, 543
Marx, Karl, 43, 68, 543
Mason, Philip, 465, 468, 490, 543
mass media, 49, 54–63, 131, 251–252,
    298–299, 355, 366–367
Massey, Douglas S., 26, 239, 281, 315, 543
Masters, Stanley H., 239, 543
Mathews, Tom, 407, 543
Mathisen, James A., 135, 543
Matthiesson, Peter, 178, 543
Matza, David, 128, 207, 543
Mayer, Egon, 422, 426, 543
Maykovich, Minako Kurokawa, 46, 385,
    390–391, 543
Means, Russell, 177–178
Medicine, Beatrice, 166, 543–544
*Meek* v. *Pittinger*, 140
Meier, August, 193, 196, 278, 280, 544
Melendy, Howard Brett, 333–334, 354, 544
melting pot, 27, 34, 496
Mencarelli, James, 174, 544
Mendoza, Fernando S., 297, 544
Menominees, 162–163, 176
*Meritor Savings Bank* v. *Vinson*, 444
Merton, Robert K., 18, 39–41, 207, 544
Metzger, L. Paul, 122, 544
Mexican American Legal Defense and
    Education Fund (MALDEF), 280,
    288–289
Mexican-American Political Association,
    287–289
Mexican-American War, 20, 275–276
Mexico, 105, 275
Meyers, Gustavus, 408, 544
Mezzogiorno, 130, 133
Miami, 219, 262–267
Michalek, Laurence, 61, 544
middlemen minority, 344, 346, 351, 496–497
Middleton, Russell, 45, 60, 544
migrant farm workers, 284–287
migration, 18–20, 34, 194, 311–312, 497
millenarium movement, 153, 183, 497
Miller, Arthur G., 46, 65, 440, 544
Miller, Herman P., 442, 564
Miller, Joanne, 435, 544
Miller, Kelly, 193, 544
Miller, Randall M., 146, 544–545

Miller, Robert Stevens, Jr., 82, 545
Miller, Stuart Creighton, 98, 545
Miller, Walter, 366, 545
Mills, C. Wright, 14, 133, 280, 314, 545
Min, Pyong Gap, 333, 545
Mindel, Charles H., 146, 545
Mineta, Norman, 379–381, 545
minority group, 5–6, 34, 397–398, 497
*Miranda* v. *Arizona*, 283
Mirandé, Alfredo, 290, 296, 302, 545
*Mitsuye Endo* v. *United States*, 384–386
mitzvahs, 418
Miyamoto, S. Frank, 385, 545
Mizio, Emelica, 319, 545
Model, Suzanne, 346, 545
model minority image, 340–349, 351, 413, 497
Mohl, Raymond A., 266–267, 545
mojados, 280–281, 300–301, 497
Molly Maguires, 96
Molotch, Harvey L., 239, 545
mommy track, 440, 460, 497
Monfort, Franklin, 291, 549
Monroe, Sylvester, 472, 545
Montagu, Ashley, 10, 13, 35, 399, 545
Monterey Park, 329, 360
Montero, Darrel M., 386, 389–390, 538, 545
Montgomery, Paul L., 365, 546
Moore, Gwen, 76, 127, 404, 501
Moore, Joan W., 146, 272, 274, 276, 282, 285,
    288–289, 291, 294, 299, 321, 525–526, 541,
    546
Moquin, Wayne, 276, 278, 287, 302, 546
Morales, Royal F., 334, 546
Morawska, Ewa T., 126, 129, 556–557
Morgan, Joan, 222, 546
Morgan, Robin, 461
Morin, Richard, 26, 546
Morley, Morris, 311, 546
Mormons, 142–144
Morris, Aldon, 201, 546
Morris, Michael, 73, 546
Morrow, Victoria P., 253, 546
Morse, Samuel F. B., 95, 546
Moskos, Charles, 198, 546
Mosley, Leonard, 377, 546
Moss, Alfred A., Jr., 188, 196, 203, 215, 522
Moynihan, Daniel Patrick, 124, 127, 129, 233,
    314–315, 319–320
Moynihan Report, 233, 294
Mufson, Steven, 487, 546
mulatto escape hatch, 465–466, 491, 497
Mullen, William, 163, 546
Mullins, Marc, 2, 546
multinational development, 483, 491, 497

Muñoz, Daniel G., 293, 546
mutilated marriages, 354, 371, 497
Muto, Sheila, 390, 547
Mydans, Seth, 108, 289, 332, 547
Myers, Samuel, 319
Myrdal, Gunnar, 16, 18, 124, 322, 432, 547

Nabakov, Peter, 283, 547
Nagata, Donna K., 388–390, 547
Nagel, Joane, 173, 178, 547
Nakamaru, Robert Tsunco, 388, 547
Nakanishi, Don T., 334, 387, 547
Nash, Manning, 15–16, 547
Nation of Islam, 25, 211–212
National Advisory Commission on Civil
    Disorders, 208, 226, 547
National Association for the Advancement
    of Colored People (NAACP), 128, 194,
    196, 199–201, 214, 243, 288
National Congress of American Indians
    (NCAI), 173, 176, 178
National Jewish Population Survey, 398
National Organization for Women (NOW),
    438, 453
national origins system, 100, 102
National Women's Political Caucus, 456
Native American Church, 179
nativism, 95, 97, 114, 497
naturalization, 95, 99
Navajo-Hopi land dispute, 159–160
Navarro, Armando, 285, 548
Navarro, Mireya, 308, 548
Nee, Victor G., 333, 366
neocolonialism, 23, 34, 497
Neoricans, 313, 323, 497
New Progressive Party (PNP), 307
*New York State Clubs Association* v. *City of
    New York*, 82
Newman, William M., 27–28, 31, 548
Newton, Huey, 210
Ng, Johnny, 337, 375, 548
Niagara Movement, 194
Nicaraguans, 268–269
Niebuhr, H. Richard, 135, 548
1990 Immigration Act, 107
Nineteenth Amendment, 436
Nisei, 375, 377, 383, 387, 389, 391–393, 497
Nixon, Richard, 175–176, 355
Noble, Kenneth B., 246, 549
Noel, Donald L., 187, 549
Nordheimer, Jon, 265, 285, 311, 549
Northern Ireland, 473–476, 489
noshrim, 403, 425, 497
Novak, Michael, 122, 127, 129, 549

Nugent, Neill, 472, 549
Nuyoricans. See Neoricans.

Oberschall, A., 204, 549
O'Dea, Thomas F., 143, 549
Odo, Franklin S., 327, 549
O'Driscoll, Patrick, 139, 549
Oehling, Richard A., 355, 549
Ogletree, Earl J., 252, 318, 549
O'Hare, William P., 73, 228–229, 347, 549
oil backlash, 411
O'Kane, James M., 131, 549
Okimoto, Daniel, 390, 549
Olson, James C., 153, 549
O'Neill, William, 436, 549
Order of the Sons of America, 281
*Oregon* v. *Alfred Smith*, 179
O'Reilly, Jane, 438, 549
Orfield, Gary, 163, 271, 291, 549–550
Organic Act, 337
Organization of Afro-American Unity, 212
Orlov, Ann, 268–270, 549
Orthodox Jews, 416–420, 422–424
Ortiz, Vilma, 311, 316, 550
Oskamp, Stuart, 53, 550
Ostling, Richard N., 136, 550
Ottaway, David S., 484, 550
out-group, 6
out-group vices, 405, 425, 497
Owen, Carolyn A., 51, 550

Pachon, Harry, 272, 274, 276, 282, 285, 289,
    294, 299, 321, 545
Padilla, Felix M., 274, 390, 550
Padilla, Raymond V., 276, 550
PADRES, 290
padrone, 130, 145, 497
Page, R., 46, 509
Paik, Irvin, 355, 550
Palestine, 477–481
Palestine Liberation Organization (PLO), 410,
    479–480
Panamanians, 268–269
pan-Indianism, 173–179, 182–183, 497
Parenti, Michael, 125, 550
Park, Jeanne, 340–341, 550
Park, Robert E., 29, 49, 121, 550
Parker, Linda S., 351–352, 550
Parks, Rosa, 200
Parsons, Talcott S., 434, 550–551
pass laws, 482, 491, 497
Passel, Jeffrey S., 108, 114, 521, 550
Patterson, Orlando, 465, 550–551
Patterson, Sheila, 469, 551

pay equity, 445–446, 460, 497
Pear, Robert, 112, 260, 551
Peddler, Sophie, 72, 551
Pentecostal faiths, 320, 323, 497
peoplehood, 125, 424–425, 497
Perlmutter, Philip, 65, 551
Peroff, Nicholas, 163, 183, 551
Persian Gulf War, 1, 61
Peters, Victor, 141, 551
Petersen, William, 20, 384–385, 388, 551
Pettigrew, Thomas F., 14, 45–46, 48, 60, 65,
    248, 551–552
peyote, 178–179
Phillips, Leslie, 308, 552
Pido, Antonio J. A., 333, 352, 552
*Pierce* v. *Society of Sisters,* 140
Pileggi, Nicolas, 127, 552
Pine Ridge reservation, 177–178
Pinkney, Alphonso, 193, 208, 210, 212, 219,
    235, 241, 247, 249, 552
Pitcairn Island, 27
Pitt, Leonard, 276, 552
Pitts, James P., 210, 552
*Planned Parenthood* v. *Casey,* 454
Pleasant, William, 249, 552
*Plessy* v. *Ferguson,* 191–192
pluralism, 31–34, 156, 214, 247, 271, 390, 489,
    497
Poland, 20
Polish Americans, 127–128
Political Association of Spanish Speaking
    Organizations, 287–288
politically correct, 5, 34, 497
politics, 53, 55, 245–247, 256–257, 306–308,
    320–322, 363–364, 387, 415–416, 454–456
politics of accommodation, 193
Polzin, Theresita, 126, 552
Popular Democratic Party (PPD), 307
Porter, Jack Nusan, 29, 58, 219, 413, 416, 552
Portes, Alejandro, 264, 287, 552
Poussaint, Alvin, 234, 552
poverty, 73, 226–227
Powell, Enoch, 469, 552
Powell, John Wesley, 150, 552
Powers, Charles H., 387, 552–553
Pradt, Mary A., 404, 413, 426–427, 560
prayer, school, 139–140
prejudice, 37–65, 126–130, 298–299, 338,
    366–370, 468
principle of third-generation interest, 123, 145
Prokesch, Steven, 475, 553
Protocols, 407–408
Public Health Service, 172–173
Puerto Ricans, 70–71, 251–253, 262–267, 270,
    289, 296, 303
push and pull factors, 20, 93
pushouts, 170, 183, 495

Quan, Katie, 359, 553
quilombo, 464, 491, 498
Quintana, Frances Leon, 276, 553
quotas, 88

Raab, Earl, 412, 553
Rabaya, Violet, 334, 553
Rabinove, Samuel, 415, 553
race, 7, 14
Rachlin, Carol, 168, 553
racial group, 7–9, 34, 498
racism, 12–14, 35, 187, 385, 457, 459, 558
Radelet, Michael L., 243, 554
Radzialowski, Thaddeus, 135
Rainbow Coalition, 246
Rainwater, Lee, 233, 249, 554
Ramirez, Anthony, 340, 554
Ramirez, J. David, 258, 554
Randolph, A. Philip, 196, 198, 203, 554
Rapson, Richard L., 339, 554
Raspberry, William, 270, 554
Rawick, George P., 190, 554
Raybon, Patricia, 61–63, 554
Raymer, Patricia, 163, 554
Raymond, Chris, 58, 554
Raza, 274, 286, 301, 498
Raza Unida Party, 288
Reagan, Ronald, 88, 270, 386
Reardon, Patrick T., 73, 554
Rebelsky, Freda, 450, 554
Reconstruction, 191
Red Cloud, 152
Red Guards, 365–366
redlining, 238, 248, 498
Red Power, 174
red summer, 197
Reed, Adolph, Jr., 211, 554
Reed, Veda, 268–270, 549
Reese, Michael, 447, 554
Reformed Jews, 417–420, 423–424
Refugee Act of 1980, 112
refugees, 108–112, 262–266, 334–335
*Regents of the University of California* v. *Bakke,*
    84–85
Reid, John, 225, 247, 554
Reimers, David M., 103, 183, 554
relative deprivation, 29, 35, 67–68, 89,
    206–207, 215, 498
religion, 9, 118–121, 133–145, 189, 211–212,
    233, 266, 289–290, 319–320, 330, 361–363,

399, 416–423
Removal Act, 151
Reorganization Act, 156–157
repatriation, 277–278, 301, 498
reservations, 157–164, 174
respectable bigotry, 126, 131, 144–145, 498
restrictive covenant, 197, 215, 498
*Reynolds* v. *United States*, 143
Rhodes, Golbert, 389, 538
Rice, Berkeley, 359, 366, 555
*Richmond* v. *Cronson*, 85–86, 228
Ridgeway, James, 65, 260, 555
Riesman, David, 334, 351
riff-raff theory, 205, 215, 498
riots, 1, 56–57, 95–97, 218–219, 279–280, 362,
    470
rising expectations, 206–207
Ritterband, Paul, 396, 555
Ritzer, George, 226, 555
Rivera, Monte, 278, 280, 315, 323, 532
Roark, Anne C., 85, 555
Roberts, Alden, 335, 562
Roberts, D. F., 10, 555
Roberts, Steven B., 448, 555
Robey, Bryant, 345, 351
Robinson, Tracey, 467, 555
Roche, John Patrick, 123, 125, 555
Rodgers, Harrell R., Jr., 461
Rodriguez, Clara, 306, 311, 314–315, 317–318,
    324, 555
*Roe* v. *Wade*, 453–454
Rollins, Bryant, 245, 555
Roman Catholics, 95–97, 118–121, 127,
    131–132, 134–138, 266, 289–290, 319–320,
    333, 457
Romo, Ricardo, 302
Roof, Wade Clark, 136, 555
Roos, Philip D., 178, 555
Roosevelt, Franklin D., 80, 196–197, 378, 381
Rosaldo, Renato, 296, 457, 555
Rose, Arnold, 15, 558
Rose, E. J. B., 42, 469, 491, 555
Rose, Peter, 32, 555
Rose, R. S., 465, 555–556
Rosen, Sanford Jay, 280, 556
Rosenberg, Morris, 58, 556
Rosenblatt, Gary, 422, 556
Rosenhouse, Harry, 265, 556
Rossi, Alice S., 88, 436, 449, 461, 556
rotating credit association, 330
Rothman, Nancy Sacks, 29, 556
Royce, David D., 233, 556
Rubien, David, 362, 556
Ruble, Diane N., 438, 511

Rudwick, Elliot, 193, 196, 556
Rule, Sheila, 472, 556
Ryan, William, 16, 35, 294, 349, 556

Sabogal, Fabro, 296, 556
Sactre, Sara, 446, 556
Sadker, David, 448, 556
Sadker, Myra, 448, 556
Said, Edward W., 477, 556–557
*St. Francis College* v. *Al-Khazraji*, 82
Salholz, Eloise, 342–343, 454, 557
Samuels, Frederick, 339, 557
*San Antonio Independent School District* v.
    *Rodriquez*, 79
Sanchez, Sandra, 254, 270, 557
sanctuary movement, 111–112, 114, 268, 271,
    498
Sanders, Alvin J., 333, 557
Sanders, Irwin T., 126, 129, 557
Sansei, 378, 385, 389, 391, 393, 498
Sapino, Virginia, 461
Sargent, Edward D., 241, 557
Sawyer, Jack, 438, 557
Scanlan, John A., 102, 557
scapegoat, 44, 64, 498
Schaefer, Richard T., 27, 48, 51, 53, 60, 63, 71,
    73, 79, 97, 196, 210, 221, 223, 235, 317,
    334, 435, 438, 441, 469–471, 473, 557–558
Schaefer, Sandra L., 334, 469, 558
Schermerhorn, R. A., 20, 490, 558
Schlozman, Kay Lehman, 128, 558
Schmidt, William E., 160, 412, 558
Schmitt, David E., 474, 558
Schramm, Wilbur, 23, 558
Schrieke, Bertram J., 98, 558
Schulman, Sam, 411, 559
Schultz, Ray, 418, 558
Schultz, Terri, 453, 558
Schuman, Howard, 55, 65, 558
Schwartz, Felice, 60, 439–440
Schwartz, John, 239, 558
Schwirian, Kent P., 265, 558
Scott, Robin Fitzgerald, 279, 558–559
Seale, Bobby, 209–210
Sears, David O., 207, 559
secession, 24–25
secessionist minorities, 140, 145, 498
second shift, 452, 460, 498
segregation, 25, 26, 128, 239–240, 291, 315,
    339, 498
self-esteem, 57–58
self-fulfilling prophecy, 17–19, 35, 48, 498
Selzer, Michael, 407–408, 559
Selznick, Gertrude J., 45, 559

Seneca Falls, 435
Senior, Clarence, 306, 559
Servin, Manuel P., 276, 559
set asides, 228, 248, 498
setoffs, 159, 183, 498
Severin, Steve, 174, 544
Severo, Richard, 127, 559
sex discrimination, 81–82, 439–456
sexism, 432, 449, 457, 459–460, 475, 498
sex roles. See gender roles
sex-typing of jobs, 440–441
sexual harassment, 443–445, 460, 498
*Shaare-Tefila Congregation* v. *Cobb,* 82
shadchan, 421
Shaeils, Merrill, 254, 559
Shaheen, Jack G., 60, 559
Shames, Deborah, 163, 559
Shannon, Lyle W., 294, 559
Shapiro, Harry L., 27, 559
Shapiro, Laura, 409, 559
Shapiro, Leon, 397, 559
Shapiro, Walter, 75, 559
Shaw, Susan M., 451, 559
Sheatsley, Paul B., 51, 53, 526, 561
Sheinberg, Sheila, 411, 559
Sheler, Jeffrey L., 226, 559
*Shelley* v. *Kramer,* 198
Shenker, Israel, 418, 424, 559
Sherif, Carolyn, 63, 559
Sherif, Muzafer, 63, 559
Sherman, C. Bezalel, 402, 559–560
Sherry, Linda, 357, 560
Shin, Linda, 329, 560
Shipler, David K., 404, 560
Shipp, E. R., 211, 560
Shorten, Linda, 184
Shreve, Anita, 455, 560
Shribman, David, 103, 560
Sigall, H., 46, 560
Silberman, Charles E., 170, 412, 423, 560
Silk, James, 112, 560
Silva, Helga, 264, 560
Silva, Nelson Dovalle, 466, 560
Simkus, Albert A., 239, 560
Simmons, Roberta G., 58, 555
Simmons, Jerry L., 467, 560
Simpson, George Eaton, 411, 560
Singer, Audrey, 219, 560
sinophobes, 98
Sioux Indians, 152–153, 161, 170
Sites, Paul, 141, 560
situational theory. See structural approach
Six Chinese Companies, 356
Skidmore, Thomas, 465, 492, 560

Sklansky, Jeff, 174, 560
Sklare, Marshall, 413, 415, 418, 422, 426,
    560–561
Skocpol, Theda, 88, 561
Slagle, Alton, 153, 561
slave codes, 187–188, 215, 498
slavery, 20, 186–192, 464, 482
Slavin, Stephen L., 63, 404, 413, 426–427, 561
Sloan, George, 367, 561
Smith, M. Estelli, 167, 561
Smith, Thomas, 38, 136, 410, 561
*Smith* v. *Allwright,* 197
Snipp, C. Matthew, 166–167, 173, 184, 561
Snyder, Eldon E., 135
Sochen, June, 436, 561
social clubs, 82, 339, 415
Social Darwinism, 12, 35, 498
social distance, 49–51
Sorensen, Annemette, 239, 561–562
Sorkin, Alan L., 166, 562
South Africa, 6, 46, 481–489
South-Central Los Angeles riots, 1, 218–219,
    228, 241, 331–332
Southern Christian Leadership Conference
    (SCLC), 201, 208
Spearman, Diana, 469, 562
Spector, Michael, 358, 562
Spencer, Samuel R., 193, 409, 562
Spicer, Edward, 163, 562
Spiegel, Don, 36, 411, 562
Spiegel, Irving, 414, 422, 562
Spindler, George, 163, 562
Spindler, Louise, 163, 562
split labor market, 71
Spreitzer, Elmer, 135, 562
Spuittieri, Tom, 467, 476, 562
Srole, Leo, 28, 121, 127
Stampp, Kenneth M., 188, 216
Stan, Robert, 464, 562
Stanley, Alessandra, 349, 562
Stanton, Elizabeth Cady, 435
Staples, Brent, 219, 562–563
Staples, Robert E., 232, 249, 562
Stark, Rodney, 120, 136–137, 146, 411, 564
Starr, Paul, 335, 563
states' rights, 81, 89, 498
Steinberg, Stephen, 45, 73, 411, 413, 563
Steinem, Gloria, 456–457, 563
Steiner, Stan, 166–167, 174, 255, 317, 563
Stember, Charles Herbert, 411, 563
Sterba, James P., 182, 563
stereotype, 17, 35, 46–49, 51, 58, 60–61, 98,
    155, 298, 343, 349, 376, 404, 435, 498–499
Stevens-Arroyo, Antonio M., 315, 563

Stewart, James H., 166, 563
Stockton, William, 313, 563
Stoddard, Ellyn R., 254, 276, 279–280, 293, 563
Stone, Andrea, 219, 563
Stonequist, Everett V., 29, 563
Stouffer, Samuel A., 60, 563
strain-reducing mechanisms, 29–30, 499
stratification, 14, 35, 499
Strauss, Herbert A., 427
Strober, Gerald S., 411, 416, 563
structural approach, 45–46, 65, 499
Stuart, Reginald, 142, 309, 320, 563
Student Non-Violent Coordinating Committee (SNCC), 208
Studler, Donley, 469, 563
Stump, Roger W., 139, 563
Suarez, Manuel, 308–309, 563
subordinate group. See minority group
Sue, Stanley, 342, 346, 352, 563
suffragists, 436, 460, 499
Sullivan, Cheryl, 166, 169, 487, 563–564
Sullivan Principles, 485, 487, 491, 499
Sung, Betty Lee, 344, 356–357, 359
Suro, Roberto, 290, 564
Sussman, Barry, 232, 245, 564
Suter, Larry E., 442, 564
Sutherland, Elizabeth, 456, 564
*Swann* v. *Charlotte-Mecklenburg Board of Education,* 221
Sweet, Jill D., 167, 564
Swinton, David, 226, 564
Swoboda, Frank, 85, 565
symbolic ethnicity, 125, 133, 145, 499

Tachibana, Judy, 344, 565
Tachiki, Amy, 352
taco circuit, 298
Taeuber, Alma F., 128, 239, 565
Taeuber, Karl E., 128, 239, 565
Taiwanese, 93, 329
Takaki, Ronald, 333, 340, 352, 360, 366, 565
talented tenth, 194
Tang, Joyce, 346, 565
Tannenbaum, Frank, 464, 565
Tasmanians, 23
Taylor, Dalmas A., 248, 565
Taylor, Frank J., 385, 565
Taylor, Robert Joseph, 51, 565
Taylor, Ronald A., 233, 565
Taylor, Stuart, Jr., 82, 112, 243, 565
Taylor, Theodore W., 163, 565
Telles, Edward E., 466, 565
ten Brock, Jacobus, 385, 393, 565

Tercheek, Ronald J., 474–475, 565
Termination Act, 161–163
Terry, Clifford, 126, 565
Terry, Wallace, 216, 565–566
Thernstrom, Stephen, 36, 566
third-generation interest principle, 123, 145, 389, 499
Thomas, Barbara Boston, 207, 566
Thomas, Clarence, 444
Thomas, Curlew O., 20, 566
Thomas, J. O., 476, 566
Thomas, Melvin E., 235, 566
Thomas, Piri, 314, 324, 566
Thomas, Robert K., 178, 566
Thomas, William Isaac, 17, 566
Thompson, John L. P., 476, 566
Thompson, Morris S., 108, 566
Thornton, Russell, 51, 153, 576
Thurow, Lester C., 226, 566
Tienda, Marta, 252, 315, 566
Tijerina, Kathryn Harris, 170, 566
Tijerina, Reies Lopez, 283, 288, 299
Tinker, John N., 389, 566
Tirado, Miguel David, 282, 288, 567
Title IX, 449
Toner, Robin, 190, 566
tongs, 355, 357, 366, 371, 499
Tostado, Ricardo, 257, 289, 567
total discrimination, 68–69, 89, 235, 499
tourists, 166–167, 360–361
tracking, 317, 323, 499
Trail of Tears, 151
Treaty of Guadalupe Hidalgo, 20, 254, 275
Treaty of Medicine Creek, 174
Treen, Joseph, 482, 567
trekkers, 482
Triandis, Leigh M., 50, 567
Triandis, Harry C., 50, 567
Trillin, Calvin, 144, 567
Trimble, Albert, 178, 567
triple jeopardy, 10
Trottier, Richard W., 350, 567
Truman, Harry, 80, 198, 307
tsu, 355–356, 371, 499
Tsuchigane, Robert, 442, 567
Tuch, Steven A., 55, 567
Tule Lake, 383, 567
Tumin, Melvin M., 314, 567
Turner, Eugene James, 35, 268, 312, 501
Turner, Gladys T., 232, 556
Turner, James, 210, 567
Turner, Margery, 88, 91, 567
Turner, Wallace, 338, 567
Twining, Mary Arnold, 190, 567

Tyler, S. Lyman, 156–157, 162, 166, 568

Ujlaki, Vilma E., 252, 318, 549
Ulster, 473–476
underclass, 72–75, 89, 294, 315, 499
underemployment, 226, 248, 499
underground economy. See irregular
    economy
undocumented immigration, 104–108
UNESCO, 10, 12–13
Ungar-Sargon, Julian, 400–401
Unified Black Movement, 466
United Farm Workers Union, 284, 286–287,
    290
United Jewish Appeal, 411, 415
*United Steelworkers of America* v. *Weber*, 84–85
Urban League, 196
Usdansky, Margaret L., 26, 567
U.S. English, 260–261

Valentine, Charles A., 294, 567
van den Berghe, Pierre, 7, 22, 492, 567
Vander Zanden, James W., 207, 567–568
Van Doren, Charles, 276, 278, 287, 302, 540
Vanneman, Reene, 234, 568
Van Valey, Thomas L., 239, 568
Vasquez, Enriqueta Longavex Y., 293,
    456–457
Vass, Winifred Kellersberger, 190, 568
Vaughan, Mary, 309, 568
Vecoli, Rudolph J., 122–123, 568
Vega, William A., 296, 568
Veidmanis, Juris, 102, 568
vendidos, 282
vicious circle, 18
victim discounting, 243
victimization surveys, 241, 248, 499
Vidal, David, 254, 568–569
Vietnamese Americans, 326, 334–336, 342,
    345
Vigil, James Diego, 282, 289, 569
Volsky, George, 265, 422, 569
Voorhies, Barbara, 434, 542
Voting Rights Act, 203, 208, 246
voucher plan, 222

Waddell, Jack O., 166, 569
Wagenheim, Kal, 306, 309, 313, 321, 324
Wagley, Charles, 6, 569
Waite, Juan J., 111, 569
Waitzkin, Howard, 244, 569
Walker, Jack, 208, 500
Walker, Lewis, 476, 490–491, 530
Wallace, Walter L., 245, 513

Wallerstein, Immanuel, 23, 569
Walters, Robert, 308, 569
Wang, L. Ling-Chi, 342, 569
Warner, Sam Bass, Jr., 96, 569
Warner, W. Lloyd, 28, 43, 121, 127, 569
War Relocation Authority, 382–383
Warren, Earl, 199, 384
Washington, Booker T., 192–194, 196, 570
Watanabe, Colin, 366, 570
Waters, Harry F., 435, 570
Watson, O. Michael, 166, 569
Watson, Russell, 417, 570
Wax, Murray L., 150, 152, 156–157, 162, 166,
    169, 178, 184, 570
Waxman, Chaim I., 414, 570
Webb, Susan L., 444, 570
Weber, Max, 14, 34, 133, 234
Webster, Peggy Lovell, 467–468, 570
*Webster* v. *Reproductive Health Services*,
    453–454
Weed, James A., 128, 526
Weglyn, Michi, 378, 570
Weicher, John C., 240, 570
Weigel, Gustave, 143, 570
Weil, Frederick D., 60, 570
Weil, Thomas E., 570
Weinberg, Richard A., 11, 570
Weisberger, Bernard A., 115, 570
Weiss, Melford S., 357, 359, 570
Weissbach, Theodore, 49, 65, 507
Weisskopf, Michael, 284, 570
Wells, Robert N., Jr., 171, 570–571
Wenneker, Mark B., 244, 571
Weppner, Robert S., 164, 571
Westfried, Alex Huxley, 314, 324, 571
Westie, Frank R., 42, 50, 571
wetbacks, 280–281, 300–301, 497
Weyr, Thomas, 272, 571
Wheeler-Howard Act, 156–157
Whipple, Thomas, 433, 514
White, O. Kendall, Jr., 144, 571
White backlash, 53, 65, 499
White primary, 192, 215, 499
Whitman, David, 271, 570
Whyte, John M., 474
Wikler, Norma Juliet, 449, 571
Willhelm, Sidney M., 43, 571
Williams, Franklin H., 359, 389, 571
Williams, Jenny, 69, 571
Williams, Robin M., Jr., 204, 249, 571
Willig, Ann C., 258, 571–572
Wilson, David S., 284, 572
Wilson, James Q., 67, 129, 572
Wilson, William J., 90, 222, 228, 235–237, 243,

249, 482, 492, 572
Wilson, Woodrow, 100
Winch, Robert F., 422, 572
Winkler, Karen, 294, 572
Winsberg, Morton D., 265, 572
Wirth, Louis, 420, 572
Witt, Shirley Hill, 156, 173, 572
Wolf, Allen, 228
Wolfe, Ann G., 43, 573
Wolfe, Thomas, 367, 573
Woll, Allen, 293, 573
women, 9–10, 49, 77–78, 81, 88, 137–139,
    231–232, 295, 319, 330, 362, 398, 430–461
women's liberation movement, 437–439,
    458
Wong, Bernard P., 359, 372, 572
Wong, Charles Choy, 359, 539
Wong, Eugene F., 340, 346, 573
Wong, Jade Snow, 372
Wong, Morrison G., 342, 349, 529, 573
Wood, Robert C., 125, 573
Woodrum, Eric, 387, 573
Woodward, C. Vann, 191–192, 573
Woodward, Kenneth L., 210, 212, 422, 573
Wounded Knee, 153, 177
Wozniak, John, 61, 541
Wren, Christopher, 488, 573
Wright, Michael, 313, 573
Wright, R. Mary Bowen, 334, 573
Wright, Roosevelt, Jr., 146

Wright, Susan, 73, 573
Wrong, Dennis H., 124, 573
Wu, Cheng-Tsu, 355, 365, 369, 372, 573
Wuthnow, Robert, 404, 573

xenophobia, 95, 114, 499

Yamamoto, Joe, 390, 573
Yamamura, Douglas S., 339
Yancey, William L., 122, 134, 233, 249, 553,
    573
yarmulka, 399–400, 418
Yee, Min S., 359, 366–367, 573–574
yellow peril, 98, 354–355, 371, 499
yeshivah, 418
Yiddishkait, 420, 425, 499
Yinger, J. Milton, 122, 23, 411, 560, 574
Yoder v. Wisconsin, 141
Yonsei, 375, 385, 393, 499
Young Lords Party, 315
Yu, Elena S., 334, 574
Yuan, D. Y., 359, 574

Zellner, William M., 140–141, 144, 146, 534
Zhou, Min, 358, 574
Zinsmeister, Karl, 41, 574
Zionism, 416, 421, 425, 477, 491, 499
zoning laws, 240, 248, 499
zoot-suiters riots, 279–280, 301, 499
Zweigenhaft, Richard L., 413, 574